ANTOINE DE SAINT-EXUPERY

# Antoine de Saint-Exupéry

## CURTIS CATE

PARAGON HOUSE

NEW YORK

First paperback edition, 1990

Published in the United States by

Paragon House
90 Fifth Avenue
New York, NY 10011

Library of Congress Cataloging-in-Publication Data

Cate, Curtis, 1924–
   Antoine de Saint-Exupéry / Curtis Cate.
      p.   cm.
   Includes bibliographical references.
   ISBN 1-55778-291-1
      1. Saint-Exupéry, Antoine de, 1900–1944—Biography. 2. Authors,
French—20th century—Biography. 3. Air pilots—France—Biography.
I. Title.
PQ2637.A274Z6355   1990
848'.91209—dc20                                                     89-25530
[B]                                                                  CIP


Manufactured in the United States of America

To the Memory of

PIERRE  MASSENET

# Contents

# Contents

# Illustrations

# Introduction

A BIOGRAPHY is almost always a risky undertaking when it concerns someone who has not been dead for a good fifty years or more. But far fewer than that are needed, alas, to decimate a generation which, like all of us, is not growing any younger. So it is with Saint-Exupéry. Though he died a quarter of a century ago, it will be years, and more likely decades, before the many intimate letters he wrote—to persons still living as to others dead—are published; but long before then most of those who knew him in his lifetime will no longer be around to share their reminiscences. The risks involved are thus intrinsic to an enterprise which from the start was a kind of rescue operation—aimed at garnering these precious recollections while there was yet time.

It was never my good fortune to meet Antoine de Saint-Exupéry. When he was in New York in 1942 I was still an undergraduate at Harvard, and the subsequent fortunes of war took him to North Africa, while I was shipped to England with the U.S. Army. This book is not, therefore, the work of an "eye-witness"; it is the work of a historian who has sought to fill out what has been written (relatively little in English, but a great deal in French) with glimpses of Saint-Ex at different moments of his existence obtained from close to a hundred of his contemporaries, kinsmen, and companions.

On one point, I feel reasonably sure, most of them would immediately agree: that Saint-Exupéry was as striking a personality as he was a writer. Nothing is more difficult for someone condemned to write at "second hand" than to convey a particular human being's charm or spell, above all when exercised by someone who was literally a magician. A magician whose heavy peasant hands could execute card tricks on a level with the great Houdini's. André Maurois once compared his story-telling gift to that of Scheherazade. John Phillips, the former *Life* photo-reporter, has called him a twentieth century Pico delle Mirandola. Others have likened him to Leonardo da Vinci and the omni-curious if not omniscient men of the Renaissance. "*Saint-Ex?*" General René Bouscat one day said to me, handing me a caricature "Pépino" had drawn of himself. "*Mais il savait tout faire*"—there was nothing he couldn't do. One of his closest friends,

Dr. Georges Pélissier, wishing to write an appreciation of him after his death, could find nothing better than the pentagonic title, *Les Cinq Visages de Saint-Exupéry*—the five "faces" or facets of his personality being Saint-Ex the Flyer, Saint-Ex the Writer, Saint-Ex the Man, Saint-Ex the Inventor, and Saint-Ex the Magician. Even so, the spectrum could have bee n extended and he could just as justifiably have entitled his book, *Les Sept Visages de Saint-Exupéry*, throwing in Saint-Ex the Humorist and Saint-Ex the Thinker, for good measure. For Saint-Exupéry, who "read little but understood everything" (to quote Pélissier), was in the deepest sense a thinker who used card tricks, word puzzles, chess games, and comic drawings to mask his innermost preoccupations.

With so many attributes and such an adventurous career it was inevitable that this pioneer of the sky should become something of a legend. In his own country Catholics and others in search of "a hero for our times" were tempted to stress the "Saint" in his name and to place him on a pedestal. The circumstances of his life did not always support such an exalted image, but his writings did; and for good or ill, Saint-Exupéry must in the end be judged by what he wrote.

Virtue, as we all know without having to read Dante, to say nothing of Gide, François Mauriac, or Graham Greene, is almost invariably less glamorous than vice. The warning was there, but Saint-Exupéry characteristically refused to heed it. Unwilling to be tempted, he devoted all his written work to a questioning study of such basic human virtues as courage, determination, perseverance, responsibility, generosity, self-sacrifice, loyalty, and love. This was asking for trouble in an age of universal unbelief, above all from a new generation of sub-Sartrian Cartesians who, whatever else they may do in life, are determined not to be the dupes of good intentions. "*Saint-Ex, c'est du scoutisme!*" as a petulant young *Parisienne* exclaimed to me not so long ago. A French Kipling, if not a Baden-Powell, who wrote half a dozen books, all of them variations on the theme of "If". Jean-François Revel has scoffed at his "prop-driven platitudes" and called him the "cou-cou man who replaced the human brain with an airplane engine." Jean Cau, that *enfant terrible* of French journalism, has dismissed his work as "the great imposture of our times", a "heroico-humanistic bric-à-brac, a chaplet of hollow ideas culminating in a purely sentimental idealism". Georges Fradier, writing five years ago in *Le Figaro Littéraire*, was forced to confess he couldn't stand little princes—"Princes in general. But above all little princes, with their blond curls, their flutelike voices, their charming caprices, their suave sighs, and their beautiful deaths". Another critic, Jean-Louis Bory, has even raised the question: *Can One Save Saint-Exupéry from Saint-Ex?* His chief objection being the cult that had been made of "this divinity in blue uniform, whose name has been shortened for the convenience of the daily service . . . this rapt profile made for pious medallions like those which proper young men of the good Catholic bourgeoisie hang against their skin at the root of the neck".

It is not the purpose of this book to answer these accusations, which really tell us more about their authors than they do about Saint-Ex. But that his work, twenty-five years after his disappearance (somewhere between Corsica and the Alps, in July 1944), should continue to arouse such controversial heat is a tribute to its abiding impact; for it is only a "dead" book which inspires no debate. It is also a tribute to his many-sided personality which has consistently baffled those who like to be able to classify people in neat pigeon-holes as, for example, "rightist" or "leftist", "arch-reactionaries" or "authentic revolutionaries". Born of a noble family that had a privileged access to *la vie de château* of the early years of this century, Saint-Exupéry was one of those blessed "children of the Gods", as Thomas Mann liked to call them; but those who most fascinated him were not such heroic prototypes as Goethe or Tolstoy, they were Dostoevski and Nietzsche, "the children of the Night". This was only one of the many paradoxes which distinguished this paradoxical being. He was a man of action who hated exercise, a poet who deliberately turned his back on rhyme and limited himself to prose. He was a mathematician of no mean talent who ended up condemning the cult of mathematics; an unbeliever who wanted desperately to believe in God. In his actions he was more profoundly committed than Jean-Paul Sartre has ever sought to be, but the word "*engagé*" occurs only twice, or perhaps three times, in all his writings. He became one of the great French stylists of this century, but he was not and did not wish to be a *professional* writer. This, of course, was and remains an unpardonable affront to those "sub-intellectuals"—as Eugène Ionesco likes to call them—who instinctively recognise in him what they most resent: the intrusion of the gifted outsider, whose life happened to be—oh insult! oh injury!—so much more glamorous than their own. As Gilbert Cesbron wrote, a couple of years ago, à propos of these detractors: "Saint-Exupéry, you see, was basically a flyer, nothing more. Why then did he busy himself with writing? Did he not realize that this is a terrain reserved for those who live off it, for those squids attached to their rock who have only their ink to defend themselves with, for that envious and venomous tribe upon whose territory it is unwise to venture? Their sacred hexagon is marked out by Gallimard, *L'Express*, the *Nouvel Observateur*, the Brasserie Lipp and the Café de Flore. This is their jungle and their paradise: *Terre des Hommes de Lettres.*"

Less discriminating than the mandarins who would like to dismiss Saint-Exupéry as a second-rate writer of "unreadable books", the general reading public, both in France and abroad, has recognized him as one of his country's great authors. Neither Marcel Proust, nor Louis-Ferdinand Céline, nor André Gide, nor any of the eight Frenchmen who have won the Nobel Prize for Literature in this century—with the single exception of Albert Camus—have been able to match the sale of his books abroad. In France his success has been even more extraordinary; for according to a best-seller list recently compiled by the *Quid* almanach, Saint-Exupéry is the only French writer of our century who has been able to place three books in the first ten (*Vol de Nuit* in fourth place, *Terre des Hommes* eighth, *Le Petit Prince* ninth. See Notes and Acknowledgements, page 575.)

Popular judgements are notoriously fallible and fickle, but it seems unlikely that some new vogue or "wave" will now be able to alter the position Saint-Exupéry has won for himself as a French classic. His popularity beyond the borders of France is all the more remarkable, in that— unlike Sartre, Malraux, or Camus—he wrote in a lyrical, poetic style made to tax the best translator. The difficulties were compounded for Anglo-Saxon readers, ill accustomed to the historic present, which comes so naturally to the French.

"It is a matter of indifference to us whether a book be written in a library or a house of ill fame, but we are unwilling to have it emanate from a group of sterile poseurs who have never lived in a truly valid manner", Richard Aldington wrote more than twenty years ago, at a time when Jean-Paul Sartre and Paul Valéry could only get themselves read by a handful of American intellectuals, whereas *Wind, Sand, and Stars* and *Flight to Arras* had been read by hundreds of thousands. "As we all know, Saint-Exupéry was a pioneer of the heroic days of flying, an already distant and legendary period. Here too there was a danger. There is a lot of aviation literature written by aviators, some of it good, but most of it mediocre and the product of paid scribblers, of that proletariat of popular literature. I feel that we should class Saint-Exupéry among the finest writers, not only because he transcribed his own experiences with such fidelity, rejecting even the most legitimate inventions, but because his moral and intellectual aims conferred a sense and a dignity to his acts. This is the difference between an adventurer and a hero."

Aldington, admittedly, had an axe to grind—as he demonstrated later in his book on T. E. Lawrence. But the distinction he here established is vital. I shall leave it to the reader to decide just what Saint-Exupéry was, but of one thing I am certain: he was much more than an adventurer.

                                                                    C.C.

ANTOINE DE SAINT-EXUPÉRY

# 1

## The Lindens of Saint-Maurice

INSIDE the cockpit it was uncomfortably hot. But such had been his experience with each new sortie. Decidedly this was a job for winter rather than the dog-days of late July. For the take-off at any rate. The heat at this hour of the morning—a little after eight—was still relatively mild, but the padded flying-togs he had just climbed into were enough to induce a clammy sweat. Burdensome too was the Mae West he wore around the waist, like the oxygen flask strapped to his left shin which he would need if forced to bail out at thirty thousand feet. A charming prospect for someone who could hardly close, let alone open his cockpit cover!

The one thing he had managed to shed was the 45 calibre revolver he was supposed by regulations to carry, in case he were shot down over enemy territory. Like his companions, who had done the same, he hardly saw himself in the role of a Hollywood hero, successfully shooting it out with a company of German soldiery. It would be miracle enough if he survived the fall. He had ceased to believe in miracles, but the flask was another matter. Unlike the revolver it was a symbol of salvation, a life-buoy designed for stratospheric heights. It was an encumbrance he had to wear to preserve appearances and to reassure himself as much as others that he was playing the game. It was the tribute he had to pay to those rites without which—be it war or peace—nothing in this transitory life has solid substance or structure. A tangible elixir, it felt more like a prisoner's ball and chain, the onerous reminder of how fragile was his fief. For once in the cockpit he was no longer free. He was, as he had once written, like a pipe in its pouch. As cramped as a crustacean. He was the prisoner of his body, and his body was the prisoner of this metal carapace. As bound to its caprices as a captain to his ship's.

Crouched on the plane's left wing, Lieutenant Raymond Duriez, the Acting Operations Officer, made a final check of the parachute straps, the mouth-phone, and the oxygen flow. The functioning of the camera shutters

I

was verified. Nothing must be left to chance, though as Duriez well knew, chance in such cases often had the final word.

All seeming in order, he helped lower the cockpit cover, something the pilot had trouble doing unaided—the accident he had suffered in Guatemala making it difficult for him to raise his left arm above shoulder level. This done, Duriez slipped off the wing and nodded to the mechanic. The first and then the second engines were started, with sudden coughing roars and gusts of gaseous wind which flattened the grasses like invisible scythes. Harnessed into his gear like a Percheron into its traces, the pilot could feel the machine begin to strain at the leash. His eyes swept the mass of dials in front of him, his forehead furrowed into that rigid concentration which was so often his when he was alone with his thoughts and not doing card tricks or laughing at the tribulations of his squadron mates, forced to sit stoically at table while pitcher-fulls of water were emptied over their heads.

Finally he raised his hand to the microphone beneath his chin.

"Colgate, here is Dress Down Six calling . . ." he began in an awkward, barely intelligible English, ". . . may I taxi and take off?"

"O.K. Dress Down Six. You can taxi and take off."

The unmistakably American voice came from the control-tent, located half a mile away on the edge of the strip.

There was a brief wave from the pilot, to which Duriez replied with a wave of his own as the mechanic pulled away the wheel-blocks. The Lightning— No. 223 of the 2/33 Photo Reconnaissance Group—bumped its way over the dirt and the grass towards the end of the field, where began the perforated metal strip which served as a runway for the Spitfires flown by the British and the Lightnings flown by the French and the Americans. It had taken the war to transform what had once been a small field for air enthusiasts into something more ambitious, and, planes excepted, a shack off to one side and near it a single hangar were the only indications that this was an airfield at all.

A minute or two later the Lightning was airborne, soaring up over the coast like a throbbing bird of prey. At high noon its twin-tailed shadow would have flitted across the stagnant waters of the Biguglia lagoon, now spread out below like a clouded mirror. To the left the rugged mountains rose in wrathful splendour, cradling ochre-hued fortress-villages which the harsh wisdom of the centuries had perched atop their foot-hills a respectful distance from the Saracen-infested shore. Bastia, with its Genoese campanile, slipped backwards and out of sight, its formidable ramparts as vulnerable from the air as an oyster in its opened shell. Off to starboard the rocky mass of Elba and the Ligurian archipelago rose softly from the sea.

Ahead, just thirty minutes distant on the map but already forty-four months removed in time, was the land of France he had left in 1940.

"I have aged so much I have left everything behind." That was four years ago, when he was playing hide-and-seek with Messerschmitts and braving the flak. Beneath him, ten kilometres down, he had spied a dark spot in the landscape which from this elevation had meant absolutely nothing to him. Yet it could well be a large country-house such as he had once known . . . with two uncles pacing up and down a dusky vestibule and "slowly constructing in the consciousness of a child something as fabulous as the immensity of the seas". And for a moment his thoughts had fled back . . . "When I was a small boy . . ." It was like a tale beginning: "Once upon a time . . ." "When I was a small boy . . . I am going back a long way in my childhood. Childhood—that vast territory from which each of us has come!" And he, where was he from? And the answer had come back with the sureness of an echo: "I am from my childhood." *Je suis de mon enfance comme d'un pays*. From a land as small as a dark hallway and yet as large as the universe. From a land . . . from a land over which he would soon be flying at the same abstract altitude of thirty thousand feet. Gently it would come out to meet him, rolling the flat expanse of water into faintly iridescent ripples, with glimpses of white beach showing like a slip beneath its undulating folds and Porquerolles and Hyères drifting out to sea like drugged leviathans. Beyond, lost in its valley of scrub oak and firs, he would sense the invisible presence of the Château de la Môle. La Môle, with its soft pink creeper and the old tiled tower where Dumas' Chevalier once played host to Queen Margot, and Paula, their Tyrolean governess, had charmed them with her bedside tales.

And here, hopefully unobscured by clouds, would come the Esterel, with Agay planted like a gem on one of its knuckled coves. Agay—the very name spelled joy!—where Consuelo had dazzled the family with her dark-haired radiance and the blood-red roses she had tucked into her hair beneath the bridal mantilla. If he was lucky, he might be able to distinguish its old sea-fort walls, but only for an instant, as inexorably it slipped behind and out of sight, pulled out from under him like a rumpled carpet. Rolling back in waves, the hills would build into mountain chains and ridges, angrily heaving up their knife-edges towards him, and as he neared Annecy he would have to keep himself from straining down for a distant glimpse of Saint-Maurice and its dark lindens, now reduced to a smudge. Saint-Maurice, which his debt-crippled mother had been forced to sell a dozen years before . . . For here too only memories remained. Memories of picnics on the banks of the Ain, with its mountain-green waters swirling and gurgling their way down to the Rhône. With Lyon a few kilometres farther on, trapped in its branchwork of rivers. Lyon, the most solid, most bourgeois of French cities . . .

They had first left the apartment when he was not quite four, and here even the memories were blurred. Save for Fourvières, with its basilica built high up on the hill, where they would go for Sunday Mass, hauled up by a clanking funicular. Walking on through the tunnel and the turn-stile, he would gape up at the walls plastered with advertisements for "Girardot's Linen Sheets—sovereign soother of aches, pains, and wounds". Strange that those words should have impressed themselves so deeply on his infant imagination. Thirty years later they had surfaced from the sub-terranean depths of his subconscious when his friend Guillaumet had returned, long after he had been given up for lost, like a ghost from the land of the dead. "And shortly afterwards I brought you to Mendoza, where the white sheets flowed over you like a balm."

A balm for the body. A balm for the soul . . .

\*    \*    \*

The wartime landing-strip has long since disappeared beneath the broad expanse of concrete on which Air France planes from Nice and Paris now take off and land several times a day. A gleaming new airport building has similarly replaced the small orange-hued control-tower which was built not long after his disappearance, and today the only momento of his passage is a slab in a hedge-girt flower-bed recalling that "from here the writer-aviator De Saint Exupéry flew off on 31 July 1944 on his last war mission".

The memory of his Lyon birthplace has been better preserved, for the house at No. 8 Rue Alphonse-Fochier still stands. An oval plaque above the modest doorway informs us that "Here was born Antoine de Saint-Exupéry, 29 June 1900." The street was then known as the Rue du Peyrat, after a Lieutenant-General of François Premier's Sénéchaussée whose memory, the city fathers decided in 1909, had less rightful claim to recognition than that of the eminent obstetrician for whom it is now named. Situated on the corner of the Rue du Plat, the house was originally the dependency of a *maison-forte* where the king's soldiery were quartered, and the curved and triangular lintels of its windows are, even more than the grime obscuring them, genuine products of the seventeenth century.

His parents occupied the third floor, and it was here that Antoine spent the first years of his life. What memories he may have garnered were all but totally effaced by the more vivid impressions of later years, and he never seems to have developed any particular attachment to the city of his birth. Neither of his parents was Lyonnais, and their temporary settling here was something of an accident. His father, Comte Jean de Saint-Exupéry, had been brought up in Le Mans and might never have met the young lady who was to become his wife had the Compagnie du Soleil, the insurance company he worked for, not sent him to Lyon as inspector in 1896.

Antoine's mother, born Marie Boyer de Fonscolombe, descended on her father's side from a family which had long formed part of the aristocracy of Aix-en-Provence, while her mother, *née* Alice Romanet de Lestrange, came from an old Vivarais family, different branches of which had produced an archbishop, a Papal Nuncio, a reformist Trappist abbot, an ambassador, a court chamberlain, a number of Knights and even a Marshal of the Order of the Maltese Cross. The Vivarais—the local name for that hilly region which stretches down the right bank of the Rhône between Vienne and Valence, lies closer to Lyon than to Aix or Marseille: which may explain why Alice de Romanet's aunt, Gabrielle de Lestrange (Marie de Fonscolombe's great aunt and thus Antoine's great great aunt) chose to marry a nobleman from the region, Comte Léopold de Tricaud. The marriage brought her a country-house situated some twenty miles northeast of Lyon and also an apartment on the Place Bellecour where, not long after his arrival in the city, Jean de Saint-Exupéry was introduced to Marie de Fonscolombe.

It was but a few yards from the corner house on the Rue du Plat to the spacious square, with its shaded centrepiece of trees and its fine seventeenth and eighteenth century mansions. One of the finest was No. 1, whose ornate overhanging balcony and flat brown-tiled roof recall the proud façades of Italy or Spain. Here, on the second floor, the Comtesse de Tricaud lived on a scale and with a style which made hers one of the fashionable salons of Lyon. Wednesday night was traditionally "open house", when anyone fortunate enough to have the proper introductions was welcome to dinner.

Fifteen years before Antoine's birth Gabrielle de Tricaud had lost her husband, and to add to her sorrows her only daughter had died of diphtheria at the age of three. She loved youth and was happy to have the void filled by her goddaughter and great niece, Marie de Fonscolombe, and—after her marriage to Jean de Saint-Exupéry—by her expanding brood. For Antoine was preceded by two sisters—Marie Madeleine (born in 1897) and Simone (born in 1898)—and followed by a brother, François (born in 1903). The youngest sister, Gabrielle, was not yet born when in March of 1904 Jean de Saint-Exupéry died after a protracted illness culminating in a stroke. A common adversity now strengthened the bonds between widowed aunt and widowed niece, whose family the older lady now adopted as her own. During the winter months Antoine and his sisters thus had the run of her salon on the Place Bellecour; and when, shortly before Easter, the Comtesse de Tricaud closed her Lyon apartment, it was with her great niece and her infants that she moved out to the country estate at Saint-Maurice-de-Rémens.

The trip in those days was made by *omnibus*—a puff-puffing local composed of gaily-painted carriages (yellow for second class) into which one climbed directly by tugging at the large brass handle of the compartment door. Over the same tracks now used by diesel-powered *autorails* these quaint old coal-burners would chug their way past the Brotteaux marshalling-yards and the northeastern suburbs of Lyon. Beyond Meximieux the *omnibus* rattled across the metal viaduct spanning the green waters of the Ain and ground to a halt three miles farther on at the little station of Leyment, where the ticket-collector also acted as *gardien* for the raising and lowering of the level-crossing barrier. A landau would be waiting with Henri Jeanton, the coachman, to jog them the remaining mile up the straight road, hedged with berry-bushes, which led to the property at Saint-Maurice.

Built on a slight rise overlooking a broad valley of clovered pastures and wheatfields, the village of Saint-Maurice-de-Rémens has added electricity, tarred roadway, and a few circumambient houses but has otherwise changed little over the past sixty years. The old tiled roofs with their huge overhanging eaves link it to the Savoie rising to the East, but under the spreading chestnut on the square—an irregular expanse of ground flanked by light-barked plane-trees—the locals still gather to play bowls, as in any village in Provence. Immediately behind the Hôtel Restaurant de la Place—which fails to rate a fork or even a bedspring in the Michelin Guide—the road leads up an incline towards the southwestern end of the village where, hemmed in by barns and farm buildings, is the entrance to the property where Antoine de Saint-Exupéry spent the happiest months of his youth.

To the right of the gate, as one enters the front court, the tall-roofed carriage-house is still to be seen; but to the left the tiny chalet which Jean de Saint-Exupéry made into his office and which his widow Marie later used as a studio for her paintings has disappeared. As has the verandah which screened the entrance and where the Comtesse de Tricaud liked to enjoy the late afternoon sun and the view beyond the gate over the valley to the ridge of Chalamont and Bublane. From this side the house, with its greyish walls and rather ungainly slate roof, looks more forbidding, as though the architect had deliberately intended it to turn its back to the road. In fact, this rear façade was added during the nineteenth century to an ensemble which, when viewed from the garden or park side, reveals the graceful symmetry of a Louis XVI mansion. Adorned with a curved centrepiece—to break the line of the roof—and two terraced wings in the flat Palladian style which became the fashion in eighteenth century France, this older portion was originally built to provide a suitable residence for a second son. For the Tricaud family's principal seat, located four miles up the valley at Ambérieu, was and remains a far grander edifice, with a proud stone balcony running the entire length of the façade and not less than thirteen first-floor windows which stare sullenly out over an ivy-covered wall. The view from here is also more spectacular, for the château at Ambérieu sits on a hill commanding the entrance to the rocky gorges which meander eastward towards Culoz, the Lac de Bourget, and Aix-les-Bains. Embarrassed, like so many other noble families, by the revolutionary upheavals which put an end to the *ancien régime*, the Comtes de Tricaud were forced for part of the nineteenth century to relinquish the mansion built at Saint-Maurice; but under the Second Empire they had regained enough of their pristine affluence to be able to reacquire it some time before Comte Léopold's death in 1885. An ardent traveller, the Count was often absent for months at a time, whereas the Countess was never happier than when at home; and being a hospitable person who liked to preside over a comfortably full house, she had made Saint-Maurice a second home for her goddaughter and great niece long before the latter's marriage to Antoine's father.

Only after one stepped from the verandah past a glass-paned door into the luminous vestibule beyond did the house begin to exercise its rustic charm. Warmed in the morning by transversal rays of sunlight flooding in over the black and white marble floor through the French window at the farther end, it would slowly cool through the hot summer afternoons, as the sun veered towards the west. With nightfall it would sink into a brooding darkness—haunted by a flickering oil-lamp—that was both mysterious and faintly chill; yet the children, with that impassioned desire to be grown-ups which is the secret yearning of all youth, would tarry here in the leather armchairs or on the oak chests after dinner, listening to their uncles converse about a world which seemed all the vaster for being so unknown. Far more than the dining-room, to which they were only admitted during meal-time, or the salon, to which the grown-ups retired to play bridge while they were sent upstairs to bed, the cool hallway was their domain. Its four chests of carefully beeswaxed oak, each two feet high and three yards long, which ran along the walls were just the right height for them to sit on and were used for storing toys as well as books and music scores. Some of these toys were home-made and not above rebelling against their lot—as happened one day when the children opened a chest and recoiled in horror at the sight of doll faces (made from potatoes) that had sprouted hallucinating noses.

For the most part the furniture at Saint-Maurice was nondescript, in keeping with the questionable taste of the period. But this is something a child would only begin to perceive much later; and in the eyes of the young Antoine the dining-room, to the left of the hallway, with its ceiling carved of walnut woodwork squares and its ponderous Italianate buffet, was rich with gothic mystery.

At the other end of the vestibule, by the stone steps leading to the upper storeys, were three ground-floor rooms occupied by Marie de Saint-Exupéry and her two eldest daughters. The salon was across the hallway to the right, and its shuttered windows likewise looked out on to the park. Beyond it was the library and then a billiard-room. A dark corridor, to which one gained access through a small door carved in the ceiling-high oak panelling in the middle of the vestibule led through to a smaller salon, the "almoner's room", the sacristy, and finally to the chapel, the triplet window of which was surmounted by a tiny tympanum representing two angels holding a small child over a replica of the château and the inscription: *"Eamos et Nos"* (Let us also go). For at Saint-Maurice, as in most French families at the time (particularly in the country) vespers after dinner were part of the daily ritual. While the servants filed in from the court outside, the Countess' personal maid would send her little granddaughter in to the salon to announce: *"Madame la Comtesse, on va à la prière."* Candlestick in hand, the Countess led the procession into the chapel, where she alone was entitled to a cushion, the gift of an orphanage she supported in Lyon, while the rest of the company had to be content to kneel on hard oak pews or wooden chairs. Some of the prayers were said in Latin, which she recited with a dowagerial disregard for grammar and vocabulary, which in any case meant little to her, while her singing, often brazenly off-key, was also the source of much hidden merriment. The children, being children, were amused and one of their impish delights was trying to eavesdrop on her confessions:

*"Mon père*, I cannot forgive myself for having uttered an oath."

"Oh, *Madame la Comtesse* doubtless had her reasons."

Far from being irksome, this respect for form seems to have impressed the young Antoine. Here was first born in on him the importance of rites and rituals which give a structure to the otherwise haphazard chaos of existence. *"Il faut pour exister, autour de soi, des réalités qui durent"* he was to write in his first book. Enduring realities to which this Mother Protectress paid homage every evening out of a sense of patrician duty and responsibility. One can find her, transmogrified, in the figure of the Berber chieftain, the Old Testament Patriarch, the Philosopher-King, whose son Saint-Exupéry imagined himself to be in his last work, *Citadelle*. "And the rites are in time what the home is in space . . . Thus I walk from fête to fête, from anniversary to anniversary, from grape harvest to grape harvest, as I walked, yet a child, from the Council Chamber to the chamber of rest . . . in the depths of my father's palace, where every footstep has a meaning."

Palatial the home at Saint-Maurice may not have been, but it was roomy enough to allow for several contiguous realms. Thus the first floor was reserved for the countess and her faithful maid-servant, the "Veuve Grandjean", more familiarly known as "Nana". The second floor was reserved for the children. The scale up here was smaller, the low square windows being barred with grillwork to keep the young ones from climbing out on to the balustrade and falling off the roof. Here the young Antoine, his younger brother François, and his still younger sister Gabrielle occupied two adjoining rooms walled with gaily coloured paper. The boys' room was heated on colder days by a tiny porcelain stove whose cosy "snoring" was to remain one of the most precious memories of Antoine's youth. It was in this room, by the light of a large oil lamp suspended from the ceiling, that he began to cover sheets of paper with the first drawings which were later to flower into the charming illustrations for *Le Petit Prince*. Here too he kept a little tapestry-covered casket into which, as his mother would wistfully remark years later, "he often stuffed letters he forgot to send me"; but that was after he had learned to write and when the fairytale world of youth was already beginning to succumb to the insidious assaults of reality. For the casket began by being a magic treasure chest where the little blond-haired boy would solemnly hide his charms and his secrets. And like Bluebeard, or what he thought was Bluebeard in the tale he had listened to, he would open the casket and say to his mother or his nurse: "Madame, here are the chests where I have laid the dying sunsets to rest."

They made a spirited trio, and particularly the two boys—"Tonio" and François—who were forever scrapping and romping. "They were, one must admit, unbearable", Simone, the older sister, recalls "but as two boys brimful of life are apt to be when there is no father around to keep them in line. They fought and obeyed no one. In the mornings their floor resounded with mad scamperings. Antoine would refuse to take his bath and wriggle himself clear of his fearful governess's grasp. Without a stitch on he'd gallop up and down, making fun of her. Or, because François refused to listen to his stories, saying: '*T'es bête, Flonflon, t'es bête!*' he would jump on him and the fisticuffs would start all over. They used to take their meals separately with their governess and their youngest sister, but usually piercing cries and vehement refusals—'No, I won't eat any carrots!'— would trouble the digestion of the grown-ups. Occasionally my exasperated mother would decide to bear down on them, giving them a thrashing—with a slipper. But wielded by a hand which was anything but fierce, this inoffensive weapon, far from hurting them, only made them roar with laughter."

The governess who had so much trouble keeping these rambunctious children in order was called Marguerite Chapays. In the village of Saint-Maurice everyone called her "Mademoiselle Marguerite," but Antoine and his sisters preferred to call her "Moisy"—a childish distortion of "Mademoiselle." Her sighs and her "*Quel malheur!*"—a source of endless amusement to the children—later reappeared in *Terre des Hommes* (*Wind, Sand and Stars*) in a famous passage where the ageing governess is described, trotting "like a rat" from one "solemn wardrobe to the next, ever checking, unfolding, refolding, recounting the bleached linen and exclaiming: '*Ah Mon Dieu, quel malheur!*' at each new sign of wear threatening the house's eternity, immediately scurrying to strain her eyes under a lamp, to resew these torn altar-clothes, to restitch these mainsails, to serve I know not what greater than herself, a God or a three-master."

This notion of the house, launched like a vessel on the seas of time, a notion which recurs throughout Saint-Exupéry's work, seems to owe much to his youthful visits to the attic. "On rainy days," his sister Simone recalls, "we used to play charades or we would explore the attic. Heedless of the dust and falling rubble, we would scour the cracks in the walls and tap the beams, searching for the *treasure*, for a treasure exists, we thought, in every old house. This hidden treasure which we were sure was there cast its spell over the whole of Antoine's existence." Or, as he himself put it in his first book, "we would take refuge among the attic's beams. Enormous beams defending the house against God knows what. But yes, against time. For there was the enemy. We kept it at bay with traditions and the cult of the past. But only we, among those enormous beams, knew that this house was launched like a ship. Only we, visiting the holds and the bulwarks, knew just where she was leaking. We knew by which holes the birds crept in to die. We knew each crack in the timbering. Down below the guests conversed and the pretty ladies danced. What a deceptive security! No doubt liqueurs were being passed around. By black-clad waiters with white gloves. While we, up above, watched the blue night pour in through the cracks in the rooftop and saw a star, just one lonely star, drop on us through a tiny hole."

When it had rained and the air was specially clear the children on the second floor could gaze out over the firs, the lindens and the chestnuts at the end of the garden and glimpse the distant blue-grey peaks around Grenoble. Nearer by the forest of La Servette, on its dark green ridge, beckoned to them with its quaint square-towered castle, nestling among the trees. The scent of wet grass and fresh cowdung would waft in from the fields, born by

the wind, sighing through the pines and carrying the sound of the village
bell. But much as they liked to venture out for walks, going to wade as they
grew older in the brook waters of the Albarine or in some sheltered pool of
the swiftly flowing Ain, the park, two hundred yards long by as many wide,
provided them with a kingdom vast enough for their youthful fancies to
roam in. Each child had his moss, leaf, and branch built "house" in a separate
clump of lilac bushes at the farther end of the park; and they were even
fitted out with rustic hearths, made of stones, over which—in clouds of
smoke and flame which threatened at any moment to ignite their fragile
constructions, they would vie with each other in the frying of pancakes or
the baking of potatoes. The boys shinned up the trunks of the lovely dark
pines and built huts on the lower limbs. Mimma—a nickname for the eldest
daughter Marie Madeleine—and Simone ran rabbit races through the rose
arbours. And then there was the vegetable garden, to the left of the house and
beyond the avenue of lindens, which alone covered over three or four acres.
Here Eugène Bouchard, the gardener, helped the children plant "their"
vegetables which they later sold—at exorbitant prices—to the grown-ups.

A particular fondness for animals and flowers was shared by all of the
children, beginning with the eldest, Marie Madeleine, who stopped picking
flowers because she did not want to see them "suffer." Later she even wrote
a delightful children's book called *Les Amis de Biche*—"Biche" being another
of her nicknames, and her "friends" including the hoot-owl, the fox, and
the ferret.

Their love, as so often happens with children, was almost embarrassingly
possessive. A "tame" tortoise was hooked up with a lead string so that it
could be taken out for walks. "Tell me Paula," the little Antoine would say
to their Tyrolean governess, "what was it like when you were a bear?" Or a
lion? Or an elephant? And Paula would have to describe her previous
incarnation as a pachyderm. Even the humblest creatures were the objects
of a particular solicitude. One day, when his mother walked unexpectedly
into the upstairs playroom, the little François silenced her with a finger:
"Mama, don't speak—I'm listening to the music of the flies."

The morning of her birthday—always a big event—there would be a knock
on the door. It was the children bringing their gifts. This time it was a book,
offered her by "Biche" (Marie Madeleine) and "Monot" (Simone). François
came with a lovely white stone, and "Didi" (Gabrielle) with a pin-cushion
into which, with the help of the housekeeper, her little fingers had sewn ten
stitches. Antoine presented her with a poem:

> *Dieu t'a donné la grâce et la beauté*
> *Et tu nous chéris, quelle félicité!*

She kissed them with tears in her eyes and told them that there would be a picnic that day—under the chestnuts in the wood. They would hold a snail race with the little horned creatures Antoine and François had been busy training for the past week. Then they would all go to friends for tea. The picnic was delicious, Marie de Saint-Exupéry recalls, "but when the start was given the snails refused to budge. To tell them apart they had been painted different colours, and this had probably asphyxiated them."

Seated outside on the lawn or in the cool shade of the lindens, her dark hair hidden by the billowing brim of her straw hat, Marie de Saint-Exupéry would work at her easel while her children played and gambolled about her. A charming group photograph, taken around 1905, shows her holding her infant daughter Gabrielle in her arms, while Antoine, casually lolling in a wheelbarrow, leans his thick mop of blond hair back against his sister Simone and Marie Madeleine looks on with a disapproving pout. Another photograph from about the same period shows the young widow with her long hair piled up over her head and spilling down over the forehead, the elegant frilled dress rising straight up to the dark bow in the back and the neckband under the chin, as she might have appeared in a portrait by Renoir. Dark haired and dark eyed, she was both slimmer and taller than her great aunt, and to the natural grace of her features was added a veil of inner long-suffering wrought by the early death of her husband and the tribulations of her eldest daughter, plagued as she grew older by recurring fits of epilepsy.

Her children, beginning with Antoine, worshipped her; for she was all love and found it difficult, no matter how badly they kicked up, to utter a reproving word. "When she wanted to paint us," recalls her daughter Gabrielle, "she would say: 'Sit still, and I shall tell you a story.'" And the restless child would sit quite still while the mother, who was a poet as well as a painter, would hold him (or her) in thrall for as long as she wished.

Headstrong as ever, the young Antoine could not wait for his share. Pierre Chevrier, who got to know him intimately in later life, has left us a charming picture of the five-year-old boy, so golden haired that he was sometimes called "*le roi soleil*", laboriously dragging around a tiny green satined armchair, so that he could sit down by his mother's side the moment she found a seat. "*Maman, Maman, racontez-moi une histoire.*" And the harried mother would find herself obliged for the twentieth time, to repeat the story of Joseph and his Brothers or of Rebecca and the Well. Great was the merriment among the grown-ups when the story, often charmingly transformed, was then proudly related to the other brothers and sisters: as on the day when the young François was overheard relating; "And then spake Isaac unto Abraham and said: 'My father, where is the beast? I see none readied for the sacrifice.' And Abraham replied unto him: 'My son, thou art the beast'."

Poet and painter, Antoine's mother was also a musician of some distinction. In her youth she had played the guitar while her brother Hubert and her governess played the mandoline. Her father, Charles Boyer, Baron de Fonscolombe, had become a composer of some talent, and her grandfather, Emmanuel, who played the organ at Aix-en-Provence, had composed masses which are still sung today. Both Marie and her younger sister Madeleine (likewise a frequent guest at Saint-Maurice) had inherited the family gift and were composers as well as pianists. They also sang (Marie contralto, her sister soprano) in the all-feminine choir of the village church, where Antoine's mother played the harmonium for the Sunday Mass.

Once a week a young music teacher by the name of Anne-Marie Poncet, would journey up from Lyon in the *omnibus*, to be met at Leyment by the family coachman. Her father, very much a man about town and at one time the director of the Lyon opera, had staged the premieres in that city of *Lohengrin* and *Die Walküre*—by oil lamps and candlelight, electricity being still unknown. A frequent guest at the Comtesse de Tricaud's "Wednesday Nights," she had been tutoring her niece in the art of singing Schumann *Lieder* and the *fin-de-siècle* airs of Reynaldo Hahn, which then enjoyed a great vogue. At Saint-Maurice it fell to her to tutor not only Marie and her sister Madeleine (who was unmarried) but also the children. Antoine, almost as a matter of course, was brought up to play the violin as well as the piano; and an amusing photograph (from a later period) has been preserved of him dressed in an incongruous pair of jodhpurs and riding boots while sawing away dreamily on a fiddle. There seems to be general agreement that his competence was moderate and that he never approached the virtuosity of his brother François, who inherited the Fonscolombes' musical gift. Though he could work out melodies on a piano, he preferred in later life to entertain the company by rolling oranges or apples up and down the keyboard and saying: "Now tell me if that doesn't sound like Debussy." And no less typically, where his mother loved Schumann and his *Lieder*, Antoine's favourite composer was Bach.

There was one passion which did possess the young Antoine and that was poetry. Here too one can detect the influence of his gifted mother; for it was not from the good Paula, the Tyrolean governess, nor from the devoted but literal-minded "Moisie" who succeeded her, that he could have acquired a precocious taste for odes and sonnets. He was only six when he wrote his first poem, and by the age of seven he was already sketching the outline for a five act opera! One night, his sister Simone recalls when the children were all in bed and it was past eleven o'clock, there was a knock on the door. It was Antoine, dressed in a shirt and with something which looked like a blanket, or it may have been a table cover, draped around his midriff.

"I have come to read some verses," he announced to his startled sisters.

"But Tonio, we're sleeping . . ."

"Never mind. Wake up. We're going to Mama's."

"But Mama's sleeping too."

"We'll wake her up. You'll see. It will be all right."

Mama protested for form's sake, but Antoine had the last word. It was a long word, for the young bard kept the little circle of nodding heads and sleep-swollen lids awake until one in the morning with the reading of his inspired stanzas.

Inspired though he may have been, he had a rival in his sister Simone, of whom their mother later remarked: "It was *she* who had the ideas." She was two and a half years his senior and this gave her an edge—at least in the early years and until Antoine began going to school to acquire a "classical" education in his turn (for the mother insisted on Simone's getting instruction in Latin, much to the horror of her kinsfolk and in-laws who felt this was a pernicious waste of time in the proper upbringing of a young lady). Fairy tales, short stories, novels—anything would do to provide them with "scenes" to be acted out as charades or as "playlets" for the entertainment of the older generation. If, as often happened, there were cousins staying at the château, they would be put to work as additional "stagehands." Anne-Marie Poncet recalls one occasion when Antoine, with his sisters and cousins, decided to put on a play called "The Telephone." Antoine was playing the leading role—that of a husband who, while taking coffee with some friends, rings up his wife, only to discover that their villa is being plundered by bandits. The directions called for "coffee and liqueurs", which the children decided to follow to the letter. Saint-Maurice had a famous stock of brandy and *marc*, including a family speciality known as "*Eau de Vie Lestrange*". When the second act began, there was a bottle of it on the tray, next to the coffee. Just as Antoine was embarking on his hideous discovery—that his wife, back at the villa, was being assaulted by the bandits—up went a cry from the audience. "Why, they've taken my *eau de vie*!" Springing up from her salon armchair, the Comtesse de Tricaud brusquely invaded the "stage" and marched off with the liquor—totally ruining the crestfallen actor's suspense.

A short plump lady with a round fattish face, the Comtesse de Tricaud was not as severe as the T-headed cane she walked about with might have led one to suspect. The twinkle in her bright blue eyes betrayed a robust wit, but unlike the celebrated Marquise de Créqui—that eighteenth-century optimist who once defined "*le savoir-vivre*" as "the art of giving wit to sots", she had little patience with fools or bores. Colonel de Saint-Didier, a card-playing neighbour who lived on the other side of the valley, was finally reduced to coming over without his wife, whom the Countess found "*ennuyeuse à mourir*"—mortally boring. "I see that I am destined to be your last gigolo" the Colonel would twit her, and the Countess would lean back beneath her broad-brimmed hat swathed in muslin and laugh uproariously.

Another assiduous visitor to the château was the *curé*, Father Montessuy, who was appointed to Saint-Maurice-de-Rémens in 1899, one year before Antoine's birth. He was a far cry from the rustic prelate which so small a village should logically have had, and he hardly merited the naughty refrain with which the children used to greet him:

> *M'sieur l'curé, cirez vos bottes*
> *Pour venir nous marier*
> *Car chez nous l'amour, i'trotte*
> *Comme les rats dans un grenier.*

He did not need to be told to wipe his shoes before entering a salon, for he was well versed in the ways of the world and had spent much of his life in Paris, even living through the siege of 1870—an experience he could, if called upon, describe in harrowing detail. A chronic throat ailment had caused him to be "banished" to the healthier air of Saint-Maurice-de-Rémens, where the Comtesse de Tricaud was not long in discovering that he made an excellent bridge partner. Almost too excellent, for one day she could not refrain from upbraiding him: "You earn your living well, Monsieur le Curé. You eat well, you drink my *eau de vie*, and you win at cards." Touched to the quick, the *curé* refused to return to the château and it was the Countess' turn to be mortified. Despairing of ever being able to re-constitute the old quartet, she finally sent one of her favourite nephews, Hubert de Fonscolombe, to inform the offended curate that a particularly succulent collation would be prepared if he consented to come back. The choice of envoy was admirable, for as a young boy Hubert de Fonscolombe had charmed his aunt by the drolery of his Christmas cards—"Dear aunt, the snow covers the earth, but it doesn't manage to freeze my heart," or—to thank her for a more than usually generous gift—"You did not vainly water an ungrateful plant." The young emissary succeeded brilliantly in his mission. Quite disarmed by his quaint speech and the succulence of his message, the mollified Father agreed to come back to the château.

To return to the crowded apartment in Lyon after a summer spent at Saint-Maurice was inevitably something of a let-down. But following her husband's death in 1904 Marie de Saint-Exupéry was invited by her mother to spend the winters at the Château de la Môle, the property of her husband (Antoine's maternal grandfather), Charles de Fonscolombe. Located some twenty miles inland from the bay of Saint-Tropez, in the heart of the wild, sparsely populated region known as *"la chaîne des Maures"*, this château was older and in many ways more picturesque than the property at Saint-Maurice. The foundations of its two round towers (originally there were even four) went back to the twelfth century, when the monks of the Abbaye de Saint-Victor in Marseille had set out to build a refuge where they could rest undisturbed by the fierce Saracen pirates preying on the coast. From the monks it had passed into the hands of various noble families until, just before the French Revolution, Joseph Jean-Baptiste de Suffren, Marquis of Saint-Tropez and of Saint-Cannat, had relinquished it to Emmanuel Honoré Hippolyte Boyer de Fonscolombe. Its most celebrated occupant was the Chevalier de la Môle whom Dumas immortalized in *La Reine Margot*; and in honour of Henry IV's fickle queen, whom her lover sheltered here for a while, one of the castle's old towers to this day is known as *"la tour de la Reine Margot"*.

One can see it today, as one drives up the highway from Saint-Tropez, proudly overlooking the grounds which slope sharply down from its eminence. From a distance it looks slightly naked, though the pale stones and tiled turrets are shaded in the afternoon by the splendid sycamore which Antoine's mother planted there more than sixty years ago. The lovely pink and white creeper which used to cover the façade has gone, and with it the trees and shrubs which used to shield the terrace where Saint-Exupéry played as a child. But in the salon, quaintly vaulted over as is so often the case in old Provençal homes, one can still admire the famous portrait Van Loo painted of a Fonscolombe ancestor.

Here, in his bed at night, the little Antoine could listen to the pitter-patter of the rain drops whipped against the creeper-covered walls by the wet East wind or hear the fierce gusts of the Mistral tug at the restless shutters as it swept away the clouds and filled the night with icy stars. If the weather was fine, the children would climb gaily on to the family's *diligence* to be driven by the coachman down to the junction of La Foux, where they would board the *petit sud* local and chug the remaining few miles into the little port of Saint-Tropez, in those days an obscure fishing village dominated by a ruined Saracen castle. Learning that his name too was Antoine, the engine-driver agreed to let the four-year-old boy ride with him in the locomotive-cab. For days thereafter every scrap of paper or cardboard in the Château de la Môle became a train. This discovery of the marvels of modern locomotion was quickly followed by another, and the next year every rock around the château was transformed into an automobile, which Antoine straddled as though he were riding a horse.

Particularly tender was his memory of the youthful joys of Christmas, when "the light of the Christmas tree, the music of the Midnight Mass, the softness of the smiles enveloped the presents in a special effulgence". For if the day, with the sun and the bees and the flowers, was full of joyous surprises, it was as nothing to the mysterious magic of the night. "And when the moon rose", he wrote in his first book, "you would take our hands and tell us to listen, for those were the sounds of the earth and they were reassuring and they were good. You were so well sheltered by this house, with its sweeping robe of earth. You had concluded so many pacts with the lindens and the oaks and the flocks that we called you their princess. Gradually your face softened as the world was laid to rest for the night. 'The farmer has brought in his beasts.' You knew it from the distant lights of the stables. A hollow sound—'they're closing the sluices.' All was in order. Finally the seven o'clock express stormed through the twilight and disappeared, cleaning your world of all that is anxious and mobile and uncertain—like a face at the window of a sleeping-car. And dinner followed in a dining room that was too large and ill-lit and where—for we were watching you like spies—you became the Queen of Night."

It could have been his mother, a sister, a cousin, a transient guest, or his first childhood love. No matter; but we can recognize the place as Saint-Maurice-de-Rémens. Years later, after a crash landing in an Argentine prairie, Antoine de Saint-Exupéry was startled to be received in a ramshackle mansion where snakes slipped in and out through a hole under the dining-room table. Someone of a less bohemian disposition might have taken fright, but not Antoine, who was suddenly transported back to the enchantments of his youth. "From one room to the next, as though perfumed by incense, I breathed in that smell of an old library which is worth all the scents in the world. Above all I liked the carrying about of the lamps. Real heavy lamps, carted from one room to another, as in the times of my remotest childhood, and which moved marvellous shadows across the walls. We lifted bouquets of light and swept the ceilings with black palms."

As the evening light drained out of the sky and the frogs began their croaking, the *garde champêtre* of Saint-Maurice would shuffle down the street with his little rod and his ladder, lighting the oil-lamps one by one. He too was not forgotten when the young Antoine disappeared within the adult Saint-Exupéry. Years later he reappears as the anonymous lamp lighter of *Le Petit Prince*. And when asked by the Little Prince why he does what he does, he replies with a simplicity which the Comtesse de Tricaud would instinctively have understood: "*C'est la consigne.*" Those are the orders.

In the beginning was the Word; but the Word was an order, and Man's first duty is to obey.

# 2

# Poet and Prankster

---

IN the autumn of 1909 Marie de Saint-Exupéry left Saint-Maurice-de-Rémens and moved with her five children to Le Mans. Antoine, who had received his first notions of French grammar and arithmetic in a day school in Lyon, was now nine, and the time had come to send him to Notre-Dame de Sainte-Croix, the Jesuit school his father Jean had entered in 1872 and his uncle Roger in 1877. His grandfather, Fernand, had settled down here after his forcible retirement from administrative life in 1871, and Le Mans had also become the home of several of his aunts.

Originally the family came from much farther south, even though the exact beginnings—if one can speak of a genealogical beginning (short of Methuselah)—are lost in the depths of the Dark Ages. The first to bear the name was Saint-Exupère, or more exactly Exuperius, a fifth century Bishop of Toulouse whose remains, or what purport to be his remains (including a mitre) are buried in the crypt of the red brick basilica of Saint Sernin (which dates from some centuries later). He was apparently on good terms with Saint Jerome, who dedicated his Commentary on the Book of Zacharias to him, and he also maintained an enlightening correspondence with Pope Innocent I. Whether he left any progeny is immaterial, for his was in the most literal sense a Christian and not a family name, as was also the case with an earlier Exsuperius who served as tutor to the nephews of Constantine the Great. The name's Latin derivation (*ex-superius*, excelling, or to go further back, *ex-superans*, conquering) is obvious, as was true of so many of the earlier French saints—like Sernin (a contraction of *Saturninus*), Sylvius, Hilaire (the jovial), and that blessed Fidis (Faith) of Agen who went on to become the Sainte Foy of Conques and the Santa Fe of New Mexico. Though he never became the object of a comparable cult, Saint Exuperius was long held in equal veneration with Saint Sernin, the first Bishop-martyr of Toulouse; and four or five centuries later the memory of his good works was still strong enough to inspire the parishioners (or at any rate the priest) of a community located roughly midway between Vichy and Limoges to choose him as their guardian—in that chaotic *Sturm und Drang* period which followed the disruption of Charlemagne's empire.

If the good villagers thought that the auspicious nomenclature of their patron saint would be enough to insure their township against wrack, ruin, and destruction, they were alas mistaken. It was too much to hope for in such a dark and violent age, and the *bourg* of Saint-Exupéry (as it came to be called) had the misfortune to end up in the highly unsettled borderland between the Limousin and the Auvergne. Located on a plateau two leagues from the town of Ussel, it was considered of sufficient strategic interest to be incorporated into Henry II of England's realm, after his marriage to Eleanor of Aquitaine; with the result that it was fought over for several centuries between French and British knights. A castle was built on the strategic height, but curiously enough, none of its occupants—from 1248 on—bore the name of Saint-Exupéry. One of them, a certain Marcel Amérigot, having gone over to the British and used the fortress to store his ill-gotten booty, was captured by the French and executed in Paris in 1392. The castle was sacked by the conquering party and again put to the torch (for roughly the same reasons) in 1454. Restored and embellished by later generations, it received its definitive come-uppance in 1791, when the Phrygian-bonneted revolutionaries of Ussel demolished everything but the stones, later used for the building of a more modern habitation.

So much for geography. Historically, the first mention of a country squire by the name of Saint-Exupéry is to be found in an inventory established by the monastery of La Saulière, in the bishopric of Brives, in which it is stated that "in 1235 Raymond de Saint-Exupéry, chevalier, conceded and gave to the Prior of La Saulière the fountain of Loderie and the authorization to have the water pass over the land". Subsequent documents indicate that he and his descendants made themselves the master of lands located in the parishes of Saint-Féréole and Saint-Germain-les-Vergnes, a good fifty miles southwest of the original township of Saint-Exupéry, from which presumably they had sprung. According to one of these parchments, Raymond's grandson Guillaume de Saint-Exupéry received 740 *sous* from his brother Hugues and his sister Pétronelle, to whom he bequeathed all his possessions, "*per visitar lo sepulcre de Nostro Senhor*"—as it is quaintly written in the *langue d'oc* (to this day spoken by the locals). There is no other evidence to prove that he actually made the pilgrimage to the tomb of Our Saviour in the Holy Land, but it was enough to permit later generations to claim that the family descended from the crusaders—in France the *sine qua non* of noble aspiration.

Not that any of this really matters. A later Saint-Exupéry acquired the castle of Miremont, near Mauriac, which was closer to their original home. But the subsequent generations seem to have continued the same south-westerly drift, away from the Limousin and the Auvergne into the Périgord and the Dordogne. In the seventeenth century a Jean Balthazar de Saint-Exupéry could boast the proud title of *"Seigneur de Rouffignac"*—which has since become a mecca for grotto-loving pilgrims. One of the family castles, which has been in its possession for five centuries, is located at Le Fraysse, which is even closer to Lascaux and its prehistoric frescoes. Antoine's great great grandfather, Georges Alexandre Césarée, was born at Moissac, and for several centuries the eldest sons of this particular branch of the family could call themselves Comtes de Saint-Amans and occupy a castle in the region of Cahors.

For the most part they seem to have been unexceptional specimens of rural gentry, content to lord it over lands which were anything but rich in this stony, cave-riddled region of Aquitaine. Tradition (or more likely legend) has it that a prelate by the name of Saint-Exupéry enjoyed consider-able influence at the court of Marie Antoinette, where the charm of his conversation was much prized. The charmer in any case was not one of Antoine's forebears. Not so the gallant Georges Alexandre Césarée de Saint-Exupéry, who boarded the *Triton* in 1779 and saw action against Rodney in the Antilles. He turned up a year later at Yorktown in time to witness Cornwallis' surrender—an event he wrote up for his commanding officer, the Duc de La Rochefoucauld (a descendant of the famous author of the *Maxims*). His exploits as a "Veteran of the American Revolution" failed to help him in 1793 when he was arrested by Robespierre's henchmen and jailed for nineteen months near Bordeaux—along with his wife, the daughter of a French naval captain, who insisted on sharing his captivity. Later they moved to Paris, where their son Jean-Baptiste was appointed an officer in the Military Household of Louis XVIII. The courtier was also a businessman, as he proved by getting rid of the unproductive castle at Saint-Amans in exchange for a property near Margaux, in the Bordeaux wine country. What chagrin he may have felt at losing a title and a couple of turrets was thus comfortably drowned in butts of vintage "Malescot-Saint-Exupéry", justly esteemed by connoisseurs as eminently potable.

Jean-Baptiste César de Saint-Exupéry's only son, Fernand, was Antoine's grandfather. Abandoning the sun-warmed vineyards of Bordeaux after Louis Napoleon made himself Emperor of the French in 1851, he served several of his Ministers of the Interior and was appointed *sous-préfet* of four different departments. Having linked his fortune too closely with those of the Second Empire, he found himself constrained to bid good-bye to administration in September of 1870, on the eve of his thirty-seventh birthday. After the Franco-Prussian war he retired for a while to the Touraine, where his grandmother, a Taschereau, had inherited a property. But being still in the prime of his manhood, he cast around for something less precarious than politics or war and finally found the occupation he wanted in an insurance company with the cheerful name of Compagnie du Soleil. The job may have lacked glamour, but it offered security in what must have seemed to the crestfallen imperialist a highly shaky and dubious republic. He established residence in Le Mans, while his son Jean (Antoine's father) was allowed to sow his wild oats during a term of service with the *Dragons* in Tours. But by and by, as the glamour of spurs and epaulets began to pall, the moustachioed sabre-dragger yielded to sober parental councils and consented to throw in his lot too with the gilt-edged Compagnie du Soleil, leaving it to his younger brother Roger to pursue the foot-slogging career he had begun at the officer training school of Saint-Cyr. Fate may have predestined him to meet and wed the dark and vivacious Marie de Fonscolombe; but it took an insurance company to post Antoine's father to Lyon.

As a younger man Fernand de Saint-Exupéry had sported a thick dark spade beard, of the kind which came into fashion with the generation of Abraham Lincoln and Garibaldi. It had since turned completely white, as had the shrinking islands of hair over and behind his ears which combined with a massive head to give him a decidedly patriarchal mien. He tended to be imperious, as was to be expected of an aristocratic *père de famille* who had sired a family of seven children and served in the administration of the Second Empire. Brought up in a predominantly matriarchal milieu, the young Antoine was not used to this kind of authority and it made for frequent trouble when they met. "My grandfather and Antoine", one of his cousins later recalled, "had this in common, that both being from the Midi, they enjoyed talking a great deal, but my grandfather was intimately persuaded that only grown-ups should hold the floor, while the children listened obediently without saying a word. Antoine was not at all of the opinion that silence is suited to youth. This conflict of opinion was the cause of many recriminations and reproaches, for Antoine always had stories to tell and long explanations to offer".

Marie de Saint-Exupéry seems to have found it equally difficult to adapt herself to her dead husband's family and the dreary, provincial town of Le Mans. The grey stucco house she and her five children inhabited on the corner of the Rue Clos-Margot and the Rue des Fontaines was just one room deep (though several rooms long) and not much roomier than their Lyon apartment. Behind was a postage-stamp garden, with just enough space for some rambler roses, a couple of fruit trees, and twenty yards of lawn—a far cry from the spacious park at Saint-Maurice.

A hundred yards up the street was the house of Paul Gaultier, a day student who used to accompany Antoine to the Collège de Sainte-Croix. As it was a good twenty to twenty-five minute walk to the school, the boys were supposed to join up at 7.30 in time for the start of the 8 o'clock class; but almost every morning, between 6 and 6.30 a.m., the doorbell would ring, and on hearing it the Gaultiers' Breton maid would say: "That must be Monsieur Antoine." She would open the door and the little schoolboy with the unruly mop of hair and the faintly drooping right eyelid would ask: "Excuse me—what is the time?" occasionally adding apologetically, "We don't have a clock at home." In fact, the little corner house on the Rue Clos-Margot had a clock, but the young Antoine was too embarrassed to admit that it didn't work.

Gaultier, who sat for two years on the same school bench, recalls him as "round-faced with a turned-up nose, smiling and at the same time surly, ill-combed, his hair in disorder, the stiff collar of his uniform and his tie as often as not askew—in a word, the untidy student who, like so many others, has ink-spots on his fingers." His schoolmates called him "Tatane"—derived phonetically from "Antoine"—a nickname he minded less than "Pic-la-Lune", later given to him for his upturning "sky-aimed" nose and the moonstruck reveries he could lapse into when daydreaming.

Two youthful letters have been preserved from Antoine's first year at the Collège de Sainte-Croix. The second is worth reproducing, for the quaint perceptiveness of its description of a visit to the Benedictine abbey of Solesmes offers a faint foretaste of his budding literary flair. It was written in the early summer of 1910 at a time when his mother had gone back to Saint-Maurice-de-Rémens, leaving him in the care of a governess and his aunts Anais and Marguerite, his father Jean's sisters who lived in a pleasant Directoire house not far from his mother's.

Dear Mama,
I would like so much to see you again. Aunt Anais is here for one month.
Today I went with Pierrot to the home of a boarder of Sainte-Croix. We had tea and lots of fun. I took communion this morning at the school. I am going to tell you what we did during the pilgrimage: we had to be at the school at a quarter to eight. We formed up to go to the station. At the station we got on to the train as far as Sablé. At Sablé we got into carriages. As far as Notre Dame du chêne there were more than 52 persons per carriage. There were only schoolboys and there were some on top and inside, the carriages were very long and were each dragged

by two horses. In the carriage we had lots of fun. There were five carriages two carriages for the choir boys and three for the school boys. Reaching Notre-Dame du chène we heard the Mass and we lunched afterward at Notre-Dame du chène . . .

After lunch we went to visit the holy sepulchre and we went into the Fathers' Shop and bought things for ourselves. After that the 1st and 2nd division and I went on foot to Solème.

Reaching Solème we continued the walk and we passed by the foot of the abéi it was immense only we couldn't visit it because we didn't have time. At the foot of the abéi we found pieces of marble in great quantity. There were big ones and small ones. I took six and I gave three away and there was one which was about 1 metre 50 and 2 metres long so I was told to put it in my pocket. Only I couldn't even move it and it was too big. Afterward we went and had tea on the grass at Solèm.

I have written you eight pages.

Afterward we went for the blessing and we formed up in rows for the station. Reaching the station we took the trains to come back to Le Mans and we got back to the house at 8 o'clock. I was 5th in Catechism composition.

Goodbye my dear Mama. I kiss you with all my heart.

Antoine

This excursion to Solesmes was an exceptional treat, offering an escape from a drudgery the young student found irksome. About half of the 250 boys attending the Collège de Sainte-Croix were boarders, but Antoine was not one of them, and his hypersensitive nature seems to have suffered from the latent scorn with which boarders tend to treat day students. The class-room discipline was strict and he was regularly punished for his lackadaisical ways, the ink blotches on his fingers, his lack of concentration during study hall, and the unbelievable sloppiness of his desk, so crammed with books, notebooks, and assorted papers that the lid would scarcely shut. His Jesuit teachers, beginning with Abbé Perroux, a gimlet-eyed martinet who drilled Fifth Formers in Latin, Greek, and French, had little use for his reveries and diversions, which were often rudely interrupted. Years later the memory of these humiliations was still vividly with Antoine when he wrote to his mother that "you are the only consolation when one is sad. When I was a child I used to come home with my heavy satchel on my back, in tears at being punished—do you remember at Le Mans?—and simply by taking me in your arms and kissing me you made me forget everything".

The Fourth Form year was less trying, the intractable Perroux giving way to Abbé Margotta, who was less of a disciplinarian and more of an inspirer. The boys called him "Boa" because of his occasional inability to stifle the most colossal yawn, but there was little yawning in his classes. A humble carpenter's son, he had managed to work his way up to the top of the academic ladder (obtaining the "*licence*" required to teach), and in the process he had developed a fervour for literature, and particularly French literature, which he readily communicated to his students. Max de Villoutreys, another of Saint-Exupéry's schoolmates, can still vividly recall his enthusiasm for the French seventeenth century and his "inexhaustible" expatiations on the subject of Molière.

Abbé Launay, who took care of the Third Form, was a classicist whose formidable erudition had won him the nickname of "César". In a photograph taken in 1914 and in which he is shown surrounded by sixteen Sainte-Croix boys (including Saint-Exupéry) in their stiff Eton collars, Lavallière cravats, and Prussian blue uniforms with gold buttons, there is not the faintest flicker of a smile on the grim-jawed face which stares out uncompromisingly under the close-cropped hair. Yet we can be grateful to this unsmiling Father for having once had the wit to set his pupils an unusual subject for composition: "Relate the Tribulations of a Top Hat." The thirteen-year-old Antoine attacked the subject with relish, and the imaginative result offered the first clear sign of his future talent.

### The Odyssey of a Top Hat

I was born already long ago in a large hat factory, where hats of all kinds were manufactured. For several days I underwent all sorts of transformations, not to say tortures: I was cut up, I was stretched, I was varnished. Finally one evening I was sent with my brothers to the largest hatter in Paris. There I was placed in the window; I was one of the handsomest top hats in the display; I was so shining that the women who spied me did not fail to admire themselves in my varnish; I was so elegant that no distinguished gentleman passed by without throwing me a covetous look. I lived in perfect peace waiting for the day when I would make my appearance in the world.

One day a distinguished and richly dressed gentleman walked into the shop. Full of solicitude, the merchant had him admire my brothers, then he showed me off rather longer than the others: was I not the handsomest? At last the client took me, turned me over, looked at me, and finally bought me. From his pocket he pulled a wallet so well garnished that the merchant sold me for twice my real worth: for his maxim in life was never to let slip opportunities . . . or bank notes.

The next day I enjoyed a brilliant outing. My owner, a most elegant gentleman, put me on to go to the Club. All his friends admired my eight reflections, my elegant form, and my other virtues. For several months I thus led a delightful existence. With what care I was kept and dusted! A faithful man-servant, entrusted with Monsieur's wardrobe, took flattering care of me. I was polished every evening, repolished in the morning.

One evening I learned that the coachman was going to get married. My owner, who wanted to give him a present, gave me to him: and from that moment on I sheltered another cranium. Alas! my existence changed completely. The first day I rolled three times in the dust and mud, and oh cruel fate! I was not even wiped off. Filled with a righteous desire for vengeance, I shrank; so much so that the coachman could no longer put me on his head! Then one day he put me under his arm and sold me for six *sous* to a vulgar clothesman. This old gentleman was a frightful Jew; his slightly crooked nose set off a face that was false and spiteful. After being cleaned I was once again placed in the window, but this time I was exposed to public view casually hung on a dirty string. "Mathew! Come here! . . . you need a hat for big occasions; well, here's one that would do perfectly!" And Mathew bought me, while Caroline, his wife, went into raptures over my splendour. I only went out on Sundays; and even then only when the sky was serene; for the price of two francs forty-five paid for me won me a special care.

But one day as Caroline and Mathew were strolling along the quay of the Seine, a furious gust of wind whisked me off with the birds. After several seconds of frightful anguish I landed on the river, and there I floated along quietly in the company of the fish, who looked with fright at this new kind of boat. Suddenly I felt myself being hauled in by a long pole and deposited upon the bank. There a vulgar ragman laid avid hands upon me and soon I underwent new tortures in a dark, dirty shack which turned out to be the shop of the chief hatter supplying Their Majesties the Kings of Africa.

Once again I was packed up; and for several days I travelled thus, wrapped in tissue paper and cardboard. Then, one fine morning, I opened my eyes to the light and was horrified to see some dark beings most of whose faces were taken up by enormous lips, and whose only clothing were outmoded bathing trunks and rings hanging from their noses and ears. Seated off to one side on a case of biscuits, one of these strange men held in his hand a sceptre made from a duster which had lost its feathers, and over his back he wore the skin of a lion he had once doubtless slain with a bravery equal to his girth. I was respectfully seized by two black hands: I started with horror and was only reassured on seeing that the dye did not rub off. Then I was deposited on the summit of the black mass making up the king. And here I have spent some more happy days. Sometimes the overly hot sun has melted my varnish, and the practical sense of my master has occasionally caused me to be used as a saucepan . . . but I still live peacefully enough, adorning the head of the terrible Bam-Boum, the most powerful prince in the land.

I write these lines in my declining days, hoping that they may reach the French; they should know that I live in a country where never will it be the fashion to do without a headpiece; and on the contrary, that when at last I have outlived my usefulness, I shall hope to be venerated as a relic for having once graced the pate of my illustrious owner, Bam-Boum II, King of the Niger.

Antoine de Saint-Exupéry

Abbé Launay was apparently beguiled by the charm of this quaint tale, for he began by according it a grade of 13, later knocked down to 12 (out of 20), adding the dry comment: "Good. Too many spelling mistakes. Style occasionally heavy-handed." Exaggerated it doubtless was and interwoven with the prejudices to be found in an upper class school; but the sureness of perception and the latent humour were already there—as in the description of the gust of wind simultaneously unsettling the top hat and the birds, the duster sceptre which had lost its feathers, and those advancing hands whose awesome blackness did not rub off like dirt or dye.

As might be expected of a boy who was born the son of a count and whose grandfather had served under an Emperor, Antoine de Saint-Exupéry was brought up in a catholic and monarchical tradition. His aunt Anaïs was lady-in-waiting to the Duchesse de Vendôme (King Albert of Belgium's sister) while the French Red Cross circle to which his mother belonged and which was run by the mother of one of his schoolmates (Madame Chapée) was in effect the charitable appanage of an aristocracy which had far more faith in "Throne and Altar" than in the fortunes of a *faute de mieux* republic. The old order throughout most of Europe was still monarchical or imperial, and France was the radical exception rather than the traditional rule. It was also a house divided against itself—not only by the Dreyfus Affair, which was bad enough, but also by the triumph of a militant anti-clericalism which led the Combes ministry of 1905 to decree the disestablishment of the Church.

The consequences were everywhere felt, and not least of all at the Jesuit Collège de Sainte-Croix, which lost the lawsuit it had started as a kind of delaying action. This setback which occurred during his second year, probably caused the young Saint-Exupéry no chagrin; it meant evacuating the barrack buildings the school had occupied on the Rue Notre-Dame (which became the headquarters of the Fourth Military region) and taking refuge in the leafy grounds of a former Capucin monastery. But it would have been asking a lot of the Jesuit fathers who ran the school to feel any particular sympathy for a godless régime which had brought on such vexations; and the same anti-republican prejudices were shared by the majority of the boys at Sainte-Croix, almost all of whom came from upper class families. They were just as naturally shared by the young Antoine, who even undertook to found a royalist committee, of which he made himself the chairman. One day, when asked to contribute to Paul Gaultier's autograph book, he picked up his pen and wrote, as might have done the Chevalier Bayard: "*Pour Dieu, pour le Roi, pour Ma Dame*" (For God, for the King, for My Lady).

The six years Saint-Exupéry spent at Le Mans were far from being the happiest of his life. One of the few bright memories he later retained was of the monthly outings his family would make to the Château de Passay, fifteen miles northeast of the city. Climbing on to the little *tortillard*—the "winder", as the children dubbed the train which snaked its way across the landscape—they would get off at the village station of Sillé-le-Philippe and be driven to the château. It was an imposing tall-roofed edifice, with two splendid wings in the classic Louis XIII style, surrounded by spacious grounds and a little lake on which the children would sally forth, screaming and laughing, in row-boats or engage in mock naval battles. Its owner, the Comte de Sinéty, had several grandsons who had been or were attending the College de Sainte-Croix, as well as a grand-daughter, Odette de Sinéty, a lovely fairhaired girl with bright blue eyes and a captivating smile.

She was something of a beauty for her age, and whenever she turned up for Sunday Mass at the Collège de Sainte-Croix chapel, she was the cynosure of boyish eyes and the cause of much undominical palpitation. As the boys filed in in their Sunday best, she would lean over to Antoine's youngest sister Gabrielle, sitting next to her on the pew, and say: "Let's see if Xavier (or Jean-Claude or Pierre) . . . is going to turn around and look at me." And when, unable to restrain his adolescent yearning, the young man did, the two girls would giggle with mischievous delight.

Though Odette de Sinéty was a good two years his senior, Antoine succumbed in his turn and spent hours in her company reciting poems and talking to her of that marvellous new invention, the "aeroplane". A charming photograph has been preserved of her sister Renée dancing a pavane with Antoine in her mother's garden in Le Mans—she dressed up in a Marie Antoinette *bergère* costume mostly made of paper, he in an eighteenth-century wig and *jabot*, added to his schoolboy uniform, while her younger brother Elzéar stares out impishly between them in his wig

and his brooches. "Antoine loved nature", Odette de Sinéty recalls, "and
he could spend minutes at a time watching a moth or a butterfly. He had
a great intensity of feeling for all animal life. He would never dream of
killing an animal, and if he saw a bird hopping about, he would say: 'Now
what do you suppose he's thinking about right now?' "

In the little drawing book which it was then the fashion for young ladies
to keep, Antoine dedicated two poems to her—one (*La Mort du Cygne*)
describing a swan's dying song, the other (*L'Hallali*) the death of a stag.

> *Le son du cor s'élève et baisse lentement*
> *Fait résonner les bois d'un long tressaillement*
> *Et sur le sol sanglant*
> *Le cerf meurt, et le cor prolonge son beau chant*
> *Tandis que l'Homme heureux d'avoir vaincu la bête*
> *Se dresse plein d'orgueil et relève la tête.*

It was a far cry from Gérard de Nerval or even Lamartine, but the two
final verses describing the hunter proudly lifting his head "happy to have
vanquished the beast" already anticipate the dim view Saint-Exupéry was
to take of bull fighting in the famous section devoted to courage in *Terre
des Hommes*.

This first youthful "passion" seems to have stimulated his literary as
well as poetic verve, for later that same year (1913) he decided to put out
a private magazine called *L'Echo de Troisième*, made up of contributions
from various classmates. Carefully penned on sheets of handsome paper,
they were pasted together to form a small volume. According to Claude
de Castillon, who was one of its "illustrators", it even imitated contemporary
newspaper advertising in carrying extravagant kitchen recipes and advertisements like: "No more reversed nails or strings to hold up your trousers.
BUY X —— Braces!" Several Saint-Exupéry poems were included in the
first issue, which also proved to be the last. "It was passed around from
hand to hand" recalls Max de Villoutreys, "and as it caused a lot of merriment and was read during study hall, it was not long before the secret was
out. It was seized during a study period by the Abbé Desroberts, who
couldn't stand Saint-Exupéry—the 'instigator', he used to call him, of
student prankishness. The issue was confiscated and we never saw it again.
No one knows what became of it."

\*    \*    \*

On June 28, 1914 Archduke Franz Ferdinand of Austria was assassinated
at Sarajevo with his wife, and within six weeks the five major Powers of

Europe were at war. The event transformed the life of the continent, touching off repercussions felt in the humblest homesteads. Before the month of August was out Antoine's uncle Roger de Saint-Exupéry was dead—killed leading his infantry battalion at Maissin. Two of his mother's cousins, Guy and Roger de Lestrange, whom the villagers of Saint-Maurice-de-Rémens had often been able to admire riding around the countryside on horseback, rode off to the war from which they never returned. She herself, having received Red Cross training at Le Mans, was appointed head nurse at the station hospital set up at Ambérieu. Hardly had she taken up her duties when a letter reached her from a sculptor friend she dearly loved. "I am leaving for the front, carrying in my heart all that has slept there for so long." As she stood there with tears in her eyes, the station-master came up and said: "Madame, a train full of wounded is due in at any moment. There's a request for stretchers—tetanus cases." She never saw her sculptor friend again. The international catastrophe later known as the First World War had begun.

It affected her two sons, as it affected everyone else. Wishing to have them closer to home, Marie de Saint-Exupéry entered them in mid-October in another Jesuit school—the Collège Notre-Dame de Mongré, at Villefranche-sur-Saône, northeast of Lyon. They liked it no better than they had the Collège de Sainte-Croix in Le Mans, and after thirteen unhappy weeks there both Antoine and François were withdrawn.

The fact would hardly be worth mentioning but for the reminiscence of this brief passage through the school preserved by two fellow students who went on to become priests. "He was not first in his class nor brilliant in his studies." Father Louis Barjon told Helen Elizabeth Crane in 1951. "He was a nice fellow, yes, liked by everybody, but not that much noticed among the rest. He was above all a dreamer. I remember him, chin in hand, gazing at the cherry tree beyond the window. We called him 'Pique-la-Lune'. I have the impression of someone modest, of someone who was original without being bookish. All of it mingled with occasional explosions of joy, of exuberance. Antoine wrote verses. I recall above all a poem about the death of a swan, visibly inspired by Lamartine. These verses of course were those of an adolescent, full of romanticism and a certain naiveté. We admired this poem very much."

Alban de Jerphanion, another of his classmates at Mongré, later remembered him as having been "a very gifted boy but perhaps not very methodical in his work. I remember that . . . he composed epic poems with a lot of verve, about the war and particularly about Wilhelm II, backing them up with caricatures—caricatures that were original and full of life. He had an extraordinary facility for composition and drawing" . . .

One of these poems about the Kaiser has been preserved, though not unfortunately the drawings which originally accompanied it. In it the German Emperor is depicted as exulting over the spectacle of Reims in flames.

> *D'un maréchal d'Empire, il est accompagné*
> *Et brusquement lui dit : "Qu'avez-vous épargné?"*
> *—La Cathédrale, sire." "Et l'hôpital?" "Il brûle."*
> *—C'est fort bien : votre armée?" "Ah Sire . . . elle recule."*

The news that his army is in full retreat while Reims Cathedral has been spared throws the Kaiser into a dark rage. "Haggard, he draws himself up in the frightful night" and orders the hideous bombardment.

> *Sa lèvre se crispe, son front se fit plus pâle . . .*
> *Vous me bombarderez, demain, la Cathédrale!"*

The sentimentalism of Lamartine has here made way for the heroic beat of Victor Hugo, but the results were hardly more auspicious.

In February 1915 the young bard and his brother were sent back to the Collège de Sainte-Croix in Le Mans and lodged in their Aunt Marguerite's pleasant Directoire house. Tonio won a third prize in French composition, but his anemic health, perhaps abetted by wartime malnutrition, caused him to be sent home in June, three weeks before the presentation ceremonies.

The school to which Antoine and his brother were next sent was the "Villa Saint-Jean", in Fribourg. The war had drained the *lycées* and even the Catholic *collèges* of teachers, and Marie de Saint-Exupéry rightly felt that her two sons would fare better in the neutral climate of Switzerland. Unlike Sainte-Croix du Mans and Mongré, both run by Jesuits, the Villa Saint-Jean was run by fathers of the Marianist order who maintained close links with the famous Collège Stanislas in Paris. Many of its teachers— beginning with Father François-Joseph Kieffer, its founder—were Alsatians who had preferred to emigrate to France or Switzerland rather than go on living within the confines of the Wilhelmian Reich. The idea had originated with a book written at the turn of the century and entitled: *A Quoi tient la Supériorité des Anglo-Saxons?* The French were still suffering from the defeat of the Franco-Prussian war, to which was added in 1898 the humiliation of Fachoda. If the British were doing so well and the French so badly, it must be because of some inherent superiority in the Anglo-Saxon educational system. French educational methods needed revitalizing through contact with another culture, and Fribourg, situated at the confluence of two languages (German and French), seemed ideally suited to the experiment.

The cure, as so often happens, had little to do with the original diagnosis. The country-club architecture of the Villa Saint-Jean's pavilions—with their geranium red roofs and rust-hued timberwork and balconies—paid homage to certain recent Public Schools, like Matthew Arnold's Rugby. So did the first floor dormitories with their porcelain ewers and wash basins and their pitch-pine cubicles (forty cubicles for forty boarders, each with a bed, a bolster, and a bed table with a chamberpot in the bottom drawer). But for the rest the school owed more to the genial personality of its founder. He was a trim little man who wore his hair short and whose chin, in an age of beards, was clean shaven. The metal-rimmed glasses which never left him could not obscure the spark of kindliness in the blue, squirrel-sharp eyes; for if Father Kieffer was a firm, he was also a not unfriendly pedagogue. He believed in a maximum of contact between teacher and pupils—whether at the "German" or "English" tables in the refectory (where French was only supposed to be spoken with the dessert) or on the playing field, and he himself was not above swinging a racket on Sundays, hopping nimbly about the court in his soutane. His office was always open to any boarder who had a problem on his mind or a grievance to unload, just as there was no fence or wall hemming in the school and the grounds from the surrounding suburb to which, if he really wanted to, any truant could escape. The idea, paradoxical as it might sound, was not to impose discipline but to get it liked and thus painlessly accepted. It was summed up in the school motto, one Kieffer had adopted years before from the Chevalier Bayard: "*De Toute Son Ame*" (With all one's Soul), a motto Saint-Exupéry later took an ironic delight in contrasting to the "*Esto Vir*" (Be a Man)—the solemn Stoic maxim common to all the Jesuit schools he attended.

Situated on the airy heights of Pérolles, the school pavilions looked out across the deep cut of the river to the quaint town of Fribourg, with its old burgher houses, its squat Cathedral tower, and the William Tell forts standing watch over its bridges. To the north and east, when it was clear, the snow-covered peaks of the Bernese Oberland basked dreamily beneath a crisp blue sky. Woods full of fragrant pines and elms beckoned from just beyond the soccer field and tennis courts, and anyone who wished to could explore their meandering paths or zigzag down the steep, slope-gripping forest to the lazy green waters of the Sarine, cake-frosted in winter with ice thick enough to skate on.

Yet Saint-Exupéry was not easily won over. Laden with harsh memories of Le Mans and Mongré, he turned up at the Villa Saint-Jean in a defiant mood. The late Paul Michaud, who was in his class, has left us a vivid description of his first encounter with Saint-Exupéry which, though almost certainly inaccurate in two respects, is still highly worth quoting.

"It was between 9 and 10 p.m. one night—in early January of 1915—that I found myself on the station platform of Fribourg. I had eaten several sandwiches in the train, but I felt a lump in my throat as I joined the other schoolboys who had got there before me. A supervisor accompanied us on foot as far as the school.

"I was immediately led up to a large dormitory lit by a pale nightlamp and shown the pitchpine cubicle I was to occupy. It was my first night as a boarder and I was a bit upset. I climbed right into bed and was about to doze off when I saw a dark shape rise up from the cubicle next door and peer down at me.

"You are new here?"

"Yes."

"Where do you come from?"

"Chambéry."

"Have you been a boarder before?"

"No, never."

"Worst luck. This place is a dump. There are two horrors here—the 'Skull' and the 'Lobster'—they're the supervisors. You'll see, really grim and—" Before he could get further a white curtain was ripped back in one corner of the dormitory and I heard one of the supervisors say: 'Saint-Exupéry, you'll be punished tomorrow. Leave your neighbour alone'."

The dark shape vanished back into its cubicle, but a minute or two later it popped up again. "Did you see?" he whispered, leaning over the partition, "that was the 'Skull—a real death head'. . . ."

Memory plays strange tricks, and when Dr. Paul Michaud wrote up this experience, in April of 1966, Saint-Exupéry was more than twenty years dead and the school they had once attended was one half century distant. In fact, Saint-Exupéry did not turn up at the Villa Saint-Jean until November 1915, by which time Michaud had already been there one year. It was thus infinitely more likely that it was Michaud who undertook to initiate the newcomer about the "Skull" and the "Lobster" rather than the other way round. Whatever the truth, one may be certain that there was frequent occasion for Saint-Exupéry to be reprimanded for disturbing the nocturnal slumbers, or pseudo slumbers, of his neighbours.

The "Skull's" real name was Guiot, a humourless mathematics teacher with hardly a hair left on his head. Not long before a student had been expelled for remarking that he had the "skull of a Jesuit," but the nickname had stuck. As for the "Lobster", he answered to the delightful name of Clad. He taught English and his rabid Anglomania was so far fetched that he spoke French with an English accent, affected stiff and what he thought were "very British" manners, and exhibited, over his brown beard, an extraordinary pair of whiskers, protruding horizontally past his cheeks like a crustacean's antennae.

Neither of these two disciplinarians turned out to be quite as fearsome as Saint-Exupéry may first have feared. Any more than proved to be the others, beginning with Abbé Guilluy, who taught philosophy to the seniors. Known as "Zizi" because of his way of pronouncing "s's" like "z's," he would turn apple red whenever one of the boys asked him an embarrassing question. There was the "*Père Simon*," the drawing teacher, who would content himself with a casual glance at his charges' doodlings while he tugged at a wayward hair in his George Bernard Shaw mane; and there was Fritsch, a genial fellow with a shock of hair as thick as his huntsman's moustache, who taught physics and chemistry and helped the boys build radio sets. There was Wahl, who taught German as well as Natural History, a broad-shouldered Austrian with an Henri IV goatee who was said to have entered the Marianist Order and helped Father Kieffer launch the school in 1903 after an unfortunate love affair in Vienna; known as "Papa", he was very popular with the students whom he would take out on long walks, entertaining his listeners with a flow of learned talk about flora and fauna which would sometimes continue unchecked around a table in a local tavern. And there was the tireless François-Xavier Friedblatt, an Alsatian jack-of-all-trades who taught physics, mineral and organic chemistry, as well as astronomy, who drilled and led the chapel choir, and who single-handedly or double-leggedly trained the more sportive types in soccer, basketball, hockey, tennis, swimming, skating, and sledding.

Saint-Exupéry, who enjoyed strolling through the woods, was as indifferent to most of these sports as he was lackadaisical in his studies. He had developed into an unusually tall big-chested boy, but if anything this sudden spurt in his growth only accentuated the feeling of physical awkwardness he had begun to suffer from at Le Mans. His schoolmates had often had occasion to laugh at his inability to replace a slipped bicycle chain or to repair a punctured tyre, and once he had lost his balance so badly that in falling the brake handle had opened a gash in his right cheek, leaving a tiny scar which remained with him thereafter.

Among those whom the young Antoine quickly befriended at the Villa Saint-Jean was a boy called Charles Sallès, who came from Lyon like himself. Sallès' grandparents, by a curious coincidence, owned a house at Châtillon-la-Palud, situated on the ridge across the valley which the Comtesse de Tricaud could admire as she sat drinking tea in her verandah at

Saint-Maurice Sallès had even been sent, like Antoine, to get private tutoring in Latin from the same curate of Bublane (next door to Châtillon) who used to spoil his summer pupils with the pears in his garden. Yet the two had never met—until the day when Saint-Exupéry walked into the refectory at the Villa Saint-Jean and sat down next to him.

Unlike his new companion, Sallès was a good, hard working student who regularly made the *Livre d'Or*—the Golden Book—in which the best students at Saint-Jean had their names inscribed. He cannot remember ever having been struck by Antoine's academic record in any field—not even in French, of which he was later to become a master. The school records bear this out, partially at any rate. For in his first year at the Villa Saint-Jean Antoine actually managed to be second (out of 25) in French composition and fifth in Latin; and in his final year he was second (out of 10) in Physics and Chemistry and third in Philosophy. But these "honourable mentions", the only ones he was able to obtain, were virtually nullified by the poor showing he made in other subjects.

At the Villa Saint-Jean First Formers with good scholastic records were granted the coveted privilege of leaving the dormitory of "*La Sapinière*" (literally the "Pine-Wood", as the House reserved for the top two forms was called) and ascending to the second floor, where they could enjoy individual rooms next door to certain masters'. If their work or their behaviour deteriorated, they had to return to the dormitory, a process of forcible demotion known among the boys as "*descendre du salon*"—descending from the drawing-room. If Saint-Exupéry does not seem to have made many such descents during his first year, it was for the simple reason that he rarely made the "drawing-room". For most of this period he was near the bottom of his division (the upper two forms) in regular classroom work: 38 out of 39 in November 1915, 40 out of 40 in March 1916, 38 out of 38 in June; and this lacklustre performance was even carried into his second year, for the school books list him as 48 out of 48 in November 1916, and 37 out of 40 in May 1917. But this being his last year—known as "*Philo*" (Philosophy)—he was able at last to gravitate upstairs to a room of his own, a privilege automatically accorded final year students.

Study hall behaviour counted for a lot in these monthly gradings, and here too the school records are revealing; for where a mark of 70 or 75 rewarded an exemplary studiousness, Antoine's systematic lack of application usually won him a rock-bottom 50. At table his mulish reluctance to speak German was regularly graded as "insufficient", and he was repeatedly being recalled to order for leaving bread all over the place and answering back in French. Even the 9 (out of 20) he was awarded for the year 1915–1916 in French composition he had to share with six others, and in any case it was not particularly spectacular; whereas—and this comes as a surprise for someone later destined to navigate over large areas of the globe—his 4 in Geography was the lowest awarded anyone for this subject. In 1916–1917 his grade of 11 (out of 20) was above class average in Physics and Chemistry, average for Philosophy, and below average in Religious Instruction; but his 7 for Natural Sciences and History and his 6 for Geography were again the lowest in his class.

It is clear that for much of his time at Fribourg his thoughts were on other things. Just where we may judge from a breathless letter he dashed off to Anne-Marie Poncet during his second term. With it came the first verses of a libretto for an operetta—*Le Parapluie* (The Umbrella)—for which, he fondly hoped, his old music teacher would compose the score. The plot was childishly simple: the hero, a young man, enters a café and seeing a dainty umbrella in the *vestiaire*, he assumes it must belong to a young girl whom he imagines to be not only beautiful but sweet, frail, bashful, and kind-hearted. He sits down at a table near the cloakroom to be sure not to miss the radiant apparition, and half of Paris—beginning with a swashbuckling Colonel and a slew of *midinettes*—sweeps past the expectant youth until . . . oh, horror of horrors! a tub-shaped creature with a hairy lip and bilious green hat appears, seizes the umbrella, and charges out under it into the rainy street.

The plot must have struck the author as being a trifle thin; for when the curtain rises, it is not on a dreamy young man, but on a chorus of "august" topers draped over the wicker chairs of a boulevard café.

> *Nous sommes les consommateurs* (they bellow at the audience)
> *Augustes, ponctuels, et graves*
> *Et nous devons tous nos couleurs*
> *Au soleil qui monte des caves.*
> *Voyez en nous de braves gens*
> *Paisibles, doux, humanitaires.*
> *Comme les poules vont aux champs*
> *Nous venons ici boire un verre.*

It is possible that some atavistic influence was at work in the depths of his subconscious; the jolly association of the "sun" with the "cellars it comes up from" harking back to his great grandfather's vat-fulls of "Malescot Saint-Exupéry" and his grandfather's life-saving employment with the Compagnie du Soleil. But Antoine had clearly been reading too much Rostand, and this first boisterous stanza was still a long whip-crack behind Cyrano's cuckolding cadets.

> *Co sont los cadots de Gascogne*
> *De Carbon, de Castel-Jaloux,*
> *Bretteurs et menteurs sans vergogne . . .* etc

But to return to *The Umbrella* . . .
A waiter, summoned to take the topers' orders, is frightened away when they all sound off at once. Whereupon they intone:

> *Nous fumons là béatement*
> *Regardant passer les p'tites femmes*
> *Et ruminons paisiblement*
> *De la vie appréciant les charmes*
> *Nous attendons sans déplaisir*
> *En citoyens démocratiques*
> *Des garçons qui doivent nous servir*
> *Daignant—*

but the rest is illegible, which is perhaps just as well. "These pages complete the first part", the librettist informed the future composer. "We've reached the point just before the entrance of Aglaé and the Colonel. Write me if I must recopy it without altering anything, or if there will be time to do this at the start of the holidays. I'll be arriving on Palm Sunday." He went on to ask if she liked the beginning, had composed the music, could read his script, and "where, when and how will it be played?" The answer, of course, was that the composer hadn't written a bar; but the rollicking doggerel amused her so much that she preserved these still-born pages long after their author had vanished from the face of the earth.

The half dozen poems of Saint-Exupéry's which have survived from this period—largely thanks to Dr. Paul Michaud—attest the tremendous impact made on his youthful imagination by the tragedy of the 1914–1918 war. As a welcome change from the strict régime of the Collège de Sainte-Croix at Le Mans, from which newspapers had been rigorously banned, the students at Saint-Jean were allowed to read the papers. Daily communiqués from the front were even pasted up on the notice-board in the games room of "*La Sapinière*". These dispatches were avidly and anxiously read, and hardly a month went by without bringing news that some graduate had fallen in battle. The feeling in the school was emphatically pro-French; and whenever a trainload of internees passed through Fribourg the boys would turn out en masse to greet the *poilus* and the officers who had accidentally strayed across the Swiss border or managed to escape from some

German *Stalag*. General Pau, when he passed through, was given a delirious welcome. Martial heroism was very much the order of the day, and one of Antoine's poems, entitled *Amertume* (Bitterness), expressed a youthful feeling of frustration at having to sit out the epic struggle on a quiet school bench rather than being in the thick of the fray.

> *Il est dur étant jeune encore*
> *De n'avoir plus comme idéal*
> *Que de murmurer "je t'adore"!*
> *Ce mot romanesque est banal . . .*
>
> *Cette vie est par trop servile*
> *Je me révolte et je dis "non"!*
> *Je préfère aux chants de la ville*
> *La voix farouche du canon.*

These verses, written before he was sixteen, constitute the first stammering statement of the Spartan ideal—hardship as the essence of human existence, as opposed to the siren-like "chants of the city"—which he was later to develop at length in his books. But this boy, who was a poet to the finger tips, was at the same time too sensitive to beauty and to those *"trésors de douceur"* which make up a civilization not to be appalled by the hideous cost of the carnage. In a poem entitled "Disenchantment" a twenty-year old French sentinel, gazing out into the night, stands transfigured by the flash of a howitzer, followed by darkness. So it is with man's dreams:

> *Et le soldat soupçonne en son âme confuse*
> *Qu'en plein essor, noyés dans l'ombre qui les suit,*
> *Nos rêves trop souvent s'éteignent dans la nuit!*

Another poem, *Printemps de Guerre*, (Wartime Spring), which describes the fighting on the Yser river, ends with the line

> *O, pourquoi sur des fleurs faut-il que l'on se tue?*

—an echo of the Canadian poet John McRae's lament: ". . . on Flanders Fields, where poppies grow." And in yet another poem entitled *Soleil d'Or* the blood redness of sunset is linked to the idea of a world which is dying:

(A Canadian lady who read my biography wrote in to ask me to remove Rupert Brooke's name and put in the name of the real author of those lines. I stand corrected, assuming that she's right.)

*Tu refais chaque jour l'histoire, ô soleil d'or*
*Et le matin jeté par quelque discobole*
*Tu sembles te lever sur un fond d'Acropole,*
*Naissant d'un peuple jeune et qui rêvait encore . . .*

. . .

*Or voici que le monde est proche de sa mort.*

The cadence of these lines betrays the influence of Baudelaire. A "*poète damné*"—as he described himself in his lifetime—Baudelaire naturally did not figure on the literary curriculum of the Villa Saint-Jean. But clandestine copies of his poetry passed from hand to hand and his verse was even openly discussed during out-of-class hours with Father Goerung, a liberal-minded young priest who taught French literature to the senior form.

The first book the young Antoine had really come to love was Hans Christian Andersen's fairy tales. Later he discovered Jules Verne. But as he confessed years later to an interviewer from *Harper's Bazaar* "I have never had much taste for pure fiction, and have read comparatively little of it. The first novels that attracted me were Balzac's, with *Le Père Goriot* my favourite. At fifteen I came across Dostoevski, a tremendous revelation to me; I felt at once that I had entered into communication with something vast, and proceeded to read everything he had written, one book after another, as I had done with Balzac. I was sixteen when I discovered the poets. Of course I was convinced that I myself was a poet, and for two years composed verses madly like all youngsters. I worshipped Baudelaire, and must admit shamefacedly that I learned all of Leconte de Lisle and Hérédia by heart, and Mallarmé as well. But even now I won't go back on this last."

Years after he had left Saint-Jean he could still throw a dinner table or a salon into fits of laughter by reciting Victor Hugo or Mallarmé in the hob-nailed accent of the Fribourgeois. But gradually his own poetic passion spent itself. One evening at Saint-Maurice after he had read some of his poems to a friend of his mother's, she quietly remarked: "You say them well. But now I must read them." Antoine was hurt. Later when another family friend, Dr. Geniès, took him to task for sacrificing precision of meaning to the artificial needs of the rhyme, he realized they were right and bid good-bye to poetry. But the instinct was too strong to be dammed; with the result that his prose, when it finally burst forth, glowed with a poetic phosphorescence.

\*　\*　\*

Saint-Exupéry's final months at Fribourg were clouded over by the increasingly ill health of his brother François, afflicted with rheumatic fever. He was brought back to Saint-Maurice-de-Rémens, where in July 1917 he finally succumbed. Sensing that the end was nigh, he called Antoine to his bedside, explaining with a youthful blush: "I would . . . like to make out my will." A will? For a boy who was hardly fourteen? But he put so much gravity and such "manly" pride into this last request that years later his elder brother could not think of it without being moved. "Had he been a father, he would have turned over his sons to my teaching. Had he been a war pilot, he would have turned the logbooks over to my safekeeping. But he was only a child. All he could entrust was a steamboat, a bicycle, and an air-gun."

He was buried in the little cemetery of Saint-Maurice-de-Rémens, by the tabernacle built over Comte Léopold de Tricaud's grave and where, just three years later, Gabrielle de Tricaud was to be laid to rest in her turn.

For a change of air Antoine and his sisters were sent that August to Carnac, on Brittany's southern coast, where their father's sister Amicie had a villa. Her husband, Major Sydney Churchill, notwithstanding his English name and rank, was really more French than British. The living embodiment of the *Entente Cordiale* (which he anticipated), he descended from an English grandfather who had been captured during the Napoleonic wars and ended up marrying a French girl. Born in France and brought up by the Jesuits in Paris, Sydney Churchill was three quarters French and would doubtless have chosen to make a career in the land of his maternal ancestry had the Saint-Cyr Military Academy not rejected him for poor eyesight. The British, less fussy for once, admitted him to Sandhurst; after which he had seen action in Burma, South Africa (against the Boers), and finally the Western front. His had been the kind of adventurous life the young Antoine was dreaming of—save that his own aspirations encompassed the sea rather than the land. His hero of the moment was Captain Némo, and like his creator, Jules Verne, there was nothing he so ardently desired as to travel and to see the world. It was sunny and Antoine, who rarely indulged in sport, enjoyed swimming in the Atlantic; but to his intense disgust his aunt, fearful of one more family tragedy (after what had happened to François) would not let him go out in the sailboats with the fishermen.

The taste of brine was still with him when he journeyed up to Paris that autumn for the resumption of the school year. The living hell of the trenches had cast a blight on the attractions of the military profession, and his ambition at this point was to be a sailor. At Fribourg he had specialized in the classics—Greek, Latin, and Philosophy—and done well enough in these subjects to pass his baccalaureat exams. Indeed, when Paul Creyssel, during a period of home leave from the front, was introduced to him in Lyon, he was amazed to find the young man as interested in discussing Kant, Bergson, and Thomas Aquinas as he was in interrogating the former dragoon about the new air branch he had just joined. The two years at the Villa Saint-Jean may not have made a scholar out of him, but they had at least aroused an interest in philosophy which was to grow with the passage of time. But Antoine's immediate needs were more pressing, and neither the great Dominican scholastic nor the pensive sage of Koenigsberg were of much help to him for the new career he envisaged. To enter the Naval College at Brest he needed training in higher mathematics—*hypoflotte* (elementary) and *flotte* (advanced), as the two year course was known in the jargon of the schools. He accordingly registered as a boarder at the Lycée Saint-Louis, located on the Boulevard Saint-Michel, across the way from the Sorbonne; and soon he was being drilled in calculus and logarithms by a formidable taskmaster called Pagès, better known to his pupils as "QQ Prime".

To judge by the letters he wrote to his mother at Ambérieu and to his friend Charles Sallès (who had meanwhile been inducted into the French army), the drill was intensive, amounting to some ten hours of maths a day. Antoine's new habitat was a far cry from the airy spaciousness of the Villa Saint-Jean, and he found it painful during recreations to be crammed into a quadrangle which—with typical exaggeration—he wrote Sallès was just "ten metres by ten". In fact, it was large enough to include eight plane-trees, though it could not have been more than fifty yards across by as many wide: which meant that even if there weren't 1800 students to fill it (another saint-exuberant exaggeration), it wasn't a place where one could indulge in such luxuries as soccer or tennis. "But", he consoled himself, "we can exercise our wit on each other, repeating every ten seconds: 'Hey, you blockhead, can't you see I've got feet?' We can also toss water bombs from the windows or launch 'raids' on the study hall of the 'taupins' (Poly-technique) or of the 'pistons' (Centrale) and mess all their things up in the secret hope of coming back and finding that they've done the same to ours. War after all is war."

At the Lycée Saint-Louis students were grouped into different divisions according to the higher institution or academy for which they were being readied. Saint-Exupéry's division consisted of some forty candidates headed, like himself, for the Naval Academy and thus known as *flottards* ("floaters", though the term was also a play on the word *flotte*, meaning "fleet" and in *argot* "water"). Those destined for the Military Academy

of Saint-Cyr were known as *cyrards*; in addition to which there were the
hard-working "moles" (*taupins*) of the Ecole Polytechnique and the hard-
driving "pistons" who had set their sights on the Central School of Engineering. Each group had its distinctive *esprit de corps*, but as all shared the same
cramped "quad", the struggle for *Lebensraum* took the form of a lively
"battle of the services"—made all the keener by the fact that many of the
"moles" were headed for a later career in the Artillery and many of the
"pistons" for duty with the Engineers.

One day, as they were milling about the quadrangle, a towering brute
of a *cyrard* began bullying a *flottard* called Henry de Ségogne, who though
more than six feet tall, found himself dwarfed by the giant. Ségogne's
prospects seemed grim and it looked as though he was in for a sound pasting
when a long arm and a burly torso interposed themselves between the
combattants. It was Antoine de Saint-Exupéry, whose six feet and one inch were
almost a match for the bully's. Daunted by the sudden doubling of the enemy's
forces, the *cyrard* sulkily withdrew, leaving the two *flottards* masters of the terrain.
The incident was trivial, but it sealed a friendship which was to be one of the
firmest and warmest of Antoine's lifetime.

Antoine, as usual, proved an unruly subject and his refractory ways won
him many a punishment from his teachers ("You will copy out the phrase
. . . two hundred times" etc.). He complained about one of them in a
letter to his friend Sallès, describing the "slavedriver" as a "regular tyrant
(tyrannus, tyranni, tyrannum). To get out of six hours of copy work I sent
him a telegram the other day urgently summoning him to a fake address
the other side of Paris during the study hall period." The stratagem seems to
have worked, and the exultant truant followed up this first success with a
barrage of anonymous missives mailed by co-operative friends in Lyon,
Le Mans, all over. "He's slowly going out of his mind with terror," he went
on, "and the charming proof of it is that he's been doubling and tripling
the punishment." Sallès in his turn was asked to slip a bogus summons
into the letter-box at Grenoble but if any effect it had, it was probably to
quadruple the volume of the punishment.

The need for distraction at the Lycée Saint-Louis was understandable,
and not just for reasons of pedagogical tyranny and recreational crush. The
normally ebullient Latin Quarter was now shrouded at night as by a pall.
Paris had yet to be acquainted with the total obscurity of the Second World
War, but the "blue-out" was already here. "The evenings are now dreary,"
Antoine wrote to his mother, "all Paris is painted blue. The trams have
their blue bulbs, the corridor lights at the Lycée Saint-Louis are blue, it's
all quite eery . . . When one now looks out over Paris from a high window
it looks like a large ink stain, there's not a splash of light nor a glow, for

sheer non-luminosity it's amazing. There's a fine for anyone with a lighted window on the street, and there's been a rush for huge curtains."

Grim though the war was, Paris still retained much of its old spark and spirit. The tumultuous goings-on in the Senate and the Chamber of Deputies (which resulted in Clemenceau's return to power) were aped by the students of Saint-Louis, who engineered a "ministerial crisis" of their own. In the new "cabinet"—largely thanks to the influence of his friend Henry de Ségogne—Antoine was appointed P.D.M. (*Préfet des Moeurs*). The chief purpose of this new "government" seems to have been to stimulate the activity of the C.D.O.—the *Chef d'Orchestre* (*sous-entendu* of the "*chahut*")—which is to say, of the classroom Hell-Raiser-in-Chief.

Nor was Paris any less perilous to the virtue of young adolescents now that it had become the "*Ville Non-Lumière*". The very murkiness of the nights enhanced the predatory charms of ladies whose shopworn looks might have been put to a rude test in daytime; and the presence of so many men at the front made what young bucks remained behind a highly prized commodity. The professionals now faced competition from amateurs, ready to do their patriotic bit "*pour la patrie*". The temptations were often too charming to be resisted; and to judge by one of his letters, several of Antoine's schoolmates succumbed. The good Madame Jordan, asked by his mother to keep an eye on the threatened morals of her son, was assiduous in the distribution of moralizing booklets which Saint-Exupéry dutifully passed on to his school chums, who read them with hoots of laughter and genuine "stupor". Well they might, for Venus took care of the problem in her own imperious fashion, quietly spreading the bane which bears her aphrodisiac name. Paris, Antoine finally wrote home, "is, I've come to the conclusion, a less pernicious city than many provincial dumps, in the sense that certain of my fellow students who were really sowing their wild oats in their home towns have grown relatively sedate here because of the danger to one's health of playing around in Paris."

In the spring of 1918 most of the senior students were evacuated from the cramped premises on the Boulevard Saint-Michel and sent to occupy the tree-lined campus of the Lycée Lakanal, in the southern suburb of Sceaux. Big Bertha was in action and there was always the danger that one of her massive shells might land squarely on the Lycée Saint-Louis and obliterate several hundred *flottards* or *cyrards* in one blinding flash. There was also an urgent need to put an end to the *lycéens'* deplorable habit of climbing out on to the roof to watch the night-time fireworks. Sceaux, as it turned out, was only slightly less vulnerable than the Latin Quarter, for random shells kept dropping. "It's almost like being in the middle of a regular hurricane, of a storm at sea", Antoine wrote to his mother, who must have been a bit perturbed to be told "it's wonderful. Only you mustn't stay out of doors, because pieces of shrapnel keep falling all over the place, and one of them would be enough to flatten you. We've found some of them in the park."

The times were not particularly conducive to concentrated study and the eighteen-year-old Antoine does not seem to have developed more taste for it in Paris than he had in Le Mans or Fribourg. His fertile imagination was kept busy devising new forms of scholastic terrorism—like the explosition of fire-crackers in study hall. "During these war years," as Henry de Ségogne has recalled, "our *lycées* and *collèges* were buffeted by a wave of singular indiscipline. Encouraged by the dearth of teachers, dragged off to the front one after the other, and by the relaxed surveillance of parents beset by weightier sorrows and anxieties, stirred by the exploits of our brothers and a desire to show what we were capable of, we too applied a kind of heroic genius to the devising and execution of our dissipations. I doubt that anyone in professorial memory has seen classroom uproars to equal those of 1918." The most mammoth of these sprees was touched off by news of the Armistice on November 11, 1918; and according to Ségogne, he and Saint-Exu (as he was known to his classmates) were the most turbulent of the lot.

The advent of peace seems to have done little to dampen this taste for turbulence. The cellars beneath the "Bastille" on the Boul'Miche were found to debouch into a large sewage tunnel where the hell-raisers could indulge a subterranean passion for bridge games. It was linked by a manhole to the Rue Cujas, on the far side of the boulevard. As a means of escaping hours of punitive study hall it was made to order. Groping his way along the tunnel, Saint-Exu had only to clamber up the metal rungs, and with a bit of outside help the heavy manhole cover could be removed and he was free to enjoy an hour or two of truancy. One day they were busy heaving and tugging at the heavy metal plate when Ségogne, who was up above, realized that they were no longer alone. One of their teachers had come up the street with his daughter and was watching the performance with morbid curiosity. Letting go of the cover, Ségogne took off down the street, while Antoine, anxious to know what was up, thrust his head up through the half-opened aperture. Fortunately dusk was falling and the teacher did not have time to recognize the strange apparition, which dropped back through the hole like a jack-in-the-box. Later, when a check was made, Saint-Exu was at his usual place in study hall, his brows knit in ferocious concentration.

In January 1919 Antoine was transferred from the Lycée Saint-Louis to the Ecole Bossuet, on the other side of the Luxembourg Gardens. His mother may have decided that he needed stricter discipline and that the

Jesuit fathers who ran Bossuet were better fitted to dispense it than the lay teachers of the Lycée Saint-Louis. Since Bossuet did not offer any instruction itself, he continued to go to class at Saint-Louis, but it was at Bossuet that he slept, took his meals, and sat through the long study-hall periods (the first of which began promptly at 7 a.m.). Ségogne remembers his friend as being "timid, a bit wild, given to moodiness, now bursting with life, now morose and shut up in a world of inner meditation. He did not make friends easily, and it pained him, for he liked to be liked".

In the large study hall at Bossuet he and Saint-Exu were allowed to have individual desks, whereas most of the others had to content themselves with benches and long tables for their home work. This favouritism may have been designed to mollify the infectious truculence of the two hell-raisers, but more probably it was due to their age; for Ségogne and Saint-Exupéry were finally obliged to spend three full years slaving away at mathematics. Undisciplined as ever, Antoine made his desk a model of disorder. The sight of this gaping woodwork, vainly seeking to swallow the inordinate mass of paper and printed matter that was crammed down its gullet, was too much for Abbé Genevois who, after repeated remonstrances, ordered Saint-Exu to take his place at the table with the others. The next hour or two were devoted to extra-curricular versification, for when the Abbé came back after study hall he found the blackboard whitened with a couple of curious stanzas. The "Odyssey of a Top Hat" had now made way for "The Ode of a Small Desk":

> *J'étais dans le fond de l'étude*
> *Un petit bureau sans valeur*
> *Je faisais la béatitude*
> *De mon illustre possesseur.*
> *Noir comme un citoyen d'Afrique*
> *Usé par d'austères travaux*
> *J'étais discret et pacifique*
> *Le plus paisible des bureaux*
>
> *Bien au frais sous la fenêtre,*
> *Gonflant mon dos comme un lézard*
> *J'étais gratifié par mon maître*
> *D'un beau désordre, effet de l'art.*
> *Ma paix ne fut que passagère*
> *L'ennemi troublant mon repos*
> *Me ravit à l'ami si cher*
> *A ses travaux, à ses propos.*

Several more verses followed, but the essence of their message was contained in the plea: "Prince"—the name given to the Abbé by his pupils—"Give me back my little desk."

The good Father was callous enough to have another schoolboy erase the immortal scribblings on the blackboard. He might well have taken umbrage at being termed the "enemy" who had interrupted the "austere labours" the little desk had witnessed, and as for the artistic genius which had gone into the making of the chaos beneath the lid . . . the less said the better. But he lived up to his princely appelation by generously allowing the disconsolate Antoine to regain his swollen-backed "lizard".

There is a penalty for lack of application and in the end the two friends had to pay for it. Ségogne who, for his sins, had previously been exiled to a provincial school in Brittany, came a cropper with the Naval exams, and so did Saint-Exu. The results had hardly been announced when pandemonium swept the Lycée Saint-Louis. "Fire! Fire!" someone shouted as the *pompiers* invaded the premises. They turned the place upside down but could find no trace of a blaze. Understandably. The phone call they had received was Antoine's last schoolboy coup, the grand finale in the series of pyrrhic battles he had fought with his superiors.

The setback was predictable enough, but later—after fame had overtaken him—the same irrepressible prankster could not resist the temptation of playing tricks with his own history. In reality, he had passed the written tests but failed in the orals. But to nourish the illusion that geniuses are infallible—for otherwise they wouldn't be geniuses!—it was explained that he had failed his exam in French composition by handing in a blank page in answer to the question: "Describe the tribulations of an Alsatian who returns after the war to his native village." Not being an Alsatian, Saint-Exu felt it was dishonest to reply to such a question. And this from the bard who had so movingly described the tribulations of a top hat and the bereavement of a desk!

Henry de Ségogne, who should know, claims the Alsatian story is poppycock. As was another delightful *canard* Saint-Exupéry helped spread one day during a conversation with a young journalist. "Is it true" the newspaperman asked him, "that in your naval exams you only got a 1 in French composition?" Since 20 was the maximum, 1 could hardly have been lower. The idea struck Saint-Exupéry as so drole that he answered: "Why, yes." And the story was off at a gallop.

All of this, of course, was later—after he had established himself as a master of French prose. For at the time his failure was anything but a joke. He had devoted three years in a vain effort to become a sailor, and now in his twentieth year he was debarred by age from making one more try. Brusquely forced to cast around for another career, he signed up in the autumn of 1920 as a student in Architecture at the École des Beaux-Arts. He spent five inconclusive months here, lodged in a cheap hotel room on the Rue de Seine, not far from the Boulevard Saint-Germain. But his real headquarters, when he was not bent over a drawing-board, were established chez Jarras, the café on the corner of the Rue Bonaparte and the Quai Malaquais. Here almost every day he would meet Bernard Lamotte and other Beaux-Arts students for a sandwich lunch. Though his mother sent him what she could—she was anything but an affluent widow— his meagre allowance never lasted out the month and there were days when, too poor to pay for ham, he would have to content himself with two quarters of a *baguette* liberally sprinkled with mustard. "Have some bread to put around your mustard", was a standard Beaux-Arts joke.

Fortunately there were relatives, like his mother's second cousin, the Duchesse de Trévise (*neé* Yvonne de Lestrange), who were only too glad to offer him a free meal, though he disliked taking too much advantage of their hospitality. There was also the occasional odd job which brought in a welcome pocketful of change. With his friend Ségogne he got himself hired as an extra in Jean Noguès' opera *Quo Vadis?* Ségogne, as a "red guard", took a sadistic delight in falling on his friend Antoine (acting the part of a "Christian") with a wooden sword. But later, when Ségogne was banished to a remote corner of the stage, Antoine got a sweet revenge (as a "black guard") by moving in on the luscious body of Sainte Blandine, a terribly tempting "martyr". It was not great opera, any more than would have been *The Umbrella* he had set out to write with Anne-Marie Poncet. Nor was it great theatre. But like *The Telephone* he had staged for his mother and his aunts at Saint-Maurice, or the role of Diafoirus he had played at Fribourg in Molière's *Le Malade Imaginaire*, it was fun. A brief interlude in weeks of unconvincing drudgery.

Antoine loved to draw and he had a gift with the pencil, but he wasn't really sure he wanted to be an architect. If he had felt the call of the sea, it was for the sense of vast adventure it brings with it. If he was fascinated by cathedrals, it was because of the mysterious space they enclose and the vast skies they point to. The rest was routine, which he abhorred.

It was interrupted in the spring of 1921 by a routine of a more imperative nature, when he was called up for military service in the army. For someone with no warlike aptitude or bent, it could have meant two years of bondage. Instead, it was a liberation.

# 3

# Baptism of the Air

---

ONE day at Saint-Maurice-de-Rémens a panic-stricken Antoine burst in on his mother and his sisters shouting: "He's dead! He's dead!" Everyone rushed out to see what was amiss, and there in the court was François, blood streaming from his face, being held under the pump by the governess. The two brothers had been experimenting with a steam engine which had blown up, knocking François over and opening a small gash in his forehead. But otherwise he was very much alive.

Saint-Exupéry's interest in mechanical objects seems to have been aroused at a very early age; for his music teacher Anne-Marie Poncet remembers him as being a "*bricoleur né*"—a born tinkerer, fascinated by boilers and pistons. He would spend hours drawing diagrams of imaginary engines, then pester the Curé, who had once taught mathematics, to find out if he thought they were all right. Still a child, he hooked up wires and boxes and built himself a rudimentary telephone. But his most ambitious "invention" was a flying machine he put together by stretching a pair of old sheets over a frame of bamboo struts, attached to the handlebars of his bicycle. None of the grownups were supposed to know anything about it, but the children who gathered to witness the dramatic "take off" down the alley of the lindens were more amused than impressed; there was a lot of furious pedalling, but to get the tyres off the ground Antoine had to build a ramp.

Exactly when the young Antoine first began to take an active interest in the "aeroplane" it is impossible to say. Twenty years of experimenting with "horseless carriages" had at last given rise to the "automobile", and in 1905 the "aeroplane" was not very far behind. Gasoline had overtaken steam, providing man at last with what Daedalus and Leonardo da Vinci lacked. A period of mad experimentation followed in which for one giddy moment it looked as though anything was possible. "An impressive number of experimenters and scientists"—to quote Gabriel Voisin, who was one of them— "had conceived and often built, with the most varied means, machines that

48

were utterly incapable of flying". One of these experimenters, a genial crackpot named Florencie, insisted that Voisin build him an engine connected by piston valves to a pair of flapping wings; and even Louis Blériot, who went on to make aviation history, lost much precious time working on a wing-beating machine which he called an "orthoptère" (the family grasshoppers belong to). Some designs called for two, others for three, still others for four wings. Octave Chanute, who was anything but a crackpot, designed a six-wing glider and then an eight-wing "multiplane," soon superseded by a job (designed by Ecquevilly) which deserved to be called a "maxiplane", since it had not less than twelve wings strung from concentric elipses. Many of these exotic contraptions were little better than flying kites, like Voisin's first cellular creations, themselves inspired by the Australian Lawrence Hargrave's nineteenth-century adaptations of earlier Chinese models. A few perspiring optimists even hoped to take to the air without motors or propellers on their "*aviettes*"—the new name coined for the wing-flanked bicycles which competed at the Parc des Princes in 1912 and by which the young Saint-Exupéry may well have been inspired in his own aero-velocipedic try outs.

The one thing we can reasonably be sure of is that this youthful interest in flying machines was greatly stimulated by his family's move to Le Mans in 1909. In July of the previous year Wilbur Wright had crossed the ocean and set up shop in the Léon Bollée automobile works at Le Mans. The emigration of this Yankee pioneer was a handsome compliment paid to a country which had contributed as much to the development of aviation as it had to that of the automobile. There are still Frenchmen who claim that the first man ever to get off the ground in a heavier-than-air machine was neither Wilbur nor Orville Wright, but a visionary genius called Clément Ader, who in October 1890 actually managed to rise a foot or two above the earth while charging across a field in an extraordinary bat-winged machine pulled by a steam driven propeller. The claim will probably continue to be endlessly debated, even though Ader merits posthumous acclaim for other reasons—like his coining of the word "aviation" (as opposed to "aeronautics"), which attests a prescient interest in birds as opposed to ships. What cannot be denied is the help the Wright brothers received in their pioneering efforts from Octave Chanute, a French engineer employed by the Baltimore & Ohio railroad who maintained a fruitful correspondence with Ferdinand Ferber, the first European to get a monoplane off the ground (May 1905) in a machine powered by a combustion engine.

This early enthusiasm for aeronautics was hardly surprising in the land which had given the world Jules Verne, the bicycle, black and white photography, radium, the Montgolfière balloon, and even more pertinently, the first aerodynamic "laboratory"—established at the Chalais-Meudon air-field near Paris, where Colonel Charles Renard devised rudimentary instruments for measuring propeller thrust and the weight-lifting capacities of inclined surfaces. A typical by-product of this enthusiasm was the Aéro-Club de France, which was established even before the old century was out (1898) in fashionable premises looking out over the Place de la Concorde. Its foremost celebrity was a dashing Brazilian by the name of Alberto Santos Dumont who led his fellow members—a mixed bag of affluent industrialists and well-heeled sportsmen—a merry chase in the construction, inflation, and crippling of an impressive number of airships and balloons. Another was Comte Georges de Castillon de Saint-Victor, uncle of both Claude (Saint-Exupéry's classmate) and his elder brother Raymond de Castillon, who was two years ahead of them at the Collège de Sainte-Croix. Like most of the early members of the Aéro-Club de France, the Count was a fervent *aérostier*—the exotic name then coined for the cloud-challenging emulators of Phileas Fogg—and among his exploits he could number a stratospheric voyage which took him all the way to Kiev and another which dropped his leaking balloon in mid-Mediterranean, from which he was fished out in time by an escorting vessel.

With the obstinacy that any passion is likely to develop, the *aérostiers* could not bring themselves to believe that there was any future to that aeronautic newcomer, not to say upstart, the "heavier-than-air" machine. The feeling was shared by the young members of the local "Aéro-Club" which the boarders of the Collège de Sainte-Croix established in imitation of the one in Paris. Its founder was Roger de Legge, whose mother was a rich Brazilian heiress—a fact which may well have encouraged the young school-boy to look forward to the day when he too, like Santos Dumont, would be piloting inflatable balloons. Virtually all of the members of this fledgling club were likewise convinced that the future lay with airships and dirigibles—with the significant exception of a boy called Ronsin, who spent his spare time trying to construct a bat-like contraption obviously inspired by Ader's. Though he was well aware of its existence, Antoine de Saint Exupéry was not a member of this club—first because he was two or three years younger than its founder, but more importantly, Raymond de Castillon recalls, "because he was not a boarder, which would have ruled him out in any case." The exclusion was probably no misfortune and may even have been beneficial—in directing the young Antoine's interest in a less fashionable but more enterprising direction. As a day student he was not bound by the iron rule which forbade the reading of newspapers by inmates of the Jesuit Collège; and the very fact that his enthusiasm first blossomed in 1909—*after*, rather than before, Wilbur Wright's epoch-making performances at Le

Mans—doubtless made it easier for him to pin his faith on heavier-than-air machines.

Their chief advocate in the Aéro-Club de France had been Ernest Archdeacon, a wealthy promoter who had helped Serpollet launch into the manufacture of steam-driven automobiles. His interest aroused by the information Octave Chanute was able to send him from the United States about the Wright Brothers' machines, Archdeacon had had a glider built at the Chalais-Meudon field as far back as 1903; but feeling too old to pilot it himself, he had turned the job over to a twenty-three year old jack-of-all-trades named Gabriel Voisin, who had accumulated considerable experience flying his Hargrave gliders in the valley of the Saône.

From then on, though the Wright brothers probably did not realize it, the French were in the race. In March 1905 Ernest Archdeacon drove his car across the field of Issy-les-Moulineaux (in the southern suburbs of Paris) with a Voisin-designed glider in tow. As the automobile gathered speed the glider shot up thirty feet into the air, lifting a 100 lb. sack of gravel placed in the centre for ballast. The upthrust proved so great that the tail was torn from the wings, and the glider came down with a crash. Archdeacon prudently decided to conduct subsequent tests on the Seine; and in June of this same year Voisin's Hargrave glider, pulled by a motorboat with a 28 h.p. motor, soared forty feet into the air and remained there as he piloted it over a distance of 600 yards. The proof had once and for all been given of the extraordinary ascensional force possessed by slightly inclined surfaces once they attain a certain speed. That day Santos Dumont, who had been watching from the bank, gave up airships and turned his sporting attention to aeroplanes. Louis Blériot, who was also a spectator, put in an order with Voisin for a model of the same cellular design.

Within months there were half a dozen French constructors in the field, and it was touch and go as to who would walk off with the coveted Archdeacon-Deutsch de la Meurthe prize (50,000 francs, or $10,000) promised to the first man to fly a heavier-than-air machine over a closed circuit of one kilometre. Santos Dumont, the first to get into the air (in November 1906), thrilled a chic crowd at Bagatelle, in the Bois de Boulogne, by covering 220 metres at a height of 12 to 15 feet, only to come a cropper. The problem of landing, it was clear, was just as important as getting off the ground. Abandoning floats, which caused too much water drag, Gabriel Voisin equipped his next model with wheels—for the first time in aviation history—and in March 1907 his brother Charles successfully took off and landed the strange cellular contraption after a short flight of 80 yards. The following autumn another Voisin biplane, fitted out with a Levavasseur "Antoinette" engine capable of developing 40 horsepower for only 70 kilograms, covered 350 yards; and in January 1908 the noted auto racer and mechanic, Henry Farman, flew his Voisin around the 550 metre course at the airfield of Issy-les-Moulineaux in 1 minute and 28 seconds. The coveted Deutsch-Archdeacon prize was won, and a new era—that of practical aviation—had begun.

By the time Wilbur Wright turned up at Le Mans in the summer of 1908 there was little he could teach the French. The "secrets" of climbing, veering, banking, maintaining equilibrium in the air, descending, and landing were no longer secret; and the basic problem was one of developing engines giving more horsepower to the kilogram and more robust frames to carry them.* Ferdinand Ferber even took Wright to task for equipping his two-propeller machine with a forward rudder which he said (quite rightly) was both unnecessary and dangerous.

Even so Wilbur Wright's first flights at Le Mans created a sensation. The fame of Thomas Edison's compatriot had preceded him, and a crowd of air enthusiasts was on hand to watch the pioneering Ohioan make his French début on August 8. Timed, among others, by Louis Blériot, it lasted 1 minute and 15 seconds. Each of his subsequent performances was an improvement on the last; but his style being cramped by the excessively small dimensions of the Hunaudières race-track which forced him to bank every twelve seconds, Wright obtained permission to move his two-winged machine to the military camp of Auvours, a couple of miles to the East, where pylons, placed five kilometres apart, were erected to measure the exact distance of his flights. Léon Bollée, the automobile manufacturer and also the president of the Aéro-Club of the *département* of the Sarthe, personally drove Wright's wheel-less aeroplane (which took off on wooden skates and a runner) to the new field where, on September 3, Wright took his machine aloft for 11 minutes. Three days later the sculptor Léon Delagrange flew his Voisin for almost half an hour over the field of Issy-les-Moulineaux, only to see his record shattered within less than a week by Orville Wright, who stayed aloft for 57 minutes in a demonstration undertaken to impress the U.S. Army Signal Corps at Fort Myers. Not to be outdone, Wilbur Wright destroyed his younger brother's record eleven days later (September 21) by remaining in the air for an unprecedented 1 hour and 31 minutes. The flight, witnessed by a gala crowd which included the American Ambassador, the airship pioneer Paul Tissandier, and many other dignitaries, won Wilbur Wright the 1908 Michelin Cup—20,000 francs ($4,000) plus a bonus of 5,000 francs presented to him by the Aéro-Club de France. The gravity-

---

* The first wings were made of sail cloth, and the Wright Brothers' 1901 glider had a wooden frame made of spruce and ash. Santos Dumont's famous "Demoiselle" (which succeeded the Bagatelle crack-up) was partly made of bamboo, and not until the eve of the First World War did the first plane with an all-metal frame appear.

defying airman was duly wined and dined a couple of days later at a lavish Le Mans banquet attended by Louis Blériot and Comte Georges de Castillon, uncle of Saint-Exupéry's classmate Claude.

Though none of these staggering events was actually witnessed by the young Antoine, they were still the talk of the town when he moved to Le Mans the following year. Roger de Sinéty, the cousin of the fair Odette, had ridden out with the bonneted and bowler-hatted crowd which flocked to the Auvours camp on horseback and in carriages to watch one of these epic demonstrations. "A horse was harnessed to the aeroplane" he recalls, "to pull it as far as the field. It was a most curious sight, with Wright, who looked as though he was sitting on the wing, steering his incredible machine as it glided along past the pines and the scrub brush. But the funniest part of it was the spectacle of elegant gentlemen in top hats getting down on their hands and knees to see for themselves if the runners of Wright's machine actually left the ground."

That same autumn Wilbur Wright shattered all flying records with disconcerting ease. On October 10 he took Senator Paul Painlevé up for one hour and nine minutes, establishing another "first". Shortly before Christmas he logged 99 kilometres in 1 hour and 53 minutes, then climbed to a record height of 460 feet. At this point in the air race it looked as though the Americans had established an insuperable lead; yet so keen was the competition from the French that in less than two years every Wright record was pulverized.

Wright's prestige was still close to its zenith when the young Antoine entered the Collège de Sainte-Croix, and we have Roger de Sinéty's word for it that he made several trips to the historic airstrip (now marked by a monument) at Auvours. His first cousin Guy de Saint-Exupéry (son of Antoine's uncle Roger), who was one class ahead of him at Sainte-Croix, claims that he was so struck by Wilbur Wright's trial runs that "he spent hours trying to devise a stabilizer—which for a boy of ten is unbelievable! His enthusiasm was inexhaustible. He used to show me his designs, launching into long explanations which meant nothing to me, but which left me spellbound by their impetuous assurance."

The doubting Thomases of Roger de Legge's "Aéro-Club" might look down their noses at these "impossible" contraptions, but it was already clear that there was an immense future for heavier-than-air machines. The 1908 Salon de l'Automobile in Paris had already paid homage to the future by roping off a section of the Grand Palais for the display of sixteen different models of aeroplanes; and when Louis Blériot succeeded in crossing the Channel some nine months later, both aviator and pioneering craft (with its wings folded up) were offered a state procession up the Avenue de l'Opéra of the kind normally reserved for royalty; after which the weather-beaten machine was trundled off to the Conservatoire des Arts et Métiers—that Pantheon of French mechanical genius—to be preserved as a memento to posterity. That same summer (1909) 150,000 fans turned out for the "Semaine de Champagne" air rally, held near Reims, and cheered themselves hoarse amid a deafening cacophony of penny whistles, bicycle trumpets, and automobile horns as they watched Henry Farman outdo Paulham and Latham by flying 180 kilometres non-stop. Even Glenn Curtiss' triumph in winning the Gordon Bennett Cup (the last such trophy to be won by an American for many years) was powerless to stem a ground swell of public interest which reached such heights at the Juvisy airshow in October that the trains could no longer handle the furious mobs, which came near to lynching engine-drivers and conductors.

It is not difficult to imagine the youthful fervour such feats must have aroused in Antoine de Saint-Exupéry. The wildest expectations of Jules Verne were being realized and in some respects surpassed. Claude de Castillon remembers having seen him spend many an hour at school (when he should doubtless have been concentrating on more "serious" subjects) engaged in "learned calculations concerning the weight-lifting properties of wing sufaces." The first and only issue of *L'Echo de Troisième*, which he put together in 1913, appeared with a spectacular cover showing a luminous plane roaring through a dark night. Odette de Sinéty, when she was not being showered with poetic recitations, was also treated to rapturous harangues about the "areoplane"; and when Antoine turned up at the Villa Saint-Jean in November 1915, the very first words he uttered, as he sat down next to Charles Sallès, were: "I've been up in an aeroplane. You can't imagine what it's like. *C'est formidable!*"

It had happened during the summer holidays of 1912. Several miles to the east of Saint-Maurice-de-Rémens a small airfield had been opened on a flat and barren stretch of ground overlooked by the wooded hills surrounding Ambérieu. Climbing on to his bicycle, Antoine would pedal over a dusty path past the haystacks and the clover and burst impetuously on to the field, where the first tent-like sheds were beginning to spring up to offer protection to the planes.

Here he would spend hours watching the mechanics labouring over their engines and the apprentice pilots being taught the A.B.C. of flying by a Lyonnais called Maurice Colliex. One day they were joined by a dark, beetle-browed sportsman with a rakish handlebar moustache who, in the manner of the champions of the period, wore his checkered golf cap back to front, with the vizor down over the top of his turtleneck sweater. A one-time mechanic, Jules Védrines had become a national celebrity overnight, and the object of a hero-worship equal to that enjoyed by Beaumont (the winner of the first Buc-Rome race of 1911) and Roland Garros. In May of 1911 he had been the only pilot to finish the first and probably most gruelling race ever held between Paris and Madrid—which proved fatal to the French Minister of War and came near to costing Garros his life. Védrines had followed up this feat in December by establishing a new world speed record of 167 kilometres an hour in a fleet Deperdussin monoplane. For the young Antoine, just turned twelve, this energetic winner of trophies must have looked like a demi-god. But he had the courage to approach him; and the demi-god, amused by the young boy's starry-eyed interest, heaved him up into the cockpit behind him. A few moments later they were in the air, droning over the lengthening shadows of poplars and wheat sheaves and cattle barns, caught in the golden rays of a sinking sun.

The event moved Saint-Exupéry so deeply that he composed a poem about it. It was apparently turned over to the Abbé Margotta to be published in a kind of summer holiday journal which he was in the habit of compiling about the *collégiens* of Sainte-Croix. But like the ill-starred *L'Echo de Troisième*, it has vanished—save for three verses:

> *Les ailes frémissaient sous le souffle du soir,*
> *Le moteur de son chant berçait l'âme endormie,*
> *Le soleil nous frôlait de sa couleur pâlie . . .*

Three fragile pillars from a ruin which has disappeared. Almost certainly it was somewhat less than great poetry; but the line about the "chant of the motor . . . lulling the sleeping soul" already bespeaks the sense of mystic rapture which was to be his every time he climbed into a cockpit.

\*          \*          \*

The First World War, like so many conflicts before and since, proved a great stimulus to technology—and not least of all in the new realm of aeronautics. In 1913 the Séguin brothers had come out with a souped-up version of their famous "Gnome" motor—so called because of its admirably compact form—and in 1914, on the very eve of hostilities, Clerget and Salmson had produced an aero-engine also capable of developing 200 horsepower. Most aero-engines up until then had hovered around the 50 to 70 horse-power level, and the general feeling when these new "giants" appeared was that they would shake any plane they were put into to pieces. There was some ground for these apprehensions; for the "Gnome"—a rotary engine which revolved with the propeller around a static crankshaft—had an occasional tendency to "fly off the handle", whirling itself loose with the propeller blade, to the understandable dismay of the pilot who (if he missed being hit by it) suddenly found himself trying to steer a glider. But the early doubts were forcibly resolved in favour of the heavyweights, and before the war was over Mercedes and Hispano Suiza were both producing engines developing 200 horsepower or more, the Séguin brothers and Louis Renault were bringing out motors of 300 horsepower, and the flamboyant Ettore Bugatti (who had helped Roland Garros design the first trans-propeller-firing machine-gun) was experimenting with a twin-block 16-cylinder monster capable of developing 400 horsepower.

Necessity, once again, proved the mother of invention. For by 1914 the hard-working Germans, who were busy shattering Roland Garros' altitude records by climbing up to 23,000 and 24,000 feet, had so far outstripped the French and British that they entered the conflict with 251 front-line planes compared to the British Army's 63 and the French army's 156. If the Allies were not swept from the skies in the opening months of the war, it was largely thanks to the skill of Adolphe Pégoud, who may be regarded as the father of aerial acrobatics. Not until 1917 did a French engineer named Béchereau, working for the Société pour la Production des Appareils Duperdus-sin (SPAD for short) succeed in producing a biplane capable of doing more than 200 kilometres an hour—a fabulous speed in those days—which the Germans were able to match one year later, with the appearance of the Fokker D VII. Even so, the aura of glory which enveloped "aces" like Georges Guynemer and René Fonck was due above all to their virtuosity as pilots and gunners.

Overnight the French Army's air branch—one could not yet speak of an "air force"—became the most glamorous of the services, outshining the once prestigious cavalry; but so young was it that it could not even produce a common uniform, with the comic result that whenever its pilot officers and non-coms had to dress ranks for a parade, they would present a motley front of multicoloured caps and tunics—ranging from the dark grey of the *chasseurs à pieds* (to which Roland Garros belonged) to the horizon blue of the infantry. Undisciplined they looked and most frequently were, partly because the service had to be improvised from scratch, partly because of the man-to man nature of the first aerial dog-fights, but not least of all because of the foolhardy esprit de corps with which the new branch was imbued—every bit as reckless as the wild panache with which the white-gloved cadets of Saint-Cyr and the epauletted sabre-swingers of Saumur had charged into battle in August 1914.

The glamorous confusion of the war years was still very much in evidence in April 1921 when Saint-Exupéry was inducted for his two-year term of compulsory military service. At his request he was assigned to the new air branch, and sent to join the Second Aviation Regiment, then based at Neudorf, in the southern suburbs of Strasbourg. As a conscript he could not theoretically qualify for flying instruction, reserved for "pilot officers" who had enlisted; he was condemned to be a *rampant*—a "crawler" or "ground-hugger," as it was picturesquely called in the new jargon of the airfields' messhalls. He was private second class and the humbleness of his status was emphasized by the official classification of his unit—S.O.A. (*Section d'Ouvriers d'Aviation*)—the aviation "workers" in question including machine-gunners as well as ground crew and mechanics.

His basic training began with the usual potato peeling and guard duty routine common to all armies. An extravagant amount of time—so it seemed to Saint-Exupéry, who was not exactly a sportive type—was devoted to calisthenics, leap-frogging contests, and soccer games, all of them under the baleful eye of hard-bitten sergeants who took a sour pleasure in consigning "loafers" to the guardhouse, where a cell strewn with damp straw replaced bed and barracks. It was a rougher and tougher kind of boarding school and Antoine began by treating the whole thing as an amusing lark. "My dormitory companions are a sympathetic lot", he wrote to his mother. "Pitched battles with bolsters. I've become one of the boys, which is something, and dish out more bolster blows than I receive."

The régime does not appear to have been inordinately inhuman, probably because of the newness of the aviation branch. The set-up was so casual that it was days before Saint-Exupéry could be issued a uniform. "They don't have the togs for us yet", he wrote home. "We wander around in civilian clothes, looking utterly idiotic." The effect, when he was finally decked out, was hardly an improvement: his jacket was so short that his lanky arms protruded from the sleeves several inches above the wrists, while his baggy breeches drooped pitifully over the unevenly rolled puttees. The French uniform of the period, as one of his fellow conscripts, Marcel Migeo, later wrote, was grotesque enough; but on Saint-Exupéry it looked positively goofy.

The day began at six in the morning, but there was a break from 12 to 1.30 in the afternoon, and another from 5 to 9 p.m. when the novice "aviation workers" were free to do what they liked. After a hasty supper in the canteen, Saint-Exupéry would hop into Strasbourg on the tram. One of his first cares had been to rent a room in the "choicest street in town" from a friendly Strassburger called Harry Mayer who couldn't speak a word of French! Here Antoine would take a bath, brew himself a cup of tea, and enjoy a pensive smoke—far from the rough-and-tumble of barrack-room bawling and brawling, to which he had to return by 9 p.m. The room on the Rue du 22 Novembre had hot running water, two wardrobes where he could hang his civilian clothes, and that unheard of luxury—central heating—which he appreciated more in the cool April evenings than later on in June, when Strasbourg was smothered by a sultry Rhineland heatwave.

From the outset his military status was ambiguous and his position privileged. It was not normal for someone with a baccalaureat degree to find himself with "other ranks"—as the British charmingly call them—and particularly for someone of noble birth who could, if he had wished, have called himself a Count. Two of his officers, Captain de Billy and Major de Féligonde, being themselves aristocrats, were sensitive enough to the anomaly of the young private's situation to decide that his "superior" education might at least be put to productive use. Since he had been a better than average student in school physics, had had advanced training in mathematics, and was clearly a fanatic about flying, he could begin by taking on a course in aerodynamics and the physics of combustion. "Just think", Antoine wrote back to his mother, "I'm going to become a professor while waiting to become a student pilot . . . What a laugh! Do you see me as a professor?"

As a way of escaping potato-peeling sessions and the dreary hours of guard duty it was at least a *pis aller*; but the prospect of spending hours in front of a blackboard held no charm for his restless soul. The one thing he wanted to do was get into the air—like the war veterans and the "aces" who spent their time looping and twisting over the Neudorf airfield in their Nieuports and Spads. The wartime training most of them had received— at the airbase of Pau, in the Pyrenees—was in a very literal sense a "crash programme" designed to plug the gaps in hideously decimated squadrons. It consisted of sending the apprentice pilot aloft after a few hours of flight training and having him put his machine into a climbing "stall" at a height of 6,000 feet. As the nose began to drop the novice airman had to kick the left or the right rudder-paddle in, while keeping the stick back, then, as the plane began to spin earthwards, kick in the opposite rudder-paddle and press the stick fully forward. As the plane went into a dive he began gently pulling back on the stick, gradually opening the throttle to regain level flight. Those that managed it, as Marcel Migeo has written, became fighter pilots; those that didn't became corpses. And those who balked at the prospect of a vertical immolation and preferred to come down in a gentle glide became bomber pilots or aerial observers.

As Istres, near Marseille—selected by the Army as the principal training base for new pilots because of its generous Provençal sunshine—the same brutal standards prevailed. The training was so rugged and the crashes so frequent that by 1921 the base had acquired a sinister renown as a "penitentiary for dead ducks". The new airfield at Neudorf, dating from late 1918 (after the French reoccupation of Alsace), had at first been granted the right to train its pilots on the spot; but after an accident in which a monitor had been killed, the right to train new military pilots was limited to Istres and to certain bases in Morocco (where flying conditions were even better than those in southern France). This left Saint-Exupéry with a choice of two courses: he could volunteer for service in Morocco, or try to obtain a civilian pilot's licence by tripling his flying experience during "off duty" hours. The first, which would not have cost him a penny, would have obliged him to serve the additional year of military service required of all volunteers; the second meant investing 2,000 francs (about $200) in a three-week cram course, the outcome of which was anything but certain.

Typically enough, Saint-Exupéry seized the dilemma by both horns. He began by passing the medical aptitude tests required of all pilots, albeit with some difficulty; for if Marcel Migeo is to be believed, on coming before the regimental doctor—a genial duffer with a walrus moustache who asked: "Now, tell me, what is the colour of my trousers?" (crimson with a black sideband)—Antoine could not resist turning to the next-in-line and whispering (audibly enough for the whiskered medic to hear): "Say, what colour is it?" "Colourblind"! exploded the Major, putting a brusque end to the prank. (When a sheepish Saint-Exupéry appeared before a second, more authoritative jury, he was careful.) Next, he volunteered for service in Morocco—preferring, if he had to, to spend three years flying rather than spend two of them on the ground. Finally, with the agreement and encouragement of his officers, he arranged to get private instruction from a civilian pilot employed by a local air transport company, which then shared use of the Neudorf field with the Air Force. To put up the necessary sum, he had to make several urgent appeals to his hard-pressed mother, who came through just in time—having borrowed the money from her banker.

Saint-Exupéry's daily life now took on a hectic tempo. To meet the requirements for a civilian pilot's licence he had to squeeze close to 100 flights into a period of about three weeks—which meant three to four flights a day, in addition to the hours he spent in the air learning to swivel a machine-gun behind the back of a veteran piloting their two-seater Spad-Herbemont fighter. The first of these extra-curricular flights was normally accomplished shortly before sunrise, when the soggy marshland grass was still thick with dew. "I fly on mornings which are soft and calm", he wrote to his mother. "We land in the dew and my kind-hearted instructor picks daisies for 'her.' Then he sits down on the wheel hub, content with his bucolic vision of the world." Compared to the breath-snatching, stomach-turning loops and spins of the Spad-Herbemont, the Compagnie Transaérienne's slow moving Farman would lumber slowly into the air, taking pupil and pilot up on "*père de famille*" outings "when not a leaf is stirring and when"—he couldn't help adding, "the motor deigns to turn". For as often as not it balked and precious hours were wasted while the impatient novice fretted . . . "Prudent and majestic turns. Soft effortless landings—neither spins nor loops", he wrote in a tone of disgust, "but wait till I pilot the Herbemont, instead of forever being its passenger . . . Ah! what a plane!"

For taking a two-minute breather when he should have been scalping potatoes, he got several days of wet straw in the guardhouse and was consigned to the base for two weeks. His accelerated schedule now left him little time for quick runs into Strasbourg for a hot bath and a cup of tea. He was to have left for Morocco in mid-June, but the combined influences of friends in Paris and the approval of his officers at Neudorf caused the transfer to be postponed for several weeks to give him a chance to finish his civilian training. Even so it was a close shave. "I've spent my pre-transfer leave here in an effort to get my licence by doubling the hours", he wrote to Charles Sallès. "But my plane's constant breakdowns cause me to lose hours in pointless waiting, while I gnash my teeth in rage."

It was probably these repeated breakdowns which gave rise to an incident destined to become one of the favourite "stories" in Saint-Exupéry's repertoire. According to its most apocryphal version, it took place early on, after the novice pilot had put in just one hour and twenty minutes of actual flying. More probably it occurred towards the end of his three-week cram course, by which time he had already acquired a certain *maîtrise*. One morning he turned up in front of the tent-like Bessonneau hangar, under which the Compagnie Transaérienne de l'Est kept its two planes, but without his instructor. It may be that the instructor was ill that day, or that knowing that the Farman was once again out of order, he simply did not bother to turn up. Next to the Farman was a Sopwith biplane which—according to the story at any rate—Saint-Exupéry had never flown. The mechanic, apparently satisfied that the fledgling pilot was quite capable of handling the unfamiliar machine, helped him pull it from the hangar; after which he carefully explained the Sopwith's idiosyncracies—an engine which rotated with the propeller and a two-knob throttle control which had to be hand-adjusted to provide for a proper mixture of air and fuel.

When the time came to give the propeller a whirl, the engine burst quickly into life, unlike the mulish Farman. And Antoine was off—on his maiden solo. It was an unorthodox solo, for it lasted longer and took the pilot higher than should normally have been the case. He later told his friend Sallès that once in the air he suddenly suffered a "blank" and could not for the life of him remember what he had to do to land. "Every time I looked down and saw the earth coming up at me so fast, I pulled back on the stick and went back into a climb."

The controls in all likelihood were more sensitive than the buglike Farman's and took some getting used to. Then there was the two knobbed fuel control which, if not properly adjusted, stalled the motor through lack of fuel or choked it for lack of air. Fearful of stalling, which could have proved fatal, Saint-Exupéry apparently fed the motor too generous a mixture, inducing a hiccup of frightening backfires accompanied by puffs of black smoke. "I still don't know how I managed to return to earth", he later confessed to Sallès. But come back he did. The plane survived the ordeal, as did the pilot, who may at one moment have thought he was on fire and that his last hour had come. His instructor may even have been on hand to witness the landing; but as time wore on and the story improved— not unnaturally with someone of Saint-Exupéry's talent—it was none other than his commanding officer, a "Colonel", who greeted the miraculous survivor with the remark: "Saint-Exupéry, you will never kill yourself in an aeroplane, for it would already have happened!"

The "exploit", in any case, had a happy ending; for the novice got the licence he was so anxiously seeking.

\*　\*　\*

In early July, after a three-day leave in Paris, he sailed from Marseille to Casablanca. He was more than ever bent on qualifying as an air force pilot, and in Morocco the holders of civilian licences could be admitted to flight training without first having to undergo the murderous punishment of Istres.

After Strasbourg—with its timbered taverns, its museums, and its Cathedral—it was something of a shock to find oneself dumped down on the dusty periphery of a city which had just begun to expand under the impact of French rule. Saint-Exupéry's initial reaction to Casablanca was one of fascinated repulsion. He sent his mother photographs of the barren surroundings: sea, rocks, "and the only trees hereabouts: big, sad cactuses. Didi (his sister Gabrielle) would be happy here. The place is crawling with vile yellow curs. They wander over the countryside in single file, looking nasty and stupid. But for them I'd go have a closer look at the *douars* with their mud-and-straw dwellings hemmed in behind a crumbling wall. In the evening one can see splendid men and small shrivelled women. They stand out darkly against the red sky and slowly go to pieces like their walls. The yellow curs howl. Opinionated camels graze the pebbles and horrible little donkeys dream. There would be some beautiful photos to take, and yet none of this is worth the little red villages of the Ain, where there are hay wagons and green grass, full of homely cows."

"The first rains fall, and a rivulet trickles past your nose while you're trying to nap . . . Open to the four winds, the shack groans like a ship, and with the rain belting us in with lakes, its a bit like Noah's Ark.

"Indoors everyone is silently bedded down under his white mosquito net, so that the place looks like a young girl's seminary. You finally get used to the idea and are about to grow timid and bashful and charming when you're rudely awoken by a few stout oaths."

"Casablanca", he wrote to Charles Sallès, "is a mushrooming city with towering buildings and sumptuous cafés, peopled with rapacious settlers, street-walkers, and pimps. Casablanca disgusts me profoundly.

"Fortunately the Arab town is there. Surrounded by a high wall, it shelters its gay little booths and its multicoloured displays, its cake hawkers roaming through the streets with big brass trays and offering you bright red meringues or blue nougat."

To his mother he waxed even more lyrical in describing his first visits to the medina. "I've bargained away treasures from white-robed Jews. They grow old amid the golden babouches and silver belts, their legs crossed under them, incensed by the 'Salaam Aleikum's of their multicoloured clients. . . .

"I saw an assassin being driven through the street. They kept cudgelling him so that he would bawl out his crime to the grave Jewish merchants and the little veiled fatmas. His shoulders were bowed and his head was staved in. It was very edifying and very moral. He was red with blood. His torturers howled about him. All the fabrics they drape themselves in leapt up and down, each violently proclaiming its hue. It was barbarous, it was splendid. The little babouches were not the least moved, any more than were the silver belts. Some were so small they would have to wait a long time to find their Cinderella, some were so rich they were only fit for a fairy. . . . But what lovely little feet they should have! And while the little babouche was telling me her dream—for golden babouches only tiled mosaics will do—a veiled stranger bargained them away from me. All I could see of her were two immense eyes . . . I only hope, oh golden babouches, that she is the most youthful of princesses and lives in a garden full of murmuring waters."

The tone of these letters is deliberately playful, and across each page there falls the smiling shadow of Hans Christian Andersen, the author of the first book the young Antoine really and truly loved. The desolate view from the barracks would fill him with nostalgia for the green grass and the green trees of Saint-Maurice. "Green offers moral nourishment", he wrote home, "it upholds the softness of manners and the quietude of the soul. Suppress this colour from life, and you will quickly dry up and turn nasty." But once through the gates of the medina, and all the asperities of the *bled* are forgotten. "If only I knew how to paint watercolours", he wrote ecstatically to his mother, "what colour, what colour!"

The ecstacy was as heady as ever when he was up in the air, as Captain René Bouscat, who then commanded an air force unit at Taza, had occasion to notice one day as he came down to land on the Casablanca airfield. To his astonishment he saw a Bréguet 14 biplane being put through a number of loops at the hair-raising altitude of 1200 feet. Not only was the plane not made for acrobatics, but the normal altitude prescribed for this kind of stunt flying was 6,000 feet, where the pilot had a chance of pulling his craft out of a dive if anything went wrong.

"Who on earth is that madman?" he asked on landing. The reply he received was: "A young corporal trainee—fellow by the name of Saint-Exupéry." Little did the Captain guess that he would hear a great deal more about him later and that one day they would be friends.

These antics do not seem to have kept the young corporal trainee from receiving his longed for promotion. It meant leaving Casablanca for the far more regal and picturesque city of Rabat, where he spent a week taking his officer cadet exams. With Marc Sabran, whom he had been to school with at Fribourg and in Paris and who was now an officer in the French army, he went to call on a Captain Priou, who had chosen to inhabit an old Arab house in the medina. Its milky whiteness was a source of unvarying enchantment. "One might almost be at the pole, walking about in the snow, so silken in the moonlight is this part of the Arab town. . . . The Captain's house, lost in the white labyrinth of Arab dwellings, backs up against the Oudaias mosque. The minaret looks down on its inner courtyard from the open sky and in the evening when one goes from the salon to the dining-room and looks up towards the stars, one hears the muezzin chanting and one sees him as from the depths of a well."

Even the landscape gradually lost its harshness, as the heat of summer cooled to the languid warmth of autumn, which at this latitude anticipates the spring. "Now that Sabran is in Casablanca—with our leaving every Saturday night for Rabat, from which we return Monday evening—life flows by easily and softly in this flowering country. For Morocco, that awful wilderness, has suddenly decked itself out in bright fresh green and shimmering prairies: dotted with red and yellow flowers, the plains light up, one by one . . ."

"Three hundred kilometres more to cover tomorrow morning", he wrote in still another letter. "The afternoons are spent sleeping, given the fatigue. The day after tomorrow, a long trip to the south. I'm going to Kasbah-Todla. Almost three hours of piloting (that's a lot of kilometres) to get there, and as many to return. What solitude it will be . . . I'm waiting with impatience.

"This evening, by the peaceful light of a lamp, I learned to steer by compass. The maps spread out before him on the table, Sergeant Boileau explains: '. . . When you get this far' (and our studious foreheads bend over the crisscrossing lines) 'you veer 45° west. . . . There, you see, a village— leave it well to your left, and don't forget to correct the wind drift with the movable needle of your compass. . . .' I begin to dream. He wakes me. 'Pay more attention . . . now 180° west, unless you'd rather cut across here . . . but there are fewer landmarks to go by . . . the road here, you see, is easy to follow.'

"Sergeant Boileau offers me some tea. I drink the cup in tiny sips. If I lose my way, I think, I'll land in rebel territory. How often have I been told: 'If you climb out of your tin-trap and find yourself in front of a woman and kiss her on the breast, from then on you're sacred. She'll treat you like a mother, they'll give you oxen, a camel, and they'll marry you off. It's the only way of saving your life.'

"My trip is still too simple for me to hope for such surprises. Still, this evening I am full of dreams. I would like to take part in long desert missions."

Ever a night owl, Saint-Exupéry still had energy enough, after the evening session with the sergeant, to pen a long letter to his mother. This time it was seated on a cot in the barracks; another time it was from Captain Priou's "adorable Moorish salon, buried in large cushions, a cup of tea in front of me and a cigarette between my lips. . . ." Later it was aboard the Navigation Paquet steamer which brought him back to France the following January. "I've installed myself in the dining room and am watching with amusement as the waiters lay the tables. What a worthy occupation! Unfortunately the dinner will come to an end during the sunset and this will spoil my dessert . . . I really can't complain about Morocco. I spent days of fearful boredom in the depths of a rotting shack, but now I look back on it as a life full of poetry."

Antoine de Saint-Exupéry was twenty-one and had spent nine months in the service. They had taught him more about the rough-and-tumble of the adult world than all his years at school. They had also unlocked the rudimentary mysteries of card tricks and sleight-of-hand, into which he had been initiated at Strasbourg by a fellow "ground-hugger" who was a conjuror in civilian life. He was not yet a full-fledged pilot, nor was he a full-fledged writer. But in his random scribblings to his mother and to Charles Sallès the glimmerings of genius—like desert landmarks—were now clearly discernible.

# 4

# Adrift

FROM Marseille Saint-Exupéry first proceeded to Istres, the grim *"bagne des élèves morts"* (penitentiary for doomed greenhorns) where novice pilots were put through their paces on antique Caudron trainers whose flabby cloth wings had a disturbing way of bending in mid-air. The training he had received in Morocco dispensed him from such menial chores as clearing the landing strips of stones (concrete runways had yet to be invented) and he was able to pass his final flight tests without killing himself in the process. Promoted to the rank of corporal in early February of 1922, he was sent to another airfield at Avord, near Bourges, where he spent six more months in pilot officer training. He emerged a second lieutenant in October, and after putting in a brief stint at another base not far from Reims, he was posted to Versailles and thus within easy reach of Paris.

The French Air Force was still in a highly formative stage, having yet to develop the vertebra of a ministry or the brain of an *Ecole de l'Air*. The idea that someone could become an officer in this new fangled service without going through the four-year grind at Saint-Cyr (infantry) or Saumur (cavalry) was still too novel to be easily accepted by the top brass. But the situation being as fluid and full of loopholes as a Gruyère cheese, General Barès, who had risen to become one of its senior officers, promised Saint-Exupéry that his temporary reserve commission would be "assimilated" if he wanted to pursue a career in the air force. Though Antoine had no particular love for military life as such, the prospect of continuing to fly was too tempting to resist, and it was with something close to joy that he now found himself transferred to the 34th Air Regiment, based at Le Bourget.

The régime he was subjected to during this probationary period was anything but tough. He had to put in an early morning appearance at the field, and to keep his hand in he was allowed to take a plane up once or twice a week; but for the rest of the time—often the better part of the day—he could do as he pleased. From Le Bourget it was an easy hop in to Paris, where Antoine

65

was delighted to renew the friendships he had made at the Lycée Saint-Louis and the Ecole Bossuet. Henry de Ségogne, having also failed to make the Naval Academy at Brest, had finally opted for a post with the Cour des Comptes. At the time he was still living in his mother's apartment on the Rue Pierre 1er de Serbie; and it was here, for lack of a better place to hang his pilot's cap, that his friend Antoine would repair whenever he had a few hours to kill. He apparently had many, for Ségogne's mother was soon complaining about the huge corpse-like form which was to be found day after day draped awkwardly over the canapé which, like so many of the beds he tried, was a size too short for his long legs.

Another friend whom Antoine and Ségogne had got to know in their final year at Bossuet was Bertrand de Saussine, better known to his companions—in the algebraic lingo of *"hypoflotte"*—as BB or *B Carré* (B squared). Their friendship had been cemented one day during a strike which had momentarily paralysed the capital. To break it, the Government had asked for volunteers and as one man the *flottards* of Saint-Louis had risen in response. Patriots all, they were more than ready to accept the sacrifice of a first-class spree. Ségogne, who had somehow acquired a nodding acquaintance with motors, was entrusted the wheel, while Antoine and BB punched tickets. It was a memorable morning (beginning at 7 a.m.) and before Ségogne was through with his desperate gear-grinding, he had managed to upset a cart full of oranges, which scattered generously across the Boulevard Saint-Germain. The Three Young Musketeers were still laughing about it when the youngest, B Squared, brought his two starving busmen-in-arms back home for lunch.

The Saussines' apartment was located in a magnificent town-house at No. 16, Rue Saint-Guillaume. Known as the Hôtel de Créquy—after the wit-loving Marquise who had lived there in the eighteenth century—it was one of those palatial residences with a spacious forecourt and magnificent *porte cochère* of which the Saint-Germain quarter is so full. The literary tradition had outlined the gay Marquise, for Lamartine had made his home here and also Ernest Renan, the philosopher-historian. Marcel Proust had haunted its drawing rooms and gardens, as had his friend Reynaldo Hahn, whose dreamy tinkling on the grandpiano in the drawing-room could arouse Proust's spirit to heights of Edwardian ecstasy. Count Henri de Saussine was an amateur composer whose musical evenings were appreciated by such connoisseurs as Ravel, Poulenc, and Gabriel Fauré. The drawing-room even contained an upstairs loggia, reached by an inner staircase, over whose balustrades the guests could ogle pianist and singers through their mother-of-pearl lorgnettes. In the process of Victorian "modernization"—undertaken to make the muses feel completely at home—the old Louis XVI *boiseries* had all but disappeared behind a flourish of draperies and a maze of Chinese screens alive with birds and flowers. The walls dripped with a Parnassian waterfall of paintings, the corners bulged with rock gardens of lacquered tables, the sofas swooned in pools of heavily frilled lamplight—in short, it was every crowded inch the kind of refuge which Robert de Montesquiou (the model for Proust's Baron Charlus) and other arbiters of *fin-de siècle* elegance could languidly approve of. Nudity being at that time one of those exquisitely defended virtues which had to be draped—on the beach, as elsewhere—even the ceiling had been clothed—with an immense tapestry, into whose lush, medieval depths the soaring listener could plunge, while listening to Schumann, with no further discomfort than a twinge of cramp in the neck. The crowning touch was the chandelier which, since it could not be hung from the scissored centre of all that brilliant woof, was suspended on a chain from the tip of a halberd, slanting out from the wall as though held in the iron grip of an invisible Vatican guard.

The last-born of five children, Bertrand de Saussine had been preceded by four sisters, of whom only the eldest, Blanche, had known the "heroic" pre-war period when Proust had frequented the house. But his ghost, to say nothing of his friends, still haunted the premises. The youngest sister Renée, who was a year or two older than Antoine, was something of a virtuoso on the violin and frequently performed at the musical soirées which her father was still fond of giving. On one of these occasions, which must have occurred about the time Saint-Exupéry was getting to know the family, a trio had been formed with Yvonne Lefébure at the piano and Louis Fournier seconding Renée on the violin. A Madame Chalandon, from Lyon, was to sing some Ravel compositions which the ageing maestro had kindly volunteered to coach her in. As Ravel was then living at Montfort l'Amaury, some twenty miles west of Paris, the concert was held earlier than usual at 5 o'clock, to give him time to get home that same evening on the train. The concert was barely over when there was a dramatic opening of doors and in past the butler swept the Comtesse de Greffuhle, feathers, veil, and gloves a-flutter, in an *entrée* which Renée de Saussine recalls as "utterly proustian". Ravel, who had not yet left, was still seated in the front row talking to Henri de Saussine, who jumped up with considerable dismay.

"Oh, but how sad, Madame! The concert is just finished."

"Oh, I don't care about the music," said the grand old lady, giving him her bony hand to kiss. "It's for you I came, dear Count."

Contrary to the idyllic portrait Proust painted of her in the character of the Duchesse de Guermantes, the Comtesse de Greffuhle had once again exhibited her real-life talent for saying the wrong thing. Ravel was much amused by her subsequent effusions—"Oh, *cher Maître*, I had no idea you

were here!"—and the incident became a favourite story among the Saussines
and their friends.

Another, and in some ways even more picturesque household which
Antoine had got to know while at Bossuet was that of the Vilmorins. Unlike
the Saussines, they were people of financial substance who owned an
exquisite seventeenth-century mansion, the oldest wing of which had been
built by Louis XIV for Mademoiselle de La Vallière in what was then the
rural village of Verrières-le-Buisson but which has since become a southern
suburb of Paris. They also occupied a venerable townhouse on the corner of
the Rue de la Chaise and the Rue de Grenelle—within easy walking distance
of the Ecole Bossuet. One of the "pistons" who was at the Lycée Saint-Louis
at the same time as Saint-Exupéry was Honoré d'Estienne d'Orves, who was
related to his mother's family through the Léstranges. Estienne d'Orves'
mother was a Vilmorin, and Antoine himself was thus distantly related to the
family. Whether it was he or Bertrand de Saussine who first brought Saint-
Exupéry to the house on the Rue de la Chaise matters little, for as a matter
of fact a whole cluster of Bossuet schoolmates found their way there. At
times it resembled a boyish stampede, which would start the moment the
last afternoon class at Saint-Louis was over and before the evening study
hall at Bossuet began. It became such routine that Abbé Dibildos, the
Basque prelate who ran the Ecole Bossuet (and who cared little for Saint-
Exupéry, be it said in passing), was once heard to ask, as he raised a quizzical
eyebrow: "I wonder what there is *chez* Madame de Vilmorin which causes
all these boys to rush over there all the time?"

The *ambiance* which reigned at the house on the Rue de la Chaise was
made to appeal to schoolboys eager to escape the severity of classroom
pedagogues and Jesuit superintendents. It was elegant but not stiff, affluent
but not vulgar, with a tinge of the libertine and a touch of the decadent
which made the family *esprit*—gay, uninhibited, and witty—as maliciously
cynical as Voltaire's. The Vilmorins, who liked to point out that they were
descended from a great nephew of Joan of Arc's, had saved themselves from
the penury which overtook so many of the better families in the eighteenth
century by developing an interest in botany which successive generations
had transformed into the most flourishing seed-producing enterprise in
France. A persistent curiosity allied to a readiness to innovate and experiment
had turned the garden at Verrières-le-Buisson into a horticultural marvel, a
kind of miniature Kew Gardens filled with rare species of African shrub and
Himalayan pine and strange oriental arbours. Philippe de Vilmorin, who
died shortly before Antoine got to know the family, had inherited and
extended the family interest in botanical genetics—a photograph has been
preserved of him holding a magnifying glass over an ear of wheat—and he

had travelled over large parts of the world in search of hybrids. A friend of Sacha Guitry and Paul Claudel, he was at home with poets and playwrights and being as handsome as he was cultivated, he had, almost *malgré lui*, made numerous feminine conquests.

In this respect, at least, his wife Mélanie was every bit his equal. Dark haired and dark eyed, she was a dazzling beauty with an oval face which came close to having the classic perfection of a Giorgione or an Ingres. Her family, the Gaufridy de Dortans, were if anything even more aristocratic than the Vilmorins, and as her daughter was later to write of her: "She was born, thanks to her ancestors, into a forest of genealogical trees fluttering with armorial leaves: titles to the left of her, titles to the right of her, titles behind and above her crowding around to fill her with a faint nostalgia at having to abandon all those rich shadows in order to live with a family of grain merchants and bring children into the world." One of her sisters, who had married into a perfume fortune, was known as *"la jolie parfumeuse"*; but for someone as radiant as Mélanie de Vilmorin nothing less than *"la belle jardinière"* would do. Bringing six children into the world in as many years had done nothing to cloud the perfection of her looks; and after her husband's death, when she moved into town with her brood, it was a very merry widow who ruled the house in the Rue de la Chaise. Ambassadors, ministers, and even royalty vied ardently for her favours and it was a rare day on which one did not encounter—in an antechamber if not in the dining-room—some prominent politician or man of the world. "I have never deceived my husband," the beautiful Mélanie was once heard to remark, adding a moment later in a no less wistful tone: "Kings, after all, don't count."

Split up into a number of small apartments, with back staircases, rambling corridors, *demi-étages* and *entresols*, where the muffled laughs and whispers were lost behind ancient walls and fine old doors, the house on the Rue de la Chaise was made—even more than that of Saint-Maurice-de-Rémens—for the co-existence of charmingly disparate worlds. That of the *jeunesse*— four boys and two girls—began on the second floor, where the merriment and the mischief and the incessant intrigues were secretely abetted by Léon Hubert, the concierge, who handled the clandestine mail (which Mama was not supposed to see) and from whose loge the children could telephone outside. But the worlds, though different and contiguous, often merged at mealtimes, when the children were treated on a *pied d'égalité* with ministers and politicians, amused at their groping efforts to fathom the mysteries of diplomacy and public affairs. Paul Painlevé, the mathematician-prime minister and an early aviation promoter, the stately Léon Bérard with his quaint Béarnais passion for Latin and Greek quotations, Daniel Vincent with his fierce black bush of a moustache, Edouard Herriot, the Mayor of Lyon and a rising star in the Radical Socialist party—all were *habitués* of the Rue de la Chaise. And there were many others, too numerous to name. Sometimes the *va-et-vient* was so intense that it led to comic encounters, frigid bows, and a stiff tipping of hats in the staircase.

Such was the extraordinary household which Antoine first discovered during his period at Bossuet and which he sought out again in the autumn of 1922. Along with the four brothers—Roger, Henry, Olivier, and André—there were two daughters, the younger of whom, Louise, was, like Saint-Exupéry, something of a poet. She was tall, had auburn hair and hazel eyes, the kind of pale "transparent" skin which appealed to him, and if she did not have her mother's almost flawless beauty—her face and particularly her teeth were a shade too equine—she made up for it with that indefinable quality which can only be called "*le charme Vilmorin*"—a captivating mixture of verve, irreverent fancy, and uninhibited caprice. Jean Cocteau, when he got to know her a dozen years later, described her as a "tall, ravishing girl with a husky voice and somewhat loose-jointed schoolgirl gestures, a laugh which wrinkles the skin of her nose and lifts a cruel lip above flashing teeth . . . a trusting, perfectly simple, uncultured being . . . Madame de Vilmorin has a red balloon which carries her up from the earth and takes her wherever she wishes to go." The description is probably a fair one for the younger "Loulou" Saint-Exupéry befriended in the early 1920s. She made no attempt at a bogus erudition, and it was precisely this absence of cultural pretence, the surprise and appetite she brought to the discovery and enjoyment of each new thing, the carefree spontaneity with which she seemed to say or do whatever happened to pass through her head at the moment which made her so irresistible. Few of the boys introduced to her failed to succumb to her spell. Bertrand de Saussine was smitten, and so in turn was Antoine de Saint-Exupéry, who had the advantage of being several years his senior.

It was, as one might expect, an ardent courtship and one to which—to her brothers' considerable surprise—"Loulou" responded. For lack of roses, which he was usually too poor to bring her, he smothered her in odes and sonnets which she received with the reclining grace of a Madame Récamier, listening to a younger Chateaubriand. A serious infirmity of the hip had come near to crippling her while Antoine had been away in Morocco, and even now at the Rue de la Chaise she was forced to spend much of her time in bed. The ailment, far from impairing her charms, only spurred on the ardour of her young suitors, who would climb up to her room, past the prim eye of Mademoiselle Petermann, her governess and *dueña*, to pay their stammering homage to her gracefully recumbent being. But the others were soon eclipsed by the fervent young Antoine, and as her brother André was later to describe it, "she felt for him a sort of passion which can be explained by the great fascination he exercised and by his way of talking of the poetry of others and already of his own". Most of these poems seem to have been lost, and it is possible that Saint-Exupéry deliberately destroyed them later when he turned resolutely from verse to prose. One was called "*La Ville*" (The City) and in it, Henry de Ségogne recalls, the lights at night were compared to a constellation.

> *Hâtons nous de rêver car voici que se dresse*
> *L'ombre qui dès midi campe au revers des monts.*

are two of the verses which have survived. The *Carpe diem* of Virgil was here transmuted into a *Carpe somnium* and Ronsard's "*mignonne . . . Cueillez, cueillez votre jeunesse*" into an invitation to cull dreams from the bright hillsides of high noon.

To the perplexity of her brothers, who could not understand what she saw in this big, lumbering pilot, Louise succumbed to the poetic barrage and agreed to give her "cousin" her hand. The mother, who understood not a word of all this poetic talk and who found him a bore and what was worse, a relatively impecunious bore, took a dim view of the affair from the start. But they became engaged and the *fiançailles* were even officially announced. Antoine's mother sent the hard-pressed suitor an old family heirloom, complete with sapphire and tiny diamonds, to give to Loulou as an engagement ring; but the gift, painstakingly and critically inspected by the brothers, did little to thaw the ice which had begun to form around this particular relationship. The Vilmorins were used to living on a lavish scale, and if one thing was obvious, it was that Loulou's fiancé was closer to the penniless sort. And what a profession, being a pilot! And worse, a pilot's wife! With all of the anxieties and none of the wild joys. Moving—who could tell?—from one dreary base to another, from one insipid garrison town to the next, at the whim of some distant and, as likely as not, dim military authority. At the risk, furthermore, of being a widow. For once in the air nothing seemed able to restrain the exuberant young pilot. To dazzle his friends, who would troop out to Le Bourget to watch him, he would do a few wild loops and then hedge-hop over the countryside with a hair-raising élan which he later enjoyed communicating to his listeners. For the Vilmorins, as for the Saussines he was the "*condamné à mort*"—the already condemned to death. A macabre appellation which came within an ace of being fulfilled one Sunday in early 1923. Antoine's engine failed as he was flying over the Le Bourget suburbs and he crashed on to the edge of the field.

He was pulled unconscious from the wreck and driven to the Guillemin hospital, where it took him several weeks to recover from a fractured skull and frequent spells of dizziness.

To Louise de Vilmorin and her family, the moral was clear: if she was to continue being engaged to him, Antoine de Saint-Exupéry would have to choose a less neck-breaking profession. Reluctant to break the news to him personally, she sent her elder sister Marie-Pierre ("Mapie") to the hospital to deliver the message, which hit him like an ultimatum. It was a severe blow to Antoine, for whom flying was a rare joy. At first he refused to believe she was in earnest; and once out of the hospital he climbed back into the cockpit, anxious to prove to himself that his mishap had not undermined his nerve and that he could still fly, in rain or sunshine, through fog or cloud, without a weakening of the will. But at the Rue de la Chaise he found a resolution as firm as his own. He was forced to choose and it was an agonizing choice; but for Loulou what wasn't he prepared to sacrifice? So finally, after much soul-searching, he agreed to abandon his flying career and to resign from the Army.

The ex-pilot was now faced with a critical dilemma. He was almost twenty-three and to resume his interrupted architectural studies at the Ecole des Beaux-Arts at this late age was virtually out of the question. It would mean three years of study, eked out on the pittance which was all his hard-pressed mother could possibly send him as an allowance. To rely on the bounty of his fiancée's family was unthinkable. He had to find a job, but here at least the Vilmorins could help him. It was in fact one of Mélanie de Vilmorin's admirers, the Minister Daniel Vincent—"that friend of poets and who recites their verses so well", as Léon-Paul Fargue was to say of him—who got Antoine a job as "production supervisor" with a tile-making company run by the Société Générale d'Entreprise. Situated a short distance from the Elysée Palace and the British Embassy—at 56, Rue du Faubourg Saint-Honoré—it boasted an excellent address; but this cubby-hole office, barely five yards square, up on the fifth floor was as depressing as the gloomy inner court it overlooked and the job he was given of scanning reports and checking figures. There would be a wild moment of euphoria at the beginning of each month when he received his pay check. Prodigal as ever, he would invite his friends to Prunier's, a short distance down the street, where, very much the *grand seigneur*, he would treat the assembled gourmets to a spartan diet of caviar and champagne. A few days later the euphoria would give way to near despair, as a distraut Antoine found himself delving into an empty pocket-book, and one more flustered letter would go off to Saint-Maurice, with a pathetic appeal to his mother for more funds.

In August Louise suddenly felt the need for fresh mountain air, and leaving

Verrières with the faithful Mademoiselle Petermann to chaperone her, she
went to Renonvilliers in the Bernese Jura mountains. Was it to "recover from
a bout of flu", as she explained, or a secret desire to get away for a bit from a
family which was silently hostile to the match and to which she was, nonthe-
less, almost umbilically attached? Probably it was a bit of both, and with
that sylph-like instinct which so often guides the feminine heart she may
have felt the need for a trial outing *à deux*, where they would be alone by
themselves on a kind of pre-nuptial honeymoon. It being the middle of
the summer vacation, Antoine had no trouble taking leave of absence from
his job; but penniless as ever he had to sell his camera to be able to join his
beloved, who had found a place to stay in the chalet of the local priest. The
dog-days were already on the wane and in the lush greenness of the mountain
valley where they took long walks, the air had a fresh tingle to it even at
midday. They picked gentians and made bouquets of their blue, violet, and
yellow flowers. For it was August 25, the Feast of Saint-Louis—which had
always been celebrated at Verrières with presents and bundles of beribboned
wrappings, like a late summer Noël. But let us listen to Louise de Vilmorin
tell the story in her own twittering flight of words:

"Oh, the lovely bouquet! . . . Saint-Louis, my Saint's Day. Oh, the
lovely promises! I reply to them, I answer for them. Are they rustic, living,
everlasting? Yes, they are everlasting.

Like all fiancés, we live at once in the present and the future. To be sure,
we make plans, but often all Antoine has on his mind is flying. He talks to
me of sublime or terrifying moments spent between heaven and earth, while
I, who am thinking of how we're going to furnish our future home, interrupt
to ask him if he likes studded upholsteries.

'A canapé in front of the fireplace is always very nice, isn't it? Particularly
in winter, and even more in the autumn, when the wet wood sizzles.'

'Yes . . . Yes . . . But come.'

'Where do you want to go?'

'On a trip. You'll see.'

And we steal away. For a few *sous* we take a tiny train. I'm careful in
sitting down not to crease my skirt, I take off my white cotton gloves, and
while he's looking at the birds, the clouds, and the celestial currents, I look
at the chalets, the neatly looped curtains, the little gardens and the plants
on the embankment. Then gazing into each others' eyes, we share our
observations and reach Bienne. The weather is grey, the waters of the lake
are dull with black reflections, the hour is dark with forebodings and under
the trees it's chilly.

'To warm up a bit let's buy some chocolate, let's have a smoke, and let's
go sit inside the station where the posters are so pretty', he says to me.

People about to part don't hesitate to kiss each other in stations. The locomotive whistle is the signal for impassioned embraces, and at the moment of parting the lovers cling shudderingly in each others' arms. It's what we do, even though we know we're cheating.

Already Antoine is beginning to lose his hair. It worries him and me too. There are, it seems, elixirs for the hair which work wonders and which can be found in the lovely pharmacies of Geneva. September is near. Alas, September is here. Goodbye to the Bernese Jura, goodbye to Monsieur le Pasteur. We are returning to Paris by train.

'Let's make a detour', says Antoine.

'A detour? What folly! And why a detour?' cries Mademoiselle Peter-mann, who's been having trouble chaperoning us. I answer: "Uh . . . Uh . . . hair lotion . . . important . . . baldness . . . disaster . . .' And with these words we're off to Geneva, where we lunch by the lakeside.

'Listen, isn't that the sound of a military band?' asks Antoine, leaping to his feet and dragging me across the street. Military music! Like all the young born before 1914 we are patriots. Our governesses used to sing: '*Sentinelles ne tirez pas, c'est un oiseau qui vient de France.*' We know the words to *Sambre et Meuse* and the *Marche Lorraine*. Military music brings tears to our eyes. We tremble at the thought of the French flag and the frontier of the Rhine and the crêpe-veiled statue of the City of Strasbourg on the Place de la Concorde in Paris, piteous reminder of the East. *Ran, pan, plan!* The music draws closer, sweeps over me, overwhelms me, and I cry: '*Vive la France*' through my sobs—only to see the Swiss flag. Oh, shame on me—a traitor to my land, . . . It was a Geneva regiment returning from manoeuvres in the field."

It was a blissful idyll, but brief, and with autumn already upon them it ended on a melancholy note, like a hunter's dying horn. Back in Paris nothing had changed and the atmosphere at Verrières was as politely disapproving as ever. Meanwhile something was changing inside Louise. Almost two years younger than Antoine she was emotionally not yet ripe for marriage. She was still too chained to Verrières, too attached to the "Vil-morin family spirit" to be able to face a separation. Years before her mother, without realizing how attached she was to it, had given away her favourite doll to the daughter of a friend, and the loss had marked Loulou with a feeling of inconsolable bereavement—comparable to the pain felt by Orson Welles' Citizen Kane on the loss of his *Rosebud* sled. But now it was not a doll, it was Verrières she was threatened with losing. And the Rue de la Chaise, where the conversations were so witty and the dinners so lively that the waiters were known to have had to hurry back to the pantry with their dishes to keep from splitting their sides with laughter in the presence of the guests. To go off with a husband who did not quite fit in, who was not a member of the clan, and who could hardly support himself, let alone a wife.

The break, when it came, took the form of a flight. One day, when Antoine turned up at the Rue de la Chaise, Louise was no longer there. She had left without a word. Only later did he learn that she had fled to Biarritz. It was a cruel blow from which it took him weeks to recover and, as we shall see, it left its clawmark on his writings. Later they made it up, and he became a friend once more. He even wrote her a number of letters imbued with a philosophic comprehension which was penetratingly lucid—about her as much as about himself: "You have such a need for a world where no gesture leaves a trace, you feel an almost animal anxiety at leaving your footprint in the sand", he wrote to her. After which he added, in a change of metaphors which would have pleased Hans Christian Andersen: "You are made to inhabit the ocean depths, whose crystal no movement disturbs."

So different from his own world, where everything was in a state of flux.

\* \* \*

That October his sister Gabrielle was married at Saint-Maurice-de-Rémens to a young country gentleman from the Esterel called Pierre d'Agay. The homecoming for this festive occasion, which his friend Charles Sallès attended, was one of the few bright spots in an otherwise dismal year. He was delighted with his sister's choice of a husband, but the fruitful outcome of her engagement inevitably cast its melancholy shadow over the less happy evolution of his own.

His one consolation was his friends—beginning with Yvonne de Lestrange, his mother's second cousin. Twelve years older than he, she was like an elder sister to Antoine, who found frequent refuge in her charming apartment on the Quai Malaquais, next door to the French Institute and Mazarin's palatial library. There was his old friend Priou, from Morocco, in whose apartment near the Buttes de Chaumont he camped for a while; and there were his friends from Bossuet, Henry de Ségogne and Bertrand de Saussine. The latter's name of "*B Carré*" (B Squared) now seemed more appropriate than ever, with the bell-bottom trousers he wore as a naval cadet—for unlike Saint-Exu and Ségogne he had worked hard and gained admission to the Naval Academy at Brest—though his appearances in Paris were now limited to occasional home leaves. But at No. 16 Rue Saint-Guillaume Antoine could be sure of a warm welcome, if only from his sisters. Renée, to beguile him would pull out her violin and charm him with Bach, his favourite composer. Or they would walk out of the gate and down the street to the right as far as the Boulevard Saint-Germain, where they could stop to gorge on *babas-au-rhum* at the fashionable patisserie of "A La Dame Blanche" or empty a bock or two of beer at the Brasserie Lipp.

"I recall one of his gestures", Renée de Saussine wrote of him years later, "perhaps the most familiar of them all: a cigarette between the index and the third finger, he would hold the box of matches with the same left hand. Struck with his right hand, one of them would flare up, lighting him from underneath, then flicker and die. His athlete's body and face—like Watteau's *Gilles*—emerged, then disappeared in the darkness. It was long enough to start a phrase or a sonnet, defend a position in a vehement albeit muffled voice, too brief to conclude. Besides, he never finished, no one ever being of the same opinion. And Antoine's act would start again, the ashtray soon spilling over with matches which formed a tiny brazier under his untouched cigarette".

On the subject of Saint-Exupéry the family was divided. "What a splendid boy!" the father would say. But Renée's mother and her two older sisters (the third was already married and away) were surprised at his frequent taciturnity. It was a rampart he put up, as so many adolescents do, to protect his inner self from an incomprehensible world. But the rampart could be scaled by those who took the trouble to know him better, and occasionally the drawbridge was lowered and out it came—like a flood.

We have a written record of one such occasion in the very first letter he wrote to Renée de Saussine and which she was generous enough to publish, with a whole batch of others, some years after his disappearance. The occasion arose as the result of a talk Henry de Ségogne had given at the Club Alpin to a roomful of dowagers. For his tour of duty in the army Ségogne had chosen to serve with the *chasseurs alpins*, and the vertigo of the heights had remained with him. "He kept the packed hall on tenter-hooks", as Antoine later recalled it, "by telling how one scales peaks as spiked as church steeples. He rattled off his heroism with a negligence which had the old ladies trembling." Their well-gloved applause and their velvety compliments were still ringing in their ears when the lecturer and three of his friends—including Saint-Exupéry and Bertrand de Saussine—sallied forth to celebrate the triumphal termination of a somewhat tense *séance*. They visited first one and then another of their favourite bistros in the vicinity of Saint-Germain-des-Prés, and soon they could no longer remember how many joints they had cased. When the time came to break up the party, several of them could still manage to hiccup "Sainte-Geneviève"—the name of the humble *pension* where Antoine was then living—but none of them could remember, still less articulate, "Poniatowski", the tongue-twisting name of the boulevard on which the *pension* was located. There was no use appealing to Saint-Exu, who by this time was way beyond all that . . . So Ségogne, who had not completely lost his bearings, finally volunteered to drag him back to his mother's apartment, where the limp bulk was deposited on the carpet. Afraid he might be sick, he put a basin with a little water in it under Antoine's head, then went back to the kitchen to brew some tea. When he returned, he saw that his friend's face had slipped into the water, from which strange noises were emanating. "Help! Help!" came the gurgle, "I'm drowning!"

It was perhaps to prove—if only to himself—that he had been as sober as a bishop throughout this festive evening that Saint-Exupéry later penned a letter to his friend Renée de Saussine which was in effect a piece of literary criticism, inspired among other things by a short story of her sister Laure's he had been carrying about absent-mindedly in his pocket for some days. The Saussine household had also been upset by a recent death, and Antoine must have felt that his bleary-eyed presence was something they could dispense with for a day or two. So he sat down at a café and began writing, and as he did so, he couldn't help poking fun at his friend Henry's exuberant rhetoric which was still ringing in his ears—with all those "sublime summits" to which, in the euphoria of a rosy-fingered dawn, he had given "sweet jam-like colours, like gum drops. The pointed peaks were pink, the horizons milky, the rocks all honey-hued and golden in the first fires of morning. The landscape seemed edible. Listening to him, I thought of the soberness of your story. One must work, Rinette. You are very good at bringing out the particularity of each thing, that which gives it a life of its own. . . ." And he went on, in a credo which Vladimir Nabokov would gladly have endorsed: "One mustn't learn to write but to see. Writing is a consequence. When the vision is absent the epithets applied are like layers of paint: they add arbitrary ornaments but they don't bring out what is essential. . . . One must ask oneself: 'How am I going to render the impression?' And the objects come to life through the reaction they evoke in us, they are described in depth. Only it's no longer a game. . . ." After which he added—something which would have gotten Nabokov's back up: "Look how the most incoherent of Dostoievski's monologues give one an impression of necessity, of logic, and hang together. The link is internal. . . . One doesn't create a living character by attaching qualities and defects to him and deducing the plot from them, but by expressing felt impressions. Even a simple emotion like joy is too complex to be invented if you're not content just to say of your hero 'he was joyful'—which expresses nothing that is individual. One joy doesn't resemble another. And it's precisely this difference, the individual life of this joy, which must be conveyed. But one mustn't be pedantic in explaining this joy. It must be expressed through its consequences, through the reactions of the individual. And then you won't even need to say: 'He was joyful.' This joy will arise of itself, with its own individuality, like a certain joy you feel and to which no word exactly applies."

Poets, who are in effect the higher mathematicians of language, are more conscious than others of the limitations of vocabulary, and here it was no longer the literary critic but the poet who was speaking. In reading these lines Renée de Saussine may well have smiled, recalling to mind one of her first literary "sessions" with the young Antoine. It was while he was still a boarder at Bossuet. He had spent his idle hours, and probably quite a few of those in study hall, composing a piece of verse drama in which brigand princes roamed like Robin Hoods through a legendary Maeterlinckian realm. A tuft of dark hair, loosened by the fervour of his recitation, had fallen over one of his eyes, combining with the paper cutter he held in his hand to fashion an image of exalted banditry. But that was three, four years ago . . . and in the interim he had changed. The ballads and the epics had been tucked away and forgotten, and now it was with the first fragments of a novel that the aspiring author was struggling. He wanted to convey the strange impressions he experienced every time he took to the air . . . and also the even stranger unreality of the return to earth.

For increasingly he felt chained up, like a dog on a leash. His job was so menial that it hardly earned him enough to pay for an occasional train trip back to see his mother at Saint-Maurice. Desperately he began casting around for other openings.

He was tempted by the lure of journalism, but shrank from having to put together factual articles for the "Information" section of *Le Matin*. Hearing that there was a shortage of pilots in China (of all places!) he toyed for a moment with the idea of proceeding to the Far East—"perhaps to run a flying school", as he wrote rather breathlessly to his mother. "It would be a magnificent pecuniary job", he added, as a mournful postcript to his present impecuniousness.

Nothing came of this dream, though Saint-Exupéry still occasionally managed to take to the air on Sundays, when he could get away from his cramped office and go up on practice flights at Orly, then a small and relatively minor airfield. "I adore this profession", he wrote to his mother after one Sunday outing. "You can't imagine the calm, the solitude one finds at twelve thousand feet in a *tête-à-tête* with one's motor. And then the charming camaraderie down below, on the field. You cat-nap on the grass, waiting for your turn. You follow your friend's gyrations with your eyes, waiting for your turn to go up in the same plane, and you swap stories. They're all marvellous. Stories of engine failures in mid-country close to unknown little villages where a flustered and patriotic mayor invites the airmen to dinner . . . and fairy tale adventures. Most of them are invented on the spot, but they are listened to with hushed awe and when one takes off in one's turn, one is keyed up and full of hope. But nothing happens . . . and on landing one finds solace in a glass of port, or by explaining: 'My motor was heating up, *mon vieux*, I was in a dither. . . .' But it was heating up so little, the poor motor."

One day his employers decided to put his aeronautical experience to work by having him take aerial photographs of their factory lay-out. Elatedly the young enthusiast suggested that the experiment be expanded into a full-fledged enterprise specializing in the aerial mapping of factory installations. While his employers made a show of seriously weighing this project, Saint-Exupéry was offered a brief diversion by being sent to preside over the company's exhibit at the Paris Fair. He sat in a hut, receiving the visits of hundreds of strangers and of a few friends, who trooped out to the fair-grounds to goggle at his mock gravity and serious mien. But the respite was brief and soon he was back in his "cage" where, as he wrote Sallès, "there's not a friend to take pity on me. . . . Life is decidedly melancholy." He continued to buy lottery tickets in an effort to make it a little less predictable. But here too his hopes were dashed and he won nothing. "It's a bit like the chagrin of love, it keeps one occupied", he remarked philosophically, only to add more fretfully: "I would so much like to change jobs and offices. I've been doing the same thing now for so long. I'm the most discouraged fellow in the world." He could not even risk napping when he wasn't busy with his figures; for one day his employer had walked into his cubbyhole with several "big wigs" and he had surprised them (and himself) by waking up from a nightmare crying: "Mama!" Eyebrows had risen, and they had solemnly marched out, convinced the poor boy was mad.

In November of 1924 he was forced to move yet again—his third displace-ment since the Pension Sainte-Geneviève. This time he holed up in a dingy room in a cheap little hotel on the Boulevard d'Ornano, behind Mont-martre. He no longer had a place where he could invite his friends, as he had been able to do in Priou's apartment on the Buttes de Chaumont, and the added burden of having to pay for his room made him more broke than ever. His "novel", which he had confidently thought half finished the previous summer, now showed signs of bogging down for lack of inspiration; and to compensate for his own feeling of inadequacy, he was reduced to lecturing to his friend Marc Sabran (who had been to the Villa Saint-Jean and then to the Lycée Bossuet, one year behind him in each case) on how to write, or rather, on how *not* to write and *not* to think. "I have noticed", he wrote to his mother, "that when people speak or write they immediately abandon all thought to go in for artificial deductions. They use words like an adding machine which is supposed to spew out a truth. It's idiotic. One must learn not to reason, but to stop reasoning. One doesn't need to go through a series of words to understand something, or else they falsify everything."

There was more than a hint of Bergson in this apologia for intuition, but it was not just a casual notion he had picked up at school; it appealed to something fundamental within him. "I detest those people who write to amuse themselves, who strive for effects", he wrote home. "One must have something to say." But that was just the trouble. Cooped up in his "cage", he felt he had nothing to say. He wanted to write but he had not yet lived. He was increasingly impatient with the dainty prattle of salon conversation, and he took it out on those around him, girls as well as boys. "I'm waiting to meet some young girl who is pretty and intelligent and full of charm and gaiety and relaxing and faithful", he wrote to his sister Gabrielle, ". . . and so I shall not find her. And I go on monotonously courting the Colettes, the Paulettes, the Suzys, the Daisys, the Gabys who are all mass produced and bore the life out of one after a couple of hours. They're waiting-rooms, no more." And when his mother undertook to upbraid him for his mulish behaviour, he replied: "I can no longer bear not finding what I want in someone, and I'm always disappointed as soon as I discover that a mind I thought interesting is simply an easily disassembled mechanism; and I feel disgust. I then have it in for that person. I have been eliminating many things and many people from my life—I can't help it."

From this tedium and despondency he was rescued in the late autumn of 1924 by a change of job. From the manufacture of tiles he moved to the manufacture of trucks. He bade goodbye to the little office on the Rue du Faubourg Saint-Honoré, rising every morning at dawn to go to work at the Saurer truck factory at Suresnes. His job was to be that of a salesman, but two months of preparatory apprenticeship were required. It meant getting up at six and taking a bus across the Bois de Boulogne, just as the pallid sun was beginning to rise in the East. At ten o'clock there would be a break for the "*casse-croûte*", and he would eat his sandwich lunch with the other workers. Ten hours of work a day, plus the three more he needed to get to his place of work and back. "I come home exhausted and fall asleep while standing", he wrote to Sallès. "But, *mon vieux*, I'm not the least bit bored. Gloriously decked out in a set of blue overalls, I spend my days under the trucks. Sometimes I go out on one of them and roar around the highways. I bawl out the chauffeurs of Hispano Suizas. I cry: '*Salaud, et ta droite?*' They look at me with a distant air and I enjoy a quiet laugh."

The rough humour of the workshops amused him and he found the mechanics and electricians "positively adorable. They bawl each other out with a wit which delights me. 'Well, maybe you could make some thunder, but you'll never be able to create a spark'." Time now flew instead of shuffling along with the jerky limp of the second-hand he had spent vacant hours contemplating in the Faubourg Saint-Honoré office. He was made to draw each engine part he disassembled before fitting them back into position. It gave him a feeling of creative responsibility, and as he wrote gleefully to Sallès: "I am already capable of demolishing your Citroën completely."

The months were thus consumed, as rapid as they were ruinous. For whenever the hotel porter failed to wake him in time—and waking Saint-Exupéry at 6 a.m. required an inordinate amount of door pounding—he would have to race downstairs with his shoelaces untied and make it out to Suresnes in a taxi. It would have been a serious drain on a better garnished purse, but for Saint-Exupéry's lightly lined wallet it was downright catastrophic. A good half of the 350 francs (about $35) a month he earned went into paying for his room, and for anything like clothes or even the fare money needed for a trip to Saint-Maurice, he had to fall back on the hard-pressed generosity of his mother.

It was still winter when he set out to explore his new bailiwick: the three *départements* of the Allier, the Cher, and the Creuse—over which it was his job to roam as travelling salesman for Saurer trucks. The money his mother had promised him for a little car of his own having failed to materialize in time, he had to take the train to Montluçon, a rather uninspiring township northwest of Vichy which was to be his headquarters. He reached it at 9 o'clock in the evening and found the town empty and asleep, behind closed shutters. In the little salon of the Hôtel Terminus a self-satisfied country squire was holding forth with an assurance which had quite cowed his captive audience—to the disgust of the newcomer, who had hoped to get away from the platitudinous pontifications he had so often been exposed to in Paris.

A couple of days later his friend Charles Sallès drove over from Lyon in his 5 horsepower Citroën and this being a Saturday night they decided to explore the local dance hall. It was a far cry from what these sophisticated urbanites had been led to expect. "No barman, no cocktails, no jazz," Antoine wrote back to Renée de Saussine. "A *bal de sous-préfecture* where couples danced beneath the severe eyes of their mothers. 'And your lady?' they said, 'and your girl how are they?' The 'ladies' formed a square around the hall. The old guard, ruminating peacefully. In the centre the 'young girls' in pink and sky blue turned in the arms of cyclists. The mothers looked like a jury. The cyclists had climbed into stiff, new dinner jackets which smelled of mothballs. They kept staring at themselves in the mirrors. They tugged at their sleeves and wiggled their necks where their stiff collars scratched them. They were happy."

So too was Saint-Exupéry—in his off-duty hours, when he was not trying to work up a synthetic enthusiasm for his lumbering merchandise. Argenton-sur-Creuse, which he reached by train, turned out to be a lovely village whose only commotion, every four hours, was caused by the noisy passage of a steam-driven tram, gliding like a toy on miniature rails. Elated by the blue sky and the snow-white clouds and the rich smells wafting from the hairdressers and the groceries, he sat down on an old stone bridge, filled with a marvellous sense of freedom. It was shared by his hat which he had casually placed on the parapet beside him and which, as he wrote to his friend Renée, "is now sailing towards America. I saw it move slowly away, take the curve with skill, and disappear. I wasn't even furious. I was melancholic."

He went to buy another and fell on a hatter who was also a *modiste*—a quiet, gentle little girl. Seated on the table Antoine began flirting with her. She spoke to him of her "aunt" and of her "cousin" as though they were old acquaintances. "Is she old, your aunt?" asked the hatless visitor. "Now look . . ." she began. "I hadn't even guessed that her aunt was young," as he wrote back to Paris. "I asked no more questions, simply nodded and said 'yes' with an understanding air."

In another village—that of Dompierre-sur-Besbre—to which he was driven by Sallès, the local *jeunesse* had put on a "*grand spectacle*" at the *mairie* when they drove up in their snow-powdered car. But the two white shouldered pilgrims were greeted by the locals like old friends. "Wedged in between a bulky groceress and the pharmacist, it didn't take us five minutes to learn the chief singer's name, all about the capers of the Assistant Mayor's daughter, and the local accent. What trust! We throbbed in this atmosphere to each patriotic refrain. An old stock of sentiments which we had to come here to find, intact with their charming outmoded vocabulary. 'The Teutons', 'the barbarous warriors', 'the knavish emperor'. Then a visit to an antique shop where we marvelled to find the rococo jewellery of our grandmothers."

"And a real band, Rinette, with a forest of brass! Pimply schoolboys blowing into them so hard one feared for their cheeks with each *fortissimo*. And then—a power failure—and out came the candles and the stifled laughs, and the cries between the actors on the stage and the parents in the hall . . . 'Oh, it's you, Marcel! Yes, my beard's falling off!' And it's pasted back *en famille* . . . We left at midnight . . . happy to have stolen up on Dompierre like traitors: happy not to have come in via the station and the Hôtel du Lion and the smile of an immigrant manager."

As a salesman Antoine de Saint-Exupéry was no great shakes—he managed to sell one Saurer truck in fifteen months of effort—but his delightful

vignettes of country life already revealed that tenderness of vision which
was to mark all his books. "Montluçon is a charming town," he wrote to
Charles Sallès, seated as usual at a table in a public place, "but the Café
Riche is full of old gentlemen who play whist and croak at each other in the
corners". He was charmed by the quaint accent of a small woman of whom
he asked the way, but chilled by the blank look in her eyes. The provincialism
of the local shopkeepers "who do twenty yards in their lives" amused him,
while simultaneously arousing a nostalgia for the vivacious company of
friends in Paris. He read Montherlant's *Chant Funèbre pour les Morts de
Verdun*, admiring its classic severity of style and worked desultorily on his
novel. The previous summer, at Saint-Maurice-de-Rémens, his enthusiasm
had been such that when his friend Charles Sallès got off the *omnibus* at
Leyment, Antoine was there to meet him with a sheaf of newly written
pages which he insisted on reading to him, seated on the roadside a few
yards from the level crossing, before they walked on together to the château.
The "reading" had continued after dinner in the vestibule, under the cheery
glow of the lamp and to the inner glow of a fine old tea, brought back from
China by one of Antoine's relatives. But the élan of the summer had since
given way to wintry doubt.

Even his Zédal "Sigma"—the "poor man's Hispano", as it was sometimes called, because of the rumble-seat posterior which belied the stately
front—failed to alleviate the tedium of his professional obligations, though
he did his best to "beef up" his acquisition by installing a powerful Ballot
engine. "My life is made up of curves I take as fast as I can," he wrote to
Renée de Saussine, "of hotels which are all exactly alike, and of the little
square of this town"—Guéret, in the Creuse—"where the trees look like
brooms. I feel a bit low. Paris is so far away, and I'm undergoing a cure of
silence".

Whenever he could, he would break the cure and come racing back to
Paris for a revivifying contact with his friends. The old as well as the new.
At the Cour des Comptes, Ségogne had befriended Robert de Grandseignes,
who was engaged to the sister of a charming young lady with pure blue eyes
and gay blond hair. Which is how Antoine liked them—though his friend
Ségogne liked her even more. Her name was Lucie-Marie Decour, and she
lived with her parents in an elegant townhouse on the Rue François 1er,
where even as late as ten or eleven they were always welcome to drop in for
a late evening snack of sausages and cheese (which Antoine particularly
relished). Moody as ever, he would usually remain tight-lipped if there were
too many others around, only unlimbering slowly as the "mob" drifted
away. Then, stretched out in a comfortable armchair by the crackling fireplace he so enjoyed, he would begin to speak—especially when they were

finally *à deux*—and the speech would build into a torrent. The older generation heard almost none of it, it was reserved for his contemporaries, and
more than once Lucie-Marie Decour heard the same reaction which had
greeted Louise de Vilmorin and Renée de Saussine: "I honestly don't
understand what you can see in that big fellow." But she knew what she was
seeing, or rather, hearing, and her insight was not proved wrong by the later
letters he wrote to her—out of gratitude for those warm fireside evenings on
the Rue François 1er and at the family property at Rolleboise, forty miles
from Paris.

And then there was Renée de Saussine, his "literary manager", as he
liked to call her. One evening they were seated with her sister Laure at the
Dame Blanche pastry shop indulging in the usual banter (*"Vous êtes un port
pour moi, Rinette"* *"Un porc ! Saint-Antoine ?"* *"Ça, c'est trop fort !"*) when
the subject of Pirandello came up. The Pitoëffs, who had already made a
sensation with *Six Characters in Search of an Author*, had followed it up by
staging *Chacun sa Vérité* at the Comédie des Champs-Elysées. The play
was the talk of the town. But at the mention of Pirandello, Saint-Exupéry
flushed, and when Laure de Saussine unguardedly went on: "It's quite
simple—one has to go back to Ibsen to find something as interesting," there
was an explosion.

"Pff!" exclaimed Antoine. "How do you dare compare them? *Your*
Pirandello . . . is . . . is . . . the metaphysics of a concierge!"

He got up brusquely and a teaspoon fell to the floor with a hollow tinkle.
Outside on the Boulevard Saint-Germain there was an awkward shaking of
hands. "One can't argue with Tonio," his friend Henry de Ségogne had said,
and here he was proving it again. Stricken with remorse Saint-Exupéry
spent the rest of the evening and part of the night composing a letter of
explanation which is worth quoting at length because it is something of a
private literary manifesto: "I can't bat ideas around like tennis balls," he
wrote to his literary manager. "I'm not made for society. Thinking is not
something one plays at. So that when conversation happens to turn to a
subject I have very much at heart, I grow intolerant and ridiculous . . .. But
Rinette, one has no right to compare a man like Ibsen with a man like
Pirandello. You have on the one hand an individual whose preoccupations
were of the highest. He had a social role, a moral role, and influence. He wrote
to make people understand things they didn't want to understand. He
tackled the most intimate problems and in particular, and I think in a
marvellous way, that of woman. Finally, whether or not he succeeded,
Ibsen was not seeking to provide us with a new game of lotto but with
genuine nourishment. . . .

"On the other hand there's Pirandello, who is perhaps a remarkable man of the theatre . . . but who comes to amuse society people and to allow them to toy with metaphysics as they were already toying with politics, 'general ideas', and scandals of adultery."

There followed a long dissertation on the nature of truth, subtly abused, the epistler claimed, by Pirandello's metaphysical juggling—which enthralled a public avid for anything singular and new. "What they want is not to understand a thing, but to feel all their previous notions turned upside down. Then they say: 'How odd!' and feel a faint chill in the spine . . .

"Several years ago it was the unfortunate Einstein who was seized upon by these society people for exactly the same reasons. They wanted to wallow in incomprehension, experience a profound dismay, feel the 'wing-brush of the unknown'. Einstein for them was a kind of fakir . . .

"This is why one must like Ibsen, who at least represents an effort at human understanding, and reject Pirandello and reject all fake vertigos— which is not easy. What is obscure is more tempting than what is clear. Between two explanations of a phenomenon people will instinctively go for the occult. Because the other, the true one, is dull and simple and doesn't make one's hair stand on end. A paradox is more tempting than a veritable explanation and people prefer it. Men of the world use science, art, philosophy as they use sluts. Pirandello is a kind of slut. . . . Society people say: 'We have stirred up a few ideas' (*Nous avons remué des idées*) and they disgust me. I like people whose need to eat, feed their children, and finish out the month have bound more closely to life. They know more about it. Yesterday on the bus platform I rubbed elbows with a straggly-haired woman with five children. She had a lot to teach them and me too. Society people have never taught me anything." And further on, he added, à propos of the "scenes of music-hall gigolettes: All this is very much 1880, garish melodrama. Human distress serves their emotions in the same way as the metaphysics of Monsieur Pirandello. Which are not even in fashion any more."

On this last point he was mistaken; for what he was blasting away at in this tirade was the Dadaist and Surrealist wave which had swept over France in the wake of the First World War, proclaiming the absolute sovereignty of the arbitrary, the irrational thrill of the *acte gratuit*, the sublime beauty of the pistol shot, elevated from the gutter and the underworld to the eminence of a "creative act". From these sentiments Saint-Exupéry never wavered, and more than fifteen years later, in New York, he was still ready to cross swords with André Breton, the cranky prophet of the new cult. Yet the real target of his broadside was less Pirandello than those salon intellectuals who got a well-groomed kick out of his dazzling paradoxes. Drawing-room chatter—and with a name like his he was exposed to quite a bit of it—bored him prodigiously. There was something too tinkling and artificial about such conversations, which he would either boycott in boorish silence or lumber into and destroy at a blow, like a Prince Myshkin upsetting a china vase. "I can no longer stand such people," he wrote in a letter to his mother, "and if I marry a woman and then discover that she likes this kind of world, I shall be the unhappiest of men".

In all this there was a strong dose of post-adolescent petulance, but it was nourished by a sure instinct as much as by the natural intransigence of youth. Charlie Chaplin's "The Pilgrim" delighted him, as did the first part of "Public Opinion"—because of the great comedian's extraordinary sensitivity and gift of observation; but for anything less than excellence he felt nothing but abhorrence. After seeing a bad film "with falsified emotions and without underground continuity", he wrote to his mother in disgust; "Outside it's biting cold. The light in the shop windows is hard. I think one could make a fine film of street impressions like this. The people who make films are cretins. They don't know how to see. They don't understand their instrument. When I think that it would be enough to catch ten faces, ten movements to convey dense impressions, but they are incapable of this synthesis and all they achieve is photography."

Eisenstein would have agreed, so too would Jean Vigo, to say nothing of Nabokov. For once again it was the author speaking, the self-appointed critic who had defined writing as first of all an aptitude for seeing. He had been giving these matters a considerable amount of thought, stimulated not only by his hours in the air—when one's normal visual horizon changed completely—but also by the literary talk he heard in the salon of his cousin Yvonne de Lestrange. Unlike Marie-Blanche de Polignac and other patronesses of arts and letters, Yvonne de Lestrange did not maintain one of those weekly "salons" where the privileged of the literary world were welcome to drop in to sample the champagne and the biscuits if the spirit moved them. But the dinner parties she gave in her flat on the Quai Malaquais often included editors, critics, and *hommes de lettres*—to whom she was only too glad to introduce her cousin as an "aspiring author". One of them was Jacques Rivière, who had teamed up with the scion of a Protestant banking family, Jean Schlumberger, and with Jacques Copeau, the brilliant *metteur-en-scène* of the Vieux Colombier theatre, to launch the *Nouvelle Revue Française*, the sophisticated literary monthly around which Gaston Gallimard and André Gide were rapidly building up the most important publishing company in France. Another habitué of her dining-room was Ramon Fernandez, who aside from being an extremely cultured man and a brilliant conversationalist had inherited from his Mexican father a talent for dancing the tango which made him a much fought over prize for salon hostesses and affluent heiresses eager to find a worthy human cause on which to bestow their largesse.

It was through Fernandez (who also contributed to the *Nouvelle Revue Française*) that Saint-Exupéry made the acquaintance of Jean Prévost, who was responsible for his literary début. He too was of exceptionally robust build, but unlike Antoine, he made a fetish of it. In his youth he had been a fat and, as he later confessed, a "ridiculous" little boy, and to overcome this tendency to obesity he had developed a strenuous interest in athletics. Every Sunday he went out to the suburbs to play soccer, and if challenged he could run 100 metres in 11 seconds. He was proud of his physique and not least of all of the toughness of his cranium, and often, on wandering into Sylvia Beach's bookshop on the Rue de l'Odéon, he would knock his head against an iron pipe running up the wall, causing both pipe and bookseller to shudder—while he felt nothing! "You might just as well have punched an iron bar as Prévost's head," she wrote years later in that delightful book of reminiscences, *Shakespeare and Company*, and it was no exaggeration: as Ernest Hemingway one day discovered when he broke his thumb during a boxing match with Prévost which his favourite bookseller had organized.

The Rue de l'Odéon, to which Saint-Exupéry was introduced by Prévost, had become in the early twenties one of the literary centres of Paris. It was dominated by two bookshops and two women, all of them remarkable, not to say unique. Located at No. 12, Sylvia Beach's lending library, Shakespeare and Company, was a favourite meeting place for American and English writers like Scott Fitzgerald, Robert McAlmon, Archibald Macleish, William Carlos Williams, Ezra Pound, James Joyce, and of course Hemingway, whom she fondly dubbed her "best customer". Across the way at No. 7, Adrienne Monnier's "little grey bookshop" was frequented by a no less distinguished galaxy of French authors, beginning with Gide, Paul Valéry, and André Maurois, and which included most of the leading literary lights, whose signed photographs and etchings were hung, two, three, or four high, above the shelves of books. There was a constant stream of human traffic between the two establishments, for their owners were intimate friends and their shops, which in winter had the cosy warmth of stove-heated studies, were literary workshops as well as bookstores. It was at Sylvia Beach's Shakespeare and Company that *Ulysses* first saw the light of day; and it was at Adrienne Monnier's Maison des Amis des Livres that Joyce's French admirers, led by the industrious Valery Larbaud and the encyclopaedic Léon-Paul Fargue—whose command of French slang was positively Joycean—would meet to discuss how the book's more intricate passages were to be translated into the language of Rabelais.

It is intriguing to reflect that at a time when Saint-Exupéry was being introduced to Adrienne Monnier and her literary circle, Hemingway, Thorton Wilder, and Scott Fitzgerald, to say nothing of Joyce, or Ezra Pound, or Ford Madox Ford may well have been conversing at Sylvia Beach's bookshop across the street—though there is no record of his having met any of them. The two women showed a fondness for velvet jackets, Adrienne Monnier's being more like a bolero. But where Sylvia Beach was slim with a "lively, sharply sculptured face, brown eyes that were as alive as a small animal's and as gay as a young girl's" to quote from *A Moveable Feast*—Adrienne Monnier had the plump form, the round nose, the healthy pink cheeks, and the plainly brushed, almost flaxen hair of a peasant. Her long grey skirt, which came down to her ankles, smacked a bit of the nunnery and a great deal of the chickenyard, and rustic too was the appetite with which she would dig into a *truffe sous la cendre*. She came of rugged mountain stock—her family was from la Ferclaz, above Chambéry, in Savoie—and though she was extraordinarily vital and curious, being perfectly at home with aesthetes like Gide or Valéry, it was probably the latent peasant instinct within her which caused her to choose Prévost—the healthy outdoor type— to help her run the literary monthly she founded in 1925.

It was called *Le Navire d'Argent*—the Silver Ship—a delicate name, delicate enough to presage a relatively early shipwreck. For the venture lasted exactly one year. But it was a lively year which saw, among other things, the first French translation of T. S. Eliot's *Prufrock* and the publication of "Anna Livia Plurabelle" from Joyce's *Finnegan's Wake*. In March of 1926 the two enterprising editors flung caution to the winds and came out with an all-American issue which included offerings from Robert McAlmon and William Carlos Williams, an extract from E. E. Cummings' *Enormous Room*, and Ernest Hemingway's *The Undefeated*, the first of his stories ever to be translated into French. The effort was superhuman and this issue practically a swansong. In a desperate effort to keep her little vessel from foundering Adrienne Monnier sold a large part of her private collection of rare books (many of them signed and dedicated to her by their authors). But the strain on her time—for she was still running the bookshop—and her resources was too great, and the next issue, published in April of 1926, was also the *Navire d'Argent's* last. The fact would not merit special attention here had this final number not included a first offering called *L'Aviateur*, written by an unknown author whom Jean Prévost was glad to introduce to the readers.

Gifted with a prodigious memory—he could recite thousands of verses by heart—Jean Prévost had been a brilliant student at school. At the Ecole Normale Supérieure, where the cream of the French teaching profession was trained, he had been wont to awake at 4 o'clock in the morning and to read

Plato until 8 a.m. in the original Greek! The unusual combination in him of physical strongman and hyper-intellectual caused him to develop an acute interest in the physical sensations one experiences in different sports; and it was this interest which was immediately aroused when he heard Saint-Exupéry trying to describe the singular sensations of flying. In his editorial note accompanying *L'Aviateur*, Prévost introduced Saint-Exupéry as a "specialist of aviation and of mechanical construction" and praised the "direct art and the gift of truth" which had gone into the composition of these fragments: fragments extracted from a larger work to which the author had given the tentative title, *L'Evasion de Jacques Bernis*.

The eight fragments published in *Le Navire d'Argent* gave the reader scant feeling of just what it is Jacques Bernis is fleeing from—unless it is that feeling of not belonging, of being an "outsider", that feeling of being a "stranger in the big city" which was Saint-Exupéry's every time he returned to Paris. Bernis is a flying instructor and he has a pupil called Pichon whom he is teaching to fly. Happy when in the air, he succumbs to an overpowering feeling of sadness the moment he touches down. "He lowers his forehead, looks at his hands shining with oil, feels suddenly limp, and abysmally sad. . . ." He rings up his friends to find out what they are doing that evening, but they are all busy. And tomorrow? Tomorrow we'll be out on the links playing golf, but come on out anyway. But Bernis doesn't play golf, so he has to settle for dinner. And thus alone, once again, he "walks up the boulevards. Upstream he pushes, through the crowd, as though against a current. So many faces to be breasted. Some hurt him like the very image of repose. That woman conquered, and life would be calm . . . calm. . . ."

We have no trouble detecting the autobiographical note, the wistful plaint left by the memory of Verrières and the Rue de la Chaise. Or in what follows: "He walks into a dancehall, keeping on his coat, thick as an explorer's among all these gigolos. Within this precinct they live their life like carp in an aquarium, doing a turn on the floor before coming back to drink. In this flabby milieu where he alone retains his reason, Bernis feels as heavy as a stevedore, his legs as straight and solid as pins, his thoughts of a leaden dullness. He advances through the tables towards a free place. The young men move flexibly aside to let him pass. The eyes of the women he touches with his own shift and flicker out. Thus, as the duty officer makes his round on the night watch, do the cigarettes fall from sentries' fingers."

This last sentence, better phrased in French, was of such a perfection that he carried it over unchanged into his first novel. For the rest *L'Aviateur* is full of sharp descriptive flashes, through which there gleams the softly humorous touch: as in this description of the crowd which rushes up to Pichon, the student pilot who (like Saint-Exupéry at Le Bourget) has just crashed his plane. "The pilot is finally dragged out, with a green face, a huge left eye, and broken teeth. He is stretched out on the grass and a circle forms around him. 'We might perhaps!' begins the Colonel, 'we might perhaps . . .' says a lieutenant as a non-com undoes the wounded man's collar—something which does him no harm and sets everyone's mind at rest. 'The ambulance? Where's the ambulance?' asks the Colonel, professionally determined to be decisive. 'It's coming,' someone answers, just to say something, which is enough for the Colonel. 'While I think of it . . .' he exclaims, and then walks rapidly away, where to he has no idea."

The most spectacular lines were those in which Saint-Exupéry sought to describe the visual sensations experienced during a session of aerial acrobacy. As in this description of a loop, begun after the plane has picked up sufficient speed: "The horizon drops, the earth recedes like a tide, and the plane points into the sky. Then, at the height of the parabola, he turns over on himself, hovering like a dead fish, with his stomach in the air. . . . Drowned in the sky he sees the earth stretch out above him like a beach and fall, vertiginously, with all its weight. He cuts the ignition, and it jells vertically, like a wall. The plane dives. Bernis pulls it gently out until in front of him once more is the calm lake of the horizon."

As though this were not dramatic enough, the author has Bernis' wing snap in mid-flight. Whereupon "the horizon goes over his head like a sheet. The earth envelops him and, like a merry-go-round, begins to turn, carrying its woods and its steeples and its plains. The pilot sees a white villa go by, as though shot by a sling. And like the sea towards the diver, the earth comes up towards the assassinated pilot."

The finale was a bit too melodramatic, not to say gratuitous, in style as well as content. But it could not mar the striking vividness and quality of the whole. As a first literary solo it was unquestionably a success.

\*     \*     \*

To be published in *Le Navire d'Argent* was a modest triumph for a young man not yet twenty-six, but it did nothing to improve Saint-Exupéry's professional situation. In fifteen months of prospecting he had only managed to sell one truck, and this seemed to his Saurer bosses too unsubstantial an achievement to warrant his continued employment. Professionally he was a misfit, geographically he was outcast: as much a stranger at the Hôtel Terminus at Montluçon as he was an outsider whenever he got back to Paris. "I'm up here for a brief stopover," he wrote to his mother, "because of trouble with my car. I feel a bit like an explorer returning from Africa. I put in telephone calls to see who's around. This one is busy, that one is away. Their life continues, while I've just arrived . . . What I ask of a woman, Mama, is to appease this disquiet. That's why one needs one so much. You cannot imagine how heavy one is, how useless one feels one's youth is. You cannot know what a woman can give, what one could give. I'm too lonely in this room."

His mother knew—and probably better than he—but there was little she could do to help. He was adrift and both knew it. He was no more made to sell trucks than he was to supervise the manufacture of tiles—"which fits me as well as a wedding-train", as he had wistfully remarked. His one wish was to return to the air, and fortunately here he had at least one mentor who was in a position to help him. This was Abbé Sudour, the assistant director of the Ecole Bossuet, who had taken as much of a fancy to the young Antoine as Abbé Dibildos had developed a dislike. In Sudour, Saint-Exupéry had a confidant he could always go back to see. He did, with increasing frequency. Impressed by his young protégé's passionate interest in flying, Sudour used his influence to land him a job as an instructor for novice pilots with the Compagnie Aérienne Française. Saint-Exupéry was delighted, and he got a particular kick out of giving his friends—like Henry de Ségogne —their baptisms of the air. But the job seems to have lacked regularity— piloting was still considered a neck-breaking sport—and just to complicate matters the family was passing through a very painful moment. His eldest sister Marie Madeleine, whose epileptic fits had been growing steadily more serious, finally died in June, leaving his poor grief-stricken mother exhausted and everyone upwrought.

It was not a happy summer for any of them and the autumn, which found Antoine casting about once more in shiftless desperation, promised to be no better.

It was Sudour again who came to the rescue. During the war, while serving as chaplain in the trenches of the Somme, he had gotten to know an Italian by the name of Beppo de Massimi, who had volunteered for service as a pilot in the French army's new air branch. They had spent many an hour in the dugouts swapping ideas and talking literature and philosophy, and the memory of these exchanges had remained so vividly with the airman that after the war he had entered his son at the Ecole Bossuet. He was now general manager of the Latécoère air company, which maintained an office in Paris though its headquarters were in Toulouse. Informed by Sudour that Saint-Exupéry was an excellent pilot as well as an aspiring author, Beppo de Massimi agreed to receive him.

The meeting took place on October 12th. Massimi was immediately struck by the young man's timidity and by the awkwardness he seemed to feel at "being so big and taking up so much space in his armchair".

He was even more struck by a kind of exaggerated modesty which kept the young man from making any claims about himself that might have sounded favourable and which even seemed to induce a strange forgetfulness about past "achievements". Only when the conversation veered away from himself to the company's operating methods and to the life of its pilots did his interest seem to brighten. All he could do, Massimi explained, was to pass on his recommendation to Toulouse. There he would have to prove himself by passing the flight tests. If he did, he would be allowed to pilot the mails—for a period to be determined later.

"And then?" asked Saint-Exupéry in an anxious voice.

"And then? . . . Well, our Operations Director needs to be seconded."

It was a flattering compliment to pay a young man whom he had never seen before, but the reaction was immediate and violent.

"But Monsieur," protested Saint-Exupéry, flushing heatedly. "I want to fly above all . . . all I want to do is fly . . ."

"And," as Massimi later described the scene in *Vent Debout*, "he put such feeling into the plea that I was moved. He could not have guessed the pleasure it gave me—I who had been solicited so often by blasé airmen wanting cushy jobs."

"When do you want to leave for Toulouse?" Massimi asked him.

"This evening, if you want," was the immediate reply.

"I'll put in a call to Monsieur Daurat, our Operations Director," said Massimi. "It's to him you'll have to report."

In the end he did not leave that evening, and it was agreed that the summons from Toulouse would be sent to Agay, so that Saint-Exupéry could stop off to see his sister Gabrielle on his way south. The last hours in Paris were spent emptying his little hotel room of his belongings. Packed into trunks, his books were carted over to the Quai Malaquais for storage in the cellar—along with an extraordinary collection of odds and ends (an engraving press, a machine for making cigarettes) which at the last moment he simply was unable to part with. He said good-bye to his friends—to Henry de Ségogne, who took off for Fontainebleau; to Rénee de Saussine, who went off to a concert; to another friend, who went to see a film. Yet they were staying on, while he was leaving.

Beyond the windows of the drawing-room the light was fading over the poplars along the quay and the tall chimneys of the Louvre. Beneath him he watched the passers-by hurrying or ambling past, oblivious of his existence. It reminded him of a railway station—with everywhere a whispering exchange of secrets to which he would never be privy. That woman passing by—he followed her with his eye—ten more steps and she would disappear from his ken. Out of sight and out of time. Yesterday they wore a living tide, and he had felt himself borne on their flood amid their tears and their laughter, but now, as he gazed down, they seemed to glide past like a procession of ghosts. Beings from a world he no longer belonged to. He sat down in one of his cousin Yvonne's armchairs, feeling suddenly awkward in his raincoat and hat. Awkward and alone. The telephone was silent and there was no one he could call. One by one the shore-lines linking him to Paris had been loosed and in a moment he would be on his own. Just what it would bring he did not know, but a new life was beginning.

# 5

# The Mail Carriers of Toulouse

---

FLANKED by sturdy plane-trees and the wooden telegraph poles of the Toulouse-Narbonne railroad, the Montaudran airfield spread its mangy wilderness of weed west of the southern outskirts of the city, in a broad valley cut by the Canal du Midi. To the left a branch spur led to a cluster of reinforced concrete buildings where had been manufactured the railway cars, and during the First World War the Salmson biplanes, which had provided the basis for Pierre Latécoère's fortune. Three years before Saint-Exupéry's arrival forge and carriage-works had been sold off to keep the airline going, but the remaining workshops and offices, scattered through a dozen private houses, barns, and converted stables still gave the establishment a quaintly rustic air. Gone were the old Bessoneau tents beneath whose canvas spread the first Latécoère planes had found shelter from the elements, replaced by a line of concrete hangars with huge sliding doors. The rows of petrol drums which had once lined the field like markers had made way for a fuel pump connected with a buried tank; and instead of the muddy pathway over which the veterans once tramped to reach their *moulins*, there was now a cement apron on to which the "windmills" could be rolled by simply picking up the tail and pushing. Gone too was the old Bréguet packing case (used for factory disassembled fuselage and wings) in which the first customs men had bivouacked, like gypsies, in a makeshift trailer mounted on bricks with stove and jutting pipe for the noonday *popotte*; dismantled in favour of a shed where a hall for passengers now adjoined another reserved for pilots. Only the field, with its tufts of grass and its dirt, was more or less the same—dusty when dry and hot, a swamp when it rained. The field and the main offices, located in a country house graced by a twin-branched curving staircase and ceremoniously referred to as the "château". It too had stubbornly refused to change, paying homage to a perseverance which made the Compagnie Latécoère—with seven years of operation behind it—the oldest continually operating airline in the world!

A few old-timers could still recall the memorable Christmas Day of 1918 when Pierre Latécoère had turned up on the field in a dark winter coat, a felt hat with a broad band on his head, his pince-nez set firmly on the nose above the dark moustache—as though this were a day like any other and he were on his way to the office. The Armistice had been signed just six weeks before, but already the strong-willed industrialist's sights were trained on the future. Climbing into the waiting Salmson, while a crowd of curious gapers watched in evident disbelief, he had calmly given the signal for the pilot to take off. Destination—Barcelona. It had been too much for a couple of veteran airmen, who had hurried up at the last moment in an effort to avert the catastrophe. "Don't go—you'll never make it!" they cried. "We've made enough wartime flights to know that one can't fly in just any kind of weather."

"People write every day," the bundled passenger had replied. "Postal airplanes won't make any sense until they take off every day."

The Salmson two-winger had buzzed down the field and fluttered up and away over the trees, safely landing on the Barcelona hippodrome a few hours later. On his return to Montaudran the following day Latécoère had been greeted by the two doubting Thomases, now won to the cause. "If you want us . . ." they had said, a trifle sheepishly, "we're with you". The doughty Toulouse industrialist had gained his first two volunteers.

Not the least curious thing about this extraordinary faith in the future of aviation was that it animated a man who was not himself a flyer. His father had made his mark by building up a small steel works and a forge at Bagnères-de-Bigorre, in the Pyrenees, while the son was sent to the École Centrale in Paris to get a degree in engineering. There Pierre Latécoère had made friends with Beppo de Massimi, like himself a rabid bibliophile he kept bumping into in Left Bank bookshops. A common love of Stendhal and Maurice Barrès helped to cement the friendship between the fiery and opinionated Pyrenean and the urbane Neapolitan with the well-trimmed moustache. With the outbreak of the 1914 war the latter had volunteered for flying service under Captain Watteau, the French aerial observer who spotted von Kluck's wheeling movement, thus helping Joffre and Gallieni win the First Battle of the Marne. Handicapped by poor eyesight, Pierre Latécoère had volunteered for the artillery, only to be sent back to manufacture high explosive shells by a front-line general who was bowled over by the novelty of his ideas. From there it was but a step—albeit a momentous one—to the manufacture of Salmson warplanes, which Latécoère launched into in 1917. The aeonautic "bug" which had bitten his friend Beppo de Massimi now got under his own skin; and soon the panelled walls of his office on the Boulevard Haussmann were covered with diagrams of flying machines, tacked up next to quaint old prints. And every time Massimi came back on leave from the front, it was about the future of flying that they would talk.

In May of 1918, by which time his Toulouse workshops had already turned out 600 Salmson warplanes, Pierre Latécoère was already looking ahead to the abrupt cut-back in orders to be expected with the cessation of hostilities. Determined to stay in aeroplane production he now evolved an audacious plan aimed at linking France to her African possessions. Flight conditions at this time—in open cockpits—made passenger transport an uncomfortable, hazardous, and financially uncertain operation; but this need not be true of the mail, which might be lost in transit but which was not subject to air sickness. A letter posted in Paris by ordinary mail had to travel to Marseille by rail, be loaded there on to a ship bound for Morocco, unloaded a few days later in Casablanca and carried by rail up to Rabat. In summer all this took a week; in winter eleven days. But by flying down the Mediterranean coast all the way to Gibraltar, Latécoère calculated that the 1,850 kilometres separating Toulouse from Casablanca could be covered in 13 hours of actual flying time (the planes available having an average speed of only 140 kilometres an hour). Nine more hours were needed for a letter to reach Toulouse by train, and another nine had to be added for refuelling and an overnight stop-over in Alicante; but all told, a letter mailed in Paris could be flown down to Rabat in 31 hours in summer and 48 hours in winter. Five and a half days shorter than surface mail in the first case; nine days shorter in the second.

But for the far-sighted Pierre Latécoère this was only a beginning. The 2,850 kilometres separating Casablanca from Dakar could be covered by aeroplane in a day and a half—three days less than the fastest cargo vessel. And beyond Dakar lay South America, which exchanged 2,000 tons of letters a year with Europe (almost three times as much as between Europe and Asia). It took 17 days to reach Brazil by boat, 23 days to reach Argentina; so that someone mailing a letter in Paris could not expect an answer back from Buenos Aires in much under fifty days. By sea-plane, on the other hand, the 800 kilometres separating Saint-Louis-du-Sénégal from the Cape Verde islands could be covered in six and a half hours; the 2,200 kilometres from the Cape Verde islands to Noronha in three days by small rapid steamers; the 650 kilometres from Noronha to Recife in another five hours by sea-plane; and the final two laps—Recife to Rio de Janeiro (1,950 kilometres) and Rio to Buenos Aires (2,100 kilometres)— in a little more than one day. The total distance of 12,400 kilometres could thus be covered in seven and a half days—cutting more than two weeks from the fastest boat time in either direction.

Though the plan called for nothing as ambitious as flights of 1,000 kilometres, it was dismissed out of hand. "Utterly utopian!" was the comment of the Under Secretary of State for Aeronautics, to whom it was presented in September 1918. The brain-child of a madman! A dream worthy of Jules Verne!

Pierre Latécoère was not a man to be deterred by a bureaucratic rebuff. The guns had hardly cooled on the western front when he founded his airline. On Christmas Day of 1918 he flew off to Barcelona. Beppo de Massimi was next sent down to scout and negotiate for landing fields at Barcelona, Alicante, and Málaga—laps of 450 to 500 kilometres being needed for aeroplanes of a highly limited range. Massimi returned to Toulouse thinking he had succeeded, but when he and Latécoère took off for Morocco a couple of months later in two Salmsons piloted by former flying officers, they got a rude surprise. The Frenchman who had undertaken to fix up the Alicante field, having confused metres with square metres, had prepared a 50 yard by 50 yard landing strip that was about as big as a tennis court. Massimi's Salmson ploughed into a stone wall, smashing the propeller; his head went through the windshield and he emerged furious and swearing, with a bloodied nose. The other pilot, who had lost his goggles, landed with the wind behind him at Tarragona, up-ending his Salmson and leaving Latécoère suspended in mid-air.

A less enterprising individual might have been willing to call it a day, but not Latécoère. He took the train back to Toulouse, shipped down a new motor for the stranded plane at Alicante, and flew down a few days later in another Salmson. The tennis court by this time had been enlarged, and they were able to land without smashing more wood. That same evening at five o'clock Pierre Latécoère climbed out of the Salmson on to the airfield at Rabat and handed Marshal Lyautey a doll's sized hat box filled with violets. They had been picked the evening before at Toulouse for Madame Lyautey, but the flight, beginning at dawn, had been accomplished in a little more than twelve hours. A new epoch had dawned, as the astute Marshal realized, and his Postal Director was ordered to advance Latécoère an initial subsidy of one million francs.

"I've done some calculating," Latécoère later told the man who was to become the pillar of the airline, "and they confirm the opinion of the specialists. Our idea is unachievable. There's only one thing left for us to do: achieve it."

It was not simply a *boutade*—even though Captain Watteau, when Beppo de Massimi showed him the calculations, replied: "Your project makes sense." On paper it did; but flying has never been a question of paper, or even of maps. To begin with, there was the weather, which

came close to swamping the project at the outset. Of the three routes open
to him, Latécoère had been obliged to veto the one via the Balearics and
Algiers because of the inexistence at this time of truly reliable seaplanes
capable of covering a 350 mile hop over the water without risk of engine
failure. He had to eliminate the shortest route—over the Basque country
to Madrid, Sevilla, and Tangier, because of the frequency of storms and
the turbulence of the air over the uplands of Castile. The only route left
was down Spain's Mediterranean seaboard. But the autumn of 1919, when
the airline was inaugurated—with just twelve pilots and eight planes—was
exceptionally stormy up and down Spain's eastern shore. One aeroplane
coming in to land near Perpignan was simply pushed back on its haunches.
Engines were drowned in torrential downpours and wooden propellers
literally eaten away by the rain, with a frightening loss of air speed. (Thereafter they were given metal edges.) Rodier, though a veteran flyer with war
experience—like all of the company's first pilots—came near to ditching
his plane and passengers into the sea near Valencia at the end of a terrible
battle with a storm which had Latécoère and Massimi hanging on grimly
to the fuselage cross-bars to keep their safety-straps from ripping. Another
war veteran, Didier Daurat, put them down at Alicante during a cloudburst
flood which claimed ten lives, set chairs and tables afloat in their hotel
dining-room, and aroused the muttering of superstititious locals: "It's
those diabolical machines that are upsetting the weather."

Half a dozen pilots cracked up within the first fifteen months—the
beginning of a toll that was to claim 121 lives in all. One of them, who
had taken a Salmson up from Mountaudran on a practice flight, went into
a spin over Toulouse and came crashing down into a suburban street in
full view of a petrified populace. Not fit to stand the strains it was subjected
to, the wartime Salmson was discarded in favour of the Bréguet
14 (which had a 300 horsepower Renault motor); but it was years before
the airline could develop an aeroplane fully equipped to meet the rugged
test.

Engine failures, recurring on an average of one every 12,000 miles (once
in every five round-trips between Toulouse and Rabat), were accompanied
by all sorts of vexations on the ground. When a rumour spread that the
pilots were smuggling in Moroccan dope, the prefectoral authorities in
Toulouse insisted on dismantling returning planes to see just where the
*kiff* was being stowed. Notwithstanding an agreement signed with the
Madrid Government in December 1920, the Spanish authorities did their
best to hamstring the airline at every turn. The airfields at Barcelona,
Alicante, and Málaga were not allowed to stock spare parts (so that the
succeeding mail planes would have to bring down a new motor or propeller),

and for the first four years communications with Toulouse had to be maintained through white carrier pigeons! The overflight of Cartagena was forbidden because of the presence there of a munitions factory; and for the same reason the French were kept from installing radio-receiving-and-transmitting sets on the fields, lest these be used for espionage and the preparation of an airborne invasion! Forced to crash land near Almería, one Latécoère pilot was arrested by a pair of *Guardia Civils*, and his mail confiscated by the local governor. Another, forced down at Lorca, was kept under custody for eight days and only released after Beppo de Massimi, who had been sent to Madrid to butter up the Spanish authorities, had moved heaven and earth to set him free.

The root cause of the trouble lay in Madrid, and more particularly at the Court where, beginning with Alfonso XIII's mother, who was Austrian, the prevailing sentiment was emphatically pro-German. The feud between republican France and monarchical Spain was, in effect, only a modern version of a rivalry as old as that between Francis I and Charles V; and as often as the more liberal politicians in Madrid would take steps to smooth things out for Latécoère, their efforts would be stymied by the unobtrusive malevolence of some all-powerful bureaucrat in the Foreign Ministry or the Ministry of the Interior, or by the colonels and generals who were more or less openly working for Dornier, Junkers, and the Germans, or who had thrown in their lot with de Havilland and the British. To deal with this concert of intrigue, Beppo de Massimi was finally forced to spend most of his time in Madrid, and his later description (in his book, *Vent Debout*) of the Venetian wiles he had to employ to outfox his enemies reads like something out of the Renaissance.

A more favourable wind began to blow with the coming to power of General Primo de Rivera in September 1923. The man whom the German philosopher Hermann von Keyserling once described as the "Sancho Panza of modern Spain" was hard-headed enough to realize that his country needed France's help in liquidating Abd-el-Krim's spectacular uprising in the Rif, and from his visits to the front during the First World War he had come away with an undisguised admiration for Pétain, Foch, and their embattled *poilus*. But even he could be circumvented and at times reduced to impotence by other generals of his junta who made no secret of their Germanophilia.

Stumble it might, and did, but stubbornly the Latécoère airline struggled and survived. One by one all of its early rivals fell by the wayside. The Paris-Lille line, started in February 1919, expired three weeks later. The Paris-Bordeaux line, like the Paris-London line, lasted a mere three months (mid-March to mid-June of 1919). Paris-Strasbourg hung on grimly for four months only to collapse on July 17, 1919. By September 1920 Latécoère alone was still in operation, able to guarantee two mail flights a week between Toulouse and Rabat. Yet it too came very close to foundering.

If it managed to survive, it was due not only to the gritty tenacity of Pierre Latécoère and the Neapolitan finesse of Beppo de Massimi, but above all the the iron hand of Didier Daurat, who was appointed Operations Manager in the autumn of 1920. Small and stocky, he had the stoop-shouldered wiriness of a terrier, with a pair of uncompromising eyes and a dark bush under his nose which barred his face like a hedge. From his father, a chaffeur-mechanic employed by the Paris gas company, he had inherited some of the earthy grittiness of Auvergne. Sent to the Ecole d'Horlogerie et de Mécanique in Paris at the age of fifteen, he had developed a youthful interest in astonomy as well as clockwork, solid geometry, engineering design, and metal resistances. Then had come the war, with its sombre funeral train of horrors. He had lived through most of it with a ferocious intensity which had prematurely aged him. Freezing nights in barns where the fear of death was painted on stubbly faces lit by flickering candles; winter trenches and icy dug-outs hollowed out behind parapets of frozen corpses; trunk-to-trunk battles in the charred vestiges of forests; the endless, rolling, deafening bombardments of Verdun chewing up a lunar landscape pockmarked with touching craters—he had seen and lived through it all. One day, in the ruins of what had once been a church, he had come upon a solitary general who had ordered him to advance single-handedly and free his captured brigade. "Advance, keep advancing, and you'll come to it!" he had cried with a moon-struck gesture—which to Daurat had seemed to epitomize the lunacy of the war.

Evacuated to Vichy with a few pieces of shrapnel in his head and heel, Daurat had first taken a dim *poilu's* view of the heavily bemedalled airmen whose passage through the salons was followed by a ripple of shining eyes and a flutter of femine hearts. But curiosity had got the better of prejudice, and the next thing he knew, he too had volunteered for service in the air. At the airbase of La Cheppes, near Chalons-sur-Marne, where he was sent to fly aerial photography missions over the German lines for French heavy artillery, he met Beppo de Massimi, whose Latin polish was matched by unusual reserves of courage. It was Daurat who had put the erstwhile *boulevardier* to work assembling and disassembling machine-guns and learning the rudiments of aerial observation; and though Massimi was a good ten years older than himself, he had responded to the stimulus by developing a firm attachment.

The war in the air, Daurat soon discovered, was almost as lethal as the war on the ground. Once attacked by five Fokkers, he brought his bullet-riddled aeroplane back to base, only to discover on climbing out that his observer was dead. In a Bréguet 14 A biplane he one day flew over the Kronprinz' headquarters château and saw fifty German fighters rise in a vain effort to attain his own 15,000 feet. Later, during a night observation flight, he spotted the brief flash of Big Bertha, helping to locate the monster that had begun shelling Paris. Sent to bombard German pontoon-bridges during the Second Battle of the Marne, he had emerged after four night-marish days the sole survivor out of 64 pilots! After shooting down a German plane, he was jumped by five enemy fighters, who had made a sieve of his wings and fuselage. One bullet had grazed his skull, another had torn through three fingers of his right hand. Weakened by loss of blood, he had taken refuge in a cloud, then groped his way home, with just enough strength left to hold his wounded hand up above the cockpit to stem the haemmorrhage.

Such was the man who joined Latécoère and Massimi in August of 1919 and who one year later became the airline's Operations Director. He was barely twenty-nine, but he had crammed enough human experience into the past six years to last him a couple of lifetimes. He needed it all that sombre autumn, when within three days two messages reached him that Rodier (who had once piloted Latécoère and Massimi) had disappeared into the sea off Perpignan and that Genthon, another veteran, had burned to death while crash-landing his plane on a rocky field between Valencia and Alicante. A mood of deep discouragement had settled on the airline, fanned by the feeling that the obstacles were too formidable and the odds too murderous. "Reasoning had taken the place of courage and scepticism had replaced intelligence," Daurat himself described it years later in his admirably sober autobiography, *Dans le Vent des Hélices* (In the Wind of the Propellers). "I regretted having to fire a number of colleagues whose value I knew and to whom I was bound by a genuine friendship. But they had become a danger to the enterprise. Having lost their faith and begun to spread a destructive critical spirit, they now used their experience in reverse: to corrode the enthusiasm of others. Some of them had developed the habit of not turning up at the airfield as soon as the wind began to whistle behind the Venetian blinds of the Hôtel du Grand Balcon, which they had made their headquarters."

An old Ford bus was hired to bring the bedroom aviators out to Mon-taudran, and those who failed to make it in time were summarily fired. Pilots' wives and mistresses who had taken to flocking out to admire their menfolks' skill in acrobatic stunts or to plead with them not to take off in the wind and rain were henceforth barred from approaching the field.

The "heroes" and the "aces" who refused to bow to the new régime were quietly sent packing. To replace them Daurat had to hire other wartime pilots—at the time he had nothing else to choose from—who were first put through the mill, as he had done with Massimi at La Cheppes. "To break the carapace of pride which characterized most of them, I imposed a probationary period in the workshops. To some of them unscrewing bolts, cleaning motors, and turning up on time seemed intolerable vexations. They left very quickly, simplifying my problem of selection."

The results of this no-nonsense attitude were soon apparent. Instead of high-hatting the mechanics, hitherto regarded as an "inferior" breed, pilots developed a feeling of comradeship with men whose job it was to keep their engines going and, as so often happened, to bail them out when a mechanical failure forced them to crash-land on a beach or a prairie. The image of the company began to change from that of a group of daredevil adventurers bent on tempting fate to that of a serious mail-carrying enterprise which made a point of flying not with, but against, the weather. Flight standards came to be regarded as about the toughest in the trade, and admission to Latécoère a gilt-edged privilege.

Almost perceptibly there grew up a new esprit de corps which became the airline's most precious, though intangible, possession. It was shadowed by a burgeoning mythology, as the "veterans" became protagonists of an ever growing list of "stories". There was, for example, the case of Jean Mermoz, destined to become the most famous pilot of the line, who came near to being rejected when he turned up at Montaudran two years before Saint-Exupéry. Ushered into Daurat's office, a sparsely furnished room with little more than a desk and a large map of Spain criss-crossed with multicoloured pencillings, Mermoz had confidently pulled out his flight record and his military certificates. A cigarette protruding from underneath his bristling moustache, Daurat glanced briefly at the papers. The muscles around his jaw betrayed not the slightest flicker of expression.

"I see," he finally remarked, his dark eyes staring coldly into those of the young Mermoz, "so far you've done nothing."

"But I've done six hundred hours!" Mermoz protested vehemently. A French general had even written him an unusually warm letter of recommendation.

"That's nothing . . . nothing at all," muttered Daurat. He looked Mermoz up and down, noting the unusually broad shoulders, the unmistakably athletic torso, the suit the poor fellow had spent hours brushing, and the long hair, sleekly groomed back behind his ears.

"You have nice hair, don't you?" he remarked, with a faint trace of sarcasm. "But you don't have the head of a worker."

"But I've come here to be a pilot!"

"Here, if you want to be a pilot, you start by being a worker. You'll follow the usual procedure, like everyone else. I'm hiring you as a mechanic. Go see the foreman and ask him for a pair of overalls."

"All right, *Monsieur le Directeur*," Mermoz had said, swallowing slightly. ". . . but when shall I be able to fly? . . ."

"Here one doesn't ask questions . . . You'll be told in due course when you can fly . . . if you fly," Daurat added meaningfully.

And for the next three weeks Jean Mermoz and six other beginners had roughened up their hands scrubbing down cylinders in a potassium wash. After which they had been put to work assembling and disassembling motors. "I was beginning to find life atrociously monotonous," Mermoz later recalled, "when one evening Monsieur Daurat growled at us, as he walked by: 'You'll report on the field tomorrow at 6.30 a.m.' "

Overjoyed, Mermoz had turned up the next morning, only to find half a dozen *anciens* (old-timers) gathered to watch the fun. They included an Alsatian named Doertlinger, a 1914–1918 war "ace" who had shot down thirteen French planes while flying for the Germans.

The aeroplane which the "apprentices" were to fly was a Bréguet 14, a square-nosed biplane driven by a 300 horsepower Renault engine. If ever there was a plane which looked like a "flying crate", it was this ungainly machine, with its large rectangular radiator and a thing which looked like a boot stuck on top of it just behind the propeller. Often referred to as the "rhinoceros horn", it was simply the exhaust stuck up there in front to expel the fumes out over the upper wing and the head of the pilot, who sat not far behind in an open-air cockpit directly beneath the wing's rear edge.

Having made shaky take-offs and landings, the first two candidates were summarily dismissed by Daurat; after which it was Mermoz' turn. Still smarting from the Boss' nonchalant dismissal of his 600 flying hours as "nothing", Mermoz took off, determined to show him a thing or two. The workhorse of the line, the Bréguet 14 was more like a Percheron than a thoroughbred racer and not made for the stunt flying which had one day so startled Captain René Bouscat; but Mermoz' blood was up and like Saint-Exupéry at Casablanca, he was going to impress the crowd with what this crate could do. Blithely throttling it down the field as hard as he could, he waited until the very last moment before pulling back on the stick, then put the lumbering biplane into a spectacular climbing bank, after which he rolled through a breath-taking series of loops before landing the craft plum on top of the white circle that had been chalked out in the middle of the dirt runway for high precision tests.

Pleased as Punch with his performance, Mermoz climbed confidently out of the Bréguet, only to find that Daurat had vanished. The "old timers" were still there, looking on sardonically, cigarette butts dangling from their lips, their hands thrust bulkily into the pockets of their leather jackets. They looked totally unimpressed.

"You needn't bother to try and find him," one of them finally spoke up, in a disarming Marseille twang. "You can go pack your bag."

"So you're pleased with yourself?" said Daurat, suddenly emerging from a hangar with his felt hat and raincoat already on.

"Yes, *Monsieur le Directeur.*"

"Well, I'm not. Here we don't hire acrobats. If you want to be a circus performer, you can go show off elsewhere."

Tearing off his leather flight helmet, Mermoz had rushed to the locker room and started stuffing his few belongings into a bag, determined to shake the dust of Montaudran from his feet forever. But suddenly there was Daurat behind him, watching him in enigmatic silence.

"So you're leaving," he finally remarked, as he pulled a packet of Caporal cigarettes from his pocket.

"Yes," answered Mermoz shortly.

"Hm . . . You're not disciplined . . . You're pretentious . . . You're pleased with yourself . . . Mmm . . . Naturally . . ."

"Yes, I'm pleased with myself."

"And you answer back."

"Of course, since you ask questions."

"You've got a bad character."

"No, *Monsieur le Directeur*," began Mermoz, "but I hate injustice. I know I piloted well."

"Just as I thought . . . pretentious . . . *On vous dressera*," added Daurat. And with that, hardly believing his ears, Mermoz was ordered to take the Bréguet up again to 600 feet, make a slow horizontal bank, and then bring it back for an easy, long-angle landing. Daurat did not even bother to witness the conclusion of this second flight, which Mermoz executed as instructed; but to rub the lesson in, he sent the fretful pilot back to the workshop for another week of screw-driving in order, as he later put it, "to instill in him a more exact notion of his responsibilities as a flyer".

When Saint-Exupéry reached Montaudran a couple of years later, he already knew what to expect. The recommendation from Beppo de Massimi carried some weight, but as the one-time *boulevardier* had warned him, it was Daurat he would have to impress. Daurat's first impression was not favourable. "His flying credentials were pretty thin," he later recalled. "He had a soft voice, a modest bearing and a look of concentration on his face. But little by little, as the conversation progressed, he began to warm up, and the answers he made to the questions I put to him revealed a young man endowed with a real flyer's temperament as well as an inventor with a fertile imagination."

Like Mermoz and the other apprentice flyers who had preceded him, Saint-Exupéry was first put to work scrubbing cylinders and taking engines to pieces. He had already been put through this kind of drill by the Saurer truck company, so that this was no particularly new or humiliating experience. He was treated at first with a kind of amused scepticism by his fellow mechanics, who didn't know quite what to make of this tall, big-chested fellow with the aristocratic name who had suddenly popped up among them. As a mechanic, he was about as clumsy as he had been as a young boy fumbling to retooth an unslung bicycle chain; but as time went on it became obvious to everyone, including Daurat, that a certain aloofness and reserve in his behaviour stemmed less from a feeling of well-born disdain than from a deep-rooted diffidence, exacerbated by the realization that until now he had been a failure in most of the things he had attempted. His dimpled grin, like his gay laugh, was infectious, but there were moments when a cloud would seem to pass over him, abruptly blotting out the sunshine and reducing him to sullen silence, which he would repair to a café to nurse.

Like his colleagues, he put up at the Hôtel du Grand Balcon, where one could then get a room for as little as four francs a day and a meal for two and a half. The wrought-iron balcony which ran along three sides of the building above the tall ground floor arches was the only grand thing about this rather scruffy hostelry, but Saint-Exupéry, not unnaturally, wanted to be with the others. Rumour had it that the sisters who ran the establishment were in secret cahoots with Daurat, who liked to concentrate his pilots in one place where he could keep an eye on them. It was an understandable precaution on the part of a man who could not be everywhere at once and who practically lived at Montaudran, which he often reached before the earliest of his flyers and would only leave long after them at night. Married to a concert pianist who had charmed Albeniz and Granados during the year he had put in for Latécoère at Málaga, Didier Daurat was anything but a misogynist; but he knew from experience the disorder a passionate attachment could introduce into the life of a pilot, and this was one of the things he kept quiet track of in forming his estimate of a flyer's reliability. He made no bones about it, sometimes remarking with brutal candour that "a pilot who gets married loses three-quarters of his value".

The régime was deliberately spartan. At the Hôtel du Grand Balcon those on duty were expected to board the old Ford bus which came by every morning at exactly four o'clock. Woe to those who missed it! Daurat would never wait, even for a minute; and if a late-riser missed the bus, he would have to get out to Montaudran on his own. For a night owl like Saint-Exupéry this new life had its hardships, but the letters he wrote back to his mother and his friends in Paris betray no trace of regret. Only at times a feeling of *dépaysement* before the strangeness of a life so radically different from what he had previously known. "My hands are full of oil," he wrote to Renée de Saussine, "and I'm the only one to find them beautiful."

Even the homesick feeling began to disappear once he had taken and passed his first flying test. We have Daurat's word for it that he was not fully satisfied with this initial performance, but Daurat was a perfectionist, and he was willing to give Saint-Exupéry a chance to prove himself. Apparently he did, for after several weeks spent taking up new Bréguets for short test flights in all kinds of weather, he was allowed to make his first trip down to Casablanca. "Rinette," Antoine wrote back to Renée de Saussine, "do you know that aviation is a lovely thing? Here it's not a game and that's the way I like it. Nor is it a sport, as it was at Le Bourget, but it's something else, something inexplicable, like a kind of war. It's a lovely sight to see the mail take off into the grey dawn, under the rain. There's the night shift, nodding with sleep, the mist over the Pyrenees, the storm the radio has reported from Spain and which will wake the pilot up. And then the take-off, with everyone dispersing in the mud while he's left alone up there to wrestle with his problems."

His maiden flight to Morocco was undertaken not as pilot but as passenger of the mail-carrying Bréguet. Behind the pilot's cockpit was a second one or "rumble seat" which could accommodate two passengers. It was protected from the wind by a hump in the fuselage which won the Bréguet the nick-name of "camel". Often the "hump" was occupied by a mechanic, and if there happened to be no traveller courageous enough to make the open-air flight, the rest of the space would be stuffed with mail bags, which were otherwise transported in two trunks slung under the lower wing like floats. Bitter experience had demonstrated the necessity of initiation flights for new pilots, for oil leaks and bursting radiators were frequent mishaps which could force them to land precipitously on the nearest field. But if some fields were havens, others concealing rivulets or rocks, were traps. Nodding their heads with condescension, the old timers would look pityingly at the newcomers and say: "The fellow who doesn't know the line, stone by stone, and who runs into a blizzard . . . I feel sorry for him . . . real sorry."

For the first part of the flight Latécoère's pilots were guided by the natural landmarks of the Canal du Midi and the Toulouse-Narbonne railway. Shortly before Narbonne they would have to turn south, flying over Salses and Perpignan towards the eastern extremity of the Pyrenees. It was here that the real problems began. If the weather was fine, they could cut in past the left shoulder of the 8,000 foot Canigou, flying up the Le Perthus pass—900 feet at its highest point—the route used by Hannibal when he penetrated ancient Gaul in 218 B.C. But if the mountains were fogged up, they would have to swing out to sea around the promontory of Cadaqués, following the Costa Brava down to Barcelona. All down the Mediterranean coast were beaches where planes could put down with relative security, but between Valencia, surrounded by treacherous rice paddies, and Alicante, the shortest route lay straight over the 5,000 foot Carasqueta range, and from here on the pilots had to be familiar with the topography of the hinterland.

The equipment was still so primitive that pilots were often obliged to carry spare altimeters tied around their necks—to insulate them from the infernal throb of the pistons. Compasses regularly went haywire, and lacking anything resembling reliable meteorological forecasts, Daurat forbade above-the-clouds flying over mountainous areas. On seeing the clouds banking up under him, the pilot was expected to plunge through the first opening and to continue flying, if necessary, at tree-top level.

The evening when Saint-Exupéry was finally called in to be told that the next morning he would be piloting the mail-plane to Casablanca, Daurat added, after a moment of silence: "You know the instructions?" He let the words sink in, then added deliberately: "It's all very well to navigate by compass over Spain, above the sea of clouds, it's very dashing, but . . ." There was a significant pause, ". . . just remember: below the sea of clouds begins eternity."

That night, at the Hôtel du Grand Balcon, Saint-Exupéry sought out Henri Guillaumet, a pilot who had joined Latécoère some twenty months before him. No one could have seemed more different from himself than this sturdy, blond, brown-eyed son of a Champagne peasant who, as Saint-Exupéry later wrote of him, "spread confidence as a lamp spreads light". Some mysterious attraction, probably nourished by an element of rustic simplicity in each, had brought them together, and it was instinctively towards Guillaumet that Saint-Exupéry now turned.

"Yes, I heard the news," Guillaumet greeted him with a smile. "Are you pleased?" And going to the cupboard, he pulled out a bottle of port and two glasses. "This calls for a drink. You'll see, it will go off fine."

Fearing he might have forgotten some vital warning, Saint-Exupéry unfolded his map of Spain and laid it out beneath the lamp. Seated next to him in shirt sleeves, Guillaumet then treated him to a curious lesson in geography—the subject which had most bored Antoine at school. The peninsula suddenly ceased to be a geographical expression and became a friend. Watersheds and hydrographic data, population statistics and livestock figures gave way to something different and infinitely more pertinent. Guadix, for example . . . he could not forget the little town, but those three orange trees there, bordering a field . . . "Watch out for them, and mark them on your map." And Saint-Exupéry marked them: three trees suddenly grown to be as big as the Sierra Nevada. And that solitary farmhouse near Lorca. With its farmer . . . and his wife. Ready, like lighthouse keepers, to sally forth under the stars to help someone in distress. "And thus from their oblivion and their inconceivable remoteness," he later wrote, "we drew details unknown to all the geographers in the world. For only the Ebro, which waters the large cities, is of interest to geographers. But not this stream hidden beneath the grasses to the west of Motril, this father provider of five and twenty flowers. 'Watch out for that stream, it spoils the fields . . . Mark it too on your map'. Ah! I would remember the serpent of Motril! How inconspicuous it looked, softly murmuring away to a few enchanted frogs, but it slept with one eye open. Stretched below the grasses across this paradise of green, it lay there in wait for me fifteen hundred miles away. And given half a chance it would change me into a fiery sheaf of flame."

What sleep he got that night was brief. He was woken the next morning at three, and half an hour later he was seated on his little bag by the hotel's front entrance, watching the rain patter dismally on the pavement. At last the antique bus rounded the corner, with an angry growl of gears, and Saint-Exupéry climbed in with the rest. Wedged in between a drowsy *douanier* and a couple of office workers, he felt a mounting thrill, mingled with anguish, at the prospect that his hour had come at last. He recalled the terse answers he and his fellow novices were apt to receive whenever a weather-beaten pilot would tramp into the canteen, his flight jacket streaming with water. How had it gone? "Hmm . . . And their brief replies conjured up a fabulous world, full of snares and traps and suddenly looming cliffs and whirlwinds that would have uprooted cedars. Black dragons defended the entrance to the valleys, sheafs of lightning crowned the crests. . . ." Soon he too would be battling the same sombre giants, the same faceless demons. But seated there in the creaky bus amid hushed exchanges and the luminous dots of cigarettes, he felt a strange elation at the idea that while those around him were chained to their dulling routine, he in a moment would be free.

Neither the dark dragons nor the Medusa-headed crests could keep him on this first flight from reaching Barcelona and putting down a couple of hours later in the brilliant sunshine of Alicante. But he was less fortunate on the return trip. Surprised by ground mist and the rapid onset of the wintry dusk shortly after flying over Carcassonne, he held on for as long as he could before crash landing on a field some miles short of Montaudran. Alerted by a telephone call, Raymond Vanier, Didier Daurat's second-in-command, went out to look for him with Touyaret, the chauffeur of their old open-air Peugeot. For hours they groped through the thick fog until at last some helpful villagers put them on the right track. "Saint-Exupéry was waiting for us," Vanier recalls in his book *Tout pour la Ligne*, "wrapped in his fur-lined suit and seated under a wing in the moist grass. 'Monsieur,' he said to me, 'the plane is intact. I apologize for not having fully completed my first mail flight: I did my best . . .' "

Two laps were all a pilot was normally expected to complete before turning over his Bréguet to the next flyer; and Alicante being the half-way stop between Toulouse and Casablanca, a steady stream of Latécoère pilots would stop over for the night in a humble *pensión* run by a plain but not unsympathetic woman called Pepita. But as nothing about the Latécoère line was normal, Saint-Exupéry soon found himself being called upon to fly the mail all the way from Toulouse to Tangier in a series of four hops. "Strange trips," he wrote to Renée de Saussine, "giving me no time to adapt myself either to Spain or Morocco. The Arabs and their camels looked as though they had just come out of a circus. . . . It's odd to enter a country, as though from within. No station signs going by with differently sounding names, no ticket collectors and porters and cab drivers to do one the honours of the country. Still half-dazed, one is plunged into the little life of the little town, without transition."

Yes, it was a curious sensation—as curious as finding oneself suddenly above those treacherous white plains of cloud Daurat had warned against— "remember, underneath . . . is where eternity begins". But the temptation was there, and up above them he was filled with a sense of isolation "which I think it is difficult to attain—and which is almost marvellous. You would not recognize the flying of Le Bourget, or the mentality of Le Bourget. Here it is something else. Something tougher but better."

One day, as he was coming down from a height of 9,000 feet, he heard an ominous sound and was persuaded that his tail-elevator wire had snapped. Bit by bit he felt the plane slipping from his grip, dropping helplessly down with controls which no longer responded. Convinced that he would end up in a spin, he pulled out his pen and wrote in ink on one of his dials: "Snapped controls. Check. Impossible avoid fall."

"I didn't want to be accused of having killed myself though imprudence," he later wrote, "the idea tortured me. It was a new experience for me. I felt myself going white, all glossy with fear. A fear without depth but not awful. A new indefinable understanding."

The experience was relatively banal, though unnerving for a novice pilot. His plane had been caught in a strong downdraft, such as one occasionally encounters without the slightest warning in a cloudless sky. The air suddenly loses its resilience and one has the sickening feeling of being relentlessly sucked down and of falling, falling . . . as fatally and irreversibly as a stone—an impression rendered all the eerier by the deceitful placidity of the heavens. Particularly in a slow-moving craft like the Bréguet the sensation could be prolonged for seconds, even minutes of anguishing suspense. "But nothing had given," he went on to admit, "and I managed to hold on until landing. When I jumped out of the plane I said nothing. I was disdainful of everything and thought no one would understand me. . . . What a world I had crept into by fraud! A world one doesn't come back from to describe. . . . How describe those fields and that calm sun. How was one to say: 'I understand the fields, the sun. . . .' And yet it was true. For a few seconds I had felt, in all its plenitude, the dazzling calm of this day. A day built as solidly as a house where I was at home, where I was well installed, and from which I was about to be ejected. A day with its morning sun, its deep lofty sky and that earth across which fine furrows were being softly woven."

The mystic note, one which was to echo with more and more insistence through his books, was already being sounded here, in this letter written to Renée de Saussine shortly before Christmas of 1926. What San Juan de la Cruz once called, in a beautiful phrase, "the sonorous silence of solitude", was exactly what he felt in these strangely exhilarating moments when, behind a groaning engine labouring forward at seventy to eighty miles an hour, he found himself suspended half a mile above a strangely immobile earth.

The homecoming, after such moments, brought with it a sense of triumph edged with a feeling of let-down. The world, and particularly Toulouse, was suddenly a bit too humdrum, too set in its ways, too much governed by an inalterable routine. "I trace my little provincial path," he wrote to Renée de Saussine. "I pass to the right of this lamp-post and at the café I sit down in this chair"—for already he seldom wrote anywhere except in cafés, where his sonorous surroundings seemed to stimulate his introspective solitude. "I buy my paper at the same kiosk and each time I get off the same phrase to the woman vendor. And the same companions, Rinette . . . until, Rinette, I feel an immense need to escape and to be new. Then I shall emigrate to another café, or another lamp-post or another kiosk, and I shall invent a new phrase for the newspaper vendor. One far more beautiful."

The wound left by the abortive romance with Louise de Vilmorin had not yet healed. He needed a confidant, someone he could pour his heart out to, someone he could love—as passionately as, a child, he had loved his mother. He had left Paris thinking it could be his friend Rinette, whose faithful presence had come to fill the aching void—somewhat to her astonishment, to judge by the bitter tone of reproach in some of his letters. It was not easy to reciprocate his own intensity, and also she was a year or two older, and he was still something of an adolescent—and a pilot to boot. "*Le condamné à mort*," they had called him, with a faint shudder and a smile. Who could say where he was headed or what would become of him now that he had left Paris? Toulouse was so far away . . . and beyond was Casablanca and Dakar. He had already felt his isolation during those sudden returns from Montluçon, when the telephone failed to answer or it was one of his friends telling him: "Not tonight, *mon vieux*, I've got a concert, I've got a dinner, I've got"—a neatly filled agenda which made him feel like an outsider. But from the distance of Toulouse or Alicante this sensation of exile was even worse. He had made fun of his friend Henry de Ségogne's "comestible" landscapes, he had argued fiercely for Ibsen and Einstein against Pirandello and the salon mandarins, but how he missed this cultural fencing now—as he sat amid the coffee cups and bocks of beer of the Café-Restaurant Lafayette in Toulouse. "And these companions," he burst out in a letter to his friend Rinette, "who always think alike bore me stiff, and for this reason I have only two or three friends—with whom I am at peace". One night in Alicante he sat down to write to her, tearing up three letters in succession. Then in desperation, he telephoned her long distance.

Solitude. Cosmic solitude! The expression wasn't his—it was Nietzsche's, but how it fitted his feelings! He had brought several of his books along with him and each reading aroused a mounting admiration. "*J'aime ce type immensément.*" No wonder! The redoubtable thunderer of Sils Maria could not but strike a responsive chord in a young man who had chosen to live dangerously. Forced down over Perpignan by engine trouble, he wandered up in its ancient streets, depressed by the sight of so many *merceries*, dispensing their traditional thimble-fulls of buttons, thread and lace. "They sell three *sous* worth of thread, two *sous* worth of needles, with no hope of ever owning a Hispano Suiza. Those who buy from them spend their lives glued to their lace-curtain windows. With the same eternal decoration adorning the mantlepiece in their rooms. Their lives are composed of habits. A prison. I have such a fear of habits . . ."

A few days later he was forced down near Rabat, managing to emerge unscathed from his wrecked machine. On the return trip to Toulouse he had to battle a nine-hour storm which bounced him about like a tennis ball. On New Year's Eve he was back in Alicante, white beneath a warm winter sun, a bright blue sky, and the undulation of its date-bearing palms. He took a ride in an open cab and watched delightedly while a laughing boot-black slapped and caressed his shoes. A beggar who approached him radiated such joy that he gave him three cigarettes "just to preserve that face".

Two nights later he was in Casablanca, listening to the gale rattling the window panes. And suddenly the half-stifled forebodings were back, tugging at his conscious mind like ghosts. "Sometimes I suffer a faint anguish when I lie in bed with my eyes open. I don't like it when they forecast mist. I don't want to come a cropper tomorrow. The world wouldn't lose much by it, but I would lose everything. Just think of what I possess in the way of friendships and souvenirs and sunshine in Alicante. And that Arab rug I bought today, which weighs me down with the soul of a pro-prietor, I who was so light and had nothing.

"Rinette, I have a colleague whose hands have been burned. I don't want my hands to be burned. I look at them and like them. They know how to write, lace shoes, improvise operas, which you don't like but which are a balm to my soul—all of which demanded twenty years of exercise. And sometimes they capture a face. A face—just think of it." For, as usual, his letters were covered with drawings, executed with coloured pencils over the pages of the hotel or café stationery he used in writing to his friends.

During a brief stop-over in Tangier he had made the round of the bars in a vain effort to find some painted beauty who could tell him about his friend Marc Sabran, who had died there a few weeks before. A week later he was back in Casablanca, battered by another bruising struggle with the elements. "I'm dreaming of white linen, Eau de Cologne, and a bath-room," he wrote Renée de Saussine. "I could do with a good ironing. I'm drenched in oil and wrinkled with fatigue." Pulled down by a relentless down-draft, he had had to bank away from mountains higher than himself, only to be tossed about "like an omelette in a frying-pan" as he fled down the valley. Five times he had been lifted bodily from his seat, rising a full head above the upper wing, specially curved to keep the pilot from knocking himself silly. As for the poor woman passenger behind him, "she was about nine-tenths passed out. It's not exactly Le Bourget any more."

After one such exhausting flight he lay down for a "nap" and without realizing it slept twenty-four hours. On meeting his friends he began a description of "last night's storm" and they stared at him puzzled. "But last night it was clear," they said. "There was no storm." His sleep had been so phenomenally deep that he had simply skipped one day.

No, it wasn't Le Bourget any more. Nor was it the same Antoine. The Rue de la Chaise was not yet forgotten, any more than was the Rue Saint-Guillaume. But the hard knocks to his body, after the wounds to his sensitivity, were making a man of him, and imperceptibly but surely he was shedding his youthful immaturity. And with it the stiff, slightly stand-offish diffidence it had taken Didier Daurat a little time to fathom.

# 6

# Sea and Sand

---

FOUR thousand kilometres in four days. Eight hours of storm from Casablanca to Alicante; nine hours of tempest from Alicante to Toulouse. "I didn't believe an aeroplane could take such blows without breaking into pieces," he had written to Lucie-Marie Decour some days before after a dizzying thousand metre drop which had finally bounced him on a solid cushion of air, a bare hundred feet above the ground. It was what the old timers had told him about down-drafts, but he had had to live through one to believe it. Just as he had had to live through the blizzard which had trapped him in a mountain valley near Lorca to experience the helpless anguish of the blind. Miraculously—there was no other word for it—he had groped his way out and made it on down to Alicante; and only then could he measure just what he had been through. On the ground the welcoming faces were relieved yet grave. Pivot, they told him, bound for Casablanca with the mail from Toulouse, had been forced back on hitting the stormy mountain stretch between Orihuela and Murcia. He had been tossed about like an omelette in a skillet—a favourite phrase with Saint-Exupéry—until suddenly he had sensed something was wrong. He had turned in his seat and his blood had run cold: for there, caught on the tailfin wire, was the rear cockpit blanket, hysterically flapping in the wind. He had lost his passenger, ripped from his harness by a stomach-emptying lurch into the void.

A marsh to landlubbers it might seem, but seldom had the mud of Montaudran been more welcome to Saint-Exupéry than on this windy mid-January afternoon, when he heaved his aching body out of the Bréguet. Drunk with fatigue, his bones and muscles still battling nervously with the elements, he stumbled over to the office where there was news for him. This was practically his last flight on the Spanish run; he was being transferred to Dakar, to pilot the mails up and down the African coast. Two thousand miles of desert, a good half of it a no man's land where blue-cowled camel drivers greeted the passing planes with musketry and fell on grounded airmen with ropes and knives. The Sahara, he had been told in Casablanca, was in a state of effervescence, and "the next pilots forced down with engine trouble will get themselves massacred by the Moors". Said with a kind of jaunty fatalism, the phrase had run in his head. Massacred by the Moors! It was enough to keep him awake at night and to make him "nervous as a hare".

Back in his lodgings on the Rue Alsace-Lorraine—for he had moved in the interim from the Hôtel du Grand Balcon—he began packing up his things until his room, clogged with trunks and crates, had the forlorn air of a dockside. The world, his world, was being turned upside down once more—save for the mantelpiece, where a humpbacked *zouave* and a petticoated shepherdess remained smilingly aloof to the chaos. For weeks he had fought a silent battle with his ageing landlady, stuffing the two porcelain figurines away in a closet, only to find them, on his return, carefully redusted and re-enthroned, deafly fending off his protests with their exasperating bonhommie. In the end he had given up the struggle, allowing the two champions to reign over the cosmic desolation of his quarters. It took him back ten, fifteen years and made him feel like a schoolboy again. The holidays were over and his memories, like his belongings, were being rolled up and crated. It was *Au Revoir* to Toulouse and the Café-Restaurant Lafayette. *Adiós* to Alicante, with its beaming beggars and the plump Pepita whose "comely chassis"—pilots being only human—had been the source of such ribald admiration. Goodbye to Peñiscola and the fishing boats drawn up on the beach which his friend Guillaumet had warned him to watch out for if ever he had to land there in a hurry. Goodbye Tarifa, goodbye Tangier and the mushy landing field near which, a few weeks before, he had seen a solitary burnoused Arab, patiently hoeing the African earth. It was dustier and drier, but it was the same deep red-brown earth of Andalusia which gave nourishment to olive trees and orange groves. Whereas where he was going now there was not a blade of grass in a hundred miles, not a hoe or a cabbage patch in a thousand.

\*　　\*　　\*

It was familiar ground as far as Agadir, beyond which began the desert and the mirages. Here, never having made the run before, he left the mail plane he had piloted down and climbed in as passenger in another Bréguet. 2,300 kilometres separated the white-walled Moroccan town from Dakar: 2,300 kilometres of almost uninterrupted beach, where an aeroplane, in case of trouble, could land. At any rate in theory: for sea mists could

play devilish tricks with the most experienced pilot, and as for sandstorms
. . . God help one! The tide too made a difference, for where the strand
was too wet the wheels would sink in on touching down, causing the plane
to topple over. Elsewhere seaside rocks, looking like mere pebbles from a
distance, could cripple the landing gear. Often it was safer to crash land
on the wind-polished tops of plateaux rising almost sheer, five hundred or
a thousand feet up from the sea. Here one risked rapid capture by the
Moors or slow death from heat and thirst. Pilots were under strict orders
not to lose sight of each other, and if one of the Bréguets was forced down
by engine trouble, the other was supposed to circle overhead until the
grounded pilot had reconnoitred the spot where the second plane could
safely land. The stranded flyer would be hoisted aboard with the mailbags
from his plane, while the Moorish interpreter (if there was no room to spare)
was left with the provisions to make his way back to the nearest base by his
own means.

Unlike the French, who periodically patrolled the Saharan hinterland
with camel-riding *méharistes* (*mehara* is an Arabic word for a particularly
swift breed of dromedary), the Spaniards who ruled over the 1,200 kilometre
stretch of the Rio de Oro, were content to limit their sway to three coastal
forts, situated at Cape Juby—480 kilometres southwest of Agadir—Villa
Cisneros—610 kilometres farther on—and La Guerra—340 kilometres
beyond that. The first French outpost was not reached before Port Etienne,
40 kilometres south of La Guerra on the northern limit of French Mauretania. From here it was nother 620 kilometres to Saint-Louis-du-Sénégal,
where the governor of Mauretania was stationed. Since the small garrison
of Port Etienne, with seventy Senegalese riflemen, was untrained for desert
sweeps, and inasmuch as the Spaniards did not go in for them, this meant
that for a distance of 1,200 kilometres Latécoère's pilots were flying over a
lawless wilderness at the mercy of camel-riding nomads. Often the heat was
such that radiators would boil over or oil seams burst before the pilots
could climb with their Bréguets to 6,000 feet or higher where they might
hope (not always successfully) to find cooler air. Breakdowns were thus even
more frequent here than over Spain—the average being one in every six
round trips between Juby and Dakar.

For the Moors the slow-flying Bréguets were more than fair game.
The same biplanes had been used in the Rif war against the warriors of
Abd-el-Krim and in southern Morocco during the drive Lyautey launched
to extend French sovereignty as far as the river Dra. The wilderness beyond,
since it officially belonged to Spain, was off limits to French *méharistes*
and thus a refuge for hostile tribes and African deserters from French
colonial forces. The older Moors could still remember the pre-1908 days

when the territory south of the Atlas was lorded over by the dreaded Blue Sultan of Kerdous; and General Mangin's entry into Marrakesh in 1911 was still too recent not to nourish a lingering hope that the hour of sweet revenge might strike and the pale-faced *"roumi"* be driven from the sands. For these desert marauders, who lived to fight and plunder, a mail-plane was as strange and incomprehensible an object as an ambulance; and persuaded that the float-like mail-trunks slung beneath its lower wings were bombs, they would open up on each passing Bréguet with everything they had.

For Saint-Exupéry, who had spent weeks looking forward to this moment, it must have been a singular sensation to see the chalk-white walls of Agadir recede like dice into their apron of orange groves and gardens. Already the air was different, its blossomed fragrance overwhelmed by the damp breath of the sea. As they soared past the red cliffs like two angry buzzards, the frightened livestock scattered wildly down the hills. Beneath them a restless ocean rolled its white foam against the rocks. Closed in behind their prickly palissades of thorn and bramble, the last Berber villages clung like sea-urchins to the coves. Off to the left the gaunt peaks of the High Atlas rose nobly through the haze, dwindling in an unbroken chain to the last mauve ripple ahead: a geographic frown where died the smiling greenery of the Sous. Suddenly men, beasts, and trees disappeared as the landscape flattened into a measureless expanse. A gash of green cactus amid the bone-white stones and wisps of nomadic tent-smoke signalled the approach of Ifni. The little garrison town floated past, followed soon by the parched gorges of the Noun. Then came the dunes, rippling forward in ceaseless waves. Undulating chains of sand, forged into horseshoes by the hammer-hot blast of the *simoun*, blowing out of the Sahara as though from a furnace door. Though it was early February, pith-helmets and sun-glasses were needed to resist the heat and the glare.

The minutes passed, with nothing but an occasional tremor in the motor to relieve the monotony of sea and land. Beneath them, like a gleaming scimitar, they could now admire the *"Playa Blanca"*—the "white beach" on which Rozès and Ville had been forced down by engine trouble several years before. Surprised by a throng of armed Moors shortly after the second Bréguet had landed, Rozès had rashly assumed that he could charm these dark-faced strangers into letting him transfer the mailbags out of his crippled machine into the other. Casually walking up to them, he had begun by addressing them in French, then harangued them in Spanish, and when neither made the slightest impression on the closed, cowled faces, he had delivered himself of a few guttural sounds in what he hoped might pass as Arabic. But the Moors, taking this smiling oratory for a sign of weakness, had rushed angrily forward and laid hands on the jovial Toulousain, while his companion Ville found himself surrounded by a howling mob threatening him with knives. In the ensuing fracas Ville had shot down several Moors with his pistol, giving Rozès a chance to break away from his captors. The get-away had been every bit as spectacular as the most implausible Western—with Rozès vaulting into the cockpit after shooting a Moor who was drawing a bead on them with his rifle from the other side of the fuselage. Furiously gunning the engine, which Ville had fortunately left idling, he had thundered down the beach as his companion clambered in behind him, braving a hail of Moorish bullets fired at them from the dunes.

The incident had created diplomatic havoc. Colonel Bens, the easy-going Spanish governor of Cape Juby, had immediately closed the base to further Latécoère flights. In Madrid Captain Ramón Franco (Francisco's younger brother) took up the hue and cry, angrily demanding that the right to overfly the Rio de Oro be permanently denied to the French and granted to the Germans. To add to Latécoère's troubles, the pilots in Casablanca, impressed by Rozès' vivid descriptions of Moorish savagery, went on strike. The African service beyond Agadir, they said, was too risky, and they were damned if they were going to risk their lives to bring a few sacks of mail from there to Dakar and back.

It would have been the death of the line and of all Pierre Latécoère's dreams had the man who was really running it not been Didier Daurat. Without wasting a moment he had himself flown down to Casablanca from Toulouse. He had only a few words for the group of pilots who were sheepishly assembled on the field to welcome him. But they were enough. He was going to Rabat to solicit Marshal Lyautey's help. As for the mail, since the others found the job too risky, he would fly the next plane down to Dakar himself. Jumping into a taxi, he was driven to Rabat, where late that same evening he was received by Lyautey. "You carry the French flag," the Marshal declared, after Daurat had explained their plight. "It's natural that I should back you up." He then wrote a personel note to Colonel Bens which he sealed into an envelope.

When Daurat got back to Casablanca, the pilots, made to feel like cowards, were vying with each other for the privilege of accompanying the *patron* south. The strike was over. But not until he actually put down at Juby the next day was Daurat sure they would not be greeted with a burst of gunfire from the Spanish. Walking up to the fort, he handed Lyautey's letter to the sentinel, who took it to his commander. Just what the letter contained, Daurat never did discover; but a minute or two later the gate was thrown open and the French pilots were welcomed in. They were received by

Colonel Bens with a bottle of champagne, and from then on every time a French plane landed the Spanish colours were hoisted in its honour.

An agreement, subsequently reached with a number of tribal chieftains at Tiznit, in southern Morocco, promised a substantial reward to any Moor bringing back captured pilots and untouched mailbags. It was also decided that Schleu (which is to say Berber) interpreters would accompany the pilots over the northern part of the run, from Agadir to Cape Juby; while Moorish interpreters from the southern tribes (who spoke completely different dialects) would fly on with them from Juby to Port Etienne. Cupidity, it was hoped, would prevail over hatred of the infidel intruder and time gradually temper the cruel spirit of revenge aroused by Ville's and Rozès' gun battle with the locals.

It was months before these hopes began to materialize, but the resort to interpreters proved of decisive importance. Many of them were former mechanics who had picked up a smattering of basic French while working for Renault or Citroën in France. Being allowed to go up in a Bréguet, so much faster than a truck or a donkey, was a highly coveted privilege which made their dark eyes gleam and their chins rise with pride. Often they would have to be stuffed into the same compartment with the mail-bags, but used to sitting cross-legged, they bore their cramped lot with genial equanimity. The pilots too were happy to have them along, and not simply to intercede on their behalf when forced down among the Moors. Experience revealed that they were often more reliable than compasses in enabling a lost pilot to regain his bearings; for as life-forsaken as the desert might seem to the untutored eye, it was rare that it did not yield a landmark the interpreter could identify.

There was one of them in the other plane, and whenever they were close enough, Saint-Exupéry could see his cowled head just behind the pilot's. Agadir by now was two hours behind them and they had overflown the stony estuary of the Dra. Gradually the African coast began pushing towards the west, the line of flight shifting almost as imperceptibly as the shadow of the struts on the Bréguet's lower wing. Shreds of sea mist still blanketed the coast—a blueish blur over the water, a tawny fuzz over the land. From this height—several thousand feet—there was not a sign of life as far as the eye could see. An ocean of sand to the left as monotonous and vast as the ocean to the right. A pampered humanity used to softer climes had abandoned this barren stretch of planet. In appearance, at any rate. For the solitude was deceptive, the wilderness not empty; merely sleeping, wrapped in a fitful slumber it needed only the drone of a motor to disturb. With half an ear it lay there listening—like passenger and pilot . . . listening for the sudden cough in the cylinders, for the wild flutter in the engine's heart-beat that could bring the desert miraculously to life. A desert as pale and angry as a hornet's nest. It wasn't so much a fear as a kind of insidious anxiety which preyed upon the ear with the insistence of a mirage. The throbbing would pile up into a strange cumuli of sound, the skipped beats into quivering swoops of silence, until he was sure . . . yes . . . this was it! Even veteran pilots were known to have succumbed to the spell. Like someone hearing voices, they would suddenly put down on some barren stretch, anxious to anticipate the unavoidable; the plane would lumber to a halt and only then, with the pistons still thumping and the propeller obstinately turning, would they realize that it was they, and not the motor, which had succumbed to a fever of the ear.

Another hour passed and the sea mist thinned as the sun rose ever higher in the fiery sky. Then, far ahead, the blue sea suddenly appeared beyond the surf-washed rim of land. On a piece of island rock, a mere seagull's swoop from the foaming shore, the British had built a fort, long since transformed into a Spanish penitentiary. "*La casa del mar*"—the house of the sea—they called it. Facing it across the foam, on its promontory of dry land, was the fort, with its adobe huts and low quadrangular wall, its crenelated citadel, and a two storey barrack-building staring glumly out across the desert. From the air nothing could have looked more toy-like and fragile, but to Jean Mermoz nine months before those stern white walls had risen up over the dunes like an unbelieved Jerusalem. His Moorish captors had dropped him off, after pocketing the 1,000 peseta ransom, just short of the last desert encampments. Saint-Exupéry could see them now, off to the left, where the tawny earth was pockmarked with dark triangles of shade. To the right, separated from the tents by tiers of barbed wire, was a canvas Bessoneau hangar large enough to shelter four Bréguets. They had reached Cape Juby, the first Spanish outpost in the Rio de Oro.

Here Saint-Exupéry had his first close-up glimpse of the "dreadful Moors". Robed in dark blue burnooses, their chins and even their noses wrapped in a *rezza* or shawl which swept on up over their dark heads like a turban, they crowded round the Bréguets in silent awe. Occasionally one of them would leap elastically into the air, straining for a better view into the cockpit, while the others, squatting at a respectful distance, were content to look on with unflagging curiosity. For hours they would squat thus, waiting for the magic moment when one of these winged monsters would take off noisily to the air; turning slowly on their haunches as it circled overhead and following the prodigy with their eyes as long as it was visible. A low, guttural "*Barrak Illah!*" (Praise be to Allah!) would usually greet the arrival of a mail-plane, but more as a matter of form than from any deep felt sentiment. For when Didier Daurat, a year and a half before, had dazzled his audience by demolishing an impressive number of bottles with a Winchester carbine, he later heard that his Moorish admirers had silently prayed for his Bréguet to crash on taking off so that they might recuperate the magic weapon.

To house the pilots at Juby a wooden shack had been built against the citadel's northern wall a bare twenty yards from the sea. Although in theory it was covered by the Spanish sentinel posted on the terrace above, in practice there was nothing to prevent the Moors from invading the premises, particularly on moonless nights when the sound of their footsteps was lost in the wash of the surf. Rather than maintain a night-long vigil, like that of the Spanish sentries above, an ingenious French mechanic had mounted a propeller on the roof, faced into the prevailing wind, and hooked it up through a magneto to the metal door handle of the shack. Anyone touching the handle without previously disconnecting the wire thus got a rude shock— sufficient to jolt the jauntiest Moor. Whether Saint-Exupéry, on his maiden visit to Juby, was given the "treatment" we do not know; but most likely he was. For on hand to greet him for the welcome meal was his friend Henri Guillaumet, who was not averse to this kind of horse play.

Saint-Exupéry's personal log-book has unfortunately been lost, along with so many other of his belongings; but Guillaumet's, which has been preserved by his widow, shows that they took off from Juby on February 7, 1927—presumably at dawn—bound for Villa Cisneros, 600 kilometres to the southwest. Guillaumet's Bréguet (No. 238) carried most of the mail, with the interpreter stuffed in on top of it, while Saint-Exupéry took his place in the passenger cockpit behind René Riguelle, who had also been flying for some months on the southern (Juby-Dakar) part of the run.

The first hours were uneventful, as they flew down the African coast. Thirty miles beyond Cape Bojador they spotted the sinister stretch of flat ground, hemmed in by dunes and beach, where Gourp and Erable had been forced down by engine trouble just three months before. Erable had taken off with the transferred mailbags, only to fly hurriedly back on spying some sinister shadows among the dunes. He had landed just in time to be riddled by a Moorish salvo, which had also killed the Spanish mechanic who was working on Gourp's motor. The interpreter emerged unscathed, but Gourp was left with a gaping wound in the leg. The Bréguets having been sacked and gutted, the Moors had started arguing over the wounded pilot. One of them, a swarthy ruffian who answered to the name of Ould Haj'Rab, had drawn his dagger, determined to finish him off there and then. He had developed a fierce hatred of the "*roumis*" while serving under French officers and non-coms in a Moroccan *goum*, from which he had eventually deserted. But his companions, being more interested in getting their hands on the bags of *duros* they could obtain from the ransom, finally prevailed on him to sheathe his terrible blade. The wounded Gourp was heaved on to a camel and strapped down like a sack of meal. For two days the caravan had trekked across the desert, Gourp groaning with every step the camel took. Unable to endure the torture any longer, he had asked the interpreter for the medicine chest and suddenly gulped down a bottle of phenic acid and another of iodine. His captors, now burdened with a dying man, had hastily dispatched one of their warriors with Ataf, the interpreter, on swift *méhari* camels to Juby. If Gourp died before they could engineer the ransom, they knew they would get nothing. For four tense days Mermoz and Ville had flown vainly up and down the coast in search of the vanished flyers, narrowly missing capture in their turn as the result of another engine failure. When Ataf and his fellow Moor reached Juby a ransom of 5,000 pesetas was agreed upon. It was Riguelle (now flying the plane Saint-Exupéry was riding in) who had flown them back and covered his fellow pilot Lassalle with a rifle as he sallied forth across the sand to cut the agonizing Gourp from his saddle ropes. Wracked by internal haemorrhages, his wounded leg a dark gangrenous mass, the semi-conscious Gourp had been flown post-haste to Casablanca, only to die in his hospital bed a few hours later.

The charred, beetle-black remains of the two Bréguets were all that was left to mark the scene of the slaughter, as they flew on over the Elbow Cape and the rocky mass of the Roca Cabrón del Norte to Villa Cisneros. Like a dark brown birthmark, a large waterless depression, known in those parts as a *sebkha*, preceded the jutting finger of land. Protected on two sides by water, the ochre-hued field lay beyond the Spanish fort which barred the neck of the peninsula like a Chinese Wall. Here they tarried just long enough to have their planes refuelled. They downed cups of hot chocolate while the same sunburnt faces and dark gollywog heads which had greeted them at Juby stared at them wordlessly from under their blue cowls. Neither openly hostile nor ostentatiously friendly, their inscrutable expressions were as full of mystery and menace as the desert behind them.

Climbing back into their Bréguets Guillaumet, Riguelle, and Saint-Exupéry continued down the coast, overflying Cape Barbas and the white strand of the Bay of Saint Cyprien. Bits of wreckage still marked the spot where the French freighter *Falcon II* had run aground eighteen months before and where Deley and Collet, landing on the wet sand in two Bréguets, had packed skipper and wounded crewmates into cockpits and mail trunks and snatched them in the nick of time from thirty Moorish camelmen. The small Spanish fort of La Guerra came into view, perched on the craggy rim of all this desolation, and then, lost in a featureless expanse of dunes the southern boundary of the Rio de Oro passed invisibly beneath them as they came down over Port Etienne. Its elongated neck of land, thicker than at Cisneros, burrowed into the sea with the nosey sleekness of a greyhound—the animal for which its bay (Baie du Levrier) was named. A good half mile separated the airstrip of hard sand from the tiny wharf and the concrete sheds where the fish were hung and dried, but the imposing blockhouse looked reassuringly solid, dug in to resist the desert winds rocking the rust-coloured sails of the lobster boats in the bay.

It was noon. They had been in the air for almost six hours, but the longest lap—the 625 kilometres separating Port Etienne from Saint-Louis-du-Sénégal—still lay ahead. It took them out over the bay and down the coast past the island of Arguin, famous for the marine disaster Géricault immortalized in *The Wreck of the Medusa*. A curse to the mariner, its reef of white sand had been a boon to Guillaumet when forced to crash land on it shortly before Christmas. Now they were flying south—over Cape Tafarit and the Tidney Islands and the jutting promontory of Cape Timiris, the last prominent landmark for almost 300 miles. In an effort to find cool air Riguelle climbed to 8,000 feet, from where the white-caps on the water looked like faint ripples on a tranquil expanse of blue. Guillaumet, off to the left, was hugging the coast, whereas Riguelle, preferring to avoid the heat and turbulence of the desert, was now several miles out to sea. Saint-Exupéry couldn't repress a faint twinge of alarm on seeing the coast recede to a white line on the horizon. "Why on earth is he flying so far out?" he thought to himself. "If anything happens now, a nice fix we'll be in." But Riguelle flew on unconcernedly, and by and by Saint-Exupéry dozed off.

His nap was rudely interrupted by a terrifying noise, like a mad hammering of skillets, while the plane was seized with trembling. Wisps of smoke snorted briefly from the motor, which lurched into an eery silence with a final unnerving thump. They had burned out the crankshaft bearings. "Damnation!" cried Riguelle. "Serves him right!" thought Saint-Exupéry, momentarily forgetting that he too was in the soup.

There was nothing they could do but bank towards the shore, which at this point rose from the seaboard in cone-shaped cliffs of pumpkin-coloured sand. Beyond the eroded dunes was a fairly level stretch on a kind of plateau, several hundred yards inland. Riguelle made for it as best he could with a feathered propeller, losing height all the time. Realizing he was going to fall short of the plateau, he steered the Bréguet in between two humps of sand. The plane touched down with a crump, shattering a wing and the landing-gear.

"Are you hurt?" cried Riguelle.

"No," answered Saint-Ex, who had braced himself for the shock.

"That's what I call piloting!" added Riguelle jovially.

Saint-Exupéry said nothing, preferring not to say what he thought of it. But any way, they were alive!

As they climbed out of their stricken craft they were overwhelmed by the immensity of the silence, into which their voices disappeared as into a blanket. "And there we were," as Saint-Exupéry recalled it not long afterwards, "with three cans of corned beef, a few litres of radiator water, and above all two pistols. Two pistols with which to ward off the desert. And the silence beginning just thirty metres away."

The silence was soon broken by the welcome drone of Guillaumet's Bréguet, circling back to look for his companions. Having spotted them, he made a safe landing on the plateau, a few hundred yards from the shattered plane. It took them some time to transfer what mailbags they could from one Bréguet to the other; but a few being left over and the plateau's sandy surface too soft for an overladen plane, it was decided that Saint-Exupéry would be left behind to guard what remained, while Guillaumet and Riguelle flew off to the nearest French outpost to unload the rest.

"Here, you made need them," were their parting words, as they handed Saint-Exupéry their pistols and a few cartridge clips.

While the two veterans flew off, Saint-Exupéry took up a defensive position amid the dunes, ready to blaze away at the enemy. But not a single blue turban, not a furtive dark shadow troubled the silence of that long afternoon, broken only by the silky sigh of the wind across the sand. As soundless as a ghost the silhouette of a gazelle appeared for one fleeting instant, then vanished back into the waves of sand.

The desert was already tinted with the gold-dust of evening when Guillaumet alighted. He was greeted by a bright-eyed Saint-Exupéry.

"You see, they didn't come!" he cried, pointing proudly to the mailbags.

Guillaumet grinned, shook his head, and then burst into a mischievous laugh. "You needn't have worried . . . We forgot to tell you—we left the danger zone some way back. The tribes around here are friendly."

The accident had fortunately occurred not far from Nouakchott, today the capital of an independent Mauretania. In those days it consisted of nothing more than a fort, staffed by a French sergeant and fifteen Senegalese soldiers. On seeing Guillaumet coming down to land, the sergeant had them line up outside and then snap to attention. The sight of those fifteen dark-faced soldiers drawn up as stiffly as Grenadier Guards in the middle of all this sand struck Saint-Exupéry as marvellously incongruous, like a wild flourish of "geraniums or lettuce" in the centre of the Sahara.

"Ah, you don't know what it does to me to see you!" the sergeant greeted them, with tears in his eyes. Twice a year a boat would stop by and they would stock up with provisions. And then the months would pass without his seeing another white man. Until the anxiously awaited day when the lookout on the terrace would spy the first flurry of dust on the horizon and over the dunes would softly pad the camel-borne *méharistes* of Atar. Sometimes it was the lieutenant, occasionally the captain. As had happened last time when, to the sergeant's eternal shame, he had seen him leap lithely from his mount and mop his wet brow . . . only to be given the dreadful news: "*Oh, mon Capitaine, c'est terrible! Je n'ai plus de vin à vous offrir. On a tout bu.*" The cellar was dry, they had drunk all the wine, even run out of tobacco. It had so mortified the sergeant that he had written to offer his resignation.

This time they were luckier. There were treasures in the basement. Lovingly, as though he were uncorking the noblest of vintages, the sergeant poured out the precious reserves of his hospitality. Visitors from France! What a gift from Heaven! That evening, as the sun went down in a blaze of hidden glory, they talked and they talked. And the sergeant who had been away from home so long, unable to speak like the others of the blonde from Chaville or of the brunette from Bourg-en-Bresse, spoke with moving tenderness of those who, once or twice a year, peopled his solitude for one prodigal night. "*Comme me disait le Lieutenant . . . comme m'a dit le Capitaine! . . .*"

The visitors were given blankets, but not wishing to sleep with the others inside the fort, they rolled up on the sand. In the middle of the night they were woken by the penetrating desert cold, biting enough to make their blankets seem transparent. While the sergeant slumbered down below, the three pilots sat out the rest of the night on the terrace above. The sky was ablaze with stars, many of them strange stars Saint-Exupéry had never seen before. It was a new sky he was looking at—with the Big Dipper pushed off into one tiny corner of Heaven. And up there, in the constellation of Taurus, was the star towards which, at some vertiginous speed, the Earth was speeding. While they chatted three stars streaked silently down the night. Three fleet-footed stars . . . stealing softly away before the sleeping sergeant could catch them. Saint-Exupéry was so moved that he found himself making three wishes, as though he had just seen the first sliver of the crescent moon. The first was that this star-filled night might last for a thousand years. The second was that this wish might be heard. And the third . . . the third . . . was that all women might be tender!

\*　　\*　　\*

Entertained though they were by his scintillating conversation and his uncanny skill with cards, Saint-Exupéry's fellow pilots had not failed to notice his penchant for reverie and a vagueness with regard to mechanical objects which often presented risks—to pilot as much as motor. He proved it once again the following morning when his companions got ready to start Guillaumet's Bréguet. The cool night had induced a massive condensation of vapour in the cylinders and it took many turns of the propeller to dry them out. The job had to be done by hand, since the Bréguets had no self-starters, and Riguelle and Guillaumet were soon sweating profusely as they tugged and heaved at the large wooden blade. "*Contact!*" they would cry, as the propeller came up to the vertical position, and Saint-Exupéry, who was in the cockpit (for his own security), would switch on the ignition. The blade would come down with a cough from the engine, and they would shout "*Coupez!*" when it failed to take fire. The process would be laboriously repeated to refill the cylinders with fuel. Up . . . *Contact!* Down . . . *Coupez!* Up . . . down, on . . . off! Up . . . Contact! Down . . .—until with a sudden surprising roar the motor sprang to life. Guillaumet and Riguelle left nimbly aside, whereupon Saint-Exupéry, whose thoughts were elsewhere, cut the ignition, as he had done so many times before. One can imagine the swearing in the silence that followed. . . . But later how they all laughed at his chronic absent-mindedness! It became a favourite yarn with the pilots of the line, one of the first of many anecdotes in the "Saint-Ex legend".

*        *        *

Dakar, after this first exhilarating taste of the desert, proved a dismal disappointment. Beyond Saint-Louis-du-Sénégal, where the orange-tinted dunes of the Sahara gave way to greenery and gardens and the watery embankments of Central Africa, alive with dugouts and black paddlers, the landscape grew progressively less dessicated, more fertile, and to that extent more human, yet to Saint-Exupéry less exalting. The terminus was Dakar, the capital of French West Africa, where a typically provincial French colony had been superimposed on a teeming African society. In four years there had occurred a radical change in the attitude of the governor, who in 1923 had refused to lift a finger to help Latécoère's first exploratory mission, on the grounds that he was not authorized to advance credits for "sportive manifestations". That these flyers were sportive types there was now not the shadow of a doubt: they were even crazy enough to fly the weekly mail in and out through every kind of weather, and right through the four storm-drenched summer months when the French Army's pilots preferred to hang up their dripping raincoats and pith helmets in the vestibule and to lounge around the Club. But it did not take the locals long to appreciate the benefits of Daurat's iron discipline; for they could now write home and receive a reply in two weeks instead of six. There was a glamour about these new heroes, these "knights of the air" which made them the objects of considerable attention. Particularly for someone with a name like Saint-Exupéry's all doors were open; and as he wrote back to his mother: "I have been received just about everywhere, and even made to dance! I had to come to Sénégal to go out in the world."

It was at a *café-dancing* frequented by Latécoère pilots that Noëlle Guillaumet (the wife of his friend Henri) first caught sight of Saint-Exupéry. He was dancing with a girl a whole head shorter than himself, and there was a luminous smile on his face as he pranced about in a state of wrapt oblivion, dragging a fallen garter with one of his bearlike feet. He was going through the motions just to be "one of the boys" and to enliven the evening; for Saint-Exupéry was painfully aware of his outlandish size and did not particularly relish dancing—"a sport for gigoos", as he sometimes called it.

Several weeks of this régime were enough to inspire a deep disgust which he tried, not altogether successfully, to conceal from his companions. They were accustomed to his moodiness and were not too much surprised to see him one evening in a Dakar nightclub bury himself in a copy of Plato's *Dialogues*, deaf to the rhythm of the band. "*C'est bien de Saint-Ex!*" they would say, with a wink and a knowing nod, something to be expected of an intellectual who was definitely an "*original*". The mood would descend on him suddenly, and then there was nothing doing: he had to draw a curtain between himself and the world. "People here are so stifling," he complained to his mother, "they think of nothing and are neither sad nor happy. Sénégal has simply emptied them of themselves." To others he was even more explicit in decrying the "trash dump" of Sénégal and Dakar, which he termed "the most loathsome of suburbs". Everything so insipid, second-rate, banal; everyone so off-hand and shameless, addressing Negroes with the condescending "*tu*"—enough to make him shudder!—vegetating in front of Dubonnet advertisements, and—oh, intolerable promiscuity!—giving each other rendez-vous in the cathouse! "I who am so leery of people, and who only understand an individual when I am alone with him!" as he wrote back to Charles Sallès.

It was with distinct relief that he could at last resume piloting the mails after several weeks of enforced immobility. At Saint-Louis-du-Sénégal he made the acquaintance of his first ostriches and marvelled at their inexhaustible appetite for watches, silver spoons, mother-of-pearl buttons, bits of glass, for anything that shines and sparkles. Taking advantage of a "gap" of free time in the weekly mail service, he went off into the interior on a four-day lion hunt. Travelling in weather-beaten roadsters, he and his companions cruised through the brush "like tanks", bagging an impressive number of jackals and wild boar. They even ventured into the desert, where the dust-raising gyrations of their groaning machines spread panic, then admiration through the Moorish encampments. When he finally came face to face with a lion, the encounter was a disappointment. He fired and wounded it, at which point his Winchester jammed. The wounded beast might have given his tormentor trouble had Saint-Exupéry not thought of frightening him away with a long push on the horn. The exploit was nothing to crow over, and it was somewhat shamefacedly that he later wrote to Lucie-Marie Decour to say that "contrary to the rules the lion didn't jump me. It went off in disgust, its trot upset by the wound, like a cow."

In addition to the routine job of piloting the mail, he was made a kind of roving ambassador and instructed to establish contacts with the Moors. He had himself introduced to the robed Sheikh of Boutilimit, who invited him to visit his desert fastness—a white-walled oasis fortress floating like a ship on a billow of tangerine-hued sand. More than a day's distance by camel, it was a short hour and a half from Saint-Louis by plane. Each foray into the desert increased his admiration for the lords of the desert "where one finds a people which remains itself . . . where one is received under tent-cover by splendid Moors, and where one crosses classic caravans which look a thousand years old, bound, one imagines, for some distant Baghdad".

At Villa Cisneros he was put up inside the Spanish fort, with nothing to write by at night but a sputtering candle sizzling with burnt flies. Outside he could hear the hollow pounding of the sea and the lugubrious cries of the sentinels upon the roof.

"*Alerta, Sentinela?*" followed by the ritual reply—

"*Sentinela, alertado estoy.*"

Each sentry would in turn take up the cry, and question and answer could be heard dwindling into the distance like an echo.

"A strange life I'm leading," he wrote to Lucie-Marie Decour, "with two thousand kilometres of Sahara for a boulevard, one thousand of them in dissident territory. From here to Juby—tomorrow's flight—we'll be shot at like partridges by innumerable encampments. The danger is slight because the Moors haven't learned how to readjust their fire against a plane; but when the motor begins to falter, it's more worrying. Like descending into a bear pit."

He was back in Dakar in early March when four Uruguayan flyers, led by Commander Taddeo Larre-Borges, were forced down into the sea some distance from Juby in the seaplane with which they had intended trying to fly the South Atlantic. Capsized by a floating breaker, they swam into shore, only to be surrounded, seized, and stripped by a mob of howling R'Guibat warriors. Mermoz and Ville, flying north with the Dakar mail, spotted the shattered seaplane near a river mouth, and Guillaumet and Riguelle, who were at that moment at Juby, were sent to look for the survivors. They finally located them, a good distance inland, strapped to the humps of several R'Guibat camels. Not long afterwards Reine and Antoine flew up from Juby with an interpreter and managed the delicate job of negotiating the ransom.

For Saint-Exupéry, thirsting for adventure, all this was most frustrating. The accident had occurred when he was at the Dakar end of the line, and he only reached Juby after the rescue was over. He heard the Uruguayans' hair-raising account of their tribulations—with the Moors taking aim several times and menacing to shoot them down like dogs. Had they been French, not one of them would have survived.

It was also during this stopover at Juby that he had his first taste of a sandstorm and came close to being shot. Thinking that the night, as black as pitch, and the wind, as thick as soot, offered complete protection, he stepped out of the pilots' shack after dinner, unaccompanied by the usual sentinel. Suddenly he heard footsteps stealthily approaching and his blood froze. Blinded by the storm and without even a revolver to defend himself, he groped his way towards the wall of the fort. A sharp challenge from the Spanish sentry rang out above him. "*Amigo . . . viejo amigo . . . Amigo . . . de enfance!*" spluttered Saint-Exupéry, desperately summoning all the pidgin Spanish he could muster. Crouching down on all fours he crawled hastily towards the shack. The shot went off behind him just as he pushed through the door.

One day, not far from the Sénégal river, his motor failed and he put down near a remote village which had never seen a white man before. He was offered a mat to sleep on and even a hut, and in return he presented his hosts with a pot of jam, which they ate with white-eyed wonderment. At three o'clock in the morning, as the moon rose over the palms, two native guides accompanied him on horseback on a long ride to the next settlement. It made him feel like an "old explorer", like a latterday Livingstone; but he was ill prepared for the excursion and in the village he caught cold. By the time he was back in Dakar he was shaking and half-paralysed with fever. He was admitted to the hospital and given an upper bunk above that of a poor woman dying of yellow fever.

He spent the next month fighting the mosquitoes, as well as his fever, and watching the other inmates of the ward wander around in their convict-striped pyjamas. Spring had passed, giving way to summer—the dreadful, sultry Senegalese summer when a veil of heat lies across the sickly sky, sudden tornado gusts rip the tops from the palm trees, when dark cataracts of water drench the steaming earth and those Europeans who cannot make it home with their families sit in their moist clothes, sweating like sponges. There was talk of the plague, of a new wave of yellow fever—like the one that had decimated Dakar three years earlier. "She's not yet dead," remarked the Negro attendant one day, nodding at the fever-wracked creature beneath him. Just to cheer him up! He weighed himself and found that he had lost fifteen pounds—"from boredom", as he amusingly put it. A letter he received from Charles Sallès brought with it the sad news that their old friend, Louis de Bonnevie, of the Villa Saint-Jean, had just died. In Morocco—like their friend Marc Sabran the previous September. There was a pox on this continent and whatever happened Sallès must remain in Europe. "I'm beginning to grow superstitious. Even though Morocco is soft and sweet next to this dustbin of Sénégal! The fellow opposite has a strange malady. Worms, long red worms keep crawling out of him from all over—it's horrible. . . ."

Saint-Exupéry finally pulled through, but he was given several months of sick leave to recover his strength completely. He flew back to France, marvelling at the greenness of the grass, the lushness of the cattle browsing off the golden alfalfa near Saint-Maurice, the softness of the evening breeze at Agay, where he spent several weeks with his sister Gabrielle and her husband Pierre. What a change, this soft lapping of a tranquil sea, from the restless surge of the Atlantic!

He was still convalescing when he received a telegram asking him to proceed immediately to Toulouse. It was Daurat who broke the news to him when he walked into his office. He was being appointed *chef d'aéroplace* at Cape Juby.

# 7

# A Year among the Moors

THE situation at Juby had deteriorated steadily since the departure, at the end of 1925, of the affable Colonel Bens, a Catalan who had shown himself on the whole favourably disposed towards Latécoère's pilots. To secure the right to overfly the Rio de Oro, Beppo de Massimi in Madrid had hit on the ingenious scheme of forming a Spanish company, the *Aero-Española*, under the auspices of Francisco Bergamín, a former Spanish Minister of Foreign Affairs. In theory the company was supposed to assure an aerial mail service from San Sebastián, in the north, down through Madrid to Sevilla, then across the Straits to Morocco, and on down the African coast. A regular mail service to the tiny outposts of Juby and Cisneros being more a luxury than a necessity to the Spaniards, the *Aero-Española's* charter had been drawn up to include the far more important community of the Canary Islands. From Juby it was only a couple of hundred miles due west across the ocean to Las Palmas or Tenerife, so that on paper at any rate they could all be linked in one extensive network. In fact, the *Aero-Española* never took to the air, its sole purpose being to stake out claims for overflying and airport landing rights. No one, either in Madrid or on the spot, was taken in for a moment by the purely fictitious nature of the scheme; but it offered a sop to Spanish pride in maintaining the flattering illusion that when flying over Spanish territory Mermoz, Guillaumet, and their companions were piloting for a Spanish company. To sustain the fiction a Captain Cervera, formerly of the Spanish Army, was stationed at Tenerife as the *Aero-Española's* "permanent representative". He proved himself most adept in buttering up the governor of the Canaries (under whose jurisdiction the forts of Juby and Cisneros fell), and he was to boot a personal friend of Colonel Bens.

Bens' departure was thus a double loss to Latécoère. It was with his active co-operation that the ransom system had been set up for the retrieval of French pilots captured by the Moors; and though he had been willing to pacify the wild tribesmen of the interior with pesetas and sacks of grain and sugar, he had generally refrained from buying them off with what these desert cavaliers most cherished—guns and ammunition.

His successor, Colonel de la Peña, had fewer scruples. He harboured no particular sympathy for the French or for Cervera, the Spaniard who was working for them. His appointment to Juby, furthermore, coincided with Lyautey's withdrawal from Morocco. To subdue Abd-el-Krim and his Rif rebels, the French had brought in ten full divisions under Marshal Pétain, and the concentration of all this manpower north of the Atlas mountains was used by pro-German elements in Madrid to sound new fears and alarums. If the French were so anxious to have bases at Juby and Cisneros, it was not, they claimed, out of any philanthropic concern for the mail; in reality, they were preparing a take-over of the Rio de Oro, hemmed in already by the *méhariste* outposts at Fort Gouraud and Atar.

The Germans had other reasons for wishing to deny the Spanish Sahara to French pilots. A chain is no stronger than its weakest link; and if the chain of Latécoère bases could be severed in the Rio de Oro, the company's operations in Latin America, where the French were making dramatic headway, would be doomed. Barred from aircraft production by the Treaty of Versailles, the Germans, led by Dornier, had set their sights on America's southern hemisphere and were busily trying to build up an industry in Spain. Their leading advocate in Madrid, Captain (later Major) Ramón Franco, had already made the headlines in January of 1926 by flying a seaplane across the Atlantic from Cadiz to Buenos Aires. Elaborate plans were being laid to link Europe and South America by zeppelins; and it looked as though the Germans had a comfortable head start when news reached Madrid in January 1927 that Latécoère had signed a mail contract with Argentina. Ramón Franco sent off a furious telegram to his officer friends in the Argentine army, asking them to issue a massive protest against this favour shown to the French. Primo de Rivera, to punish him, ordered his arrest and a two-month prison sentence, but a few days later the hothead aviator left quietly for Germany on a "study tour"—proof of the powerful support he enjoyed with other generals of the junta.

Such was the situation when Saint-Exupéry was assigned to the Dakar-Juby run in the spring of 1927. A couple of German agents had been operating out of Ifni and were known to have supplied the Moors south of the Dra with guns and ammunition. It was with German Mausers that Erable had been shot and Gourp critically wounded; and it was with German, if not Spanish, bullets—so more than one Latécoère pilot believed—that they were being fired on almost daily as they flew over the Moorish encampments up and down the coast.

The suspicion seemed dramatically confirmed one morning in March 1927 when Ould Haj'Rab—the former Moroccan *goumier* who had led the assault on Gourp and Erable—rode boldly up to Cape Juby with fifteen camels and forty R'guibat warriors armed with French carbines and German Mausers. Twice admitted to the fort, where he was received by Colonel de la Peña, the dagger-belted nomad had the satisfaction of seeing his camels loaded with heavy bundles brought out from the fort and which seemed to the French pilots and mechanics to contain weightier material than the tea, cloth, or sugar the Moors were wont to barter against the wool of their sheep. As the caravan rode past the Bessoneau hangar, wildly acclaimed by a frenzied Moorish mob, Ould Haj'Rab turned in his saddle and made a scornful throat-slitting gesture, aped by his warriors who shook their fists and aimed their weapons at the French.

After their departure the Moorish interpreters informed Jean Mermoz and his companions that the caravan was headed south for an attack on Port Etienne, one thousand kilometres distant straight across the burning sands. It was too much for Mermoz, galled by the mockery he could now read in the eyes of the emboldened Moors. He took off shortly afterwards, as though on a routine Bréguet-testing flight, and furiously buzzed the R'Guibat encampment, actually managing to flatten a few black tents in the slipstream of his propeller. This quixotic action did not keep Ould Haj'Rab and his desert pirates from pursuing their southern trek. But subsequent reconnaissance flights kept track of the caravan's advance, and when the assault on Port Etienne was finally made ten weeks later, the garrison was ready. So were the *méharistes* of Atar, who fell on Ould Haj'Rab's warriors from behind and slaughtered them to a man.

For Mermoz and his companions it was a sweet revenge for the "massacre" of Erable and Gourp, but it did nothing to improve their strained relations with the Spanish, ever prone to accuse the French of "stirring up the desert". The situation at Juby was complicated by the presence of an *escuadrilla sahariana* which the Spaniards, not to be outdone by the French, had stationed there to keep an eye on their vast empire. The flying actually accomplished by its officer pilots was limited, and as the months passed they grew increasingly unhappy to see Latécoère's flyers taking off and landing all the time while they themselves were sometimes grounded by lack of fuel for weeks at a stretch. Airmen are men of action, not diplomats, and Mermoz and his companions, who had more than one grievance against the Spanish, could not always conceal the condescension they felt for the "soft life" of their military brethren. All this made for bad blood, maliciously envenomed by intriguing Moors.

At Villa Cisneros, where the French had been debarred from putting up a hangar or even so much as a toolshed, one of Latécoère's ace mechanics finally succeeded in mollifying the Spanish governor by repairing his Ford car, restoring a local water pump, and even shoeing his horse. But at Cape Juby, where relations remained unpleasantly tense, someone more impressive than a mechanic was needed to tackle the prickly Colonel de la Peña. Back in Toulouse Didier Daurat shrewdly calculated that Saint-Exupéry might have just what was needed: a name likely to impress a Castilian aristocrat who fancied himself, with the hereditary weakness of his calling, a gentleman as well as an officer, and the sense of finesse which occasionally distinguishes the better born. The line had a number of seasoned flyers for the routine chores, and Saint-Exupéry's unpredictably erratic talents could be put to better use than in simply piloting the weekly mail. The instructions Daurat issued him were characteristically laconic: he was to improve relations and establish close ties with both Spaniards and Moors. The choice of method was up to him. With that Saint-Exupéry was told to pack his things and to leave on the next flight. The departure was so hectic that he did not even have time to write a farewell letter to his mother.

*        *        *

Joseph Kessel, who visited Cape Juby a few months after Saint-Exupéry's tour of duty there was over, has left us a harrowing description of this desert outpost, as it then was. "Strands of barbed wire protected the fort over a distance of two kilometres. During the day they marked the limits of the safety zone, which shrank at night right up to the fort walls. A fort peopled by dejected and godforsaken men. Juby was used by the Spanish as a penitentiary, and the soldiers who guarded the jailbirds were hardly distinguishable from their charges. In their tattered uniforms and sandals, their gaunt faces sometimes going for weeks without a proper wash or shave, they wasted away in idleness and silence. Even the officers had trouble resisting the erosion of sand, solitude, and sun. I spent one whole hour in a kind of pillbox which had been turned into a canteen, listening to the monotonous roll of dice. It was the only sound to be heard in this assemblage of phantoms. Not a voice spoke. The faces were devoid of expression."

In Saint-Exupéry's subsequent writings and even in his letters there is hardly a word about these walking ghosts. Only in his first letter written from Juby to his mother is there a fleeting reference to them. "For the moment I have been doing a bit of boating, I breathe the pure air of the sea, and I play chess with the Spaniards who've been won over by my dazzling recommendations." Just what these last words mean is not clear, for there is no trace of such "dazzling recommendations" in the residual archives of the Latécoère company, which were all but scattered to the winds during the last war. Presumably Beppo de Massimi had bestirred himself in Madrid with his customary skill. It is also possible that José-María Quiñones de León, the Spanish Ambassador in Paris, who had already helped Latécoère get started in South America, had put in a good word on behalf of the new *chef d'aéroplace* at Juby with his friend King Alfonso XIII. The Spaniards, though obliged as a matter of policy to be lukewarm to the French, were probably not unhappy to see a refreshingly new face turn up among them and particularly one belonging to a someone who was as adept at chess as he was at card tricks. They may also have derived considerable amusement from Saint-Exupéry's exchanges with the older Colonel de la Peña; for the Colonel's knowledge of French was as rudimentary as Saint-Exupéry's command of Castilian, which he generously peppered with the Provençal he had picked up as a boy from his mother.

With the Moors his success was more spectacular. He began by lengthily interrogating the Moorish interpreters about the Cape Juby region and the tribes that inhabited it. The Izarguin, he discovered, were the least hostile—to both French and Spanish—and the readiest to co-operate; the chief troublemakers were the Ait Oussa, the Ait Gout, and the fierce R'Guibat, who warred as often among themselves as against the pale-faced infidel. He expressed a desire to reconnoitre the surrounding wilderness and to acquaint himself with the language of its inhabitants—something no Latécoère pilot before him had shown much interest in doing. The request aroused a mild sensation. The interpreters, being for the most part illiterate, were clearly not up to the task; but it did not take them long to dig up a *marabout*, or itinerant holy man, who agreed to trudge in every day from the desert and give Saint-Exupéry a lesson. Word soon spread that at Juby there was a "*roumi*" of a new and curious sort who was willing to spend hours every week covering sheets of paper with the looped characters of Islamic script. Every time he stepped out of the Latécoère shack he would be besieged by beggars, hobbling over from the nearby well, and by a throng of bright-eyed urchins who danced barefootedly around him, imploring bits of chocolate. The little girls in particular intrigued him, with their big black eyes and their tiny arms. Though dressed in rags, they moved with the grace of Hindu princesses, and the way they heaved up their tinier brothers and sisters was preciously maternal.

Curiosity getting the better of their hostility, the blue-shawled chieftains came to view the prodigy who was taking an interest in their tongue and their ways. Soon they were being invited to drink glasses of steaming tea with the "*roumi*". In lieu of the imposing desk and the high-backed chair which Colonel de la Peña occupied when receiving visiting delegations in a kind of "throne room" inside the fort, all Saint-Exupéry had was a makeshift table made of a door slung across a couple of empty fuel barrels. But the Moors, who would squat down on the floor before him, seemed to appreciate this lack of pretension. In the desert the rites of hospitality are sacred, and while one may with impunity slit the throat of almost anyone provided he is in "alien" territory, the guest one has invited under one's tent is sacrosanct. It was not long before Saint-Exupéry was being invited to visit the chieftains in their tents; an escort of Moorish horsemen offering him protection as they rode a mile or so inland—in that wild *terra incognita* no Spaniard had yet ventured to explore.

"Stretched out on their carpets," he wrote back to his mother, "I can see from under the bulge of the tent-cloth this calm, rounded sand, this humped earth, and these sons of sheikhs playing naked in the sun, with the camels anchored near the tent. And I have a strange impression. Not of remoteness, nor of isolation, but of a fleeting game." He was in the "bear pit" at last, but the local "bears"—for the moment at least—were tame. With the help of the interpreters he even managed to teach some of them the *Marseillaise*!

Gradually he began to fathom the unwritten rules of the desert. The Moors were basically more contemptuous of the Spaniards, holed up in their fort, than they were of the French, who lived in a shack beyond the battlements, with nothing to protect them but a whirling propeller and a door handle charged with a mysterious, repelling power. Occasionally a Moorish rifleman would sink a bullet into the wall of the fort, less with the specific intent of killing one of its sentries than to remind the barbarians cringing behind those fortifications that he, the bedouin, was still lord of the desert. Many a Moor, on crossing paths with a European, would turn aside and spit into the dust—to show that for him the "*roumi*" was not an object of hatred but of scorn. "You are lucky," Saint-Exupéry was gravely informed by a chieftain who had mustered three hundred rifles, "in France you are lucky to be more than one hundred days' march away". "You eat salad, like goats, and you eat pork, like pigs," a stern blue-veiled Moor once said to him, seated beneath his tent like a judge. And the tone was one of infinite contempt.

One day two of Saint-Exupéry's fellow pilots, Henri Delaunay and Marcel Reine, after crash landing on a beach, managed to fly out in their two Bréguets. A dozen bottles of Perrier water were emptied into one of the radiators, which had started to boil, but to lighten the load all of the provisions as well as the two interpreters were left behind. The following day the two hardy Moors reached Juby after a long march, their eyes gleaming as brightly as the silver pommels of their daggers. Before retiring to their tent, they were invited into the shack by the pilots to sip tea and chew biscuits. Finally, after a good bit of prodding, one of them described how they had been overtaken by a caravan headed south. Ever on the qui-vive for booty, the camel drivers insisted on about-facing and being guided back to the seaside spot where the two Bréguets had landed. Scorning the few bottles of wine—alcohol being forbidden by the Holy Book—they had emptied out the two sacks of vegetables and amused themselves kicking the cauliflowers and the lettuce all over the beach.

It was a strange feeling to live wedged in like this between sea and sand, like a high-water barnacle. At high tide the water would lap right up against the shack, and Saint-Exupéry could almost touch it by thrusting his arm out through the barred window. On the other side all one could see was desert; and at night the spectral shadow of the Bessoneau hangar, housing the base's four planes. To sleep on there was a board and a mattress filled with a thin layer of straw. A water-jug, a metal basin, a typewriter, a handful of books, and the dossiers of the line completed the sparse décor. There was another bedroom for transient pilots, and a "common room" decorated by pin-ups which beckoned temptingly from the walls in the evening under the pioneer glare of a hissing Kerosene lamp. Often it would sound as though rain were falling outside, but the pitter-patter on the corrugated roof was simply due to the nocturnal condensation of moist air. For entertainment there was an old gramophone with a broken spring which had to be turned by hand—to the frequent discouragement of the turner, who would give up in mid-record. When there was company Saint-Exupéry would entertain his friends with card tricks, which grew steadily more sophisticated as he delved into successive magicians' manuals. He also organized telepathic sessions, which occasionally left the others spell-bound by the acuteness of his intuition. When alone, he often read, but it was rarely a novel. It could be Plato or Aristotle, Bergson or Nietzsche, or some scientific treatise, for which he had an insatiable appetite.

At Juby his three principal companions were the mechanics Marchal, Abgrall, and Toto. A formidable workhorse, Marchal in a pinch could carry on for forty-eight hours non-stop. Toto was somewhat different. He had an incurable weakness for Pernod and red wine. Daurat, who had first run into him in his First World War squadron, had finally had to fire him at Montaudran for being too frequently *dans les vignes du Seigneur*. Some weeks later he had come upon the disconsolate mechanic hammering down crates in a remote warehouse: doing odd jobs for a subsidiary com-pany. Touched by this fidelity to Latécoère, Daurat rehired him, but to keep him from corrupting the newcomers at Montaudran, he had exiled him to Juby. Here, between bouts of *gros rouge*, he supervised the cooking, skilfully applying a blowtorch to the pans every time the burners on his stove were blocked by flying sand. He was aided by a majestic *maître d'hôtel*—a tall, bearded Moor whose desiccated frame was enveloped in flowing robes. He was known as Attila, and everything had to be explained to him in gestures, since he understood not a word of French.

The other "boarders" included a cat, a dog, a chimpanzee which conversed in bird-like chirps, and even a hyena, which had to be tied up outside during meals. Occasionally a gazelle would pad noiselessly out of the night and press it's soft nose against the window pane. Saint-Exupéry also caught and tried to tame a sand fox, a tiny creature with huge ears; but it proved too wild to be domesticated, and as he wrote to his sister Gabrielle, "it is as savage as a beast and it roars like a lion".

Henri Delaunay, whose secret hobby was writing plays and whose book, *Araignée du Soir* (Evening Spider), merits a place on any bookshelf of "flying classics", has left us a gay picture of this extraordinary community, as he saw it one evening when Saint-Ex (for how else could one possibly call him?) was acting host to his friends. We are shown Guillaumet engrossed in drawing puzzles at the table: word and picture puzzles which, in their down-to-earth simplicity, would give way like a trap-door beneath Saint-Ex's wary but overly sophisticated tread. We are shown Mermoz bare chested—and what a chest it was!—in a pair of black *méhariste* pantaloons, leaning back pensively in his chair, to one strut of which Riguelle is busy tying a string. A string hooked at its other extremity to the collar of Mirra, the dog, who can be counted on to bound forward—and with what a crash!—when the meat dish is brought in. Just how this particular prank ended and how hard Mermoz hit the dust Delaunay neglects to tell us; but there is a succulent description of Kiki, the chimpanzee, going through the motions of swallowing a razor blade in order to cadge another banana from his gullible providers.

On the 20th of each month a mast and a jib-sail would appear over the blue, and the 100 ton motorized sloop which brought in supplies from the Canaries would heave to beyond the bar. The sight of this sail—"all white and clean and pretty like fresh linen"—as he wrote to his mother—brought to mind the fabulous cupboards of his youth, opened with a venerable creak by the faithful Moisie. "And I think of those ageing house-maids who spend their lives ironing white table cloths which they pile up on the shelves and which are like a balm. And my sail sways softly, like a well ironed Breton bonnet, but the softness is brief." It was indeed, for what from a distance was sweet food for the poet's eye was in the next instant a stormy challenge to the man of action's muscles. The cape being without a harbour and the surf too strong to put in close to shore, the sloop would have to cast anchor beyond the bar, over which Saint-Exupéry had to steer the punt-like tender. Everything the outpost needed for its subsistence— from amunition crates and barrels of fresh water to fuel drums and crates of fodder—had to be floated in, while the livestock were simply pushed into the surf and forced to swim ashore. Occasionally a steer would be carried by the current beyond the fort's barbed wire perimeter, and it would fall into the grasping hands of the Moors. But a day or two later, lacking the hay to feed it or a stable in which to house it, they would trade in the lowing beast for reams of cloth or a few bales of barley.

Towards Christmas a kind of fever took possession of the desert, as the neighbouring Izarguin girded their loins for an attack from other Moorish tribes. There was a smell of powder in the air and at night nervous sentries would send up flares, shedding a strange, artificial glow over the rose-tinted sand. "It will end like all these large Moorish manifestations," Saint-Exupéry wrote to his mother, "—by the theft of four camels and three wives". But it was a mournful Christmas nonetheless. Though his friend Guillaumet turned up with the weekly mail from Dakar, the boat supplying them was overdue and they had only canned food for supper. "It was such a melancholy evening," Saint-Exupéry wrote back to Lucie-Marie Decour, "that we were all in bed by ten o'clock."

Almost every morning, as the sea mist evaporated under the rays of the torrid sun, he would take up one of the spare Bréguets which were stationed at Juby for emergency operations. Such flights were necessary to clear the cylinders of condensation and to keep the spark plugs from rusting. They also gave Saint-Exupéry a chance to reconnoitre the hinterland. Sometimes he went with an interpreter, or he would take up a Moorish chieftain whose pride he wished to humble. Having never seen the earth from anything higher than the hump of a dromedary or the crest of a palm tree, the haughty warrior would be overawed by the crushing spectacle of his doughty camels and his black tents reduced to insignificant dots beneath him. More than once Colonel de la Peña had occasion to start fretting at the inordinate length of some of these "test flights". During one of them, south of Juby, Saint-Exupéry swung inland and followed the jagged escarpments of the Seguiet-el-Hamra for a good hundred miles until, over a lip of parched ground, he spied the verdant blush of S'mara the mysterious, with its virgin ruins as forbidden to the white man as Timbuktu.

His relations with Colonel de la Peña were soon cemented by an incident involving a Spanish flyer who was forced down by engine failure a dozen miles from the fort and made prisoner by the Moors. At the Commandant's request, Saint-Exupéry took off with several veiled warriors from the opposing tribes of the Izarguin and the Ait Oussa, landing them in carefully selected spots to negotiate the captured officer's release. He was finally returned—after payment of a solid ransom; but to recover the stricken aeroplane's motor, the Spanish were obliged to muster 300 armed Moors and to back them up with a man-of-war dispatched from the Canaries.

And so the months passed, the dry desert winds of winter and spring giving way in June to the moist breezes of the ocean. One night Saint-Exupéry was awoken around two o'clock in the morning by the unusual sound of a motor overhead. Night flights, with which Daurat had begun experimenting in Toulouse, had not yet been introduced along the African coast; but the airline's bases were equipped with ground flares for emergency landings after sundown. The flares were now hurriedly lit and to Saint-Exupéry's astonishment a large monoplane put down. It was the new Latécoère 25, bigger and safer than the Bréguet 14 since it had a cabin capable of holding four (radio operator and two passengers as well as pilot). Three men climbed out of it. Two of them were strangers, but Saint-Exupéry had no trouble recognizing the round, red-cheeked face of Marcel Reine, the jovial Parisian whose choice *argot* was one of the joys of the line.

"You might at least have radioed you were on the way," Saint-Exupéry complained. "We've been fogged in here for weeks and this is the first night it's lifted."

"There was a full moon at Agadir, so I decided we'd carry on and do a bit of night flying," answered one of Reine's passengers. He was a senior Latécoère inspector and obviously pleased with himself. The other passenger was Edouard Serre, the head of the airline's new radio department, who was making his first inspection tour of the African bases.

While the Latécoère 25 was being refuelled by the mechanics, Saint-Ex offered his guests a meagre snack of eggs and chocolate. The inspector, who had decided to remain at Juby, insisted that Reine and Serre should fly on without delay.

"But Cisneros has gone off the air," Saint-Exupéry protested. "They're no longer monitoring, for they think the mail is still at Agadir."

The inspector refused to listen to reason, and not long thereafter Reine and Serre climbed into the Laté 25 with a Moorish interpreter and took off into the night.

Early the next morning, while the inspector was still slumbering, Saint-Ex got up and had the radio operator call Villa Cisneros. Had Reine and Serre arrived? The answer was No. There was the same reply from Port Etienne, the same from Saint-Louis-du-Sénégal. Cisneros, furthermore, was completely fogged in.

At ten o'clock, no one having seen a trace of the airmen, Saint-Exupéry took off to look for them. The coast was still blanketed in mist, but though much of it had burned away by the time he turned and started back, he could spot no sign of a crashed plane. At Juby he found the inspector busy spraying his office with fly-tox, surrounded by a mob of beggars with whom, he airily explained, he was "negotiating" the organization of caravans to hunt for the vanished flyers. Saint-Ex sent them packing, then called on his Moorish chieftain friends, asking them to dispatch swift emissaries across the desert —with the promise of a generous reward.

Toulouse having been alerted, Verneuilh, the *chef d'aéroplace* at Agadir, was sent south to fill in at Juby, while Saint-Exupéry undertook a second exploratory mission. At Port Etienne he teamed up with Bourgat and Riguelle, who had flown up from Dakar to join in the search. They took off in three planes, following the coastline on parallel courses a mile or two apart, so as to cover the widest possible area inland without losing sight of one another. As they flew north Riguelle, dogged again by bad luck, burned out his piston bearings and had to crash land near Cape Bojador—near the fateful spot where one year earlier Erable and Pintado had been assassinated by the Moors. Bourgat, after putting down, discovered that his Bréguet had developed an oil leak which had to be repaired before he could hope to take off again. When Saint-Ex landed in his turn, shortly before sunset, it was to be told that they would have to spend the night there—in the heart of a "dissident" desert, bristling with Moorish guns.

The tense night which followed was to remain in Saint-Exupéry's memory as one of the most moving he had ever lived. While Jean-René Lefèbvre, the Villa Cisneros mechanic, went to work on Bourgat's motor, the others hauled crates of food and canned goods from the three fuselages. Since this promised to be their last night on earth, they might as well make the most of it. The emptied crates were each filled with a candle, protected by the wooden slats from the buffeting of the wind. "Thus in mid-desert, on this naked crust of planet," as Saint-Exupéry was later to recall it, "in an isolation as pure as the first days of the Creation, we built a human settlement. Grouped for the night in our village square, on this patch of sand over which our crates threw a trembling light, we waited. We waited for the dawn which would save us, or the Moors. There was something about this night which had a taste of Christmas. We told stories and reminisced about the past, we joked and sang."

While Didier Daurat in Toulouse stood grimly by his office window staring out over the expressionless obscurity of an airfield which now seemed desperately barren, half a dozen jovial Frenchmen were living it up among the dunes. In a couple of days the line had lost four planes and as many pilots— vanished from the face of the map! Along with the head of the new radio service, the ace mechanic who had patched things up at Cisneros, and the lanky aristocrat who at Juby had reversed the hostile tide. For Daurat it was one more sleepless night, one more cross he had to bear alone, on his rounded shoulders, in the mournful silence of an empty office. For Saint-Ex and his companions the vigil was more festive but no less sleepless; he amused them all when the time came "to go to bed" by announcing that he was going to curl up in one of the mail trunks. But try as he might, he was no longer the little blond-haired Antoine who had once gaily clambered into fair-ground gondolas, and unable to wedge his bulk into the open float, he finally took refuge in the cockpit.

When dawn rose they were half frozen but alive. The resourceful Lefèbvre having successfully plugged the leak, Bourgat was able to take off in his Bréguet and Saint-Exupéry in his. Their arrival at Cisneros was greeted with almost delirious relief. A Moorish emissary had just come in with the news that Reine and Serre were still alive: their plane, which had gone off course during that fogbound night, had ploughed into a plateau some distance inland, and they were now prisoners of the fierce R'Guibat tribe. The Moors were willing to let them go—for a million camels and a million rifles . . . and the liberation of all the "dissident" warriors the French had captured in their part of Mauretania.

Four months of tortuous negotiations were needed to secure the release of the two flyers, who were harshly treated and almost lynched by their captors. Weeks were spent simply trying to locate them, for as news of the R'Guibats' "fabulous haul" began to spread across the desert, other tribes mustered guns and camels, determined to lay hand on the prey. Soon the whole desert was aflame, with ambushes and skirmishes and wild nocturnal flights, as Serre and Reine were roughly moved by their kidnappers from one hide-out to the next.

For Saint-Exupéry this was a period of intense activity. He flew up and down the desert, dropping off Moorish emissaries to contact the R'Guibat caravan. The job was anything but easy, given the varied nature of the terrain. Latécoère's pilots had learned to be wary of the crusty surfaces of saline depressions, which could prove as deceptive a trap for their landing-gear as the moist sand of the beaches. Far firmer were the flattened tops of the plateaux, often strewn with millions of minute shells deposited from a paleolithic age when the Sahara was an ocean floor. Many of these plateaux, Saint-Exupéry discovered, were hemmed in by vertiginous cliffs, like those of Utah or Arizona. One day he came down on one such upland, only to find that there was no way of getting the Moorish emissary down the almost vertical walls of rock. They were resting on a desert island floating on a desert sea. "No Moor could have assaulted this impregnable castle," as he was later to write in *Terre des Hommes*. "No European had ever explored this territory. I was treading a sand that was infinitely virgin." As he stooped to pick up a smoothly polished aerolith, quite unlike the other stones around it, a sense of rapturous wonder swept over him: it was the dark residue of a meteor, fallen from outer space like a raindrop from the stars.

The search for Reine and Serre had been going on for a month when in mid-July another mishap occurred much nearer to home. On his way up from Villa Cisneros the unlucky Riguelle was once more forced down by engine failure, this time just twenty miles short of Cape Juby. He was picked up by his companion Dumesnil, but the paralysed Bréguet had to be left behind. Standing orders from Toulouse forbade rescue operations aimed at recovering planes in "dissident" territory, where the danger of ambush was too great. But the proximity of this mishap was such that Saint-Exupéry felt it warranted an exception to the rule. The seaboard cliffs south of Juby ruling out all possibility of getting the Bréguet back by boat, he decided to attempt an overland salvage. First, he had Marchal and his fellow mechanics put together a two-axle plane-wheel chassis, on top of which was mounted a cradle strong enough to support the weight of a spare motor. A special harness, almost thirty yards in length, was next fashioned so that the four-wheeled cart could be hitched to camels. Robed in his dressing-gown, which he wore like a *jellaba*, Saint-Exupéry then called on several Moorish chieftains camped in the vicinity and besought their assistance. They were more than dubious when they heard of his incredible proposal; but finally Ataf, the interpreter who had survived the martyrdom of Gourp, volunteered to recruit six mounted warriors to escort the expedition.

The extraordinary caravan—composed of three camels (two for pulling the cart and a third loaded with picks, shovels, and spare wheels), two donkeys (carrying food supplies and water), eight mounted horsemen (including Saint-Ex and Marchal), two guides and seven other Moors (armed with rifles as well as spades)—set out from Juby late one afternoon and reached the stricken plane the next morning after an all-night trek. Saint-Exupéry had hoped to be able to drag the disabled Bréguet to a smoother stretch of ground, but a cursory inspection of the rock-strewn vicinity made it clear that the take-off would have to be attempted on the spot. The Bréguet, furthermore, was in worse condition than expected; for the piston-rod in wrenching itself loose of the crankshaft had smashed one of the engine mounts.

A camel-riding guide was hastily dispatched to Juby to bring back a new set of motor struts, while the Moorish workers got busy flattening out a runway, 90 metres long by 8 yards wide. Saint-Exupéry took his turn with the shovel, helping to reduce the hundreds of rocks protruding through the sand to gravel-like rubble, while Marchal, the mechanic, struggled to dismount the Bréguet's crippled motor. At sundown there was still no sign of the camelman who had been sent to Juby for the engine-mounts, and Saint-Exupéry was beginning to get worried.

"They must have killed him," remarked Ataf, the interpreter, cheerfully. By "they" he meant members of the Ait Oussa tribe, whom he held in great awe. Saint-Ex began to have second thoughts about the wisdom of his bold initiative; but it was too late now to turn back. If the worst came to the worst, they would have to risk a take-off without the new engine-mounts.

The onset of night was punctuated by wild alarums. The camp-fires were hastily snuffed out while the Moorish riflemen filled the night with bullets. "It was magnificent," Saint-Ex later described the show to a senior airline official; even more thrilling than his first desert night at Nouakchott.

Shortly after midnight there was a new scare, as a Moorish rider galloped up in great agitation. He was an Izarguin, like the other Moors who were with them.

"What's wrong?" asked Saint-Exupéry, seeing everyone scramble to their feet in a wild babble of excitement.

"Order from Colonel . . . Come back quick . . ." explained Ataf in his pidgin French. "Ait Oussa *rezzou* chasing us . . . everyone killed!"

In less time than it takes to say "*Barak Allah!*" Saint-Ex was heaved on to a camel, along with Marchal, and they were off across the desert behind their camel-driver. Headed north, towards Juby. No speaking, no smoking—there was not a sound from their ghostly procession save for the faint clop of horses' hooves. The very silence breathed panic and this mad scramble through the night struck Saint-Exupéry as "lacking in serenity".

They had been jogging along for close to three hours when he began to grow suspicious. The horseman who had first brought the message had ridden off to help the neighbouring Izarguin round up their livestock. Saint-Exupéry began questioning Ataf, who finally admitted that there had been no message from the Colonel at Juby; the "messenger" had simply taken it upon himself to order them back post-haste.

"Stop!" shouted Saint-Exupéry in a rage.

He slid off the camel with Marchal and they hurried up to the leader of the Moorish escort.

"What's the idea?" cried a furious Saint-Ex, "running away from an enemy no one has seen? . . . Tell him," he ordered Ataf, "tell him what a fine group of 'warriors' he and his men are—since they don't even wait to see the enemy before taking to their heels!"

There were some angry mutterings from the "warriors", but the only ɪeply from their chief was a grunt and one more motion of the head—in the direction of Juby.

"Too bad!" exclaimed Saint-Exupéry, in a tone of deep disgust. "I should have got myself an escort of women. We would have been better defended."

Stung by the taunt, the horsemen wheeled about. An acrimonious discussion ensued. Saint-Exupéry insisted they return immediately to the plane. The Moors no less stubbornly refused: it was too dangerous, they said, at night they could easily be ambushed. Finally a compromise was reached. They would hide out for the rest of the night, then proceed back to the Bréguet at dawn. The sea being not far away, to the west, they took refuge in a gully formed by the erosion of the cliffs.

Marchal, like Saint-Ex, made no attempt to hide his disgust, while Ataf was his usual cheerful self.

"It will be sad . . ." he said, shaking his head. "Gourp, Erable . . . I tried to save . . . No good . . . But you? . . . it will be more sad . . ." He made a gun-firing gesture. "Ait-Oussa kill everybody . . ." he added philosophically.

At dawn, the horizon failing to reveal any murderous silhouettes, the caravan resumed its march towards the south. Just as they reached the Bréguet—shortly after sunrise—two planes from the *escuadrilla sahariana* flew over and dropped a message—a real one this time—from Colonel de la Peña. It was brought to Saint-Exupéry, since none of the Moors could read. The enemy was closing in, read the message, they must return to Juby forthwith.

"Fine!" nodded Saint-Ex, folding the note into his pocket.

"What is it?" he was asked.

"A note from the Colonel," he answered genially. "Just to cheer us up."

With that everyone went to work again. To nip further mutinies in the bud Saint-Exupéry informed the Moorish workers that they would receive the pay promised to the escort if the others decamped. The workers redoubled their pounding while the horsemen chafed at the bit. Swearing and sweating profusely, Marchal struggled to install the spare motor on what was left of the mounts.

Towards noon camels appeared on the horizon and the Moorish horsemen galloped off, firing wildly in front of them. A few bullets sailed overhead and the remaining Moors hit the sand—all except Ataf who "retained a semi-dignity . . . by walking on all fours," as Saint-Ex later described it. The camels disappeared, Ataf rose proudly to his feet, and they were able to eat their lunch in peace.

While Marchal worked desperately to bolt down the spare motor, Saint-Exupéry had a springboard of banked earth built at the end of the runway to help the Bréguet get off the ground. The space beyond was also cleared of stones, in case the machine came down and had to be bounced into the air again. At five o'clock that afternoon the job of bolting in the motor was still far from finished, but Saint-Ex decided they could delay the take-off no longer. The sun was setting fast and they could not risk a third night in the desert. They would have to chance it.

A few turns of the propeller and the engine burst into action. While Marchal climbed in behind, the Moorish workers held the Bréguet by the tail, since it had no brakes. With a wave Saint-Exupéry gunned the engine and the Moors let go. The Bréguet lumbered heavily down the track, climbed the earth springboard and lurched drunkenly into the air. For an instant it seemed as though they were going to bang right down again, but no, the cushion of desert air sustained them and they were off. A quarter of an hour later they put down at Juby, where the Spaniards were as relieved to see them as Toto, the mechanic-cook, who had prepared a special feast for the occasion.

Once he had slept off his fatigue, Saint-Exupéry took to the air again in a determined effort to locate Serre and Reine. Their plight seemed increasingly desperate; and the letters which were brought back to Juby by Moorish messengers spoke of a likely assassination if they were not soon delivered. The fault was largely Serre's: thinking to impress his captors, he had let it be known that he had friends in high places who would move heaven and earth to free him. Their imaginations fired by the belief that they had laid hands on an important French "chieftain", the Moors upped the ransom, which at one giddy moment reached the preposterous figure of a million rifles, a million camels, and a million pesetas!

Not until early September—by which time Saint-Exupéry had put down four times and suffered one breakdown in hostile territory—did they finally discover where Serre and Reine were being held. Pretending he was leaving on one more routine mission up the coast, Saint-Exupéry took aboard a Moorish chieftain known for the boldness of his desert coups. He was also, as it happened, a good friend of the R'Guibats. Saint-Ex put the Moor down on the floor of a dry wadi, half a day's march away from the R'Guibat camp. He was given money with which to buy two camels, if the prisoners' lot was so desperate that an immediate escape had to be risked. He was also given flares to light—to signal that the coast was clear—when Saint-Exupéry flew back four days later.

Getting out of the wadi was no mean feat in itself; Saint-Exupéry had to bounce his Bréguet three times over logs and ditches and then fly up between two vertical cliff faces. The return journey proved unnecessary, when it was learned that the R'Guibats had agreed to climb down from their astronomical demands. Which was just as well; for the Moorish chieftain in the wadi, mistaking the Casablanca courrier for Saint-Exupéry's Bréguet, fired off his flares prematurely and could not have given the "all clear" signal. But the episode was typical of Saint-Exupéry's hardy initiative. Unwilling to engage any but his own responsibility, he had paid the Moor out of his own pocket for the purchase of the camels. Only subsequently was Toulouse informed of the venture, warranted, he felt, by the plight of his companions; but a venture which the airline, like the Spaniards, would have had to veto if consulted.

\*   \*   \*

Originally Saint-Exupéry had hoped to obtain home leave in August. But it was not until September that Reine and Serre, looking like haggard skeletons, were finally turned over to the Spanish authorities at Villa Cisneros. Four weeks later a new crisis arose when a Spanish plane was brought down by Moorish gunfire 180 kilometres south west of Juby. At Colonel de la Peña's request Saint-Ex took off with a Spanish observation officer and a companion plane flown by a sergeant-pilot of the *escuadrilla sahariana*. Near Cape Bojador they located the gunned craft and its wounded lieutenant-pilot, who had been miraculously rescued by a force of friendly Moors after being manhandled by a smaller group of R'Guibat marauders. Forced to relinquish their prey, the latter had gone off angrily in search of reinforcements but might at any moment surge back over the dunes in a wild blaze of musketry. The Spanish sergeant-pilot, after landing, found himself with a hopelessly stalled engine, and Saint-Exupéry was left to fly back the wounded lieutenant. Half an hour after landing at Juby, he took off again in his hastily checked and refuelled Bréguet, this time with a Spanish mechanic. At Bojador two hours of tense work were needed to get the Spanish sergeant-pilot's plane going, but they were able to take off without having to run the gauntlet of R'Guibat bullets. The Spanish Air Force gratefully offered to make up the cost of the operation: an offer Saint-Exupéry characteristically rejected on the grounds—*Noblesse oblige!*—that the rescue of two pilots, a plane, and an officer observer was more than enough to justify the burning of a thousand litres of fuel.

Altogether it was a harassing autumn for the *chef d'aéroplace* at Cape Juby. "Never have I landed or slept so often in the Sahara, nor heard more bullets whine," he wrote to his mother. "And yet sometimes I dream of an existence where there is a tablecloth, fruit, walks under the lindens, perhaps a wife, where one greets people amiably instead of shooting at them, where one doesn't lose one's way at 200 kilometres an hour in the mist, where one walks on white gravel instead of eternal sand." What he purposely neglected to add, for fear of upsetting his mother, was that his eyes were giving him trouble. One day, while flying over the desert, he had lost his goggles and the glare of the midday sand had practically blinded him before he could make it back to his base.

Early in November a message from Daurat in Toulouse informed him that he was being transferred to South America. But once again his departure was delayed by an unforeseen mishap. Vidal, appointed to replace him as *chef d'aéroplace* at Juby, had taken off from Agadir in the mist and disappeared —with his Moorish interpreter and the monthly pay for the base personnel at Juby and Cisneros. The pilot, in blindly following the seaboard cliffs (all he could see in the fog), had inadvertently flown up a wadi riverbed and crashed into a slope. He and his interpreter were ransomed back to the French by their Moorish captors, but in the process much of the monthly pay was lost.

Three more weeks and at last Saint-Exupéry could fly home, bearing in his baggage more than 150 pages of manuscript he had burned much midnight oil writing—with a scratchy nib dipped into an ink bottle he had to keep tightly screwed down against the sand. "I dream of exploring the dissident zone for the airline," he had written to Charles Sallès from Villa Cisneros, while overhead the sentries filled the night with their echoing cries. "I think I could hit it off with these fellows without getting myself plugged. It's a risk worth taking. Not for the gratitude it might bring me— I couldn't care less—but for myself. Because I can't imagine some understanding not arising from a human contact, and because this is the only thing that has passionately interested me all my life . . . I feel there's a certain way of placing oneself on the same plane as others. And that if one doesn't understand other races, it's because one brings one's own vocabulary and categories of sentiment. Rather than a humble attention."

That attention he had applied with such skill and finesse that he had secured the grudging respect of the Moors, finally persuaded that the mail-carrying Bréguets were messengers of peace and not the bomb-laden warplanes they had first taken them for. With the Spaniards he had been less successful—as he made clear in a report on the Rio de Oro he drafted for Latécoère on his return to France. But even if he had failed to mollify Colonel de la Peña, who had maintained the veto on night lighting and strip markers after the Reine–Serre fiasco, he had at least limited the damage and won the private esteem of Spanish governor and pilots.

For himself these thirteen months had proved an unforgettable experience. He had ridden under the stars through the wild anarchic night; he had seen the stilted shadow of the camel caress the sun-flushed dunes; and he had felt the pale shiver of the moon upon the sand. He had learned to love as well as fear the Sahara; but it had left him with an uneasy foreboding. "My greatest melancholy," he wrote to Charles Sallès, in reply to a letter announcing his old friend's impending marriage, "my greatest melancholy is to have tasted of a form of life, something like that of the 'gentlemen of fortune', one of austerity, destitution, and adventure. I no longer know if I am capable of being happy. The effort needed to be happy discourages me. The patience it takes! Never for more than a month will I now know the *douceur de vivre* . . . I have tasted of the forbidden fruit."

Painful, lonely, and nerve wracking it had often been, but in a way this torrid hell of the desert had been a paradise; and now, as he winged homeward, he was turning his back on a kind of Eden.

# 8

# Southern Mail

THREE years had passed since Saint-Exupéry's first literary offspring had appeared in *Le Navire d'Argent*, and in the interim much had happened. The Rue de l'Odéon, with its two enterprising bookshops, still remained a literary centre, but the focus had gradually shifted away from magazines and publishing, even though for much of 1928 Adrienne Monnier was kept busy helping Auguste Morel and Valery Larbaud (assisted by Stuart Gilbert and Léon-Paul Fargue) prepare a French translation of *Ulysses*. In the *Crapouillot* of November 1927 André Rouveyre, as savage a writer as he was a cartoonist, had opened an onslaught on Paul Valéry—"that poet of duchesses"—who had just been elected to the French Academy in the traditional green velvet costume, exquisitely tailored for him by Madame Jeanne Lanvin as though for a "belated gigolo". There was indignation in the salons and a smell of powder in the dining-rooms which did little to cloud the lustre of that galaxy of essayists and poets—Claudel, Valéry, Léon-Paul Fargue, and Saint-John Perse—who had helped make Princess Caetani's *Commerce* perhaps the foremost literary quarterly in Europe and who were already contributing to the rise of the *Nouvelle Revue Française*.

If Saint-Exupéry now took the same direction, it was largely thanks to the persuasive drive of Jean Prévost, who had for some time been contributing articles of literary criticism to the N.R.F.—as the *Nouvelle Revue Française* was more familiarly known. It was he who introduced his friend Tonio to Gaston Gallimard, its publisher. The interest taken in Antoine's first effort had encouraged him to finish a short story called *Manon, Danseuse* which he had hoped before leaving for Toulouse to get published in the N.R.F. The reams of paper he had covered in his neat, birdlike handwriting during his "exile" at Montluçon had seemed sufficiently impressive—in bulk as well as quality—to support the highest hopes; and Gallimard had accordingly made him an offer for a book if he could but add a third "short story" to the two others, or weld them together into a large whole.

The story of Manon, the Dancing Girl was destined to remain still-born. Later Saint-Exupéry could explain to the rare friend who was allowed to read it that it was a "youthful and immature work" which he did not wish to see published. But if *L'Aviateur* is any kind of guide, there was probably another reason. Whole chunks of that "story"—if such it can be called—were carried over into the novel he set about writing during his year at Juby; and in the same way it seems reasonable to suppose that parts of *Manon, Danseuse*—directly inspired by his unhappy love affairs in Paris—were preserved and imbedded in the 170 pages of text he brought back with him from Africa. The title he gave them—*Courrier Sud*, or "Southern Mail" —taken from the markings he had seen on a Toulouse mailbag destined for Dakar—was at least superficially misleading; for many more of them are devoted to a frustrating romance than to a pilot's airborne vicissitudes. Though what emerged was presented as a "novel", it was in fact a highly autobiographical projection of his own deeply divided psyche; and if he was less than successful in sewing the two—the world of feeling and the world of action—together, it was as much due to the split nature of his existence as to his inexperience as a writer.

No one was more painfully aware of it than Saint-Exupéry, who had spent many a sleepless hour wrestling with a problem that was as insubstantial and yet as omnipresent as the surf he could hear rolling in long metallic shudders along the bar outside his window. In a letter sent to his mother from Dakar in which he mentioned the "big thing" he was writing for the *N.R.F.*, he was already admitting that he was "bogging down a bit" in his story. Writing is as much a catharsis for an author as painting for an artist or composing for a musician, and the young Saint-Exupéry was too acutely introspective not to realize it. There was something he had to get out of his system, there was a psychic skeleton rattling in the closet of his subconscious which had to be exorcized by a process of literary "sublimation"—to speak like the Freudians; and much as he might embroider or seek to embellish it with moongilt and stardust, it had the dark lining of a troubled dream. To reassure himself he would read passages to certain of his pilot friends during their stop-overs at Juby; but though Mermoz dabbled in poetry and Delaunay amused himself writing plays, they were only amateurs and not the literary professionals he now had to impress. This explains the trepidation with which he brought his manuscript to Gallimard and the anxious blush with which he would await the reaction of the reader. The spiritual tribulations of Bernis—the central figure of *Courrier Sud*—were of course his own, and in describing them he was, to a painful degree for so sensitive a person, stripping himself naked and laying bare his soul.

His misgivings, as it happened, were exaggerated. His novel was accepted and the prevailing sentiment on the Rue de Grenelle—where Gallimard was then located—seems to have been succinctly expressed by the opening lines of the book review Jean Prévost subsequently wrote about it: "It is difficult not to like this book." Not only did they like it; they wanted more.

As an author Saint-Exupéry was quite unknown, even though as a flyer he belonged to the glamorous company of the Aéropostale, whose exploits were beginning to make the headlines. It was consequently felt, as the proofs were being readied, that he could do with a send-off from some writer better established than himself. Jean Prévost, who had introduced him to the readers of *Le Navire d'Argent*, had volunteered to review the book for the *N.R.F.*, so that there could be no question of his also writing the preface. Gallimard finally suggested that Saint-Exupéry call—"*de ma part*"—on André Beucler, another young author who belonged to that up-and-coming literary group which Jean-Paul Sartre (six to eight years their junior) later dubbed the "Club of the not yet Thirty Year Olds". When Saint-Ex asked the reason for this suggestion, Gallimard replied quite simply: "Because I know you'll hit it off." Probably he reckoned that being two years older than Prévost and Saint-Exupéry, Beucler—who already had three published books to his credit—could speak of *Courrier Sud* with the authority of a "veteran" and the sympathy of a contemporary.

Asking a complete stranger to preface a first novel was a new and unnerving experience for Saint-Exupéry, who turned up at the Beuclers' apartment without a word of warning and bashfully rang the bell. He was greeted warmly by the family—Beucler himself was out—but try as they might, they were unable to keep him from dropping off the proofs and vanishing as unexpectedly as he had appeared. When Beucler came home three hours later he was given a vivid description of the tall young man who had dropped out of the blue with his "joyous eye and diffident upper lip" and an amusing trumpet nose which was forever quivering, with the sensitivity of an insect's antennae. Fortunately the novice author had jotted down his address before decamping, so that the two writers were able to meet a day or two later.

The encounter took place at a café on the Avenue Wagram, and for Beucler at any rate it was friendship at first sight. Saint-Exupéry had turned up with an armful of newspapers—"destined not to be read"—and three books which lay sprawled over the marble-top table: André Gide's *Un Esprit Non-Averti*, Colette's novel *Sido*, and *Scènes de la Vie Future*, that blistering attack on American mores which Georges Duhamel dashed off after a brief, frustrating visit to the land of Calvin Coolidge. There was also a mechanical mouse, or it may have been a clockwork rooster, that Saint-Ex had bought for the amusement of some child—a detail which struck Beucler so forcefully that he could still vividly recall it twenty years later.

"I am a Nietzschean," Saint-Exupéry declared to Beucler, once the preliminary greetings were over, "a Nietzschean and at the same time a Marxist". Just how he reconciled these diametrically opposed philosophies is anything but clear, at any rate from the radio broadcast account Beucler later gave of this initial encounter. All Beucler could recall was that Saint-Ex felt that "the mediocre must be organized—which is why I'm a Nietzschean", adding "*je ne peux rester en cave*"—I can't remain in the cellar. This is why he had chosen aviation, he went on to explain, a fertile field for individual expansion and ascension, since it offered everything: a sense of team spirit, comradeship and sacrifice in the presence of shared hardships and dangers, and the invigorating stimulus of emulation.

Once launched they found it difficult to stop talking. What a joy for Saint-Ex, who had been starved of it in the desert, to be plunged back into the cultural and intellectual bath of Paris! The Paris of the late twenties, jumping and kicking to the gay beat of the Charleston, captivated by the boulevard refrains of Chevalier, mesmerized by the dark legs and swansdown of Josephine Baker and drunk on the sobbing chords of Russian tzigane orchestras which a revolution had forced to take to the road. A Paris warmed by the convulsive embers of Dadaism and the fiery quarrels of the Surrealists; a Paris of Voisins and Hispano Suizas where only a couple of months before an armada of well-gloved hot-rods had roared up the Champs-Elysées with Frédéric Loiseau, the madcap cavalryman who had just raced across the Sahara in a dusty but still fire-spewing Bugatti.

The previous summer had been hot, the grape harvest magnificent, and the wines of 1928 offered a promise which was to be surpassed by the even nobler vintages of 1929. France had seen nothing like it since 1911 and the sweltering summers immediately preceding the First World War. Now as then the world was dancing on the rim of a volcano, and the Wall Street Crash of September was as remote and imperceptible as a tiny cloud, the size of an infant's hand. The movies were about to break the sound barrier, the lustrous star of Greta Garbo was beginning to rise in the cinematographic firmament, and—as Beucler later noted—the pioneers of aviation were chalking up fabulous new triumphs in the sky. Yancey and Williams had recently flown from the United States to Santander in thirty-two hours and those two dare-devil Britons, Harry Ulm and Kingsford Smith, had joined Sydney to Croydon in record time. The troublesome issue of war reparations had been solved, superficially at least, by Young; Briand and Kellogg had produced a pact ensuring everlasting peace; and the scholarly Dr. Brüning was Chancellor of a pacific Weimar Republic. All seemed for the best in the best of possible post-war worlds—and nowhere more so than at Montparnasse, now the home of Picasso and Kisling, where the recently opened

Coupole, with its *entresol* orchestra and dancing girls in waistless dresses and cloche hats, was rapidly supplanting the Closerie des Lilas, dear to Hemingway and his friends. Louis de Broglie, who dared challenge Einstein on his own ground, Georges Bernanos, the fire and brimstone scourge of a corrupted Christendom, and Tagore, the oriental sage and mystic, were the talk of the town. "Paris was smiling, a trifle smugly and a shade too self-assuredly," as Beucler later recalled the climate of the moment, "and Saint-Ex was delighted to be alive. In his glance as in his arms there was a joyful readiness to embrace everything."

The preface Beucler went on to write for *Courrier Sud* attests the impact made upon him by this "hero", this "man of action", this "soldier" who could still find time to write amid a hundred and one adventures in the desert, and this even though "Saint-Exupéry is not a writer". Later he may well have regretted the phrase, which was a trifle hasty, but at the time it simply echoed Saint-Ex's own opinion of himself. He was a flyer, not a writer. Jean Prévost, when asked why he wrote books, had answered bluntly: "In order to make a living"—an answer that had greatly shocked the young Jean-Paul Sartre when he heard it. What the latter first mistook for a facile cynicism was, he later realized, essentially a determination to be honest in a period glittering with fanciful hypocrisies. Yet honesty can sometimes be deluding if it is over- or misapplied. With his athletic gifts and magnificent physique Jean Prévost was better fitted for a life of action than Saint-Ex, to whom all exercise was basically repugnant; and with his poet's soul it should logically have been he rather than Prévost who looked upon writing as a primary activity. But this Saint-Exupéry could not do. For if writing, as he had once observed, is a consequence of seeing, it is just as much a consequence of living. And living for Saint-Exupéry meant more than sitting at a desk darkening sheets of white paper.

A preface is not usually a critique, and it was thus left to Edmond Jaloux, the most influential French critic of the day, to put his finger on the weakness of the novel when it was published early in July. Heroes—he was willing to take Beucler's word for it—did not usually write well and often committed glaring errors of syntax and style; but such was fortunately not the case with the author of *Courrier Sud*. What then, he asked (in the July 6th issue of *Les Nouvelles Littéraires*), "is so fetching about this little book?" The answer was "Almost nothing . . . a romantic adventure, of which we have hundreds, but situated in such a modern setting that one doesn't see the romantic as much as one sees the modern. Its charm consists in the perpetual contrast between the decisiveness, the healthy brutality, the energy of this man of action and the internal world, made of roses and fairies, which he carries within him. In truth, roses and fairies for him are one and the same thing, summed up in a single being, Geneviève . . . his childhood friend, so beautiful and touching."

In *Courrier Sud* the author narrator is the bosom friend of the hero, Bernis: the same Bernis of *L'Aviateur*, save that here he is no longer a flying instructor but a pilot of the southern mail. The narrator, who has played the role of elder brother or Guillaumet to him in the past, is based at Juby, where Bernis is due to land with the mail some time that night. Bernis' take-off from Toulouse in the early dawn is described, and later a storm over Spain which is a literary embellishment of what Saint-Exupéry had once sought to evoke in a letter to Renée de Saussine. Beyond Valencia the clouds clear and Málaga appears, like a bright pearl in the depths of an aquarium, with thirty thousand feet of clear blue air above it. Night will catch him as he overflies Gibraltar, and until he spies the luminous beacon of Tangier there will be nothing for him to do in the gloaming save glance now and then at his instrument panel . . . and dream. In a long, elaborate flashback, the two months Bernis has just lived through flicker past his eyes like a film. The train trip to Paris and the rediscovery of a world which seems oddly static—"like those Breton sailors who come home to their picture-postcard villages and the inordinately faithful fiancée who has hardly aged a day. As unaltered as an engraving in a children's book. Seeing everything so properly in place, so well ordered by fate, we take fright as from something mysterious and obscure. Bernis inquired after a friend. 'Oh, the same as ever. His business not doing too well, though. Well, you know . . . that's life.' They were all of them prisoners of themselves, held back by a hidden leash, and not like himself—this fugitive, this poor child, this magician."

As Georges Mounin was later to remark, these three curious nouns could be applied just as aptly to the young Rimbaud, suddenly turning his back on poetry and fleeing a Europe which filled him with despair. If Bernis is a "poor child", it is because his riches are the stuff that dreams are born of, and if he is a magician, it is because he has made good his escape from a world that threatened to stifle him. The world of his remembered youth, which is also that of the narrator, who shared it with him . . . and Geneviève. She was fifteen when he and Bernis were just thirteen. Grave, a secret smile upon her lips, a fairy goddess, the Queen of the Night. But the boys, with that cruel curiosity which characterizes youth, could not wait to pry the secret open . . . eager to know (the narrator is talking) "if it was possible to make you suffer, to crush you in our arms to the point of suffocation, for we felt in you a human presence which we wanted to bring to light. A tenderness. a distress we wished to bring into your eyes. And Bernis would take you in his arms and you would blush. And Bernis pressed you tighter and your eyes grew bright with tears . . . without your lips being sullied. And Bernis told me that those tears came from the suddenly filled heart, more precious than diamonds, and that he who drank them would live forever. He also told me that you lived in your body, like a fairy beneath the waters, and that he knew a thousand spells to bring you to the surface, the surest of them being to make you cry. . . ."

But the breathless fairy, like a bird, had flown away, the years had passed, Bernis and his friend had gone off to become pilots and Geneviève, no longer Queen of the Night, had married a pompous and insensitive brute of a businessman named Herlin. They have a child, but the child grows sick, begins to vomit blood, and finally, despite the efforts of doctors and nurses, dies. Driven half out of her mind by the loss of her child and her husband's ponderous reproaches, Geneviève flees their Paris apartment and knocks in the middle of the night, at her friend Bernis' door. "Jacques, Jacques," she cries, "take me away".

From Cape Juby, where he has been receiving letters from his friend Bernis, the narrator sounds a warning note: "I have thought a lot about your letters and your captive princess. Yesterday, walking on the beach, so nude, so empty, so eternally sea-washed, I thought we resembled her. I don't really know if we exist. Often of an evening, in the half light of tragic sunsets, you have seen the Spanish fort sink in the glowing sand. But the reflection of a mysterious blue is not of the same stuff as the fort. Yet it is your realm. Not very real, not very sure . . . But let Geneviève live.

"Yes . . . in her present disarray? I know. But in life dramas are rare. There are so few friendships, so few tendernesses or loves to be liquidated. Despite what you say of Herlin, a man does not count for much. Life, I think, is based on something else."

"Those customs, those conventions, those laws, everything you do not feel the need of, everything you have escaped from . . . that's what gives her a framework. To exist one must have about one realities which last. But absurd or unjust, all that is but a language. And Geneviève, carried off by you, will no longer be Geneviève.

"And then, does she know what she needs? That habit of fortune, of which she's unaware. Money is that which permits the conquest of goods, external agitation—and her life is internal—but fortune . . . is that which makes things last. It is the invisible subterranean stream which for a century feeds the walls of a house, one's memories, the soul. And you are going to empty her life as one empties an apartment of a thousand objects whose presence one no longer noticed but of which it was composed."

And so it happens. Bernis takes Geneviève away on an impossible evasion which turns to disaster. As they drive out to the country in a car she is taken ill and they go from one hotel to the next desperately seeking a berth for the night. The next morning, after a night as mournful and distracting as a vigil, he drives her back to Paris, sadly decided to release the captive who did not have the strength to flee.

There is static in the air, radio communications are upset by noisy interference from the Canaries (this is one of the best passages in the book), but Bernis, who seems for a moment to have been swallowed up by the night after taking off from Agadir, puts down safely at Juby a couple of hours later. During the brief stop-over he tells his friends the end of the adventure. On his way back to Toulouse he had stopped off to see her once more—in that "realm of legend asleep beneath the waters" where in an hour Bernis had the impression of having lived for a century. The house is mortally still, the hallway dark, no one is expecting him. He hears voices discussing in hushed, worried tones. Something is wrong. Geneviève is ill. He creeps into her room, and in the dim light of dusk she stirs, stares at him, says "Jacques".

"She clung to his sleeve like a drowning person seeking to grasp not a presence, nor a support, but an image. She looks at him. And now slowly he appears to her a stranger. She no longer knows that wrinkle, that look. She grips his fingers to call him, but he can be of no help to her. He is not the friend she bears within her. Already weary of this presence, she pushes him away and turns her head."

Bernis, without a word, creeps out of the darkening room, leaves the silent house as quietly as he had entered it, slips through the trees and jumps the garden hedge. "You see," he later explains to his friend, while the mechanics are refuelling his Bréguet by the small Juby hangar, "I tried to drag Geneviève into a world of my own. Everything I showed her turned dull and grey. The first night was of an utterly nameless depth. I had to give her back her house, her life, her soul. One after the other all the poplars of the highway. And the closer we got to Paris, the less thick was the distance between the world and ourselves. As though I had wished to drag her down below the sea."

With that Bernis climbs back into the cockpit and flies off towards Dakar. He lands at Villa Cisneros, goes on to Port Etienne, but disappears before reaching Saint-Louis-du-Sénégal. They eventually find the wreckage of his plane, shot down by the Moors, not far from the little Saharan fort of Nouakchott where—unknown to the reader—the author had spent his first enchanted night under the cold desert stars.

In reviewing the book, Edmond Jaloux complained of a regrettable obscurity in the description of Bernis' complicated relations with Geneviève. "All this remains very literary and superficial. One doesn't explain psychological moods with poplars. As lyrical as one may be, one must seek to remain sober and clear in certain moments, and we would have preferred something simpler after the final separation of Bernis and Geneviève."

The criticism was well taken, and the clearest proof of it is that in his next book Saint-Exupéry was careful. But precisely because it lacks this discipline, *Courrier Sud* rings with a kind of springtime rapture which has its own youthful charm. As in this passage which Georges Mounin later singled out as a good example of his "external surrealism":

"Tangier, that little nothing of a town, was my first conquest. It was, you see, my first theft. Yes. Vertically at first, and from so far off. Then, during the descent, this flowering of meadows, plants, and houses. Up into the daylight I was bringing a sunken city warmed by the breath of life. And suddenly, five hundred metres from the field, this marvellous discovery: an Arab hoeing the ground, whom I pulled towards me, whom I made into a man on my own scale, who was really and truly my booty, my creation, my game. I had captured a hostage and Africa was mine.

Two minutes later, on the grass, I was young, as though put down on some star where life begins again. In a new climate. On this ground, under this sky I felt like a young tree. I stretched my flight-strained muscles with a marvellous craving. I took long flexible strides to unlimber from the piloting, and I laughed at having rejoined my shadow on landing."

This was not the fluxive dream-world of Joyce, nor the wild poetic jungle which André Breton and Tristan Tzara wanted to explore in the name of the untrammelled "metaphysical freedom" of the human imagination. Saint-Exupéry had little taste for the cosmic anarchy of the Surrealists, but he was fascinated by their experiments with language. In leaving the earth man was entering a new universe of experience in some ways as strange as Einstein's fourth dimension or Picasso's deliberately kaleidoscopic puzzles. The problem was one of describing the objective reality in vividly subjective terms: terms unaffected by the conventional language of science, images undulled by the corrective wisdom acquired at school. For this new dimension, for this new frame of vision, he felt, a new set of poetic images and symbols was needed. It could be objected that many of them were not as fresh as he naively supposed: also that the lyric strain within him was so strong that it kept overflowing its bounds and running away with him. In this he was yielding to external influences as much as to his personal bent. For if the rapturous description of Geneviève and her "enchanted realm" is a lyrical attempt to evoke the vanished joys of his youth, it owes less to Proust (who was more analytical) than it does to the florid style which Jean Giraudoux had developed in novels like *Simon le Pathétique* and *L'Ecole des*

*Indifférents*, which had impressed the young Antoine by their metaphorical exuberance.

Marine images abound in *Courrier Sud*, as Jaloux might have noted instead of speaking of "fairies and roses", of which there is scant mention. And they are not there by virtue of some passing poetic whim. Seen through thousands of feet of air, as though through a transparent substance or crystal (an image he actually uses), the earth can seem to lie at the bottom of an atmospheric ocean, with trees and rocks and grasses like the stonebed of an aquarium. Up there, as for the mariner on the surface of the waves, all is storm and stress; but in the depths below all is, or seems to be, of an eery stillness. It was this artistic screen of images which, in describing Geneviève, Saint-Exupéry was imposing on his abortive passion for Louise de Vilmorin. He had sought to drag her from her enchanted kingdom—the magic garden of Verrières, the old town-house on the Rue de la Chaise—and like Bernis with Geneviève, he had failed. He had lacked the money needed to maintain that "external agitation" which to many who have it is the elixir of life, and he had had to fall back on the threadbare fortune of his dreams. And from the depths of his creative unconscious there had arisen the distant memory of Hans Christian Andersen's pathetic Little Mermaid: that golden-haired nymph who to join her dark-haired Prince was forced to lose her tongue and suffer agonies of pain with every step she took on dry land. "Oh, my love!" sighs Bernis' partner. "She clings to him, her head thrown back and her hair tangled, as though dragged from the waters." The allusion could not have been more transparent.

In its original form, as a short story, it had been entitled *L'Evasion de Jacques Bernis*. What Bernis was fleeing from was not simply Geneviève; it was also the enchanted kingdom of his youth he had hopelessly outgrown and which, as though shrivelled by a witch's spell, had shrunk to dwarf dimensions. A kingdom which, victim of the Proustian dilemma, he could neither properly re-enter nor totally forget. Down there, in those windless depths it lay, as inaccessible as a drowned forest, as inviting as a sunken cathedral. "And we would come back towards the house, heavy with secrets, like those divers of the Indies who have fingered pearls."

For Saint-Exupéry the feel of those pearls was unforgettable, and, as he was later to write: "In the end memories are all that are left us." From the strictly literary point of view *Courrier Sud* deserved the treatment Jaloux gave it. As a first novel it fell short of being a *chef d'œuvre manqué*. But autobiographically, it gleams with sunken treasures.

# 9

# The Winds of Patagonia

HIS first book had just gone to the printers in April of 1929 when Saint-Exupéry bid good-bye to Paris and took the train to Brest. Six years of laborious experimentation in Toulouse had at last brought forth a new series of Latécoère monoplanes which promised to make night flying a less than suicidal venture. Henri Guillaumet, like Jean Mermoz before him, had been recalled from the Dakar–Casablanca run to undergo night-flight training, but for Didier Daurat this was only a first step. Faithful to Pierre Latécoère's old dream, he was looking forward to the day when they could span the South Atlantic by air. Hydroplanes at the time seemed the only feasible solution for tackling the central 2000 mile stretch (between Saint-Louis in Sénégal and Natal in Brazil) which, with the engines then available, could not be covered in less than twenty hours. Which meant that part of the crossing had to be done at night. Almost alone among his colleagues, for the most part a simple lot, Saint-Exupéry had received instruction in higher mathematics: enough, Daurat decided, to warrant his being entered for a course in sea-plane piloting and celestial navigation at the Naval Air College in Brest.

The *Cours Supérieur de Navigation Aérienne*—as it was officially known—had been allotted several barrack classrooms inside the mediaeval ramparts of the old Breton citadel. To reach it one had to climb the streets of the *vieille ville*; and it was here, at a sidewalk café called the Continental, that Saint-Exupéry and his fellow students held their first informal meeting. There were eleven of them, of whom only two—including Saint-Ex—were civilians, the rest being army lieutenants graduated from the Ecole Polytechnique or from the Academy of Saint-Cyr. Their instructor, Lionel Chassin, a naval lieutenant who was hardly older than they, had decided to break the ice by arranging an initial encounter around a couple of marbletop tables. The last to turn up, typically enough, was Saint-Exupéry who, after finding himself a furnished room near the tree-filled promenade of the Cours Dajot, had managed to lose his way in the meandering streets of old Brest.

To Chassin this "hulking unruly-haired devil of a fellow" seemed as gauche as he was massive with his "Mickey Mouse nose, his slightly bulging black eyes, and his luminous forehead". But he lost no time making himself one of the boys. Chassin had brought along another naval lieutenant named Créhalet, whose job it was to give the students practical flying instructions to supplement their theoretical training. "The first round of drinks was on me, as was only natural," Chassin recalled years later. "Then Captain Bizouard, the oldest of the students, returned the compliment by offering the next round, which was also normal. Créhalet then declared that he had the right and the duty to 'wash the pavement' with his brothers-in-arms; whereupon Saint-Exupéry, in the name of the civilians present, asked to be allowed to offer a round in his turn. From that moment on everything went to the dogs, each feeling himself obliged to offer his round of thirteen Noilly-Cassis . . . I seem to recall the day's ending—we had to eat, after all—with some bacchic songs which must have left my students with a curious opinion of their future instructor."

No less curious must it have felt to Saint-Exupéry to be back at school with a former *flottard* for instructor and a handful of erstwhile *taupins* and *cyrards* for fellow students. The moment they learned that he was recently returned from the Rio de Oro, where he had been *chef d'aéroplace* at Cape Juby, they dubbed him "Juby"—the name he was known by for the remainder of the course. "Juby" seems to have made up in verve what (as usual!) he lacked in studious application; for almost twenty years later Chassin could still vividly recall his stories—not only of his desert adventures, but of his schoolboy pranks at the Lycée Saint-Louis . . . of how, for example, he had once acted a bit part and practically broken up the play by tramping on to the stage in a Roman tunic wearing spectacles and garters, and sent squeals through the audience by "accidentally" dropping his spear and bending down in his Pretorian mini-skirt to pick it up!

At night, when the sky was clear, they would troop up to the castle gates, to which they were admitted by a bosun's mate with the wonderfully Breton name of Pennaneach, who would drag wearily up the cold stone steps behind them jangling his enormous keys. They would take a bead on the stars with their Favé quadrants, inscribing the results in their Bertin notebooks; and the session completed, would come tumbling out and flow on down to the dancehalls of the Ermitage or the famous Brasserie de la Marine, where the discussions, once started, often went on for hours. Seemingly absorbed in fashioning a cornucopia from a strip of silver paper, "Juby" would suddenly pull out a pencil and jot down a few formulas and figures.

"Now what do you think of that?" he would ask Chassin. And Chassin, marvelling at his inventiveness, would have to explain that the navigational device he had just thought up already existed. It reminded him of Pascal, reinventing the basic theorems of geometry before finding them in Euclid. "His genius lay in detecting the invisible links between two orders of phenomena which at first sight are very different, and in combining them to solve a problem more easily."

This genius was less evident in the classroom, and particularly in his practical work. Excellent in theoretical mathematics, "Juby" could be frighteningly clumsy when it came to application. Chassin was amazed to come upon him one afternoon in a state of agitated sweat over a compass reading which was fantastically off course. During a test flight when he had to take a vertical bead on the ground, he managed to drop and smash his Favé quadrant on the floor of the plane. One spring morning Chassin took him out on a seaplane instruction flight. After carefully explaining that one of the major differences in taking off with a seaplane was that one pulled back on the stick rather than pushing it forward (to get the floats out of the water), he turned over the controls to Saint-Exupéry; after which, as Chassin amusingly described it, "he forgot my instructions . . . and we disappeared in an eddy of churning water".

A far more serious mishap overtook him a few days later as he was landing a two-motor Latham flying-boat. The plane was equipped with a drift-meter which Saint-Exupéry and his fellow students had used during experimental flights made with Captain Bonneau, the base commander. The drift-meter hatch being difficult to close, Chassin had instructed the students not to touch it during test flights. But "Juby" had opened it and then forgotten to close it. As soon as the flying-boat touched down it began to ship water. Chassin, standing on the wharf, saw Saint-Ex throw up his hands and make frantic signals while gunning the engines to keep up the front of the plane. A cutter reached the stricken craft just in time to tow it in to the dockside, where it was heaved drippingly out of the water by a crane.

These lapses, as Chassin quickly realized, had a specific cause. Anxious by nature, Saint-Exupéry was doubly so now in anticipation of the appearance of *Courrier Sud*. The Gallimard page proofs reached him while he was in Brest, and much of the time he should have spent on his homework was devoted to correcting them. Eager to test the reaction of his "reading public", he gave his companions different passages to look at. The general reaction seems to have been favourable, and according to Chassin, the opening lines were so admired that they were almost learned by heart:

*Un ciel pur comme de l'eau*
*Baignait les étoiles et les révélait*
*Puis c'était la nuit.*
*Le Sahara se dépliait*
*Dune par dune*
*Sous la lune.*
*Sur nos fronts cette lumière de lampe*
*Qui ne livre pas les objets*
*Mais les compose,*
*Nourrit de matière tendre*
*Chaque chose . . .*
*Et nous marchions nu-tête,*
*Libérés du poids du soleil.*
*La nuit : cette demeure . . .*

As published, these opening lines, though imbued with the breath of poetry, came out as prose: "A sky as pure as water bathed the stars and brought them out. And then night fell. Dune by dune the Sahara unfolded itself beneath the moon. Its light, falling on our foreheads with the softness of a lamp blending forms instead of sharpening them, enveloped everything in its tender sheen . . . And bareheaded we walked, relieved of the weight of the sun. In that dwelling place—the night . . ."

Even in the English translation, so much more ponderous than the French original, the euphony of certain words—like the Sahara unfolding itself "dune by dune . . . beneath the moon"—carries a poetic ring that is unmistakable. The young author could even have been blamed for overdoing it, had it not been for the carat lightness of the touch. Unlike Monsieur Jourdain of Molière's *Le Bourgeois Gentilhomme*, who spoke prose without realizing it, Saint-Exupéry could not help threading poetic gems on the simplest descriptive sentence.

In a commemorative article written three years after Saint-Ex's disappearance, Lionel Chassin recalled that "despite his absent-mindedness and the clumsiness displayed in his exams . . . Saint-Exupéry obtained a diploma he hardly merited and which allowed him several years later to become a seaplane test pilot for Latécoère". The truth, as Chassin himself later had occasion to explain, was less simple. Saint-Ex finished the aerial navigation course ninth out of eleven. Satisfied with his students' proficiency, Chassin was for passing them all, but the Colonel who had been sent down to Brest to supervise the exams was having none of it. "Your course enjoys great prestige in the Air Force," he explained to Chassin. "It must keep it.

The final certificate must have the reputation of being difficult to obtain. Which means—some have got to be flunked!"

Chassin protested vainly against this absurd reasoning—to this day typical of the French pedagogical mentality—but in vain. At least two of the students, the Colonel declared, had to be flunked. "All right," said Chassin wearily, "they're your charges, after all, not ours"—he meant the Navy's; and with that he gave the name of the two who had received the lowest marks. One of them was a lieutenant who had until then seemed headed for an impeccable military career. What? The Colonel was appalled. Nothing doing!

"Give me the name of Number Nine," he thundered.

Reluctantly Chassin gave him the name—Antoine de Saint-Exupéry. Saint-Exupéry? . . . Hmmmm . . . Who's that? A civilian? . . . Splendid! Just what's needed! So Number Nine was flunked. And the Colonel returned happily to Paris, pleased with the ingenuity he had shown in reasserting the intellectual superiority of the military branch.

*     *     *

His less than brilliant showing in this course probably confirmed Didier Daurat in what he may have begun to suspect: that Saint-Exupéry was not the man he needed to fly the first hydroplane across the southern Atlantic. The new Laté 25, with a cabin for four, contained the answer to the problem confronting him. If it could hold a radio operator, it could also include a navigator—which meant that the pilot could be dispensed from having to undergo extensive training in celestial navigation.

At Toulouse, which Saint-Exupéry reached after a brief stopover in Paris, he was put to work piloting the new Latécoère 25 and 26. The appearance of these new monoplanes was in the process of transforming the airline. Fitted with a 450 horsepower Renault engine, in place of the 300 horsepower motor which had powered the Bréguet 14, they could carry one ton of merchandise and average 500,000 instead of 20,000 kilometres per breakdown: enough to reduce the hazards of overflying the Rio de Oro to one twenty-fifth of what they had been in the "heroic" period which Saint-Exupéry had known. These results owed much to the introduction of regular night flights, which did more than simply halve the time of mail delivery. The night air, over hot areas like the Sahara, tended to be less turbulent for pilots and infinitely less wearing on engines, chronically upset by boiling oil and bursting radiators in the blistering heat of midday. The ground mist was no more blinding at night, and for most of the way down the African coast pilots could be guided by the luminous phosphorescence of the strand, strewn with millions of microscopic sea fish left there by the restless pounding of the surf. The new Latécoères also eliminated the necessity of flying over the Saharan stretch in pairs; for even the cabinless Laté 26 had three open-air cockpits, placed one behind the other, which could accommodate an interpreter or a mechanic as well as a radio operator.

Saint-Exupéry's apprenticeship on these new planes seems to have been limited to practice flights on the Toulouse–Casablanca run. In his wonderfully vivid book, *Araignée du Soir*, Henri Delaunay recalls a trip they undertook together during the August dog-days to salvage a Latécoère which had crash-landed on a beach near Valencia. They set out from Alicante one evening with two mechanics and drove right through the night—preferring the cool of the stars to the merciless heat of the Spanish sun. On reaching the stricken plane Delaunay would have liked to stretch out under one of the wings while the mechanics went to work on the motor, but Saint-Ex, who seemed not to have felt the all-night drive, insisted on dragging him into Valencia for a look at the "sights". Hounded by flies and beggars, Delaunay grew increasingly irritable as they wandered through the baking streets—emptied of their evening animation—pausing to gape at shadowless façades and dazzling walls. "At a wooden booth all they could offer us was lukewarm beer, and I didn't know if the water in the fountains was drinkable." Only that evening, when they were back at Pepita's *pensión* in Alicante, did Delaunay begin to realize all they had seen and heard on listening to Saint-Ex's description of their excursion. The plaintive wail of a hidden guitar, streets echoing with the jingle of orange-laden donkeys, the broad shadows of the palms mirrored in the rippling basins of street-corner fountains—his candid gaze and seemingly vacant ear had registered them all. "Listening to him I regretted having been more attentive to the clink of glasses inside a *bodega* than to the façade of the cathedral, where he had noted some amusing details in the sculpture. I found myself readmiring the old rampart towers which had so long defied the assaults of men only to yield to the coquettish embraces of climbing vines and creepers. I was amused by those ragged urchins, pulling tragic faces as they stretched out their palms and then rippling into peals of laughter the moment they got what they wanted."

\* \* \*

Early in September Saint-Exupéry was informed that he was being transferred to South America, whither Didier Daurat had preceded him. He had just six days in which to visit his sister Gabrielle at Agay and to say goodbye to his mother at Saint-Maurice-de-Rémens. In Paris he called on Gaston Gallimard and showed him a few pages from the new book he had been writing. His publisher, who seemed pleased with what he saw, urged him to carry on and finish it. If necessary, to speed things up, he could arrange to have the galleys sent back to him in Argentina by air. In any case he wanted another novel from him as soon as possible. But otherwise Antoine found Paris disconcertingly empty. His friends were still away on vacation—Yvonne de Lestrange at her château near Poitiers, Henry de Ségogne busy climbing mountains near Chamonix. "I wandered around Paris full of melancholy," he wrote a few days later to Lucie-Marie Decour, who also was away—at Juan-les-Pins, on the Riviera. He felt like Bernis, as he had described him in *Courrier Sud*, lost in a tide of strangers on the boulevard and thinking: "It's as though I weren't here."

But at Bordeaux, where he took the ship, Yvonne de Lestrange was on the dock to bid him a fond farewell. The voyage lasted eighteen days and, as he knew, he would be gone for a good two years. At Dakar, there was a letter for him from his thoughtful mother; he hurriedly replied by the same Aéropostale mail-plane which had carried it down. The heavy, pasty air brought back familiar memories, and it took the sharks and the flying fish, leaping athletically around the ship, to make him feel that he was really leaving France. "I had no idea the sea could resemble a prairie," was the way he described it in a letter to Lucie-Marie Decour. There were the usual deck games and he soon found himself playing blind man's buff and entertaining teenaged girls with card tricks and drawings. Even the captain could not resist their captivating solicitations, letting them gag his shrewd seaman's eyes and disguise his salty limbs in the outlandish attire demanded by some new charade. To Saint-Exupéry's surprise the old mariner did not bother to disembark whenever the ship put in to port. It was as though the land had ceased to count in his existence. His element was this vessel, where he was content to pace the deck while his passengers amused themselves playing cards below. Bridge and rummy were not for him, any more than books; for the only characters which interested him were inscribed up there in the zodiac.

"Now show me the Southern Cross," he would nod to Saint-Exupéry, as they leaned pensively against the rail.

To humour him Saint-Ex would point at random to some distant constellation.

"My boy," the captain would say, shaking his wise head, "my boy, you know nothing. In three days we'll show it to you. We've hidden it in the sea."

When three nights later it finally rose, the skipper made a present of it to the little girls.

"You see that?"

"Yes, Captain."

"It's a lovely jewel, it's the Southern Cross."

And the girls marvelled in silence at the necklace which the old seaman thus pulled from the ocean.

Less spectacular than the glittering constellation, Buenos Aires finally hove into view over the glaucous waters of La Plata. There waiting for him on the dock were the broad shouldered Jean Mermoz, with his flying hair and windy red scarf; his dear friend Henri Guillaumet, with his brown eyes and boyish grin; and the inimitable Marcel Reine, eager to slap his back with puckish bonhommie, a vigorous, "*Ah, les vaches!*" and a choice volley of Parisian *argot*.

There was a room waiting for him at the Majestic Hotel, not too far from the Aéropostale's offices, located in a low edifice at No. 240, Calle de la Reconquista. Beyond its wide lobby, bare save for a central counter, were a number of offices. The largest of them contained an imposing director's desk and walls plastered with aerial route maps radiating out like spokes from Buenos Aires—towards Pernambuco, Asunción del Paraguay, and Santiago de Chile. Here Saint-Exupéry found Didier Daurat, Paul Vachet, the French pilot who had done most of the spade-work in prospecting for new airfields and in opening the Rio de Janeiro–Buenos Aires line, as well as Captain Vicente Almandos Almonacid, whose office this was.

From his distant Arabic ancestry, so distant that even he professed to know little about it, Almonacid had inherited a pair of dark quarter-moon eyes and a subtle thin-lipped smile. Of medium height, he had both the trim build and the nervous temperament of a jockey. Generations, if not centuries back, an Almandoz had left Castille and an Almonacid had abandoned Sevilla for the New World. They had first settled in Chile, before crossing the mountains to Mendoza. His father had been the governor of the "distant and melancholy Rioja . . . amid whose cyclopean rocks, rough-hewn precursors of the pyramids"—to quote the poet Joaquín Gonzales, who was a good friend of the family—the young Almonacid had acquired a veneration for the Andean heights that never left him. Like Saint-Exupéry, he was a typical *enfant du siècle* who had developed an early passion for mechanics and problems of design. Expelled from the Naval College of Buenos Aires for "rowdiness", he had put his knowledge of geometry to good use as land surveyor and then gone to France to study sanitation—his ambition being to give the town of Bahía Blanca an up-to-date municipal draining system. Instead, he had been bitten by the aeronautic bug that had fatally infected Voisin, Santos Dumont, and the Farman brothers, and he had spent his spare hours devouring aviation treatises and designing stabilizers. As early as 1913 he was writing enthusiastic letters home about his plans to build an

*aeromóvil* capable of spanning the Atlantic in a single flight; and as someone
would be needed to fly this Jules Verne construction and he was not the
armchair type, Almonacid decided he had better master the fundamentals of
piloting himself.

What followed was like a sequence in a Marx Brothers film. Maurice
Farman, who had as much trouble understanding his Spanish as Almonacid
had fathoming Farman's French, thought he was dealing with an experienced flyer who had come to France—the home of the aeroplane—to obtain
an international pilot's licence. After taking him up on a brief "courtesy"
flight around the Toussus-le-Noble field, he climbed out of the plane and
let Almonacid take over. Fearful of disappointing the crowd of curious
spectators who had gathered to watch "the foreigner", Almonacid decided
he would have to take the plane up, though he had never flown in his life
before. The resulting solo, which ended with his accidentally stalling the
motor (considered the height of daring) as he came in to land, convinced
the assembled company that this was an Argentine "ace" at work. The
conviction was dramatically confirmed during his second flight when he
accidentally grazed the roof of his hotel as he came in to land—who but
an ace would dare fly so low!—not realizing that one needed to have the
wind against and not behind one.

Everything in the subsequent career of this high-strung Argentinian
had the same epic quality about it. When the First World War broke out
in 1914, he had volunteered for the Foreign Legion and seen action in the
trenches. He might well have stayed there but for his friend Gustave
Eiffel, the engineer-constructor of the famous Tower, who used his influence with the military to have Almonacid transferred from the dug-outs
to the airfields. In the new branch the "Argentine ace" soon made a name
for himself with bold night flights over the German lines; and in Argentina,
if nowhere else, he is honoured as the "inventor" of night-time bombardments. He had a number of narrow escapes which he modestly attributed
to his "lucky star" but which war correspondents were readier to ascribe
to a legendary *maîtrise*; with the result that when he finally returned to
his homeland in 1919 with the *Médaille Militaire*, the *Croix de Guerre*, and
the rank of Captain in the French Army, he was given the red carpet treatment by club presidents and politicians and fashionable hostesses eager to
brighten the bemedalled splendour of their tables.

In the interim an enterprising Frenchwoman by the name of Adrienne
Bolland had set out to demonstrate the superiority of the second sex by
flying over the Andes, something no one had yet been mad enough to want
to do. Not to be outdone, Almonacid decided that he too would fly over the
Andes, but farther north where the mountains are even higher. Furthermore

he would do it at night. He took off late one evening in a Spad fighter which had been offered to him by the French Military Mission and climbing to 18,000 feet, he soared past the moonflooded mass of the Aconcagua (23,000 feet) without bothering to use an oxygen mask. He suffered a frostbitten nose (from a temperature of 40° below), engine failure caused by lack of fuel as he was coming down on the Chilean side, and finally a crack-up as he skimmed over the beach at Viña del Mar. But his "lucky star" was still with him and he ploughed into a mound of sand just short of some iron scaffolding which could have killed him on the spot. He was helped out of his damaged machine by a sympathetic coastguard, while the incoming tide laid claim to the Spad. The Chileans, who had hoped to be the first to overfly the Andes, raised a howl of protest, claiming that their coastguard (posted there to watch for smugglers) had needlessly risked his life dragging this Argentine "pirate" from the sea. But this storm in a diplomatic tea-cup only enhanced the fame of the hero, who was given a delirious welcome when he returned home to Buenos Aires.

But for the unreserved support given them by the *condor de la Rioja* —as he was henceforth known to his compatriots—it is doubtful if the French could ever have scored the breakthrough they finally achieved in 1927. It had begun two years earlier with another incident which had added its aura to the Almonacid legend. When the first Latécoère mission flew in to Buenos Aires in January 1925, Almonacid was outraged by the cavalier way in which the two Bréguets were forced to evacuate the military airfield of Palomar by the assistant commandant, who shared the emphatically pro-German feelings of most of the Argentine military. A day or two later, at a banquet given to honour the trail-blazing French airmen, Almonacid walked up to the offending colonel and challenged him to a duel. They stalked out of the banquet hall together, and an hour or so later Almonacid returned—alone—and resumed his seat as though nothing had happened. The colonel had chosen to fight with sabres, which Almonacid had never handled in his life; but with his customary impetus he had fallen on his adversary with a furious flourish and opened a gash over his right eye before the officer knew what had hit him.

When Pierre Latécoère disembarked in Buenos Aires two years later Almonacid was on the dock to greet him. The founder of the world's oldest continually operating airline was flanked by another Frenchman, already in his early sixties, who had lent his dynamism to the cause. A pioneering business magnate who had built harbours, carved roads and railways through the jungle, and acquired vast holdings in Brazil, Marcel Bouilloux-Lafont was a kind of 1920s' Onassis: a bustling European who had made his fortune abroad and a man who was willing to take risks. Nothing at the time could have seemed more foolhardy than launching a mail-carrying airline over thousands of miles of jagged coast and jungle and the world's second highest mountain chain. But the sheer audacity of the enterprise seems to have appealed to the ageing tycoon even more than the figures and income estimates which had originally been submitted to him by Latécoère's first emissaries. The months had passed and gradually scepticism had given way to enthusiasm, to the astonishment of his entourage and perhaps even of himself. Aviation, in which Bouilloux-Lafont had had little faith until then, suddenly became a belated passion and the Aéropostale the pampered child of his old age.

Enlisting the backing of men like Bouilloux-Lafont and Almonacid must have given great encouragement to Pierre Latécoère, and at first a favourable wind had seemed to blow behind his South American venture. At the Casa Rosada, Argentina's White House, the three of them were received by the co-operative President Alvear, who let Almonacid draft the outline for a ten year contract granting Latécoère the right to carry up to 25% of all letters mailed from Argentina to Europe. Though not explicitly guaranteed, it amounted to a virtual monopoly; for never during the next ten years did letters sent by air total even 10% of all the mail exchanged between Argentina and Europe. The Germans, who had been hungrily eyeing the same market, understood it immediately, setting up a protesting hue and cry which their Spanish spokesman, Ramón Franco, loudly echoed in Madrid.

The expectation was that the Argentine precedent would be followed in Brazil, the seat of Bouilloux-Lafont's empire and influence. But the establishment of a Brazilian air company having been challenged by the local Court of Accounts, the French had to content themselves with one year contracts renewable on an annual basis. On his return to Paris Pierre Latécoère solicited the support of the French government, which was asked to underwrite the two million franc debt he had incurred in capital investments. Vexed by the indifference he encountered in official circles, worried by the situation in the Rio de Oro (from which the Spaniards seemed bent on driving the French), overwhelmed by the unexpected obstacles he now faced in South America, he gave way to mounting discouragement and in April 1927 sold out his company to Marcel Bouilloux-Lafont.

The new company, which came into possession of all the South American and African installations, as well as the repair shops in Toulouse, took the name of Compagnie Générale Aéropostale (or Aéropostale for short). Undaunted by the momentary setback in Brazil, Bouilloux-Lafont dispatched emissaries to Chile and Uruguay, where mail-carrying contracts on the Argentine pattern were successfully negotiated. The French were thus able to retain the lead they had established over both Germans, now planning to link Europe to South America by zeppelins, and Americans, who were working their way down from the Carribean. A veteran Latécoère pilot, Paul Vachet, was sent north to organize a chain of airfields up the long Brazilian coast as far as Natal, the jumping-off point for Recife and Dakar; and in December 1927, eight months ahead of Saint-Exupéry, Jean Mermoz was sent to South America as chief pilot to get the mail service into operation.

In Argentina, Almonacid explored the outskirts of Buenos Aires and found what he was looking for in the suburb of Pacheco: a reasonably flat piece of grassland, long enough to accommodate the new Latécoère 25s and 26s. He then negotiated a second contract with his friend President Alvear and the Argentine government for a purely internal mail service. Unlike Brazil, whose jungle hinterland presented a seemingly insuperable obstacle, the Argentine pampas seemed ideally suited to be overflown. The 600 miles separating Buenos Aires from Mendoza to the west, Tucumán, to the north west, and Asunción del Paraguay to the north, could be negotiated in single hops by the new Latécoère monoplanes; while a series of airfields down the heavily indented coast could at last link the capital with Patagonia, 1,500 miles distant as the crow flies. Save for an irregular boat service, the only communications linking Buenos Aires to the country's southern extremity was a morse code transmitting and receiving station operated by the Argentine Navy at San Julián, in the province of Santa Cruz; for the regular telegraphic services were frequently interrupted by furious winds and snowdrifts strong enough to snap the wires.

Little persuasion was thus needed to convince the Argentine government of what it stood to gain by the development of a domestic postal service. Affiliated with the Aéropostale, it took the name of Aeroposta Argentina. Marcel Bouilloux-Lafont became its chairman, several of his associates were on the Board of Directors, while Almonacid was named "Technical Director". The statutes, however, insisted that 75% of the personnel had to be Argentine nationals. In fact, it was a joint Franco-Argentine enterprise, relying on French capital and know-how as well as on the aeronautical experience of local enthusiasts like Almonacid and Bernard Artigau, an Argentine airman of Basque origin who had shot down a dozen German planes during the First World War.

By the time Saint-Exupéry reached Buenos Aires in October 1929, most of the pioneering work was well under way. Paul Vachet, his predecessor as "*Jefe de Tráfico*", had inaugurated the biweekly mail service between Buenos Aires and Asunción del Paraguay at the beginning of the year and laid the groundwork for the extension of the service towards the south.

Not realizing what lay in store for him, Saint-Ex reached Buenos Aires thinking he would be piloting the mail under Vachet's direction. Instead, he discovered he was replacing him as the Aeroposta Argentina's "Traffic Chief".

\*        \*        \*

The site Almonacid had picked out for an airfield at Pacheco lay four miles beyond the suburb of San Fernando. To reach it one had to bump over a primitive country road so pitted with holes that the driver of their 1927 Citroën was forced to weave in and out between them, as though negotiating a slalom. On the field two large hangars had been built—one for the Laté 26s which carried the mail over the international route between Chile and Brazil; the other for the Laté 25s (with a cabin for passengers) which were already plying back and forth between Buenos Aires and Asunción del Paraguay. A number of tin huts had sprung up to house workshops and canteens for the personnel, and two tall aerials stood guard over a chalet which served as the "brain" of the line and which was to be Saint-Exupéry's headquarters for the next fifteen months.

On October 14, just two days after his arrival, Vachet took Saint-Exupéry south on a Laté 25. The Aeroposta was due to open its southern mail service a fortnight later, and the outgoing *Jefe de Tráfico* wanted to guide his successor over the first lap before taking leave of Argentina. Their route took them southwest over interminable plains of ploughed fields and pastures, cut into rectangles by long wire fences. Saint-Exupéry was struck by the monotony of the landscape and particularly by the paucity of trees—so different from France with her poplars and plane-trees and chestnuts marching across the horizon like grenadiers. Even the *estancias*, with their primitive barns, were relatively nude, garnished only by the stark metallic obelisk of their wind-driven water-wheels. The villages, becoming scarcer the further south they flew, seemed to have drained the earth of its verdure. Though it was October, this was the Argentine spring and a parched one at that; for the fierce winds and the scant rainfalls of this year of 1929 had laid bare the sandy crust of the alfalfa fields, embellished here and there with a timid blush of green. A few cotton-dry clouds were deceptively massed over the Sierra de la Ventana, beyond which loomed the languid arm of the Bahía Blanca—the "white bay"—named after its necklace of saltpetre wastes, lining the gulf like bunkers.

On the tiny landing strip, a patch of uneven ground bristling with tufts of weed, the Argentine pilot Rufino Luro Cambaceres was waiting to greet them. Years later, he could still recall the impression first made upon him by Saint-Exupéry with "his broad shoulders and his tall build, the arms clinging to his sides and his lumbering walk, similar to that of a bear". He was even more struck by the unhappy look on Vachet's face, ill concealed by the forced smile.

"Luro," he said, "this is the Aeroposta's new Traffic Chief, who's going to take my place. He's a veteran pilot and an excellent companion, so you won't need to miss me. As for myself, I must leave immediately for Venezuela to organize the new service they want me to set up there." He stayed just long enough to have his plane refuelled, then flew back to new skies and latitudes, leaving Saint-Exupéry to complete what he had so promisingly begun.

Buenos Aires being linked to Bahía Blanca by 300 miles of track, it had been decided to bring the mail overnight by train, and to have the Aeroposta carry it on from there by air. In this way the capital could be linked to Comodoro Rivadavia, 900 miles distant, in a single day—instead of three by boat—without resorting to night flights for which the recently acquired landing strips were not yet equipped. But this was merely a beginning; for Almonacid, with the full support of his government, had his sights trained on the Tierra del Fuego and the Horn.

The southern mail service was officially opened on November 1st by Saint-Exupéry himself. On October 30th he flew out of Pacheco with Luro Cambaceres, who had helped Vachet prospect for airstrips as far as Comodoro Rivadavia. South of Bahía Blanca they flew over the Colorado river, its reddish waters pressed out like a filament of tooth-paste along the zig-zagging bed. Ahead, silvered by the transparent disc of the propeller, they could see the first inklings of Patagonia—a tangled wilderness of dark green bramble pencilled with stabs of yellowish bark. From 6,000 feet up the earth looked as though it was suffering from mange, its un-combed fur pitted here and there with bright eczematous patches. Saltpetre beds, across which there seemed to ripple undulating streaks of flame. "Flamingos!" shouted Luro Cambaceres. Saint-Exupéry peered down. Like a train of powder catching fire, long colonies of flamingos were taking to the air, startled by the throbbing bird of prey above.

On they droned, over the serpentine languor of the Río Negro, a barely visible thread of quicksilver caught in its golden coils. Here and there a village, faintly peppered with the pastel green of its willows. And then, like a threadbare coat unravelling its lining, the dark garment of green brush gave way to shimmering dunes and a line of darker sky, which spread out before them with the insidiousness of a tide. The Gulf of San Matías. It dwindled back slowly to a pale purple smudge, finally disappearing, as the earth came up to meet them, behind the tiled roofs and sheds, the boats and warehouses of San Antonio Oeste. The port's tiny airfield, where Luro Cambaceres had landed several weeks before with Vachet in a Bréguet 14, was too small for the Laté 25 and they had to put down in a dry lagoon, some ten minutes' flying time away. A few adobe huts with split corrugated roofs, a watering trough made of *chanar* trunks, and a throng of half-clad children were about all there was to mark the site of the future airfield of "Las Maquinas". The sea, though invisible as they climbed out, enveloped them in a wave of moist air, floating in over the scrub brush and the dunes.

Stopping just long enough to refuel, they took off again for the south, flying down the long gulf of San Matías and across the Valdes peninsula, with its ranches and its barns. Beneath them, like bugs, trucks laden with fruit and vegetables plied up and down the roads. Trelew, the next stop, looked more like a beach colony than a town, with its geometric grid of straight dirt streets and its tin-roofed huts. Meteorologically it was a haven, tucked down beneath the lip of the wind-blown mesa of Montemayor, which rose abruptly to the south of the Río Chubut. A vast plateau, 500 kilometres long, across which the fierce Patagonian wind rolled with the momentum of a billiard ball. Clumps of tenacious scrub, thinning as they rose, flocks of hardy guanacos, scattering wildly as they approached, were all that could hold out against the cruel slap of the wind, blowing down in gales through the chipped teeth of the Andes. An occasional village, tucked into the fold of a valley, peeped up at them through its pale coverlet of willows, not daring to venture out on to those withering heights. "A land as bumpy as an old cauldron," Saint Exupéry was later to describe this rumpled carpet of earth, worn to the very woof and scraped bare of all vegetation—save for the sombre stalks of a "burnt out forest". A forest of black derricks, poised like locusts over this crumbling fringe of land.

At Comodoro Rivadavia the late afternoon air was chill. As though galvanized by the arrival of the Aeroposta, the place had succumbed to a fever of pioneer frenzy. Tractors purred over the brown earth, turning up the dry soil. Shacks were going up on every side—workshops, administrative buildings—amid water tanks and oil wells. The road, made of trash, crinkled meanly under their tyres as they drove through colonies of workers' huts. They breasted the hill overlooking the town and for a dazzling moment were offered the vast panoramic sweep of the Gulf of San Jorge, with the shore dwindling mistily into the blue of the ocean: an ocean pricked like a reef by the Cabo Tres Puntas—the Cape of Three Points— 140 miles straight across the sound.

They put up at a hotel named (after Christopher Columbus) the Colón— an appropriate choice for such a trail-blazing community. Nine thousand oil workers, many of them hillbilly types from the northern wilds of the

Catamarca, had descended on this bony littoral like scavengers on a Klondike; and the Far West fury with which they stormed the speakeasies and the cathouses, crammed into two explosive blocks, was as elemental as the winds that came howling down from the mountains.

The next day Saint-Exupéry said goodbye to Luro Cambaceres, who was to continue down to the Horn by car, scouting for new airstrips on the way. Before flying back to Buenos Aires, he had time to explore the nearby beaches, darkened by an army of walruses. The sight of so many seals taking sun baths on the sand was too much for Saint-Ex, who would not rest until he and a helpful mechanic had captured a baby walrus, which they bundled on to the Laté with the mail for the return flight to the capital.

He had frequent occasion to return to Comodoro Rivadavia, henceforth linked to Bahía Blanca by biweekly mail flights. He was there on November 16th, together with Mermoz, a French pilot with the implausible name of Paul MacLeod, and a wiry Argentinian named Próspero Palazzo to welcome back Luro Cambaceres from his excursion to the Horn. Ostriches, guanacos, and flocks of sheep seemed to be the principal inhabitants of those austral wilds, but wherever they had encountered human beings, the welcome was invariably warm. Twice Luro and his mechanics had had to cross river estuaries by raft—the second time at Puerto Santa Cruz, where the wind was blowing so furiously that they were afraid the cables would break during the crossing. Pathetically eager to reduce the solitude which was all that most of them had ever known, teams of enthusiastic locals were already hard at work preparing four new airstrips.

Two full months were needed to complete the job, and it was not until mid-January that Saint-Exupéry could fly the whole distance down to the Tierra del Fuego. There, just as Luro Cambaceres had told him, were the two hillocks a pilot could steer by in aiming for Puerto Deseado—the "Desired Haven" Sir Thomas Cavendish and his five storm-tossed vessels had thankfully discovered, while fleeing a furious hurricane in 1586. At Santa Cruz, Saint-Ex could admire whole congregations of island penguins, parading up and down in tails like ushers at a wedding. Then Río Gallegos, where the air, becoming steadily cooler the further south he flew, was surprisingly crisp. To the right the eternal snows of the *cordillera* began horning in on him from the west, while ahead lay the straits of Magellan, beyond a primeval landscape of cooled lava, pricked by the frozen bubbles of dead craters. He flew on to Punto Arenas, even though the touchy Chileans, in whose territory it lay, would not allow the Aeroposta to land there; so that Río Gallegos remained the terminus of the line. And so back to Buenos Aires, borne on the wings of the *pampero*, blowing up from the Horn. "I have just covered 2,500 kilometres in one day," he wrote excitedly to his mother. "Coming back from the extreme south where the sun sets at ten o'clock in the evening, near the straits of Magellan. It's all green, with towns spread out on lawns. Strange little towns with corrugated roofs. And people who have grown so warm and friendly—from having to huddle around their fires against the cold."

Three more months were needed to equip the airstrips with proper hangars, without which no plane could long resist the gale winds of Patagonia. The opening of the completed line was scheduled for early April, and already the Argentine winter was upon them. To protect himself from the unaccustomed cold, Próspero Palazzo, the thin little pilot from the warm province of Tucumán, took to wrapping himself in newspaper to the great amusement of his fellow pilots who could hear as well as see him approach, bulging like a Michelin tyre-man and crinkling at every step beneath the unnaturally inflated leather like an audible Bibendum.

On March 12th Luro Cambaceres took off from Comodoro Rivadavia with Albert Auge, the Aeroposta's administrative agent, and a French mechanic named Gilbert Pellaton. As they flew south along the Gulf of San Jorge one of the engine's two magnetos began to flutter, transmitting only a feeble spark to the twelve cylinders. They flew on to Puerto Deseado, where Pellaton set out to repair the defective magneto. Some time later he appeared at the hotel, where the others were sitting down to lunch, and gave them the bad news. There was no fixing the magneto. It was finished.

"We'll continue with one," replied Luro Cambaceres calmly. After which he added: "*No hay otro.*"

This expression—literally meaning "There's no other"—had become a watchword with the pilots of the Aeroposta. It was the kind of motto which forms, almost by spontaneous combustion, wherever men are linked by a rugged team spirit in the face of fearful odds. Somewhere in Spain— so the story went—for such a thing could only have happened in the land of Don Quixote—there once lived a poor shepherd boy who used up his scant earnings wooing a damsel in a neighbouring village, even going so far as to deprive himself of a coat. One day he called on the parents who, moved by his assiduity, agreed to let him have their daughter's hand. As he tramped back over the hills, he was overtaken by a thunderstorm before he could reach his home. Seeing him trudge past, soaked to the skin and without a coat to protect him, a fellow mountaineer hailed him: "*Como, tu así, y con este tiempo?*" (What! Out like that, and in this weather?) To which the young shepherd gave the glorious reply: "*No hay otro*" (There's no other).

For the pilots of the Aeroposta Argentina, as for those of Toulouse, there was no question of choosing the days on which one could fly. The mail had to go through, no matter what, and the Patagonian weather being what it was—*no hay otro*—it had to be bucked . . . and vanquished, like the rest. There was no question of turning back. So Luro Cambaceres flew on to San Julián on one magneto and with an engine which was finally averaging a bare 100 revolutions a minute. They put down at Río Gallegos at 5.30 p.m., and Luro Cambaceres' first act was to send a cable back to Buenos Aires assuring the central office that the weekly mail service would begin as scheduled on April 2nd. There was not a word about the magneto, which might have aroused the scepticism of the locals; not a hint of an accident, which might have given the doubting Thomases and the Aeroposta's numerous adversaries a new club to beat it with.

They made it back to Comodoro Rivadavia the next day, borne on the shoulder of the southern wind. In Buenos Aires, Luro Cambaceres gave Almonacid and Saint-Exupéry a detailed account of the trip. On hearing about the defective magneto, Saint-Exupéry was aghast. "You should have turned round. You were risking an accident."

Almonacid looked at him for a moment, and then asked:

"And you, what would you have done?"

Saint-Exupéry's brow suddenly cleared and a far off, almost wistful look lit up his face. "The same thing," was the answer.

On April 2nd, exactly as planned, the first Patagonian mail plane took off for Buenos Aires, inaugurating the weekly service. Marcel Bouilloux-Lafont had himself flown down to Río Gallegos for the event in a Laté 25 piloted by Saint-Exupéry and Elysée Négrin, the Aeroposta's overall inspector. The town turned out in force for the fiesta, and on the eve of the inaugural flight the newly equipped airfield witnessed an extraordinary April Fool's Day, with an abundance of champagne and a dizzying number of baptisms of the air.

Maintaining the weekly service month in and month out proved an arduous enterprise for what could now be called "the southernmost airline in the world". To keep the water from freezing in the radiators during the bitter winter months, it had to be diluted with 25% alcohol and 25% glycerine. Years later Saint-Exupéry would entertain his friends with vivid recollections of the Patagonian winter: of how the Onas Indians, dressed like Eskimos in nothing but animal hides (in this case the guanaco), would wear it with the fur or the hide next to the skin depending on the season and the direction of the wind . . . of how the sheep of the Tierra del Fuego would sleep, bedded down in the snow so deeply that all one could see of them was a hundred wisps of steam rising in the frozen air.

Another of his stories, told with a dimpled chuckle, was about the order he had one day signed: "Pilots are forbidden from landing at Comodoro when the wind velocity exceeds 150 kilometres an hour." For the wind, even more than the cold, was the most formidable adversary in this "land of flying stones" where a gust could easily knock a man over if he didn't brace himself for the shock. Special techniques had to be devised for getting planes into and out of hangars. A twin-wheel runner was placed under the tail while twenty or thirty soldiers heaved and pulled on ropes and hooks. Often a whole hour, sometimes even two were needed to roll a landed plane into the hangar, the men straining on the ropes and digging their heels into the frozen earth like the legendary barge-pullers of the Volga. Sometimes they were forced to zigzag upwind, like a sailboat tacking, clinging in clusters to the wings to keep a gust from flipping the plane over. When the fierce West wind was howling, the plane would have to be dragged out of the hangar with its propeller already turning, to keep it from being blown off the field like a butterfly. It would be faced into the wind, the pilot at the controls gunning the engine to neutralize the force of the gale, while the local soldiery and ground crew dragged it back to the edge of the field for the take-off. A take-off which often looked like an almost vertical ascension, as the furious wind lifted the groaning machine from the ground, cables and hooks dangling, before the pilot could even give the signal for the cast-off.

The most titanic battle Saint-Exupéry ever had to wage against the elements took place one day as he was flying down from Trelew towards Comodoro Rivadavia. Nine years later, when he wrote it up for the American edition of *Wind, Sand and Stars* he confessed to his difficulty in finding the words and images he needed to do justice to this hallucinating experience. He and his fellow pilots were familiar with the rough stretch before Comodoro, where the high pressure air of the Pacific was funelled through a narrowing gap in the Andes, like water in a nozzle, and came bursting down the scrubbed surface of the mesa at 100 miles an hour. They would tighten their safety belts and brace themselves for the shock, prepared for a battle that might go on for forty minutes. But on this particular day the sky was a steely blue, like a knife blade, and the brilliance of the sunshine was unnaturally sharp. From a distance everything looked cloudless and wonderfully calm, save that close to the sloping surface of the earth he could see a veil of dust, like a flurry of ashes, rushing headlong towards the sea.

A few faint, warning bumps and then without warning it hit him. He could see the earth slide madly away to the right, at a vertiginous pace. He banked hastily into the wind, whereupon the skidding landscape slowed and grew ominously immobile beneath him. His wings could no longer bite into the landscape; his plane kept slipping its grip, like an eroded gear. For twenty minutes he fought desperately to gain 200 feet; then abandoning a hopeless struggle, he let himself be buffeted down a transversal valley in the hope of creeping out under the gale. Instead, he was lifted 1,500 feet up by a broadside which hit him with the force of a muzzle blast. Before he could bring his plane back into the wind, he was six miles out to sea, straining desperately to regain the coast, now reduced to a blurred line in the distance. The wind he was fighting was blowing at the fantastic velocity of 150 miles an hour—the maximum speed of his Laté 25—and if he had been piloting an old Bréguet, he could never have made it back. "For the first time in four years of flying for the airline," he later wrote, "I doubted the resistance of my wings. I was also afraid of ploughing into the sea, not because of the downdraughts which flattened into a kind of mattress at the level of the waves, but because of the topsy-turvy angles at which they kept hitting me."

Eighty minutes later he was as far out to sea as ever, but he had climbed 900 feet—enough to spy, some distance further south, a kind of blue river in the midst of this boiling ocean, which howling whiplashes of wind were churning into angry froth and combing into long green breakers. He let himself drift southwards towards that auspicious patch of blue, where the force of the gale seemed less ferocious, and then, like a punch-drunk boxer who feels his opponent weakening, he tightened his grip on the controls, dug in his heels, and began painfully pushing toward the shore. Below him the sea shuddered and shattered into fans of flying spray, but slowly he could feel himself inching his way back. One hour it took him to regain those six lost miles. The blurred line became a shore, and then gradually a cliff, under whose protective lee he sought shelter from the hurricane. Veering south, he struggled on towards Comodoro Rivadavia. The worst was over. But the wind was still howling so furiously when he came in to land that 120 soldiers had to be mobilized to help drag his Laté 25 towards the hangar. One hour of dogged heaving and pulling, and at last—they were in.

That night, in his hotel room, when he collapsed into bed, his cramped muscles were still battling a storm which, with desperate and unabating frenzy, moaned at the eaves and rattled the corrugated roof above him.

# 10

## *Hijos de Francia*

---

THE year Saint-Exupéry spent in South America was also a momentous one for the Aéropostale. By introducing night flights between Rio de Janeiro and Buenos Aires in the spring of 1928, Jean Mermoz had cut mail delivery between the two capitals from five days by ship to a single day by air. Similar progress had been made on the Toulouse–Dakar run, where the new night-flying Latécoères made it possible to bring the mail down in a day and a half. In all, the 6,000 miles from Toulouse to Dakar, on one side of the Atlantic, and from Natal to Buenos Aires, on the other, could now be covered in four days, or even less. But the time gained over the land was lost on the sea, the coastguard cutters that plied back and forth between Dakar and Natal needing five, six, and sometimes seven days to cross the 2,000 miles of the South Atlantic. Strive as they might to drive their vessels across the ocean at a full speed of 18 knots, the valiant crews and skippers of these corvettes were frequently slowed by rough seas and their steam-turbine engines plagued by bursting pipes. Diesel-powered cutters were tried on an experimental basis, but the improvements were not striking enough to warrant a greater capital investment in their purchase. With the Germans already experimenting with airships and flying-boats, it was simply a question of time before they would overtake their rivals in the airmail race—unless the French could meet the challenge in this field too. The Aéropostale, to retain its lead, would have to cross the ocean by air.

Toulouse had recently brought out a Latécoère 28, with a 480 horsepower engine, that was more reliable than anything the line yet had in operation. By giving it a 650 horsepower motor manufactured by the celebrated Hispano Suiza works and fitting it with floats, Didier Daurat produced a sea-plane that could carry ten passengers at an average speed of 140 miles an hour. What was more, he claimed it could span the 2,000 miles between Saint-Louis-du-Sénégal and Natal in a single hop. The French aviation "authorities" refused to believe it; whereupon he recalled Mermoz from South America to prove it.

In Buenos Aires an enthusiastic crowd turned out to see the famous airman board the *Lutétia* for the homeward trip. Over the past two years he had pulverized record after record with a regularity which recalled the early years of the Wright Brothers and Roland Garros at the peak of his renown. He had linked Asunción to Buenos Aires and been the first to fly from east to west across 1,200 miles of Brazilian jungle, where the slightest engine failure would have spelled catastrophe. He had been the first to pilot the mail over the *cordillera* separating Chile from Argentina, and the sensational escape he and his mechanic Collenot had engineered from an inaccessible mountain ledge in the Andes had seemed so unbelievable that the Chileans had first refused to believe it. As he went from one triumph to the next, his exploits were followed in the press like those of a torero. Saint-Exupéry, along with Guillaumet and Reine, was among those who accompanied him to his cabin. Mermoz, they realized, was about to tackle the greatest challenge of his career, and on its outcome would depend their own continuing success.

The *Lutétia* sailed on January 20, and one month later Mermoz was in Toulouse, ready to take delivery of the Laté 28. Equipped with floats, it was shipped to Perpignan, where Mermoz put it through its initial tests. While he went off to the Lac de Berre, near Marseille, to obtain his seaplane pilot's licence, a few final modifications were made. Then, on April 11, he took off with a navigator and radio-operator and flew the Laté 28 on a triangular course between Toulon, Marseille, and Béziers to establish a new world record: 4,300 kilometres covered non-stop in thirty hours. "Just think," Mermoz exulted to Didier Daurat, "1,200 kilometres more than we need to cross the South Atlantic".

In Paris, the aviation authorities who were subsidizing the Aéropostale were not so easily impressed, and it took days of bureaucratic wrangling to overcome their misgivings. Finally, with that discreet heroism which is the salient virtue of stoolpigeons, they agreed to have the flight permit *airmailed* to Natal, in northeastern Brazil, so that it could travel in Mermoz' seaplane. If, as these hardy deskmen feared, the pilot failed to make it, the official authorization from Paris would sink with him beneath the waves, clearing the boys at the top of any awkward responsibility!

The date for the inaugural flight was set for May 12, so that a generously full moon could light Mermoz through the sombre hazards of the night. Unwilling to leave anything to chance, Daurat flew down with him as far as Saint-Louis-du-Sénégal. There, as they were putting the Laté 28 through a final revision, a cable from Rio de Janeiro brought them the disastrous

news that Julien Pranville, the bright young engineer who had served as
Daurat's second-in-command at Montaudran before being sent down to
head the Aéropostale's operations in South America, had just drowned after
an aeroplane accident off Montevideo. Marcel Bouilloux-Lafont had
originally intended flying up to Natal to greet Mermoz at the conclusion of
what promised to be an epoch-making flight, but at the last moment he had
changed his mind and delegated Pranville to replace him. Saint-Exupéry
had seen him off from the airfield of Pacheco in a Laté 25 piloted by Elysée
Négrin, the former Toulouse test pilot who had helped him open the
Patagonian service. It was a foggy night and as Négrin came down below a
fog bank hoping to glimpse the lights of Montevideo, his wheels ploughed
into the murky waters of the Plata and his plane plunged to a shuddering
halt. May in the southern hemisphere is like November in the north, and
the water was so cold that one by one they succumbed of exhaustion. Of the
five persons on board only one survived—a Brazilian army lieutenant who
managed to keep his mattress afloat for two and a half hours by blocking the
leaking air valve with his thumb. His account of how the three Frenchmen
(including Pranville) sacrificed themselves for their two Brazilian passengers
made the headlines all over South America, further raising the prestige of
Saint-Exupéry's companions.

It was a cruel loss which affected everyone: Marcel Bouilloux-Lafont,
who now bitterly regretted his insistence that Pranville leave Buenos Aires
in the middle of the night; Saint-Exupéry, who mourned the pilot who had
flown down with him a few weeks earlier for the Río Gallegos fiesta; Mermoz,
whom Négrin had seconded on the first non-stop flight between Toulouse
and Saint-Louis-du-Sénégal (23 hours in a Laté 26); and above all Didier
Daurat, who had lost six pilots and three radio operators over the previous
fifteen months and who now found himself deprived of his chief aide in
South America. A less determined man might have faltered at this point, as
had Pierre Latécoère three years before, and bowed to adversity. But
Daurat had suffered—often in silence—through other calamities without
giving in. This was not the moment to toss in the sponge. Instead, he ordered
a final, meticulous check-up of the Hispano Suiza engine.

Early on the morning of May 12 almost 300 pounds of mail, flown in relay
by three pilots, were dumped on to the wharf at Saint-Louis-du-Sénégal
exactly twenty-five hours after leaving Toulouse—in itself a new record.
One hour later, laden with bouquets presented them by the governor of
Mauretania and the members of the French colony, Mermoz and his two
crewmates—the navigator Jean Dabry and the radio operator Léo Gimié—
climbed into the seaplane and took off towards the west. The first part of
the flight went off without a hitch. Dabry, a merchant marine officer, had

made a number of crossings on the Aéropostale's corvettes and knew the exact location of the three rescue vessels that had been posted across the South Atlantic at 500 mile intervals. But as evening fell and they approached the legendary "*pot-au-noir*", Gimié's efforts to maintain radio contact with the light-ships were thwarted by intense static in the thunder-charged air. The horizon disappeared in a universal rout, as black as ink and thick as soup. Torrents of equatorial water beat upon the cabin roof, seeping in through cracks and flooding the floor, while Mermoz and his companions sat there, stripped to the waist, the sweat running down their backs in rivulets. The blinding flashes burned out Gimié's antenna, but in the dark intervals between, Mermoz spied a viscous glow to the north west. Abruptly altering course, he made for the faint crack in the darkness and shortly thereafter they came out upon a landscape of hallucinating grandeur. How many ancient mariners had strayed into these windless waters with sails as lax as sheets, only to succumb to the infernal stew-pot heat, their phantom vessels with their cargo of despairing corpses doomed, like the Flying Dutchman, to drift across a phantom ocean? A gigantic still-life cyclone, of a sombre immobility. An eery kingdom of waterspouts, as motionless and dark as "the black pillars of a temple", as Saint-Exupéry was later to describe them in a memorable page of *Terre des Hommes*. Their swollen stems, like giant toadstools, held up "the low, sombre vault of the tempest, but through the cracks in the vault shafts of oblique light streamed down, and the moon shone between the pillars on the cold flagstones of the sea. And Mermoz pursued his course among these uninhabited ruins, veering from one channel of light to another, swerving around these giant pillars . . . towards the exit. And the spectacle was so overpowering that only after he had cleared the Black Stew Pot did Mermoz realize he hadn't been afraid."

Others were to do it after him with the same routine regularity they had shown in learning to defy the mists and the mirages of the Sahara and the shattering gales of Patagonia. But Mermoz was blazing a new trail across the equatorial sky and his exploit was both a test and a portent. A portent made all the graver by the disaster which had overtaken Pranville and Négrin. A second mishap at this critical juncture and the prestige of the Aéropostale would have sunk like a stone. But the fifth pilot to take over was another veteran of the same resolute mettle—Raymond Vanier, like Didier Daurat a survivor of the epic air battles of the First World War. The same dark-browed, dark-whiskered airman who had driven out from Montaudran in the old open-air Peugeot to look for Saint-Exupéry on that fogbound night when he had crash landed short of the field on his first flight back from Barcelona.

From his base at Rio de Janeiro, Vanier was to have flown up to Natal with Pranville and Négrin. Now he had to cover the 1,500 miles alone. He reached Natal in plenty of time to pick up the three large postal bags which Mermoz had brought over in his sea-plane and which contained letters destined for Brazil, Uruguay, Argentina, Chile, Paraguay, and Bolivia. A bare hour after Mermoz had landed, Vanier was in the air, headed back for Rio de Janeiro. At one stop he was forced to change from his closed Laté 25 to an open cockpit Laté 26, and for a long agonizing moment it looked as though he would never make it. Violent thunderstorms and rain had closed in on the Brazilian capital, and the weather report from the Aéropostale's radio shack at the Los Affonsos airfield was that visibility was nil and a landing out of the question. But Vanier sailed right through the storm like a boxer, banking away from hills which kept looming out of the night like fists. His radio antenna grilled by a thunderbolt, the operator crouched down in the open cockpit behind to keep from being forcibly ejected into the diluvial darkness, Vanier finally touched down in the middle of the night at Rio, after circling for five minutes at beach level to avoid hitting the famous Sugar Loaf. He had flown more than 37 hours in the past 72.

At dawn the jovial Marcel Reine took over for the next lap to Buenos Aires, where Saint-Exupéry was overjoyed to see him land towards the end of that afternoon. A quick shift of mailbags and Henri Guillaumet was off in his turn on the final leg of the marathon. He reached Mendoza well before midnight but had to wait for the weather to clear over the Andes, and not until late the next morning could he thread his way through the mountains. When he landed at Santiago it was 1.30 p.m., May 15, 1930. The first completely airborne mail from France to the Pacific Ocean, as Didier Daurat wrote later, "had required four and a half days. Twelve years earlier, amid a general incredulity and while the guns were still thundering, a man had drawn up a detailed plan of the impossible and declared: 'I shall carry the mail from Toulouse to Buenos Aires in seven and a half days.' Pierre Latécoère's dream had been surpassed."

\*     \*     \*

It took Mermoz eight days to reach Buenos Aires as he and his two companions were wined, dined, and toasted at gala receptions in Rio de Janeiro, Montevideo, and every city in which they stopped. Enveloped like newlyweds in streamers, they were paraded around in open cars for the acclamation of the public. In Buenos Aires they were greeted like national heroes, invited to stately balls, and asked to officiate at the openings of sport clubs and stadiums. They could not stroll through the streets without being

recognized and surrounded by enthusiastic crowds which would break into
the *Marseillaise*. Mermoz, in particular, became the object of a frenzied
cult. His virile profile, with the romantic shock of hair, was stamped on
cigar cases and perfume-bottles, made a brand mark for cigarettes, pasted
on match-boxes, engraved on lighters. The idol of an infatuated femininity,
he was stormed by breathless victims eager to immolate their residual
virginity on that herculean chest. In Paris, on the eve of his epic flight, a
mistress had committed suicide at the prospect of losing him. The wild
twenties had still not succumbed to the dismal thirties, and in the land which
had given birth to the tango, the same impassioned *señoritas* who swooned at
the sight of Rudolf Valentino and quivered to the throbs of Carlos Gardel's
guitar, could not wait to throw themselves and their bouquets at this radiant
French flyer.

For Saint-Exupéry, as for all the pilots of the Aéropostale, these were
glorious days, the fruit and apogee of years of unrelenting effort. It was
heartening to feel that one belonged to an enterprise which had broken
record after record and systematically tackled the impossible. But the
euphoria, he knew, was transient, destined to blow away like a whirlwind as
Mermoz and his companions moved on, like conquerors, to Chile and
Bolivia.

After a brief sojourn at the Hotel Majestic, Saint-Exupéry had found an
apartment in the Guemes building, then Buenos Aires' tallest skyscraper,
not far from the port. More than once Bernard Artigau, the Argentine
pilot, was amused to see him appear on the Calle Florida in a ludicrous pair
of overalls several sizes too small for his bulky frame and which barely
covered his knees. Saint-Ex would have put in a full day's work at Pacheco
and then come home, unconcerned by the comic figure he cut amid the well
brilliantined youths of the evening *paseo*.

His friend Guillaumet had rented an apartment near the Colón Theatre,
where he was joined by his wife Noële, whom he had met and married during
his term of service in Dakar. Knowing little of the reputation of this quarter
—Serrito—and underestimating the enterprise of the caretaker, Madame
Guillaumet was surprised by the repeated phone calls she received at
night from unknown men forever asking the standard question: "*Cuanto
cobra?*" It was weeks before someone from the company undertook to
explain that what they were asking was how much she charged; and the
idea that his friend Henri's wife was being "tarted" amused Saint-Exupéry
no end.

Only too glad to get away from his desk at the Avenida de la Reconquista,
Saint-Ex would seize on any pretext to pilot the mail himself. He would
appear without warning, suddenly ringing the bell at the Guillaumets'

apartment and then flopping down on the couch, where he would regale them with vivid accounts of his latest adventures and tribulations. "He would talk and talk," recalls Noële Guillaumet, "until completely worn out, he would suddenly collapse and fall asleep. And what a sleep! Henri would have to take him down in the elevator, open the door, and literally pour him into the taxi, where he was quite capable of dozing off immediately without the driver's knowing just where to take him."

As *Jefe de Tráfico* for the Aeroposta Argentina, Saint-Exupéry was at once exacting, daring, and ingenious. A local pilot called Rose was once bawled out for landing in the pampa next to Saint-Ex's plane, which had been forced down by engine trouble. "I fine you two hundred pesos, Rose, to teach you proper respect for the mail." What the well-meaning pilot should have done, in the best Daurat tradition, was fly on to the next port of call and unload the mail-bags before returning to help Saint-Ex.

Mermoz one day saw Saint-Exupéry coming down to land on an unusually short strip in Patagonia. Realizing that the telephone wires ahead would make him overshoot the field, he gunned his engine, soared up, banked, and came down this time *under* the wires for a virtuoso landing.

Finding the right person to staff the remoter bases was not easy, for life in the Patagonian wilds was harsh. At one base (probably San Julián) the monotony was such that official after official soon asked to be relieved. Saint-Exupéry finally decided that the person for the job was a young Argentinian who led such an orderly, upright life that every evening after work he dutifully went home to his mother's. The young man was sent south; but soon strange rumours floated back to Buenos Aires and Saint-Ex had to fly down to see what was amiss. The airstrip was vacant—save for a young lad who led him into town, where he found his virtuous subordinate comfortably boarded in the local brothel! Tired of shuttling back and forth between airstrip and "boarding-house", the windblown youth had found it simpler to transfer the airline agency to his quaint abode. But most extra-ordinary of all—and with what relish Saint-Ex would lead up to this crescendo when recalling the episode—the young man was still a virgin!

On another occasion word reached him that the representative at Bahía Blanca was raiding the till. It was awkward news, for he happened to belong to one of the town's better families. But the ingenuity "Juby" had displayed in the Rio de Oro was as present as ever in the *Jefe de Tráfico* in Buenos Aires. Informed by cable that the *Jefe* would be flying down on a certain day on an inspection tour, the suspect till-raider was given ample time to borrow the missing sum. When Saint-Exupéry finally appeared, he went carefully over the books, then asked to see the cash-box. Sure enough, it was full; there was no trace of a deficit. "Fine," nodded Saint-Ex quietly.

"I'm going to take it back with me to Buenos Aires." And with that he flew off, leaving the crestfallen felon to make it up with his creditors.

\* \* \*

The euphoria induced by Mermoz' triumphal passage through Argentina had hardly had time to wane when it was brusquely clouded by bad news, which Saint-Exupéry received on landing at Pacheco with the Patagonian mail. His friend Guillaumet, on one of his biweekly mail flights, had failed to put down at Mendoza two and a half hours after taking off from Santiago. He was missing—somewhere over the Andes—and this in mid-June, which in the southern hemisphere is as cold as a northern Christmas.

Fatigued though he was by his return flight from the south, Saint-Exupéry took off immediately for Mendoza, 600 miles to the west. Guillaumet had flown out of Santiago the previous Thursday, only to be forced back by snow. He had taken off again the next morning—Friday the 13th—and disregarding an unfavourable weather forecast he had disappeared into the mountains. The blizzard only cleared on Sunday, the day Saint-Ex reached Mendoza; but no trace of Guillaumet's plane could be found anywhere along the trans-Andean railroad, the route Daurat had recommended for the crossing of the *cordillera*. The top of its pass, marked by a gigantic statue of Christ, was not quite 13,000 feet high, well within the capacity of the Potez 25, a high-altitude plane that had a ceiling of 20,000 feet. Guillaumet had evidently chosen another route, but there was no telling which nor just how far into the frozen chain he had gotten.

The Aéropostale, just to complicate matters, had only one other Potez 25 available. It was piloted by Pierre Deley, who took off for Santiago to explore the Chilean side of the range. Saint-Ex was left to probe the western slopes in an open-cockpit Laté 26 which could barely climb to 15,000 feet, well below the icy peaks towering into the blue sky above him.

The days passed, followed by freezing nights, and with each new sundown Saint-Exupéry's heart sank. Up and down the massive chain he flew, threading his way up the valleys as far as he dared go, banking steeply away from soaring cliffs, and all the time craning his neck down in the biting cold for a glimpse of his lost friend. But the snows were all bafflingly virgin, the valleys inhumanly empty, frozen into a silence of eternity. Back at Mendoza he would stagger half frozen out of his plane, only to be greeted by long faces: "The Andes, *compañero* . . ." and there would be a grave nodding of heads, ". . . in winter . . . you've no idea what it is!"

Monday passed and then Tuesday. The frontier guards paid to keep an eye on the contraband flourishing in warmer months, had nothing to report.

A flyer lost in the *cordillera*? They had seen no one. In his desperation Saint-Ex even contacted several mountain smugglers, seeking to induce them to go out on exploratory missions. *Hombre!* In the dead of winter? *No, Señor*. They'd be risking their lives, and what for? To find a corpse? "The Andes in winter don't let their victims go."

In Santiago, whither he flew to join Deley, there was the same reaction. The Chilean officers they spoke to advised them to abandon a vain quest. Even if Guillaumet had survived the crash, which was doubtful, he would have perished of cold the very first night. "Up there the night, when it catches you, turns you into ice."

Wednesday came and went without a sign of the lost flyer. That made five days. Five days in mid-winter. No one in living memory was known to have spent more than four days in the Andes and to have lived to tell the tale. There was no use insisting: Guillaumet was lost. But still they searched, with a hope born of numbed despair. Thursday passed, again with no result. What was a man, or even a plane among these monumental pyramids of ice? The spectacle of all these peaks, drawn up in their white-plumed battle-dress, was so overpowering that Saint-Ex had the impression that "a hundred squadrons flying for a hundred years could not have finished exploring this enormous chain. . . ." In a letter written to his mother not long after he spoke of the wonder with which he had watched the "birth of a snowstorm" from a generous altitude of 20,000 feet. "The peaks were spouting snow like volcanoes and it seemed to me that the entire mountain was beginning to boil. A beautiful mountain with summits 7,200 metres high (poor Mont Blanc!) and two hundred kilometres wide. As inaccessible, of course, as a fortress, at least in winter (and we're still in winter alas!) and up above it in a plane a sensation of prodigious solitude."

And so Friday dawned, greyer and more hope-drained than ever, A week to the day since Guillaumet had vanished. After a morning spent in further fruitless probing, Saint-Ex was bolting down a mournful lunch in a Mendoza restaurant when someone burst in with the news: "Guillaumet . . . Guillaumet's alive!"

Saint-Exupéry rushed out. Behind him a spontaneous cheer went up— for days the newspapers had been talking of nothing else—and friends and strangers embraced in an explosion of spontaneous joy. The incredible, the miraculous had happened!

Twenty minutes later Saint-Exupéry was in the air, with two mechanics —Avry and the same Jean-René Lefèbvre who had repaired Bourgat's Bréguet that memorable candle-lit night near Cape Bojador. The telephone call Lefèbvre had received had come from a police-station in the town of San Carlos, some distance to the south, to which the husband of the shepherd woman who had found Guillaumet had ridden to report the event. Saint-Exupéry had no map of this region, but by flying at tree top level above a dirt road he reckoned that they could not miss their bearings. And sure enough, they had not been in the air for long before they spied an unusual concentration of automobiles and horsemen on the road. The gauchos waved at them frantically as they passed overhead, and without hesitating a moment Saint-Ex "hopped" a line of poplars and came down on the nearest field, managing to stop just short of a ditch.

"No sooner had we landed" Lefèbvre recalls, "than we all ran like mad, but mad with joy, to hug Guillaumet. . . . Normally so calm, even he couldn't hold back his tears." It was an exhausted, stubbly-faced Henri around whom Saint-Ex threw his arms, a weather-beaten tramp in a borrowed overcoat and split shoes. His hollowed cheeks were creased with frostbite and fatigue, and his rough, chilblained right hand had barely the pulse of life left in it to press and express his gratitude. "What I've done," was all he could blurt out, "what I've done, I swear, no animal would have gone through".

"I could see you but you couldn't see me," Guillaumet said to him later, recalling the plane he had seen flying above him in the mountains.

"But how did you know it was me?"

"Because no one else would have dared fly so low."

As Saint-Ex sat by his friend's bedside nursing him back to health, the incredible story came out in pieces, like ice on a thawing river. Blocked by a storm which heaped fifteen feet of snow on to the Chilean slopes of the Andes, Guillaumet had given up the trans-Andean route and attempted a crossing farther south. Some days before a group of French guanaco hunters had told him of another route via the Laguna Diamante, a crater-lake some 10,000 feet up dominated by the icy cone of the Maipu volcano. He was well into the mountains flying at the Potez' maximum height of 20,000 feet when he was suddenly engulfed in a whirling blizzard. "Rolled around like a hat" —as Saint-Ex later described it—his plane kept dropping . . . dropping. . . . Thirteen, twelve, eleven thousand feet. . . All he could do was let go of the controls, hang on grimly to the cross-bars to keep his harness-straps from ripping under the strain of each new air pocket, and wait for the inevitable crash. Then suddenly, through a veil of whirling snow, he spied the inky waters of the Laguna Diamante directly beneath him. Warmed by hidden currents welling up from its volcanic depths, its dark waters never froze, providing the blinded pilot with a landmark, with something solid to cling to in this maze of scudding flakes.

The wind howled, the snow blew, but for the next hour and a half, like a kite whirling on a string, he flew round and round the rim of the dark pool

below, vainly waiting for the storm to lift. The trappers had assured him
that the lagoon's snow-covered shores were flat enough to land on, but when
he finally was forced to risk it, his wheels and propeller dug into the snow
and the tail flipped straight over his head. Thus the Potez came to rest,
upside down on the snow like a shattered insect. Using an emergency exit
panel, he dug himself a pit under one of the wings, lined the bottom with
his parachute silk, and then bedded himself down with the mailbags and food
supplies for the next forty hours. Sunday morning the sky cleared at last
and he saw a plane above him—Deley's Potez! But before he could light
the first flare it was already disappearing over the ridges. The smoke, in the
midst of all this snow, was white—as invisible from the air as his crippled
plane, with its white wings, its white fuselage, and its exposed white under-
belly.

In the Andes blizzards tend to last three to four days and to be followed
by as many days of good weather. The Mendoza plain, he reckoned, lay
forty miles to the east, but the slopes in that direction were less steep than
on the Chilean side and he would have the afternoon sun to warm his back
rather than to blind him. So he set out for Argentina, sinking with each step
into drifts from which he would have to fight his way free. Without warning
deep snow would give way to glare ice, and before he could brace himself
he would be off down the mountain. On one such slide he went for half a
mile before he was checked by a snowdrift, but without letting go of the
suitcase into which he had packed an alcohol stove, a half bottle of rum, a
packet of biscuits, and several cans of beef and sardines.

It took him all Sunday and far into that night to climb the 12,000 foot rim
of the Laguna Diamante crater. After a painful climb up a mountainside, he
found himself staring down an impassable abyss and had to back-track. His
feet started to swell and he was forced to shed his lacerated flying-boots.
He spent the second night working his way up another mountainside by the
light of the moon. To thaw his frozen feet he took refuge in a gully, removed
his shoes and warmed his toes with his woollen scarf. When too exhausted
to continue, he would sit on his suitcase for a few minutes, listening to his
erratic heartbeat, then continue. The important thing was to keep going,
keep going . . . to rest occasionally, but never for long. In *Le Grand Silence
Blanc*, a book he had recently read about Alaska, Louis-Frédéric Rouquette
had explained that one had to keep going, no matter what, or the cold would
steal up on one softly, quietly. And the next moment one was frozen. Solid.

The third day Guillaumet had to descend into a riverbed and wade
through a torrent of icy water up to his knees, then continue at night with
the aid of a flashlight until the moon rose over the frozen peaks above.
Twenty-four hours of effort during which he managed to advance exactly

two and a half miles! Burdened by the weight of his flying suit, he finally shed it.

The next day (Wednesday) he slid down the slope of a ravine, and was only stopped by a large rock. His right side was severely bruised and his flashlight and suitcase knocked from his grasp by the force of the shock. They slid on down the slope and disappeared from sight. At this point he felt the game was up. Why go on struggling? He was a goner. Without food, without a light for the darkness he could not survive another night. And how restful to lie here, quietly, serenely, without having to steel one's exhausted muscles in one more terrible effort. Even the cold now seemed a comfort as it stole over him. . . . And then he thought of his wife Noëlle . . . and of his friends. If they knew he had given up the fight like this? And like a vision from the past suddenly engulfing the mind of a drowning man, he saw the phrase in his insurance contract which specified that death could not "legally" be certified if the body could not be found: in which case his widow would have to wait four years before being able to make good her claim. Above him was a rocky ledge; if only he could reach it, his body would be safe from avalanches of thawing snow which in the springtime were likely to sweep him off this protective rock into the abyss.

Once on his feet again, he decided to carry on—past the ledge and beyond. To the point of total exhaustion. He could only limp, for one of his ankles was now severely cut, and his feet were so swollen that he had to slice open his shoes with a penknife. But on he struggled, clambering over rocks like a bear. While crossing another torrent, he was almost swept away.

Thursday. No food. Nothing but the water he managed to scoop from a mountain stream, whose downhill course he was now desperately following. He was oppressed by a sensation of immense fatigue, of mounting weakness. Reduced to eating blades of grass in an effort to gain strength. Grass? So the snows were ending. Or were they? For all was now a blur, as he staggered on. Where was he? But no, it was the sun up there ahead of him, shining on something miraculously green and no longer blindingly white. A green valley, with lingering patches of ice. He came upon some mule tracks, and their welcome sight revived the waning heartbeat within him. A refuge? A mountain hut? A rancho? He could not tell, for everything was turning, turning around him. But it was a woman, an Indian woman who was holding him by the chin and forcing a hot liquid between his cracked lips. She had taken fright on seeing this grizzly, wild eyed creature totter down the valley towards her, and taking him for a mountain brigand she had jumped on her donkey and hastened to jog away. But something in the creature's feebleness of gesture and in the oddness of its attire had impressed her young son sufficiently to stop her. The news had gone out to all the frontier posts that there was an airman lost in the mountains, for whose recovery a substantial reward was offered. "*Aviador! El aviador!*" cried the little boy, tugging at his mother's sleeve. When she finally looked back, the abominable snowman had stumbled and fallen. The leather helmet about his ears made it clear that he was not a brigand, but when he opened his mouth to speak, the only sound that came out was a rasp.

\*     \*     \*

In Mendoza the exhausted Guillaumet was put to bed, while Saint-Exupéry telephoned to his wife Noëlle in Buenos Aires to say that her husband had been found. She was to have flown up to Mendoza to join them, but at the last minute the trip was cancelled; and it was in their humble Serrito apartment that the joyful reunion took place. Saint-Ex was in such high spirits that at the end of the meal he lay down on the couch and burst into song:

> *Les filles de Camaret se disent toutes vierges*
> *Mais quand elles sont dans mon lit*
> *Elles préfèrent tenir mon vit*
> *Qu'un cierge, qu'un cierge . . .* (etc)

It was a baudy Breton fishermen's song and one of his favourites. Undaunted by the melodic gusts pouring from Saint-Ex's heaving torso, Looping, the Guillaumets' fox terrier, leaped on top of him, much to their amusement. Saint-Exupéry looked down for a moment, smiled as he reached to caress him and then let his head fall back with his nose more than ever in the air.

*M'sieur le maire de Camaret a acheté un âne* (etc)

And on it went, in mingled bursts of song and laughter, until Noëlle Guillaumet finally got up, wondering why Looping had grown so silent. While his amiable massager was bawling his melodic obscenities, the terrier had decided to have himself a meal and had already chewed up several inches of sleeve before his mistress put an end to the feast. Shaken by this sartorial disaster, Saint-Ex let the priest and the mayor and his republican ass and all the harlots in Brittany founder in mid-stanza and walked out in a huff.

But his ill-humour was short-lived. He would gladly have sacrificed all the suits and shirts he possessed to get his friend back from the icy tomb into which he had fallen. Henri was alive and it was the talk of the town.

"GUILLAUMET SAVED!" screamed the headlines, as though announcing an international event.

Mermoz was not forgotten, but a new French hero had now sprung up to share his fame. His grinning schoolboy face adorned no ashtrays or lighters, but soon by the campfires at night the gauchos of Chile were strumming a new ballad on their guitars. A ballad in gay waltztime:

*Que eres hijo de Francia has probado*
*Demostrando tu enorme valor*
*Y hoy el mundo te dice admirado*
*"Guillaumet es el gran aviador."*

*Y le hiciste la cruz a la muerte*
*Caminaste valiente, no más*
*Porque habiendo une gota de vida*
*Un Francés no se rinde jamás.**

* For you've proved by your glorious courage
The stout son of France that you are
And the world now cries out in homage
"Guillaumet, what a pilot you are!"

And to death you turned a cold shoulder
Struggling on through thick and through thin
For as long as there's breath in his body
A Frenchman will never give in.

# 11

## *Ma Sorcière*

IT took Saint-Exupéry some time to reconcile himself to his new habitat; for if he could later write to Luro Cambaceres that the fifteen months he had spent in South America were among the happiest in his life, such was not his feeling at the time. At Cape Juby there was nothing but barbed wire and a sombre flourish of Moorish tents between himself and the desert; but between himself and Argentina there was the city of Buenos Aires, which he disliked almost as cordially as he had Dakar and Casablanca. He moved into a furnished apartment in what was then the highest building in town, a kind of concrete eyrie which failed to satisfy the nightbird he was. As a nest it was high but not high enough; for though eight floors up, there were seven more above him—"with an enormous concrete city round about", as he wrote to Renée de Saussine. "I would have the same impression of lightness in the middle of the Great Pyramid. I would have the same impression of lovely walks to take. Unfortunately here there are also the Argentinians." He made allowances for his fellow pilots, to whom he was bound by the *camaraderie* of his profession, but for the rest he found the Argentinians as flamboyant, shallow and demonstrative as he had found the Moors proud, secretive, and aloof. He even found fault with the landscape, and in a letter written to his mother he advised her against making a trip to Argentina (advice she finally disregarded) on the grounds that there was no countryside for her to paint. "Beyond the sprawling city limits there are only square treeless fields, with a shack and an iron water-wheel in the middle. That's all one sees in a plane for hundreds and hundreds of kilometres."

In one respect Saint-Exupéry had not changed: he was sick for home— for his country, for his family, for his friends. Vulnerable as he was to what one might call the complex of Orpheus—unable to resist a backward glimpse at his beloved—he now looked back over his past with the same sense of loss and irretrievable nostalgia with which, after he had left it, he was to regret "his" Argentina. There was the paradise lost of his youth, so frequently evoked in his letters to his mother, and the lost Eden of "his" Sahara. Even Paris, where he had so often felt himself an outsider in those frustrating post-adolescent months, now seemed touched with gold, and forgotten were the implacable tedium of his tile-counting job and the desperation of his failure to arouse a provincial enthusiasm in the virtues of the Saurer truck. An unexpected letter from Renée de Saussine which reached him in January 1930 was enough to unleash the "invasion of a thousand adorable and forgotten things. Glasses of port, the gramophone, evening conversations after our visits to the cinema. The waiter Chez Lipp, Ségogne, and the charming misery which I regret because the days had different colours varying from the beginning to the end of the month. Each month was a beautiful adventure—and the world was magnificent because, unable to have anything, I desired everything. . . . But now that I have bought the handsome leather suitcase I dreamed about, this extra supple felt hat, and this three-handed timepiece, I have nothing left to hope for."

As usual, he was exaggerating. Financially his situation had taken a dramatic turn for the better. As Flight Director of the Aeroposta Argentina, he received a monthly salary of 25,000 francs (more than a thousand dollars) which permitted him at last to send periodic sums back to his mother, from whom he had borrowed so freely in the past. But if his "end of months" were less desperate than they once had been, sparing him a spartan diet of *croissants* and coffee, the beginning and middle of each month were as prodigal as ever. The idea of saving up for a rainy day was utterly alien to his being; a being which, as Daurat once remarked, "had a deep-seated scorn for money and an equally desperate need of it." This scorn, if not directly atavistic or aristocratic in origin, almost certainly owed something to the relatively impecunious years he had known at Le Mans, when he had had to walk every morning to school, whereas a boy like Roger de Legge, whose family fortune—it was whispered—exceeded 100 million gold francs (a colossal sum at the time), could have himself driven up to the door in a luxurious limousine driven by a Negro chauffeur. The sub-conscious, notwithstanding our best intentions, is wracked by the most fearful jealousies; and as modern psycho-analysis has shown, the complexes first formed in youth, even though suppressed, can continue to exert a subterranean influence far into adult life. Being relatively poor for the person who is not rich—and it had been Saint-Exupéry's condition for years—can easily be made the virtue of necessity; and it probably explains the condescending phrase in *Courrier Sud* according to which "Money is that which permits the conquest of goods, external agitation"—a declaration which was anything but a literary pose.

Paradoxical as it might seem, the malaise induced in him by the sudden filling of his wallet was almost as great as that he felt the moment his pocketbook was empty. The need to "burn it" as quickly and as brightly as possible was, indeed, an almost metaphysical necessity. In Paris it had taken the form of reckless invitations to champagne and caviar lunches at Prunier's; in Buenos Aires the diet was the same, but the means being substantially greater, the "external agitation" induced by a monthly flood of cash enveloped the ladies he frequented. Some years before in Toulouse he had come back one day to his lodging to find his girl friend of the moment seated quietly in a chair darning his socks. This appallingly bourgeois spectacle was too much for him, and he had promptly sent her packing. Poverty was something he preferred to endure in solitude—even though he often complained of it in public—and he was not going to have his Cinderella blackening her hands with the coal scuttle. For his friends— the finest champagne and the choicest caviar; for those he happened to be courting—the most sumptuous bouquets . . . and more; for humble as might be their provenance, he wanted them to be dressed like queens.

"He was very much the *grand seigneur*," recalls a friend who was in Buenos Aires at the time. "I remember one night when we had gone out to a nightclub restaurant called the Ermenonville. Among the dancers on the floor was a strikingly good-looking girl, tall, blond, and beautifully dressed. She turned out to be French and was employed there as an *entraîneuse*. Saint-Ex, who cared little for dancing, sat there watching, and only when we got up to leave and realized he wanted to stay on and talk to her, did we suddenly understand why it was she was so handsomely clothed."

Invariably French-speaking—for he was lazy about learning Spanish— these casual conquests tended to be tall and blond, natural for someone of his dark-haired build. One was a pretty French journalist who was heavily smitten; another was the wife of a Belgian businessman who embarrassed Saint-Exupéry one evening by coming up to him at a ball and declaring in an impassioned voice: "*Vous avez brisé mon coeur! . . . Vous êtes l'homme de ma vie!*"

Fortunately there were people among the French colony in Buenos Aires whom he found "delightful"—friends, as it happened, of the Vilmorins and to whom he was introduced by one of Louise's brothers, who was in South America at the time. "I shall certainly find others," as he wrote to his mother, "who like music and books and who will make up a bit for the Sahara. And also for Buenos Aires, which is another kind of desert." The months passed and in due course his expectations were confirmed; and out of this desert—the desert of Argentina—there blossomed two roses.

\*    \*    \*

He came upon the first by the most curious of accidents. There were fifteen airfields in the Aeroposta Argentina's network which he had to oversee; but it was also his job to prospect for secondary airstrips. One day he took off from Buenos Aires with an Argentine mechanic and headed for Concordia, some 180 miles to the north on the air route to Asunción del Paraguay. He came down not far from the city on a level piece of ground which seemed made for emergency landings. As ill luck would have it, there was a hole in the middle of the field, hidden by tufts of prairie grass, and into it, unerringly as a billiard ball, he rolled, wrecking one of his wheels. They climbed out and were examining the damage when two girls rode up on horseback. There was a brief exchange in Spanish and then, without warning, they addressed him in French. Saint-Exupéry was surprised . . . and delighted. No, they were not French but Argentine—their grandfather had come from Alsace.

"And what are you doing here—in the heart of South America?"

"We live here." They waved across the prairie grass towards a nearby hill. "And you?" they laughed.

"I'm a flyer. We were looking for an airfield, and this is the result."

They looked sadly at the tilted plane.

"We'll tell Papa," said one of them finally. "He'll come down for you in a car." And they rode off through the grass.

Their father's name was Fuchs, and in memory of his native Alsace his two daughters, like his son, had been brought up to speak French. He came down for them in an old Ford jalope, bumping through the waving grasses, and as they wound their way up the hill, an extraordinary baroque mansion came into view, girdled by stone balustrades and terraces which the burning sun had bronzed to an amber-rose patina. A sunburnt castle, visited upon this grassy height by some nostalgic settler with a head full of dreams. The place had gone to seed, in the best hidalgo tradition, and the town of Concordia had finally inherited it after the demise of its quixotic constructor. At a loss as to what to do with the stately encumbrance, the city fathers had gladly leased it to Papa Fuchs in the hope that he could keep it from going completely to pieces. He had done his best in what was only a delaying action: there were venerable fissures in the walls and venerable gaps between the polished floorboards; the woodwork was crumbling, the door-jambs were flaking, the chairs were wobbly, but everything shone as though it had just been waxed and to Saint-Exupéry, who had the soul of a bohemian, this tender solicitude and this venerable decomposition only added to the fairy-tale enchantment. What a restful change from the windblown wastes of Patagonia, this view from the terrace over the sloping grasslands and the silver green of the olives down to the sparkling blue waters of the Río Paraguay! And the library with its secret treasure of French books!

Saint-Exupéry flew back, and soon he was one of the family. The mother adored him and so did the daughters whom he playfully called his "princesses". "Be careful", he would warn them between card tricks, "or one day some horrid little husband will come along and lead you off into captivity". The two girls would nod gravely and smile, assuring him they would be careful. They were, and still are free . . . and unmarried, charmed by a phrase which had the force of a spell. Today the *castillo* of San Carlos, which was gutted some years ago, extends its roofless arms to the moon; but the memory of this "oasis", with its two "silent fairies" and the magic hole under the dining-room table where the vipers had their nest, has been preserved forever in *Terre des Hommes* (and in *Wind, Sand and Stars*).

\* \* \*

If time is such a healer of human quarrels and sorrows, it is, as a philosopher once noted, "because one changes, one is no longer the same person". Saint-Exupéry did not need to read Pascal—one of his favourites—to know that he was no longer the young man who had suffered so much in Paris. The anguish he had once felt was a spent anguish, and if it had left a mark on his soul, it was like a scar which one can still feel after it has ceased to hurt; it was like a chip in an old piece of furniture which, with the passage of the years, adds its imperfection to the rugged charm of the patina.

"I hope I shall come back to you a marriageable man", he had written to his mother from Toulouse, on the eve of his departure for Dakar. The problem had preoccupied him for years after the abortive engagement to Louise de Vilmorin, and to judge by his letters to his mother (for hers have disappeared) it was the subject of considerable correspondence between them. Time, that patient healer, had gradually soothed the wounds left by that affair and literature had done the rest. Renée de Saussine, who had unwittingly succeeded her, had proved more difficult to forgive. He had left Toulouse determined to banish her from his mind—as a punishment for her failure to reciprocate his feelings—and the days, followed by the weeks, had gone by without his putting pen to paper. And then one day, while he was in Dakar, a letter had reached him in which she had sounded a plaintive note: why had he stopped writing? "Send me quickly some more letters, I like your letters so much." Meant as encouragement, that phrase had cut him like a whiplash and frozen him into sullen silence. The idea that his letters were items in a collection, objects for the exquisite delectation of a connoisseur, was more than he could bear. It had taken him two years to get over it: two years during which he had torn up innumerable letters in a determined effort to obliterate the past. Fortunately those years had been so eventful that though the past kept knocking on the door, he could now look back on it all as though on a dream, like something which had happened to someone else and not to the person he had since become. Even the word had disappeared from his letters to his mother, and the idea of marriage, which had troubled his nights in Paris and Toulouse, now seemed to this traveller, to this restless Sinbad, of a picturesque implausibility. A blessing which might overtake him in Paris, in his own country, but not in this distant, alien land of Argentina.

The ways of Providence are mysterious and so are those of the soothsayer. His mother's brother Jacques had married a Russian, and one day in their Paris apartment a friend of hers, who was also a Russian and a palm-reader to boot, had predicted that Antoine would marry a young widow whom he would meet within the next eight days. The eight days had passed, the young widow had failed to materialize and a bemused Antoine had since had seven or eight years in which to cultivate his celibacy.

Probably the incident was not even a memory when Benjamin Crémieux turned up in Buenos Aires in the late summer of 1930. The descendant of an old Jewish family from Avignon, Crémieux had made a name for himself in the French literary world by translating Pirandello. His "sad myopic eye and his faintly Assyrian beard" to quote Nino Frank—had long been a familiar sight on the Rue de l'Odéon, where along with that other eminent translator, Valery Larbaud, he had befriended Joyce, who in turn had introduced him to the Triestine writer Italo Svevo (in real life Ettore Schmitz), one of the chief sources for the Jewish lore to be found in *Ulysses* and a model for the character of Leopold Bloom. Crémieux, who advised Gallimard on contemporary Italian writing, was one of the more international members of the *Nouvelle Revue Française* as well as a founder of the French P.E.N. Club; and it was as a kind of literary ambassador that he was sent to South America in 1930 on a lecture tour sponsored by the Alliance Francaise.

In Buenos Aires he had looked up Saint-Exupéry, whom he had got to know in Paris as a member of the *N.R.F.*; and at a literary reception which the Alliance gave in his honour he introduced his friend Tonio to Señora Gomez Carrillo, an attractive dark-haired young lady whom he had met on the ship coming over. Her husband, Enrique Gomez Carrillo, had died a few years before, leaving her an apartment in Paris, a villa in Nice, and also —which explains her coming to South America—considerable holdings in Argentina. A native of Guatemala, Gomez Carrillo had spent his youth in San Salvador—like herself—before moving on to Europe, where he had risen to become an editor of the Madrid paper *El Liberal* as well as correspondent for *A.B.C.* In Paris he had met Mata Hari—for he was a journalist with a marked taste for adventure—and he had even written a book about her which had caused him momentary trouble with the French authorities towards the close of the First World War. Not content with that, he had married the famous Spanish singer Raquel Meller (*La Violetara* and so on). It was his second marriage and while it lasted, for it finally ended in divorce, it seems to have been a tempestuous affair. At the Café Napolitain and the Cardinal, not far from the Opéra, the two spots habitually frequented by the Latin-American colony in Paris, he was known as "*el gran sablista*" (the sabre-happy duellist) for his readiness to cross swords with any critic daring to question his wife's vocal genius. When somewhat later he met Consuelo Suncín de Sandoval, he was already a white-haired man of forty-nine while she was barely seventeen—that May time in the life of so many Spanish women. Her radiant dark hair and vivacious dark eyes were irresistible—at any rate to the hot blooded adventurer—and to everyone's surprise, including perhaps her own, he married her.

Consuelo Gomez Carrillo may not have had the seductive languor of a Mata Hari, but her temperament and exotic imagination were certainly the equal of Raquel Meller's. When her husband died in 1927 she sculpted his death mask in a strange plaster (or papier-mâché) mixture which apparently acquired a mysterious after-life. Placed upon a pedestal in the small two-room flat he had left her near the Madeleine in Paris, it would startle her visitors by emitting ominous cracks "whenever Consuelo flirted or said something out of place . . . I was nineteen at the time," recalls Xenia Kouprine (the daughter of the Russian novelist Alexander Kouprine), "and she was a little older, perhaps twenty-five, though she seemed very young. She was typically South American, small, graceful, supple, with beautiful arms and hands. She had expressive black eyes that shone like stars and an adorably smooth skin."

On a large table in one of the rooms in her cluttered Paris apartment, which played host to a bohemian invasion of writers, journalists, actors, and lawyers who would troop upstairs with cheese and sausages and unceremoniously plonk themselves, their loaves of bread and bottles of wine down on to the newspapers covering the floor, was exhibited another plaster cast —of her late husband's hand. Like the mask, it too was imbued with a life of its own, for Consuelo insisted that it wrote . . . at night! "I can't say I ever actually saw it write," Xenia Kouprine admits, "but I did see a manuscript". She also saw doors which would suddenly open in the middle of the night, as though pushed open by a family spirit! The atmosphere was so charged with mysticism and her friend Consuelo's imagination so endlessly fertile that the "moment would finally come when one lost all notion of true and false".

In her wilder moments she was quite capable of saying that through her mother's family (Sandoval) she was descended from the Dukes of Toledo—a title which happens to belong to the Kings of Spain; and extravagant as it might sound, one was prepared to believe it. For nothing seemed too implausible for this extraordinary creature—a poetess who sculpted, or was it a sculptress who wrote verse?—whose fancy was as restless and as moving as the west wind and the clouds. "I come from a land of volcanoes and revolutions," she would say, and the story that followed was as revolutionary as it was volcanic. No less extraordinarily, it was never quite the same, like a sunrise refusing to parody the splendour of yesterday's dawn. As I first heard it, a good twenty years ago, from someone who had known her in New York, it was a wild birth which had coincided most awkwardly with an earthquake in her native San Salvador. A village had been engulfed, a family decimated, a hideous carpet of lava had flowed down the mountainside, and in the panic-stricken confusion of the escape the prematurely born child had had to be stung to life by wild bees, attracted to the still-born flesh by a Negro mammie and her supernatural voodoo powers. Apocryhal it almost certainly was, for the story had changed hands at least once and probably improved in the telling; but like a floodwave gathering momentum through the gorges, it bore witness to what, way back, must have been a spectacular cloudburst.

Her late husband Gomez Carrillo had, by virtue of the same tireless magic, been transmuted into an Ambassador to France. In more prosaic fact he had gone to Argentina and acquired its citizenship in order to become Argentine Consul in Paris. A prolific writer who tossed off more than a score of books in his lifetime, Gomez Carrillo had also written regular columns for two Buenos Aires papers—*La Nación* and *La Razón*—both of a more or less "liberal" persuasion, and more important (for the incidence it was to have on Saint-Exupéry's life) he had become an active member of the Radical Party which then held power in Argentina and through whose influence and patronage he had acquired considerable holdings in that country. It was, so far as one can ascertain, to look into these matters—the inheritance being disputed by an illegitimate daughter Gomez Carrillo had had by another woman—that his young widow Consuelo had decided to come to Argentina in this fateful month of September 1930.

Such was the small, vivacious person whom Benjamin Crémieux now introduced to Saint-Exupéry. Like many other French pilots, he had found the social life of the Argentine capital a constricting change from the freer atmosphere of Paris. An almost Spanish severity maintained the public separation of the sexes, and even in the most fashionable bar in town there was a *salón para caballeros* for the men and a *salón para la familia* to which women were admitted if they came with their husbands. The bikini, of course, was unknown and at Mar de la Plata, southeast of Buenos Aires, men were obliged to wear a kind of skirt, like a Scotsman's kilt, above their bathing trunks. Puritanism had no part in Saint-Ex's make-up and for someone who had known the wild Paris of the twenties, these taboos were particularly irksome. He found it simpler to cultivate the French colony in Buenos Aires, where he was spared the pains of having to master a new language.

It was thus with a surprise verging on delight that he made the acquaintance of Consuelo Gomez Carrillo, who chattered away at him in a brittle but extraordinarily picturesque French which amused him no end. She was dark and petite—not his type at all—but there was a wild beauty in her dark eyes and a wild wind in her speech which held him spellbound. So he was an *aviateur?* How marvellous! How wonderful it must be to look down on the earth from up there, how small, how strange everything must look! But alas, she had never been up in a plane.

"Then I shall take you up," cried Saint-Exupéry. "It will be your baptism of the air, and I shall be your parent, your godfather, and your priest."

She was delighted. Why not? She was not an Argentinian and there was no family *dueña* or jealous husband to interfere with the fun.

Saint-Ex was as good as his word. They drove out to Pacheco, where he took her up in a Laté 25, making sure she was carefully strapped into the seat next to his. A few thousand feet up, he said to her with a grin: "Now I shall show you what this plane can do." And with that he put the plane through a series of sharp banks and glides which utterly unnerved her. "Stop! Stop!" she cried. "Please, please!" But the game continued, and with each swoop she grew more frightened. "Please . . . please . . ."

"All right," said Saint-Exupéry. "I'll stop—if you promise to be mine . . ."

He reduced the speed of the motor and pushed forward on the stick. The nose of the plane went down and to Consuelo's horror the earth started coming up at them, growing larger with each terrifying second. "Stop!" she wailed, "stop!"

"Say 'yes'," shouted Saint-Ex, who was enjoying himself hugely.

"*Oui, oui, oui!*" she cried, covering her eyes.

He pulled back on the stick and the sky, which had disappeared over their heads, dropped gently back into place. Ouf! They were saved. He gave her a broad dimpled grin, but it was not until they had landed that she was prepared to smile again.

With the passage of the years this episode, which is true and no figment of the imagination, likewise developed a venerable patina. Not long ago I heard an amusing version of it—according to which the plane included not only

Saint-Ex and Consuelo but also a number of startled passengers and, as luck would have it, a priest who to appease the dare-devil pilot agreed to wed them on the spot—which is to say in mid-air! This is an amusing example of the telescoping of reality. There were only two of them in the plane for this strange baptism of the air, but it did end in marriage. Probably neither had much inkling of what lay in store at first, and certainly not Saint-Ex who only meant it as a joke. But three days later one of those revolutions which she had talked about in her native San Salvador overtook the sister republic of Argentina. The Radical party to which her late husband had belonged was rudely unhorsed by a conservative general named José Evarista Uriburu, and from one day to the next Gomez Carrillo's properties were confiscated by the new masters of the country. His widow suddenly found herself practically without a penny—in an alien country, far from home. Feeling himself responsible—he had after all asked her to be his—Saint-Exupéry took pity on her plight, and stretching out his arm, he took her under his wing.

Several months later Consuelo sailed back to Europe, while Tonio stayed on in Buenos Aires to greet his mother, who took the ship from Marseille in mid-December. Anxious to know if she had made it safely aboard the *Flandre*, he put in a long distance call from Buenos Aires to the Marseille town-house of one of his Fonscolombe cousins: the call was received by his sister Gabrielle in the concierge's lodge (where the telephone was located) and it caused quite a sensation. His mother spent that Christmas on the high seas and the New Year was already upon them when she finally tripped down the gangplank on to the Buenos Aires dock. January—the Argentine mid-summer. To amuse her Antoine flew her up to Asunción, 600 miles to the north, but she was so sickened by gas fumes and the smell of oil that she barely had the strength to climb out of the plane, looking "utterly wrinkled and exhausted". It took her three days to recuperate in a delightful hotel, where she drank iced pineapple juice (for the weather was very hot) and painted a lovely landscape of green palm-trees and red earth.

After six weeks spent in Argentina, she embarked with Tonio for the voyage home. They were accompanied by a small puma, which he insisted on bringing back as a "present" for his younger sister Gabrielle. He took it for daily walks on the deck, keeping it on a tight leash in his strong hands. At night, instead of going to bed, he would sit down to work at a novel he had been writing for most of the past year. Often at 3 or 4 in the morning he would rouse his sleeping mother, just as the little Tonio had once woken his protesting sisters at Saint-Maurice-de-Rémens. His mother would protest once again, but always in vain: he had to read her what he had just written; and while she blinked pathetically at the light, he would say: "Yes, Mama, but it's under the shock of awakening that one's mind is most alert." She may have thought differently, but her son's need of attention was as tyrannical as ever. And as usual, he had the last word.

At Cadiz he disembarked to join Consuelo, while his mother was left to cope with the puma, which was soon tugging her all over the deck. One day the animal got loose and bit an officer in the leg. The Captain took a dim view of the assault and Tonio's harassed mother was finally persuaded to sell the embarrassingly wild cat to a breeder of chipmunks who happened to be on board. Gabrielle, probably to her relief, never saw the "present" her brother had been so intent on foisting upon her.

Consuelo, meanwhile, had returned to Paris, where Xenia Kouprine one day got a telephone call from her, anxiously beseeching the young film actress to come to see her quickly . . . because something dreadful had happened! On reaching her apartment on the Rue de Castellane, Xenia found her dressed in black. The light had gone out of her eyes and her face was red from weeping. She was desperate, she told her young friend in what the latter has described as her "telegraphic" style. In South America she had met the most wonderful man, who had saved her from fear and despair. "You know, I was alone, in the mountains . . . lost . . . in danger . . . it was dark. . . . And then he came, big, strong, and beautiful. . . . He took me away and saved me . . ." But not for long . . . for a revolution had broken out and—oh horror!—he had been shot before her eyes! "And his scarlet blood flowed over the white stones in the blinding sunlight . . ."

If Xenia Kouprine is to be believed, Consuelo at this point was ready to take her life. Apparently—her young friend only discovered this later—some grave misunderstanding had cropped up between Consuelo and Antoine, reducing her to this pass. She was prevailed upon to move out to a bungalow by the lake of Enghien, north of Paris, where Xenia Kouprine spent three agitated days trying to keep her from opening her veins or swallowing poison.

The third day, however, a telegram arrived and suddenly a radiant Consuelo was dancing about like a bird.

"What's up?" asked Xenia. "What is it?"

"He's coming!" cried Consuelo, waving the telegram.

"Who's coming?"

"He, him, the man I love!"

"But you told me they shot him in front of your eyes!"

"Oh, you know," answered Consuelo lightly, "I didn't want to love him . . . and I thought he had left me and been unfaithful to me. And so I imagined him dead."

Both she and Tonio were very much alive when they met in Madrid and took the train back to Paris. Here she was introduced to his friends, some of whom, familiar with Tonio's tastes, had trouble believing he could seriously be contemplating marriage to someone so curiously petite and dark. And then, she was not French but Latin-American! His aunt Anaïs, who had been lady-in-waiting to the Duchesse de Vendôme, wanted to have the wedding announcements printed up in Paris, but Tonio had set his mind on a marriage in Provence. The idea appealed to Consuelo, who was anxious to revisit her villa in Nice.

After several days in the capital, during which Antoine had time to show the manuscript of his new novel to Gaston Gallimard, they boarded the train for the Riviera. At Agay, on the Esterel, his sister Gabrielle and her husband Pierre were waiting to greet them in the old square-walled castle on the point which Antoine loved so much. Originally built as a fort according to a design of Vauban's, it had long been the residence of the governors whose duty it was to guard this stretch of coast from the incursions of Barbary pirates; but the eighteenth-century windows which had been pierced in the rose-hued walls had turned it into a charming Provençal mansion. A fine dinner was given in Consuelo's honour, and Tonio, normally so bohemian, insisted on its being as elegant as possible—with nothing but the finest in silver and crystal.

The rest of this month (March) was spent commuting between Agay and Cimiez, the residential suburb above Nice where was located the villa, with its enchanting little garden, which Consuelo had inherited from Enrique Gomez Carrillo. There was a garden party at Agay, to which everyone of importance in the village was invited and at which their betrothal was officially announced. As luck would have it, it was a beautiful spring. Yvonne de Lestrange, who was holidaying on the Riviera with her son, came over to see them, as did her friend André Gide, who happened to be spending a few days in Agay. She had first met Gide during his visit to the Congo in 1926, at a time when she was working as a bacteriologist for the Pasteur Institute; and they had even travelled on a river steamer together up as far as the Ubangui. It was the beginning of a friendship which brought him frequently to the little apartment on the Quai Malaquais, where Antoine had been introduced to him in the spring of 1929, during one of his periodic escapes from the Celestial Navigation Course in Brest.

Tonio now brought over the manuscript of the new novel he had been working on in Argentina, and it was at the Hôtel de la Baumette, where Gide was staying, that he read *Vol de Nuit* (*Night Flight*) to him in several long sittings. Over the dinner table at the château, where Gide was a guest for meals, Antoine talked to him for hours about his experiences in South America. Gide was so enthralled that on returning to Marseille a day or two later he devoted several pages of his Journal to Tonio's graphic account of

Guillaumet's adventure in the Andes. He was also impressed by the new novel, noting in his Journal in his usual dry style: "Great pleasure seeing Saint-Exupéry again at Agay, where I spent several days with P. Had been in France barely a month. From Argentina he's brought back a new book and a new fiancée. Read the one, saw the other. Congratulated him warmly; but for the book in particular. I hope the fiancée proves as satisfactory."

The wedding was held a few weeks later (April 12th) in the chapel at Agay, reached by a footbridge spanning the cutting of the railroad tracks. At Antoine's urgent request his old schoolteacher and mentor, Abbé Sudour of the Ecole Bossuet, journeyed down from Paris to wed them, sending him off into matrimony just as five years before he had helped launch him on a new career with Latécoère. The weather was flawless and the sun sparkled gaily on the water. The bridegroom looked very happy in his dark double-breasted suit, exhibiting a quaintly avuncular solicitude for his two tiny nieces (Didi's daughters) who gripped two bridal bouquets in their little clenched fists. Instead of a white veil Consuelo wore a mantilla, and the roses in her dark hair made her look more than usually dazzling. The garden and the château terrace, where they posed for the photographer, were heady with the scent of flowers, there was laughter in the air, and at the luncheon which followed at the Roches Rouges—Agay's finest gastronomic establishment, where the chef did his Provençal best to rise to the occasion—even the sceptics pretended to be enchanted by the bride's exotic looks and speech.

The honeymoon was spent at Agay, with occasional trips to Cimiez and Beaulieu (just beyond Nice), where Consuelo introduced her new husband to the playwright Maurice Maeterlinck, whose actress wife had been a friend of hers and of Gomez Carrillo. While her volubility exasperated some, it enchanted others, and there was even a dinner where Consuelo was so irresistibly droll—among other things, she got up and did an imitation dance in the middle of it—that the host, who had long been plunged in a state of deep depression, ended up laughing like his guests till tears came into his eyes.

Just why this vivacious "*oiseau des îles*"—this island bird from the tropics —had chosen to settle on Tonio no one quite knew. An accident of fate? A stroke of destiny? Who could tell? But she, at any rate, was sure it was predestined. A soothsayer back in her native San Salvador had predicted it all, her entire life, before laying eyes on her. He was a strange little fellow who had insisted on living outside the village under a large tree. To those who asked him why he chose such a singular habitation, he would reply "because of the lightning". For if ever he moved, it would strike him dead. People shook their heads and went their way, but one day, during a storm, he came out from under his tree and was struck dead by a thunderbolt.

Saint-Exupéry himself did not seem to know quite what to make of her. Was she fire or was she water? The sun or the moon? She seemed to embrace all the elements and all the moods. Changing? Like the tide. Capricious? Like any woman. Unpredictable? That was part of her charm. Fascinating? Beyond a doubt. Her name was Consuelo—"consolation" in Spanish—but as often as not he called her "*mon poussin*"—my chick. Next to his huge bulk she looked so small, so fragile; and one day in a playful mood he called her his "*papavéracée*"—the family poppies belong to. She retaliated by calling him "*Papou*" and the name so delighted Didi's children that from then on he was known as *l'Oncle Papou*.

But there were other names, for neither of them was lacking in imagination. Once, after a mysterious absence of three days Tonio received an unsigned telegram from some remote village in the Alps which read: "Don't you hear the jingle-bell of your little lost lamb?" They had been expected to lunch at an aeroplane manufacturer's, but in the end Antoine turned up alone. He arched his eyebrows and shrugged his shoulders in a helpless gesture. Consuelo? He had no idea what had become of her. And he added with a disarming smile: "*J'ai perdu ma sorcière.*" My sorceress! And as his friend Henri Jeanson was later to remark, no one knew which of the two it was who had bewitched the other.

# 12

# Into the Night

---

ON the 11th of March, 1931, a few days after Saint-Exupéry's return to France and a bare month before his marriage, three of the Bouilloux-Lafont banks which had been financing the Aéropostale were forced to close their doors in an effort to halt a massive run on their deposits. A communiqué issued at the end of a long directors' meeting explained that they had been driven to this extreme by the French government's unwillingness to ratify the "conventions" which the Air Ministry had signed with the Compagnie Générale Aéropostale and which would have permitted the three banks to recoup most of the 70 million francs they had invested in the airline. In effect, the momentary suspension of operations and the banks' refusal to continue financing the Aéropostale amounted to a declaration of bankruptcy.

The news hit pilots and ground crews like a thunderbolt, spreading dismay and consternation up and down the line; for virtually no one—from Toulouse to Santiago—had had the slightest warning of the storm into which the Aéropostale was now suddenly plunged.

Unlike Pierre Latécoère, whom he had bought out in 1927, Marcel Bouilloux-Lafont had always been involved in politics, and the score of enterprises he had built up in South America—embracing banks, ports, roads and railroads before he added aviation—had all been developed with the help of official contracts obtained from this or that government. Years of pioneering effort in the tropics had convinced him of the truth of Robert Walpole's dictum that "every man has his price" and induced an excessive reliance on the persuasive *propina*. "If you want to succeed in this country," he had said to Prince Charles Murat (who headed the first Latécoère mission to South America) one day in 1924 as they were having a drink in a Rio de Janeiro hotel, "you must have a revolver in one pocket and a newspaper in the other". A revolver to intimidate one's enemies, a newspaper to anticipate the latest speculative possibilities on the stock market and, no less important, to know which were the influential palms which might have to be greased tomorrow.

Nothing is more potentially deluding than success, and an unbroken series of successes in South America had ended up persuading Bouilloux-Lafont that what was good for Brazil or Uruguay must also be good for France. To succeed in business one needed to have political backing, and this he was confident of having obtained in 1928 when his brother Maurice was appointed Vice President of the French Chamber of Deputies as well as chairman of its Military Affairs Committee.

Profitable though his Latin American enterprises were, they were unable to cover the immense costs involved in the development of the Aéropostale, whose operations now spanned three continents and an ocean. The French government's subsidy, averaging out at roughly 22 francs for every kilometre flown, fell far short of covering the equipment of new airfields, the purchase and operation of ocean-going vessels (for the South Atlantic), to say nothing of the Laté 28s which were ultimately due to replace them. Still more money was required if the airline was to go on expanding, but the hard pressed banks could no longer provide the needed capital. It would have to come from the government, which meant some degree of outside interference, or from a loan. Bent on remaining the master of what he had bought up and expanded, Marcel Bouilloux-Lafont rejected a series of government proposals aimed at reducing his own holdings in the Aéropostale in favour of the French state's. Instead, he undertook to launch a 200 million franc loan which was purported (quite fancifully, as it happened) to have been "approved" by the Air Ministry and to enjoy the backing of the state.

Age often induces a hardening of the character as well as of the arteries, and at sixty-eight Marcel Bouilloux-Lafont had turned into a truculent white-haired old man. Whenever he turned up at Fouquet's, the swank Champs-Elysées restaurant that was patronized by Boni de Castellane, Philippe de Rothschild, the flamboyant Ettore Bugatti, members of the Jockey Club, real and fake countesses, and all those who in this age of waning elegance were as impeccably bowler-hatted as they were richly gloved and fanned, the waiters, on a signal from the *maître d'hôtel*, would line up in a row, their white napkins over their sleeves, as though presenting arms for a visiting monarch. It was a reassuring scene, but not one made to quicken a sense of modesty which was as alien to Marcel Bouilloux-Lafont's imperious nature as it was to that of his son André, who—unfortunately for both—had inherited copiously of his father's conceit but very little of his flair. Maurice Bouilloux-Lafont was head of the Chamber of Deputies' Military Affairs Committee, and the Finance Minister in the Pierre Laval government which took office in January 1931 was Pierre-Etienne Flandin, who in the past had acted as legal adviser for one of Bouilloux-Lafont's Latin American concerns. With this kind of support he assumed—rashly, as it turned out—that he had no need to change his high-handed ways and that the government would in the end agree to underwrite the loan he had so brazenly launched.

It was a catastrophic miscalculation. The France of this period was still the thrifty, penny-pinching France of Raymond Poincaré; and though the doughty Lorrainer had just fallen from power, his belief in financial integrity and circumspection was still shared (though not always practised) by most of the dominant bourgeoisie. It was shared in particular by Jacques-Louis Dumesnil, the Air Minister, and by his able assistant, Emmanuel Chaumié, the Director of Civil Aviation, who felt, not unreasonably, that if the Ministry was going to underwrite the Aéropostale's operations, it had a right to have a look at its books. To the Bouilloux-Lafonts, used to fewer scruples abroad, this seemed like an intolerable intrusion into family matters. An unpleasant tug-of-war ensued which built up into a crisis when two inspectors Chaumié had sent to South America to look into the Aéropostale's situation, returned to Paris with a rather critical report which revealed, among other things, that the capital holdings of a country bank in the *département* of the Eure-et-Loir had been used by Bouilloux-Lafont to buy land and shares in South America. When the simple-minded provincials discovered the profitable use to which their savings had been put, they made a rush on the bank, which had to close its doors. Already hard hit by the 1929 Crash, other banks were unwilling to come to the rescue, and the Bouilloux-Lafonts soon found themselves embarrassingly short of liquid cash. Their decision to suspend operations in three of their Paris banks was, in effect, a final desperate attempt to blackmail the French government into coming to the rescue. But the government refused to be panicked and the crisis was on.

Delighted to have a weapon with which to bludgeon the Laval government, the left-wing press seized on the "scandal" to demand the expropriation of the owners and the nationalization of the Aéropostale. In the Chamber of Deputies Jacques Doriot, the Communist, and Léon Blum, the Socialist, rose in righteous wrath to denounce the "conflict of interest" involved in the Finance Minister's links with Bouilloux-Lafont; and though Flandin and Laval displayed sufficient sang-froid to heap ridicule on their adversaries, their purely forensic victory did little to alleviate the plight of the Aéropostale, now caught in the cross-fire of partisan polemics.

By the time Saint-Exupéry reported back for service in May, after a two month leave of absence, the confusion within the Aéropostale had reached unprecedented heights. Many pilots had continued flying though they had not been paid for weeks. No one knew any more just who was boss—least of all Daurat, who had had a falling out in his turn with the Bouilloux-Lafonts.

One day, in Toulouse, Daurat had received a telephone call from Chaumié, the director of Civil Aviation, asking him to come up immediately to Paris. At the Air Ministry he had been taken in to see Jacques-Louis Dumesnil, the Minister. "What we are afraid of," Dumesnil had explained to him, "is that the Bouilloux-Lafonts will simply close down the airline and suspend all operations. This must be avoided at all costs. We'll advance you the funds needed to keep going, month by month, but what we want from you is a pledge that you'll keep the line going."

Daurat, who had no desire to see twelve years of heroic effort simply flushed down the drain, immediately gave his word: he would carry on in Toulouse as though nothing had happened.

On emerging from the Minister's office, shaken by what he had just learned, he had a moment of hesitation. Should he or should he not call on Bouilloux-Lafont, his hierarchical superior, and inform him of this conversation? Finally he decided against it. Dumesnil and Chaumié had become such *bêtes noires* for the Bouilloux-Lafont clan that if they learned that Daurat had been to see them, there would be a terrible scene. So he took the train back to Toulouse.

Hardly was he back when the telephone rang in his office. This time it was André Bouilloux-Lafont on the line. "You must come up to Paris," he said. "There are problems that have got to be talked over." So Daurat took the train back to the capital. When he was ushered into the vast presidential office on the Boulevard Haussmann, both Marcel Bouilloux-Lafont and his son André were on hand to greet him. The reception was glacial.

"You have been to see Dumesnil at the Ministry," cried the sexagenarian, shaking an accusing finger and a shock of angry white hair.

"Yes," answered Daurat, wondering just who had tipped him off. There were Bouilloux-Lafont spies even in the Air Ministry. "I was asked to remain at my post and to keep the airline going—that was all. I promised I would."

But the old man refused to be appeased. All this, he thundered, was part of a plot in which Daurat was secretly conniving. Dumesnil had tried to win him over to use against him. Dumesnil was in cahoots with Pierre Latécoère, and the object of the manoeuvre was to get rid of him, Marcel Bouilloux-Lafont, and to reinstate Latécoère (who still owned 7% of the Aéropostale's stock) as the airline's chairman. Hardly believing his ears, Daurat denied the charges and vainly sought to belittle the accusations.

"When Latécoère sold me the airline in 1927," Bouilloux-Lafont finally exploded, "the only element of value he sold me was yourself. Today, in this affair, you are my greatest disappointment."

What was Daurat to say? For a man who had conceived a belated passion for aviation at the age of 62 and who had invested vast sums of time and money in it, this was an astonishing statement. Particularly for someone who had developed a personal fondness for Jean Mermoz, who had piloted him all over South America: Jean Mermoz, now consigned to the dustbin as worthless!

The debate went on in this acrimonious vein for two entire days. Daurat was wined and dined at Fouquet's as the two Bouilloux-Lafonts sought to pressure him and Mermoz into making a broadcast over Radio Paris (a private station) attacking Dumesnil. Daurat refused. He had never taken part in cabals and he was not going to begin now. Mermoz, who asked him what he should do, was given the same advice. The Aéropostale stood to gain nothing by being involved in plots and vendettas. Mermoz, who respected Daurat almost as much as did Saint-Exupéry, took the advice and refused in turn. He went back to his seaplanes while Daurat returned to Toulouse.

"You will see what I'm capable of!" were Marcel Bouilloux-Lafont's parting words as they took leave of one another. It did not take Daurat long to feel the force of this threat. Ever since his period of captivity with the Moors—back in 1928—Edouard Serre had harboured a simmering hatred for Daurat who, he was convinced, had allowed him to languish for four months in the hands of his captors before making any serious effort to have him freed. An electronic technician who had been appointed head of the Aéropostale's radio communications service, Serre was something of a crack-pot the moment he stepped beyond the boundaries of his particular speciality. For the length of his captivity he had only himself to blame: one of his first acts on being made prisoner had been to write letters to his "friends"—for he was a rabid socialist—Vincent Auriol and Léon Blum. The letters had been brought by a Moorish emissary to Colonel de la Peña at Cape Juby, who had sent them on to Madrid. This appeal to two prominent French "Reds", far from cutting any ice with the conservative government of Alfonso XIII, had only encouraged Madrid to muddy the waters still further. The suggestion relayed back to the Moors was—agree to the liberation of Serre and Reine in exchange for twenty Moorish prisoners who had been captured by the French *méharistes* of Atar and Port Etienne; or ten Moors for one Frenchman. It had taken the French—and that meant the Quai d'Orsay, among others—three full months of haggling to scale these demands down to something more reasonable. Daurat had played only a minor part in these negotiations, with which Beppo de Massimi in Madrid was far more directly concerned; but Serre had concluded quite irrationally that it was all Daurat's fault.

Serre's dislike was also fed by a feeling of frustrated superiority. He was a graduate engineer of the prestigious Ecole Polytechnique in Paris, whereas all Daurat could boast was a diploma with the Ecole d'Horlogerie et de Mécanique. Yet within the Aéropostale it was Daurat who was really "*le Patron*", the Boss. Though Serre's radio communication service was independent of Daurat's administrative control, limited to pilots and mechanics, it was Daurat, who had been with the airline from the beginning, who enjoyed all the prestige and most of the authority. There had been growing tension for some time between the two services—the radio communication service on the one hand and Daurat's *Service d'Exploitation* on the other—and the previous summer (1930) Serre had asked Roger Beaucaire, an engineer who worked for the main Aéropostale office in Paris, to broach the matter to his friend, André Bouilloux-Lafont, who was slowly taking over the reins from his father. Beaucaire did so, only to get this astonishing reply: "Look, I haven't time to concern myself with these kitchen quarrels. The chef wants one thing, the chauffeur wants another—I'm not going to get involved in these petty squabbles."

That had been before the crisis had come to a head in March 1931 and Marcel Bouilloux-Lafont had accused Daurat of betrayal. Serre may at one time have thought of resigning, but the situation now was dramatically changed. Taking advantage of his rival's fall from favour, Serre pressed for a general wage rise throughout his department. He was a socialist, whereas Daurat was a conservative, if not a "fascist", and now at last he could prove the superiority of his ideological convictions. This was hardly the moment for the Aéropostale to add to its operating costs, but André Bouilloux-Lafont was willing to endorse Serre's proposal. It was time to favour the chauffeur since the chef had failed them, and much as he disliked "kitchen politics", perhaps this sop thrown to a socialist who was on such good terms with Blum and Auriol could serve to persuade the latter to call off their parliamentary dogs.

If such was the calculation, it was once again misguided. Within the Aéropostale Serre's wage rise brought on chaos. Veteran mechanics were incensed to find their earnings frozen while radio technicians who had served for fewer years were awarded generous advances. Overnight what had once been a closely knit unit, animated by a genuine esprit de corps and spirit of self-sacrifice, was transformed into a hornets' nest of animosities and grievances, a warring camp of cliques and clans. Didier Daurat was no longer master of his ship, now cleft in twain, as he was later to write, by "two policies, two leaderships, two states of mind".

To save the enterprise from foundering completely a "committee of liquidation" was set up, composed of four members headed by Raoul Dautry, an enterprising engineer who had made himself a reputation running the *Chemins de Fer de l'Etat* and who went on (later) to unify the French railway system. His stewardship brought only a momentary respite, for by this time the worm was in the apple. A policy of rigorous retrenchment was introduced and the Aéropostale's operations were henceforth limited to the Toulouse–Buenos Aires–Santiago de Chile run. The projected hook-ups between Chile, Peru, Bolivia, Argentina and Paraguay were abandoned, as was the mail service scheduled to span the vast rain forests and highlands of Brazil. In Venezuela Paul Vachet managed to keep the airline going with local government support, but the service from Natal to the French Antilles islands was sacrificed. Left to fend for itself, the Aeroposta Argentina had to suspend the Patagonian service, which Saint-Exupéry had laboured so hard to develop; and only the following October was it resumed, when the company—now wholly Argentine—was renamed the Aeroposta Nacional. Within a matter of weeks the strenuous efforts of half a dozen years were reduced to nothing and the Aéropostale ceased, virtually overnight, to be the leading airline in the world.

Marcel Bouilloux-Lafont may not have had the energetic genius of a Ferdinand de Lesseps, but the catastrophe which overtook the Aéropostale bore a distressing resemblance to the Panama scandal. For Saint-Exupéry it could hardly have come at a more awkward moment. He now had a wife to support—just when the post he had recently occupied in Argentina had ceased to exist. Mermoz, alarmed by the disaster which had overtaken the company, had also made a beeline for Toulouse, where Guillaumet, who had not flown since mid-April, joined them. All three of them were present on June 15 when Raoul Dautry came down from Paris on an inspection tour with André Bouilloux-Lafont. To Dautry's question: "What improvements would you like to see?" Mermoz, speaking for all three, replied: "Nothing —except to retain Monsieur Daurat. For then the improvements will come of themselves."

If Dautry, a capable and honest man, had been completely free to act, this is what he might have done. Unfortunately, he knew nothing about aeronautics and he felt forced to heed the counsels of André Bouilloux-Lafont, who was also a member of the "Committee of Liquidation". And André Bouilloux-Lafont was out to get even with Daurat, no matter what.

A sensational new charge was now trumped up against Daurat by two pilots whom he had dismissed for professional failings and a telephone operator whom Serre had just appointed Secretary General of the central office in Toulouse. Daurat, they claimed, was a pyromaniac who had sat up many a night in Toulouse burning instead of delivering the mail. They could vouch for what they said, for they had seen him at it—with their own eyes! The charge was grotesque, but in the impassioned climate of the moment, it was enough to make the headlines and to raise a new clamour from the baying bloodhounds of the left-wing press. The Moors, whenever they captured an Aéropostale plane, first fell on the mailbags, out of which they could cut themselves burnouses. Next they would slit open the envelopes in the hope of finding money, scattering everything that failed to interest them to the winds. What letters it could recuperate, the Aéropostale brought back to Toulouse, where they were turned over to the local post office. Daurat had nothing to do with the ultimate fate of such missives; but with his usual thoroughness in foreseeing accidents, he had stuck envelopes together and then plunged them into water or put a match to them to see how best they might resist the perils of fire and sea. These were the pyrotechnic sessions this criminal had secretly indulged in! Absurd? For Saint-Ex, as for Guillaumet and Mermoz and most of their fellow pilots, they were utterly unbelievable. But not for Daurat's enemies now led by André Bouilloux-Lafont. Shocked by such vindictive pettiness Beppo de Massimi, the Aéropostale's General Manager, resigned. Daurat—over the vain protests of Mermoz, Guillaumet, and Saint-Exupéry—was fired.

It was a shock to all of them suddenly to find themselves on their own, no longer guided by the *Patron* they had served so eagerly for years. But they were too attached to the Aéropostale to be prepared to give up there and then. The accusations against Daurat were too fatuous to be upheld in a court of law, and probably they hoped that once they were exposed for what they were—calumnies and lies—Daurat would be reappointed to his post. So they went back to their piloting, little realizing the devastating havoc which the blindness of André Bouilloux-Lafont was still to visit on the company.

From Toulouse Saint-Exupéry was sent to Casablanca, where Consuelo joined him a little later, flown down in her turn by the company. Tonio was already on the job, off piloting the Dakar mail, when she arrived, and she found herself at the Hôtel Excelsior having to lunch alone. Attracted by her vivacious dark looks, a Frenchman seated at the next table engaged her in conversation and was much amused when she said, as though it were the most natural thing in the world: "I have come from the sky, and the stars are my sisters."

Saint-Exupéry's job, which had changed like his status, was to fly the Dakar-bound mail over the central stretch of the African run. Instead of the Bréguet 14, which he had once flown in daytime, he now piloted a Laté 26, taking off from Casablanca around 4 o'clock in the afternoon. He would touch down at Agadir shortly before sunset, and the rest of the flight would be done by the light of the moon or the stars. Port Etienne, the terminus, would heave into view at dawn, just as the huge orange globe of the sun began to rise over the rosy dunes to the east.

Usually his only companion was the radio operator, who sat in the open cockpit behind him, taking down the messages he received through his earphones and passing them up to Saint-Ex on slips of paper, which could be read by the light of the instrument panel. Open to the four winds, the Laté 26 was not built to transport passengers. But there were occasional exceptions; as happened one hot July afternoon when Saint-Ex walked into the dispatcher's office at the Casablanca airfield only to be informed that this time he was to carry a passenger.

"What?" cried Saint-Exupéry. "I'm being landed with a passenger for the flight over the desert? And at night?"

"I have orders," answered Julien, the *chef d'aéroplace*. "From Paris."

"But a passenger, that's one hundred litres less fuel—with the loss of more than one hour's flying time. If we run into mist, we risk running out of fuel and then what will become of the mail?"

Julien made a helpless gesture. Those were the orders, he could do nothing about them. It was at that moment, as the prospective passenger later described the scene, that the pilot suddenly spotted him. "He examined me as though he were weighing me, curious to know what odds my weight stacked up against the mail. A few minutes later, seated on a crate and holding on to the cross-bars, I saw the white terraces of the Moroccan city disappear behind us. Up front Saint-Exupéry hid the instrument panel with his bulk, occasionally turning round towards the radio operator seated next to me."

The passenger was Jean-Gérard Fleury, a young journalist who was on his way to South America to write a series of articles on the Aéropostale. At Agadir they took on a Schleu interpreter, and a little later as the sun sank, Fleury watched in fascination as an arabesque of shadows moved gorily across the sands: a caravan of camels plodding their way down the coast. "And suddenly night fell, dense and hostile. My eyes, ill accustomed to this blind flight, could barely make out the thin, pale line of the surf separating the two equally dark immensities of ocean and desert. By the light of an exhaust-pipe hooked to the wing Abdallah, the Schleu, watched me, flames darting across his shining eyes."

A rectangle of red field-lamps marked the emplacement of the Cape Juby airstrip. They had hardly touched down when to Fleury's astonishment a troop of tall Moors, draped and veiled in blue, hurried up to Saint-Exupéry, seizing his hand and raising it to their dusty lips. "*Labès*," answered

Saint-Ex, who seemed more embarrassed than pleased to receive this desert homage. "All followed him in silence as far as the shack, where we went to drink a glass of water, that precious water which a steamer brings once a fortnight from the Canaries. While one of the Moors, squatted before a flickering red grate, poured oil and broke eggs into a pan for a hasty meal, other veiled men came hurrying up. After observing a long moment of respectful silence, the veiled warriors suddenly broke into speech, punctuated by expressive gestures. Saint-Exupéry listened to them, nodding his head, silencing this one, pointing to another to speak, like a caid among tribal chieftains."

So it looked to an outsider, for whom all this was strange and exciting. To Saint-Exupéry, however, it was routine—like the clouds into which they plunged shortly after leaving Juby. "Often, as we pitched and rolled in the storm,"—this is Fleury writing—"I saw the faint landmark of the surf disappear. But then the sky cleared and the desert was dotted with flickering lamps—the fires of nomad encampments."

On his return to Casablanca, Saint-Ex would find Consuelo waiting for him with Dr. Henri Comte and his wife—friends who had been recommended to him by the daughter of a French senator from Lyon. The Comtes occupied a villa in the hilly suburb of Anfa, but as often as not they would meet up at a sea-side *bistrot* called "Chez Zézé", where two mechanical pianos were ready to spring noisily to life at the drop of a fisherman's coin. It amused Tonio to maintain the honky-tonk atmosphere for as long as he could, but his reserves of change exhausted, he would finally dip into his own slightly more sophisticated repertory of old French folksongs; and out would come a quaint ballad about a pretty girl who seduces a poetic cobbler (*Aux Marches du Palais*)—in those "good old days" when all the King's horses could drink from his village stream and four periwinkle clusters beflower the corners of his bed.

Between bouts of singing Saint-Exupery would entertain them with descriptions of his latest experiences in the air, groping, as he talked, for the words needed to convey these new and unfamiliar sensations. How easy, how effortless it all sounded years later when, in *Terre des Hommes* (*Wind, Sand, and Stars*), the reader found himself reliving one of these tense, uncertain moments—like the memorable night (in October 1931) when Saint-Ex and Jacques Néri, his little Corsican radio operator, suddenly found themselves hopelessly off course and far out over the Atlantic as they were flying south west towards Villa Cisneros. It was the hour of the setting moon, which meant that in addition to going deaf (the radio stations, disoriented by voices coming from all points of the compass, had ceased their goniometric transmissions) they were also going blind. "The moon was fading like a glowing ember into a snow-white bank of mist. Above us, in its turn, the sky was clouding over, and from now on we were navigating between those clouds and this mist in a world emptied of all light, of all substance."

Later, after several harrowing hours spent trying to regain contact with a completely fogbound shore, Saint-Exupéry sat down at Port Etienne and wrote a letter to Benjamin Crémieux in which he sought to transcribe what he and Néri had just lived through in artistically meaningful terms. He began by saying how amazed he had been to learn, from certain book reviews of *Courrier Sud*, that he was a disciple of Tagore, that he was "gratuitous", and that one cannot write about one's job. "The job seemed to me simply the sum total of its most deeply felt experiences. Must one then be a eunuch in order to speak about love? And not be a literary critic in order to know how to talk about a book? Mr. B's blacksmith might well write an idiotic book about his anvil, but I doubt that he would do better in making château life his subject."

During his most recent flight, he went on, he had found himself lost over the mist, with his radio out of action. "The night was moonless and I was navigating between the mist and thick clouds which made the night even darker. The only material thing left to me in all the world was my plane. I was 'outside of everything'. And then I spied the first flash of a light on the line of the horizon. I took it for a beacon. Imagine the joy you derive from a small brilliant point which contains everything! So I headed for this light, but it was a star." After nibbling vainly at a number of such decoys "I suddenly felt angry and surprised myself thinking: 'Won't I ever find the one I'm living in?' I was really lost in a kind of interplanetary space. And if I were to speak in some book of the only habitable star, would this be literature, this reflection made more by my flesh than by myself? Wouldn't it be truer, more honest, more complete than any other explanation? The essence of my experience that night, its human core was not some technical gesture, but this new scale of values and dimensions which suddenly imposed itself. And I imagine that even the simplest yokel, when he's in the throes of action and hasn't time to pick and choose his words but simply lets his flesh think for him, doesn't think in a technical vocabulary, but in something beyond words, in symbols. Later he forgets them, as though waking from a dream, and in their stead he substitutes a technical vocabulary; but the symbol contained everything. And it wasn't literature."

This realization—that thought is essentially symbolic, associative, and in a supra-Kantian sense "synthetic"—was, of course, nothing new, and Saint-Exupéry had not read Proust for nothing. He complained a little further on in the same letter of the needless sloppiness of certain expressions —like "a bus caught in a traffic jam", a classic example, he felt, of a false analogy, since what a bus (or for that matter any) driver feels in a crowded street is not one of being stuck like a fly in a pot of jam, but of being hemmed in by solid objects, like stones. A writer's first obligation, if he is effectively to describe what he experiences, must therefore be to dig beneath the worn stereotypes of language which hamstring our speech to that "consciousness which lives on in sleep and which one sometimes surprises on waking— telling the story in its own way". He had surprised it on this particular night over the clouded ocean weaving its own imaginative web around those three stars he had sought to keep just above his starboard wing. "I was doing a trapeze act. The stars were a trapezium. There was the same void beneath me, the same problem of balance, the same muscular attention, the same upward motion of the head, and even the same luminous points as in a firework display or at a country fair. And as I emerged from this kind of reverie, I found myself saying: 'I'm doing a trapeze act among the stars.'

"Here is an example of a very precious, very literary image, but unusable because it appears to be just that, and yet which was neither precious nor literary—a peasant has as many precious dreams every night—and which expressed everything so well that it was the one my body had chosen."

There is a strong tinge of Bergson in this apologia for "unconscious thinking", though many others—Joyce, Kafka, Freud and the Surrealists, to name but those—were also fascinated by this mysterious *terra incognita*, the subconscious or dreamworld of the spirit. As a nightbird and a poet who was never happier than when roaming the high seas of fancy, Saint-Ex was understandably intrigued by that tireless spinner of tales, that industrious Penelope, that unsleeping Scheherazade who continues to beguile the human brain during one's hours of doggish slumber. But how is one to dip into this secret subterranean language we carry within us when even our dreams are influenced by the collective stereotypes of everyday speech? Mallarmé, in his famous tribute to Edgar Allen Poe, had called it the poet's mission to free himself from the *"mots de la tribu"*—the parlance of the tribe—and Gide may well have commented on the fact during their talks at Agay, when Tonio was trying to find the images he needed to convey the individual intensity of Guillaumet's experiences, to say nothing of his own. For already in his Journal Gide had had occasion to note how not only the thoughts but the sensations and emotions of the simplest human beings are influenced and moulded by the pat formulas and conventional phrases with which and inside of which they live. He and Jean Schlumberger had been offered dramatic proof of it one day during the First World War when they had gone to visit a convalescent hospital for wounded soldiers recently withdrawn from the front; they had been dumbfounded to hear these same soldiers "from whom we'd been expecting true accounts at last, naively reciting back to us phrases one could read every day in the papers: phrases they'd obviously read themselves . . . It was by means of them that they had seen, felt, experienced. . . . Not one of them had been capable of furnishing the least original reaction."

It was precisely this originality—in its oneiric spontaneity—that Saint-Exupéry was seeking to recapture. But finding the words to evoke it was another matter. The trapeze imagery applied to his night-flying experience appealed to his youthful memories of acrobats and circus-strings of bulbs, but it was far too earthy to convey that sense of lostness he had felt in the cold unreality of this moonless night. This particular image was thus ruthlessly scrapped in the later, definitive account—in favour of something which curiously anticipates (by some forty years) what Borman, Lovell, and Anders were to feel on their return from the glacial immensity of infinite space towards the small but glowing welcome of "the good earth".

\*     \*     \*

The reward for these poetic travails overtook him sooner than expected, a bare month after this unearthly night when the stars, like celestial anglers, had baited him with the golden glimmer of their sinkers. On December 4th twelve of the eighteen lady members making up the jury voted to award the 1931 Fémina Prize to Antoine de Saint-Exupéry's second novel, *Vol de Nuit*. The news, flashed to Toulouse and relayed from there on down the line, caught up with the author at Cape Juby. He was immediately granted permission to fly back to receive the prize; but his first obligation being to the line, he was given the South American mail to fly back up. When he finally put down at Toulouse, after twenty-four hours of piloting, André Dubourdieu, Daurat's old companion, had to look twice to be sure just who it was. "A three-day growth of beard was gnawing at his face and retaining the black filth (which had been) spit from the motor's exhausts. . . . Who would have recognized his aristocratic hand in the coalman's paw he stretched out towards me? Shod in old sandals and dressed in trousers that were grease-spotted and tattered at the cuffs, all he had on was a blue ratteen overcoat which he wore over his bare chest and which was tied around his waist with a string. Two hours after his arrival at Montaudran he boarded the train for Paris, having barely found time to slip into a dirty shirt and rumpled suit pulled out of a suitcase he had left in Toulouse on an earlier trip."

Hopping into a taxi as soon as he reached the Gare d'Orsay, Saint Ex
raced to the Hôtel Lutétia and plunged into a hot bath. A barber was
summoned to his room to deal with the grizzly mane, and while he sat under
the razor in his warm bathrobe, the bellboy was sent off to procure a new
shirt from the nearest haberdasher and to bring his rumpled suit back
from the presser's.

While the Fémina Prize was won on the novel's merits—and probably
more justifiably than that year's Goncourt Prize (which went to Jean
Fayard's *Mal d'Amour*)—there is little doubt that *Vol de Nuit* was enor-
mously aided by the preface André Gide had generously agreed to write
for it. He began by noting the essential fact that the introduction of night
flights had been the decisive innovation which had made it possible for
aeroplanes to compete successfully with trains and ships. The risks involved
in tackling the "perfidious mystery of the night" were thus anything but
gratuitous, and heroic in the deepest sense of the word. Even more than
by the pilot Fabien, Gide was impressed by Rivière, the airline manager,
"who without being dehumanized rises to a superhuman virtue. . . . His
implacable decision tolerates no weakness, and the slightest lapse is punished
by him. But it is to his imperfections that it applies, and not to the man
himself whom Rivière seeks to mould. In his portrayal of him we sense the
author's intense admiration. I am particularly grateful to him for bringing
out a paradoxical truth which seems to me of great psychological importance:
that man's happiness lies not in freedom but in the acceptance of a duty.
Each of the characters in this book is ardently, wholeheartedly devoted to
what he must do, to the perilous task in the sole accomplishment of which
he will find the repose of happiness."

In the article which Edmond Jaloux devoted to *Vol de Nuit* in the November 7th issue of *Les Nouvelles Littéraires*, he declared that this preface would
"surprise many of its readers, for Monsieur André Gide is rarely understood, even by his followers." And after quoting the above passage he
added: "Let no one accuse him of disavowing himself: M. André Gide
has always oscillated from this sentiment to one which could be termed
'menalquism'. " Jaloux was right. As Jean Prévost was later to write:
"How can one compete with Gide's sincerity? We have but one and he
has twelve." This was a scathing exaggeration, but there were at least two
different personalities behind that balding Tibetan mask and that kindly
but at the same time tortured gaze. The self-proclaimed apologist and
follower of Oscar Wilde was the same austere Protestant who agreed with
Dostoevski—to say nothing of Immanuel Kant—that freedom can induce
a profound metaphysical anguish, a kind of psychic void which it takes a
faith to fill; the kind of collective faith which he thought—for Gide's love

affair with Communism was still platonic and he had not yet visited the workers' and peasants' paradise of the East—was causing the people of the Soviet Union to move mountains.

In its original conception Saint-Exupéry's second novel was intended as something more than a story of night flying or a study of courage, heroism, and leadership. The universe of the moon, the stars, and of dreams had always fascinated him, perhaps even more than it had Proust, and *Vol de Nuit* was first of all meant to be a paean to the Night. "I don't know why I'm thinking this evening of the cold vestibule of Saint-Maurice," he had written to his mother from Buenos Aires in January 1930, at a time when he was immersed in his novel. "We used to sit on the chests or in leather armchairs after dinner, waiting for the hour to go to bed. And our uncles paced up and down the hallway. It was ill-lit, we heard snatches of phrases, it was mysterious. As mysterious as darkest Africa. . .

"The 'kindest', the most peaceful, the most friendly thing I have ever known was the little stove in the upstairs room at Saint-Maurice. . . . Whenever I woke up at night, it was snoring like a top and casting soft shadows on the walls. For some reason I used to think of a faithful poodle. The little stove used to protect us against everything. Sometimes you came upstairs, you opened the door and you found us enveloped in a lovely warmth. You would listen to it swiftly purring and then go down again. I have never had such a friend.

"What taught me the notion of immensity was neither the Milky Way nor flying, nor the sea, but the second bed in your room. It was marvellous luck to be sick. Each of us yearned to be ill in turn. It was a boundless ocean to which one gained access through the 'flu. And there was also the crackling fireplace." He went on to add, a sentence or two later: "I am writing a book about night flying. But in its intimate meaning it is a book about the night (I have never really lived save after nine o'clock.)

"Here is the opening, it's the first recollections of night:

'Nightfall would find us dreaming in the vestibule. We were waiting for the passage of the lamps: they were carried like clumps of flowers and each moved beautiful shadows across the walls like palms. Then the mirage wheeled and the bouquet of light and dark palms was locked into the drawing-room. For us the day was now over and in our children's beds we were launched towards another day.

'Mama, you would lean over us, over this flight of angels, and so that the journey might be peaceful, so that nothing would disturb our dreams, you would smooth the sheet of this rumple, this shadow, this wave . . . For a bed is smoothed as a divine finger smoothes the sea.'

"After which there follow journeys through the night which are less well protected, the aeroplane . . ."

In the final version most of this was scrapped; Saint-Exupéry rightly understanding that it was far too proustian in tone for the kind of book he was trying to write. The bouquet-bearing lamps made their appearance later in the "Oasis" interlude in *Terre des Hommes*, just as the uncles in the twilight vestibule of Saint-Maurice haunt the pages of *Pilote de Guerre*. Only two of these metaphors finally survived in *Vol de Nuit*. The first—that of the sickbed—occurs in sentences like: "Somewhere out there the mailplanes were struggling. Their night flights dragged on—like an illness needing to be watched over." Or as in this description of the Flight Manager, leaving his office for a change of air. "On the pavement he was jostled, but he thought to himself: 'I'm not going to get angry. I'm like the father of a sick child, walking with small steps in the crowd.' " The second, Neptune image was applied to the pilot's wife, gazing fondly at her sleeping partner: "He lay there in the calm bed as though in a harbour, and lest anything disturb his sleep, she smoothed out this rumple, this shadow, this wave with her finger, stilling the bed as a divine finger does the sea."

There is nothing particularly abstruse about this association of ideas—between the dark mystery of the infant bedroom and the opaque mystery of night flying, between the heart-warming flash of a beacon and the purring flicker of a stove. Like *Courrier Sud*, *Vol de Nuit* begins with the onset of evening; seen this time by the pilot Fabien, who is flying the Patagonian mail northward. Like a child he is launched on to the dark immensity of the night, while in distant Buenos Aires the Traffic Director—a kind of solicitous "mother-figure"—maintains an anxious vigil. The name Saint-Exupéry gave him—Rivière—may have been the result of sheer accident; but it seems more likely that it was chosen for some perhaps not altogether conscious connotation which appealed to the author's mind. One of the four pilots who figure in *Vol de Nuit* is called Pellerin—which is to say "pilgrim". A pilgrim of the air headed for the distant port or sanctuary of Buenos Aires, whose beacon or lantern (the image of the inn is actually used at one point in the book) is kept bright and watched over by the Traffic Director, Rivière. Rivière? "River" in French, to be sure, but derived etymologically from that which binds it, the Latin *ripa* or in French *rive*, which means "bank". And Rivière is just that: the old mariner on the bank whose job it is to haul his sailors safely in to shore.

The plot of *Vol de Nuit* is of a deceptive simplicity. Three mailplanes are flying towards Buenos Aires, where they are due to land around midnight, and from where a fourth plane is due to take off with the transferred mail-bags bound for Europe. The first to land is Pellerin, the pilot of the mail from Chile, who battles his way through an Andes snowstorm described, as Edmond Jaloux the critic wrote, with a genius worthy of a Conrad or a Kipling.

"Then everything began to sharpen. Crests, peaks grew razor sharp, cutting into the hard wind like bowsprits. And it seemed to him that they were veering and drifting around him like ships-of-the-line taking up their battle stations. The air was suddenly powdered with dust, which billowed softly like a veil along the snows. He looked back to see if, in case of need, there was still an avenue of escape behind him, and a shiver ran up his spine: the entire *cordillera* behind him was now in seething ferment.

'I'm lost.'

From a peak just ahead of him the snow suddenly began to rise: the fume of a white volcano. Then from a second peak, slightly to the right. And, one after the other, all the peaks caught fire as though successively touched by some invisible runner . . ."

Heaved up by a mysterious air current which lifts him to 21,000 feet and over the last peaks, Pellerin drops safely down over the level Mendoza plain. He reports on his flight to Rivière and to Robineau, an inspector whose uninspiring job it is to issue reprimands and penalties for all delays in plane departures, even for those due to weather conditions like fog. For the fog is not a valid reason for delaying a take-off.

If the pilot suffered engine failure over a forest and smashed the plane, it was too bad: it should have happened elsewhere. For orders are orders. "Orders," reflects Rivière, "are like the rites of a religion which seem absurd but which are what mould men".

While Rivière leaves the airfield to visit company headquarters in town, Robineau, a newcomer who feels the need for human companionship, asks Pellerin to have dinner with him. He is rudely summoned back to the airfield by a message from Rivière, who is of the opinion that an inspector's place during a night on duty is at his desk and not in a hotel dining-room. So he's on friendly terms with Pellerin? . . . No, that's nothing to be reproached with . . . only"—and this is said with a sad smile—"Only you're the boss . . . You must stick to your role . . . Tomorrow night you may have to order this pilot out on a dangerous take-off. He will have to obey." A little later, still pacing up and down his office with small, precise steps Rivière adds: "If it's because they like you that they obey you, you are deceiving them. You yourself have no right to ask a sacrifice of them. . . . And if they think your friendship will spare them certain disagreeable

chores, you are also deceiving them. For they will still have to obey."
Forcing Robineau to sit down at his desk, he has him take down his dicta-
tion: "Write: 'Inspector Robineau imposes such and such a penalty on the
pilot Pellerin for such and such a reason . . .' It's up to you to find the
reason." "*Monsieur le Directeur!* " Robineau protests, only to be silenced.
"Act as though you understood, Robineau. Remember—like the men who
are under your orders. But without telling them."

Such is Rivière, stern but not inhuman—as is made clear by the "sad
smile" with which he says to Robineau: "Only—you are the boss." But
the slightest weakening of the will and the entire enterprise could founder.
"It is curious," reflects Rivière, "how easily events can get the upper
hand"—like tropical vegetation which, if not ceaselessly combatted, will
topple a temple. For a slip-up he demotes a veteran mechanic, Roblet,
while gazing with pity at his honest, work-roughened hands. He rouses
the pilot who is to fly the Europe-bound mail and ticks him off for a failure
of nerve in the face of a storm. When the pilot—one of the bravest, as he
knows well—starts to describe the hallucinating obstacles that were looming
up before him—Rivière silences him crisply: "You have too much imagination."

It was the sort of thing Didier Daurat must have had frequent occasion
to say to his pilots. But this particular passage in *Vol de Nuit* was no less
directly inspired by a book of Jules Verne's Saint-Exupéry had read and
greatly admired when still a boy—*Les Indes Noires*, the story of an abandoned
coalmine near Edinburgh where an old foreman, Simon Ford, comes upon
an overlooked vein. Summoning back the engineer under whom he had
once worked, he and his son dig their way into a fabulous subterranean
grotto which turns out to be warrened with coal. A new company is formed
and an underground city—only Verne could have conceived of such a
thing!—springs up in an atmosphere of jubilant prosperity troubled only
by the periodic "manifestations" of some malevolent spirit who clearly
wishes Simon Ford and his family no good. The troubling phenomena,
far from being the supernatural work of the legendary sprites and demons
haunting the Scottish lakes, are finally revealed to be the work of a half-
crazed "penitent"—the name then given to the scout whose job it was to
explore a new seam on all fours holding a candle (which would begin to
blaze in the presence of leaking carbon gas) above his cowled head. In
Verne's novel the cowled "penitent" is blind just as are the night-flying
airmen of *Vol de Nuit*, and the step from that word to "pilgrim" (Pellerin,
the pilot) seems once again too short to be purely accidental.

One of the most gripping scenes in Verne's novel occurs when Simon
Ford's son descends into a deep, unexplored well with nothing but a miner's

lamp to guide him. Miners' metaphors occur more than once in *Vol de Nuit*—
as when Fabien, who is bringing up the Patagonian mail, plunges into
black clouds, forerunners of the storm which is about to engulf him. "And
as he could no longer see anything of the world but the red cockpit bulb,
he shuddered at the thought that he was descending into the heart of the
night, with no one to help or protect him save for his little miner's lamp . . ."

The moral of Verne's novel is that resolution and courage and hard
practical sense can in the end get the better of crippling mysteries and a
supernatural belief in irrational phenomena. The same faith moves Rivière
in *Vol de Nuit* to reflect, after reprimanding the airman who is to fly the
Europe-bound mail: "I am saving him from fear. It's not him I'm attacking,
but through him that resistance which paralyses men in the face of the
unknown. If I listen to him, if I feel sorry for him, if I take his adventure
seriously, he will think he's returning from a land of mystery, and mystery
alone is what one is afraid of. There must be no more mystery. The men
must descend into this dark well, and then come up again saying they've
found nothing. This man must descend into the innermost heart of the
night, in all its depth, and without so much as that small miner's lamp which,
though it only lights up the hands or the wing, keeps the unknown at arm's
length."

So much for Jules Verne and the childhood memory of that friendly,
glimmering little stove which had helped chase away the demons of the
night. If they provided the foundations for the novel, the rest came from
Saint-Exupéry's own experience with the Aéropostale.

To the north of Buenos Aires the sky is clear and the mail plane from
Asunción will soon be landing. But meanwhile Fabien, piloting the Patagonian mail, has been swallowed up in a huge cyclone which—defying the
weather forecasts—has come raging down from the Andes, knocking out
telegraph communications and filling the air with static. He throws out a
flare and to his dismay he spies the sea beneath him through a cleft in the
clouds: the gale winds have pushed him out over the ocean. He turns and
heads due west in an effort to regain land. Blinded by the stormy night,
his hands sore from gripping the buffeted steering-wheel, he suddenly
sees a rift in the clouds above him and the lustrous twinkle of several stars.
He spirals upwards and gradually the clouds shed their "muddy shadows"
and grow increasingly white and pure.

"His surprise was extreme: the brightness was such that it dazzled
him, and for several seconds he had to close his eyes. He never would
have thought that the clouds at night could dazzle. But the full moon and
the constellations changed them into waves of radiant light.

"In a single bound, as it emerged, the plane had entered a calm which seemed wondrous. There was not a wave to rock him, and like a ship passing a jetty he was entering into sheltered waters. He had found refuge in some uncharted spot of sky, as hidden as the bay of the Happy Isles. Beneath him, nine thousand feet deep, the storm formed another world, shot through with gusts and cloudbursts and lightning flashes, but which turned towards the stars a surface of snowy crystal."

Fabien has succumbed to the fatal lure of the stars; he has eaten of the forbidden bait, but this deceptive taste of paradise promises to be brief, for—as his last radio message received in Buenos Aires explains—he now has just half an hour's fuel left. Rivière, down below, suddenly feels tired and old. Half an hour's fuel and nowhere to land; for by now towns and airports are completely blacked out by the diluvial fury of the cyclone. What can he say to the pilot's poor wife who, realizing that her husband is overdue, comes out to his office to see him? The moment he most dreaded—having to face a woman, a brave woman to be sure, whose terrible distress is betrayed by the faint tremble of her lips. Rivière is full of pity for this frail, pathetic creature of a wife, but inevitably she is the enemy and he must not show his pity. Her world of domestic quiet and stability, of white sheets and china and roses, is the contrary of his; a world of storm, strife, and challenge. It is the classic theme of passion versus duty—as old as Corneille and Racine, as old as the Greeks. But Saint-Exupéry has given it a new philosophical twist. For it is the trembling distress in this woman's face and the impression it makes on Rivière's entourage which suggests the answer to the problem that had been plaguing him. Were all these risks really worth it?

At Cape Juby one day Saint-Exupéry had surprised his fellow pilot Henri Delaunay by taking him aside and asking him in an anxious voice: "Tell me, why have we accepted this kind of life—with all its risks?" And Delaunay, quite baffled by the question, had stared at him for a long moment and then replied, with marvellous simplicity: "Don't ask me. Frankly, I couldn't tell you." More than thirty years later, in recalling this moment in *Araignée du Soir*, Delaunay still had the honesty to add: "And if the question were put to me again today, I'd given the same answer."

It was the simple truth, but for someone as metaphysically curious and tormented as Saint-Exupéry it was not enough. In *Courrier Sud* he had sought to give a halting answer to the question: each Aéropostale plane was carrying 30,000 love letters, shortening the anguished suspense of separated lovers. It was too melodramatic an answer to ring true—

even though Daurat had instilled a respect for the mail, for its speed and regularity of delivery, which amounted to a cult. In *Vol de Nuit* Rivière sets himself the question, after hearing the pathetic voice of Fabien's wife come over the telephone and not knowing what to answer. "Is the sacrifice of a pilot really worth it?" One day an engineer, bent over the squashed face of a construction worker, had said to him: "Is this bridge worth this squashed face?" If the question could have been put to everyone in the vicinity beforehand, all of them would doubtless have agreed to go on making the detour via the next bridge. Yet people went on building bridges.

If, Rivière reflects, human life has a price, we always act as though there were something surpassing human life in value . . . But what? "Perhaps there is something to be saved in man which is more durable; and perhaps it was to save this part of man that Rivière was working? Otherwise the action would have no justification." Later he recalled—but where had he read it?—that the justification lay in making men eternal. Like the Inca temple he had seen in Peru, built in honour of the Sun God.

"In the name of what harshness, of what strange love, did the leader of men of yore force his throng to drag this temple up the mountain, thus compelling them to construct their own eternity? And there rose in Rivière's mind the image of those crowds in provincial towns strolling in the evening around their bandstands. 'What happiness there is in that simple harness.' But the leader of men of yore, if he felt scant pity for man's suffering, felt a boundless pity for his death. Not for his individual death, but pity for the species, doomed one day to be erased like footprints on the sand. And he drove his people to erect stones which the desert would not bury."

As an answer it was too superhuman, too neo-romantic—good enough for Malraux, who has remained in this respect a Nietzschean, but not good enough for Saint-Exupéry, who cared more for the vital spark of the present than for the sombre ruins of the past. A somewhat different answer thus occurs to Rivière, suddenly riveted by the look of distress on the face of Fabien's wife. "We don't ask to be eternal: what we ask is not to see acts and things suddenly lose their meaning. The void surrounding us then suddenly yawns on every side." Beyond his office door, in the large room where the secretaries and telephone operators were seated, the pace was already visibly relaxing. The mail flight to Europe had been postponed—indefinitely, they seemed to think—in view of the fate which had overtaken Fabien the pilot. A laxness seemed to have descended on everyone and everything. "Death, there it is!" thought Rivière. His work was at a standstill; the tautness had gone out of his enterprise, now limp as a sheet—"like a sailing ship becalmed upon a windless sea".

When Robineau enters his office with the idea of offering him a few words of sympathy for the misfortune that has overtaken him, Rivière gives him a long, penetrating stare which causes the fumbling inspector to stiffen. The words of sympathy wither on his lips; instead, he hears himself blurt out: "I have come to take your orders." Rivière, as though expecting just this, pulls out his watch and says: "The mail plane from Asunción will land at 2.10. Have the mail plane for Europe leave at 2.15." The line might have lost a pilot, but night flights would continue.

To the casual reader all this might sound exaggerated and far fetched; yet in this case fiction was only paying its poetic homage to reality. It was this clockwork precision in real life which had made the Aéropostale what it was in its prime; the fastest and most punctual mail service in the world.

No particular discernment is needed to appreciate how much *Vol de Nuit* owed to its author's own experiences. The book was dedicated to Didier Daurat, to whom Saint-Exupéry actually read some pages one windy night in November of 1929, in the primitive iron-roofed hotel of Comodoro Rivadavia. Rivière was Daurat, transferred from Toulouse and made Operations Director in Buenos Aires. The mechanic Roblet, for whose experienced hands Rivière felt such pity, was a literary reincarnation of Toto the mechanic, whom Daurat had fired for drunkenness and then rehired, moved by his fidelity to Montaudran and the Latécoère firm. The loss of Fabien and his radio operator was the kind of painful experience Daurat had had to endure through many a nocturnal vigil at Toulouse—for in all 121 persons lost their lives to make the Aéropostale what it finally became. Indeed, if there is one criticism one can make of *Vol de Nuit*, it is that the circumstances of the novel's climax were less dramatic than what had actually occurred. When Jean Mermoz decided that the Aéropostale had to adopt night flights if it was going to survive, the general reaction of his colleagues had been: "You're crazy!" "On the Spanish and African runs," Mermoz explained to Julien Pranville, the Operations Director for South America, "individual will power made up for the inadequacy of the material. We created commercial aviation before there were commercial planes. We'll practise night flying with our men while waiting to do it with instruments."

"It's a terrible risk!" Pranville had pointed out; only to hear Mermoz retort: "All right, I'll take it. I'll fly the first courrier through myself. And if I can pull it off, others will do it after me." And he had taken off and conquered the night—without meeting Fabien's fate.

The person who had met Fabien's fate was the pilot Elysée Négrin; and it was the disaster which overtook him and Pranville, when they ditched down just short of Montevideo in the dark waters of La Plata in May of 1930, which was the real-life precedent for the plot of *Vol de Nuit*. In this accident Daurat lost a veteran flyer who had once been his chief test pilot in Toulouse as well as his second-in-command. In real life the loss of a Fabien would have been relatively banal; but if Mermoz had gone down on his maiden flight across the Atlantic, it would have been a blow from which it would have taken the Aéropostale years to recover. But Daurat still had the fortitude to send Mermoz on his way. Later, in his autobiography, *Dans le Vent des Hélices*, he humbly begged off, explaining that Rivière was "an admirable figure of a chief", but that he, Daurat, was not Rivière. He was right—but for a reason which his modesty forbade him from adding: that he was greater than Rivière.

The virtues of *Vol de Nuit* are also its limitations. Its extraordinary concision puts it in the category of those taut French classics—of which Benjamin Constant's *Adolphe* is perhaps the supreme example and Françoise Sagan's novelettes unwittingly spectral caricatures. The four hundred pages Saint-Exupéry accumulated during his stay in Argentina were ruthlessly winnowed out and reduced, in the final Gallimard version, to a scant 150 pages of text. But one cannot help regretting that so much was jettisoned; for the very rigour of the pruning made plot and protagonists at times a trifle too schematic. For this, of course, there was a reason, one which Saint-Ex had almost certainly begun to suspect. He was not a novelist but a poet and, as Daniel Anet was later to write, *Vol de Nuit* "is a work which gets as close as it can to a poem stretched out into a book of prose". Or, to put it more comprehensively, it was a treatise on leadership written in the form of a novel in the language of a poet.

Occasionally in *Vol de Nuit* a metaphor was strained, as the author succumbed to that sentimental lyricism in which *Courrier Sud* is drenched. But on the whole the discipline was admirable, breaking down only in the finale. "And Rivière went back to his work, walking slowly past the secretaries cowed by his stern gaze. Rivière the Great, Rivière the Conqueror, bearing his heavy burden of victory." It would doubtless have appealed to Carlyle, it might even have appealed to Nietzsche, by whom it was more directly inspired; but this final lurch into hero worship was a literary *faux pas* which was to get Saint-Exupéry into hot water with at least one critic. The phrase reveals how powerful was still the influence of the fulminating Teuton, even though his histrionic spell was beginning to lose its force. For to the fire and brimstone of *Thus Spake Zarathustra*, to the "Live Dangerously" of the thunderer of Sils Maria, Saint-Exupéry was already beginning to oppose a humbler but profounder ethos, partly drawn from his own experience.

In his preface to *Vol de Nuit* André Gide quoted from a letter Antoine had sent to his cousin Yvonne de Lestrange from Cape Juby a year or two before and in which, after describing his Bréguet-recovering venture, he had written: "For the first time I have heard bullets whining over my head. I now know what I am under such conditions: far calmer than the Moors. But I also understood something which had always puzzled me— why Plato (or Aristotle?) places courage on the lowest rank of the virtues. It's not a composite of very pretty feelings: a touch of rage, a tinge of vanity, a lot of stubbornness, and a vulgar sportive thrill. Above all, the exaltation of one's physical strength, though this really has nothing to do with it. One folds one's arms across one's open shirt and breathes in deeply. Yes, it's rather pleasant. When it happens at night, one has the added feeling of having committed some huge tomfoolery. Never again shall I be able to admire a man who is only brave."

It is curious to see the luminous thought of Plato rise like a moon over the landscape of Saint-Ex's meditations and begin to dim the effulgence of Nietzsche's shooting stars. And it is even more curious to note that this very quotation—from *The Laws*, a work of Plato's old age—figures in Julien Benda's *La Trahison des Clercs*. That blistering critique had first appeared in 1927 and immediately stirred up a hornet's nest in French intellectual circles; and it would surprise me greatly if it did not figure among the books Saint-Ex kept requesting from his friends and family during those lonely months in Africa.

What Benda was attacking in his famous diatribe was not the generals and the soldiers for whom war, after all, is a professional—and to that extent legitimate—concern. It was the intellectuals, those who had donned the toga in preference to the sword and who in extolling the cult of arms and martial virtues had betrayed their calling. Nietzsche, with his exaltation of the "superman"; Georges Sorel, with his justification of violence; Charles Péguy, the proclaimer of a patriotic *mystique* which was a law unto itself; and the ineffable Maurice Barrès, ever ready to unsheath his academician's sword—the only sabre he ever wielded—and to cry in a language the Duke of Plaza Toro could certainly have envied him: "Sons of France, advance! I am ready"—from the safe distance of two hundred miles—"I am ready to fight to the last *poilu*!"—these were the "clerics" who had betrayed their trust, which after all was to defend civilization against barbarism. And if Benda used the word "clerics", it was because Barrès and Péguy, not to mention Father Sertillanges, had posed or were posing as the defenders of Christian civilization while preaching a narrow nationalistic credo which had made possible the scandalous miscarriage of justice known as the Dreyfus case and which was now inspiring the grotesque posturing and strutting of Benito Mussolini and his Fascist admirers.

It is not difficult to imagine the impact which a book like Benda's must have had on someone as impressionable as and morally preoccupied as Antoine de Saint-Exupéry. Like most of his contemporaries, he had throbbed and thrilled at the role of martial drums and the glorious unfurling of French flags; and at one moment his adolescent exaltation had even been carried to the point of lauding the heroic boom of the cannon. But his family had suffered too much from the horrors of the First World War for him not to sense the ghastly realities which lay behind all this literary smoke and impassioned rhetoric. His experience with the Aéropostale had sufficed to make him understand that even the sublime heroism of a Guynemer might not be the highest form of valour, and that there are degrees of courage perhaps just as great for being less dramatic and unsung. André Gide had understood this perfectly at Agay while listening to his friend Tonio tell of Guillaumet's death-defying exertions in the Andes. And he had noted in his Journal: "Nothing to warm oneself with, nothing to eat. . . . A terrible temptation to let oneself drop off to sleep. The inviting whiteness, the voluptuous torpor of all those fields of snow. The third day he slides to the bottom of a ravine and emerges completely soaked. But he still has the perseverance to struggle back up a 3,000 foot slope in order to dry himself in the first rays of the sun . . . No food for four days. Fearful of losing control over his thoughts, he concentrates all his will power on their choice. Courage here is not risking one's life; but the opposite . . ."

In that final sentence Gide put his finger on the nub of the problem; though he felt impelled to add a sentence or two later: "Heroism is what is most lacking in our literature today." The phrase now sounds a trifle strange, when one thinks that it was written in 1931, on the eve of one of the most terrifying explosions of bogus heroism and bravado the world has ever seen. But the truth Saint-Exupéry had stumbled on while writing *Vol de Nuit* is that there are degrees of courage just as there are categories of love, and that the spectrum runs all the way from the infra-red of the fatuous to the ultra-violet of the sublime. Admirable the lonely struggle of a pilot like Fabien may be, but even more admirable is the stoic fortitude and perseverance of a Rivière (for whom one can read Daurat or Guillaumet). Both forms are to be found in *Vol de Nuit*, which is in effect a hymn of praise for an enterprise at its apogee, but which was published—by a cruel twist of chronology—just when that enterprise, having lost its nerve and its bearings, was, like Fabien, headed down . . . into a well of darkness.

# 13

## Adrift Once More

YEARS before, at a time when Saint-Ex was trying to sell Saurer trucks, a Czech fortune-teller had predicted: "You will marry a foreigner and you will become a famous writer." To which she had added: "Avoid the sea, and after the age of forty be careful about the planes you fly." The first two elements of the prediction now came back to him, as solidly confirmed by what had happened as the third. (Saint-Exupéry's distaste for sport encompassed bathing. He was not a good swimmer and ever since his eye trouble in the Sahara, he did not like to remove the dark glasses he habitually wore whenever he was near a beach.)

Between them, André Gide's encomium and the Fémina Prize transformed Saint-Exupéry's career. Overnight he became a famous and not simply an "interesting writer with a future", and a coveted prize for the literary salons (few of which he bothered to frequent). Delighted by the success of *Vol de Nuit*, Gallimard looked forward eagerly to another book, while Gide encouraged him to build up something around Guillaumet and his adventure in the Andes. The idea tempted Tonio so much that the copy of *Vol de Nuit* which he presented as a gift to Noëlle and Henri Guillaumet carried this dedication: "As a souvenir from an old friend who has always considered their home a bit like his, their port wine like his own, and their affection as the surest of havens", adding in a moment of rash euphoria: "In anticipation of the next book, to be called 'Guillaumet', here is this small one."

The euphoria, shared by his mother who had joined Consuelo and himself at the Hotel Lutétia in Paris, was understandable, but it was soon clouded by two misfortunes. The first had occurred in Nice, where Consuelo, while driving a car, had run over a pedestrian. A messy lawsuit followed, and the damages finally awarded proved so costly that they were obliged to sell the little villa with the lovely garden at Cimiez—much to the sorrow of Consuelo and Antoine, who for a whole week before Christmas had played host there to his sister Gabrielle.

Christmas this same December (1931) was spent at Saint-Maurice-de-Rémens, and here again the joy was tinged with sadness. The cost of maintaining the château, with its spacious park, had proved increasingly burdensome to Antoine's mother, now left on her own for much of the year. Two of her children had died, her second daughter Simone had left for Saigon with a job as archivist, Gabrielle spent most of her time at Agay, and Antoine could not be counted upon to put in more than fleeting appearances. When he and Consuelo turned up again in mid-January, it was in the sorrowful awareness that this would be their last visit. Crippled by debt, Marie de Saint-Exupéry had decided to sell the property to the city of Lyon—to be made into a boarding school. The weather, as though anxious to make Antoine's last days there as happy as possible, was exceptionally fine and sunny, closer to an Indian summer than to a harsh mid-winter.

But winter finally came, if only in his heart, when his mother and Consuelo left for Megève, to spend several weeks in the snow. Antoine, who cared as little for ski-ing as he did for swimming, bade a sad adieu to Saint-Maurice, with its beautiful lindens and its attic-fulls of childhood memories, and returned alone to Paris. Fame was already tugging at his coat-tails and foreign publishers were taking an interest in his work. Eventually *Vol de Nuit* was translated into fifteen languages—including Japanese and Finnish—and a little later (as we shall see) it was made into a movie by Hollywood.

Credit for the English translation, published that same year, goes to two remarkable expatriates. The first was Caresse Crosby, who merits a place alongside Marguerite Caetani and Sylvia Beach as an enterprising patroness of letters. The Paris of the early thirties was a far more close-knit community than the dispersed, distraught, and car-crazed metropolis it has since grown into. Where there are now only one or two literary salons that are still worthy of the name—and pale ghosts at that—there were then a good dozen, aired and animated by a tang of novelty and excitement, even though they were haunted by that species of parasite which, lacking the creative spark itself, exercises its talent for scavenging in critical vivisections. The precipitous tumble of the franc, which fell to one-fifth of its pre-war value between 1920 and 1924 (and even to one-eighth in 1926, before it was saved by Poincaré), had made Paris a relatively inexpensive haven for foreign writers and artists, offered an abundance of cheap apartments by impoverished widows or parents who had lost their bread-winning husbands or sons in the fearful blood-letting of the First World War. Into this Paris Harry and Polly (later Caresse) Crosby, both poets with a fondness for bohemian informality, had nestled like swallows. They had no pressing financial cares —one of his uncles was a manager of Morgan's Bank—they had an entrée into the literary world another uncle, Walter Van Rensellaer Berry, was an intimate friend of Proust—a Crosby cousin, Nine, had married a Polignac and was thus related by marriage to the famous literary hostess, Marie-Blanche; and finally, they had found—at 19 Rue de Lille, around the corner from Yvonne de Lestrange's flat on the Quai Malaquais—a magnificent three-storey apartment in an eighteenth-century town-house. It included a library (on the top floor), an ornate Sicilian dining-room, and—for they were not surrealists for nothing—a luxurious bathroom (complete with bearskin and fireplace!) in whose voluminous sunken marble tub (big enough for four) their less well scrubbed bohemian friends could bathe and even frolic during evenings which, as Caresse Crosby later wrote, were "rather Pompeian".

From one of her forebears, Robert Fulton—inventor of the steamboat—she had inherited a taste for revolutionary innovations which produced the brassière. The traditionalists were shocked, the rebels and radicals delighted by the cloth-of-gold evening suit, cut like a man's dinner jacket, which Madame Vionnet, the supreme arbiter of female fashion, had tailored for her and which she wore with a vest of sheerest net and a big lace jabot over a short tubular skirt. One of the Crosbys' whippets was called Narcisse—in honour of the day-dreaming flower the Symbolists had made so fashionable; and black being her husband's favourite colour—he even wore a black gardenia in his dinner jacket button hole—their first publishing venture, the Editions Narcisse, was soon transmuted by surrealist metamorphosis into the Black Sun Press. It produced some memorable first editions—including forty-seven letters written by Marcel Proust to Walter Berry, Hart Crane's *The Bridge*, D. H. Lawrence's *Sun* and *The Escaped Cock*, Ezra Pound's *Imaginary Letters*, and not least of all, James Joyce's *Tales of Shem and Shaun*.

Following her husband's suicide in 1929, when the Black Sun of Gérard de Nerval's poetic melancholia became a nightmarish reality, Caresse Crosby broke with the past, and instead of rare editions, she courageously launched into the publication of cheap paperbacks selling at 12 francs (50 cents) a copy. Ten or fifteen years before the idea finally took root on the other side of the Atlantic, Crosby Continental Editions—C.C.E. for short—began spewing out avant-garde authors like Hemingway, Faulkner, Kay Boyle, and Dorothy Parker. But in keeping with the cosmopolitan spirit of their sponsor, French as well as American authors were selected. One of them was Alain Fournier's maeterlinckian classic, *Le Grand Meaulnes*. Another was Raymond Radiguet's *Le Diable au Corps*, which was translated by Kay Boyle. A third was *Vol de Nuit*, translated from the French by Stuart Gilbert.

It is a pity that in her enthralling autobiography, *The Passionate Years*, Caresse Crosby does not tell us through whom it was she first met Saint-Exupéry. But shortly before his recent, much to be lamented death Stuart Gilbert told me that it was she who brought translator and writer together. Gilbert at the time was not a professional translator. A former judge in the British Colonial Service who had served for years in Burma, he had drifted into writing much as he had drifted into marriage—to give happiness to others as well as to himself. One day on the Riviera he had bumped into a French girl, who, charmed by his quiet manner and the twinkle in his soft English eye, had agreed to become his wife. In much the same haphazard fashion he had picked up Joyce—by one day wandering into Sylvia Beach's bookshop on the Rue de l'Odéon, attracted by a curious notice in the window announcing a "little costful" (for "inexpensive") edition of a book. It had apparently escaped Sylvia Beach's harassed eye, but even Gilbert's stiff British lip must have curled ever so faintly when he learned that this gem of fractured *Anglish* had been culled by none other than Auguste Morel, then busy working on a French translation of *Ulysses*. There was, Gilbert felt, a limit to modesty, even when it was as endearing as his own, and as he happened to be an admirer of Joyce—he had read *Ulysses* in Burma—he asked if he might be allowed to savour more of Morel's efforts. The privilege was granted and it did not take the connoisseur long to pick out a few more pearls, which Sylvia Beach hastened to transmit to the Master. A meeting was arranged between the Irish exile and the refugee from Burma. Joyce, beguiled by his mouse-like modesty, his wry wit which could be as gentle and yet as sharp as his greyhound features, and—for Gilbert had more than one string to his bow—the rag-time gusto with which, if need arose, he could pound the keyboard to keep the company in rousing spirits, was delighted to appoint him Grand Keeper of the Joycean Seal. And thus it was that to save this Gallic *Ulysses* from drifting on to the rocks the former Burma judge became a kind of lexicographic policeman; an emergency pilot in that polyglotic crew which comprised Chief Engineer Morel, Captain Valery Larbaud (translator-in-chief), and—as the ultimate court of appeal—Admiral James Joyce, First Lord of the Dublin Backwaters.

The experiment might have ended where it began—with *Ulysses*—had not Stuart Gilbert one day climbed the two flights of stairs leading to Caresse Crosby's apartment on the Rue de Lille, where the hostess, taking him gently by the arm, propelled him in the direction of a tall, somewhat balding man who was surveying the company with the aloof but alert air of a faintly troubled penguin.

"Monsieur de Saint-Exupéry," she said, by way of introduction, "has just written a book which I think should be translated into English. And," she added looking pointedly at Gilbert, "I think you're just the person to do it". To Caresse Crosby, a poet, a book as rich in poetic imagery as *Vol de Nuit* was made to appeal; not least of all because it had to do with flying— for which her sun-loving husband Harry had developed a belated fancy a year or two before his death. Stuart Gilbert, little realizing what he was getting into, agreed to read the book, and then, with his customary affability, he consented to translate it. The text proved deceptively simple: for what seemed at first like facile images turned out, upon closer inspection, to have a subtle poetic depth which he had not anticipated. "And before I was through," as he told me the story, "I was taking passages to Joyce and saying: 'Now how would you translate this?' And Joyce would take a long squint and then say: 'Well, let's see . . .' And I'd get my pages back later, revised by the Master."

Irish exuberance, in the process, may well have gotten the better of English reserve; for when Desmond Harmsworth, following up on Crosby Continental Editions, brought out *Night Flight* in London shortly before Christmas of 1932, Peter Quennell, writing in the *New Statesman and Nation*, remarked that the "translation, though not eminently felicitous, allows us to appreciate the quality of the author's style, which is sensitive, subtly modulated, but clear and direct". The *Times Literary Supplement*, which devoted a couple of well packed inches to it a month or so later, noted that the "fundamental opposition between the world of action and danger which his (i.e. Rivière's) project represents and the tranquil, domesticated world symbolized by Fabien's wife . . ." though "more romantic than logical . . . endows the story with a certain rhetorical impressiveness which the author skilfully maintains." L. A. G. Strong, in the *Spectator*, was less charitable, declaring that *Night Flight* had been "liberally padded to achieve novel size"—a statement which must have come as a surprise to the author, who had chopped it to one third of the original length. Flexing one more muscle, Strong felt called upon to add that the novel was "excellently but a little too expertly told—by which I mean that the devices employed are not all literary". After which, like a magician doing an Indian rope trick, he left his eleven-line article casually suspended in mid-air, leaving the gaping reader to wonder how a book which is too expertly told can be insufficiently artificial.

The most telling critique came from the other side of the Atlantic, where *Night Flight* had been published by the Century Company three months earlier, in September of 1932. Only partially impressed by Christopher Morley's enthusiastic preface, in which he had written: "Here for the first time an airplane enters into imaginative literature," Clifton Fadiman, in *The Nation*, drove to the heart of the matter in dealing with Rivière, whom he described as "a transcendental martinet, for whom the service is a kind of mystic categorical imperative . . .

"He applies the West Point-Prussian disciplinary system to the business of transporting mail. It is not that he is inhuman or greedy: no, he kills men for the sake of a pure idea, which he is never quite able to define, even to himself. There is something in him that has gone hard and hopeless. His spirit is dead; and in order to hide from himself this deadness, this essential solitude in a world of living men, he apotheosizes Work . . . 'We behave as if there were something of higher value than human life . . . But what thing?' He never succeeds in answering the question. There is no answer. His nearest approach to it is the Conradian formula of Duty, conceived in superhuman terms, Duty performed regardless of whether or not it is understood by Rivière or his underlings, Duty apart from its personal and social significance.

"Rivière," he went on, "is a sick man, a rotting man, like all who are fascinated by the spectacle of pure power and pure efficiency divorced from beneficent ends. But the author does not admit it, does not wish to see it. Instead he holds up Rivière as the supreme mystic hero. After Rivière (though like the Russian nobleman's, his heart is breaking) has stoically endured the death of his favourite pilot Fabien, the author ends the tale: 'Rivière went back to his work and, as he passed, the clerks quailed under his stern eyes: Rivière the Great, Rivière the Conqueror, bearing his heavy load of victory'."

The same kind of argument can be used to denounce any enterprise which involves an element of risk—like landing on the moon, for example—and I personally doubt that if he had to review the book again today Fadiman would come to quite the same conclusion. But he was influenced, understandably enough, by the spirit of the times, as he made clear in the next paragraph:

"It is disheartening to see a great artist like André Gide (who has just signed Rolland's manifesto against war) praising this book in fascist terms, making a virtue of its febrile heroism, declaring that 'Man's happiness lies not in freedom, but in his acceptance of a duty'. Can he not see that Saint-Exupéry's admittedly eloquent deification of mere will and energy leads straight to Von Treitschke and the megalomania of Il Duce? Does he not see that this lurid heroic sentiment can easily be impressed into service and that by its empty witchery men can be confused, blinded, and sent straight to their deaths? This is no mere story of adventure—would that it were! but a dangerous book. It is dangerous because it celebrates a pernicious idea by disguising it as a romantic emotion. It is dangerous because it enlists a fine imaginative talent in the defence of a spiritual toryism."

The least that can be said is that this was being unfair to Gide. His statement that happiness consists not in freedom but in the acceptance of a duty owed more to Dostoevski and Kant (who once wrote a treatise on "Eternal Peace") than to anyone else; and far from feeling the slightest affinity for von Treitschke or Mussolini, Gide was fascinated by the new socialism rising in the East. It can of course be argued that Dostoevski was a "spiritual Tory" and that the various faiths or causes men choose to live by form a long chronicle of human delusion. But the experience of this century, to say nothing of others, would seem to suggest that a spiritual void or an absence of belief results in nothing so much as licence or despair. Gide, furthermore, had been careful to quote from the letter Saint-Exupéry wrote from Cape Juby and in which courage—empty bravado—was placed last among the Platonic virtues. Fadiman, had, quite rightly, detected the residual Nietzschean note in *Night Flight* and pounced upon it. What he could not know was that more decisive in the novel's construction was the author's own experience in the Aéropostale, an enterprise which was competitive, to be sure, but anything but jingoistic; and an enterprise whose decline, as events were soon to prove, was but one symptom of a catastrophic loss of national will and a cramped defence-mindedness which were to encourage the megalomaniac aberrations of *Duce* and *Führer*.

Nor was Didier Daurat, to whom the book was dedicated, the "transcendental martinet" whom Fadiman saw in Rivière. The severity of the bonus system Daurat had devised for rewarding and punishing his pilots had been introduced not to kill men but to save them. When Guillaumet, an exceptionally reliable airman, one day managed to stop his plane just short of the end of the field because he could not lift his tail off the ground, he discovered on climbing out that the mechanic had reversed the tail-fin cables! His reward for averting a serious accident was, surprisingly enough, the cancellation of his monthly bonus; but when he went in to protest Daurat immediately put him in his place: "It's a pilot's job to verify the work of his mechanic." When Mermoz, after his epoch-making crossing of the Atlantic in 1930, decided to repeat the performance by flying the same seaplane back from Natal to Saint-Louis-du-Sénégal, Daurat had cabled him to postpone the attempt until the motor had been thoroughly revised. Instead, Mermoz had gone over his head, obtained permission from Marcel Bouilloux-Lafont, and finally succeeded in getting the seaplane into the air across a windless lagoon—after 53 trial runs! Six hundred miles out a serious oil leak had developed and Mermoz had been forced to ditch his Laté 28 near one of the Aéropostale's mid-ocean watch-vessels. The three-man crew and the mailbags were saved, but a wave capsized the plane, which sank. At Dakar there was wild acclaim for the "hero" who had made it safely back, congratulatory telegrams poured in, but there was icy silence from Toulouse. At Montaudran, when he turned up for an explanation, Mermoz was allowed to cool his heels in the antechamber for a while before Daurat would consent to receive him. Exactly what he feared had happened, the Boss explained to him tersely; in obstinately trying to get the seaplane into the air during several windless weeks, he had strained the engine and the result had been his mid-ocean mishap. It was nothing to boast about. Hence no telegram of congratulation. But no less typically, having issued the stern reprimand, Daurat hastened to reassure Mermoz that he had not lost his confidence. "How difficult it is," Daurat wrote in *Dans le Vent des Hélices*, "to manage such generous temperaments for whom too strict a discipline is barely endurable! Letting them have their own way often means condemning them to death; but brutally thwarting them is occasionally enough to kill their enthusiasm."

This is not the Treitschkean language of some posturing jackanapes calling on his men to new heights of sacrificial heroism. It was the stern, down-to-earth language of a Boss who was severe because he was dealing with men who, being pioneers and adventurers, were permanently tempted to become *prima donnas*. It was Daurat's rigorous determination to cut out this kind of nonsense that had made the Aéropostale into something other than a group of circus acrobats and into a genuine brotherhood of pilots, in which there were leaders—no organization can function without them— but no *prima donnas* or "aces". None of this was known to Clifton Fadiman, even though some of it was suggested in *Night Flight*. But the author's fellow pilots knew it, and because they knew that Daurat was a greater figure than Rivière and the real history of the airline more dramatic than what one glimpses of it in the novel, many of them were years forgiving him, and some never forgave Saint-Exupéry for having written *Vol de Nuit*. The book he had intended as a eulogy of Daurat and his companions turned out instead to be a literary millstone tied around his neck. More than anything it explains why he never wrote another novel—the reality he had known being so much nobler than the fiction; just as it explains why, notwithstanding his immense poetic talent, seven more years were needed before Saint-Exupéry ventured to come out with another book.

*       *       *

In mid February of 1932, after a leave of absence which had lasted a good nine weeks, Saint-Ex reported back to work with the Aéropostale. This time he was posted to Marseille, to pilot the seaplanes the airline was now flying across the Mediterranean to Algiers. The job on the whole was routine, without the thrills he had known in the Rio de Oro and Argentina, and the fact that he was often relegated to second place as co-pilot did nothing to alleviate the tedium. At Juby, as in Buenos Aires, he had been somebody; but here he was little more than a cog in a machine.

The Aéropostale, meanwhile, was in hotter water than ever. As though Daurat's dismissal and the damage done by Serre had not sufficed, André Bouilloux-Lafont now plunged into a new and even more catastrophic venture. In his misguided zeal to serve his master, one of his assistants introduced him to a strange, shifty-eyed individual with the not exactly reassuring name of Lucco. Lucco, who claimed to be a bona fide newspaperman, assured André Bouilloux-Lafont that in the course of his journalistic explorations in the troubled waters of French politics he had made some startling discoveries. Thus, if the Air Ministry (still headed by Jacques-Louis Dumesnil) was so critical of the Bouilloux-Lafonts' managerial methods and stubbornly refused to underwrite their 200 million franc loan, it was because Emmanuel Chaumié, who headed the Ministry's Civil Aviation department, had secretly arranged with Pierre Latécoère and Beppo de Massimi to sell a chunk of Aéropostale holdings to the Lufthansa airline in Germany. Chaumié, Lucco intimated, had even been bribed by the Germans to facilitate the deal; and, as this particular story developed—for Lucco was not lacking in imagination—it was in an Amsterdam bank that a special account for him and his friends had been opened. It was a fantastic yarn, and like some Arabian Nights tale, it grew steadily bigger and more fantastic as Lucco, who knew a gullible man when he saw one, kept bringing in "document" after "document" to substantiate his charges.

Heedless of the warnings of Roger Beaucaire, who had become a kind of Public Relations factotum for the Aéropostale (and a good friend of Saint-Exupéry to boot), André Bouilloux-Lafont plunged blindly ahead, glad at last to have the "goods" with which he could sink his sworn enemies, Dumesnil and Chaumié. No attempt was made to check the veracity of the story about the special account the Germans were alleged to have opened for their French benefactors in a Dutch bank. Instead, the "documents" produced by Lucco were quietly circulated among a number of deputies, setting off rumours which were soon running up and down the corridors of the French Parliament. The Pierre Laval government had just fallen; André Maginot, the Minister of War and inventor of the famous "Line", had just died of a surfeit of oysters; and Aristide Briand, the white whiskered apostle of everlasting peace, had been forced to give up the post of Foreign Minister he had held for six consecutive years. The new government of André Tardieu, who shared Clemenceau's germanophobic feelings, was both more down-to-earth and anti-German than its predecessor; so that the news that a senior official in the Air Ministry was in the secret pay of Berlin was seized upon with malicious delight by its enemies to create havoc for the cabinet.

But André Bouilloux-Lafont had failed to reckon with General Maxime Weygand, then Chief of the Army's General Staff. The charge that Chaumié a senior official in the Air Ministry, was in the pay of the Germans was, Weygand felt, a matter interesting France's "national defence". André Bouilloux-Lafont was accordingly invited to visit the Ministry of War with the "documents" he had collected. But the canny General, after leafing through the file, quietly opened his desk drawer and locked it away. When his flabbergasted visitor asked to get it back, Weygand bluntly refused. "We shall study these documents, and if there is anything in them, you may rest assured that we shall take the appropriate action," he said, politely but firmly showing Bouilloux-Lafont the door. The action was not long in coming. A summary investigation revealed that Lucco's "documents" were simple forgeries. Weygand took the dossier to Paul Painlevé (who had succeeded Dumesnil as Air Minister), and a warrant for André Bouilloux-Lafont's arrest was issued "for the use of fakes". What had begun as a financial crisis was now a full-fledged politico-judicial scandal.

All this was most trying for Saint-Exupéry, who found the company he had once been so happy with and whose praises he had sought to sing in *Vol de Nuit* become an object of public ignominy. In June 1932 he obtained a two-week leave of absence to help his mother move from Saint-Maurice-de-Rémens to an apartment in Cannes and to help Consuelo liquidate the unpleasant aftermath of the car accident in Nice; but he was so casual about returning that the Aéropostale's management in Toulouse was obliged to write him a sharp note on July 22 reminding him that the prolongation of the leave he had requested (as of July 1st) had expired without his having bothered to telephone through an explanation.

The reprimand was enough to bring him running to Toulouse, where it was finally decided that he should go back to piloting the mail on the African run. Consuelo, after relinquishing the villa at Cimiez, joined him once again in Casablanca, where they took possession of a sparsely furnished apartment on the Rue Noly. As spendthrift as ever, Saint-Exupéry kept almost permanent open house for his pilot friends (like Guillaumet, who had been reassigned to Casablanca too), airline and other officials, and more generally to anyone of interest, Moroccan as well as French, who happened to cross his path. He had developed a passion for Moroccan *méchoui* (roast lamb) and *couscous*, which were doled out in generous proportions to his French and Moslem guests by a tall Negro manservant whom Consuelo called "Blanchette". The money for daily living expenses was kept in an unlocked casket—at one time it was even a soup-tureen—placed on the mantlepiece, where Blanchette ("Whitey"—so named because he was as black as the ace of spades) or anyone else who wanted to could help himself at will. The "run" on this particular bank proved permanent, and the haemorrhage was such that neither Saint-Exupéry's pilot's salary, substantial though it was, nor his author's royalties were adequate to stem it. This explains the plaintive note one finds cropping up again in his letters; as in this one, quoted in Pierre Chevrier's biography. "My melancholy stems perhaps from my difficult life. I spend my time settling bills and the hard life I lead serves no purpose. I have trouble making ends meet. I care so little about money that it doesn't really matter, but it's making me feel increasingly uncomfortable. There's a kind of wall in front of me. All my needs are immediate, and I'd like to have a breather."

His life as usual was irregular, for sandstorms and engine trouble could still occasionally play havoc with flight schedules. Noëlle Guillaumet recalls how one day Antoine insisted on taking her to the cinema. During the film he seemed fidgety, getting up several times and disappearing. Finally he came back with a buoyant gleam on his face, and flopping back into the seat next to hers, he relaxed at last. Only after the film was over did he tell her that he had wanted to keep her distracted because her husband Henri had been overtaken by a sandstorm, which is why he had been slipping out every twenty minutes or so to put in a call to the airfield. But Henri had come through safely and all was well.

At Port Etienne, where his friend Jean Lucas was now *chef d'aéroplace*, Saint-Ex himself had to battle more than one sandstorm. Later, in *Terre des Hommes*, he described how the Captain commanding the godforsaken outpost had had three cases of good French earth shipped down from Bordeaux so that he could cultivate his own carrots and radishes; and how, when the sand began to rise over the Sahara, his "park", as he whimsically called it, would hastily be moved down to the basement. It was here, one moonlit night, when the wind had suddenly died after weeks of insistent blowing and the dunes beyond the window were a soft silky pink, that Saint-Ex, who was shaving, was startled by two dragonflies and a little green butterfly that kept brushing against the light bulb. Fragile messengers fleeing before the storm, they had fluttered their desperate way to the sea-girt outpost, a few minutes ahead of the disaster-on-the-march which had devastated their palm-tree oasis and which any moment now would engulf them all in a blinding, choking dervish-dance of grit and sand.

And yet, though the risks were still there, just beyond the lip of the horizon, the old enchantment had gone and, he couldn't help feeling, forever. "To savour a country, a race, a milieu," he wrote from Port Etienne in mid-September, "one must admit all the conventions. They are what give one roots. There's a great melancholy in living without conventions, one suffers from a kind of absence of reality. The first time I lived here I accepted them all. The breakfast hour, the tinkle of the milkman's bell, the rheumatism one cultivates, and even vespers create this reality in whose shelter one can live. And all it takes is a single branch pushed back somewhere in a world which is rich with meaning, and the marvellously human intrigue one hatches with the young girl in the post-office . . ."

In four years Saint-Ex had changed and so imperceptibly had the desert. The magic of the sands was still there, but it was no longer the same Sahara. Slowly but inexorably the European was exercising his corruption. The untamed hinterland was being tamed, and the savage pride of the warrior was giving way, by virtue of an invisible erosion, to an attitude of cringing deference. The old thrills were rarely felt, and precisely because the Laté 26 was so much safer than the erratic old Bréguet, what had once been an adventure was turning into a job. "Cape Juby, Cisneros, Puerto Cansado, the Saguet-el-Hamra, Dora, Smarra," as he was later to reflect in *Terre des Hommes*, "have been robbed of their mystery. The horizons towards which we sped have flickered out one after another like those insects which lose their colours once they are cupped in warm hands. But he who was pursuing them was no plaything of an illusion. In chasing these discoveries we were not mistaken. Any more than was the Sultan of the Thousand and One Nights, who sought a matter so subtle that at dawn his lovely captives expired in his arms, having lost, once touched, the gold of their wings. We were nourished on the magic of the sands, others perhaps will sink their oil wells and grow rich on their merchandise. But they will have come too late. For the forbidden palm-groves, where the virgin powder of the shells yielded their most precious stuff, offered only one hour of fervour, and we it was who lived it."

\*    \*    \*

Throughout this year and whenever they could get up to Paris, Mermoz, Guillaumet, Dubourdieu, and Saint-Exupéry kept hammering away at the authorities in a concerted effort to have Daurat regain his old position with the Aéropostale. The lawsuit he had been forced to bring against his detractors—those who had accused him of being a pyromaniac—was eventually won, adding one more humiliation to the Bouilloux-Lafonts' discomfiture. But by the time the verdict was handed down—early 1933—the Aéropostale was more rudderless than ever, having become the prize of rival political theories and ambitions. Daurat's dismissal had been followed by the elimination of many of his former appointees, while at least one pilot he had dismissed for grave incompetence had taken advantage of the chaos to get himself rehired.

Such was the situation in February 1933, when Saint-Exupéry undertook to write a long letter to Raoul Dautry, the Aéropostale's interim manager, in which he made mincemeat of the grotesque "sophistries" which had been levelled at his former boss. "No matter how valid the reasons the management of the Aéropostale may have had for preferring another manager to Daurat, there is no common measure between his work of twelve years' standing and the unproved denunciation of a telephone operator and a pilot which were alone responsible for his dismissal. A board of directors always has the right to dismiss a manager when it wishes, even without a cause, but none has the right to resort to such a pretext. It has even less right to resort to a mere pretext in order to refuse a just indemnity to the person it has dismissed and to whom, as it happens, the Aéropostale owes everything."

The appeal, for all its eloquence, had not the slightest effect: less perhaps for any fault of Raoul Dautry's than for the increasingly turgid situation in which he found himself plunged. The "scandal of the Aéropostale" had long since transgressed the bounds of administrative logic to become a venomously political affair. Two governments had come and gone since the Tardieu cabinet of early 1932; a President (Doumer) had been assasinated; and the elections of that May had brought victory to the Left, borne to power on a tide of pacifistic demagogy precisely at a moment when, on the other side of the Rhine, the Nazis were gradually taking over Germany. A few days after Hitler was named Chancellor of the new Reich (January 30, 1933), Edouard Daladier formed a left-centre government in which the Air Minister was no longer Paul Painlevé, the friend of Daurat and Mermoz, but Pierre Cot, a Radical Socialist deputy from the department of Savoie. Saint-Exupéry had met him several years before through a mutual friend, but as we shall see, he refused to take advantage of this friendship to promote his own interests.

Cot, whose socialism was so radical as to be barely distinguishable from that of the Communists, decided that the time was ripe to fuse the five independent air companies which then existed in France—CIDNA, Farman, Air Union, Air Orient, and the Aéropostale—into a single whole called Air France. Mergers are almost invariably painful and only too often chaotic, and this one was no exception. To begin with, it brought forth a Board of not less than 36 Directors—or what C. Northcote Parkinson would define as a perfect prescription for paralysis. A majority of the shares in the new company were awarded to Air Orient, which though honestly run had been getting a government subsidy of 41 francs for every kilometre flown (compared to 22 for the Aéropostale) and which had yet to introduce night flying, considered too risky! Logically, the most efficient of the five air transport companies should have been favoured in the new consortium, but it was almost the reverse which happened. The Aéropostale being in a state of "judicial liquidation" was smothered, while the dominant force in the new consortium became Air Orient, itself owned by the powerful Suez Canal Company, and the dominant voice that of Ernest Roume, a former Governor General of Indochina, who had moved on to become head of the influential Banque d'Indochine.

Politics, once again, had got the better of logic—precisely at a moment when Jean Mermoz was chalking up new victories in the sky. Piloting a sleek three-engine craft designed by a brilliant young engineer called René Couzinet, he took off from Istres (near Marseille) and flew non-stop to Port Etienne (2,100 miles), crossed the South Atlantic in fourteen and a half hours, then flew non-stop from Buenos Aires to Rio de Janeiro (1,500 miles), and finally recrossed the South Atlantic—in May 1933—putting down safely at Dakar even though one of his three motors had failed. In the course of his 15,000 mile trip he established four new world records—the one for the South Atlantic remaining unbroken for the next four years! It was a striking demonstration of the superiority of multi-engined, land-based aircraft over sea-planes and flying-boats. Sikorski and Douglas in the United States, Dornier and Junkers in Germany had come to the same conclusion; but though the plane Couzinet had designed as early as 1929 was three to five years ahead of theirs, Air France, under its new management, would not order a single one!

In August Daurat was rehired, but given a purely honorific post as travelling inspector. In October the priority rights which Portugal had granted the Aéropostale several years before were quietly abandoned, whereupon Pan American and British Imperial Airways stepped in to fill the void. In December the Venezuelan airline Paul Vachet had managed to keep going after the Aéropostale's collapse was offered to Air France, only to be refused—on the grounds that it was making profits! "What!" Jean-Gérard Fleury quotes an *Air France* director as exclaiming: "an airline which makes profit? Imagine the havoc which arguments drawn from profit-making enterprises can work on the principle of subsidies!" What Pierre Cot, the Air Minister, thought about it, Fleury fails to add (in his book, *La Ligne*); but as a good socialist he probably agreed that a profit-making enterprise must, by definition, be inherently wicked and something to be avoided at all costs.

The old spark was clearly gone, and even Mermoz' heroic efforts bore a distressing resemblance to artificial respiration. No one felt it more keenly than Saint-Ex, who had been with him that memorable day in Toulouse when they had vainly argued against Daurat's dismissal. He was increasingly unhappy over the hostile atmosphere he encountered within the airline, where certain fellow pilots now treated him as a *littérateur*, a kind of literary impostor who had muscled in among them—as though there were something unbecoming in a pilot's also being an author. Things being in a state of flux, he felt he could do with a change of air; and as neither he nor Consuelo particularly fancied Casablanca, he informed the company that he was taking leave of absence. With that they moved back to Paris where her former husband Gomez Carrillo had left her an apartment at No. 10 Rue de Castellane, just behind the Madeleine.

Having written again to Raoul Dautry—to explain why he was prolonging his leave of absence "until the dust begins to settle", as he put it—Saint-Exupéry decided to apply for a job with Air Orient. The answer he received from Louis Allègre, son-in-law of the powerful Monsieur Roume, was that the final decision on his application would have to wait till the fusion of the five companies into Air France was complete (which happened in September 1933). In effect, it was a brush-off, motivated by an adverse report on Saint-Exupéry which the new Air France directors had received from an engineer who was one of Daurat's sworn enemies. Had he wished to, Saint-Ex could easily have gone over Allègre's head and made a direct appeal to Pierre Cot, the Air Minister; but this he characteristically refused to do, simply because it would have meant "abusing" a personal friendship.

Saint-Exupéry now found himself frozen out and in the cold. Financially, the situation was worrying, for he had a wife to support and the royalties from *Vol de Nuit* and its foreign editions were all too soon spent. *Night Flight*, which Clarence Brown in Hollywood made into a film starring Clark Gable and Helen Hayes, should have brought him quite a sum; but his interests in the United States, it seems, were then very ill defended and all he got out of it was a pittance.

Didier Daurat, who had not forgotten the letter Saint-Ex had written to Dautry on his behalf, now came to the rescue; and to help his friend out of his fix he got him a job as test pilot with Latécoère, who was still manufacturing planes though no longer in the mail-line business. Leaving Consuelo in Paris, Antoine took the train to Toulouse and hied himself out to Montaudran—so rich in memories!—where he was received by Jean Dombray, like Daurat a First World War squadron leader and one of the first pilots hired by Latécoère. With him was Victor Rescanières, the

Chief Test Flight Engineer, whom Saint-Exupéry had never met before. Little has been written about this part of Saint-Ex's life, and for good reason: he was not made to be a test pilot, and his record during these months was not exactly brilliant. But no less typically, he was still the same *grand seigneur* who at Cape Juby had paid a local chieftain out of his pocket for an enterprise he undertook on his own responsibility. Rescanières never once heard him utter an ugly remark about any of his colleagues, and only with the greatest difficulty could he get Saint-Exupéry to produce an occasional statement of expenses, so that he could be reimbursed for the sums spent while on company business.

In the years since he had given up the Aéropostale Pierre Latécoère had branched out into the production of two- and even three-motored planes, some of which were mounted on floats to be made into flying-boats. One day Saint-Exupéry was asked to fly a Latécoère 35 up to Paris, where it was to be examined by an Air Ministry inspection committee. Saint-Ex had never piloted a three-motored plane before, but the novelty made him all the keener. Just what happened en route is not clear, but he was forced to make an emergency landing short of Paris. No damage was done and the incident was trivial, but it was a harbinger of the more serious incidents which were to follow.

André Dubourdieu, the sober, level-headed flyer who had once served as Daurat's second-in-command at Toulouse, was now also working for Latécoère in the plane-testing department. One day, he recalls, his friend Tonio was so eager to get into the air that he refused to be put off by the coughing and spluttering of the left engine on a twin-motor prototype which was to usher in a new series of Latécoère flying-boats. "Needless to say, the splutterings got worse after the take-off and the engine kept back-firing and smoking. After banking, the plane was heading back towards the field when we were horrified to see a large piece of metal, something like a chunk of corrugated roofing, rip away from the plane and spin slowly to earth. But the plane continued its flight as though nothing had happened and a few minutes later it made a perfectly normal landing. What we had seen fall away was the door which Saint-Ex in his haste to take off had neglected to bolt properly and which, suddenly opening in mid-air, had been wrenched loose by the slip-stream."

Among the planes Saint-Exupéry was given to test were three new Laté 29s (each mounted with a 650 horsepower Hispano Suiza motor) destined for Paul Vachet's Venezuelan airline. He had to take each up to 10,000 feet, gun its engines over a 5 kilometre stretch between Muret and Saint-Clar, while jotting down any pertinent comments on the pad he carried in his lap. After completing one such test Saint-Ex climbed out of the cockpit and told Rescanières, the Test Flight Engineer, who had been watching from the Muret end of the run: "Not so good, I'm afraid. All right at cruising speed, but whenever I gave her the gas she began to tilt."

"To which side?" asked Rescanières.

"H'm . . ." said Saint-Exupéry, "let's see . . ." He faced around, as he had been flying, with the setting sun in his face, and added: "Yes . . . that's it . . . she tilted to the left."

"Are you sure it wasn't to the right?" asked Rescanières, who had noticed the plane's right wing continually dipping, as had the mechanics who were with him.

Visibly puzzled, Saint-Ex continued to face into the sun and to raise and dip his arms, as though he were the plane.

"No," he said, "it must have been to the left".

"And your flight pad?" asked Rescanières. "What did you note down?"

The pad, when produced, touched off a wave of troubled laughter. It was bare of any technical information; instead, the pilot's restless pencil had amused itself covering the page with a female silhouette.

Once the planes had been given their preliminary engine tests at Toulouse, they were flown to an airfield at Saint-Laurent de la Salanque, not far from Perpignan. Here the wheels were removed and replaced by floats, and it was across the brackish tidewaters of the Salanque (a kind of small inland sea) that the transformed craft made its first trial run as a seaplane. Try as he might, Saint-Ex could not work up much enthusiasm for the routine job he had been given, and even less for the mosquito infested flat-lands in which he and Gilbert Vergès, the chief test flight mechanic, were occasionally obliged to camp. It was a relief to return to the Hôtel de France in Perpignan, where he could relax over a glass of port, listening to the music of the café orchestra and watching the girls saunter by in a game which struck him as "inoffensive as a parade of lead soldiers". But there were days when this provincial entertainment palled. As in this letter written to a friend: "I've just returned from the seaplane base where I've made some try-outs. My ears are still throbbing and my hands are smeared with oil. And here I am alone with my drink on the terrace of a little café as evening falls, and in no mood to have supper . . . I spend my days by a kind of pond which is neither sea nor lake, but a lifeless expanse I don't like. The sea is one thing, but salt-water stretches for some reason are always sad . . . A real lake seems to me the image of happiness, lined with neat houses which look sedately at one another. If one likes the girl in the house on the other side, she is close but inaccessible and there's a wonderful feeling of adventure . . . But at Saint-Laurent de la Salanque, where I spend my days, there is nothing but rotting seaweed . . .

"An evening like this one in Perpignan," he went on, "drags on endlessly. I know nobody here and don't want to know anyone . . . These people seem to be simmering quietly away—like a stew-pot—to the end of their days. What point is there to their lives? Two friends did come to see me today: a young settled down couple, happy, I suppose, but who seemed to me a bit soured. You know—the churlishness of people who're a bit too secure. Those petty pointless scenes which lead to nothing. That groundless rancour which lurks at the bottom of happiness. After they had left I heaved a sigh of relief, and yet I liked them, but there's a certain peace I hate. Don't you think there are some people who are like a sea wind?"

In addition to the mosquitoes by which they were daily—and even more nightly—devoured at Saint-Laurent de la Salanque, there were other tribulations. In the little village of Le Barcarès they found a restaurant with the enchanting name of "La Langouste qui Chante"—the Singing Lobster. Its owner, a man with the curiously Catalan name of Got, had acquired a monopoly on the purchase of lobsters in the area, having rashly agreed to buy all the lobsters the local fishermen could bring him, no matter how copious the hauls. Saint-Ex and his companions thus found themselves being offered *langouste à l'américaine*, *langouste à la catalane*, *langouste à la provençale*, *langouste à la mayonnaise*—lobsters big and small, fat and thin and in every conceivable disguise, until the sight of one more crustacean was enough to make their stomachs quail.

A little later they found refuge from the two-pronged offensive of mosquitoes and shell fish in an almost empty beach hotel called the "Lido", which an optimistic *colon* had erected in the midst of these sandy wastes in the belief that French families returning from the colonies would want to stop over here for a few days in order to "acclimatize themselves" gradually to the less tropical conditions of their homeland. The hotel was blissfully empty of clients; but what was even more relaxing was the absence of flying creatures preying on them at night. Behind the hotel someone had had the brilliant idea of setting up a powerful light with a ventilator which sucked in a steady stream of fruit-flies, gnats, wasps, moths, butterflies, fleas, dragon-flies, and of course mosquitoes attracted by the irresistible bulb. The toll taken by this luminous vacuum cleaner was such that for several hundred yards around there was not a mosquito left to trouble the happy clients, who could sleep quietly through the night with their windows open.

A few days before Christmas Saint-Exupéry was ordered to fly a single-engine Laté 29 seaplane to the naval base of Saint-Raphaël, where it was to be put through several months of rigorous testing by technicians of the French Navy. Overjoyed at the prospect of exchanging the stagnant backwaters of the Salanque for the lovely bay of Saint-Raphaël—from where it was a short hop to his sister Gabrielle's home at Agay—Antoine notified Consuelo in Paris and a double room was reserved for them at the Hôtel Continental.

On December 21 Saint-Exupéry took off from La Salanque with three passengers. A naval lieutenant named Bataille was seated next to him up front, while a technician named Meyer, sent down from Paris, sat almost immediately behind. The fourth member of the party, Gilbert Vergès, the test flight mechanic, sat further back in the machine-gunner's cockpit which had been carved out of the fuselage midway between the nose and the tail. The flight was smooth and uneventful until they came down to land over the bay of Saint-Raphaël. Seated where he was, Vergès could see by the horizontality of the fuselage that the tail was still up as they were about to hit the water. It was, though Vergès did not know it, a repetition of the error "Juby" had made at Brest with his friend Lionel Chassin. But that was when they were trying to take off, when all they risked was bogging down in an eddy of churning water, whereas now they were landing. Had Saint-Ex, in a moment of absentmindedness, forgotten that he was flying a sea and not a ground plane, and that his tail had to go down? No one, in any case, had time to answer the question, for the moment the floats touched the surface of the sea, the water foamed over the tips, gripping them like a brake. Down they plunged and up went the tail, carried by the continuing momentum in a dizzying semi-circle right over the pilot's head until the seaplane came to a shuddering halt on its back. Lieutenant Bataille, who fortunately had not bothered to fasten his seat-belt, sailed straight through the open window panel in the upper part of the plexiglass cover above the cockpit. Meyer, seated behind, found himself bruised and upside down in a gurgle of inrushing water, while Saint-Exupéry, who had been gripping the controls, was so stunned that it took him a few seconds to realize what had happened. Vergès, fearing the worst, had braced himself for the shock, and then, without hesitating a moment, had plunged head first through the machine gun aperture in the plexiglass turret, through which the water was already pouring into the fuselage.

While a rescue launch put out from the dock, Vergès and Bataille swam around the seaplane, which was settling slowly. Reaching the door, Vergès found it closed, with the water level steadily rising. He tugged at it desperately and finally managed to open it an inch or two; then, wedging his foot into the slit, he heaved with all his might and finally tore it open. Inside, Meyer, who could not swim, had already swallowed quite a lot of water, but in a moment he was out, held up by Vergès and Bataille.

But meanwhile, where was Saint-Ex? The accident had so surprised him that instead of following Bataille's example and plunging through the open cockpit panel which was now beneath him and through which the dark green water was rushing in, he groped his way back towards the tail, where he finally found himself in a kind of air-pocket, still able to breathe above the rising water, of which he too had swallowed quite an amount. The sensation of being momentarily preserved in a kind of underwater bell came as such a sweet relief to this lover of mermaids and marine life that he almost succumbed to the treacherous spell. But then he spied a blurred patch of light farther down the flooded fuselage. It came from the door Vergès had managed to tear open. Saint-Ex, who had thought for a moment that his last hour had come, took a deep breath and plunging back into the water, he groped his way down the fuselage as far as the door, through which he swam, letting himself rise like a bubble to the surface. His three companions, who had been picked up by the rescue launch, were about to give him up for lost when he suddenly surfaced with a wild gasp and a flailing of arms.

Later, in describing this mishap, Saint-Exupéry could write: "And the water, which was icy, seemed warm. Or more exactly, my consciousness did not consider the temperature of the water. It was absorbed by other preoccupations." Once again, as at Le Bourget ten years earlier, he had had a close brush with death, and it left him with the realization that in such critical moments one does not have time to be afraid. The shuddering and shivering came later—as happened now when he was bedded down at the Hôtel Continental by a solicitous Consuelo.

When his cousin Yvonne de Lestrange, who usually waited for his calls but who had not heard from Tonio for some time, rang up that evening, he said: "So you've heard about it?"

"Heard what?"

"About the accident."

"No. What accident?"

"I almost drowned." And he gave her a vivid description of the sense of peace which surprisingly envelops one after one has swallowed many mouthfuls of water. Like Guillaumet, he had endured his moment of temptation, when it seemed so much easier just to let oneself go. But the blurred patch of light at the other end of the fuselage had signalled to him like a bell, and after vomiting all the water he could, he had taken a deep breath and plunged to his salvation.

His sister Gabrielle came over from Agay and they saw much of each other in the next few days. But the exceptionally merry Christmas Antoine had looked forward to was now inevitably clouded. All their plans had been upset by the accident, and it even affected Christmas Eve, which he and Consuelo were to have spent with Maurice Maeterlinck and his wife at Beaulieu. Instead, Tonio and Consuelo unexpectedly turned up at Agay in evening dress around ten p.m., looking awkwardly out of place during the Midnight Mass in the village chapel.

This time the accident was too serious to be overlooked, and Saint-Ex's employment as a test pilot was abruptly terminated. There was no question of their staying on at Saint-Raphaël for a couple of months, as had originally been planned, and sadly Antoine and Consuelo were forced to return to Paris. Once again he was without a job, and this time with a black mark on his record as a flyer.

More than a year had passed since Saint-Exupéry had gone on extended leave of absence from the Aéropostale, and by now—January 1934—the Air France merger was already four months old. Each time he was back in Paris Jean Mermoz would put in a good word for his friend, but the response of the bureaucrats running the new consortium remained bafflingly passive. Previously Saint-Ex had been told that his application had to wait the consummation of the merger; now he was informed that he could have been admitted if only he had applied at the time the fusion was taking place. It made no sense, it was utterly illogical, the new pretexts invoked contradicted the earlier explanations, and Saint-Exupéry felt as frustrated by this run-around as K in Kafka's *The Castle* (which struck a singularly responsive chord when he later read it.) He complained of it in a letter addressed to Air France's Directeur d'Exploitation (the job Daurat had once occupied with the Aéropostale) in which he pointed out that through his articles, books, and lectures he had done more than any of his fellow pilots to make them and their achievements known, but that his only reward was to find himself reduced to posing as a candidate for admission when for him the Airline should be something of a family.

"Please excuse the embittered tone of this letter. And please forgive me for thinking that it's not one of those employer-employee relationships which can be covered by simple contracts; but often in the South my colleagues and I assumed risks which no contract could have foreseen and no payment, to my knowledge, could conceivably repay. If nobody was astonished at having occasionally to risk his life, regardless of contract, just so that our airline could survive, it was because it seemed to us a bit our handiwork and to that extent something of our own . . ." etc.

This was the kind of language which might have appealed to Daurat, but it struck too personal a note to cut much ice with the new management of the hydra-headed combine known as Air France. Furthermore, the letter's date—February 2, 1934—could not have been more ill chosen; for

just two weeks earlier Emmanuel Chaumié, the Air Ministry's director
for Civil Aviation, and Maurice Noguès, who had been appointed to run the
Aéropostale, had been killed in an air accident. Both were friends of Daurat,
and Chaumié had also become a friend of Saint-Exupéry's.

To complicate matters the cabinet in which Pierre Cot was once again
Air Minister now found itself engulfed in a crisis which rocked The Republic
to its foundations, while across the Rhine an increasingly cocky Reich was
beginning to flex its muscles. In March 1933, following the Reichstag fire,
Hitler had been granted full powers; in October Germany had withdrawn
from the League of Nations and walked out on the disarmament conference
in Geneva; and in the carefully rigged elections of November 90% of the
voters cast their ballots for the Nazis. As frightening as the increasingly
mechanized unity of its Teutonic neighbour was the appalling disunity of
France. Paris, during this same autumn, saw two governments collapse,
while right- and left-wing deputies carried on an endless tug-of-war over a
hopelessly disarticulated budget; and this dismaying spectacle of parliamentary impotence was darkened by a series of scandals culminating in the
Stavisky Affair, of January 1934, in which the Camille Chautemps government found itself directly involved.

Saint-Exupéry was in Paris when the crisis finally boiled over in early
February, and he would have had to be both blind and deaf not to take an
anguished interest in what was going on around him. His own fate had
come increasingly to depend on the whim of highly placed bureaucrats,
while his friend Jean Mermoz was by now shoulder deep in politics. The
type of dynamism which was being exhibited in Italy, to say nothing of
Germany, appealed to a daring pilot who was a man of action ("a wiry
tough guy", to quote Caresse Crosby) in every inch of his being. Some
eighteen months earlier Mermoz had been invited down to Rome to attend
an international meeting organized by Italo Balbo, Mussolini's Aviation
Minister, for all the airmen who, like himself, had flown across the Atlantic.
Mermoz was as much taken by the ebullient Marshal as Balbo was impressed by Mermoz, and by the time the celebrations were over, they
were good friends. An Air Minister who kept his staff in physical trim by
insisting that they go up in the air, like himself, several times a year and
practise parachute jumps, was, Mermoz thought, the type of individual an
increasingly will-less France could use in ministerial office. The country
needed shaking and waking up, and the man for the job—so Mermoz was
led to believe—was a dashing officer with a handsome physique and a winning
smile, a certain Lieutenant Colonel de La Rocque, who had once served
on Marshal Foch's staff. A militant anti-Communist, La Rocque had been
named to lead a movement called the *Croix de Feu*—the Cross of Fire—

originally made up of First World War veterans who had been wounded and decorated for heroism in action. Subsequently it had expanded to include a host of young devotees—girls as well as boys—organized in local chapters all over France and who were sufficiently enthused by what was going on in Italy to think that the only salvation for an increasingly divided and "corrupt" régime was a dose of totalitarian discipline.

In the riots of February 6, 1934—the bloodiest upheaval Paris has witnessed in this century (25 persons killed, 2,000 wounded, police included) the *Croix de Feu* "militants" of Colonel de la Rocque in fact played a less active role than did Pierre Taittinger's *Jeunesses Patriotes* and the *Union Nationale des Anciens Combattants* (a kind of veterans' organization comparable to the American Legion), many of whom seem to have hoped that by storming the Chamber of Deputies and bodily expelling the "thieves" and "assassins" who had set up shop there, they could topple a corrupt republic and bring to power one of those "providential saviours" to whom the French periodically turn in moments of distress. Such a saviour was at hand, certain of these super-patriots felt, in the person of Marshal Lyautey, the conqueror and pacifier of Morocco. It was a wild and woolly notion, for the Marshal, already entering his eightieth year, was now virtually in his dotage and had but a few more months to live. But venerability has an extraordinary appeal to the French, as they proved once again by turning in this tense hour to Gaston Doumergue, a former President of the Republic and himself a ripe seventy.

To pacify the veterans and the various monarchist, bonapartist, neo-Fascist, and peasant groups which had come close to overthrowing the Republic, Doumergue chose another prestigious soldier, Marshal Philippe Pétain, to occupy the crucial Ministry of War. As an additional sop to the forces of the Right another military figure, General Denain, was chosen to replace Pierre Cot as Air Minister. This latter appointment did more than pacify the restless Jean Mermoz: it filled him with delight; for it was under his orders that he had served in Syria and it was Denain who had written the recommendation he had handed to Daurat when he had first applied for a job with Latécoère.

Whether or not there was a cause and effect relationship between Denain's occupation of the Air Ministry and Saint-Exupéry's final admission to Air France is not clear, though it seems likely. In April of 1934, at any rate, he was informed by official letter that he was being assigned to Air France's "Propaganda Service", with a monthly salary of 3,500 francs to which would be added the bonuses habitually granted to pilots whenever their lecture tours took them overseas. It was roughly one seventh of what he had been earning as Flight Director of the Aeroposta Argentina, though the difference was actually less, in view of the decline in prices which had taken place in France as the combined result of the Depression and a deliberately deflationary policy; it was far from being what Saint-Exupéry had hoped for, in some ways it was hardly more than a consolation prize, but by now he was too desperate to turn the offer down.

If he still harboured any illusions—which seems doubtful—they were very soon dispelled. The old team, not to say family, spirit he had once felt with Latécoère and the Aéropostale still existed on the airfields which made up the African and what was left of the South American runs, but there was little trace of it in the administrative offices in Paris. What Saint-Ex would have liked would have been to serve under the orders of a man like Didier Daurat, but in the cumbersome new organization of Air France, Daurat had been shunted to one side and made travelling inspector. His new job did at least afford him the cruel satisfaction of noting how, with each passing month, the lead France had once enjoyed in the air was being whittled away by a policy of passive abandonment. On his return from a six month inspection trip to the United States, Daurat was shaken to discover that the directors of Air France, disregarding his earlier protests, had purely and simply abandoned all further night flights to Berlin. They had been taken over in toto by Lufthansa, which could now offer its pilots the exclusive privilege of overflying a territory it might one day be their mission to bombard—and conquer. Nor, incredible as it may sound, was any effort made over the next five years to challenge this ominous monopoly, the Germans continuing right up until 1939 to effect all the night flights between Paris and Berlin. The same defensive state of mind which had produced the Maginot Line was now at work within Air France, causing it not to expand, but to contract. And what had begun as admiration on the other side of the Rhine was already turning into manifest contempt.

Part of the trouble was a suicidal financial policy aimed at maintaining the value of the franc at a time when other currencies had gone in for drastic devaluation or abandoned the gold standard. The price France had to pay for this *politique de prestige* was a steady decline in exports, a stagnant national income, growing unemployment, and a mounting budget deficit— at a time when Germany, pursuing a diametrically different policy, was booming. Retrenchment became not only a watch-word but a kind of ideal to which everything else had to be sacrificed; and just as the French Army, under Weygand and Pétain, saw no need to invest in new-fangled articles like tanks—after all, what was a tank when faced with a French 75?—so the directors of Air France saw no need to encourage an engineer like René Couzinet, in whose sleek *Arc-en-Ciel* Mermoz had made his record-breaking crossing of the South Atlantic. Indeed, so "retrenchive" was the

general climate that it took all the vehement desk-pounding Mermoz could
muster, backed by the journalistic broadsides of his friends Jean-Gérard
Fleury and Joseph Kessel (the novelist) to keep General Denain, the Air
Minister from caving in in his turn—which he came within an ace of doing
by giving serious consideration to a pool agreement with Lufthansa which
would in effect have let the Germans establish a monopoly on all further air
crossings of the South Atlantic. Thanks to their combined efforts the pool
idea was buried *in extremis*, and the best pilots Mermoz could recruit—
including Guillaumet—were concentrated at Dakar and trained to fly
regular weekly mail flights to and from South America.

Though Saint-Exupéry took little part in this epic battle—unlike Mermoz
he disliked button-holing politicians and arguing with ministers—he was
more than a disinterested spectator, and many were the evenings he spent
with Fleury and Kessel, discussing the uncertain future of French aviation.
But each victory Mermoz won offered only a momentary break in a general
retreat; and for Saint-Ex there was scant satisfaction in working for a
company which seemed so ready to throw in the sponge and to liquidate
what he and his friends had laboured so hard to establish.

One of the few truly happy moments he spent in an otherwise disappointing year came in July 1934 when he was sent by Air France on a study trip
to the Far East. He left Marseille on the 12th, touched down at Damascus
on the 14th, then flew overland to Baghdad and across the Persian Gulf to
India, finally reaching Saigon on the 19th. To meet him at the Than-Son-
Nhut airport was Pierre Gaudillère, one of the army lieutenants who had
been with him for the Aerial Navigation course in Brest. Saint-Ex told his
old friend that there was one thing above all he wanted to do: visit the
ruins of Angkor Vat in Cambodia. A papier-mâché model of them had been
exhibited at the Colonial Exposition which for six months had been the
talk and the marvel of Paris in 1931; but Saint-Exupéry's curiosity had
also been aroused by the scandal which André Malraux's thefts of Khmer
works of art had touched off and in which so many Gallimard authors,
including his friend Gide, had been indirectly involved, in rallying to
Malraux's defence. Saint-Ex, who read relatively few novels, had almost
certainly read *La Voie Royale*, based on Malraux's adventures in the Cambodian jungle, and he had often had occasion to meet Malraux in the
Gallimard circle, to say nothing of Verrières—for Malraux had become a
good friend of Louise de Vilmorin and her brothers, whom Antoine still
occasionally saw.

At the Cat-Lai naval air base there was, as it happened, an Air France
seaplane which had been tied up for months under a hangar doing nothing.
So after lunch they took off under a burning sun in the direction of Cambodia,

with Saint-Ex at the controls. To reduce the danger of accident involved in flying straight across country (which meant jungle), Gaudillère had his friend follow the water course of the Nha-Be and the Vaico, leading to the Mekong and Pnom-Penh. And well he did, for twenty minutes out the motor suddenly died and they had to make an emergency landing on the water. The Indochinese mechanic who was with them soon spotted the trouble and a few minutes later they were airborne again; but only for five minutes, when the motor failed once more. They splashed down at a point where the Vaico flows into the Soirap, but this time the mechanic could not get the engine restarted. The anchor they put out to keep from drifting downstream slipped along the soft mud bottom and soon they were headed for the China Sea. They finally made it to one shore, an inaccessible tangle of vegetation branching out over the crocodile and snake infested mudbank. Calmly seated in the seaplane, they watched the sun go down through the tropical tangle, turning the opaque waters into a river of gold. Comfortable in the knowledge that they would be rescued the next morning by a Navy launch, they tucked into a picnic supper, troubled only by the mosquitoes which kept droning around them. Far from sulking, Saint-Ex seemed exhilarated by the mishap, and as Gaudillère later recalled, the curious sensation of finding oneself isolated on a stretch of dark water was something new to add to his "already well stocked album of adventures". Overhead the Southern Cross rose like a brilliant four-pointed kite, while beneath them they could hear the muddy tide lapping against the hollow wooden floats as it pushed its way up the estuary from the sea. Saint-Exupéry was reminded of the plateau in the Sahara he had once landed on and which had never before been trodden by man. Here, too, they were on a kind of virgin island, too inhospitable to receive the friendly imprint of man's passage.

Then without warning he suddenly burst into song, his voice echoing strangely in the dark mosquito infested night.

> *Dans le jardin de mon père*
> *Vole, mon coeur, vole*
> *Dans le jardin de mon père*
> *Y a un pommier doux*
> *Tout doux, tout doux.*

It was an old French folk song; but because Saint-Ex had just been reading the legend of the Ramayana and had persuaded Gaudillère to talk to him about Khmer art and Cambodian customs, the paternal apple orchard was now invaded by three princesses:

*Trois belles princesses*
*Sont couchées dessous.*

Three Asparas with golden tiaras and vine-like arms and gestures, and slim legs under their silken sampots. And Rama, if he win the battle, will have my love, promises one of the princesses. Thus East was poetically linked to West and the immortal Asiatic epic wedded to a humble French folk song; so too the "mineral solitude of the desert", as Gaudillère later noted, was linked by an interesting association of experiences with the "primaeval creeping and crawling of the delta".

Finally Saint-Ex fell silent—a very long silence which seemed to Gaudillère to last a full hour. He remembered how one evening in Brest "Juby" and he had sat for a long moment watching the huge globe of the sun sink beyond the Porzic lighthouse and the jetty into the reddened sea. And suddenly he had remarked: "One ought to have an hour like this every day. I feel sorry for those who don't offer themselves this treat from time to time."

Saint-Exupéry's visit to Indochina lasted two weeks. On August 12th he was back in Marseille. He was returning to his wife and family but he was also returning to a job for which he felt scant enthusiasm. It had been a wonderful outing, a bit like a vacation, but he felt like a schoolboy coming back for a new term.

Later that same year a letter from Rufino Luro Cambaceres, the latest in a series he had not bothered to answer, suddenly moved him at long last to reply. "My departure from your country and the Aeroposta Argentina," he wrote, "was much harder for me and pained me far more than you can imagine. There is no period in my life which I prefer to the one I lived among yourselves. No comradeship ever appeared healthier than the one I knew with you. What memories, what scores of memories of our work together! The trips to the south, the build-up of the airline, the winds of Comodoro, the fatigue, the anxieties, and the joys I shared with you! In Argentina I felt as in my own country . . . But afterwards I brusquely had to leave you and this caused me deep pain. I found myself obliged to return to a company hamstrung and entangled in the intrigues of a confused and unjust policy. I realized perfectly that I would never again find the peace I had lost . . . Not only have I felt a kind of impossibility for answering, but it was still painful for me to open the envelopes and to return to my memories. If a man is hopelessly in love with a beautiful woman, to live in peace he must destroy her pictures . . . and this is a bit what I have done. Now when I think back on these things, all I feel is an amiable melancholy."

There was a touch of exaggeration in all this, as well as an elementary courtesy in disguising what he had actually felt about Argentina at the time. But the slack in his present life now made those tense, vital months seem as radiant a memory as the year he had spent in the Sahara. The premonition he had expressed in the letter written to Charles Sallès from Cisneros was coming true; and the happiness he was to taste from now on, he knew, would never be more than fitful and intermittent.

# 14

## Two Crashes

---

THE letter to Luro Cambaceres was written from No. 5, Rue de Chanaleilles. For in the meantime Saint-Exupéry had changed his habitat. Shortly after the February 6 upheavals on the Place de la Concorde he had bumped into Roger Beaucaire on the Rue Royale and they had stepped into Weber's café for a drink. Beaucaire had much to tell him about the curiously "dynamic" mentality of the *Jeunesses Patriotes* and other activist groups which had stirred up the furore. He had rung up, only to be greeted with something like a snarl: "I've been receiving a lot of phone calls lately. You're not calling by any chance because you want protection?" As though the backroom boys were already hard at work drawing up black-lists of suspects to be liquidated when they took over. Saint-Ex, after listening to him open-eyed—he had apparently not realized just how far the Fascist rot had spread—began complaining of his listless existence, made all the drearier by his having to live on the Right Bank, a step from the Boulevard Haussmann and the Printemps and Galeries Lafayette department stores. "If only we could find something else," he sighed. "I'd give anything to move to the Left Bank."

Not long thereafter Beaucaire heard of an apartment that was about to be vacated on the Rue de Chanaleilles, near the Invalides. Saint-Ex lost no time going over to look at it. Anything but spacious, it had just four small rooms located on a second floor. But the rear court, backed by an austere convent wall, was embellished by a spreading tree whose friendly branches seemed to want to shake hands through the windows. The two rooms on the street side overlooked the *porte cochère* and the coach-house roofs of the Hôtel de Chanaleilles, a charming Louis XV town-house originally built for the Duc du Maine and later inhabited by Paul Barras (Joséphine Beauharnais' protector) and the famous Madame Tallien (to say nothing of its present owner and restorer, Stavros Niarchos, the Greek shipping magnate.) Automobiles in the mid-1930s were still a luxury limited to the happy few, and the Rue de Chanaleilles—like its fashionable neighbour, the Rue Barbet de Jouy, with its leafy gardens and elegant *hôtels particuliers*—offered a restful haven for someone who had been exposed to the commercial hurly-burly of the Rue de Castellane. Consuelo needed little persuading, and in early July of 1934 she and Antoine made a new home for themselves in this tiny "fly-cage", as their friend Henri Jeanson was to call it.

"Bird-cage" would more aptly describe the quaint nest Tonio had found for his captivating *"oiseau des îles"*, for that "seductive animal whose warbling was on a par with its plumage"—to quote Jeanson again. "Very amusing, very intelligent, very lively, endlessly chirping, it painted, wrote, and sculpted with felicity. A knowing bird, a rare bird—of the race of the Consuelos—for such was and is her name. I shall never forget the way Saint-Ex used to look at her. She disarmed him, so fragile, so small, so insufferable that he was minded at times to put her in her place, which I think he did. She surprised, she fascinated him, in a word: he adored her. A bird which refused to stay still. It perched, whenever the fancy moved it, on this big plush bear, this flying bear of a Saint-Ex. They seemed to have sprung out of some Walt Disney cartoon. Saint-Ex, wrapped up in double-breasted suits which were rumpled into folds and often buttoned all askew, was careless about elegance. Nor did he care a fig for luxury, and the apartments he camped in were sometimes too large, sometimes too small. Things he happened to be occupying—like his suits."

This one was definitely on the diminutive side, and its minuteness was emphasized not only by Antoine's bulk but also by his wife's extra-ordinary ebullience. Life with Consuelo may at times have been trying, and even exhausting, but it was never boring. As she was as much of a bohemian as he, it tended to be helter-skelter—like his room, where books, ties, shirts, packets of cigarettes, and toothbrushes were as indiscriminately jumbled as the books and papers he had once crammed into his school desk. Often of an evening the guests would turn up, nine o'clock would pass, it might even be getting on towards ten when suddenly Consuelo would exclaim: "But Heavens, I've forgotten the dinner!" And before he quite knew what was happening, the most affluent looking guest would be seized by the arm and dragged away, Consuelo explaining as they went through the door: "We'll make a quick tour of the restaurants and be back." And back they would come a half hour later, laden with caviar and *pâté de foie gras* and bottles of wine and cheeses which, when the money ran out—as it had a way of doing—her companion would be asked to pay for.

For if Saint-Ex was frequently penniless, his wife was often more so, though seemingly less daunted by this recurring calamity. She would hail a taxi, without a penny in her handbag, and have herself driven to a café—like Weber's on the Rue Royale—where she would hop nimbly out, saying to the doorman: "Joseph, would you mind paying the fare?" then walk into the café with a swish of silk or fur as though she had just bought the place up. The entrée was invariably grand—but a bit too grand for Saint-Exupéry's bashful taste: particularly when the doorman appeared, cap in hand and an ingratiating smile on his face, and he would have to fumble in his pocket for the fare and the generous *pourboire* which habitually went with it.

His own means of locomotion tended to be different, though in some ways just as extravagant. The flash flood of royalties touched off by *Vol de Nuit* and the Fémina Prize had permitted him, in 1932, to invest in a pearl-grey Voisin touring car in which he had driven Consuelo and his mother around during those summer weeks when he had helped her move from Saint-Maurice to Cannes. His later impecuniousness should logically have led him to exchange it for something less luxurious, but he could not help being tempted by the glamorous machines he saw exhibited in the salesroom windows of the main Bugatti store on the Avenue Montaigne. Often, when in the vicinity, he would stop in for a chat with the "*Patron*"— as Ettore Bugatti was universally known to workers, friends, and even family—or when he was out, with Frédéric Loiseau, the madcap cavalryman whom the "Boss" had hired as "travelling inspector" and general salesman on the strength of his trans-Saharan safari.

One day, Loiseau recalls, Saint-Ex walked into his office in his usual "unassuming and charming" way but this time with a particularly dimpled grin on his face. Finding the *Patron* out, he had struck up a conversation with his secretary—about the price of a 2.3 litre model (with compressor) whose sleek lines he had admired in the window.

"For Monsieur Bugatti's friends—of whom I happen to be one—there is a reduction, is there not?" he had asked.

"Oh, of course, Monsieur."

"Have you any idea how much?"

"I think it's 10%."

"10%—for friends . . . And how much for the others?"

"Exactly the same," was the enchanting answer.

The upshot of this particular "intrigue" was the acquisition of a Bugatti roadster which had it all over the Voisin for speed and in which (much later) he came close to killing himself against a peasant's cart blocking a stretch of level highway. But the upkeep of this racy vehicle proved an added strain on its owner's shaky finances, and as time wore on the yawning hole in the rear seat, which was never fixed, and the door which had to be held shut with string, after the handle had ceased working, became as venerable additions to its décor as had been the cracks in the floor boards and the vipers' hole under the dining-room table which had so charmed him at the *castillo* of San Carlos.

Having a car in which to roam the countryside—when he could not fly over in an airplane—was almost a psychological necessity for someone who could not bear being cooped up in a room or an office. Even his writing he preferred to do in cafés, like the Deux Magots at Saint-Germain-des-Prés, where he found the hubbub a stimulus rather than a distraction to his nocturnal lucubrations. And it was not that like Georges Bernanos—another great café scribbler—he needed to be enveloped by the companionable commotion of the human voice; for one day Jean Ihler, who had been a boarder with him at the Villa Saint-Jean in Fribourg, found him pacing up and down the platform of the Perrache station in Lyon.

"And what are you doing here?" he asked in surprise.

"Ah *mon vieux*," was the answer, "I need this animation. I like the coming and going of these trains. It gives me inspiration. Then I sit down in the buffet and start writing."

It was also in the cafés, even more than at home, that Saint-Ex would meet his friends, often reading to them what he had just written in order to get their reaction. For as earnestly as he sought it—even going so far as to smoke an occasional pipe of "pot", like Coleridge—he distrusted his inspiration once the creative fever had cooled. For every paragraph, for every page he kept, there were a dozen, there were a score, perhaps even a hundred he tore up and discarded. But this labour of Sisyphus failed to daunt him, and long after midnight, when every other client had left, it would take the noisy piling of chairs on to the tables to make him realize that the waiters were closing shop—at the ridiculously early hour of two or three in the morning!—and that he would have to pick up his papers and move on.

There is a limit to perfection and by early 1935 Saint-Exupéry was beginning to feel the inevitable pinch. Joseph Kessel, a nightbird like himself who liked to drag him off to listen to gypsy violins in some Russian night-club where he would not only empty but literally *eat* the champagne glasses set before him, was so struck by the pages from his "new book" which Saint-Ex read to him that he could describe them not long afterwards as "among the most beautiful, the densest, the newest, and the most inspired which a man has written . . ."—a generous tribute from a fellow author who had some right to be jealous (Kessel's novel *L'Equipage* having failed to win as much acclaim as *Vol de Nuit*). It was also a prescient judgment, for at the time this tribute was written—early 1936—little of this new material had been published, even in an aviation weekly like *L'Aéro,* which was as interested in experimental writing ("My Finest Flying Experience") as in the development of aeronautic techniques. He did agree to write one or two prefaces—for Maurice Bourdet's *Grandeur et Misère de l'Aviation* as for José Le Boucher's *Le Destin de Joseph-Marie le Brix*; but though the agreement with his publisher gave Gallimard a claim on five books, Saint-Ex refused to be rushed into producing a manuscript which, he stubbornly insisted, was "not yet ripe for publication".

In the meantime he and Consuelo had to live—on something more substantial than hope. His job in Air France's "Propaganda Service" was little more than honorific, while the remuneration was niggardly. It required him to make an occasional speech—at which he did not always excel—but it did at least bring him into contact with many influential people, including newspaper editors who were prepared to make tempting propositions.

The origin of his first newspaper assignment, which lifted him momentarily from his financial morass, can probably be traced to a talk Saint-Exupéry gave to the Aéro-Club de France in mid-February of 1935. The talk was accompanied by a documentary film on aviation progress in Russia, and among the guests present was General Vassilchenko, the Soviet Military Attaché in Paris. The occasion was part of a Franco-Soviet rapprochement engendered by the increasingly strident militancy of the new masters of the Reich, one of whom—a Major von Helders—had created a sensation some eighteen months before by publishing a 300 page book charmingly entitled *How Paris Will be Destroyed in 1936!* Refusing to be outstripped by the Germans and the Italians, who were forging dynamically ahead, the Russians were making strenuous efforts to build up a modern air force. One of their leading engineers, Professor A. N. Tupoleff had even designed and produced a 42 ton, eight-engine monster which was the largest plane in the world. Baptised the *Maxim Gorki* on the occasion of the author's sixty-fifth birthday, this aerial leviathan was something Saint-Ex was curious to examine and it offered him one more reason for wishing to visit that vast *terra incognita*— so ardently praised by some, so bitterly denounced by others—known as the Soviet Union.

\*     \*     \*

Unlike André Malraux, whose novels were as political as his ideological commitments, Saint-Exupéry had never been primarily interested in politics. He had never actively participated in any political party, nor, like his friend Gide, had he enrolled as a member of the World Anti-Fascist Committee which Romain Rolland and Malraux had organized in a desperate attempt to combat deeds with words. But the bloody riots of February 1934, Mermoz' efforts to recruit him for the *Croix de Feu*, and the growing arrogance of the totalitarian regimes in Italy and Germany had gradually aroused a concern over what was happening both in France and Europe.

The only political group Saint-Ex frequented with any assiduity at this time was one gathered around Gaston Bergery, a liberal deputy from Mantes to whom he had been introduced by his journalistic friend Henri Jeanson. To call Jeanson a "journalist" would, of course, be demeaning to an ebullient iconoclast whose agile pen was as skilled in the concoction of diatribes as in the composition of plays and film scenarios.* Already a rising star on the satirical *Canard enchaîné*, Jeanson had made himself feared as well as famous at a time when a local Savonarola with the implausible name of Abbé Bethléem, had taken to publicly tearing up copies of salacious publications being exhibited on boulevard news-stands. Following in his footsteps, Jeanson and his friend the surrealist poet Robert Desnos had moved from one kiosk to the next, destroying all the copies of *Le Pèlerin* and other religious periodicals they could lay their hands on—a performance which had added plenty of fuel to the furore. After the February 1934 riots Jeanson had joined forces with Bergery, Georges Izard the lawyer, and Paul Langevin the physicist, to form a *Front Commun* designed to combat the right-wing monarchist and neo-Fascist movements that were threatening the Republic. All of them were emphatically anti-militarist as well as stout republicans, and their favourite targets in the weekly *La Flèche* were the international munitions barons (François de Wendel, Schneider-Creusot, Krupp, Albert Vickers, Basil Zaharof) and the muscle-flexing patriots (everyone from General Weygand to "*Arsène Lupin de la Rocque . . . Colonel de la Cambriole*"—which is to say, "Colonel Housebreaker of the Fiery Cross") whose concerted efforts, they claimed, could plunge the continent into new wars.

Their trenchant pacifism was a bit naive, but their sincerity was evident, and Saint-Exupéry was soon a frequent visitor at Gaston Bergery's apartment on the Rue de Bourgogne, located an easy five minute walk from the Rue de Chanaleilles. Essentially a free-thinker, Bergery was a political outsider who belonged to no rigid group or clan. His sympathies lay unequivocally to the left and he had even married the daughter of Leonid Krassin, the Russian revolutionary, though he himself was not a Marxist. His second wife, Bettina, was American, but he was just as emphatically opposed to uninhibited capitalism. In this kind of climate Saint-Exupéry could feel at home.

---

* He wrote the dialogues for those two pre-war classics, Julien Duvivier's *Pépé-le-Moko* and Marcel Carné's *Hôtel du Nord*, to say nothing of that comic masterpiece, *La Fête à Henriette*, also directed by Duvivier, which came later.

Probably no country at this time was the subject of such hatred and ill informed controversy as the Soviet Union. Here, too, Saint-Exupéry harboured sympathies not too far removed from those of his friend Gide, but not having been able to judge the realities of Communism at first hand, he preferred to keep an open mind. This attitude recommended itself to Pierre Lazareff, who frequented much the same milieu and to whom Saint-Ex had been introduced the year before by their common friend, Nelly de Vogüé; just as it found favour with his journalistic colleague Hervé Mille, whom Saint-Exupéry had known even longer. Still relatively young—neither was yet thirty—Lazareff and Mille were already influential editors of *Paris-Soir*, the new afternoon daily which the textile magnate Jean Prouvost was building into the most dynamic newspaper in France. "The Graphic Revolution", as Daniel Boorstin has called it, was already transforming the French press, and much of *Paris-Soir*'s burgeoning success was due to its pioneering use of flashy photographs. Its editors had also sensed that what the public wanted was not one more "journal of opinion"—quite a number of which had gone under since the First World War—so much as a paper which could keep it vividly and promptly informed about what was going on in the world. *Paris-Soir* already had a regular correspondent in Moscow, André Pierre; but the brutal realities of Stalinist Russia, with its rigid censorship of all dispatches, had taught him to be careful, and much of his reporting at this time was limited to "safe" topics like the latest exploits of Soviet parachute champions or the plans being hatched by Professor Molchanov, director of the Slutsk Aerological Institute, for putting up a winged rocket with a man inside (this in April of 1935!) for the exploration of the stratosphere.

Most of the journalistic "authorities" on Russia being either rabid enthusiasts who could find no fault with Stalin or disabused "believers" (like the Trotskyists) who had turned into vitriolic critics, Lazareff suggested to Prouvost that *Paris-Soir* might stand to gain by sending Saint-Exupéry to Moscow as an impartial observer who had no axe to grind and as a writer who already possessed a "name". The idea struck Prouvost as judicious. Hitler had just announced that Germany would no longer be bound by the military restrictions of the Treaty of Versailles, and the realists, led by Pierre Laval, the French Foreign Minister, were urging a diplomatic rapprochement with Russia. May Day was approaching—when hundreds of airplanes were to fly over Moscow, an event Saint-Exupéry could judge with the practised eye of an airman; and being politically uncommitted, he could be counted upon to avoid the pitfalls of prejudice and to give an eloquent as well as impartial description of what he saw and heard.

Flattering the offer was, but it filled Saint-Exupéry with qualms. Much as he liked to drop in at the Cadran, on the Boulevard des Capucines, or sample the Juliénas of the Caves Mura, frequented by Jeanson and other *Canard enchaîné* writers, he was not and had no desire to be a journalist. Travel writing, of the kind Paul Morand had made so fashionable, was also something he had little taste for. But the opportunity of visiting Russia, the "motherland of Socialism", was too tempting to resist. The growing belligerence of Mussolini's Italy, visibly girding to invade Ethiopia, the goose-stepping tramp of Hitler's Germany had made Russia, in comparison, respectable.

Even so, the prospect of visiting a country with whose language he was totally unfamiliar and about which he knew so little disturbed Saint-Exupéry considerably. Late one evening he was sitting in the Brasserie Lipp mulling over the problem when in walked Léon-Paul Fargue. Fargue was then living a hundred yards further up the Boulevard Saint-Germain in a hotel calling itself (with delightful incongruity) the Palace, though actually it was a relatively modest establishment which had catered to Bertolt Brecht and Waldo Frank before being swamped by an invasion of anti-Fascist intellectuals (Alexei Tolstoy, Boris Pasternak, Thikhonov, etc.) deposited there by their French mentors—Gide, Malraux, and Aragon. A habitué of Adrienne Monnier's Maison des Amis des Livres and a close friend of André Beucler, Fargue had known Saint-Exupéry since the late 1920s. They had first met —or so at least he later claimed—in the world famous "cheese museum" run by Androuet on the Rue d'Amsterdam, where Saint-Ex's hypersensitive nose had begun to quiver at the sight of "a large disc of Brie de Melun, almost smoking with seduction and radiating with straws like needles sticking out of a Japanese hairdo, or maybe it was a Livarot in its tan leather jacket".

The style is typical of a man whose Neronian head, a mesh of dark hair brushed across the balding Roman brow, and tortoise lips belied a mind as frisky as a pony and as ribald as a rabelaisian monk's. Once he got going it was difficult to stop him, for Fargue's fund of stories and his verbal inventiveness were virtually inexhaustible. Like Joyce (of whom he was in some ways an indolently Gallic version), he felt that rules were made to be broken, language was something to be juggled with, and pat phrases should be scrambled into strange new omelettes. "*L'inciclos est dent,*" he would say, allowing the unusual sound to jar slightly on one's teeth, "is better for upwraught nerves than '*l'incident est clos*'" (the incident is closed). "An infirmemière"—a play on the word "*infirme*" or "ailing"—"is more appropriate than *infirmière*" (nurse). One of his most tongue-twisting *trouvailles* was "*Ossitoyarmezin!*" which he felt was a great improvement on the *Marseillaise*'s less muscle-bound "*Aux Armes, Citoyens!*" An incomparable monologist—as Jean Galtier-Boissière (no mean tale spinner himself) once said of him—Fargue was the joy and despair of hostesses. A joy because a dinner with Fargue was "made", a despair because of his inveterate habit of turning up a couple of hours late, by which time the roast was either ruined or coffee about to be served.

No two persons could have been more unlike than Saint-Ex, never happier than when he was on the move, and Fargue, the sedentary *pantoufflard* poet who found it an effort to climb out of his slippers into a pair of everyday shoes. Yet one quality they shared: both were night owls, members of what Fargue liked to call "*le ministère de la nuit*"—the Ministry of Night. Almost every evening between ten o'clock and midnight, Fargue would turn up at the Brasserie Lipp, sitting down on the brown moleskin seat near the wall ceramics his father had designed and fired for the brasserie's Auvergnat owner. Then he would wander on, at the play of his fancy, to the Deux Magots or to the Flore, before putting in an appearance at Le Boeuf sur le Toit (which Cocteau had helped make famous) around two o'clock in the morning; moving on from there around four to Florence, the most fashionable night-club in Paris, where evening dress was mandatory for everyone but Fargue, who had a disarming way of unconcernedly shaking hands and making quips in his soft collar and lounge suit, a suit often generously sprinkled with the ash falling from the cigarette butt which clung from one corner of his mobile lips.

Like Saint-Exupéry, too, Fargue was habitually impecunious, and countless were the stories about his ingenuity in extracting funds. He would spend his last penny on a magnificent bouquet of flowers to be sent to a hostess and think nothing of turning up in a taxi and asking the butler to pay the cabman. Settling taxi fares was a chore he found intolerably irksome; and as there was hardly a seedy nook or a back-alley cranny he had not explored in a Paris he knew like the palm of his hand, he would often retain a cab for an entire afternoon, moving from one address to another, finally giving the poor driver the slip by darting into a building with a rear exit on another street. When things got really tight, he would go and see his publisher Gaston Gallimard, who was also Saint-Ex's, and explain that he was so hard up he was going to have to sell his mother's old wardrobe (which took up an impressive amount of space in the apartment he occupied for many years near the Gare Montparnasse). The plea put in on behalf of this "old family possession" usually sufficed to squeeze a few more driblets of an advance or the last drops of a royalty out of the canny publisher, who was not a Norman for nothing; nor would Gallimard, who had a sense of humour, be unduly chagrined to learn a few days later that Fargue had tried out the same tale of woe on several other "victims".

"Should I say that we became friends right away?" Fargue later wrote of Saint-Exupéry. The answer apparently was "yes"; for Saint-Ex had a "way of attacking questions and cheeses which appealed to me. It was skilful and direct, though half hidden by an impalpable screen of negligence and fancy. He was outgoing and jovial . . . but suddenly attentive, as one is in those moments where there suddenly passes before the screen of the mind the side of something which has never been glimpsed before."

Just what Saint-Exupéry told Fargue that night at the Brasserie Lipp we do not know, but apparently his words made a considerable impression. For a day or two later Fargue turned up at Comtesse Marthe de Fels' Tuesday afternoon salon, in the fashionable sixteenth *arrondissement*, saying: "*Ah, le pauvre Saint-Ex!* He's in a state. He's being sent to Russia to do a *reportage* and he feels completely lost. What can we do to help him?"

"I have just the person," said Marthe de Fels, herself a Gallimard author and a literary hostess who numbered Valéry, Claudel, and St. John Perse among her friends. Taking Fargue by the elbow she led him over to Prince Alexander Makinsky, who was stationed near the buffet within easy reach of a canapé. A White Russian refugee who had settled in Paris with his parents, Makinsky had met Fargue but not Saint-Exupéry, whom he gladly consented to "enlighten".

Fargue got in touch with his friend Saint-Ex and it was agreed that the three of them would meet at the Brasserie Lipp around 11 p.m. a day or two later. Saint-Exupéry turned up at the appointed hour, as did Makinsky, but—typically enough—there was no sign of Fargue. Finally, after a long, fruitless wait, Saint-Ex, who had been sitting near the entrance watching the clients come and go through the revolving doors, got up and walked over to a stranger he had noticed sitting oddly still amid this human ebb and flow. Was he, by any chance . . . Prince Makinsky? He was.

What most struck Makinsky during the conversation that followed was Saint-Exupéry's almost total ignorance of recent Russian history. Events like Kirov's assassination in Leningrad (the previous December) or the bitter infighting that was going on within the Party between Kamenev, Zinoviev, Bukharin and their followers, on the one hand, and Stalin and his henchmen, on the other, had either passed him by or failed to interest him particularly. The intricacies of Soviet politics, it was clear, intrigued him far less than the predicament of the Russian people, and as a Latin, which he was—to the roots of his being—he could not help wondering how he was going to get on with the Soviet man in the street.

"Let me tell you a story," said Makinsky, "which should encourage you— I mean, things aren't always as bad as they look. It's, if you like, a Russian version of the Faust legend . . . I don't know if you know it?"

Saint-Exupéry shook his head.

"Well, there was once a man—we'll call him Ivan Ivanovich—who in a mood of despair decided to sell his soul to the Devil. So he wrote him a letter and a few days later he got a reply: the Devil would be waiting for him at such and such an hour of a certain night on the Bald Mountain—as you know, in Russian stories there's always a bald mountain around. Anyway, Ivan Ivanovich hied himself out to the wild spot but could find no trace of the Devil. He was beginning to give up hope when he spied a bearded patriarch seated silently upon a log. The last person he had expected to find out on a wild night like this was a holy man, but finally screwing up his courage, he walked up to him and asked: 'Father, have you seen anyone around here of late?'

" 'No' answered the holy man. 'Why? Are you expecting someone?'

" 'Well, yes, as a matter of fact I am.'

" 'And may I ask whom?'

"As you can imagine, there was a moment of embarrassed silence, and Ivan Ivanovich didn't know what to say.

" 'Not the Devil, by any chance?' said the patriarch.

" 'Well yes,' was the startled reply. 'But how did you guess?'

" 'Because *I* am the Devil,' replied the holy man quietly."

Makinsky paused, amused by the gleam of interest in Saint-Exupéry's dark eyes.

"And what happened then?"

" 'Why do you look so surprised?' said the holy man to Ivan Ivanovich.

" 'Because . . . because . . . well, frankly, I expected the Devil to look a bit different.'

" 'Ah!' exclaimed the patriarch, 'don't you realize that the pen has always been in the hands of my enemies?' "

Saint-Ex was apparently much beguiled by this quaint tale, though it did little to still his latent malaise. At the Gare de l'Est there was a sleeper waiting for him, but the splendid isolation it assured him for the long overland trip to Moscow brought scant relief from his brooding meditations. Why was he making this trip? What was it exactly he was hoping to find? "What I am going to look for" as he later sought to explain, "I may never attain. I don't believe in the picturesque. I suppose I have travelled too much not to know how deceptive it can be. As long as a spectacle amuses and intrigues us, it's because we're still judging it from a foreigner's point of view. It's because we haven't grasped its essence. For what is essential in a custom or a rite or in the rule of a game is the taste they give to life, it's the meaning of the life they create. But once they possess this power, they no longer seem picturesque but quite natural and simple."

Unable to sleep, he rose at one o'clock in the morning and went to explore the rest of the train. The sleeping-cars, like the first-class carriages, were empty, reminding him of those de luxe Riviera hotels which stayed open all winter long to cater to the spoiled whim of a single client, sole survivor of a dying breed. But the third-class compartments were crammed, like the corridors, with slumbering forms over which he had to step: Polish miners whose contracts had expired and who were now homeward bound. Beneath the eery blue of the night-lamps these heaps of shapeless bodies swayed and were jostled in a fitful slumber, which they clung to desperately, shifting heavily from one sore side to the other. Even the "hospitality of a sound sleep" had been denied these uprooted exiles whom the callous economic tide of the Depression was washing back to the poverty they had vainly sought to flee.

Back in the empty sleeping-car his feeling of dejection was compounded by the unreality of the luxury in which he was once again enveloped. The compartment steward swayed towards him up the corridor of the rocking train to ask him at what hour he would like to be woken. "What could have been simpler? And yet between this icy individual and myself I feel the empty spaces which separate men from one another. In the cities one forgets what a man is. He is reduced to his function: postman, salesman, the neighbour who disturbs you. It is in the desert that one best discovers what a man is. One has walked a long time after the plane accident towards the little fort of Nouakchott. It was what one was waiting for amid the billowing mirages of one's thirst. But there to greet one is only an old sergeant, lost for months among these sands and so moved by it that he weeps. And a vast night opens up in which each relates his life and makes a gift of that lot of reminiscences through which one discovers a common human kinship. Two men have met and exchange the homage of their gifts with a dignity of ambassadors."

Even here, as they rolled east and northwards, Saint-Ex was under the desert's spell. The world was levelling out, with woodlands and plains, increasingly flat and barren, as the train rattled on towards Berlin. Like the landscape, the restaurant car had changed and was now German. The waiters seemed snappier, less sloppy, as though proud of their calling. Saint-Exupéry was moved to ask himself: "Why, each time one leaves France, does one feel that something has slipped? Why in France this slightly vulgar atmosphere of electoral kowtowing? Why are people so uninterested in their functions and in society as a whole? . . . . Purely symbolic are those provincial inaugurations at which some minister, reading a speech he hasn't written before the statue of some obscure politico he's never known, pours out a torrent of praises of which neither he nor the crowd believe a single word. . . .

"But suddenly, beyond the borders of France, one feels that people are stepping into their functions. The dining car steward waits on you as impeccably as he is dressed. The minister, when he inaugurates, touches on points which really hold his listeners. His words go to the heart because of the subterranean fire they share.

"Yes, but in France this *douceur de vivre*, this feeling of universal kinship. . . . Like the cabman who takes you into his confidence, or those obliging waiters of the Rue Royale who know half of Paris and all of its secrets and who are glad to put in the most confidential phone calls or to lend you a hundred francs. . . .

"Everything is contradictory. The tragic dilemma is in having to choose or to discover which way life is moving. It's what I'm thinking as I listen to the German seated opposite, telling me: 'United, France and Germany would be masters of the world. Why do the French fear Hitler, who is a bulwark against Russia? All he's done is restore to people here a free folk's prerogatives. . . . He represents order.'"

At the next table some Spaniards, bound like himself for Russia, were growing visibly excited. Saint-Ex could hear them discussing Stalin and the Five Year Plan and all the new things that were being done there. "What a change in the landscape!" he thought. "Beyond the borders of France people are no longer interested in the spring, but they are perhaps a bit more preoccupied by the destiny of man."

Poland, with its dark, resin-scented pine woods, reminded him of the sandy forests of the Landes, south of Bordeaux, where a single spark, far swifter than a hundred glinting axes, can cause the trees "not to burn but to fly away". At the Soviet frontier post of Niegoreloy he had to pack his bags and dismount, as they transferred to the broader gauge. Where was the revolution, he could not help wondering, on seeing a gypsy orchestra fiddling away in the vast station buffet. The customs hall, too, with its ornate gilt walls, seemed decked out for a country banquet. The only proletarian touch was provided by the bearlike stolidity of the customs inspector, who pawed through his belongings with the dirty fingers of a moujik.

Judging this vast *terra incognita* was not easy for a newcomer who spoke not a word of Russian. But as the train approached Moscow across the plain, he needed no interpreter to be impressed by the 71 planes—he counted them carefully—engaged in practice flights over the city. "And thus the first visual image I receive is that of an enormous hive, buzzing with activity beneath its swarm of bees."

These reflections on his train trip to Russia were written after he had reached Moscow. On the platform to greet him was Georges Kessel, Joseph's brother, who had been in the Soviet Union for the past three months writing articles for the Paris weekly *Marianne*. Saint-Ex, who had written to him a week or two before to ask if he could find him a room, was relieved to be met by a friend who spoke Russian, and whose first action was to summon a porter! The Moscow terminus might not have a tzigane orchestra playing in the buffet, but it had porters and taxi cabs—just like the Gare du Nord or Victoria Station in London! So the revolutionaries were not as proletarian as the capitalist world had been led to believe. . . .

The taxi drove them to the Savoy, a hotel Georges Kessel had selected because it was smaller and quieter than the Metropol or the International, to which most foreigners trooped in droves. Police surveillance here was less intensive, even though Frenchmen at this moment of Franco-Soviet harmony were left relatively unmolested, Russia having yet to experience the pathological frenzy of Stalin's first great Party purge. The handwriting, however, was already appearing on the wall, and Kessel, who had actually managed to invite Kamenev's daughter to the theatre, could sense that the "liberal" interlude was drawing to a close.

Saint-Ex himself was soon to feel the iron weight of the state's heavy-handed pressure. Though he reached the Russian capital well before May 1st, he was too late to obtain a coveted place on Red Square from which to watch the May Day parade. The French Embassy, to which he appealed, could do nothing to help him, still less Georges Kessel, who had to leave at this critical juncture for a four-day trip to Leningrad. It was a detail, but one which forcefully brought home to Saint-Exupéry just how ponderous was the implacable bureaucracy which had grown up around the master of the Kremlin, whose rare appearances in public—like those of a "god being brought out of his tabernacle"—were reserved for the eyes of spectators who had been meticulously screened. There was nothing, however, to keep him from roaming the adjacent streets on the eve of the event. It was cold and there were even some flurries of snow, but which failed to dampen the ardour of teams of comrades busy draping the façades of buildings with immense red streamers which billowed in the wind like sails at a regatta.

The next morning Saint-Ex rose early, determined to see something of the show, even if he couldn't push his way through to Red Square. But he was not early enough; for he found the hotel entrance blocked by guards, who stood there woodenly repeating that the doors would be opened—at five o'clock that afternoon! Like the other unfortunates who lacked official passes, Saint-Exupéry was a prisoner in his own hotel.

He was pacing up and down the lobby like a caged beast when suddenly he heard a sound like an approaching thunderstorm, only steadier and more deliberate, more unbroken. A thousand airplanes were advancing on the city, bearing down on its domes and dwellings and teeming multitudes with a giant hand of steel. For Saint-Ex this sonorous challenge was too much.

There was still a spark of schoolboy devilry within him, and he was damned if he was going to be cooped up indoors when so much excitement was going on outside! At the Lycée Saint-Louis he had used a tunnel and a conveniently located manhole; here he used a window and a fortunately neglected terrace.

In a trice he was in the street; a street that was strangely empty save for a few children who went on playing unconcernedly. Like a tidal wave gathering momentum in its course, everyone else had been sucked relentlessly towards the beckoning vastness of Red Square. For a few minutes Saint-Exupéry leaned back against a wall, looking up at the seried ranks of metallic Vs which droned over his head as implacably as a rolling-mill. Then he walked up a number of deserted streets, only to be rebuffed each time he sought to get by the guards barring the approaches to Lenin's mausoleum. Finally he found himself in an avenue where an interminable mob, a mile-long flow of human lava, was slowly moving towards the Kremlin. Heavily muffled, they shuffled along as though for a funeral procession, notwithstanding the gay note struck by their red banners. Suddenly there was the sound of music; bored by the stalled march, a musician from one of the bands had struck up on his accordion. Others began playing, and in the twinkling of an eye this sombrely clad procession dissolved into groups of red-cheeked dancers, kicking and whirling away the tedium of a frosty morning. Saint-Ex was reminded of Bastille Day in Paris. "A stranger hailed me and handed me a cigarette. Another offered me a light. The crowd was happy. . . . Then suddenly a tremor ran through the crowd, the musicians put up their brasses, the banners were hoisted, the ranks reformed. A group leader tapped a young girl on the head with his cane to get her to resume her place. It was the last individual, the last familiar gesture. Everyone grew serious again as the march towards Red Square was resumed. Already the crowd had stiffened, it was going to appear before Stalin."

Written in what for him was a hurry, Saint-Exupéry's first article was telephoned through the next day and published in the May 3rd issue of *Paris-Soir* over a front-page article announcing the forthcoming signing of a Franco-Russian Non-aggression Pact. On the whole, it was a meritorious effort, though some readers may have been surprised by certain of the author's forward-looking speculations. After mentioning the fact that beards and grisly chins had vanished overnight in Russia, banned by a simple decree from the Master of the Kremlin, Saint-Exupéry could add: "One has the impression that the day it touches clothing, the magic wand of the Plan will at once brighten the streets of Moscow where caps and work clothes still strike a sad grey note. And it hardly seems paradoxical to imagine the day when Stalin, from the depths of the Kremlin, will decree that a good self-respecting proletarian should dress up in the evening. Russia, that day, will dine in evening clothes."

It was a good ten days before Saint-Exupéry was willing to commit himself again to paper. Did he perhaps sense that his first article was a shade too rosy-hued? It is possible, though Georges Kessel, after his return from Leningrad, seemed more inclined to regard it as surreptitious indolence. Momentarily delivered from the domestic cares which weighed down on him in Paris, Saint-Ex seemed out to enjoy a few days of truancy. At table he spread inch-thick slabs of butter on the radishes he ate, and when Kessel raised a questioning eyebrow, his friend gaily explained that it was because his doctor had told him to stay away from bread—this as much as lack of exercise being the cause of his expanding girth. As Kessel could see, he was obeying the prescription to the letter: the rich black peasant bread was left untouched, while Saint-Ex took the edge off his enormous appetite with half a pound of butter. There was something about the atmosphere in Moscow, he explained to a sceptical Kessel, that was just not conducive to writing. He suffered from the prevailing dearth of cigarettes—how could one write without smoking?—and when he felt that this particular excuse was beginning to lose its credibility, he would devour a bar of chocolate, enough to induce a headache which made all work impossible.

Saint-Exupéry's time, of course, was not altogether his own. The Russians, who were out to impress their visitor, invited them both out to watch a parachute jumping exhibition accompanied by a lavish luncheon.

"I suppose you realize," Kessel turned to him as the banquet got under way, "that you're going to have to make a speech".

"A speech?" Saint-Ex was appalled. If there was one thing he really hated, it was making speeches.

But Kessel insisted. After all, he was a famous writer, it was logical, wasn't it? The news put Saint-Exupéry off his meal completely. Barely nibbling at the caviar and leaving most of the other dishes virtually untouched, he spent the next hour feverishly jotting down ideas on scraps of paper, while Kessel preserved an admirably straight face. The repast ended, predictably enough, with vodka toasts, but no one thought of asking Saint-Exupéry to expatiate in French.

Saint-Ex took the joke in his stride, though his hungry stomach was far less amused by this diversion. But a day or two later he scored a neat revenge. Kessel had managed to accumulate a respectable hoard of English cigarettes, which Saint-Exupéry would occasionally smoke out of sheer desperation, unable to satisfy his craving for American tobacco, which he infinitely preferred. One evening he suggested to Kessel: "Let's play a game of chess." They sat down at the board and ten minutes later Saint-Exupéry was brilliantly checkmated, Saint-Ex looked glum. "All right," he said, "let's have another". A second game was started and, like the first, ended in quick defeat.

"We'll just have to play a third," said Saint-Ex grimly, "but this time let's make it more interesting".

"How do you mean?" asked Kessel.

"Well, let's say—if you win, I have to give you a packet of English cigarettes. And if I win, you have to give me a packet of American."

"It's a bargain," said Kessel, pleased at the prospect of enlarging his stock of Craven A's and Player's.

To his astonishment his lacklustre opponent now suddenly caught fire. He took the third game, and then the fourth, followed by a fifth. By the time the tournament was over Kessel found himself owing him more than a dozen packets of American cigarettes—in a city where they were almost as rare as diamonds. It was Saint-Ex's turn to enjoy a good laugh. The "poor player" had turned out to be a whiz, and to pay off his debt the harassed Kessel was reduced to filling his pockets with Camels and Chesterfields, quietly removed from the silver bowls and chalices of an American Embassy reception.

His brow wreathed once more in sweet Virginia smoke, Saint-Ex could at last get down to the job of composing his second article. It was devoted to his train trip through Germany and Poland; and by an extraordinary coincidence, his harrowing description of all those Polish miners, herded like cattle into their third-class carriages, appeared in the same issue of *Paris-Soir* which brought the news of Marshal Pilsudski's death. The lyricism this time was frankly pessimistic, in marked contrast to what Saint-Exupéry had written about May Day in Moscow; but the writing, perhaps for the very reason that it was in the minor key, was incomparably superior. What had begun as an article had turned, before it was halfway through, into an elegy: as in this description of one of these Polish miners lolling on his wooden seat in the shabby third-class compartment:

"His skull was as bald and heavy as a stone. A body folded into an uncomfortable sleep, imprisoned in workclothes made of humps and hollows. He was like a lump of clay—similar to those shapeless wrecks one can see at night sprawled on subway benches. And I thought: 'The heart of the problem is not in this poverty, this dirt, this ugliness. But this same man and this same woman one day met. And the man doubtless smiled at the woman. And doubtless, too, he brought her flowers, after work. Bashful and fumbling, he may have trembled at the thought of being spurned. But the woman, by natural coquetry, but the woman sure of her grace, took pleasure in prolonging his suspense. And the man, today no more than a machine for digging or drilling, thus felt in his heart a delicious anxiety. The mystery is how he could have turned into this lump of clay. Through what terrible mould has he passed, marked by it as though by a machine-press? A stag, a gazelle, an ageing animal conserve their grace. But why must this lovely human paste be so disfigured?"

And a little further on:

"I sat down opposite a couple. A child had somehow made himself a hollow between wife and husband and was sleeping. In his slumber he turned and I saw his face in the dim glow of the night-lamp. Ah, what an adorable face! To this couple had been born a golden fruit. Out of these heavy, worn togs had sprung a triumph of charm and grace! I bent over this smooth brow, this gentle purse of the lips and thought: 'Here is the face of a musician, this is Mozart as a child, here is a lovely promise of life.' The little princes of legend were no different from him. Sheltered, cared for, cultivated, what might he not become? When by virtue of some mutation a new rose is born in the gardens, all the gardeners are moved. The rose is isolated, the rose is cultivated, it is favoured. . . . But there is no gardener for men. Mozart the child will be marked like the rest by the machine-press. Mozart will thrill to the sound of trashy music in the stench of café concerts. Mozart is condemned. . . ."

The first *Paris-Soir* edition was about to go to press while Saint-Exupéry was still dictating his article from Moscow, so that the pressure on the typist at the Paris end was more than usually intense. But when, after an abnormally long pause, Hervé Mille walked in to find out what was holding up the next typed page, he found the poor woman in tears.

"What's the matter?" he asked.

"I can't go on," she spluttered, "I can't . . . It's too beautiful, too beautiful . . ."

Saint-Ex, at the other end of the line, may not quite have realized what was happening; but his first reader—in this case, a listener—could only carry on to the end with a handkerchief to dry her eyes.

The third of his articles, dealing with his first impressions of Russia and entitled "Moscow! But where is the Revolution?" was telephoned through two days later and published next to an article describing Pierre Laval's official visit to Moscow. But it was in the fourth, headlined "USSR 1935— Crimes and Punishments in the Eyes of Soviet Justice", that Saint-Exupéry's perplexity about the land of Lenin was most tortuously revealed. He had arranged to meet a Soviet judge who (doubtless through an interpreter) undertook to explain that the fundamental principle of Soviet justice was "not to punish but to correct. . . . If fear must be instilled because common law crimes are on the rise and the epidemic must be halted, we punish more severely. When an army is going to pieces, a few are singled out and shot by way of example. The same person who, a fortnight earlier, would have got three years of hard labour, has to pay with his life for a piece of petty robbery. But we have checked the epidemic and have saved our men."

The comment Saint-Exupéry added to this explanation was once again highly personal: "This judge does not permit himself to pass judgment. He is like a doctor whom nothing can scandalize. He heals if he can, but since he is serving society above all else, if he cannot cure, he executes. Neither the stammering of the condemned nor the tremble of the lips, nor the rheumatism which endears him to us is of the least avail in securing a reprieve. In all of this I discern a great lack of respect for the individual, but a great respect for man, for the kind who perpetuates himself in individuals and whose greatness must be forged."

The thoughts and even the choice of words had barely changed since *Vol de Nuit*; and while this may well have been the gist of what the judge actually asserted, Saint-Exupéry was unconsciously superimposing the figure of Rivière, that *brasseur d'hommes*, that moulder of men, for whom the individual was like a paste or a wax which it was up to him to fashion into a being of a higher sort. Even so, Saint-Ex was too attached to the personal and to the human not to raise a momentary protest: "I grant you, *Monsieur le Juge*, the foundations of justice. But the endless drive, the surveillance, the passport everyone must have to move about the country, the universal submission to the collective, these are what seem intolerable to us. And yet, I think that even here I understand . . . They have founded a society and now demand not only that people respect its laws but also that they inhabit it. They demand that they organize themselves socially not only in appearance but also in their hearts. Then and only then will the discipline relax. . . ."

"For," Saint-Exupéry went on, "part of the Russian people have nomads' souls and are haunted by the old Asiatic desire to take to the road, in caravans, beneath the stars. So houses are built to tempt the caravaneers. Apartments are not rented but sold. Travel permits are issued for all movements within the country. And those who raise their eyes too high towards dangerous signs in the sky are sent to Siberia, where they are put through the wringer of winters with sixty degrees of frost. And thus perhaps a new type of man is created, stable and as fond of his factory and human group as the French gardener is of his garden."

It was an idyllic vision not only of Soviet justice but also of Soviet society; and the "perhaps" in that final sentence seems to indicate that even Saint-Exupéry was a bit dubious about the soundness of his apologia. For the people sent to work camps were not simply the nomadically inclined, nor the "thieves, the pimps, and the assassins" he cited as examples and who had been banished to the North to move mountains of earth and to link the Baltic to the White Sea with a canal; they were everyone and anyone who happened to have fallen out of favour with the Powers that Be and who were consigned to the mind-numbing oblivion of concentration camps by the arbitrary order of some callous commissar or political intriguer. And it was not only expecting a lot, it was being downright naive—as so many intellectuals in the thirties were—to suppose that such brutal and indiscriminate means could, by the magic alchemy of doctrinal passion, bring forth a newer, better, purer type of human being.

Saint-Exupéry was on surer ground when he left the fetid chambers of Soviet justice to take to the air. Though the world's largest plane, the *Maxim Gorky*, had been flying for about a year, no foreigner had yet been allowed to go up in it. Saint-Ex had put in a request, asking that an exception be made in his case, but several weeks had passed and he had all but abandoned hope when unexpectedly one afternoon the rare authorization was granted. "I installed myself in the lounge located in the nose of the plane," as he later described the experience, "and watched the take-off. The machine shuddered powerfully forward, and I felt this forty-two ton monument plant itself solidly in the air, and I was surprised at the ease of the take-off."

He was even more surprised by the "walk" he took through the plane, which was divided into eleven different compartments, some of them with sleeping berths. In one compartment he came upon a secretary quietly typing away. A mechanic led him on an inspection tour through the left wing, so huge that its motors could be reached through doors opening into dens which were like miniature engine-rooms. An engineer showed him the electric power-plant, hooked up to a huge loud-speaker strong enough to broadcast to the ground above the roar of the eight engines. Saint-Ex felt as though he were exploring the bowels of a destroyer; and back in the lounge, as he gazed down on the city of Moscow, he had the impression of viewing it all from the balcony of a de luxe hotel.

The very next day a catastrophe overtook the *Maxim Gorky*. It had just taken off from the airport with its 11 man crew and 37 hand-picked members of the Aerodynamic Institute on a flight intended to take them to Leningrad and back when a stunt pilot, eager to impress the gaping crowd below, tried a couple of daring loops around the giant. As he was pulling out of the second his propeller struck one of the *Maxim Gorky*'s wings. The stricken monster shuddered, the left wing slowly detached itself from the body, engines began exploding, and within seconds the world's largest plane was plunging towards the earth. The flaming wreckage was strewn over hundreds of yards, and one of the wings plummeted down on a small wooden house which was burnt to cinders with its two inhabitants. 51 persons, including the stunt pilot, perished; and Saint-Exupéry's article, hastily altered and re-entitled "The Tragic End of the *Maxim Gorky*", inadvertently acquired a macabre topicality. Had his authorization come through one day later, he too would have been among the victims.

Quite different in tone was the last article Saint-Exupéry gave to *Paris-Soir* on the eve of his departure from the Soviet Union. Someone had told him there were still three hundred ageing French schoolmarms living in Moscow. Originally hired as governesses for the children of the better born in Tzarist times, these "little grey mice" had survived the storm of 1917 by offering their pedagogic services to the sons and daughters of the Russian revolution. A typically grey-haired specimen was Mademoiselle Xavier, who had holed up in an apartment building in the suburbs, where her un-announced visitor (Saint-Ex) had some trouble unearthing her. . . . A visitor from France? Not possible! "Just think, the first in thirty years!" And in the twinkling of an ageing spinster's eye the cabinet was opened, the glasses set noisily down upon the table—for the door was open and she wanted the entire building to know of her good fortune—and her big bearish guest, his cheeks a-dimple with pleasure, was treated to a rare feast of cakes and madeira.

Saint-Ex's impromptu visit became the occasion for a fête, as ten other "little grey mice" flocked to the newly painted apartment of one of Made-moiselle Xavier's friends to greet this extraordinary apparition from their homeland, who brought them a lavish stock of port, wines, and liqueurs. Soon they were all a wee bit drunk and singing songs and kissing their "Prince Charming".

But then—"A gentleman of infinitely grave mien makes his entry. A rival. Each evening he comes to sip tea, speak French, and nibble at the cakes. But this evening he sits, austere and acrimonious, by a tiny table."

"He's Russian," the "little grey mice" informed him, "and do you know what he's done?"

Saint-Ex had no idea.

"Tell our Frenchman what you did in 1906," they cried, harrying the newcomer, who now assumed the modest air of a *grand seigneur*. Negligently he fingered his watch-chain, deliberately dallying. Finally, yielding to their entreaties, he turned and casually remarked, but carefully stressing each syllable: "In 1906 I played roulette in Monaco."

The little old ladies clapped their hands in triumph.

"Towards one o'clock in the morning it is time for me to go home. I am accompanied in great pomp to the taxi. I have a little old lady on each arm, two little old ladies who keep crossing their steps. Today I am the *dueña*.

"Mademoiselle Xavier whispers in my ear: 'Next year I too shall have my apartment, and we'll meet in my place. You'll see how pretty it will be. I'm already embroidering the hangings.'

"Mademoiselle Xavier leaned closer to my ear. 'You'll come to see me before the others. I'll be the first, won't I?'

"Next year Mademoiselle Xavier will be only seventy-three years old. She will get her apartment. She will be able to start life at last."

                              *       *       *

The tone of these articles was so fresh, so original, so sparkling that they caused something of a sensation among newspaper readers. The questions Saint-Exupéry had touched upon were fundamental even if the answers were not always satisfactory, and Madame Larosa—for such was her name—had not been misled in breaking down over her stalled typewriter. For the passage about the Mozart child was of such imperishable perfection that it could still be used four years later as the finale for *Terre des Hommes*. Everyone was pleased—Prouvost, the publisher of *Paris-Soir*, for having "annexed" an eminent man of letters; Pierre Lazareff and Hervé Mille for having picked a winner; and not least of all Saint-Ex, who could now pay the arrears on his rent and look forward to a month or two of affluence.

The respite, predictably, was brief, even though he now found himself besieged by journalistic offers. In July he finally let himself be talked into giving the liberal weekly *Marianne* (which his friend Gaston Gallimard had helped found) an article on Jean Mermoz; but it was more to praise the "*pilote de ligne*" who had spearheaded the battle to save something from the wreckage of the Aéropostale than it was to fill his own pockets at his friend's expense. The article ended on a typically anti-chrematistic note which alone sufficed to make this clear. "The night flight and its hundred thousand stars, this serenity, this sovereignty of a few hours, money does not buy. This novelty of the world after a difficult lap; these trees, these flowers, these women freshly coloured by a life which has just been granted you at dawn, this concert of little things which are given back to you and are your just reward, money does not buy. . . ."

Overtures were also made to him by *L'Intransigeant*, *Paris-Soir*'s chief competitor in peppy journalism. Though not quite as entertaining as *Paris-Soir* (its owners were less ready than Prouvost to invest large sums of money

In their paper), *L'Intransigeant* was making a desperate effort to vie with its rival's practice of hiring celebrated authors to write article series. Its new editor-in-chief, René Delange, had also befriended Saint-Exupéry and was most anxious to conscript his talents. But for what? That autumn, as the storm began to break over Ethiopia, there was talk of sending him to East Africa to rival the coverage which that swashbuckling adventurer, Henry de Montfried, was providing *Paris-Soir*; but the idea of getting dragged into a kind of journalistic duel failed to excite Saint-Ex, and in the end it was a regular *Intransigeant* reporter, Emmanuel Bourcier, who was sent out to report on Mussolini's dismal "war against barbarism".

Saint-Exupéry, besides, was now engrossed in another project which was to bear charming fruit. For this indefatigable scribbler who was never happier than when doodling with coloured pencils (his caricatures, though often erratic, were frequently comic) the cinema was too rich a medium of expression not to have provoked a fascinated interest. He had shown it in the early twenties by the passionate fervour aroused in him by Chaplin; and what his fellow pilot Henri Delaunay later took to be indifference—each time he saw him walk out of an Alicante movie-house after fifteen restless minutes—was in reality a highly critical reaction to the cheap, ill conceived, sloppily composed, and unimaginatively directed films he was constantly being exposed to. For every Chaplin or Eisenstein, for every René Clair or Jean Renoir there were a hundred mediocre hacks, but it was they alas! who kept the market well supplied. One of Saint-Ex's more savage annotations in the little leather-bound notebook he had taken to carrying around in his inside pocket and on which he liked to jot down whatever happened to occur to him, states: "Thus in the film, from the loveliest clay in the world"—his way of speaking of the flesh—"is born the empty and abysmally stupid star. An animal of such hollowness I doubt she's even bored. . . ."

During his year in Argentina he had put his critical interest to the test by beginning a film scenario entitled *Anne-Marie*. He apparently did little about it after his return to France, perhaps because the crisis within the Aéropostale put him in no mood to peddle a pilot's fantasy that was essentially gay and light-hearted. But by 1935 he felt less hamstrung by this kind of inhibition, and he was lucky enough to meet a film director, Raymond Bernard, with whom he immediately hit it off. His illustrious father, the playwright Tristan Bernard (to whom Antoine was also introduced), was one of the great wits of the day. His son may not have inherited his formidable facility with words, but he had inherited his sureness of ear; and his ear was enchanted by the droll story of *Anne-Marie*.

It is to be hoped that the text will one day be included in Saint-Exupery's complete works; for though it was substantially reworked between author

and director, the original scenario is unmistakably *exupérien*, full of those
quaint flashes of whimsy which were already brightening his letters twenty
years before he wrote *Le Petit Prince*. Dumas' Three Musketeers were four,
but in *Anne-Marie* there are five inseparable companions. Flyers all, they
are so inseparable that each time one of them bursts into the pilots' common
room, his first query is invariably: "Where are the others?"—as though
no one else could be meant. The most imposing of them is "The Detective"
—so called in the text—whose two specialities are card tricks and a Holmes-
like talent for unravelling mysteries. The second is "The Peasant", so
named for his duck-raising passion (at his little place in the country) though
in the air he has the courage of a lion. (We have little trouble here recognizing
Guillaumet.) The third, "The Lover", is a twentieth-century Aramis,
constantly embroiled in amorous scrapes from which his friends are often
called upon to rescue him. Then there is "The Thinker", a silent fellow
who spends his time modelling a lump of clay he carries around in his
pocket. And finally there is "The Boxer", a small wiry type "with the waist
of a young girl and muscles of steel".

The film opens with the Boxer narrowly missing a crash as he comes
in to land on the airfield where the five are serving as test pilots and flying
instructors. One of his controls is jammed. The fault is not the mechanics';
it is patently an error of design. Solemnly the five Inseparables march into
the designers' workroom, where a hundred draftsmen and engineers are
bent over their drawing-boards. Guided from one to the next, they descend
menacingly on a bearded technician, only to discover—the world is full of
surprises!—that the culprit is not he but his neighbour, a lovely young girl.
Their hostility gives way at first to withering contempt until the Peasant,
pulling back the drawing-board behind which she is half-hiding, finds the
poor girl in tears. Immediately the stern judges become tender consolers.
Patiently they explain to her that logarithms are one thing, but that piloting
is another. Science can do a great deal, but to keep a plane in the air and
a pilot from cracking up, the humble artisan is needed to second the geometer. So why not become both—by learning to fly herself? Anne-Marie,
for such is her name, is delighted and the five Inseparables take her in hand.

The Detective is giving her her first theoretical lesson when it is
interrupted by a desperate S.O.S. from The Lover, who has gotten himself
into one more romantic fix. Jumping into a car with a sackful of equipment,
the four pilots and Anne-Marie race to the scene of the crisis. With a
sang-froid born of multiple experience, they rescue the beleaguered Don
Juan by hoisting him from a fourth floor balcony up to the floor above,
while an irate husband goes on vainly pounding at his wife's locked door.
The adventure cements their new friendship with Anne-Marie, but only

partly; for she is feminine and beautiful and thus the object of external solicitations. The Group take a dim view of a whipper-snapper who is evidently distracting "their" Anne-Marie, and several ruses concocted by the Detective permit them to identify the bounder, who is quickly made to look ridiculous in her eyes. Several other "intruders" are eliminated in the same resourceful fashion.

Anne-Marie makes her solo and obtains her pilot's licence, to the beady-eyed joy of her old sea-captain father. But her heart once again is taken, this time by a character named the Inventor, who (like Saint-Ex) spends an inordinate amount of time dreaming up improvements for things which have already been invented. But he plays Bach, has a drole sense of humour, and as often as not when the concierge knocks at the door with the mail, there he is lying stretched out on the bed. "When a sweeper sweeps", he explains, "he works. When an inventor invents, he works. I am an inventor." And his eyes return to the ceiling. But in the Design Room at the field, into which he wanders to find out what the experts think of his latest patent, his eyes come to rest on Anne-Marie's. An inventor! How glamorous! She is delighted, he is charmed, and soon the new suitor is introduced to her pilot protectors, who close ranks against the non-flying outsider. Unflustered by their barbed questions, he stymies the Detective, who asks him to pick a card, by foiling the trick and pulling the card from his sleeve. For the Inventor is also a magician.

He is also a man of honour; and when the Detective, in a despairing man-to-man appeal, asks him to stop distracting Anne-Marie with his visits and his bouquets of flowers—the world, after all, is full of lovely girls, but where else is to be found a close-knit group like theirs?—the Inventor smiles a melancholy smile but finally consents to make the sacrifice requested.

But Anne-Marie is sentimental, and something must be done to fill the void. Seated around a table, the five Inseparables decide to write her a joint love letter. The Thinker composes the first draft, to which the others suggest improvements. Anne-Marie is visibly enchanted to find a new *billet doux* from an unknown admirer waiting for her every day in her mail-box. The letters become longer and it is soon evident that the Thinker is cheating. He has taken to adding pages of his own invention to the jointly approved epistle. Poor Thinker! He in turn has been smitten. Well, let them get married, cries the Detective. But before Anne-Marie has time to open the final letter in which the Thinker reveals his identity, he is killed testing a new plane.

The days pass and there are no more letters. The Thinker's final missive is preserved unopened in a little commemorative niche in the Detective's room, along with the lump of modelling clay which never left him. Now a full-fledged pilot, Anne-Marie has set her mind on establishing a new non-stop flying record. But shortly before the take-off she chances on the Thinker's letter, and bursts into tears. She liked the Thinker, she sobs to the Detective, but those letters! . . . she was certain they came from the Inventor. It is dismaying news—the Detective was half in love with her himself—but once she is in the air, he calls on the Inventor and brings him out to the field. Speaking for his three remaining friends, the Detective explains that they have made something of Anne-Marie—after all, she's trying for a new world record—but in itself this was not enough. They had jointly sought to make up for music, stars, and roses, but had failed. She was his for the asking.

Anne-Marie, meanwhile, is in trouble. Her airplane has been overtaken by a storm and her radio antenna knocked out by a thunderbolt. Circling desperately above a nearby town, whose lights she can still see, she no longer knows where to land. The four Inseparables race to an emergency field and light petroleum flares, but situated eight miles farther north, they are too faint to be detected through the blinding rainfall. The Inventor saves the day by invading the local power plant and alternately cutting and reconnecting the current, while the Boxer takes care of the protesting technicians. From the air Anne-Marie sees the city lights oddly blinking, and realizes a message is being morse-coded to her. The message deciphered, she heads north and puts down safely on the rain-swept strip. The Detective rushes up as she climbs wetly out of the cockpit, and seizing her by the shoulders he turns her round towards the Inventor. "Kiss him," he says. "He's proved himself a man".

\*     \*     \*

The film Raymond Bernard made of *Anne-Marie* proved as delightful as the original script. Pierre-Richard Wilm, who rode around on a motor-cycle with roses on the handlebars, made a beguiling Inventor, while Annabella was a captivating Anne-Marie. At the première in Marseille, attended by Saint-Ex's sister Gabrielle, the film's dramatic ending was even greeted by a burst of spontaneous applause.

Enjoyable though this cinematographic interlude proved to be, it was too vicarious an experience to satisfy a zest for flying which had never left him. Much as he liked his Bugatti—that "*pur-sang*" of the road, as its horse-loving manufacturer liked to call it—it was too earth-bound a machine to be able to compete in Saint-Exupéry's affection with the kind of airborne "thoroughbred" which his old boss, Didier Daurat, had helped bring into

production. Fed up with the will less inertia of a company which had virtually given up night flying as too risky, Daurat had left Air France and teamed
up with Beppo de Massimi and Louis Renault (the automobile manufacturer)
to launch a new airline. Called Air Bleu, it aspired to give France an internal
postal network comparable to the one Lufthansa had so successfully established in Germany. The plane Daurat was relying on for this purpose was a
sleek, streamlined job known as the *Simoun* (after the hot wind of the
Arabian desert). Built by Caudron and powered by a single Renault 240
horsepower engine connected to a variable-speed propeller, it could cruise
at 250 to 300 kilometres an hour, or a good 50 kilometres an hour faster than
most commercial planes of the period. Saint-Ex, whose interest in aerodynamics had remained unflagging, found the *Simoun's* greyhound silhouette
too tempting to resist; and throwing caution to the winds, he used up all his
earnings (from the Moscow trip and the film rights to *Anne-Marie*) to buy
one.

For a chronically penniless person it was an expensive toy, but Saint-
Exupéry was hopefully persuaded he could turn it into an asset. The year
1935 had already produced a new crop of broken records, and in the air as
on the automobile race tracks lavish rewards were being offered to trophy-
winning "aces". In January Amelia Earhart had astounded the world by
flying non-stop from Hawaii to California; but of more immediate interest
to Saint-Ex was the Belgian Guy Hansez' triumph in September, when he
won the Wakefield Cup flying a Caudron-Renault *Simoun*. Two prizes at this
time were being offered by the French Air Ministry for long distance flights,
supposedly as an encouragement to airplane manufacturers. One was a prize
of 500,000 francs (about $33,000) for the person who could fly in the shortest
time from Paris to Tananarive, in Madagascar, before the expiration of the
year (December 31, 1935). The other was a prize of 150,000 francs (about
$10,000) for anyone who could better the record time of five days and four
hours which two Frenchmen (Lalouette and Goulette) had established for
the distance between Paris and Saigon.

Though the first of these two prizes, for obvious financial reasons, was
much the more attractive, Saint-Exupéry was tempted by the second—for
the simple reason that he already knew the course, having flown to Saigon
and back the previous year. His doubts about the first may also have been
influenced by the mishap which overtook Edouard Corniglion-Molinier, the
dare-devil pilot who had previously flown André Malraux out to Arabia in a
vain search of the Queen of Sheba's legendary capital; in September he had
crash-landed on to a ploughed field shortly after take-off and both he and
his mechanic had been seriously hurt.

Just when Saint-Exupéry first discussed the project with René Delange of *L'Intransigeant* is not clear, but it was probably in early October. Delange apparently liked the idea of a journalistic account of a Paris–Saigon "raid", and Saint-Ex went ahead with the purchase and preparation of his *Simoun*. He hired the services of a mechanic called André Prévot, but the job of readying the *Simoun* must have taken longer than expected. For the plane was still not ready towards the end of this same month (October) when Delange came up with a new journalistic proposition. Marshal Lyautey, who had died in July of the previous year, had requested in his will that Morocco, the land he had conquered for France, be his final resting place. It had taken a year to build a suitable mausoleum in the hallowed "Chellah" cemetery, just beyond the imperial walls of Rabat, but now everything was ready for the official transfer of his ashes. The date had been fixed for the final days of October, and Delange, knowing Saint-Exupéry's fondness for Morocco, asked if he would not fly down there and write up the event for *L'Intransigeant*.

The answer apparently was "Yes", though what else the agreement between them comprised is a matter of conjecture. There is no mention of any such journalistic assignment in the brief biography which René Delange later devoted to his friend, and Jacques Meyer, who was the Managing Editor of *L'Intransigeant* at the time, has no recollection of it whatsoever. Consuelo, who accompanied her husband on this trip, recalls their having flown down on a "normal" Air France flight, and this is corroborated by Dr. Henri Comte. Saint-Ex had never liked Casablanca, and it is possible that the martial pomp and circumstance which was generated for the arrival of the French cruiser *Dupleix* (bearing Lyautey's remains) irked rather than inspired him. Whatever the case, he seems to have succumbed to the same journalistic torpor which had overtaken him in Moscow, for Henri Comte heard him say one night, after dinner: "I must go to the post office and send my cable—I'm overdue as it is."

Presumably he cabled something, but just what it was it is impossible to say for sure. *L'Intransigeant* had been devoting daily articles to the event ever since Lyautey's ashes had left Nancy on October 26, but the dispatches filed from Casablanca and Rabat on the 29th and 30th were unsigned ("from our own correspondent" and exceptionally on the 30th "from our specially sent reporter".) They were straightforward news dispatches which showed hardly a trace of literary elegance or originality; and it thus seems reasonable to assume that they emanated from someone else, Saint-Ex's dispatch being quietly buried because it reached Delange too late.

Henri Comte recalls this visit of Saint-Exupéry's as having been relatively long, but it is doubtful if it lasted more than three to four days. Saint-Ex was still in Casablanca on the 31st when Jean Mermoz flew in from Paris on a new do Havilland *Comet* which he was testing for Air France. That evening they all met for dinner at Zézé's quaint bistrot by the sea, where Saint-Ex amused the company with lively recollections of his first plane-stealing exploit at Strasbourg and the acrobatic loops which had so startled Captain Bouscat over the Casablanca airfield.

Saint-Exupéry was in such a hurry to get back to Paris that he finally left Consuelo in Casablanca and returned on an earlier flight. The reason for this precipitation was probably less to see how work was progressing on the *Simoun* than to give satisfaction to his Air France employers. His job in the publicity department was anything but well remunerated, but his contract did at least guarantee him a regular pilot's bonus each time he flew a plane on official business. Most of his travelling had hitherto been confined to France; but with a *Simoun* at his disposal he could now extend the range of his lecture tours while benefiting from a parallel increase in pay. If such was one of the factors which prompted him to invest in the plane, it was a wild hope which bore little relation to the economic imperatives of the moment ("retrenchment" being the universal watchword)—as Saint-Ex was now to discover. It is not clear who first suggested the idea of his undertaking a lecture tour around the Mediterranean, but one thing is certain: the budget allotted to himself, another Air France colleague named Jean-Marie Conty, and his mechanic André Prévot, was so meagre that it barely covered the basic costs of fuel. For the rest they had to rely on box-office proceeds from the sale of lecture tickets and on whatever hospitality they could elicit from local French groups and diplomatic representatives.

Algiers was their first stop, followed by Tunis, which they reached on November 12th and where the lecture audience was particularly enthusiastic. At Tripoli Marshal Italo Balbo, who had been banished thither by Mussolini, received Saint-Exupéry with open arms; and after copiously wining and dining him and entertaining the company with droll stories which he rattled off in a colourful Mediterranean French, he would not let his guests go until he had written a postcard to his "friend" Jean Mermoz, even though it meant sending a guard to wake the nearest stationer in the middle of the night.

As a lecturer Saint-Exupéry was not particularly gifted. It often took him a long time to warm up, and sensitive as he was to the response of others, in the presence of some audiences he never quite got off the ground. In Alexandria and again in Cairo his voice gave out under the strain of a cold, and some of the meagre earnings they had saved up from previous lectures were used to buy cough medicines and pills. In Damascus, then the capital of a French-administered Syria, they were warned that they would have to obtain special permission to overfly Turkish Anatolia. On landing near the border at Adana, they thought for an anxious moment that they were headed for the nearest jail when a peasant, pointing at their bright red *Simoun*, cried, "Bolshevik!" But a call put through to Ankara by the local authorities enabled them to pursue their flight without further molestation. They reached Athens on the 22nd, where the reception once again was friendly. Originally Saint-Ex had intended flying on to Rome, but the bad blood aroused between France and Italy by the Abyssinian war was now such that he was advised by the French Ambassador in Rome to return to Paris by another route, which he did.

The trip had been enjoyable, it had been something of a lark, it had even been moderately successful in terms of "propaganda", but one thing was distressingly apparent: it had failed to make Saint-Ex one penny richer at a time when his financial plight was more desperate than ever. Though the rent for the little flat on the Rue de Chanaleilles only amounted to 7,250 francs ($480) a year, even this was proving too severe a strain on his finances. He had already let one quarter go without paying the rent, they were now well into a second, and the landlord, the otherwise affable Monsieur Laclavière, was growing understandably impatient. The fiscal authorities, irked by his failure to pay his tax arrears, had informed Consuelo that all the furniture in the apartment would be placed under official seizure if payment was not soon forthcoming. The final blow came from the gas and electric company, which cut off their supply because of their inability to settle the accumulating bills. The little flat made suddenly uninhabitable, Consuelo moved to the Hôtel du Pont-Royal, where she was spared the embarrassment of meeting her unpaid landlord on the stairs, but where the expenses of daily living were not exactly lessened. Yuti, her Pekinese, which they could not bring to the hotel with them, had to be left with Madame Boursault, the concierge at No. 5, Rue de Chanaleilles; and to overcome her obvious reluctance to accept this additional responsibility Antoine was obliged to leave her his gold watch as a guarantee that he would return, once he was in funds again, to relieve her of a small but hungry new charge.

Not one but three or four wolves were now howling at the door, and rarely had Saint-Ex felt himself in such a desperate impasse. There was one way out—establish a new record for the Paris–Saigon run. It had been his hope from the start, and now that he had flown his *Simoun* over 7,000 miles with hardly a cough in the motor or the loosening of a single bolt, he was convinced he could fly twice that distance without encountering serious trouble.

Saint-Exupéry must have been back in Paris by November 25th, but it was more than one month later before he finally took off for Saigon. Just what occasioned the delay remains something of a mystery. He may possibly have been afraid to establish his record too early, lest some other "ace" be tempted to follow hot on his heels and better his performance in the lapse of time still left. He may even have let himself be tempted by the bigger prize being offered for the record for the Paris–Madagascar run. As it happened, two veteran flyers, Gaston Génin and André Robert, were now striving to improve on their own record (85 hours) for this course, and they were trying to do it on a *Simoun*, just like his own. When they took off from Le Bourget on December 9th, they were already on their second try: as unsuccessful as their first, since they had to give up the attempt after engine trouble developed just beyond Benghazi.

On the 12th, while Génin and Robert were homeward bound, another air ace, André Japy, took off for Saigon. Four days later he touched down in the Indochinese capital, having covered the distance in 87 hours and cut more than a day from the previous record time. His plane, though also a Caudron, was powered by a 100 horsepower Renault motor which could only average 185 kilometres an hour, far less than the *Simoun*. Saint-Ex thus figured that he stood a fair chance of bettering Japy's performance, even though the reward offered—150,000 francs—was less than a third of the prize for the Paris–Madagascar run. Génin and Robert, by this time, were back in Paris, working feverishly to prepare their *Simoun* for a third and as it proved, victorious assault on their own record. The news was flashed back to Paris on December 21st that they had landed safely at Tananarive after flying 11,000 kilometres in 2 days and 9 hours—more than one day less than their previously established record time. It was a brilliant achievement which dashed any lingering hopes Saint-Exupéry might have harboured about his own chances of snaring the larger prize. But the smaller could still be his if he were willing to make the try.

There were now just ten days left before the year was up, and as Saint-Ex knew, his *Simoun* needed to undergo considerable transformation, with the installation of extra fuel tanks, etc. But he was by this time so desperately poor that not only could he not pay for these indispensable preliminaries; he could not even pay for the fuel they would need for the trip. Little was needed, however, to persuade René Delange to foot the bill. The previous March, when a revolution had broken out in Crete, *L'Intransigeant*, not to be outdone by *Paris-Soir* (which also had a plane and a pilot in action) had sent Corniglion-Molinier flying down in a Farman 430 in a race to get its own man there first. If *L'Intran*—as it was familiarly known—was willing to finance a flyer who was no great shakes as a writer, why would it not be willing to finance his, Saint-Ex's, record-breaking flight to Saigon? He would repay the newspaper's advance by writing up the experience in a series of articles. The expense of the trip, entirely covered by the advance, would cost him nothing; and if, as he confidently assumed, he broke Japy's record, the 150,000 francs would be his, and he could return to the gas- and lightless flat on the Rue de Chanaleilles with a generous handshake for the landlord and a handsome *pourboire* for Madame Boursault, as relieved to return the Pekinese as she would doubtless be sorry to relinquish that elegant gold watch.

The idea appealed to the editors of *L'Intransigeant* far more than it did to Didier Daurat, whose help Saint-Exupéry needed to get his plane ready. On paper, Daurat was forced to admit, it made sense. With its superior speed the *Simoun* could cover the distance from Paris to Saigon in 70 hours —17 less than Japy's time, or enough to provide a margin of safety for such unpredictables as contrary head winds. But the project left him cold. These highly publicized "raids"—as they were called in France—were far too much like the circus aerobatics he had sternly discouraged in Toulouse. Besides, there was barely one week left in which to ready the plane, which meant rushing things through over the Christmas holidays. Saint-Exupéry, further-more, was in a visibly agitated state of mind, hardly an ideal condition for someone about to embark on a physically exhausting test. But his friend was so insistent and seemed so downcast at the idea of letting slip this "golden opportunity" that Daurat finally relented, and his mechanics were put to work transforming the *Simoun*.

Why Saint-Exupéry himself was so casual about the final preparations is not clear. Consuelo had taken an instant dislike to the scheme and kept nagging at him to give it up. Christmas Day, a Wednesday, went by, followed by Thursday and Friday, and still the departure was delayed. Bad weather may have been one reason, and even more likely the *Simoun* was not yet ready. But that Friday evening, at a little *bistrot* on the Avenue de Clichy where he and Consuelo dined with Raymond Bernard and his wife, Tonio showed himself as dead-set as ever on making the flight.

"Walk down with me to the pharmacy," he said to Bernard, after they had finished eating. "I want to buy some benzedrine to keep from falling asleep in the air."

On their way down the street Saint-Ex caught sight of a sign in a doorway advertising the occult powers of a Madame Anastasia (or some such name) "Astrologer and Clairvoyante", who could predict the future to anyone willing to come up to her chambers.

"Wait here a moment, would you?" he said to Bernard. "It won't take a moment." A couple of long strides and he disappeared up the stairs.

When he came down a minute or two later he was visibly shaken by what the soothsayer had told him. Bernard looked at him inquiringly, but all his friend would volunteer was an irritated exclamation: "Oh, nothing! The usual *cartomancienne* nonsense. Please forget it, forget it. It was ridiculous of me to give way to an impulse like that." He changed the subject, and not until one month later, when Bernard saw Saint-Ex again, did he learn that the crystal gazer had predicted that his enterprise would fail.

The next day, Saturday, Saint-Exupéry, accompanied by his friend Jean Lucas, the former *chef d'aéroplace* of Port Etienne, went to call on Monsieur Viaud, the head of Le Bourget's weather bureau. He had decided to take off the next morning (December 29th) and he wanted to find out what sort of weather to expect on the way. Upstairs, in the meteorological room, the two airmen were confronted with a huge ochre-coloured map of the world, over which the wind currents had been pencilled in like tendrils bristling with tiny thorns.

"This one," said Viaud, putting his finger on an anti-cyclone, "will hit us on Monday."

Over Russia and Norway the winds were curled up like demons, tense but not yet unleashed. But just north of the Persian Gulf a tiny dervish was whirling.

"Is that sand?" asked Saint-Exupéry, already feeling the hot, gritty breath of the desert blowing furiously in his face as, blinded, he groped his way down towards Basra.

"Sand?" said Viaud, slowly shaking his head. "No. . ."

It was all Saint-Ex needed to fix the take-off for the next morning.

Late that same evening Lucas was summoned to the Hôtel du Pont-Royal by a telephone call. "I need some help—on the mapping," his friend explained.

On reaching the suite, Lucas found the maps spread all over the table, but not one compass reading or flight measurement had yet been made. Saint-Ex shrugged his shoulders with a sad, helpless smile, and then asked: "*Mon vieux*, would you mind doing them for me? . . . I have to talk to Consuelo."

Lucas sat down with ruler and angle, and working across the accordion of stuck together maps, he calculated the time estimates and compass bearings—while Saint-Exupéry retired behind a curtain to the other half of the suite, where the arguing, so it seemed to Lucas, went on for hours.

At four o'clock in the morning Lucas shook Saint-Ex awake. Looking haggard and more than usually heavy-lidded, he dragged himself to his feet and was shown the markings. The moon here, a thin sliver of a crescent, would keep him company that evening till 10 p.m. Here were the sunrises and the sunsets, in Greenwich Mean as well as local time. And here were the maps, with the distance measurements and compass reckonings.

Downstairs Henry de Ségogne was waiting in the lobby with two other friends—Léon Werth and his wife Suzanne (of whom more will be said in a later chapter). As they drove out to the airfield someone asked Saint-Ex where he'd put the thermos bottles with the coffee. Heavens! He'd forgotten them. Luckily they found a pharmacy which was open, where they bought a couple of flasks. They had them filled at a café, which the owner was just lighting up.

At Le Bourget Didier Daurat was already on the field, together with André Prévot, the mechanic who had accompanied Saint-Ex on his Mediterranean junket. The *Simoun*, when it was dragged out of the hangar, was barely visible in the grey light of dawn under a nagging drizzle. Saint-Exupéry walked around the plane, running his hand over the wingspan and the fuselage, like a rider caressing a horse. He was proud of his "*pur-sang*", which had held up so well over so many thousands of miles. The thermos bottles and the two small travelling bags were stuffed into the cabin, after which Prévot and Saint-Ex climbed in. It was still dark enough for the instrument panel to glow in front of him, like a constellation. Soon it would be all they had to go by; for to give it a maximum of speed and range, the *Simoun* had been stripped of everything that was not absolutely essential. Even the radio had been jettisoned since a choice had to be made between operator and mechanic: which meant that once in the air they could not communicate with the ground. But this did not bother Saint-Exupéry. The previous winter he had taken eleven and a half hours of P.S.V.—*Pilotage Sans Visibilité* or "blind flying" instruction—at the training school Henry Farman had set up at the Toussus-le-Noble airfield; and for the rest he felt he could rely on Lucas' diligent map work.

To Ségogne, at least, the take-off—a few minutes after seven—seemed terribly prolonged, as though the fuel-laden *Simoun* would never leave the ground. But a moment later it was up, rising over the houses and the trees and off—everyone hoped—to Saigon. "I avoid Paris," as Saint-Exupéry later described it, "with a kick to the rudder-paddle. Melun. I am flying very low between showers, looking for the Loire valley. Nevers. Lyon. . . . We're shaken about a lot in the Rhône valley. The Ventoux is combed by a snowstorm. Marignane, Marseille . . . Today is a day when time flies. . . ."

They were already some distance out to sea, headed for Sardinia, when Saint-Exupéry noticed a stream of misty vapour over the left wing's fuel gauge. He had his mechanic check the fuel level. "We've used up more than 200 litres," Prévot reported. Just what he feared—a leak. They'd already lost 70 litres, flown to the wind.

There was nothing for it but to turn back to Marignane, where Saint-Ex, while waiting, drank a *café au lait*. The minutes ebbed by, as inexorably as a haemorrhage. At last the leak was plugged and they could pursue their course—across a wind and rain swept Mediterranean. A misty spread of green, and there was Tunis.

While they were refuelling and as he was coming out of the airport office, Saint-Exupéry heard a dull crunch: an ugly sound which reminded him of an explosion he had once heard—in a distant garage where two men had been killed. He felt a twinge of ominous premonition . . . But they took off —into the golden dusk and the night. Benghazi, the next stop, was swallowed in a well of inky darkness until four lines of rubies suddenly outlined the rectangle of its airfield and a long flute-like searchlight probed up towards them like a luminous antenna. Twenty minutes to refuel—and what a helpful ground crew!—and they were off again on the next lap, bound for Cairo and the Nile.

The Libyan coast, along the approaches to Egypt, was now off limits— one more deplorable result of the Abyssinian war. But by flying straight across the Tripolitanian hump on a course aimed midway between Alexandria and Cairo, Saint-Ex reckoned that any drift due to a change of wind would push him either towards the luminous glow of Alexandria to the left or towards the bright dots of Cairo and the Nile to the right. At Benghazi they had told him he would be helped along by a 20 to 25 mile an hour tail wind. At a cruising speed of 190 miles an hour he could count on having to fly three hours and twenty minutes to cover the 600 miles of desert ahead of him; or three hours and three quarters if the tail wind died. He climbed to 6,000 feet, there where he had been told that the winds were likely to be most favourable—and for the next three hours he flew straight ahead on the course he had set, crossing what he later called "the great black valley of the fairy tales, the valley of ordeal. No help to hope for here. No pardon for errors. We are yielded up to the discretion of God."

Three hours out and the red lamp on his right wing began to flicker strangely, and then blossomed into a rosy bouquet. They had entered a cloud and a halo had formed around it in the mist. Saint-Exupéry climbed to 7,500 feet, then dropped to 3,000 in a vain effort to shake it off. The halo disappeared for a moment but soon returned as they plunged into another cloud. . . . A strange green star now appears ahead of them, supernaturally bright, like the lodestar of the Three Kings. Four hours . . . they've been flying four hours and five minutes, and there's not a sign of Cairo or the Nile. If they continue on their present course they risk flying right over the Nile, hidden by the clouds, and on into the Sinai desert. Saint-Exupéry changes course towards the North, hoping to come out over the sea and to see the lights of Cairo off to his left. He slows the engine and starts a gradual descent until he comes out under the clouds. But underneath there's nothing but darkness. 1,200 feet. He daren't drop any lower until he has a clearer idea of exactly where he is. A slight bank to the right—North North East—to avoid another cumulus looming over there on the left. . . . And then—just as he and Prévot cried: "A lighthouse!" at the sight of something glinting 900 feet beneath them, a mighty shudder tore their world to pieces. For seconds the shocks and shuddering continued, as Saint-Ex waited for the "purple star" of an explosion to send them to kingdom come. But there was no star and no explosion, only a sudden dizzying rotation, as a wing struck the ground and the stricken craft was pivoted violently about and their cigarettes sailed straight through the smashed window. Travelling at 170 miles an hour the *Simoun* had grazed the top of a plateau, scraping off bits and pieces as it ploughed over 250 yards of wood and metal-littered ground "with the tail-thrashing of a reptile". Normally they should have been blown to bits, but miraculously they were still alive—with nothing to complain of more serious than one sore knee.

The full account of the harrowing ordeal which followed—as later described in a series of newspaper articles and then in *Terre des Hommes*—is too long and elaborate to be repeated here. Their water tank, like their fuel tank, was shattered, and here they were—with one orange, a few uneaten grapes, a quarter of a litre of white wine in one thermos, and a half litre of coffee in the other badly damaged flask. Lost in a wilderness where, by the light of his flashlight and after a brief reconnaissance, Saint-Exupéry realized there was not a blade of grass, not a sign of life.

"Our situation was not exactly brilliant," he later wrote in the official report he drafted on the accident.

"We were deprived of water and incapable of pin-pointing our position over a radius of 500 miles. But we set out immediately after having scratched out our plans on the ground in huge ten metre letters. We had three-quarters of a litre of coffee left and we had to get away before the thirst got us. That day we must have covered from 30 to 40 miles, including the return to the plane. Thirty miles from the plane, atop a crest, we could still see nothing but mirages which dissolved as we advanced. We preferred to return, placing our trust in search planes. That day we finished our last drop of coffee.

"At dawn of the second day I changed tactics, leaving Prévot near the plane. He was to prepare and light a fire to attract attention to the plane in case a search plane appeared. I left on a new exploration without water. That day I walked from eight to nine hours at a fast clip: all the more tiring because of the rocky ground into which I had to dig my heels in order to have markers for the return trip.

"No plane having yet overflown us, we decided that we were outside the search area. We were beginning to feel the lack of water terribly So we decided to leave the plane and to walk straight ahead of us until we dropped in our tracks. There seemed no point in our turning back since no one was looking for us hereabouts. I remembered Guillaumet and that this was how he had saved himself in the Andes, and it was his example I followed. We didn't expect to get very far. We chose North East as our direction—for the sole reason that it was the only one we hadn't yet tried —but we had no hope in it. The next morning we were so exhausted that we could only move forward two hundred yards at a stretch."

They had seen so many magnificent mirages—oases, camels, cities— Prévot, like Guillaumet in the Andes, had even heard a cock crow, Saint-Ex at one dizzying moment had seen three dogs chasing each other, that when a mounted Bedouin finally appeared over a crest of sand they thought they were dreaming once again. They stretched out their arms towards the apparition, but unconscious of their presence it moved slowly on. They shouted, but no more than a whisper issued from between their desiccated lips. Too weak to run, they stood there gesticulating helplessly across the deafness of those hundred yards that were like a hundred miles, as slowly, deliberately, implacably the vision passed on and out of sight.

But then, from behind a dune appeared another haughty camel's neck and a second Bedouin who might also have ridden by had he not slowly, but oh, so slowly, happened to turn his head their way. The miraculous had occurred . . . and suddenly, yes, there he was, the giver of life, walking towards them over the sand "like a god upon the sea".

Placing his hands on their shoulders, he pushed them to their knees and had them lie forehead downwards in the sand. Then, using the soft feather of a bird, he unstuck their lips and gently pushed a lentil mash into their parched mouths. Time was needed to moisten their tongues and palate back to normal, to the point where they could absorb a mouthful of water without splitting the mucus membranes and dying. When at last, after a seemingly interminable interval, a basin of water was brought up, the Arab had to pull back their heads repeatedly to keep them from drowning their faces in the water.

Exhausted but revived, they were heaved on to a camel and transported to an encampment, where towards evening a carload of armed Bedouins picked them up and drove them to a soda factory which a Swiss engineer was operating near a saline deposit. At midnight they were in Cairo.

Back in Paris the days had passed amid a steadily mounting anxiety. Saint-Ex's friends, knowing that Consuelo was staying at the Pont-Royal, began collecting in the lobby, the armchairs of which were soon occupied by a contingent of journalists, who camped there day and night. Writing in *L'Intransigeant*, Peyronnet de Torres, the paper's aeronautic correspondent, claimed that two days before the take off Saint-Exupéry had told him he was planning to fly from Benghazi to Baghdad in a single 3,300 kilometre hop—which meant that the search planes sent out by the British and the Egyptians might have been looking in the wrong area. If he had crashed, it was the third air disaster in as many days; for two flyers (Pierre Pharabod and Théodore Klein) had just been killed at Wadi Halfa in a desperate last-minute try for the Paris–Tananarive prize, while the pilot of an Imperial Airways clipper, *The City of Khartoum*, had been the sole survivor of a crash caused by the sudden failure of all three engines two miles short of Alexandria.

The company at the Hôtel du Pont-Royal was now joined by Marie de Saint-Exupéry, who had journeyed up anxiously from Cannes to be with her daughter-in-law. But Wednesday, New Year's Day, passed and Thursday dawned with no news. Joseph Kessel, Jean-Gérard Fleury, Gaston Gallimard, Yvonne de Lestrange and a host of others kept surging into the crowded lobby, surprised to discover how many of Saint-Exupéry's good friends they had personally never met. A ceaseless stream of telephone calls kept the switchboard operator in a state of permanent exasperation. Thursday morning Consuelo, accompanied by several others, went to consult a clairvoyante, a certain Madame Luce Vidi, who when presented with Antoine's raincoat, informed her that her husband was alive. His plane had been smashed, but he had not been hurt. In fact, she would have news of him within the next twenty-four hours. He had been picked up by a caravan, he was very tired, and—she added as a final touch—"I see him in a hammock". Late that same evening the lobby of the Pont-Royal was more abuzz than ever when shortly after midnight the news came through from Cairo that Saint-Exupéry had been found. Uttering a theatrical cry, Consuelo swooned back into the arms of a conveniently stationed reporter. She came to just as quickly, in time to hurry to the telephone and hear her Tonio's voice. "Papou!" she cried, "Papou! . . . it's too good to be true!" "*Mon poussin*," he answered, "I can't believe myself I'm still alive. . . . Send me some shirts," he finished, "I've got nothing to wear".

In the lobby anguish gave way to wild joy, and strangers who had barely met an hour or two before marched off to a nearby apartment, where the animated discourse and the raucous singing, which went on for hours, ruined many a neighbour's sleep.

When Saint-Exupéry awoke in Cairo after a long slumber, he was surprised to find himself between white sheets, which seemed to him more than ever like a balm. The ray of sunshine pouring through the window was no longer lethal, and the honey he spread on his buttered bread had the sweet taste of nectar. But what moved him most was the telegram waiting for him from his sister Gabrielle: *"Sommes tellement heureux."* We're so happy!

At the office of *L'Intransigeant* news of Saint-Exupéry's rescue was hailed with undisguised relief. They had taken a long and relatively expensive gamble on this record-breaking "raid", and though it had ended in near disaster, something at least might now be salvaged from the wreckage. A cable dispatched to Cairo elicited a telegraphed reply to the effect that Saint-Exupéry would be leaving Egypt in a couple of days on the *Champollion* and that, as agreed upon, *L'Intransigeant* would get exclusive rights to his account of the adventure. The telegram seemed reassuring enough to René Delange, the editor-in-chief, but not to his assistant, Jacques Meyer, the Managing Editor. Familiar with Saint-Ex's lackadaisical ways, he insisted that he be made to do his writing on the spot, as he had done for *Paris-Soir* in Moscow. Otherwise, Heaven only knew when he would get the thing written! For the moment he set foot back in Paris, he would be besieged, solicited, and tempted by a hundred and one distractions and nothing would be done.

Jean Antoine, France's first radio reporter and a son of the famous French theatre director André Antoine, was accordingly dispatched to Cairo with orders to lock Saint-Ex up in his hotel room and not to let him embark until he had finished his story. The title finally chosen for his five-article series— *"Prison de Sable"* (Prison of Sand)—may have owed something to this forcible incarceration, which lasted two weeks. The *Champollion* sailed from Alexandria without Saint-Ex, whose sartorial distress was only slightly relieved by the parcel he finally received from his wife—containing one dress shirt! Ah, Consuelo! What did she think—that he would need it to be received at the court of King Fuad? . . .

It was on another steamer, the *Kawser*, that Saint-Exupéry finally reached Marseille on January 20th—two days after Rudyard Kipling's death and one day before King George V's. Consuelo was there to greet him, as were a score of reporters and photographers who swarmed aboard with pencil pads and magnesium flares. Antoine's swollen feet were still swathed in bandages, and his statement for the press was dictated from a promenade-deck bench.

Shortly after his return to Paris he rang up Henri Jeanson, who had also sent a cable to Cairo expressing his joy over his rescue.

"Allo, Jeanson?" he said. "Saint-Ex here. . . . Could you do me a great favour?"

"Of course. Where are you?"

"At the Deux Magots. I'll wait for you."

When Jeanson turned up at the café, Saint-Exupéry was with a friend whom he courteously took leave of, so that they could be alone.

"Well, what's up?" asked Jeanson.

"Well, I'll tell you . . . I'd like you to accompany me home . . . I don't dare go back . . . just think—I owe two quarterly payments . . . I don't know what kind of reception I'm likely to get from the concierge . . . But if she sees us together, she won't dare blow her top . . . Otherwise—"

"You mean you haven't seen your concierge since you got back?"

"Urr . . . of course not!"

"But my poor fellow! For six days now the papers have been carrying headlines about you. Your concierge—why she'll fling her arms around your neck, hug you, offer you coffee, wait and see!"

"Possibly . . . But come with me all the same, one never knows . . ."

"And thus," Jeanson later recalled, "Saint-Ex, who had vanquished thirst, despair, the desert, physical suffering, who had risked his life several times, and about whose exploits and young genius the papers had been raving in huge headlines, was quite simply and humanly afraid of his concierge."

Everything went off exactly as Jeanson had predicted. But there was one thing which continued to bother him.

"Tell me, Tonio, why did you pick *me* to come with you to the concierge's?"

"First, because you're the only person one can say this kind of thing to. . . . But there's something else. . . ." Saint-Exupéry paused, then added: "If I'd approached some other friend, he'd perhaps have lent me the money, whereas . . . ."

"Yes?"

"You couldn't have, even if you had wanted to."

# 15

## The Agony of Spain

A COUPLE of days after his return to Paris Tonio and Consuelo had dinner again with their friends, the Raymond Bernards. "Would you like to hear something?" Saint-Exupéry asked them towards the end of the meal. He pulled out a sheaf of papers he had been carrying in his pocket: the account he had written of his "shattered flight"—*le vol brisé*. He read it from start to finish in his rapid, somewhat muffled voice, and before he was through Consuelo, who had not heard it before, was in tears. Raymond Bernard was so moved he could hardly speak. What they had just heard bore not even a residual resemblance to journalism: it was a literary *tour de force* which placed its author at one bound in the front rank, alongside of James Montague Doughty, Richard Burton, T. E. Lawrence—in a word, of all those who from Ibn Khaldun down to Muhammad Asad (the author of *The Road to Mecca*), have written of the desert with mingled hate and love, mixed fear and admiration.

The text, as published in six successive issues of *L'Intransigeant* in late January and early February 1936, was so perfect that it could be carried over three years later with hardly a word altered into *Wind, Sand and Stars*, and in a slightly more condensed version into *Terre des Hommes*. More than four years had passed since the appearance of *Vol de Nuit*, and though Saint-Exupéry had published very little in that space of time, it was now clear that the silent gestation had born fruit; for in force of description nothing in the earlier work could compare with this hallucinating portrayal of the torments of human thirst.

The fee paid by *L'Intransigeant* to Saint-Exupéry for the six articles having been partly consumed in preparing for the Paris–Saigon "raid", not much was left over when he and Consuelo retook possession of their little "bird-cage" in the Rue de Chanaleilles. Madame Boursault, the concierge, was glad to be relieved of Yuti, the Pekinese, and to be rewarded by Saint-Ex with a generous *pourboire* in exchange for his gold watch; but the apartment owner, Monsieur Laclavière, though he finally obtained the six months' rent that was due him, had come to the conclusion that a penniless writer and also a break-neck airman was more likely to prove an immediate liability than a long-term asset. On February 9 the three-year lease was accordingly rescinded, and Antoine and Consuelo moved to the Hôtel Lutétia. Eleven days later, on the 20th, Laclavière, understandably anxious to rent the premises to a new tenant, wrote to Saint-Exupéry asking why his furniture was still at the Rue de Chanaleilles. No answer being forthcoming, he telephoned to the Lutétia on the 24th and an embarrassed Saint-Ex was forced to confess to his former landlord that he could not move out his furniture because it was "under seizure" by the fiscal authorities for failure to pay tax arrears. At Laclavière's suggestion, Saint-Exupéry finally agreed to have the furniture moved to an official *garde-meubles* (storage depot), pending the day when he could buy off the bloodhounds of the Ministry of Finance.

It was while he was at the Hôtel Lutétia, desperately casting around for some way of recouping his losses, that overtures were made to him for the filming of his first novel, *Courrier Sud*. In his near bankrupt condition he was in no mood to resist such a tempting proposition. Besides, the precedents seemed auspicious. *Night Flight* had been made into a successful movie by Hollywood and the filming of *Anne-Marie* had proved an equally happy venture. Pierre-Richard Wilm, who had played the part of the Inventor in that delightful picture, was again recruited—this time to fill the role of Bernis, the flyer. But—and here the trouble began—it was no longer Annabella but Jany Holt who was picked for the delicate part of Geneviève; and the director this time was not Raymond Bernard, with whom Saint-Exupéry had got on so well, but Pierre Billon, with whom he was soon at loggerheads.

It would have been difficult, even under the most favourable circumstances, to make a first-rate film out of something as delicately pastel-tinted as *Courrier Sud*. The central theme of the novel—Geneviève's abortive love affair with Bernis—was far too autobiographical, far too closely linked to his own idyll with Louise de Vilmorin for the unhappy author not to wince each time a new twist was added to the plot or a false note struck. Robert Bresson (who was later to achieve international fame with films like *Pickpocket* and *Journal d'un Curé de Campagne*) was hired to help Saint-Ex write a workable scenario, but he was too sensitive a person not to glimpse the inner torment it was causing the author; and before they were half-way through he prudently retired.

Had Saint-Exupéry not been so desperately broke he would probably have followed Bresson's example; but he was by now so committed to the film that he felt he had to carry on, if only to limit the damage. Determined to be helpful, he travelled down to southern Morocco with director, camera crews, and actors, and actually flew Bernis' plane in several desert sequences. In a village near Goulimine, where most of the filming took place, he struck up an acquaintance with the local Native Affairs Officer, Captain Foucher, who asked if he could do him a favour—by flying his wife back to Casablanca in his Caudron Renault plane. She had come down secretly to spend some weeks with him—in defiance of the regulations which made this troubled region "off limits" to all army wives—and he was afraid of getting into trouble if the authorities found out. Saint-Ex was only too delighted to have such a charming travelling companion for the return trip; and during the couple of days he was forced—by engine trouble—to spend in Casablanca, his friend Dr. Henri Comte was much amused to hear an eloquent Saint-Exupéry expounding the latest theories of Eddington and Max Planck to a pretty captive audience which had obviously not been much exposed to such physical and metaphysical considerations.

About the film Saint-Ex was far less happy, as he made clear to Henri Comte and also to others after his return to France. He was particularly outraged by the extravagant demands made of Jany Holt, who had to play the part of Geneviève. His friend Léon Werth, who was present at several of the filming sessions, saw him turn pale with indignation during a sequence in which the heroine, fleeing from home, was shown lost and erring on a country road. On coming suddenly upon a group of peasants, she was portrayed as recoiling in fright. "Nonsense!" he fumed to Werth, "utter nonsense!" One of the traits which marked the provincial aristocracy was the ease with which they got on with the peasantry. "That she should take fright at some suburban intersection," he complained, "all right—she's never lived in the suburbs. But that she should be terrified by the sight of a few peasants is utterly unreal."

Seethe as he inwardly might, Saint-Exupéry had to see the messy business through to the bitter end. For in the meantime he and Consuelo had to live, and elsewhere than in the relatively expensive Hôtel Lutétia. Someone—it may have been Pierre Cot, the former Air Minister, who had lived in the same building—put him on to an apartment located not far from the Rue de Chanaleilles in a modern edifice recently built by the *Assurances Sociales* —or Sickness Insurance Authority. The rent—25,000 francs a year (about $1,650)—was three times what Saint-Ex had been paying (theoretically, at any rate) for his previous "bird-cage"; but for what it offered—a magnificent duplex apartment occupying the top two floors of a six-storey apartment building on the Place Vauban—it was almost ridiculously cheap. For there, beyond the windows and the penthouse terrace, was a breathtaking vista:

the stately chapel of the Invalides, beneath whose exquisite Hardouin-Mansart dome is buried the body of Napoleon.

For a relatively impecunious couple it was a bit like jumping out of the frying pan into the fire; but the prospect of inhabiting such a magnificent apartment proved an irresistible temptation. The place was as spacious and airy as the one on the Rue de Chanaleilles was cramped, and with its panoramic vista and windows full of sky it was, to quote René Delange, "just made for an airman". There was only one trouble—it was almost too big. The few pieces of furniture they were able to get out of hock were hopelessly lost in this bare expanse of floor and walls. "Here and there in the distance," as Henri Jeanson has put it, "one spied an armchair, a grand piano, a garden stool, a small bench, a white wooden table". The description is accurate, so far as it goes—though there was also a studio couch and more than one garden chair: there were three or four of them, all painted green, lent to them by friends to help furnish the void. Consuelo took possession of the lower floor, where she now had room to spread her canvases and chisels, while Tonio made himself at home upstairs. An inner staircase led to a charming oval dining-room and a few steps higher up one came to the library or study, with a bedroom on one side and a splendid terrace on the other. The built-in bookshelves were so broad that his books failed to fill them completely; and while a few veterans fought to maintain an upright stance, many of the rest lay sprawled in a drunken heap which their owner soon gave up trying to redress. His bedroom was equally chaotic, strewn as usual with an extraordinary assortment of disparate objects—"an army canteen, a boot, ties, a compass, electric razors, binoculars, shirts all over the place, American magazines, a Negro mask, a sight-taking instrument, a pair of pincers, packs of cigarettes" and Jeanson claims, "a small parasol".

The tenants were proud of their new palace, just as they were of what came to be its most distinctive and distinguished feature—a butler named Boris, who paraded back and forth between spacious vestibule and upstairs kitchen with the dignity of a Tsarist general, which he claimed once to have been. Destitute like so many of his fellow exiles, he had been recommended by Madame Andronikov, mother of the famous Prince who to this day remains the Quai d'Orsay's official Russian interpreter. Any professional shortcomings Boris may have shown as a butler were more than compensated by his virtues as a cook: his *blinis* and *borsches* were justly renowned, while his *air de grand seigneur*, much to Saint-Ex's amusement, overawed the guests accustomed to the doll-house squeeze of the Rue de Chanaleilles.

Life, though far from rosy, was beginning to look up. For even before the filming of *Courrier Sud* was finished, Saint-Exupéry had been contacted by his friend Henri Jeanson for something which had all the earmarks of a

Madame Marie de Saint-Exupéry and her five children
*(Courtesy of Mlle. Anne-Marie Poncet)*

Antoine's father,
Jean de Saint-Exupéry
*(Courtesy of Gabrielle d'Agay)*

Antoine's mother, Marie
de Fonscolombe de Saint-Exupéry
*(Courtesy of Gabrielle d'Agay)*

Antoine with, left to right, his eldest sister, Marie-Madeleine,
his youngest, Gabrielle, his brother François, and Simone
*(Courtesy of Madame Marie de Saint-Exupéry)*

Saint-Maurice-de-Rémens
*(Photo by author)*

Château de la Mole
*(Courtesy of Madame Marie de Saint-Exupéry)*

Abbé Launay and the third form
*(Courtesy of Claude de Castillon)*

Antoine in Molière's *Le Malade Imaginaire*
(at the Villa Saint-Jean, Fribourg)
*(Courtesy of Abbé Boulet)*

**Self-portrait in letter to
Renée de Saussine**
*(Courtesy of Renée de Saussine)*

**Drawing of young girl
in letter to Rinette**
*(Courtesy of Renée de Saussine)*

**Young Saint-Ex in a bow tie**
*(Courtesy of Air France)*

Beppo de Massimi
*(Courtesy of Latécoère company)*

Didier Daurat and Enderlin
in Málaga *(Courtesy of Latécoère company)*

From post office
to airfield in
"heroic" times
*(Courtesy of Air France)*

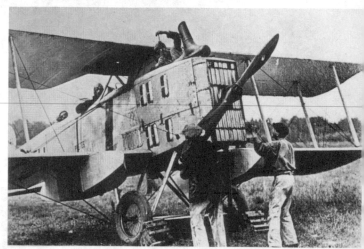

Starting a Bréguet 14
*(Courtesy of Air France)*

Saint-Exupéry at Cape Juby
*(Courtesy of Latécoère company)*

Aerial view of Cape Juby
*(Courtesy of Air France)*

The Laté 28 which Jean Mermoz piloted across Atlantic
*(Courtesy of Air France)*

Jean Dabry (navigator), Jean Mermoz (pilot), Léo Gimié
(radio operator) *(Courtesy of Air France)*

A Laté 28 overflying the Andes
*(Courtesy of Madame Guillaumet)*

The Andes, as they looked to Guillaumet and Saint-Ex
*(Courtesy of Mlle. Chardin and E. Bobrowski)*

Mon vieux Guillaumet

Tu vois par la photographie ci dessus que j'attends
impatiemment ton arrivée et on ne peut plus m'arracher
de la dune d'où je considère l'horizon

Et par le dessin ci dessous avec
quelle ardeur je t'écris — je ne
pense même plus à mettre en
l'ordre !

.ton rapport était épatant.
Il reste un fauteuil à l'académie
je te conseille vivement de
l'enlever. c'est une affaire.

enlève cette sacrée poussière.

Letter from Saint-Ex to Henri Guillaumet
*(Courtesy of Madame Guillaumet)*

Letter from Saint-Ex to Henri Guillaumet (*continued*)
(*Courtesy of Madame Guillaumet*)

**Château d'Agay (a watercolour)**
*(Courtesy of Mireille des Vallières)*

**Consuelo and Antoine on their wedding day, at Agay**
*(Courtesy of Gabrielle d'Agay)*

Saint-Ex and his mechanic,
André Prévot, posing in
front of their *Simoun*
*(Courtesy of Madame Marie de
Saint-Exupéry)*

Henri Guillaumet
and Saint-Exupéry
*(Courtesy of Air France)*

The end of the *Simoun*
*(Courtesy of Madame Marie de Saint-Exupéry)*

The hut at Orconte
*(Courtesy of Commandant Moreau-Berillon)*

Saint-Ex with a halo, at Montceau-le-Waast (to the left
Jean Israel, to the right, Captain Moreau)
*(Courtesy of R. Dutordoir)*

Self-portrait of "Pépino"
*(Courtesy of General René Bouscat)*

Saint-Ex being helped into
his flying gear
*(Photo, John Phillips)*

"Père" Rieutord in action
*(Photo, John Phillips)*

Saint-Ex in the cockpit of his Lightning
*(Photo, John Phillips)*

"very big project". Alexander Korda, the film magnate, who had just scored a hit with *The Private Life of Henry VIII*, was now preparing to embark on something even more ambitious. Nothing less than the story of aviation—for which he wanted Jeanson to write the script. The story of aviation? It struck Jeanson as a big order, but then Korda was a big producer. No peanuts for him! He wanted the works, from alpha to omega. From the first plane . . . no, from the first flight down to the most recent. From Leonardo? . . . No, from Icarus. . . .

"From Icarus?" Jeanson had protested. "But my dear Alex, the film will last a hundred hours."

"Never mind about that, *mon cher Henri*," was the grand reply.

Jeanson was no pilot and he knew little about aviation, but here, it occurred to him, his friend Tonio could help him. Just think—someone who was a pilot, a poet, and a well-established writer! Korda needed little convincing, while the idea of such a film thrilled Saint-Ex. At lunch—for they met frequently—his imagination, liberally sprinkled with Beaujolais, would take wing in all directions. Clément Ader in his steam-driven bat! The Wright Brothers at Kitty Hawk . . . Voisin in his Hargrave glider . . . Ferdinand Ferber . . . "And Blériot!" they said one day. "Just think— Blériot commenting his first flight across the Channel . . . *Magnifique!*" Yes, just what was needed.

A few days later the three of them were installed in a private projection room watching an old Pathé film recount the story of the epoch-making flight. Seated there in his white whiskers, as solemn as a bank president or a field marshal, Blériot watched the flickering screen, while Saint-Ex and Jeanson stared wonderingly at Blériot staring at his own past. The projection completed, they popped the vital question: how would he like to comment what they had just seen? The old man's eyes lit up: the idea enchanted him. Fine! They would register his voice . . . one of these days . . . When they parted Blériot gave Saint-Exupéry a particularly warm handshake, his eyes bright with emotion. Neither realized, as they took leave of each other, that the old flyer's days were numbered and that a couple of months later he would carry his commentary to the grave.

A week or so later Korda summoned Jeanson and Saint-Exupéry to London. The welcome as usual was princely. A suite had been reserved at the Savoy and that evening there were seats for them both at the theatre. The next day they went out to the Denham studios, where Korda said: "I'm going to show you what we've already filmed."

"What! The film's already under way?"

"Well, a couple of short sequences," he admitted.

The lights dimmed and to the visitors' consternation there on the screen

appeared a British Blériot with an absurdly small moustache, climbing into
a bogus plane which smelled almost visibly of Denham papier-mâché and
glue. Saint-Ex and Jeanson were so floored that for an embarrassingly long
moment they were speechless.

"Well, how do you like it?" asked Korda.

"Hmmm . . . odd . . ." was the mumbled reply.

The next fragment dealt with Santos Dumont. During the projection a
bulky individual plonked himself down on the seat next to Jeanson. He wore
an Elizabethan doublet and his nose, even for those robust days, was of an
extravagant length. Peering through the dark, Jeanson finally recognized
him:

"Hallo, Laughton."

They shook hands. Korda had signed him up—for a colossal sum—to play
the role of Cyrano de Bergerac. While Santos Dumont was landing on the
screen, Laughton filled Jeanson's astonished ear with an English rendition
of the famous ballad Cyrano declaims during his dual with de Guiche.

Santos Dumont disposed of, they walked out into the daylight, where
Saint-Exupéry was introduced to Charles Cyrano-Laughton. Before he could
recover from his sudden confrontation with that heroic proboscis Korda
sprang a fresh surprise on them.

"Do you know Wells?"

A moment later they were shaking hands with the author of *Things to
Come*, which Korda was also busy making into a film. With his whisky-red
cheeks H. G. Wells—to Jeanson at any rate—looked like a rollicking coachman, just stepped out of *The Pickwick Papers*. Wells was full of stories that
had a way of petering out into eloquent silence each time a bare-legged girl
walked past.

"Hmmm . . . did you see that?" The gleam in his eye was almost as
interested as Groucho Marx's.

A little later Jeanson suddenly spied a familiar face. "Look who's coming,"
he said to Saint-Ex. "Damned if it isn't our friend Fernand Léger! Hey,
what the hell are *you* doing here?"

"What do you think?" answered Léger. "The set and costumes for *The
World of Tomorrow*. A real brain-buster. Just think—dressing people who
don't yet exist! . . . Where are you staying?"

"The Savoy."

"Fine. From here on we stick together."

Léger had been given a studio, where he spent his time—which is to say,
the time he wished to spend—covering manikins with cellophane, wire, and
rubber. His wardrobe, since his arrival in England—all expenses paid by
London Films—had noticeably expanded, and it was an amusing sight to

see his bulky proletarian frame now warmly enveloped in the finest Harris tweed and displaced, whenever the spirit moved him—as it often did—in a shiny chauffeur-driven limousine. He was off to see his clients in the London area, of whom he had kept an elaborate list. Not born a Norman for nothing, this Léger!

During their stay in London, Fernand Léger took them on several jaunts through the East End pubs and music-halls, but one evening Saint-Ex and Jeanson found themselves on their own. One more evening to kill. They were at their wits' end.

"What if we went to have a drink at a club?" suggested Jeanson.

"But we're not members," objected Saint-Ex.

"That doesn't matter. You just walk in, sign the register, hand over a pound, and you're in. . ."

"What! In any old club?"

"No, of course not . . . But in second-rate clubs, yes."

A few minutes later they penetrated an establishment of this latter order and instantly regretted it. A few sorry-looking chairs and tables, a bench running around the wall, a shabby dance floor on which three frozen-faced couples were turning to the strains of a provincial brass band—it might have been Lunéville or some other French garrison town. But it was too late, they had paid their pound, and there was nothing for it but to drown their gloom in a mug or two of tepid ale.

They were eyeing each other dolefully across their pints when one of the girls on the floor, who had been staring at them intently, suddenly disengaged herself from her partner and came over to their table.

"Tonio!" she said in French, "you don't recognize me?"

"Paulette!" he cried.

He had met her years ago in some Dakar night-club. Suddenly the air was full of names and reminiscences. And Pierrot, the little fellow who used to whistle like a blackbird? . . .

"Dead, burnt to a crisp."

"Oh. But he whistled so beautifully! What a shame! And . . . and . . . what was his name, that big boy who used to eat cigars and who was such a wolf?"

"Lost an arm."

"And Marcel, who used to keep pulling out photos of his kids to show us?"

"He's living in the Midi."

"And Francis . . . and . . ."

She sat down with them and the questions continued in a flush of shared excitement. His face suddenly alive, Saint-Exupéry was happy, happy to have come to this dive after all. What an excellent idea! But it was less pleasing to the owner, who felt that this particular intermezzo was being unnaturally prolonged.

"Ol right, duckie," he said, nodding to the girl. "About time you got up and looked after the others, instead of wasting your time . . ."

("He had sized us up immediately," as Jeanson later noted. "We weren't interesting.")

"Well, what are you waiting for?" cried the owner, as the girl remained seated.

It was too much for Saint-Ex, the "peaceful, the kind Saint-Ex", who rose to his feet, livid, and gripped the man by the tie.

"You are going to apologize to this lady. . ."

"What!"

"Yes, apologize . . . right now!"

Again he shook him. "Don't you understand that this lady is a friend of my friends?"

"There was a bit of shoving around," as Jeanson recalls, "a brief exchange of blows, a table was upset—as in a third-rate film. But the owner apologized. So all was well. We found ourselves back out in the street, more or less intact. Between two and three in the morning. Such was Saint-Ex, the fraternal Saint-Ex, who would not tolerate a lack of respect for someone who was a friend of his friends."

\*      \*      \*

One day Korda called them in and launched into a long lecture on the history of the cinema. "We let him talk," Jeanson recalls, "without interrupting and hoping he wouldn't ask any questions. For since our arrival in London all the brilliant ideas we'd had in Paris had evaporated. We could remember nothing and were incapable of reconstituting anything. It was as though our brains had suddenly been stuffed with wool."

"And now," said Korda, more than ever the *grand seigneur*, "I have a piece of good news for you. I've found you a beautiful house in the country. Spacious grounds. A golf course. A chauffeur, servants to take care of you. You'll be much better off there for working than at the Savoy."

"No," said Saint-Exupéry quietly. "If you don't mind, we'd rather go back to Paris."

"Ah! . . . Why?"

"Because," he answered, "I don't know why it is, it's strange, but here in England we no longer have any ideas. There are no vitamins left. Shakespeare took everything."

Korda did his best to keep them, but in the end he had to let them go.

The next day Jeanson and his friend Saint-Ex flew back to Paris. At Le Bourget they were stopped by a customs inspector who took a dim view of the giant—not King but Emperor-size—matches they had bought on the other side of the Channel.

"I can't let you in with that merchandise," he declared.

"We'll pay the duty."

"No, this particular article isn't covered by our list."

"But it's a present, a present for our wives!" Saint-Exupéry insisted.

"No. What is forbidden is prohibited."

"Now look here, *Monsieur le Douanier*," said Saint-Ex finally, "how can you do this to us . . . to us? You . . . a contemporary!"

The customs inspector almost reeled under the shock.

"Ah . . . all right," he grumbled. "You can pass . . . But you should have said so earlier."

In the end Alexander Korda's "The Story of Flying", like Charles Laughton's *Cyrano de Bergerac*, never saw the light of day. The dozens of sketches Fernand Léger had made for H. G. Wells's *Things to Come* were forgotten, pushed aside, and finally disappeared—along with so much else. Years later Korda could say to Jeanson: "When I think, my dear Henri, that all those sketches by Léger were thrown away! . . . No one knows what became of them. If they were found again today and were put up for sale, we'd get infinitely more out of them than what that film cost us and what it brought in!" And he hardly needed to add—a conclusion Saint-Exupéry had reached long since—"Yes, a strange thing, the cinema!" Strange indeed!

\*     \*     \*

This slightly madcap visit to the land of John Bull afforded an amusing interlude at a time when the ominous tramp of jack-boots was beginning to worry Germany's neighbours and France's social ferment was rising to a boil. In February of that same year (1936) Pierre-Etienne Flandin, the Foreign Minister in the Albert Sarraut government, had managed to persuade a reluctant Chamber of Deputies to ratify the Franco-Russian accord which Laval had signed in Moscow the previous May, during Saint-Exupéry's visit to the Soviet Union. But when Hitler denounced it as a manifestation of "anti-German hostility" and proceeded to occupy the Rhineland, the rabbit-like reaction of the Sarraut government made it clear that the non-aggression pact with Moscow was nothing more than diplomatic hocus-pocus. Anthony Eden, the British representative in Geneva, asked the French not to act until the matter had been considered by the League of Nations; the League predictably did nothing; and by the end of March a beaming Adolf Hitler had his audacious coup endorsed by a 98% vote of confidence from an enthusiastic *Volk*.

On both sides of the Channel pacifism was in the saddle, and in Paris the popular cry now everywhere to be heard was: *"Du pain, la paix, la liberté!"*—as though more bread would automatically ensure more peace, and more peace a greater degree of liberty: which in the existing context meant liberty to forget what was going on in the rest of the world. The deflationary policy which successive French Finance Ministers had stubbornly pursued in defence of an overvalued franc and which resulted in a 30% decline in private income (partially offset by a 25% drop in prices) had aroused the ire of an ever growing number of workers, employees, and peasants, to say nothing of some 800,000 unemployed. They took it out on their "oppressors" in the elections of April 1936, which made the Socialists, led by Léon Blum, the leading party in the country, and which saw the Communists leap dramatically from 11 to 72 representatives in the Chamber of Deputies. Blum was immediately asked to form a new government in a climate of growing anarchy and violence, as red flags blossomed from the flagstaffs of provincial *mairies* and fist clenching mobs marched along the boulevards singing the *Internationale* and the revolutionary *Carmagnole*. Metallurgical plants were forced to cease production, airplane factories were crippled, rail and bus services were upset as a million workers went on strike. Hotels and restaurants, as well as the Opéra Comique, were "seized" by radical committees, and ships tied up in the Marseille docks were boarded by seamen and stevedore "soviets" apparently determined to emulate the epic heroism of a Petersburg October. For a moment it looked as though France was about to go the way of Russia, and so sure of it was Maurice Thorez, the Communist leader, that he assured an overflow crowd gathered at the Palais des Sports: "The Communist Party will soon be in power. I tell you, Comrades, soon!" The Champs-Elysées, as is the custom in moments of French political tension, became the scene of repeated encounters between Phrygian bonneted "revolutionaries" and tricolour-waving "patriots" shouting *"A bas les Soviets! . . . Blum au poteau! . . . La France aux Français!"* (France for the French— an insidious reference to Blum's Jewish origins.)

Of this turmoil Saint-Exupéry was a passive but pensive spectator— unlike his friend Jean Mermoz, who had risen to become Vice President of the *Croix de Feu* or, as it was now called, the *Parti Social Français*. The new party's "socialism" was about as suspect as that of Hitler's "National Socialists", even though its leader, the dashing Colonel de la Rocque denied any intention of adopting Fascist ideology or methods. Mermoz, who had got to know quite a few of them, had developed an understandable scorn for French politicians; but endowed as he was with more energy than acumen, he continued to place his trust in the tall, trim-waisted Colonel who, he confidently hoped, was to be the rejuvenator of an increasingly potbellied and decadent Republic. Fired with a burning desire to do something to lift his limping country out of its rut, he vainly sought to win over Guillaumet and Saint-Ex to the cause. To appease him, Saint-Exupéry finally agreed to meet La Rocque. It is to be regretted that unlike his friend André Gide, Saint-Ex did not keep a journal; for we would then have had a vivid, spur-of-the moment account of what must have been a memorable and perhaps even comic confrontation. But Roger Beaucaire recalls having met Saint-Exupéry shortly after their encounter, still seething with annoyance. "Ideas!" he cried, speaking of La Rocque. "Do you know what there is in that noodle of his? . . . A broth—with tiny *croutons* floating around in it, and those tiny *croutons* are his ideas."

The two million right-wing "militants" who—so their leaders claimed—were ready to forestall a revolutionary take-over did not in the end have to take to the streets. By obtaining substantial wage increases and by introducing legislation for a 40 hour week and a fortnight's annual paid holiday, Léon Blum pacified the strikers and the latter-day *communards*, who agreed to shelve their banners and unclench their fists and to return to their work benches and kitchen sinks. On July 14th, France's National Holiday, several hundred thousand of them locked arms and marched from the Place de la Nation to the Bastille to demonstrate their left-wing solidarity and fixity of purpose, but it was more like a peaceful frolic than a putsch. No ministry was stormed, not an armoury was ransacked, not a church was fired; and if the gutters ran with anything that day, it was with a stale residue of beer. For all the tumult and the shouting, the moderates once again were in control; and it was left to Spain, with the assassination of Calvo Sotelo a day or two later, to show the world what a nightmarish blood-bath a civil war can be.

*       *       *

Within four days of the first Moroccan insurrection *L'Intransigeant* had three correspondents on the scene, covering the conflict from Madrid, Barcelona, and Tangier. Two days later (July 23) Raymond Vanier, Daurat's former assistant in Toulouse, flew Peyronnet de Torres, the paper's aviation correspondent, down to Madrid, where they picked up the first photographs of fist-waving soldiers and rifle-carrying women to be brought out of Spain. Just one week later Emmanuel Bourcier, who had previously covered the

Abyssinian War, was asked to leave Spain by General Mola's officers in
Burgos on the grounds that his country (France) was in the grip of a godless
*Front Populaire*. They must have thought better of this attempted expulsion,
for Bourcier was back a few days later with Mola's "red berets" (the notorious *Carlistas*) whose national colours—red and yellow, as in the arms
of Castille—clashed strangely with the red banners of the proletarians. The
next day, after a dramatic eight-day odyssey which took him via Málaga to
Morocco, Gibraltar, and Algeciras, a newcomer, Gautier Chaumet, scored
another triumph for *L'Intransigeant* by turning up in Sevilla, the first
foreign reporter to reach the headquarters of the rebels' southern command.

With four correspondents now covering the struggle, *L'Intransigeant*
could have rested on its laurels. But the competition it was receiving from
its dynamic rival *Paris-Soir*, which soon had five reporters on the scene,
was such that on August 10 René Delange pulled out a new trump. A front-
page photograph, showing him standing in shirtsleeves and tie in front of a
fuselage and a propeller, was accompanied by the announcement that the
"famous pilot writer" Antoine de Saint-Exupéry had just left for Spain on
the newspaper's private plane, and that they would shortly be publishing
the first of his dispatches under the title: "*Espagne Ensanglantée*"—The
Blood Bath in Spain.

Saint-Exupéry's financial situation—with not only a wife but now a
butler to support—was too precarious for him to refuse this new journalistic
offer from his friend Delange. The hopes he had pinned on Korda had
withered like autumn leaves and Louis Blériot was dead. (He died on
August 3 of this same year.) War had no appeal to Tonio, but the conflict
in Spain was too close to France, herself deeply divided between Leftists
and Rightists, to be as easily disregarded as the Ethiopian war. The sabre
rattling could be heard all too clearly in Paris, where General Castelnau,
not to be outdone by the generals of the peninsula, was already proclaiming
in the conservative *L'Echo de Paris*: "It is no longer two factions which are
disputing the advantages of power; it is a war between Muscovite barbarism
and western civilization."

The flight down to Barcelona afforded Saint-Ex a deceptively placid view
of Catalonia. The papers for the past few weeks had been full of news from
Spain, and if one thing was clear it was that atrocities were being committed on both sides. Saint-Exupéry's sympathies lay with the Republicans,
but he had read enough stories about chapels being burned and priests
summarily shot to know that in their own rough way they could be as
violent and arbitrary as the Nationalists.

Beyond the Pyrenees he overflew Figueras, the first important town in
Spain. Beneath him a church, which he knew to be gutted, shone like a

jewel and he could see no trace of its "irreparable wounds". Already gone was the pale smoke into which its gilt treasures and its woodwork and its prayerbooks had been transmuted, rising and then melting like a smudge into the blue of the sky. Not a line in the landscape seemed to have changed, and the town beneath him sat there, at the centre of its radiating roads, "like an insect in the centre of its silky trap".

Barcelona, by the time Saint-Exupéry reached it, had been so ruthlessly purged of Nationalist sympathizers that although still haunted by patrols and disturbed by truckfulls of gun-waving militia, the city seemed curiously tranquil, as though the war here were already over. The photo accompanying his first article in *L'Intransigeant* showed two anarchists, one brandishing a rifle, the other a pistol in the right hand and a cigarette in the left, as though the whole thing were a colossal lark. But the very first evening, as Saint-Ex sat at a café watching the usual *paseo* on the Rambla, the war's stark reality was forcibly brought home to him when four armed men appeared out of nowhere and pointed their gun barrels at the stomach of the man sitting next to him. His face suddenly beaded in sweat, the poor fellow slowly rose, as did his arms, in a kind of leaden trance. He was searched by one of the militiamen, then ordered forward with a curt nod. "And the man left his half filled glass, the last glass of his life, and started off. And the two arms he held above his head seemed those of a drowning man. 'Fascist', murmured a woman sitting behind me, between her teeth. It was the only witness who dared show she had noticed something. And the man's glass stayed there, bearing witness to a crazy confidence in luck, indulgence, life . . . And I saw him move away, the gun barrels near his hips, bearing with him the invisible frontier which just five minutes earlier had run right past my chair."

The first impression was deceptive, and the closer Saint-Exupéry looked at Barcelona the more he realized it was an armed camp. At his hotel a machine gun had been mounted on the roof, but when he tried to find out why, no one could tell him. Amused by the martial appearance of his "garrison"—the hotel staff—he took several snapshots of them. One was a photo of a tall dark fellow to whom he wanted to give the developed print.

"I have his photo," he said. "Where is he?"

There was an embarrassed pause, a bit of worried head scratching, and finally he was told: "We had to shoot him. He'd denounced a man as being Fascist. So we shot the Fascist. But this morning we learned that he wasn't a Fascist, but simply a rival . . ."

As Saint-Ex remarked, in writing up this incident: "They do have a sense of justice."

It was not easy to know just what to make of the strange breed of anarchists who were in control of the city. The crazy gusto with which they careered through the streets in their newly acquired Hispano Suizas and Delages, splashing terrified pedestrians on to the pavements as they went, was reminiscent of the bullring yet a bit unnerving. No less disconcerting to Saint-Exupéry was his encounter with the anarchist leader, García Olivera, an uncompromising egalitarian who explained that he was in favour of absolute equality. There was no reason, García Olivera claimed, why a great painter should live better than a stevedore, "for if he paints better than the stevedore, it's because he's inherited a better eye. The merit isn't his . . ." Saint-Exupéry, who had been planning to write up this conversation for his *L'Intransigeant* readers, tucked it away instead in his leather-bound notebook, where he wrote: "In our society criteria other than force or cleverness intervene, for we live in a spiritual realm and the poet also constitutes a capital. But the poet at the service of the masses, why? And why the masses to serve the poet? Because the poet's power must be tempered so that human society be less rough and so that other poets may be born. But not because a poet has no merit . . . And," he added in another entry, "I couln't care less about García Olivera's point of view: 'Is it just that someone with better eyesight should be better off than a metal worker?' I don't know how to define justice. The only question is this: 'What structure will best favour creation and the spiritual life?' "

The five articles Saint-Exupéry telephoned back to *L'Intransigeant* from Barcelona were highly impressionistic, like the ones he had sent from Moscow; but if anything, in these the personal and human note was even stronger. One night he had himself driven out by three armed anarchists to the suburban railway yards where another contingent was due to entrain for the front. The spectacle was banal, but seen through his poet's eye, it was transferred into something immense and symbolic of the entire civil war. He was surprised, first of all, by the total absence of uniforms. "These men will get themselves killed in their work clothes," he thought. "In their black, mud splattered togs." Rather than soldiers leaving for the front they reminded him of vagrants preparing to bed down for the night.

"We're moving up to Saragossa," the commander of the detachment informed him, in a voice so low it was almost a whisper.

"Why does he speak to me in this low voice?" Saint-Exupéry wondered. As though they were in a hospital. Yes, there was no mistaking it: a civil war is not a war but a malady.

"These men are not moving to the attack in the heady joy of conquest, but are dully struggling against a contagion. The same is doubtless true in the opposing camp. . . . A new faith resembles a plague. It attacks from within. Its spread is invisible. And as they walk through the streets the adherents of one side or the other feel themselves surrounded by the carriers of a plague whom they are unable to recognize.

"This is why the men ,before me are departing in silence, with their instruments of asphyxiation . . . Barcelona, Saragossa are, to all intents and purposes, composed of the same human blend: Communists, anarchists, Fascists. And these men jammed in here together differ perhaps more from one another than from their adversaries. In a civil war the adversary is internal . . .

"And this is doubtless why this war has taken such a terrible form. Death here is a quarantine ward. The germ carriers are purged. The anarchists go from house to house rooting out the plague-stricken and removing them by the cartload. And on the opposing side Franco could get off this frightful phrase: 'Here there are no more Communists.' The weeding out has been done as though from an infirmary; the weeding has been done as though by a medic."

It is interesting to see Saint-Exupéry resorting to this clinical analogy ten years before Albert Camus was to use it in *La Peste* and twenty years before Eugène Ionesco was to give it a fresh and surprising twist in his *Rhinoceros*. For if there is one thing this blood-stained century has proved it is that man's inhumanity to man stems from something much deeper and more sinister than a callous indifference to the conditions of others— that readiness to treat them as "things", that *réification* of which Sartre has so often spoken and which is nothing but Marx's *Dinglichkeit* in existentialist disguise. Human exploitation has nothing particularly laudatory about it, but the ideological medicine invented to cure this bane has shown itself to be infinitely more cruel. For regarded as active "agents" men can seem far more dangerous than as passive "things". Only a mad industrialist would want to destroy his workers and machines as in an ideological war or purge the possessors of the "faith" seek to extirpate the "infidels", the "godless", and the "unbelievers". "They tire me with their shooting," Saint-Exupéry observed in his notebook of the Spanish anarchists he had been frequenting. "Firing squads are pointless, for religions should convert."

This, it can be objected, is a language better suited to the New Testament than to the harsh realities of our century. But Saint-Exupéry was making no effort to be topical—in writing for the readers of *L'Intransigeant*: "And I think of our respect for death. And I think of the white sanatorium, where the young girl slips softly away among her kin who, as though receiving some inestimable treasure, gather her last smiles, her last words. For never again will this individual achievement be recreated. Never again will one hear exactly this laugh, nor this inflexion of the voice, nor this quality of repartee . . ." And now, springing forth from this meditation as miraculously as a crocus amidst the ruins of war, came this cry, one of the most poignant, the most despairing, the most hopelessly beautiful cries to have been uttered in this desperately inhuman age: "*Chaque vie est un miracle.*" Each life is a miracle.

The crescendo, coming towards the end of his third article, was a bit too sudden, and probably startled more than one *L'Intransigeant* reader. But the doubting Thomases who may have thought he could not rise to the same level after this were destined to be dumbfounded. Hemingway, with his intense boxer's instinct, could muscle his way in among his *amigos republicanos*; Malraux, anxious to prove (with the help of his friend Corniglion-Molinier) that he too could take to the air, might fly over the enemy emptying a pistol into their trenches (was there ever in the annals of modern war a more fatuous performance?); but Saint-Exupéry was more modest. More modest and more human. Among the Frenchmen he met in Barcelona was a notoriously anti-clerical socialist to whom (in his fifth and final article) he gave the name of Pépin. Horrified by what he saw going on around him, Pépin the priest-hater had turned himself into a one-man committee . . . to rescue priests! One can imagine the surprise, and then the wild delight, with which Saint-Exupéry must have greeted the apparition of someone who, in the midst of all this carnage, was interested in saving rather than eliminating lives. In a trice they were friends, Saint-Ex accompanying Pépin, the priest-baiting saviour, through the rolling hills of Catalonia.

They stopped at a mountain village, where the local vigilantes informed them, as though it was the most natural thing in the world; "Yes, we shot seventeen of them . . ." Seventeen? Yes, seventeen "Fascists". The curate, the curate's maid, the sacristan, and . . . fourteen minor notables . . . "For all is relative," as Saint-Exupéry later explained to his readers. "When in their papers they read a portrait of Basil Zaharoff, the master of the world, they transpose it into their own language. They recognize the pharmacist or the nurseryman. And when they shoot the pharmacist, it's a bit of Basil Zaharoff who dies. The pharmacist is the only one who fails to understand."

At the café where they paused for a drink Saint-Exupéry was struck by the expression on the face of a man who was playing billiards. He was trying hard to look calm, but he mopped his brow too often. Up there on the hillside a couple of acres of vineyard were his: did this make him a land-owning exploiter? A criminal to be punished? "Does one shoot a man who plays billiards? He played so badly, with trembling hands. He was all upset, still not knowing if he was a Fascist. And I thought of those poor monkeys who dance before the boa constrictor, trying to gain its pity."

They had to leave the billiard player to his uncertain fate, for Pépin had come to the village on a specific mission. A French priest named Laporte had been living hereabouts: what had become of him? At the headquarters of the revolutionary committee, half a dozen rugged peasant faces stared in turn at the slip of paper which was passed around. Laporte? Laporte? . . . No, replied the committee chairman finally, the name meant nothing.

"But yes," protested Pépin. "A French priest . . . disguised no doubt. You captured him yesterday in the woods. Laporte . . . Our Consulate is looking for him."

He pulled out his French Socialist Party card, which passed from hand to hand, like the slip of paper. There was the same wordless gravity on those rugged peasant faces. Not hostile, no; simply inscrutable. Just what were they thinking, these stout pale-eyed yokels? "We've put our heads in the lion's mouth," Saint-Ex thought to himself. For after all, how were they to judge these two strangers who had come to save a "Fascist?" Maybe in their eyes they were just as guilty.

"I have the impression we've arrived too late," Pépin nudged Saint-Exupéry.

"Hmmm . . ." said the chairman, clearing his throat, "this morning we found a dead man on the road, at the entrance to the village . . ." There was a meaningful pause. "He should still be there."

"They've already shot him," Pépin said in a low voice to Saint-Exupéry, while someone was sent out to "verify" the dead man's papers. "Too bad. They'd have handed him over to us, they're good fellows at heart."

As they drove away Saint-Ex asked Pépin: "This is the third village we've come to on this strange assignment, and I still can't figure out if it's dangerous or not."

Pépin laughed. He'd saved dozens of lives already, but who could say? Dangerous? Not dangerous? "Well, yesterday I had a couple of tense minutes. I'd just removed a Carthusian as they were hitching him to the post. The guns were ready, there was a smell of blood in the air—so there was a bit of grumbling." But they had made it to the car and once inside, Pépin the priest-baiter just couldn't resist:

"You god-blank son of a blankety-blank monk!" he cried in delighted triumph. But the priest, who had flung his arms around his saviour's neck, could not even hear the hideous blasphemy through his sobs of relief.

Farther on they abruptly drew up by the roadside on hearing the sound of rifle shots coming from a screen of trees ahead of them, dominated by two factory chimneys. The militiamen riding in the car behind stopped in turn and unlimbered their guns. They too had heard the sound of shooting. Several of them went forward to find out what was happening. Saint-Exupéry was reminded of an evening years ago in Provence when, as he rounded a bend on a country lane, he had caught sight of a village huddled around its tiled companile against the twilight. "I had sat down in the grass and was enjoying this moment of peace when suddenly the wind brought me the sound of a funeral knell. It told me that tomorrow a shrivelled, withered up old woman would slip beneath the earth, having contributed her share of work. And this slow music, mingled with the wind, seemed to me charged not with despair but with a discreet and tender joy. This bell, which celebrated baptisms and deaths with the self-same voice, was announcing the passage of one generation to another, the story of the human species. Even over these humble remains it was celebrating life, and I felt nothing but a great tenderness in listening to this betrothal of the poor old lady with the earth. Tomorrow for the first time she would sleep beneath a royal mantle, sewn with flowers and singing crickets."

Saint-Exupéry's reverie was brutally interrupted by a militiaman's return. A girl had apparently been picked out and shot in front of her brothers. "How atrociously simple!" thought Saint-Ex. Later, in writing up this relatively banal incident—what was one life among hundreds, among thousands that were being similarly mown down?—he added: "Human events doubtless have two facets. A facet of drama, a facet of indifference. Everything changes according to one's perspective—that of the individual or that of the species . . .

"This is perhaps the explanation for the grave faces of these peasants who, one feels, have no taste for horror and who will nevertheless come back to us in a moment, having flushed out their quarry, content to have exercised their justice, quite indifferent to this young girl who stumbled on the trip-root of death, caught and harpooned as she sought to flee, and who now lies in the thicket, her mouth full of blood."

It was the contradiction that had been nagging him since *Vol de Nuit* and which, as he now confessed, "I cannot resolve. For the greatness of man is not made up of the sole destiny of the species: each individual is an empire.

"When the mine has caved in, burying a single miner, the life of the community is suspended. The comrades, the children, the women flock to the pithead in their anguish, while the rescuers beneath their feet tear with their picks at the entrails of the earth. For what? To save a unit in a crowd? To deliver a human being, as one would deliver a horse—after weighing the services it can still render? Ten comrades may perish in the attempt, but what a shoddy reckoning of loss and profit. . . . For it is not a question of saving one termite among the termites of the termite heap, but a conscience, but an empire whose importance is measureless."

That evening, back in Barcelona, Saint-Exupéry looked down from the window of a friend's apartment on to a ransacked cloister. The ceilings had been shattered and the walls breached with gaping holes, so that one could pry into its innermost secrets. But where were its secrets now? He was reminded of those termite heaps in Paraguay he used to kick over to see what was going on inside. "And doubtless for the conquerors who kicked open this tiny temple it was only a termite heap. Suddenly brought to light by the kick of a soldier's boot, the young nuns began to scurry to and fro along the walls, and the mob felt nothing of the drama.

"But we are not termites. We are men. The laws of space and numbers have no relevance to us . . . One cancer victim, woken in the night, is a focus of human suffering. A single miner may be worth the death of a thousand others. I cannot, when it is a question of human beings, juggle with this hideous arithmetic . . . A young girl shot down amid her brothers? No, it is not death that makes me shudder. It seems almost sweet to me when it is linked to life; and I like to think that in a cloister a death is celebrated like a feast day . . . But this monstrous forgetfulness of the quality of man, these algebraic justifications, this is what I cannot accept.

"Men no longer have respect for one another. Soulless bailiffs, they scatter the furniture to the four winds, ill aware that they are destroying a realm. Here are committees which arrogate to themselves the right to purge in the name of criteria which, two or three times changed, leave nothing in their wake but corpses. Here, at the head of his Moroccans, is a general who condemns entire populations to oblivion, his conscience at peace, like a prophet crushing a schism. Here people are shot just as trees are hacked down in a forest. In Spain the mobs are on the move, but the individual—that solitary universe—cries out in vain for help from the depths of his mine pit."

\*     \*     \*

As was evident from the tone of his articles, Saint-Exupéry came home profoundly shaken by what he had seen, only to find his own country more deeply divided and confused than ever. Leftists who only yesterday had been denouncing a greater military effort and the "war mongering" of the munitions barons in the name of a pacifism as categorical as it was imperative, were now just as belligerently clamouring for armed intervention in Spain. Louis Aragon, the one-time surrealist who had mocked patriotism and reviled the French flag in the name of proletarian internationalism, now suddenly took to exalting martial and patriotic virtues. André Malraux, who had had himself flown to Madrid while Saint-Exupéry was in Barcelona and Lérida, was not only talking of intervening: he was actively planning a Republican assault on rebel-held Oviedo.

The Catholic intelligentsia was no less divided and confused—between "right wingers" like Charles Maurras, Henri Massis, André Rousseaux, Thierry Maulnier, and the philosopher Gabriel Marcel, who had earlier signed a manifesto supporting Mussolini's onslaught on Abyssinia in the name of the "defence of the West", and "left wingers" like François Mauriac, Georges Bernanos, Emmanuel Mounier, and Jacques Maritain—all as stoutly Catholic as the others—who could not bring themselves to endorse Franco's "Christian crusade". Even the government of the *Front Populaire* was split down the middle between "activists"—like Saint-Ex's friend Pierre Cot, once again Air Minister and all for intervention—and "wait-and-seers", like Yvon Delbos, the Foreign Minister.

Since doing nothing is generally easier than doing something, particularly when it involves taking a risk, Léon Blum—that "Stendhalian who had strayed into politics", as the French historian Jacques Chastenet has called him—took the easy way out. Following the British lead, he proclaimed a policy of non-intervention. Though his sympathies were obviously with the Republicans, he would not lift a finger to help them. He had come to power to obtain a better deal for the French working classes, and he was not going to be diverted from this essential aim by the troublesome events beyond the Pyrenees. It was sad that Spain should bleed to death, but if that was the price needed to keep France uncontaminated, then it was worth it.

This attitude of pious abstention exasperated Saint-Exupéry—not so much on political as on moral, or perhaps one should say hygienic, grounds. Nothing is more corrupting than facility; and this national inertia, this deceptive self-indulgence were unmistakable symptoms of "entropy"—as he liked to call it—of a society that was growing flabby and degenerate. France was turning in upon herself in the name of a philosophy, if such it could be called, which was as selfish and callous as it was short-sighted. Nothing is more belittling than egotism; and as he wrote in his notebook: "Greatness springs first of all and always—from a goal outside oneself (Aéropostale): and as soon as man is closed in on himself, he impoverishes himself. As soon as he serves *himself*. This socialism which preaches individual self-indulgence exalts men less than the Fascism which preaches sacrifice for something external."

To this extent at least Saint-Exupéry was in agreement with Mermoz. He had no use for Fascism or his friend's idol, the soup-brained Colonel de la Rocque, but he understood his quest, his thirst for a cause, for a challenge which gives life an intensity and a significance without which it grows flaccid and inept. "Mermoz," he had written one year earlier in the article of homage *Marianne* had published, "is one of the rare men who do not confuse money, the symbol of wealth and possession, with wealth and possession, and who, refusing a tawdry bargain with merchants sincerely shocked to see their poor treasures spurned, takes off once more on arduous ventures for the enjoyment of veritable goods." Impetuous and misguided at times he might have been, but the same fervour that had moved him to challenge the Andes and the South Atlantic had driven him straight into the arms of the *Croix de Feu*.

But one day in December of this same year (1936) Mermoz took off on a venture which proved more than usually arduous. Saint-Exupéry got the news that same evening as he was sitting down to a dinner party. He sat for a long time hardly uttering a word, and only towards the end of the meal would he finally admit what was on his mind. Mermoz, after taking off that morning from Dakar in a four-engine Latécoère flying-boat, had radioed back when already 500 miles out over the Atlantic: "Cutting right rear motor." Silence, nothing but silence, had followed. "Saint-Ex was in such a state" recalls Alexandre de Manziarly, who was at the same party, "that he left before the evening was over".

Just what had happened neither he nor anyone else would ever know for sure. But the right rear propeller (which had shown a dangerous tendency to wobble) had probably whirled itself loose before it could be feathered and sliced through the horizontal tail-fin, shattering the plane's delicate equilibrium and plunging it into the ocean.

Immediately Saint-Exupéry was besieged by *in memoriam* requests. He began by indignantly refusing to "write up" a friend who might tomorrow be discovered on a life-raft and rescued. But after forty-eight hours had passed without yielding a trace of flying-boat or flyers, he consented to write a brief article for *L'Intransigeant*. In it he recalled how shaken Mermoz had been some months before on learning of a similar disappearance over the Atlantic of Collenot, the resourceful mechanic who had twice helped him fly his stricken Bréguet out of the Andes. "He was an old companion who had shared Mermoz' joys and reverses. His death had jarred the great pilot, and this was the only time I ever saw him discouraged. He kept looking at his hands, this time powerless to save him. And he said to me: 'Collenot should not have disappeared without me. Fate was unjust in splitting up our team'."

One week later Saint-Ex gave *Marianne* another article in which he expressed the hope that some miracle might still bring Mermoz back to "one of those *bistrots* in the evening, oh, my unbearable friend, where you would turn up suddenly, forever late and without excuses . . . And we shall then recommence our old disputes. Let us prove you wrong once more. . . . Let me fling my insults at you once again. They are tender, and I am so afraid of never again being able to vex you."

One month later, all hope now definitely abandoned, he wrote a final tribute for *L'Intransigeant*, parts of which were later included in *Terre des Hommes* and *Wind, Sand, and Stars*. "He was of that fine race which confronts the world head on. He spared himself no effort, he recoiled before no adversary. He was totally committed in his actions. He was the image of flourishing manhood. Jean Mermoz bore into the wind, like a tree."

"Mermoz, Pichodou, Cruveilher, Lavidalie, Ezan"—there were five of them on that last flight—"were men of a trade, and that was the source of their greatness. One needs a tool to enter into contact with the world. One needs a plane or a plough. The peasant, in plowing, bit by bit discovers the secrets of the earth. And this truth is universal. Through the wooden handle of his tool he learns more than from the pages of a book. And he becomes a sage. Thus did these men, through their cockpit controls, through the magic of their instruments of work, acquire a kind of peasant wisdom. They too met those elementary divinities—night, day, mountain, sea, and storm—on the self-same footing. They watched their skies, quite simply, as those earthlings would have watched their vines. It was the source of their serenity."

\*   \*   \*

Eager to recapture the taste of this serenity, denied him in the strife-torn atmosphere of Paris, Saint-Exupéry in January 1937 welcomed the opportunity offered him by Air France of prospecting a new route across the Sahara linking Casablanca to Timbuktu and Bamako. With what he had been able to extract from his insurance company, bolstered by fresh advances from René Delange and his publisher Gaston Gallimard, he had bought himself a new *Simoun*, to make up for the loss of the first. Accompanied once again by his faithful mechanic André Prévot, Saint-Ex left Paris in early February and headed south. His first stop was Rabat, where he called on General René Bouscat, commanding the French air forces in Morocco, who was amused to meet the "madman" he had once seen executing "suicidal" loops over the Casablanca airfield.

With a new navigation compass and drift-gauge to steer by, Saint-Exupéry flew straight across the desert to Timbuktu, on to Bamako, and over to Atar, where the legendary Captain Bonnafous was now no more than a memory. Instead, he was greeted by a testy colonel, who had not been warned of this civilian invasion of his military realm. But the glowering gave way to captivated wonder as the intruder, casually picking up a deck of cards from the office table, said: "Choose a card." His magician's charm had subdued one more monster.

In Dakar he was given a young lion. Like the Argentine puma he had sought to quarter with his sister Gabrielle, he just couldn't resist the idea of bringing the cub back to France. Chained up in the cramped cabin just behind the pilot's seat, it soon manifested its distaste for this aerial outing by beginning to paw wildly at Saint-Ex's back and to emit great rumbling roars which seemed about to shake the wooden plane to pieces. Prévot, struggling valiantly to subdue the restless beast, had his arms and hands severely clawed; and he probably would have been half chewed to pieces had Saint-Exupéry not found that by violently banking the *Simoun* from one side to the other he could stun his sea-sick passenger into a semi-comatose condition. On landing at Algiers, where they narrowly missed a crash due to a half jammed elevator flap, Prévot had to be hospitalized while his lustily roaring charge was entrusted to a local tamer.

So far as one can gather, Saint-Ex had obtained a new advance from René Delange to help cover the costs of this trip; the idea apparently being that he would write it up for *L'Intransigeant*, as he had done for the Libyan crash. But in getting back to Paris he seems to have decided that Prévot's mid-air wrestling match with the lion cub could make an entertaining topic for dinner-table conversation but nothing more. Delange, however, had made him a generous advance, and he felt obliged to repay him in some way or other. He accordingly gave him a written account of Guillaumet's escape from the Andes—which as a piece of literature could bear comparison with what he had written about the Libyan desert. It was what André Gide had been pressing him to write ever since he had first heard Tonio tell the story at Agay. It finally appeared in print in the April 2, 1937 issue of *L'Intransigeant* under the title: "*L'Aventure Pathétique de Guillaumet—* recordman for the crossings of the South Atlantic and the Andes Cordillera." Six years had been needed to overcome the author's scruples, and even now he felt called upon to accompany his article with an apologetic letter in which he asked his friend's forgiveness for writing up his courage!

Much as he detested petty proceedings of this kind, Saint-Exupéry was now obliged to open a libel action against another publication. In late January, just as he was taking off on his trans-Saharan odyssey, a scurrilous weekly called *Voltaire* had published an article which claimed that his Libyan adventure had been a carefully contrived hoax. Far from crashing in the middle of a god-forsaken desert, where he and his mechanic had almost died of thirst, Saint-Exupéry—the article claimed—had quietly landed near a Cairo suburb, and to fool the search planes sent out to look for him, he had heaped sand on the tricolour cockades on his wings. The charges were fatuous—if only because Saint-Ex's *Simoun*, being a civilian and not a military plane, carried no cockades. Besides, even a numbskull with a minimal acquaintance with arithmetic could have figured out that Saint-Exupéry stood to gain infinitely more by making it safely to Saigon to win a 150,000 franc prize than he could possibly hope to reap by resorting to such an elaborate artifice. The sum received from *L'Intransigeant* probably did not amount to one-fifth that amount, and even if he had played possum for three days in a Cairo suburb, all it could have proved was that the man who wrote "Prison of Sand" was an imaginative genius. The judges, in any case, lost little time making up their minds; and when the libel case finally came to court the following October, Fernand Décis, the publisher of the offending sheet, was condemned to pay Saint-Exupéry 15,000 francs in damages.

The grotesque accusations published by *Voltaire* were not untypical of the envenomed atmosphere of the moment. While the Communists, who had started out supporting the *Front Populaire*, had grown increasingly hostile to Léon Blum because of his neutrality towards Spain, the conservatives could point to the extraordinary witchhunt launched by Stalin against his enemies in Russia to justify their abhorrence of Bolshevism and their admiration for Francisco Franco. Blum's attempt to insulate France from the events in Spain was thus doubly a fiasco. It proved a failure militarily—in permitting the enemies of democracy (Fascist Italy and Nazi Germany) to dictate the future of the Iberian peninsula; and it proved a failure psychologically—in that it could not keep France from being split down the middle between anti-Communists and anti-Fascists. In the conservative *L'Echo de Paris* Pierre Cot, the Air Minister, was accused of having sold the secrets of a new airplane cannon to the Russians, with whom the French had earlier concluded a non-aggression pact. Roger Salengro, Blum's Minister of the Interior, was so hounded by two right-wing weeklies—*Gringoire* and *L'Action Française*—who accused him of having run away from the trenches during the First World War, that though publicly exonerated in a parliamentary debate, he went home and in a fit of depression shot himself. When André Gide, who had made a trip to Russia the previous summer to attend Maxim Gorky's funeral, came out with a book in which he dared criticize some of the things he had seen in the Soviet Union, Romain Rolland had him expelled from the World Anti-Fascist League as a "traitor" to the cause of peace.

Try as she might to insulate herself from the surrounding world, France in turn was succumbing to the prevailing madness. Passion was stifling reason, just as prejudice was obliterating fact. Suddenly everyone was shouting and everyone was deaf. "At the root of everything," Saint-Exupéry commented in his notebook, "is a prodigious incomprehension, an abysmal ignorance of *facts*. No Fascist has read *Sous la Schlague des Nazis*. No Front Populaire supporter has read the articles in the *Nouvelliste* about the upheavals in Spain, which are no less monstrous. . . . The incredible lack of knowledge of each other. Croix de Feu, Front Populaire. They are not fighting for nothing, but for *ways of being* which happen to be confused. If I say to them: it is shameful on your part to sully Mermoz' memory because he took a political line, and if you ask me to explain myself, I have nothing to answer. The rational here is out of place."

What Saint-Exupéry meant was that logic alone could not provide an answer to this dilemma. It could serve the critical purpose of vivisecting opposing ideologies, but it could not by itself plug the spiritual void they claimed to fill. And for him the spiritual was the ultimate criterion by which all these social upheavals and revolutions had to be judged. "Priority of the mass over the élite?" he wrote in his notebook. "Never. Priority of matter, of the standard of living over the spirit? Never. Priority of logic over a certain human irrationality? Never. Affiliation of socialist doctrine with those who burned churches and spat on the aristocracy? Never. And what enlightened French Communist would dare to defend those points of view? For whether one likes it or not, Spain, in burning her art treasures and emptying the closed world of her convents, accorded—even if only for a fleeting instant—a priority to stupidity over civilization."

In the midst of the confusion the French government was visibly foundering. The trouble with Blum's socialism was not only that it was confused; it was spineless. The *Front Populaire* had come in like a lion, but a few months of uncertain rule had turned it into a sheep. Unconsciously it had inherited the Maginot Line complex of its Radical Socialist and right-wing predecessors and gone over to the defensive. "The Communist Party," as Saint-Ex commented in his notebook, "has perhaps more an idea of greatness than the Socialist party, which is why the man who needs a faith is drawn to it". Blum in this sense was typical: a Socialist who no longer knew what he wanted. He had set out to provide a new deal for the workers, but he had shown himself to be no less attached to the sacrosanct "defence of the franc". A timid attempt at deficit financing—along Rooseveltian, Schachtian, or Keynesian lines—was tried and then abandoned in favour of "budget orthodoxy" and deflation. Wages were frozen in the name of a necessary "pause", and feeling themselves betrayed, thousands of workers went on strike. In March 1937 a protest demonstration, organized by the Communists, turned into a bloody riot.

Shorn of the last tattered remnants of its original prestige, the increasingly unpopular *Front Populaire* now added one final folly to its list of non-achievements. For some months past several acres of Seine waterfront in the vicinity of the Eiffel Tower had been reserved for the International Fair devoted to "Arts and Technics", due to open on May 1, the traditional Labour Day. While work on the foreign pavilions had forged ahead, French workers, by indulging in repeated sit-down strikes (with demands for more pay) had completely stymied the construction of the French pavilions. When the Fair was inaugurated on May Day, all the other edifices were dwarfed by the Soviet and German pavilions, while the French were in such a half-finished state that the official guests at the inauguration had to be whisked down the Seine on a boat ride intended to mask the unsightly chaos behind hastily erected board fences. The visitors who were to have been impressed by the greatness of the Popular Front were offered instead a striking demonstration of French feebleness compared to the dynamism of Europe's two most menacing dictatorships. Nor was this dismal impression much tempered by the spectacular parachute tower which was erected to provide an illusory distraction. Similar towers had been in use for years in Germany and Russia (not to mention Italy) to foment a public taste for parachuting, but in France, where it now made a belated appearance, it could only be regarded as a superannuated novelty. As one of the pioneers of French aviation, Saint-Ex, like his old boss Didier Daurat, was asked to make a public demonstration. He had never used a parachute in his life, and on reaching the top of the tower, he was overcome by predictable vertigo. Later he confessed he had never felt so frightened in his life, and that he never would have summoned the nerve to jump if someone hadn't pushed him off the platform. The parachutes were equipped with safety wires, so that the danger was minimal; but this only irked Saint-Ex the more for making the exhibition gratuitous.

*       *       *

Even before the *Front Populaire* finally collapsed in June, Saint-Exupéry had agreed to return to Spain, this time for *Paris-Soir*. The terms offered him by Jean Prouvost were almost unbelievably generous: 80,000 francs ($3,200) for a total of ten articles. Like its rival *L'Intransigeant*, *Paris-Soir* also owned a plane, piloted by a First World War ace, Major Lemaitre. But because of the French insurance companies' refusal to underwrite flights to the "front", It was in another plane, jointly owned by *Paris-Soir* and the London *Daily Express*, that Saint-Exupéry was flown south.

Madrid, which he reached in the second half of April, was under siege and Franco's gunners, dug in on the heights of Garabitas, kept lobbing in random shells which cut down casual strollers on the Gran Vía and filled the streets with glass and crumbled masonry. At the Hotel Florida, where Saint-Ex found himself lodged with Ernest Hemingway, John Dos Passos, Martha Gelhorn, Herbert Mathews, Sefton Delmer, and a small army of other journalists, an occasional chunk of shrapnel would imbed itself in a wall and stray bullets splinter window frames and mirrors. The city was beginning to suffer from shortages of food and, fearing the worst, Saint-Exupéry decided to stock up on grapefruit, which he lugged up in large numbers to his room. But his natural generosity soon got the better of his avarice when one night a Nationalist shell blew up the hotel's hot-water tank. There was pandemonium in the corridors as clients rushed from their rooms to escape the clouds of steam, but Saint-Ex had time to fill up a basket of fruit, which he was pleased to distribute on the stairs to members of the second sex, with the words: "*Puis-je vous offrir un pamplemousse, Madame?*"

Among the French correspondents whom he bumped into in Madrid was Henri Jeanson, who had been sent down to cover the Republican front for the *Canard enchaîné*. The normally placid Saint-Ex, to his friend's considerable surprise, now displayed "an extraordinary exaltation. At the name of Franco he exploded. He had no use for these rebel generals. . . . At the station of Irun, I told him, I'd gotten into an argument with André Salmon and Emmanuel Bourcier, correspondents who had chosen the other camp. Saint-Ex hugged me. A bomb exploded a few yards away. 'From here on out,' he cried, 'we're brothers' ."

According to Jeanson, Saint-Exupéry was outraged by the misery of the Spanish people, stupefied by their courage, and saddened by the colossal confusion in which they were patently floundering. He told Jeanson he would like to move around on the Republican front. Jeanson took him to meet Durruti, leader of the anarchist FAI (*Federación Anarquista Ibérica*) whom the Russians were later to assassinate along with his companions. Durruti immediately put a brand new Rolls-Royce at their disposal and gaily wished them a pleasant stay in Spain!

"The chauffeur, who had a *toro* in his tank"—to quote Jeanson again, "charged us over the pitted, cratered, ridged, and rocky roads of Spain, as though over a four-lane superhighway. A break-neck pace under a neck-baking sun. To while away the time the chauffeurs of the *Frente Popular* had invented a typically Spanish game. Whenever they saw another *Frente*

*Popular* machine hurtling towards them, they would step on the gas with an '*Olé, compañero!*' and see if they couldn't rip the mudguard off the opposing vehicle as they scraped past at one hundred and fifty kilometres an hour. The game, as can be imagined, required considerable finesse. Saint-Ex seemed to take a keen interest in it. Feeling less at ease, I suggested hypocritically to our chauffeur that he go easy on his lovely Rolls.

" 'What difference does it make?' he shrugged his shoulders. 'The car is requisitioned!'

"I dared not add that it was my own bodywork I was particularly concerned about.

" 'My friend will give you five hundred pesetas for each mudguard you rip off,' promised Saint-Ex magnanimously.

"The chauffeur gave us more gas and another verse of the *Internationale*. I mopped my brow. This particular joke promised to make me poorer."

On reaching the front Jeanson found it equally difficult not to betray an occasional quiver of the jaw in the company of *desesperados*—the name they had coined for themselves—whose favourite sport was unlatching their grenades a second or two before hurling them. One day Saint-Ex found himself in the courtyard of a building which, he was told, was being attacked by the Nationalists from the other side of the wall. The anarchist *desesperado* standing next to him had just lobbed a grenade over the wall, where it made a nice explosion. But he shook his head, displeased. "Too high," he explained to Saint-Exupéry with a gesture. Picking up another grenade he pulled out the safety pin, paused for a second and then let fly. It flew over the wall on a lower trajectory. "No . . . still not good enough," cried the anarchist, shaking his head. He let fly with another which this time barely skimmed the top of the wall—like a well placed tennis shot. If it had failed to make it, the grenade would have bounced back on their side, and they would both have been blown to bits. "Ha!" cried the anarchist, pleased at last. He had been watching his companion out of the corner of his eye to see if he was frightened. Saint-Ex smiled, thinking the ordeal was over. But no, here was the *desesperado* readying another. Just to show him that the last one was the result of skill, not luck!

Unlike his earlier articles, written on the spot in Moscow, Cairo, and Barcelona, the new series he gave *Paris-Soir* were not written until he was back in Paris. The fears which Jacques Meyer of *L'Intransigeant* had earlier expressed at the time of the Libyan adventure were now dramatically confirmed when it came to delivering "copy" to editors and printers. Saint-Exupéry's trip to Spain had begun in April and lasted until May, yet it was weeks before the first article was ready, to say nothing of the others which were supposed to follow in quick succession. Each article was endlessly written and rewritten, the author reclaiming it a dozen times after it had been turned over to Pierre Lazareff and Hervé Mille. In the final stages he even resorted to bribery to gain admission to the presses, where the flabbergasted typesetters were asked to hold everything—there was a word to be changed, a comma to be added, and in the end entire paragraphs had to be reset. In the process the articles kept getting longer, as though the mingled anguish and exaltation he had felt for the heroic defenders of Madrid could never find words enough to be properly expressed.

At last, on June 27th, the first article appeared. A luminous, almost unnaturally luminous, moon-flooded night, and here he was with a Republican lieutenant, walking up a front-line trench in a northern suburb of Carabanchel. Overhead the bullets were whining like insects, but more ominous seemed to him the periodic gurgle, like a bottle of uncorked champagne, he could hear as shell after shell finned through the heavens like "sharks towards their prey". Franco's artillerymen, it occurred to him, were like demented vandals, chipping relentlessly away at that mass of moon-lit stone, at that Sleeping Beauty of a city he could see through a gap in the embankment; Franco's cannoneers were trying to "sink Madrid as one sinks a ship". And what was the purpose of this random terror? He could see none. That very afternoon, while walking on the Gran Vía, one of these shells had landed like a thundercap. "Enough to uproot one life, just one. The passers by were still dusting the plaster from their clothes, others were running, the cloud of smoke was beginning to drift away, but the fiancé, miraculously spared a scratch, stood staring at the *novia* whose golden arm he had been clasping a moment before, transformed into a blood-soaked sponge, a packet of flesh and linen. Kneeling down but not yet understanding, he slowly shook his head, as much as to say: 'How strange!' He could recognize nothing of his friend in this scattered marvel. Slowly, with atrocious slowness, the rip-tide of despair turned its knife blade in his heart. For one more lingering second, still stunned by this ravishment, he searched about him for the light familiar form, as though it at least should have subsisted.

"But there was nothing there but a packet of mud. Fled, evaporated was the frail gilt of humanity! And while there welled up in his throat a cry which something strange deferred, he had time to understand that he had not loved those lips, but the pout, the smile of those lips. Nor those eyes, but their look. Not this breast, but its soft marine smell. He had leisure to discover now at last the cause of the anguish love may have brought him. Was he not pursuing the unseizable? It was not the body he had hugged, but the bloom, but the glow, but the weightless angel it clothed . . ."

The "law", if such it could be called, of reprisals? A battered face for a bloodied eye, a crippled jaw for a shattered tooth? The hideous law of talion was as old and as cruel as Cain and Abel, and "the first of all murders is lost in the primeval night of time". But all that mattered to Saint-Exupéry in this brief, murderous moment was that he had seen a young girl stripped, like a matador, of her *traje de luces*, her robe of light. "As for the military role of such a bombardment, I have been unable to discover it. I have seen housewives disembowelled, children disfigured, an old woman street-vendor wiping bits of scattered brain from her humble treasures. I have seen the janitor coming out of her lodge to wash the blood from the pavement, and I still fail to understand what role in a war is played by such street accidents."

Years before the analysts, the statisticians, and the autopsists of the Second World War were to proclaim what the Goerings and the Bomber Harrises were too obtuse to understand, what the Curtis Lemays and their ilk have never been able to fathom, Saint-Exupéry had put his finger on the pathetic fallacy of mass bombardments. "A moral role? But a bombardment is self-thwarting. It defeats its very purpose. Each shellburst in Madrid provokes a gradual hardening. What was wobbly indifference stiffens. A dead child matters when it is yours. A bombardment, it seemed to me, does not disperse: it unifies. Horror induces a clenching of the fists, a closing of ranks in the same shared shudder.

"The lieutenant and I clamber up the embankment. Like a vessel, like a face, Madrid is there, taking its blows in silence. But so it is with man: hardships slowly fortify their virtues."

"That makes sixty," remarked the officer to Saint-Exupéry, as one more blow descended on the anvil. Madrid was being hammered out—like a shield in Vulcan's forge.

From the general Saint-Exupéry descended to the particular to drive home the point he wished to make in the third of his *Paris-Soir* articles. The captain of a front-line unit had invited him to share a frugal repast in their basement command post, where the simple way of breaking bread and passing it around struck Saint-Ex as almost Christ-like. This promised to be the last supper he and his sergeant and their volunteers of death might well partake of before charging out at dawn without artillery support on their suicide mission. Seated round a bare table whose chief ornament was a bottle of Spanish brandy, the ten men seemed resigned to their fate, aware that even if they made it across those eighty yards of lethal no-man's-land through bursts of machine-gun fire and mortars, and even if they forced their way into the thirty houses they had been assigned to take, their quixotic charge could do little to alter the final outcome of the war.

The sergeant who was to lead the assault with the captain had lain down on an iron bedstead and dropped off to sleep: a sleep so deep as to be undisturbed by the telephone which rang to say that the attack had been called off by order of higher headquarters. What? The attack had been called off? In a trice the air was filled with grumbling. "What do they take us for—women? Are we fighting a war or what?" Their reactions awoke a sympathetic response in their guest: what, after all, could be more frustrating for a newspaperman than an attack which fails to materialize? The "story", like a soap bubble, had suddenly burst into an iridescent nothing. But this broad-shouldered, lumbering Frenchman who, like Hemingway, could down that Fundador firewater without flinching, was not just another "war correspondent", and those dark, insistent, heavy-lidded eyes—so vague and yet so penetrating—had been observing the reactions of these men with a deceptive alertness. A Curzio Malaparte might have preferred to describe the vainglorious inanities of a generals' mess, but like a George Orwell or a Hemingway, Saint-Ex felt quite at home in this humble community of men, the sacrificial cannon-fodder off which all wars feed. The attack had been called off, a new lease of life had been granted them, but now as they plonked down their elbows on the table around the early morning cups of coffee, they suddenly felt limp, as though cheated of something intangible but all-important. They had gone into the next room, where the sergeant was asleep on the bedstead, and by the light of a sputtering candle they had said: "Hey, sergeant!" put a hand on his shoulder and tried to wake him. The body had resisted—how poignantly Saint-Exupéry recognized the feeling!—refusing to ascend from the delicious dream-depths in which it was plunged, and the sergeant had rolled over again, like a stubborn animal turning its back on the slaughter-house. But when at long last he had sat up and blinked, instinctively his arm had stretched out for his rifle. "Ah, yes . . . it's time!" Only to be told that no, it wasn't time after all—since the attack had been called off.

And what was he doing here, this sergeant who in "real life" had been a humble Barcelona accountant? Could he really say, any better than had Henri Delaunay when Saint-Ex had put the question to him at Cape Juby —just why he was here? One of the accountant's friends had left for the front, followed by another and then another. Gradually it had dawned on him how insignificant, how trivial were all these figures he had been laboriously entering in his register—compared to the drama that was going on around him. And suddenly, like those tame ducks which begin to hop to and fro and to flutter on seeing the wild ducks fly over in curving arrowheads on their continent-spanning migrations, this humble Barcelona bookkeeper had felt the call of the wild.

"This call moved you, it torments you as it does all men. Whether we call it sacrifice, poetry or adventure, the voice is the same. . . . The tame duck had no idea its tiny head was vast enough to contain oceans, continents, and skies; but here it is, beating its wings, refusing the grain and the worms. . . ."

"And so you feel yourself carried away by this internal migration no one ever spoke to you about . . . Suddenly, by virtue of a midnight test which stripped you of all accessories, you discovered in yourself a person of whom you were unaware . . . Someone great and whom you will never forget. And it is yourself . . . He has opened his wings, he is no longer bound to the perishable goods of this world, he has agreed to die for all men and thus entered into something universal. A mighty breath sweeps through him. And here he is, shed of his matrix, the sovereign lord that lay dormant within you: man. You are the equal of the musician who composes, of the physicist who broadens the horizons of knowledge . . . You have reached that altitude where all loves have but a common measure. You may have suffered, you may have felt lonely, your body may have found no refuge, but into its open arms today you have been received by love."

The mystic note? Yes, it was there, unmistakable, for all to hear. Closer to a Santa Teresa of Avila than to a Hemingway or an Orwell, human as was their sympathy for the plight of a suffering mankind. Indeed, in the wartime annals of this century there is probably nothing quite like these on-the-spot recordings of Saint-Exupéry's, which are not articles in any ordinary journalistic sense, but meditations on war, on death and destruction, on the meaning of life. Even the exalted note involved a certain risk of being misinterpreted, as though in praising the stoic resignation of this Barcelona accountant Saint-Ex were also praising the war that had transformed his condition. But the truth he was seeking to expose was more universal than the war that happened to illustrate it. For in paying homage to the humble of the earth who must so often pay for the windy rhetoric of their leaders, he was exalting the memory of his friend Mermoz. Like the sergeant, he had accepted his destiny as part of his daily lot. He had made the supreme sacrifice in the name of something greater than himself.

The article which ended on this lofty note was only the third in a series originally intended to run to ten. Was Saint-Exupéry secretly afraid that the next might prove a let-down in comparison? There is no telling for sure. But after a cyclist had been sent over to the Place Vauban to pick up the fourth article, a breathless Tonio suddenly burst into the offices of *Paris-Soir* and asked to reread it. Pierre Lazareff and Hervé Mille had barely had time to glance at the copy as it was handed to them page by page by the typist, and they had just reached the point where, in Saint-Ex's latest narrative, a Spanish soldier was about to sally forth, grenade in hand. Was it the *desesperado* he was describing, the one he had stood next to trying to look calm, as he skimmed the wall with his deadly projectiles? We may never know. But suddenly and without the slightest warning Saint-Ex angrily ripped his own pages to shreds. "No good!" he frowningly exclaimed. "No good!" And without a word of explanation he left as unexpectedly as he had come. The next article was never delivered, and the *Paris-Soir* series ended in "sudden death", or—to use a more exalted image—in a trinity.

What is the explanation for this extraordinary behaviour? One day André Malraux had said to him à propos of the war which had brought his fighting energies to a boil: "You can't imagine the thrill it gives one to get behind a machine-gun and to blaze away!" Instinctively Saint-Ex had felt a shiver of horror pass through him. Doubtless there were people for whom war, like fighting, was a sport, but the "vulgar sporting thrill" he had felt at Juby under the whine of Moorish bullets was a bit different from this . . . but perhaps not too different from the casualness with which his *desesperado* neighbour had been tossing his lethal merchandise over that protective wall. War, after all, was something more serious than a sport, and there were categories in it more vital than brute feeling. As he put it in a letter quoted in Pierre Chevrier's biography and which summed up his ambivalent admiration for his anarchist friends: "The old team spirit of the Aéropostale is what I found again among the ararchists of Barcelona during the Spanish civil war. The same gifts, the same risks, the same mutual help. The same lofty image of man. They could have said to me: 'You think like us.' But they said: 'Why aren't you with us?' And I had nothing to answer which they could have understood. For they were living off feelings, and on the level of feelings I had nothing to object to the Communists, any more than to Mermoz, or to anyone in the world who agrees to risk his life and who praises the bread broken in common among comrades above every other good. But I don't believe the Catalonian anarchist is made to preside over the future of man. If he triumphs, all he will be able to pull out of his soup-tureen will be a simple vainglorius grub which interests me but little . . . Why, to get drunk on a moment of drug-like feeling, should I go ruin what I regard as my spiritual aim? . . . The spirit should dominate the point of view of sentiment."

It was the truth which had been building up within him for half a dozen years, and what he had witnessed in Spain had only acted as a catalyst. But no less typically, he was in no hurry to deliver the message, as though paralysed by the fear that once again he might be misunderstood. Poverty in the end was needed to vanquish his scruples, and as we shall see in a later chapter, what finally emerged was something of a journalistic accident. An accident yes, but also a miracle.

# 16

## Between Sickle and Swastika

WHEN Gide's book, *Retour de L'U.R.S.S.*, was published in November of 1936, Saint-Exupéry's first cousin, André de Fonscolombe (who had a Russian mother) had come to see him about it. Gide's critique, he felt, was much too mild, and he wanted Tonio's advice about the rebuttal he was preparing against it. Antoine was glad to oblige, though he limited his intervention to choice of words and style. His own thoughts on the subject were reserved for his notebooks. "There is something fine but also unpleasant in the welcome given to Gide by these masses of people. This need uneducated people have to compromise, wear out, and sully . . . If a choice has to be made between government by the individual and government by the mass, I think—as the little provincial town shows—that government by the mass is the most crushing and unjust that exists."

On this last point his sentiment was not far removed from Gide's. Gide had gone to the Soviet Union on the occasion of Gorky's funeral in the hope of finding that a radically new social philosophy had produced a radically new and better type of man. Instead, he had been upset to find that it had above all created a crushing uniformity of opinion. Like Saint-Ex, he had been exhilarated by the boyish team spirit everywhere encountered, but depressed by the refusal to accept any but the dogmatic "truths" (often patently false) which had been forcibly injected into thousands of naive heads. "What is at present asked is acceptance, conformism," Gide had written. "What is wanted and demanded is approval of everything that is done in the U.S.S.R.; what one seeks to obtain is that this approval be not resigned but sincere and even enthusiastic. The most surprising thing is that this is achieved. On the other hand, the slightest protest, the slightest criticism exposes one to the severest punishment and is immediately stifled. And I doubt that in any country today, even in Hitler's Germany, the spirit is less free, more cowed, more fearful (terrorized), more vassalized."

It was that last terrible sentence, in which Stalin's Russia was placed on the same footing as the Third Reich, which brought the storm down on Gide's head and provoked his excommunication (by its High Priest, Romain Rolland) from the World Anti-Fascist Committee. Gide, as Saint-Exupéry knew, was only telling the truth: a truth ennobled by the fact that it came from a one-time believer whose god had failed, from a proselyte who had been forced to make an agonizing reappraisal of his faith. Having never been one of the faithful, Saint-Exupéry was in a more fortunate position. "The Virgin carried through the streets of Sevilla, Stalin carried through the streets of Moscow: a difference of aesthetics, says Lévy," he commented in his notebook after a lively discussion. "No, much more . . . The greatness, the efficacy of religions is in having posed their revolutionary problem after having founded the image of the spiritual man to be attained. Once this man is created, let him organise his universe."

"The revolutionary Marxists organize the universe without considering the man this organizing creates (Divinity of the object). I fail to find that so grandiose: the Milky Way, the great silence of intergalactic space, to culminate, after millions of years, in the 'historical mission of the proletariat . . .' What a difference in the scale of reference! And what is meant by 'historical mission of the proletariat'? I refuse to admit this finality."

Saint-Exupéry's notebooks (which were only discovered after his death) are full of annotations of this kind which show that he was far more deeply concerned by these social problems than the aloof or joyous air he wore in public might lead a casual acquaintance to believe. His friend Pierre Bost, whose novel *Le Scandale* was awarded the Prix Interallié the year that *Vol de Nuit* won the Fémina, used to be amused by the diagrams Saint-Ex would sketch on random scraps of paper as they sat at the Deux Magots or some other café and which were supposed to illustrate the merits or defects of the capitalist system. Pierre Cot, the former Air Minister, came away from a number of such conversations with Saint-Exupéry, impressed by what he took to be a certain admiration for the Soviet Union. Saint-Ex talked to him at length about the régime's educational methods which had apparently impressed him, particularly its willingness to promote the sons of former aristocrats or well-to-do bourgeois families who, having started out in life with a greater cultural baggage than the semi-illiterate muzhik, could render greater services to the state. But it is more than likely that he was concealing his deeper sentiments, not wishing to offend Cot's left-wing susceptibilities. For his notebooks strike a rather different note: "The individual should not tyrannize the mass, the mass must not tyrannize the individual. Everything is discussed, as though by Tual, on a level of sentimental pleading: 'the admirable people' . . . I don't know what this means, except that those who share and suffer are generally more profoundly human than happy egoists.

But my revolution being aimed at making people happy, I can't very well wish for a society ruled by its lowest elements, that is, the scoundrel or the beggar lording it over the aristocrat, the scientist or the people raised to the rank of man."

The trouble, Saint-Exupéry realized, lay in the hopeless confusions of meaning which had accumulated around the simplest words—like "people" and "mass"—as a result of the patents of nobility which had been conferred on them by Rousseau and Marx. "Since in Russia", he argued in his notebooks, "nothing checks accession to culture and power, the *people* or the *mass* is defined as what is left over, as the least evolved, least cultivated, least refined human category—and above all the least apt to become it since selection has already played its part. Then what do the people's will, the will and power of the mass mean except the inadmissible supremacy of matter over spirit?" Where a state of total democracy is theoretically achieved, words like "people" or "mass" should logically disappear from public parlance, having lost their relevance. It was what W. S. Gilbert had suggested in a famous line from *The Gondoliers*: "When everyone is somebody, no one is anybody." Or as George Orwell was to put it in *Animal Farm*: "All pigs are equal, but some are more equal than others."

The reality, which had nothing to do with theory, was that in the Soviet Union power was wielded by an élite, as callous as that of any capitalist country, and which used words like "people" and "masses" to chloroform the captive mind into voluntary submission. For this reason alone Saint-Exupéry could not be satisfied by left-wing ideologies, which vitiated the charity inherent in the original impulse through the unscrupulous exploitation of a hypocritical vocabulary. "I know what Malraux is looking for—the pathetic," is another typical entry in his notebooks. "And he forgets the vain endeavours of his youth, to consider only greatness, the only climate he finds breathable, and struggle against imposture. Struggle against bourgeois egoism. Struggle against the hackneyed. Generous indignation against poverty. Everything which the Christianity of the catacombs has brought down to us and which, having lost in God its keystone, has trouble defining itself. For it was without doubt easier to save this contradiction with the Church and the Bible Prophets than with an anarchistic movement which, in establishing a new society, prepares effects in direct contradiction with its aims."

In writing this Saint-Exupéry had not forgotten what he had witnessed in Spain. "Can ideas be discussed under the sole angle of the massacres they provoke? . . . The end justifies the means. Yes, but only when the means do not contradict the ends. To make a leftist revolution so that man may be honoured (or what is fine in man), all right; but not through calumny, intrigue and blackmail, which represent a lack of respect for man or what is fine in man." Again, thinking of Malraux or it may have been of Gide, Saint-Exupéry could add: "He is to the left because he likes the masses. And I because I do not like them. I like the species." Recalling the ideological intolerance which had so shocked him in Spain, he wrote: "A civilization where a man is respected over and above his ideas—that is my civilization".

That too was André Gide's ideal—the *Civitas Hominis*, the Heavenly City of Untyrannized Manhood he had hoped but so notably failed to discover in the Soviet Union. But where Saint-Exupéry differed from Gide was in the latter's naive belief that in some ill-defined and miraculous way a civilization of the masses could spontaneously bring forth that exquisite artistic flowering which his fine aesthetic sense instinctively demanded. The ugliness of the monumental buildings the Russians were putting up had shocked the aesthete in Gide, but as Saint-Ex remarked in his notebook: "Only Gide can simultaneously regret the ugly object in the U.S.S.R. and wish for an even more egalitarian socialism, not understanding that this socialism amounts to mass production (only point of view from which it has concrete meaning) and the condemnation of wasted time. But we who believe that a poem, to be beautiful, may cost a full year of human life, like the chasuble embroidered by fervent female hands, like the Chinese tea-cup over which the artist has consumed a lifetime refining a single brush-stroke; we who believe in the truth of this mysterious cult and in the objects of this cult, we first of all crave a society which authorizes it. As for the problem of the beneficiary, which by definition cannot be the mob, we relegate it to the background, for it matters little to us whether it is the private Maecenas or the state. And if we incline towards anyone, it is rather towards the private Maecenas."

In taking issue with Gide, Saint-Exupéry was thinking less of public buildings than he was of paintings, grand pianos, rare books, and other products of craftsmanship. But if he defended art patrons and wealthy connoisseurs, it was not out of love for this particular species. "The disappearance of wealth, about which I couldn't care less, worries me not because of the wealthy but precisely because of the poor, who are going to be even more besotted by the manufacture of tractors or stools rather than by gilt-work, book-binding, de luxe watch-making, etc. . . . a little more doltish and a little fatter. Does the gain make up for the loss?" Apparently not, for a little further on he added this trenchant comment: "The sophistry of Gide. For the art object cannot be acquired by the collectivity. That robs it of all human meaning. And the average taste of the mob culminates in what he hates: Russia. Besides, the problem of matter will always arise:

how immoral, then, to compose these love sonnets where there is not enough wheat. Let him go cultivate the earth."

This final blast was probably every bit as caustic as the broadside his cousin André de Fonscolombe had been preparing. Long after he had visited it, the land which had brought forth Dostoevski continued to fascinate Saint-Exupéry, who felt sympathy for the fate which had overtaken its people. Though he had little taste for ideological tracts or economic treatises, he insisted on ploughing his way through *Das Kapital*. The notion of class as an absolute, unchanging category struck him as "absurd" and as out-dated as that of "industrialist exploiter" or "proletariat". Yet antiquated concepts like "Left" still dominated public talk as in the days when "Renault was building cars for Renault".

With the same rugged determination Saint-Exupéry digested Trotsky's bitter attacks on Stalin, only to note that what Trotsky was really criticizing was less Stalin than the Revolution itself. "All revolutions," he commented in his notebook, "will be betrayed, and in more than one sense (and by *betray* I don't mean as a regrettable transformation, but simply as an unpredictable transformation, possibly a happy one. It is impossible to know by means of intellectual reasoning what sort of man will emerge from a given set of conditions; one cannot think the future)."

Unlike Malraux, one of whose leitmotifs has been the idea of bringing culture to the masses, Saint-Exupéry was not convinced that civilization reposes on "the more or less easy access to museums". More important, he felt, was the "number of painters who paint" and the "activity and fervour of the schools". Here too his suspicion of the state was basic and unchanging. "In the communist system the State plays the role of feudal lord and nourishes civilization. Which brings us to another serious trouble . . . unity of doctrine. A thousand patrons favour all tendencies, the State only one: a hemmed in creativity. Above all,"—and here Saint-Ex saw eye to eye with Gide,—"a brake to conceptual creation which is by definition opposed to the prevailing system. Perhaps the utmost will be extracted from existing systems, but there will be no further progressing. Who in the U.S.S.R. would have nourished Breton and Aragon?"

\*     \*     \*

In judging the Soviet Union, as one can see, Saint-Exupéry remained what he had always been—an individualist and non-conformist. It was the quality he shared with Léon Werth, an authentic "left-winger" whose ideas and arguments he valued precisely because they were so often at variance with his own. The two might never have met had it not been for the tenacity of René Delange, the editor-in-chief of *L'Intransigeant*. One day he said to Jean Lucas (whose father-in-law had been Werth's closest friend during the First World War): "How about getting Werth and Saint-Ex together?" Werth greeted the idea coolly: Saint-Exupéry meant little to him and *Vol de Nuit* was too close to hero worship to appeal to his own anarchistic, Trotskyist, and—to use the language of present-day Marcuseans—anti-authoritarian inclinations. But Delange kept insisting, and when Werth finally consented to meet Saint-Exupéry one night at the Deux Magots, the miraculous occurred. It was anything but a meeting of minds, for they never stopped arguing; but for both Werth and Saint-Ex it was a kind of *coup de foudre*—to use Jean Lucas' expression: friendship, not to say love, at first sight.

Nothing could have been less predictable than this extraordinary amity between two persons so totally different in so many ways. Werth, to begin with, was twenty-two years older than Saint-Exupéry (having been born in 1878, at Remiremont in the Vosges). His grandfather had been a Jewish rabbi and his uncle, Frédéric Rauh, a philosopher who had risen to become the director of the Ecole Normale Supérieure in Paris. The young Léon had inherited their scholastic flair, and at the Lycée Ampère in Lyon he had walked off with the first prize in philosophy in his baccalaureat year—for all of France! Logically, like his uncle, he should have gone on from there to a brilliant academic career, but Léon Werth by instinct was too much of a rebel and a free-thinker, a trait he shared with Saint-Exupéry. Instead, leaving his parents in Lyon, he had fled from the lycée, which he found too boring, and journeyed up to Paris to try his luck in the capital. Hired as a *surveillant* (a kind of junior teacher and study-hall supervisor) in a Catholic school, he was soon expelled when it was discovered that he had been taking the seniors out on long walks along the banks of the Seine, where they were allowed to smoke as they pleased. Next he had found himself a job as private secretary to the writer Octave Mirbeau, and started work on a novel, *La Maison Blanche*, (The White House) a harrowing account of his experiences in a hospital where he had been confined for weeks with a serious case of otitis. As ill luck would have it, the novel came out in 1913—the year which saw the appearance of Alain Fournier's *Le Grand Meaulnes* and Valery Larbaud's *Barnabooth*. Each had its determined supporters among the ten Goncourt jurors who included Octave Mirbeau, no less firmly decided to vote for Werth's *Maison Blanche*. The upshot of this literary log-jam was the choice of a fourth book—Marc Elder's *Le Peuple de la Mer*—an absurd decision which should have sufficed once and for all to divest this misbegotten institution of the last shreds of its tattered prestige.

A volunteer when the First World War broke out, Werth had lived through the hell of several years in the trenches, later recorded in *Clavel, Soldat*—a novel which can stand comparison with Henri Barbusse's *Le Feu* and Roland Dorgelès' *Les Croix de Bois*, with Robert Graves' *Good-bye to all That* and Richard Aldington's *Death of a Hero*, and even with the most famous of them all, Erich Maria Remarque's *All Quiet on the Western Front*. One day Werth had seen half a dozen men quite needlessly killed because an officer had decided that the shovels they had left out in the open after a night of trench-digging had to be retrieved in broad daylight. The spectacle had convinced him, as the First World War convinced Louis-Ferdinand Céline and so many others, that nothing can exceed the stupidity of the military mentality. But no less typically, after the Pope had made a speech condemning the war, Werth had silenced an anti-clerical schoolteacher with the comment: "When for once he says something that makes sense, it's no time to criticize the Pope."

From anti-militarism it is but a short step to militant pacifism, and Werth, after the war, had been welcomed with open arms by Romain Rolland and Georges Besson when they founded *Cahiers d'Aujourd'hui*. Like many other socialist enthusiasts he undertook a pilgrimage to the Soviet Union, only to be arrested in Warsaw as a Trotskyist and to languish for a while in one of Pilsudski's jails. He was more successful in 1925, when he made a trip to Indochina (like Gide's trip to the Congo at about the same time) and published his findings in an emphatically anti-colonialist book. Later Werth served briefly as editor-in-chief of *Monde*, an "anti-Fascist" weekly which Henri Barbusse launched in 1928 with thirteen million francs that were turned over to him by Anatoli Lunacharsky, the former Soviet Commissar for Education. The job, while it lasted, was fascinating, for *Monde's* galaxy of distinguished contributors included not only Romain Rolland, but Maxim Gorky, Albert Einstein, and Miguel de Unamuno (then an exile from Primo de Rivera's dictatorship). The trouble started when the original capital ran out and Moscow began cracking the financial whip. Werth, whose revolutionary élan was above all individualistic, found it impossible to swallow the new party line and it was the beginning of a gradual break with Barbusse, Henri Wallon, and other Communists who had once been his friends.

On the eve of the First World War Werth had stopped writing for *Le Petit Parisien* when its conservative editors refused to publish an article he had written favouring the workers in a Saint-Nazaire dock strike. Later, he had refused to review books for the Communist daily, *L'Humanité*, when the editors made it clear that he was not free to write exactly as he pleased. The iconoclast in Werth made him sympathetic to Léon-Paul Fargue, who wrote a particularly laudatory article about him in the mid-twenties, just as it made him sympathetic to Henri Fabre (editor of *Le Journal du Peuple*, to which Werth also contributed), whose newspaper office was a haven for other free-thinking souls like the poetess Séverine, H. P. Gassier (the *Canard enchaîné's* first and for a long time only cartoonist), Rirette Maitrejean (of whom more will be said in a moment), and not least of all, that other Saint-Exupéry friend, the irrepressible Henri Jeanson.

Jeanson, not the sort of person to suffer bores, has described Werth as a "short, bespectacled, sharp-featured man, not the least embittered, for whom the paintings and books of others were a means of livelihood, and who could draw an entire philosophy out of his pipe". An anarchist and a free-thinker Werth may have been, but there was a solid pipe-smoker's wisdom behind it; and it was precisely this element of solidity, this absence of triviality, this intransigeant sincerity—so different from Valéry's patronizing remark to Malraux: "I am interested in lucidity, I am not interested in sincerity"— which made Saint-Exupéry feel instantly at home with Werth. The large round glasses he wore in front of the sharp, close-set eyes gave him an owlish look, and he once drew a profile of himself with a bird's beak for a nose. His large scholar's brow and the thin lips were also deceptively prim, and certain of Saint-Exupéry's friends could not help finding his deliberate mode of speech and thought a trifle too ponderous and pedantic for their own livelier tastes; but when he was in the mood, Werth, like Saint-Ex, could shock a sedate company out of its post-prandial lethargy by the lusty intoning of the bawdiest of barrack-room ballads.

Even Werth's Trotskyism was less dogmatic than instinctive. During the First World War he had sided with the *poilu* against the hierarchy. During the terrible struggle in Russia between Stalin and his enemies his sympathies automatically went out to the underdog and loser, named Leon like himself (and who spent most of 1934 in France, after his exile from the Soviet Union). The same human feeling caused Werth to befriend another victim of Stalinist oppression, Victor Kilbatchiche, better known under his assumed name of Victor Serge. Introduced by Werth to Saint-Exupéry, Serge too was soon a frequent guest at the apartment on the Place Vauban.

The author of *The Tulayev Affair* and *When It's Midnight in the Century* —which can stand comparison with Koestler's novels in their exposé of the macabre inner workings of Russian Communism—was in some ways an even more extraordinary person than Werth. Though born in Brussels in 1890, his parents were a Russian couple who had emigrated from Russia to escape the relatively mild vexations of the Tsarist police. The son, a Kropotkin—or perhaps one should say a Bakunin-style anarchist, had at the age of twenty just launched an inflammatory sheet called *L'Anarchie* when he and his girl friend, Rirette Maitrejean, were arrested as suspected accomplices of the notorious *bande à Bonnot*—a "gang" of young anarchists whom a genuine bandit (Bonnot) had recruited for his own criminal designs. Refusing to "squeal" on his fellow anarchists, though he had nothing to do with Bonnot's murderous hold-ups, Kilbatchiche (alias Serge) was condemned to five years in a French prison. After his release he moved to Spain, where he took part in a revolutionary insurrection. Arrested a second time when he returned to France in 1919, he was finally expelled to Russia, where he became a member of the Communist Party, worked with Zinoviev on the staff of the International and with Leonid Krassin in the secret police. Three years were enough to rid him of all his revolutionary illusions, and a couple of years more sufficed to win him a place on the G.P.U.'s black list. Arrested as the result of a cabal hatched against his father-in-law by a young Communist woman who wanted to occupy his Moscow apartment, Victor Serge would probably have been swallowed up in Stalin's first great Party purge had not Panaït Istrati, the Rumanian, and other socialist sympathizers in the West taken up the cudgels for him and finally engineered his banishment from the Soviet Union early in 1936.

His former jailers would probably have done better to keep him in prison, for Victor Serge was not the sort of person to keep his mouth shut about the monstrous iniquities he had personally witnessed. Hearing that he had returned to Brussels, Henri Jeanson's friend, Jean Galtier-Boissière, wrote to ask Serge if he would be willing to write up the inside story of the Russian Revolution for his quarterly magazine, *Le Crapouillot*. Serge was delighted to oblige. Entitled "From Lenin to Stalin", it appeared early in 1937, a couple of months after Gide's *Retour de L'U.R.S.S.* and exploded like a bombshell over France's left-wing intelligentsia. Froth at the mouth as they might, *L'Humanité*, *L'Avant-Garde*, and Henri Barbusse's *Monde* were reduced to vain splutterings by this devastating critique of Stalinism written not by a tourist—like Gide or Saint-Exupéry—but by an "insider". Gide, delighted to find his mildly pessimistic forebodings now dramatically confirmed, enlisted Serge's service in drafting an elaborate annex or epilogue to his recently completed "first impressions". It appeared in June 1937 under the title *Retouches à Mon Retour de l'U.R.S.S.* The "retouching job" was so devastating, the facts and figures marshalled made such mincemeat of official Soviet statistics that André de Fonscolombe gave up looking for someone to publish the rebuttal he had prepared with the help of his cousin Antoine.

Some six years later Saint-Exupéry could write in a letter to a friend: "A certain French bourgeoisie is awful, but the pure doctrinaires of Marxism are just as bad. (Read *When It's Midnight in the Century*, by my Russian friend Serge.)" Charles Sallès, who was present during at least one of their long sessions at the Place Vauban apartment, was able to appreciate at first hand the diligence his friend Antoine applied in studying this burning question—Russian Communism—not only from books but from a first hand source like Serge. The random jottings which were discovered in his notebooks after his death might lead one to believe that they were no more than the scribblings of a dilettante, unversed in the complexities of sociology or economics. To a certain extent they were, if only because Saint-Ex was personally more interested in science; but they were not the casual lucubrations of an ignoramus. The world, Saint-Exupéry realized, was sick: sick from a surfeit of inflammatory slogans, some of them so deadly that they could send millions of innocent victims to the grave. But the remedy for this malady was not easy to find, still less to apply. Man, if he is to be something more than a cabbage, needs a faith to live by, and communities a sense of purposeful mission if they are really to be bound together. But where can such a faith be found—short of those mind-numbing dogmas which reduce the individual to the collective will of the herd?

*       *       *

"It is, to put it mildly, strange," Gide had written in his Journal as far back as August 1933, "that today 'mysticism' is on the side of those who profess to be atheists and irreligious. It's in the form of a religion that Communist doctrine exalts and nourishes the young today . . ." After which he had had the courage to add, some sentences further on: "And besides, I understand the attempt to unify thought which Hitler is trying today, imitating Mussolini: but which can only be obtained at such a terrible cost of thought impoverishment! Specific and individual value yields to I know not what collective value, which ceases to have any intellectual value whatsoever."

Saint-Exupéry was too much concerned by the importance of the spiritual in human affairs not to have been similarly intrigued by the "mystique" that had brought order out of chaos in Italy and Germany. One of the things which had most depressed him in Spain had been the total lack of discipline displayed by the anarchists, who would think nothing of moving, bag and baggage, from one section of the front to another, unconcerned by the "hole" in the line their arbitrary departure might suddenly open up. As he was later to comment in his notebook: "In a military struggle, spiritual and material forces being equal, the army formed by the mystique of order will win out over the army of disorder. (And this because order is a quality.)"

In France the last vestiges of a "mystique" had foundered with the collapse of the first *Front Populaire* government, and the prevailing sentiment was well illustrated by the quip which was already beginning to make the rounds of French army messes: "What does one do when one receives an order? Answer—wait for the counter-order." The cynics of Radical Socialism had replaced the fist-clenching prophets of the new terrestrial paradise, to the undisguised relief of the conservative bourgeoisie, but the country as a whole showed scant signs of being any happier. "Look at Mermoz, and the joy of men when a great deal is demanded of them," Saint-Ex commented sadly in his notebook. Hitler in Germany, Mussolini in Italy were generating a genuine enthusiasm by calling their peoples to new efforts and sacrifices; but what was Léon Blum's successor, the bland Monsieur Camille Chautemps, demanding of his fellow citizens? Precious little, so far as Saint-Exupéry could see. Never had the Radical Socialists been more industriously negative—in dreaming up valid reasons for doing nothing. The policy of non-intervention in Spain was maintained unaltered, while the economy continued to stagnate.

What, in comparison, was the secret of Germany's extraordinary dynamism? And what was the price the Germans were having to pay for it? Both questions had long intrigued Saint-Ex, but it was not until the early summer of 1937 that chance afforded him the first inklings of an answer.

The plane in which he and Prévot had taken off for Saigon in December 1935 having fortunately been insured, Saint-Exupéry had used the refund to buy himself a new *Simoun*. One week-end in late June or early July of this year (1937) he yielded to his ever restless *Wanderlust* and took off with a friend for Amsterdam. It had been agreed that they would dine that Sunday evening in a little Rhineland village with some friends recently returned from Canada; but the weather being fine and the morning still young, Saint-Ex said: "Why don't we fly on to Berlin, and back to the Rhine from there?"

Minutes later they were in the air, headed for the German capital. The flight was uneventful until they put down at Tempelhof, where they were met by several stony-faced officers of the airport police, who demanded to see their papers. Large sections of the Reich had been decreed off-limits to unauthorized aircraft, and it was glaringly apparent that the flight of Saint-Exupéry's *Simoun* was in every way "irregular".

While the two "intruders" were detained under custody, the airport police tried to contact the French Embassy, which was closed (this being Sunday), and then telephoned to the home of Captain Paul Stehlin, the Assistant Air Attaché, who happened to be on friendly terms with Goering and his sister. Asked if he knew anything of a Frenchman answering to the name of Saint-Exupéry who had just landed on an unauthorized flight, Stehlin, who had met him once or twice before, quick-wittedly answered: "Of course. He's a very good friend." Certainly he could vouch for him. Indeed, he would come to Tempelhof immediately to clear things up.

Not until they were comfortably installed at a table in the dining-room of the Hotel Eden, to which Stehlin invited them to lunch, did Saint-Ex fully realize the gravity of his offence—in daring to fly to Berlin without first alerting the authorities. In the Third Reich whatever was not specifically authorized was *streng verboten*.

After escorting his guests back to Tempelhof and seeing the refuelled *Simoun* take off towards the west, Stehlin blithely assumed that this minor diplomatic fuss was over. Saint-Exupéry doubtless thought the same. But as he flew south west over Brandenburg and the Harz mountains, the temperature inside the cabin began rising under the impact of a blazing sun. "Smells as though something's burning," said Saint-Ex, sniffing. And indeed it did.

They were now approaching Kassel and could already see its airfield. Afraid that a fire might break out at any moment, he banked towards the field and began circling at a low altitude, ready if necessary to make a rapid landing. But though the strange smell persisted, neither he nor his companion could find the slightest trace of anything burning; and after fifteen minutes of circling, Saint-Exupéry righted his plane and flew on towards the Rhine.

His original intention had been to fly to Frankfurt. But the friends with whom they were to dine had telephoned through to say that they had seen an airfield near Wiesbaden which looked far more attractive and which was much closer to Rüdesheim, the quaint, vineyard girt village where they were to meet that evening. And sure enough, as they skimmed over the densely wooded Eiffel hills, the airfield came into view, looking marvellously green and unencumbered, just as their friends had said. If anything, it was almost too unencumbered; for as he circled around it prior to landing, Saint-Exupéry could see no trace of a hangar or a plane, only a lax windmarker, billowing lazily from its mast.

Hardly had the *Simoun* rolled to a stop on the grass when fifty bare-chested youths, all dressed in the same black shorts, came roaring out of the nearby woods. They surrounded the *Simoun* in a sea of boyish chatter, but not content with that, they heaved like a rugby scrum against the door each time a perspiring Saint-Exupéry tried to push out of the baking cabin. The sweat was running down his face in rivulets, his shirt was plastered to his moist back before the grim game was ended by the appearance of a German officer.

But their tribulations were not over. The officer's gaze was stern. Uncompromising. A gush of guttural words poured forth, a cataract of *verboten*

. . . *streng verboten* . . . *nicht gestattet* . . . which even Saint-Exupéry had little trouble understanding. They had landed on a military field, which was absolutely "off-limits". All right, Saint-Ex sought to explain in his fumbling German, he would fly on to Frankfurt.

"*Nein! Nein! Nein!*" shouted the officer. "*Sie bleiben hier!*" He was not taking off anywhere; he was staying put.

After a lot of argument, Saint-Exupéry and his companion were allowed to push the *Simoun* over to one side of the field and to sit under the shade of its wings, where the apprentice Luftwaffe pilots brought them bocks of beer to slake their thirst. This enforced immobility lasted the rest of that warm afternoon and was only ended towards six o'clock when another officer drove up in a car and explained to Saint-Exupéry in French that he was suspected of espionage—all that circling over Kassel and the exploration of this off-limits field.

The French Embassy in Berlin was contacted, and it was Stehlin once again who received word that his "good friend" was creating diplomatic havoc in the air. This time the authorities were sterner, refusing to allow the "spy" to continue to Frankfurt unless accompanied by a German police officer. The black-shorted cadets lined up to watch the take-off, and to thank them for the beer they had been kind enough to bring him, Saint-Ex put the *Simoun* into a steep bank and swooped down over their heads and outstretched arms as they chanted: "*Heil! Heil! Heil!*" The policeman maintained a grim silence, but his knuckles turned white gripping the seat next to the pilot's. Nor did his exacting surveillance relax until the following day, when the German authorities yielded to the persuasive intervention of the French Ambassador in Berlin and let the wayward airman proceed in peace.

*          *          *

This first taste of Hitlerian discipline was a bit disquieting, and particularly when the underlying efficiency was contrasted with the all too patent laisser-aller of France, which had once led the world in the field of aeronautics. In late September one of the last remaining French speed records—one Hélène Boucher had set in April 1934 flying a Caudron Renault "Coupe Deutsch" at 280 miles per hour, was shattered by Jacqueline Cochrane in a Seversky fighter plane. In November a speed record Howard Hughes had established in September 1935 (355 m.p.h.) was smashed by a German called Wurster, chief test pilot for Focke Wulf, on a Messerschmitt 109 (at 380 m.p.h.). The French were no longer in the running. At Biscarosse, south of Bordeaux, Saint-Ex's friend Henri Guillaumet was kept waiting for months before being allowed to take off in a six-engine Latécoère

flying-boat which it had taken almost ten years to produce! Even then he
was not allowed to fly the North Atlantic via the Azores and Bermuda, which
is what it had been designed for. Nor was any of this accidental: it was part
of a general pattern. The entire country was running downhill and its aircraft industry with it. Between 1928 and 1937 there had been nine different
Air Ministers and eight different Air Force Chiefs-of-Staff. The resulting
instability at the top had caused repeated havoc with work schedules lower
down. "Not a plane in our squadrons answers completely to the definition of
a first class airplane," the French aviation weekly *Les Ailes* commented
gloomily in September of this same year. "Their inferiority in speed ranges
from 150 to 200 kilometres an hour. This means that if war breaks out
tomorrow between France and Germany or Italy, for example, the Air
Force would find itself in the same situation as it was at the start of the battle
of Verdun in 1916. Then our air force, made up of Farman 'chicken coops',
Voisins, Caudrons, Nieuports, which pilots had long regarded as obsolete,
were totally submerged and crushed by the German Air Force, which had
first-class planes equipped with fuselages and the first Fokker fighters."

History was repeating itself with that genius for plagiarism it so often
exhibits. In a desperate effort to save something of France's vanishing prestige, the Air Ministry asked Saint-Exupéry (and two other well known airmen) to fly down to Bucharest, where he gave a talk on *Vol de Nuit*. Maryse
Bastié, the woman ace who had finally broken Mermoz' South Atlantic
record in 1936, was sent to Latin America on another propaganda tour.
Words were asked to cover up for deeds—though Guillaumet did manage in
November to win one more record for France by flying 3,600 miles non-stop
from Port Lyautey in Morocco to Maceio in Brazil.

It was probably the flying trip to Rumania which gave Saint-Exupéry the
idea of undertaking a South American foray. In Paris, life with Consuelo was
proving a bit tumultuous; he had a large debt to settle with *Paris-Soir* for
the seven Spanish articles he had failed to deliver; and he could not go on
endlessly tapping his friend and publisher Gaston Gallimard for more
advances on a book which he seemed somehow incapable of putting together.
He needed a change of air, and a flying trip to the New World—or so at least
he fancied—might help resolve the "contradictions" in his personal life.

The idea had first been broached to the Air Ministry in September, but
it was not until just before Christmas that he was finally given the green
light for a "raid" which was to take him from New York to the Horn, on the
southernmost point of the American continent. Saint-Exupéry, meanwhile,
had cooled to the project, which had already been overtaken by Maryse
Bastié's goodwill tour of South America; but he was not a man to turn back.

Accompanied once again by the faithful mechanic André Prévot, Saint-Ex sailed in early January 1938 on the *Ile de France*. In New York he was warmly greeted by members of the French colony and given a room on the twenty-fifth floor of the Barbizon Plaza Hotel. Perched high up amid all these illuminated signs and towers, he had the strange impression of being on an ocean clipper, with the wind sighing through the rigging, the restless night broken by the wail of sirens, and muffled sounds below, like the hollow clank of iron or rumbling of objects being pushed around in a hold.

A good week was needed to uncrate the *Simoun*, which had travelled over with them on the *Ile de France*; and while Prévot kept a watchful eye on the local mechanics, Saint-Ex had time to make a quick trip to Canada to visit Quebec and Montreal. The take-off, originally scheduled for February 1, had to be postponed several times because of heavy snowfalls, and it was not until the 14th that he and Prévot finally flew out of Newark just as dusk was falling. They were buffeted by snow for the first part of the flight, but the radio beam of the Philadelphia airport helped them on to a safe landing at Washington. They reached Atlanta at 2.15 a.m. the following morning, but were prevented by groundfog from taking off again until 11 o'clock. Houston . . . then Brownsville, where they landed that evening just before 9 p.m. A good night's rest, and at 8 the next morning (the 16th) they were in the air again, bound for Vera Cruz. Another long hop took them over the mountains to Guatemala, where they landed to have the plane refuelled.

Was Prévot a bit careless in supervising the airport groundcrew, as Saint-Exupéry's biographer Pierre Chevrier suggests; or did Saint-Ex forget to remind him not to fill the tanks completely since they were now 5,000 feet up, with a greatly reduced air density? The truth may never be known. But as Saint-Exupéry roared his *Simoun* down the kilometre long field he could sense his normally light plane straining heavily to leave the ground. By this time the plane had gathered too much speed to stop and Saint-Ex did the only thing he could: he pulled back desperately on the stick. The *Simoun* nosed into the air, barely clearing an embankment at the end of the field, only to fall back for lack of sufficient climbing speed. The plane hit the earth and turned over twice, scattering pieces of wreckage over a hundred yards. Both occupants were knocked unconscious by the crash. Prévot, when he came to, emerged with nothing worse than a broken leg; but Saint-Exupéry, who only recovered partial consciousness several hours later in the hospital, had suffered eight fractures, including a broken jaw, a cracked shoulder blade, and a shattered wrist. For days he lay in a semi-conscious coma, with just enough strength to scribble telegraphic messages with his left hand. After a week he was strong enough to have himself wheeled to a telephone for a long distance call to France, but the infection in his right forearm had by now begun to assume alarming proportions. For the next fortnight he had to wage a daily battle against the hospital surgeons who wanted to amputate his right hand.

One night he woke up feverishly to find that in his troubled sleep he had thrown off his sheets and blankets and was shivering with cold. The attendant who came to wrap him up again—for both his arms were paralysed—was astonished to hear an almost delirious Saint-Ex asking desperately to be wrapped up in the "sheet . . . the sheet that heals wounds . . ."

"A sheet that heals wounds?" The attendant was amazed. "But we don't have any such thing."

Saint-Exupéry fretted, but his conscious mind was unable to explain why he had made such a strange request. Only one year later, when he happened to be passing through Lyon and took the funicular up to Fourvières, did he suddenly realize on seeing the old, faded sign just beyond the tunnel turnstile proclaiming "Girardot's Linen Sheets—a sovereign soother of sores and burns"—that his subconscious had been at work in Guatemala.

Consuelo, who had embarked on the *Wyoming* the moment she got word of the accident, reached Guatemala on March 5, and from then on Antoine had a voluble ally who could out-talk the doctors in their own language and help her battered husband save his dear right hand. A French doctor was flown down from Mexico to check on Saint-Exupéry's slow recovery, but it was decided that for the expert medical attention he required he would have to be transferred to the United States. He reached New York a few days later, and there waiting for him on the airfield was his old friend Henri Guillaumet, who had been sent to America with another French test pilot on an Air France study trip.

Put up at the Ritz Carlton, Saint-Ex paid daily visits to a clinic where the doctors, here too, were in favour of amputation. One day he had been seated for a long time in a waiting-room when he asked a passing nurse what was the cause of the delay. "Oh", she answered gaily, "you'll just have to wait your turn. There's an operation going on in there which is taking longer than expected." What! Saint-Exupéry almost jumped out of his seat. They had been planning to chop off his hand after all! Without another word he crept out of the clinic, and refused to return until he had rallied friendly support. The director finally yielded to his insistence and let him keep his hand, but made him sign a certificate absolving the hospital of all responsibility for what might ensue. The X-rays had revealed that he would never again be able to lift his left arm above shoulder level. As for the wounded wrist, it was touch-and-go for several weeks. After removing the bandages one day, Saint-Exupéry was startled to see a tiny green plant growing in the wound, but it disappeared as the scar slowly healed.

Shortly before the end of the month he was well enough to attend a luncheon offered to his friend Guillaumet by Jean Brun, the local Air France representative, but he had to be careful about his drinks. The shock of his accident had been so great that for months thereafter he was subject to dizzy spells, his head would start throbbing, he would hear strange buzzing sounds, and his nerves would be set on edge by something as trivial as the opening of a match-box. While Guillaumet left for France on the *Normandie*, Saint-Ex remained behind in this strange airborne city where his feeling of strangeness was heightened by his total ignorance of English. He stubbornly refused to learn even a basic smattering of words, on the grounds that it would rob him of the charming "intrigues" he could hatch each time he walked into a department store and stirred up a lively commotion by asking the startled salesgirls to find someone on the floor who could speak French. "Ah! *Vous Français?* . . ." and with much nudging and laughter the beaming visitor would be offered a fleeting vision of "a young girl's grace".

Saint-Exupéry's prolonged convalescence had at least one fruitful consequence. For years he had been wrestling with the problem of the third book which André Gide as much as Gaston Gallimard had been urging him to write. He had decided long ago that it would not be a novel—the aftermath of *Vol de Nuit* was still too bitter a memory; but how was he to make a book out of a constellation of variegated experiences which made excellent newspaper or magazine "pieces" and could keep a dinner-table spellbound, but which lacked a unifying thread? Why, Gide one day objected when they were discussing the matter, why need his book be a monolithic whole? "Why couldn't you write something which would not be a continuous narrative, but a kind of . . ." Here Gide groped for an appropriate image, ". . . well, something like a bouquet, or a sheaf, grouping together into different chapters, and without regard to time or place, an airman's sensations, emotions, and reflections: something like what Conrad's admirable *Mirror of the Sea* is for the sailor?" Saint-Ex was unfamiliar with this particular book of Conrad's (which Gide had read in English), but he followed his mentor's erudite advice and read it in a French translation. It was just the stimulus he needed, and as Gide later recalled, the first fragments Tonio read to him "surpassed my wishes, hope, and expectation."

It was this "sheaf" of scattered fragments which Saint-Exupéry now had sent over to him from Paris and on which he began working during his New York convalescence. Here he was aided by two windfalls. The first was the friendship he struck up with Colonel William Donovan, a First World War veteran of the Argonne whose love of France was on a par with his love of adventure. Realizing that a suite at the Ritz Carlton was a luxury Saint-Ex could ill afford for long, he generously invited him to occupy a room commanding a splendid vista over the East River in his luxurious apartment on Beekman Place.

The other unexpected stroke of luck was the presence in New York of Jean Prévost, who was in the United States on a university grant. The generous friend who had published his first literary effort in Adrienne Monnier's *Navire d'Argent* and later introduced him to Gaston Gallimard was only too happy to promote Tonio's interests once again—this time by introducing him to Eugene Reynal and his new associate Curtice Hitchcock, a former Century Company publisher whom Saint-Ex had once raced around Paris (along with Léon-Paul Fargue) in his nerve-wracking Bugatti.

An American translator, Lewis Galantière, was recruited for the job, and before he left New York in April Saint-Exupéry turned over to him a batch of manuscripts, most of which had previously been published in French newspapers or periodicals, though none of it was known to Americans.

The title for his new book seems to have caused Saint-Exupéry a good deal of brain-wracking. A copy of the text he showed to his friend, Georges Pélissier later that same year bore the title *Etoiles par Grand Vent* (Stars in a High Wind). Another, which he presented to Henry de Ségogne, was entitled *Vent sous les Etoiles* (Wind beneath the Stars). In New York it was finally agreed between Saint-Ex and his publishers that the title should be *Wind, Sand, and Stars*—taken directly from the passage describing the festive night he had spent with Bourgat and Riguelle near Cape Bojador, when they had sat there by the crated candles wondering when the Moors would come careering over the dunes in a blaze of wild musketry. "We tasted this same light fervour one has in the midst of a well prepared feast. And yet we were infinitely poor. Wind, sand, stars. A style fit for trappist monks."

\*   \*   \*

For much of that summer, after his return to France, Saint-Exupéry carried his sheaf of material around from one place to another, as though still unclear in his mind as to the final form to give it. After visiting his sister Gabrielle at Agay and reassuring his worried mother about his physical state, he felt the urge to undertake a pilgrimage to the Villa Saint-Jean at Fribourg. He tarried for several days on the Lake of Geneva—so fraught with memories of his romance with Loulou—and cruised around on its little ferry-boats, notebook in hand, in the hope that the everchanging views of the Dents du Midi and the castle of Chillon would lift him to heights of Byronic inspiration; but when they failed to, he would disembark in disgust at the next lakeside stop.

From Fribourg he drove on to Saint-Maurice-de-Rémens, as though anxious to reestablish contact with his remotest youth; but the fleeting glimpse he caught of what was now a summer camp for boys depressed him beyond words. Rapidly he moved on to Etoile, the little village in the department of the Drôme to which *"Moisie"* (Marguerite Chapays), his mother's old housekeeper, had retired. When the shrivelled old woman opened the door in answer to his knock, she burst into squeaks of joy. But she was a bit overwhelmed by this balding giant whose head scraped her low ceiling and who had lost the golden hair (now turned brown) she had known when, as a boy, he was called *"le roi soleil"*.

Back in Paris he found himself once again beset by a host of personal problems. Consuelo's exuberant ways had begun to exhaust him, and one day he had warned her: "If you go on running around like this, you'll end up like a rose shorn of its petals." But the Rose, which kept spinning, was equally unhappy, for what she wanted above all was a place for her sculptures and she found it burdensome lugging them up and down six flights of stairs at the Place Vauban. Besides, that palatial apartment, like its principal adornment—Boris the butler—had become extravagantly expensive to maintain. So by mutual accord they separated for a while. Consuelo moved with her sculptures to a fourth floor apartment on the Rue Barbet de Jouy, around the corner from their former "bird-cage" on the Rue de Chanaleilles, while Antoine moved to a small bachelor's flat on the Rue Michel-Ange, near the Auteuil race-track. Its pale blue living-room was furnished with Louis XVI chairs and a russet couch, and in the tiny vestibule was hung a huge gilt mirror which, as Georges Pélissier was later to recall, sent back a "rosier and healthier image of oneself". On the mantelpiece was set one of Saint-Ex's prize acquisitions, one the good doctor had first brought to his attention: a Jaeger "Atmos" clock which could keep perfect time—for a thousand years, as Tonio liked to say—without ever being wound up; a temperature variation of just one degree sufficing to keep its ethyl-chloride "heart" going for four days at a stretch. But the most precious feature of his new lodgings was the terrace, past whose rambler rosebush one was offered a sweeping vista of the Seine and the heights of Saint-Cloud.

It was here that he wrote a preface to the French edition of Anne Morrow Lindbergh's *Listen, the Wind!* which offers an interesting insight into his ideas on writing.

By late August he had accumulated enough new material to be willing to leave a typescript with Gallimard before going off to Vichy for a health cure. But he was still not satisfied and kept ceaselessly correcting his text, forcing Gallimard to hold up sending it to the printers. But as the month of September wore on, with the war clouds gathering ominously over the continent, he found it more and more difficult to concentrate on his writing. Like everyone else he was paralysed by the news from Sudetenland and Central Europe. Unable to stand it any longer he came racing back to Paris— in time to live those incredibly tense and anxious hours which preceded the signing of the Munich agreement during the night of September 29–30.

Seldom, even in the tortured history of the Third Republic, had French public opinion been so divided and confused. While Bunau-Varilla, the editor of *Le Matin* was all but openly expressing his admiration for Hitler— "*plutôt Hitler que Blum!*" was the great phrase of the moment—Henri de Kerillis, in the no less conservative *L'Echo de Paris* was proclaiming that precisely because the French air force was so terrifyingly inferior to the German, Czechoslovakia had to be saved. In the conservative *Le Temps*, the organ of the Comité des Forges and of the "200 *familles*" (the plutocracy effectively running French affairs), a jurist by the name of Barthélemy undertook to demonstrate that the treaty binding France to Czechoslovakia had been nullified by the lapsing of the Locarno agreement! Pierre Bénard whose servility to the Communist Party line had precipitated Henri Jeanson's and Jean Galtier-Boissière's resignation from the *Canard enchaîné*, was piously proclaiming that nothing could be more understandable than that three million Sudetens should be allowed to become Germans so that the peasants of the Berri, the Normans, the Lorrainers, the Auvergnats, etc. should not be turned into cannon-fodder—which was almost word for word what Henri Béraud was saying in the reactionary weekly *Gringoire*. The arch-monarchist *L'Action Française* was, as might have been expected, running true to its anti-Semitic form: Charles Maurras proclaiming in his habitual dogmatic tone that a war for Czechoslovakia would be a war fought for the "*Chuifs*" (the Yids).

The Jews were no less divided; for while Georges Mandel, Colonial Minister in the Daladier government, and Julien Benda, the writer, were for intervening to save Czechoslovakia, Emmanuel Berl (the editor of *Marianne*) was employing his subtle intellect to ridicule the "war-mongers". As for the Communist *L'Humanité*, it was positively revelling in a fervent patriotism which might have sounded a bit more genuine had Stalin not let the cat out of the bag the previous May by assuring a plenary session of the Third International that a war among the capitalist countries had to be encouraged because the infallible teaching of Marx-Engels-Lenin conclusively demonstrated that "revolution will automatically ensue from a war among these states". Almost alone amid the hue and cry Saint-Exupéry's friend Gaston Bergery sought to maintain a minimal *sang-froid* (in *La Flèche*), though his pacifistic inclinations could not help but receive a rude buffeting.

For Saint-Exupéry, who had never harboured such naive illusions, the dilemma was just as cruel. In his notebook he had long since taken private issue with Bergery and Jeanson, not to mention Romain Rolland, refusing to accept the facile notion that it is the munitions manufacturers who are responsible for wars. "I realize full well that the political state of the world, carrying with it the risk of war, will favour Basil Zaharof's existence and activity. I also realize that once born, Basil Zaharof will favour the political conditions which motivate and serve him. But only as a parasite; and I have no right to say that Basil Zaharof, really so unimportant, conditions the risk of war even though his activity runs exclusively in that direction. For then it is *the risk of war* which conditions itself." At the time of the Abyssinian war he had written: "I would accept this game, which exalts man perhaps, if it weren't played with poisoned gas." And on another occasion he had noted: "What, intellectually, is more unacceptable than war? Alain realized it when he thought that to purge the world of it, it was enough to find it unacceptable."

But that was just the trouble. The war now looming over Europe like an angry black cloud could not be frightened away with a swish of logical anathemas. Nor was it the kind of game Captain Bonnafous and the camel-riding *méharistes* of Atar had played with their Moorish adversaries over vast stretches of Saharan desert: a game ennobled by a rudimentary chivalry. It promised to be the indiscriminate butchery Saint-Exupéry had personally witnessed in Madrid.

The three articles he now dashed off, under the dramatic spur of the crisis, gave eloquent expression to his perplexity. The middle one was essentially a holdover from his Spanish *reportage*, one of the seven articles he had promised but failed to deliver to *Paris-Soir*. By boxing it in between two others of a more general character, he was able to offer his friends Pierre Lazareff and Hervé Mille a philosophical triptych entitled "Peace of War?" which they were glad to sandwich into three successive issues or *Paris-Soir* (October 2, 3, and 4) between an article by Colette and another by Winston Churchill on the same topic.

"A malaise, to be healed, must be clarified," Saint-Exupéry began in the first article (entitled "Man of War, Who are You?"). "And we are certainly in a state of malaise. We have chosen to save the Peace. But in saving the peace, we have mutilated our friends. And there were doubtless many among us who were prepared to risk their lives for the duties of friendship. These feel a kind of shame. But if they had sacrificed the peace, they would feel the same shame. For they would have sacrificed man: they would have accepted the irreparable crumbling of Europe's libraries, cathedrals, and laboratories. They would have agreed to ruin its traditions, they would have agreed to change the world into a cloud of ashes. And this is why we oscillated from one opinion to the other. When Peace seemed threatened, we discovered the shame of war. When we seemed spared of war, we experienced the shame of Peace."

It was an admirable statement of what France had just lived through—save that all too few Frenchmen had really felt a deep, wholehearted shame over one of the most desperate, but at the same time sordid diplomatic deals ever perpetrated in the name of "noble" intentions. For one Bernanos, so grieved by his country's ignominy that he chose the road of exile, for one Montherlant crying: "Rave on, ye hapless, hoodwinked, and bespatted helots . . . who greet your humiliation and defeat with slavish transports of delight," there were a thousand French men and women ready to clutch at that tempting fig-leaf: "Peace with Honour!" Colette was far closer to the general mood in writing (in the October 1st issue of *Paris-Soir*) with tranquil smugness: "We did not behave badly . . . If we take due stock of the week just passed, we come out of it honourably. Each did his best." Which, of course, was true. Beginning with M. Edouard Daladier, that "bull with snail's horns"—to quote Jean Galtier-Boissière—who flew back from Munich "doped to the gills on champagne" in anxious dread of the barrage of bad eggs and rotten apples he would have to weather, only to be mobbed at Le Bourget by a sea of hysterical admirers.

For Saint-Exupéry the trouble began the moment he had stated the initial dilemma. "Why do we make war when at the same time we know it is absurd and monstrous? Where is the contradiction? Where is the truth of war, a truth so imperious that it dominates horror and death?" The contradiction, he claimed, did not arise from any concrete set of circumstances, but from differences of "language"—the word Saint-Exupéry preferred to "ideology". "Languages carry such inextricable contradictions that they make one despair of man's salvation. Franco bombards Barcelona because, he says, Barcelona has massacred priests. Franco thus protects Christian values. But in the name of these same values the Christian sees a bonfire made of women and children in a bombarded Barcelona. And he no longer understands. These, you will say, are the dire necessities of war . . . War is absurd. Still, one must choose a side. But the stupid thing, it seems to me, is first of all a language which forces men to contradict themselves."

It was not a satisfactory answer, as his friend Léon Werth had had frequent occasion to point out; even though Saint-Exupéry went on to add: "Do not object the evidence of your truths, for you are right. You are all right. Even he is right who heaps the world's misfortunes on the hunchbacks. If we declare war on hunchbacks, if we launch the idea of a race of hunchbacks, we shall soon learn to exalt ourselves. All the villainies, all the crimes, all the prevarications of the hunchbacks will be laid at their door . . . And when a poor innocent hunchback is drowned in blood, sadly we shall shrug our shoulders: 'These are the horrors of war. He is paying for the rest . . . He is paying for the hunchbacks' crimes.' For hunchbacks too commit crimes."

The phrasing of this paragraph was not altogether felicitous, if only because the exalted tone—habitual with Saint-Exupéry—was at war with the underlying irony. But the allusion was unmistakable for anyone who had been following the news. At the Nazi Party Congress held three weeks before in Nürnberg Goering had fulminated: "Those miserable pygmies"— he meant the Czechs—"are oppressing a cultivated people" that is, the Germans. "Behind them is Moscow and the eternal mask of the Jewish devil." By resorting to a euphemism—"hunchbacks" instead of "pygmies"— Saint-Exupéry was able to broaden the scope of his argument. For as the next paragraph made clear, it was against all witch-hunts undertaken in the name of a "superior truth" that he was inveighing: whether the "hunch-backs" were Slavic *Untermenschen*, Jewish "devils", or the "godless un-believers" whom Franco had decided to eliminate root and branch from the ravaged landscape of Spain. So strong were Saint-Ex's feelings on the subject that the gist of this paragraph was carried over into *Wind, Sand, and Stars*: with the curious result that when the book was translated into German (*Wind, Sand, und Sterne*) it escaped the nodding censor's eye for the first couple of editions.

"Forget then these divisions," Saint-Exupéry went on in this first *Paris-Soir* article, "which once admitted bring in their wake a whole Koran of unshakable truths and the fanaticism that ensues. One can group people into persons of the left and of the right, into hunchbacks and non-hunch-backs, into Fascists and democrats, and these distinctions are unassailable; but the truth, as you know, is that which simplifies the world, and not that which creates chaos."

The "eternal" truth he was here contrasting to the narrow dogmas of ideological fanatics was the universal truth of a Newton reducing the chaotic complexity of post-Aristotelian physics to the celestial harmony of universal gravitation. But it was precisely this kind of "simplification", applied to human phenomena, which had given rise to the blind hatreds Saint-Ex was denouncing—brought about by the arbitrary division of human beings into "good" and "evil", "noble" and "base", "Aryan" and "non-Aryan", "white" and "black", or (as in Russia) "bourgeois" and "proletarians". This was where he parted company with Werth, who shared his detestation of dogmas, but who, precisely because he was of a less scientific cast of mind and an atheist to boot, refused to believe that human quarrels and divisions could be resolved by the mere invention of a new universal language, comparable to that of the European Middle Ages. For did the universal language of a Dante or a Thomas Aquinas spare mediaeval Europe the vexations of war or "purges"?

Saint-Exupéry's second article, laboriously entitled "In the Night Enemy Voices call and reply to each other from one trench to the other", only extended the dilemma he was unable to resolve. It provided a moving description of a night-time reconnaissance on the Spanish front. When Saint-Exupéry had all too casually lit a cigarette, it had brought a swift salvo of bullets whining overhead, but a little later the most barrel-chested of the scouts he was accompanying had leaned his rifle on a stone and bawled across the valley to the enemy: "It's I, Leon . . . Antonio . . o!" The choice of names was not accidental; and in this symbolic act of brotherhood Saint-Ex was transposing the basic kinship he felt, over and above their arguments, for Léon Werth, his friend.

This type of warfare—if one can call night patrolling warfare—was still recognizably human. As human as the conduct of that gallant French captain who, having beaten off a Rif mountaineers' assault with the help of other Berber tribesmen who happened to be visiting his fort, had later returned the three hundred cartridges they had fired in his defence—well aware that they might be used tomorrow to kill his own men. That was war when it was still human, still chivalrous. But what relevance did this have to the present crisis in Europe where, as the Spanish Civil War had shown, Stuka dive-bombers and long-range guns were callously indifferent to chivalry? The answer alas! was none. Nor was much consolation to be derived from the philosophical message Saint-Exupéry went on to offer: "The truth for man is that which makes a man of him. When he who has known this altitude of human relations . . . compares this self-aggrandizement to the mediocrity of the demagogue who would have expressed his fraternity to these same Arabs by broad claps on the back, who might perhaps have flattered the individual but who would have humiliated the man in him, the latter, if you reprove him, will only feel for you a somewhat scornful pity. And he will be right."

It was the solitary hermit of Cape Juby talking, the Frenchman who had won the grudging respect of Moors and Spaniards by his *gran señor* behaviour; but again, what relevance did it have to Munich and Nazi Germany? "Do not try to explain to a Mermoz," Saint-Exupéry went on, "as he plunges towards the Chilean slope of the Andes, with victory in his heart, that he is mistaken, that a businessman's letter was perhaps not worth his risking his life. Mermoz will laugh at you. The truth is the man who was born in him as he overflew the Andes." After which he added; "And if the German today is ready to shed his blood for Hitler, you must understand that it is pointless to discuss Hitler. It is because the German finds in Hitler the occasion for working up enthusiasm and offering his life that everything for this German is great. Do you not understand that the power of a movement rests on the man it delivers?"

Here at last, in the middle of the third and final article, Saint-Exupéry gripped the fearful dilemma by both horns. But what was this deliverance that was being promised to the Germans? Essentially a false promise. "One can unearth wooden idols and resuscitate old languages which have more or less fulfilled their time, one can resuscitate the mystiques of pangermanism or of the Roman Empire. One can get the Germans drunk on the euphoria of being German and countrymen of Beethoven. One can swell their pride right down to the humblest stoker. But it is harder to make of a stoker a Beethoven. These demagogic idols are carnivorous. The man who dies for the advancement of knowledge or the healing of the sick serves life, even in dying. It is lovely to die for the expansion of Germany, or Italy, or Japan, but the adversary is no longer an equation opposed to an integration, nor a cancer resisting a serum; the enemy is the man next door. He must be confronted, but today it is no longer a question of conquering him. Each installs himself behind a concrete wall. Each, for lack of anything better, sends out squadrons which night after night torpedo the other's entrails. Victory belongs to the one who is the last to rot; and, as in Spain, both adversaries rot together."

This was the kind of thing Romain Rolland might have written from the height of his lofty neutrality. But whereas Rolland was an integral pacifist who believed the Hindu virtue of *ahinsa* (non-violence), Saint-Exupéry was still enough of a Nietzschean to feel that certain types of warfare were ennobling compared to the ant-heap existence imposed on the inhabitants of an industrialized continent. "In Europe there are two hundred million people who have lost their way and who are waiting to be born. Industry has torn them from their peasant idiom and lineage and shut them up in enormous ghettos which resemble railway switchyards, encumbered with lines of black freight-cars. From the depths of their workers' settlements they would like to be awoken."

It was what he had felt during the train trip to Russia at the sight of those poor Polish miners, it was what he felt each time he passed through a Paris suburb. For as his friend Léon-Paul Fargue remarked of him later: at heart Tonio was a country boy, not made for the city. Saint-Ex proved it at the conclusion of this final article, by recalling a typically rustic scene: three peasant sons gathered around their mother's deathbed.

"*Tout est contradictoire!*"—everything is contradictory, the Inventor had sighed at one point in the scenario for *Anne-Marie*. And nowhere was this truer than with war. It was again Fargue, writing a couple of years after his friend's disappearance, who recalled how on those evenings when they made the rounds—from Nine-la-Marseillaise to the Café de Flore, to Chez Paul, or to "some grand well-waxed-salon-lady", they would reach strangely paradoxical conclusions. "If, we thought, men differ according to intestines, mysticism, the image of God, the choice of purgatives, the form of the larynx, the lines of the hand, the colour of the gums, nerves, resistance to pain, their toes and their eyebrows, love and pleasure, they are kinsmen, cousins, brothers in war! And little did we guess in saying so just how right we were!"

\*   \*   \*

The three articles published in *Paris-Soir* did little to clear up the problems left over by the Munich crisis, but they did at least enable Saint-Exupéry to repay part of the debt he had so long owed Jean Prouvost, its publisher. During this same month of October Hervé Mille invited him to dinner at Jarot's, then a fashionable restaurant near the Gare Montparnasse, to see how the rest of Saint-Ex's debt could be liquidated. To Mille's considerable surprise—he was not used to seeing his friend looking like a businessman—Saint-Exupéry walked in with a briefcase. It contained a whole sheaf of clippings of articles which had been published in aviation weeklies like *L'Aéro*, others which he could not offer Mille because they had been published in newspapers (like *L'Intransigeant*) or magazines (like *Minotaure*), but there was also a whole batch of new material which had either never been in print or which the author had completely reworked. The whole comprised the raw material for Saint-Exupéry's new book— roughly corresponding to what he had already turned over to Lewis Galantière in New York and given to Gallimard in August.

Mille needed no special urging to accept six choice items for publication in *Paris-Soir*. They included Saint-Ex's description of the old Latécoère bus and the eve of his first mail-piloting solo in Toulouse; the night he and Néri had gotten "lost" over the Atlantic; the festive "Christmas" he, Bourgat, and Riguelle had been forced by engine failures to spend in the candlelit proximity of Cape Bojador; his solitary exploration of a desert plateau never before trodden by the foot of man; and two articles about the Arabs. Published over a period of eight days in November, under the general heading of "*Aventures et Escales*" (Adventures and Ports of Call), this second Saint-Exupéry series precipitated a news stand rush such as *Paris-Soir* had never known for articles of an untopical and essentially literary character. Quality, for once, had brought a rich dividend in quantity.

It augured well for the success of his new book, but failed to allay his restless artistic anxiety. A perfectionist if ever there was one, Saint-Exupéry wanted a perfect title, and neither the one he had agreed upon with his American publishers—*Wind, Sand, and Stars*—nor *Etoiles par Grand Vent*, which he had picked out for the French edition, satisfied him completely. With the skies of the continent now beclouded by the "gathering storm" (as Churchill was to call it), there were weightier things to focus on than the glitter of the stars. Both titles were too melodramatic for his sober taste, and might even seem misleading—the book he had put together being less about the elements as such than about Man's struggle with them: which in the last analysis meant struggle with himself. André de Fonscolombe, a frequent visitor to the Rue Michel-Ange apartment, was thus put to work reading the assembled material to see if he couldn't dream up something better. The result of their combined excogitations was a list of not less than thirty alternative titles which Tonio showed to Yvonne de Lestrange, among others. The one finally chosen, oddly enough, was not among the ones she saw: that much she remembers. Probably this was because it figured on the list their cousin André had prepared. They were going through it one evening at 52, Rue Michel-Ange when they came to "*Terre des Humains*" (Earth of Human Beings). Suddenly a light shone in Antoine's dark eyes. "*Terre des Hommes!*" he exclaimed to his cousin Fonscolombe. "That's it." And *Terre des Hommes*—Man's Earth—it was.

On the other side of the Atlantic, meanwhile, Lewis Galantière had retired to Sherwood Anderson's country place in the south west Virginia hills and was busy on the American translation. Throughout this autumn he was bombarded by a hail of letters from Saint-Ex, who wanted this changed or that eliminated. One of his excursions had taken him over to Algiers, where he had submitted his "bouquet" to Georges Pélissier's critical judgment. The good doctor had only one criticism to make: he felt that the first part of Saint-Exupéry's account of his Paris-Saigon "raid", though a fine description of a trans-Mediterranean flight, slowed down the narrative. "But I've never yet described a normal flight," Saint-Ex objected; only to agree, after a brief debate, to the amputation. But Galantière, when the idea was put to him, was more insistent; and it was the longer version, virtually word for word as it had appeared in *L'Intransigeant* three years earlier, which was included in *Wind, Sand, and Stars*.

Since this accorded with his original intent, Saint-Exupéry was secretly pleased by the decision. He was, however, less happy about his translator's insistence on retaining the articles he had written on Madrid for *Paris-Soir*; for though the times were desperately out of joint and this autumn sombre indeed, he did not wish to strike too dark a note before the anguished finale; and it was in its positive, less warlike aspects that he wished to stress the theme of human brotherhood.

Christmas, that year, was spent on the Riviera—between Agay and his mother's quaint *bastide* on the rocky mountainside of Cabris. On December 28th he took the steamer to Algiers, eager to pick the brains of his friend Georges Pélissier. The new year brought him back to Cabris; and it was here in a small family *pension* auspiciously named "Horizon"— the view over the olive trees was sweeping—that Tonio corrected the final proofs of *Terre des Hommes*, in an air heavy with the scent of January mimosa.

A few weeks later he boarded the *Normandie* and crossed the Atlantic once again. In the protracted epistolary debate he had been carrying on with his American translator, he had found Galantière reluctant to throw overboard what he later described as "a great deal of beautiful and moving writing which (in my view) he had no right to jettison". Surprised by so much stubborness—and what tribute, after all, could have been more flattering?—Saint-Ex had finally yielded to Galantière's entreaties and let him prepare a book that was considerably longer than the one he gave to Gallimard. Now he wanted to tell his translator that he was sorry for all the trouble he had caused him.

Though touched by this unexpected gesture, Galantière had to remind Saint-Exupéry that he had promised his American publishers two additional chapters which had not been delivered. "He made a face", to quote Galantière again, "and said he thought he could write one, at any rate, in a couple of days; it had been ripening in him for several years and was ready to drop. And in his room at the Ritz, in New York, he wrote what some readers believe to be the most exciting chapter in *Wind, Sand, and Stars*, the chapter called 'The Elements'."—the chapter in which Saint-Exupéry described his terrifying battle, beyond Trelew, with the Patagonian hurricane which had swept him so brutally out to sea.

The finished product, once again, revealed what Saint-Ex could do under pressure. He had planned to return to France on the *Normandie*, which was due to sail back in just four days; so that this section was written in little over forty eight hours. But for years he had been telling this particular story to his friends, each time seeking to improve it. As Georges Pélissier was later to observe: "All those who became closely acquainted with him know that Saint-Exupéry *talked* his books before writing them, and that in writing them, he tested their power on his friends, reading them passages and urgently soliciting an immediate judgment. He endured objections

or criticisms with kindness, but with a visible impatience." It depended
on the audience, for Saint-Ex, in Léon Werth's words, though "the most
lucid of men was also the most anxious." Never satisfied with what he had
written, he needed a sounding board to assuage his unsleeping anxiety.

For once even Saint-Exupéry was pleased with the anthology piece he
turned over to Galantière, whose whip cracking had sufficed to bring forth
a brainchild that had known eight years of pregnancy. Hastily he cabled to
Gallimard, asking that the printing of *Terre des Hommes* be held up to
include this choice new morsel. But it was too late. The plates had been
composed and the final pages of *Terre des Hommes* were already rolling off
the presses.

\*     \*     \*

Review copies of *Terre des Hommes* had already gone out to the critics
by the time Saint-Exupéry returned to Paris, and his little Auteuil flat was
soon crammed with piles of complimentary copies waiting to receive a
personal dedication in his neat airy hand. When Jacques Baratier dropped
in to interview him for *Les Nouvelles Littéraires*, he noticed two books on
his desk: Georges Sorel's *Réflexions sur la Violence* and an issue of *Etudes
Carmélitaines*. Saint-Exupéry smilingly handed him a special copy of his
new book which the workers of the Grévin printing shop had presented
to him as a gift: "Look at it, it's printed on aeroplane wing-cloth. What
artistry! And what work! I would like them to know how much I was touched
by their gesture!"

"You see," Saint-Ex concluded, after they had talked at some length
about his crash in the Libyan desert and his near drowning in the bay of
Saint-Raphael, "in concrete fact there are no dramas; they only exist in the
imagination". He was continuing the thought he had expressed at the end
of "The Elements", where he had written: "I could probably have shaken
you by telling you the story of some unjustly punished child. But I involved
you in a cyclone without, perhaps, tormenting you. But is not this how,
week after week, we watch the bombardment of Shanghai from the plush
depths of movie-theatre seats? Without a tremor we can admire the coils
of soot and cinders which these man-made volcanoes pour into the sky.
And yet, along with the grain of the granaries, the heritage of generations,
and old family treasures, it is the flesh of burned children which, dissolving
into smoke, slowly fattens that dark cumulus.

"But in itself the physical drama only touches us if it shows us its spiritual
sense."

These lines were written in New York; even here, in the luxury of his
Ritz Carlton suite, Saint-Exupéry's mind had been preoccupied by what

was going on in the outer world. By the time he was back in Paris Barcelona had fallen and his Republican friends were doomed. Just what new tragedy was about to descend on Europe no one quite new, but Saint-Ex thought it might be a good moment to go and see what mischief the masters of the Reich were brewing across the Rhine.

It did not take him long to find out. The trip, made this time by car and not by plane, gave him ample opportunity to appreciate the hobnailed realities of National Socialism. Germany, he was surprised to discover, was not only arrantly militant, it was healthy and in no imminent danger of starving. The inns and hotels he stopped at served generous wads of butter in a land where—so numerous Frenchmen had been led to believe—this agricultural commodity had been ruthlessly sacrificed to guns. (As though a savage twist of the udder could make a cow spew forth bullets!) So the Germans, who had been producing four warplanes for every one produced in France (800 compared to 200 a month), were having their butter and eating it too!

In Bavaria he found the roads clogged with military convoys; and through the windows of a Nürnberg beerhall he watched in horrified fascination as several hundred *Hitlerjugend* tramped past, their martial arrogance spurred on by raucous *Sieg Heils* from all sides. The waitress who had been serving him, noticing the frown on Saint-Exupéry's face, bent down and whispered: "My son is one of them, out there. They take them from you when they're still small. After that they're no longer one's children, and there's nothing one can do."

Berlin too was changed, and quite noticeably for the worse, even though this time he did not risk arrest for overflying *verboten* territory. Warmly greeted by Otto Abetz, whose official task it was to "improve" Franco-German relations, he was given a high Nazi official to guide him around the capital. The official followed him everywhere, like a shadow, to Saint-Exupéry's mounting exasperation. What were they afraid of—that he would get lost? Or see too much? . . . There was an art exhibition he wanted to see. *Jawohl*, said the official, he would be delighted to see it with him. They walked past a series of paintings, including a few Impressionist landscapes in which the official showed not the slightest interest. But suddenly he stiffened, as though touched by a live electric wire. "Ah!" he exclaimed, pointing to a specimen of Third Reich "realism", "That's the kind of painting Our *Führer* likes . . . *Heil Hitler!*" he added, clicking his heels like a wooden puppet.*

---

* Both Herve Mille and Charles Sallès remember hearing Saint-Ex tell them of an encounter with a senior member of the Propaganda Ministry. According to Mille, the official in question was none other than Goebbels himself. At one point in the conversation the dialogue went as follows:

Saint-Ex by this time was beginning to chafe at the bit. This shadow who followed him everywhere was getting on his nerves. Otto Abetz, whom he went back to see, was only too glad to help. He would like to get out of Berlin and see something of the country? Why, by all means. How about a visit to the *Führerschule* in Crössinsee, which is to say, in Pomerania? With Monsieur Henry Bordeaux, his compatriot and an author like himself? . . . Saint-Ex did not need to have the offer repeated. A Frenchman with whom he could share his impressions? What a windfall!

Shortly afterwards Henry Bordeaux and he were being led around the exemplary institution where a new generation of "model leaders" were being trained to assure the permanence of the Thousand Year Reich. The physical landscape was delightful: pleasant expanses of greenery, neat red-brick buildings, healthy outdoor athletics. But the inner landscape was bleak. To his questions: "What do you think of this? . . . What do you think of that? . . ." the answer invariably was: "Our Führer has told us . . . *So sagt der Führer* . . ." Cornered by a tricky question, one cadet answered a bit unhappily: "We don't know. Our Führer hasn't told us."

After visiting "this laboratory of the will", as Bordeaux later described it, they were led into a library where the bookshelves were crammed with works on history, philosophy, sociology, and biology.

"Are the students authorized to read books of a different point of view?" they asked. "The works of Karl Marx or Auguste Comte, for example?"

"Of course," was the reply, "they are free to do so".

"And what if they provide them with objections to National Socialism?"

"They will express them and they will be refuted."

"And what if the refutation does not seem to them conclusive?"

"They will be expelled . . . But" added the director with a condescending smile, "that never happens. Our dogma is *der deutsche Mensch*". German Man!

---

Goebbels: "But Herr von Saint-Exupéry, you must at least admit that we are a country of order, whereas France——"
Saint-Exupéry: "Superficially yes, but not fundamentally."
Goebbels: "Ah?"
Saint-Exupéry: "Let me take an example. Suppose that at noon tomorrow all the traffic lights stopped functioning and all the policemen were removed from the streets of Paris. What would happen? There would be an hour or two of confusion, to be sure, but eventually things would sort themselves out and the drivers would carry on as before. But if the same thing happened in Berlin? . . . there would be total and absolute chaos."
The curious thing in Hervé Mille's recollection of this exchange is that he remembers Saint-Ex telling him about it over a lunch-table at his apartment on the Place Vauban, which Saint-Exupéry gave up in the summer of 1938—that is, a good nine months before this second trip to Germany. It is possible that Saint-Ex may have made another trip to Germany between the flying foray of July 1937 and March of 1939. Pierre Lazareff recalls a luncheon in Paris where Saint-Exupéry used this same argument against Otto Abetz. Only this time he was more forthright. "In France, if the police were removed, there would be a few more robberies and a few more old ladies would be killed. That's all. But in Germany . . . do you really believe the régime could last?"

It was too much for both of them, and they hastened back to Berlin. There had been some talk of Saint-Exupéry's meeting Goering, who had been vacationing at San Remo and who had even driven over to Monte Carlo in his magnificent Mercedes to take part in the annual Battle of the Flowers, but Saint-Ex would have none of it. He was not going to prolong his stay for the pleasure of shaking hands with that bemedalled Gargantua whose mind, even if it was the equal of his girth, gave him no right to dismiss the Czechs as "pygmies". Besides, the war clouds were massing once again over Central Europe and at any moment the borders might be closed.

On March 14th Monsignor Tiso, who had pushed Slovakia into declaring its independence, arrived in Berlin to be solemnly received by the Führer. That evening Emil Hácha, the President of the dismembered Czechoslovak Republic, reached Berlin in his turn—in a last minute effort to change the Führer's mind. But the Führer's mind was made up: Czechoslovakia was in a state of "dangerous decomposition", and to put an end to the "intolerable terror against Germans" reigning in Bohemia and Moravia, the Wehrmacht was ordered across the borders at 4 o'clock the following morning.

After visiting the Berlin zoo (to admire its famous white bears) and calling on the French ambassador, Robert Coulondre, Saint-Ex decided it was high time to be leaving Germany. The return trip, in a Plymouth lent to him by a friend, took more than a day; but so anxious was he to be back that, on reaching the French border, he telephoned through to his friend Georges Pélissier, who in his absence had been occupying his Auteuil apartment: "I'm coming. Don't have lunch without me. I have so much I want to tell you . . ." The good doctor waited, and at 4 o'clock that afternoon a weary but anything but tongue-tied Antoine finally made his appearance.

"They're building so many planes," he told Pélissier, when they finally sat down to table, "that they haven't even had time to build hangars for them. I passed fields covered with planes parked out in the open. You don't build that many planes and leave them exposed like that to the weather unless you plan to use them. *Mon vieux, c'est la guerre!*"

He was right, it meant war—though the Armageddon was still six months off and the British could flounder around for six more weeks before resigning themselves to the inevitability of conscription. This time Saint-Ex needed no Léon Werth or Victor Serge to explain what was wrong with the system. Stalin, with notions like "class" and "proletarian", was reaping the whirlwind which Marx had sown; Hitler, with concepts like "non-Aryan" and "*Untermenschen*", was reintroducing the terrors of the Inquisition. Each, in the Führer's exquisite parlance, was bent on "decomplicating" life.

And France? What was one to think of France? When all one of his compatriots could think of doing was to "snicker over the German tendency to make the most of opportunities". Exasperated, Saint-Exupéry commented in his notebook: "What opportunities could we make the most of when we are tending towards nothing? Men? As many as you want: look at the mechanics of the Aéropostale. If oriented, we are every bit as ingenious in making the most of opportunities, in exploiting the roads offered. But what point is there in stationing oneself in the middle of the intersection if one has no desire to walk?"

# 17

# Man's Earth

MORE than a springtime swallow is needed to build a city; more than a
naive belief in human dignity to make a man. No one knew it better
than Saint-Exupéry, who for years had been struggling to define this dignity
and to determine what it really is to be a man. Like rounded pebbles worn
smooth by the oceanic tide, terms like "human dignity", "man", "the
freedom of the individual", "the pursuit of happiness", "the sovereignty of
the people", "the conscience of mankind" had been rubbed clean of meaning
in the ceaseless ebb and flow of ideological debate, as in the pan-humanist
clap-trap of politicians' banquets and journalistic rhetoric. For one thing
was patently evident: Rousseau, to whom Marx owed so much, was wrong
when he declared (at the beginning of *The Social Contract*): "Man is born
free but is everywhere in chains." The chains are still with us, as distressingly
present as under the *Ancien Régime*, but no man is born, whether free or a
slave. Man is not born a man; he is born a child. An individual *is*, but a man
only *becomes*: slowly, step by step, by virtue of ceaseless striving and self-
mastery. Were it otherwise, were the earth absolutely hospitable and man
(the Natural Man of Rousseau) fundamentally good, all our problems would
be resolved in advance. Life would lose its tension and the world be a
Garden of Eden, similar to certain Polynesian islands where the natives have
only to stretch out a languid hand and pluck the fruit generously hanging
from the limbs. But vast areas of the planet are inhospitable, and in places
uninhabitable; and by the same token life is not a gift but a predicament.
Human existence is not an effortless movement across a level plain: it is
ascent—up a slippery slope which shows no mercy when the effort is relaxed.
And without this upward striving the individual remains a shiftless individual, a drifting plank upon a drifting tide, a cypher in a sea of cyphers, an
atomic unit in an atomic ant-heap.

This is the message of *Terre des Hommes*: the golden thread which ties
its random episodes into a tight bouquet. The message is expressed in the

book's opening lines, lines which—for some inexplicable reason—are missing from *Wind, Sand, and Stars*: "The earth teaches us more about ourselves than all the books. Because it resists us. Man discovers himself when he measures himself against the obstacle."

In these three staccato sentences, which ring like hammer-blows, Saint-Exupéry resumed the sum total of his acquired wisdom. Those who later tried to make out that he was an "existentialist" were mistaken; Saint-Exupéry was never an "existentialist", even assuming that one can provide a satisfactory definition for this catch-all word. His was a "resistencialist" philosophy, to borrow a term first coined by José Ortega y Gasset who, though Saint-Exupéry did not know it, had begun hammering out just such a philosophy a quarter of a century before. The same philosophy which Arnold Toynbee was simultaneously adapting to six millennia of human history with his leitmotif of "challenge and response." Manhood is not something given by birthright, but acquired. Man is not man by virtue of what he inherits, but by virtue of what he does, what he creates. So deeply was Saint-Exupéry persuaded of this that he made this concept of "creation" the criterion or touchstone by which he judged not only man but civilization. "What a man is worth is so much what he becomes. I do not know what he is," is one of many such comments in his notebooks. "Men. Sacrifice—not to what they are but to what they can become" is another. "You offer me a more beautiful apartment building, a better car, a purer air . . . But what men to inhabit them?" is a no less typical query. And by the same token he could write, à propos of that arch-rebel André Breton: "Childhood, cuffs about the head, religion, sacrifice—are so many actions intended to make a man emerge from this little animal. Nothing is better suited to form an André Breton than André Breton's family against which he rebels."

The application of this "resistencialist" criterion to society was enough to point up the pathetic fallacy underlying absolute socialism and the ideal of "womb to tomb" security. "I am to the Left because I do not like the masses. If I were to the Left and liked them (which is to say, preferring them, since it's a question of serving them to the detriment of the privileged) I would be wary of combating the conditions of life which make them nobler (poverty, sacrifice, injustice)." Or, as expressed towards the end of *Terre des Hommes*: "What good to us are political doctrines which claim to make man flourish, if we do not know what type of man they will engender? Who is to be born? We are not a flock to be fattened up, and the appearance of one poor Pascal is of more weight than a few prosperous nonentities."

Such a conception of life, as one can see, is poles removed from Rousseau's idyllic concept of the natural goodness of man, to which he would tend to revert but for the innate iniquity of society. A typical product of eighteenth century thought, this latter notion assumes that there is within man, from birth on, something already pre-established and pre-formed, but it was precisely this facile notion which Saint-Exupéry was combating. Basically man is formless: he is like a lump of clay which it will take years of moulding to fashion into something determinate. The image runs through all of his books—from *Vol de Nuit* to his last posthumous work. But the clay is not lifeless; it is living clay, inhabited by a spark. It is like the *"gangue"*—one of his favourite words—the muddy matrix from which, after much scrubbing and polishing, the diamond emerges in all its radiance. And just as it requires an abrasive to reveal the radiance of the gem, so adversity alone (what Toynbee would call a "challenge" or Ortega a "predicament") brings out what is finest, what is latent, in human beings. The two "princesses" of the Paraguay "oasis" owe their grace not only to their poetic harmony with Nature, but to the diligence they show in preserving their cracked *castillo* from crumbling into total ruin. The human worth of Bark, the Moroccan slave at Juby, comes not simply from the "cargo of dreams" he, like any mortal, carries in his head, but from the desperate energy he is prepared to expend to reacquire his freedom, even though it may ultimately doom him to poverty. When word spreads through the desert that Captain Bonnafous, the dread *méhariste* of Atar, is going home to France, his Moorish enemies are dismayed: they are losing the adversary whose existence was the condition of their manhood, the foe whose rumoured approach could arouse the nodding shepherds from their pastoral sloth, tear indolent husbands from the soft embraces of their women, draw the sleeping swords from their scabbards, launch the pegged camels across the wastes in hot pursuit of this camel-riding "pirate" whose phantom passage, somewhere beyond the dunes, could charge the entire Sahara, like a magnetic field, with a pole of converging hatreds, strangely resembling love. Mermoz, by virtue of the same vital logic, would not have become the man he did if he had not been willing to pit his wits and his courage against the perfidious mystery of night flying or the monstrous water-spouts of the South Atlantic. Guillaumet would never have been acclaimed as an exemplary "son of France" if he had not measured his will to survive against the frozen slopes of the Andes.

But the moral in all this is not to be found only or essentially in these epic demonstrations of human heroism. *Terre des Hommes* was not intended as just one more adventure book, written about that necessarily limited élite— the mountain-climbers and the flyers, the soldiers and the Bedouins. For its central theme is summed up in an image which is neither sportive nor nomadic, but workmanlike: "There is a quality which has no name. Perhaps it is 'gravity', but the word is unsatisfactory. For this quality can be accompanied by the most smiling gaiety. It is the quality the carpenter has when he places himself face to face with his piece of wood, fingers it, measures it, and far from treating it lightly, gathers all his virtues to deal with it." And the model of human behaviour Saint-Exupéry holds up as the sum of what human behaviour should be is not just Guillaumet, crawling painfully towards the ledge which will save his body from the spring avalanches so that his wife can collect her widow's insurance: no, it is the image of the old gardener (Eugène Bouchard of Saint-Maurice, though in the book he is not named) saying, as he lies a-dying on his humble bed: " 'You know . . . at times I sweated as I spaded. I could feel the rheumatism tugging at my legs and I used to curse this drudgery. Well, today I'd so like to spade, to spade in the earth. Spading seems to me so beautiful. One's so free when one's spading! And then, who's going to trim my trees?' He was leaving an untilled earth. He was leaving an untilled planet. He was linked by love to all the lands and to all the trees of the earth. He was the generous, the prodigal, the Grand Seigneur! He, like Guillaumet, was the brave man, when he fought against death in the name of his Creation."

How well Tolstoy would have understood that feeling! But for Saint-Exupéry, who had probably never cobbled a shoe or scythed a field in his life, what mattered was the universal moral to be drawn from these contrasting examples. "To be a man is, precisely, to be responsible"—the gardener for his tree, the father for his family, the carpenter for his trade, the sculptor for his art, the skipper for his ship. This was Saint-Exupéry's mature answer to Nietzsche's "Live dangerously!", just as it was to the revolutionary heroics which are the stuff of André Malraux's novels. But *Terre des Hommes* was more. It was also, in its culminating pages—devoted to the pathetic spectacle of all those Polish miners he had seen on the long train trip to Russia—an anguished cry of distress at the creeping march of a mechanized civilization where the manhood of the pilot, the integrity of the poet or the painter find it increasingly difficult to assert itself; where the peasant is uprooted and tossed, like one more human faggot, on to the mounting wood-pile of a mind- and soulless proletariat; and where, most poignantly of all, the bright creative flame, the Little Prince, the Mozart slumbering in each growing child is snuffed out in the raucous honky-tonk of cheap café music and the spiritless distractions of an over-crowded, over-agitated, infra-human world where "there is no gardener for men".

*       *       *

"Only the Spirit, if it breathe upon the clay, can create Man." Such were the closing words of *Terre des Hommes*. But seldom had the Spirit—the spirit which had once made Europe a crucible of creative fervour—flickered more fitfully than in this sombre spring. March 1939 was hardly a propitious moment for the publication of a book aimed at exalting the brotherhood of man ("Only human operation—to reconcile," as Saint-Exupéry had written in his notebook, à propos of the Spanish Civil War, "but one can only reconcile with the aid of a new conceptual system".) Fate, once again, seemed to be mocking the author with a diabolical anachronism. *Vol de Nuit* had had the misfortune to appear six months after the collapse of the Aéropostale it was intended to extol. *Terre des Hommes* was published at a moment when the fabric of European civilization was being methodically ripped to shreds by the most fratricidal descent into barbarism the continent had experienced since the depths of the Dark Ages.

One of the first to review the book was the arch-Catholic and arch-monarchist Robert Brasillach; and by a cruel irony his critique appeared in the very issue of *Action Française* (March 16) which announced the Nazi annexation of Bohemia and Moravia. It was a curious assessment, if only because of the patently divided sentiments of the reviewer, torn between admiration for the style and a dogmatic obligation to take issue with the content. "Romanticism" he wrote, "has taught us that *sincerity* is the supreme virtue of the writer. It is a word which was much abused after the war, along with the more scholarly word of *authenticity*, which enabled those who used it to strike a lofty note in the literary cafés . . . Let us admit right away that what bothers us in appreciating *Terre des Hommes* is that everything in it is rigorously exact, rigorously *authentic*."

It was not that Brasillach was out to go the salon mandarins one better, by echoing what Valéry had once remarked to Malraux: "I am interested in lucidity; I am not interested in sincerity." If only because he was an ardent Catholic, Brasillach was less superficial than the foppish aesthete who had written *Monsieur Teste*—"who mistakes his stomach rumblings for revealed truths", as Saint-Ex (who had no use for Valéry) once acidly noted. But the bigot in Brasillach could not accept Saint-Exupéry's desperate impartiality. "The militiaman of Madrid is worth the defender of Toledo. Each obeys his 'truth'. In the same way the captive gazelle yearning to flee is not concerned by the lion or the jackals that await her. 'What do the jackals matter if the truth of the gazelles is to experience fear?' And thus heroism is reduced to an instinct."

Brasillach was equally unwilling to accept the nobility of the French Captain's *grand seigneur* gesture in giving the Berber riflemen who had helped defend his fort 300 bullets to make up for those they had expended on his behalf—on the grounds that these same bullets will be used to kill his men, for whom he is responsible. "Individual heroism is opposed to political heroism, which is to say, to the heroism of the defenders of the city.

One cannot choose to be elegant with the blood of one's own men . . . The Church" he went on, now laying down the dogma, "has always taught that it is the cause which makes the martyr. Neither M. de Montherlant nor M. de Saint-Exupéry think so: they see in heroism a means of individual perfection. M. André Malraux opines in the same sense. But this is not the sense of our soil, of our history, of our race. It is a romantic and Nietzschean deviation, basically rather oriental."

This last sentence must have struck Saint-Exupéry as odd, if by "oriental" Brasillach was including the Moslem world, whose doctrinal fanaticism ("a whole Koran of unshakable truths") *Terre des Hommes* implicitly condemned. But Brasillach, who had a religious axe to grind, was preaching to the converted. Far more important was the impartial judgment of René Lalou, whose review in *Les Nouvelles Littéraires* (March 18) could hardly have been more laudatory. "How" he marvelled, "can he speak of himself with an ease which many professional biographers might well envy him? Simply because the emotions he expresses are universal . . . he *is* 'man's consciousness' in which this marvel is reflected."

The book was considered so important that three weeks later Edmond Jaloux followed up with a second review of *Terres des Hommes* in the same literary weekly. Far from being a random collection of adventurous experiences, *Terre des Hommes*, he said, was the work of a moralist who, while not the *casanier* (stay-at-home) type, could stand comparison with a Montaigne or a Proust, since at heart he was heeding Socrates' counsel: 'Know thyself.' And though Saint-Exupéry's "firm, concise" style had a tendency to drift occasionally into the pathetic, his moral message was fundamentally that of a Nietzsche, a Carlyle, an Emerson. "One must belong to the class of 'supermen' or 'heroes' or 'representative men'. An ethic which has nothing aristocratic about it, appearances notwithstanding. Every individual can become one or the other, if he feels the vocation or desire. But life is petty if one renounces this vocation or if one fails to yield to this desire.

"It is well that a work like *Terre des Hommes* brings us back to essential truths, and that it does so with a virile and poetic gravity, without posturing or ostentation. M. de Saint-Exupéry's book is one of the most beautiful we have read in a long time."

Such was also the opinion of the French Academy, or at any rate of Henry Bordeaux, who had returned from Germany so impressed by his fellow traveller that he had decided to dedicate his next book to him. But it took all the eloquence he could muster to overcome the misgivings of his fellow academicians, who objected that it would be improper to give Saint-Exupéry the French Academy's *Grand Prix du Roman* since *Terre des Hommes* was not a novel. Technically they were right, but Bordeaux reduced them to silence by asking what other author they could produce who had shown such elegance of style, imbued his characters with so much life, and his narrative with so much zest—all of them qualities, after all, a novelist was supposed to exhibit. Floored by this mace stroke, Bordeaux's colleagues gave in, and *Terre des Hommes* received the solemn consecration of the French Academy as the best novel of the year.

\*     \*     \*

1939, even less than 1932, was a year made for euphoria; but buoyed by this unexpected acclaim and relieved at last of crippling debts and obligations to his publisher and newspaper friends, Antoine de Saint-Exupéry was prepared to forget the problems of a darkening world and to indulge in a brief moment of springtime rapture. For the Easter holidays he left Paris and drove down to Saint-Amour, famous for its wines and its *poulet de Bresse*, where Léon Werth's wife Suzanne had a country house. It was a bit like coming home, for just forty miles to the South was Saint-Maurice-de-Rémens, with its cargo of youthful memories.

One sunny morning they were driving through the countryside when Werth and Saint-Ex stopped for lunch at a riverside restaurant by the Saône. The board terrace overlooked the sleepy waters and the poplars on the farther bank were bathed in misty sunlight. As he fingered the crude wooden table, carved like a schooldesk by previous clients' knives, Saint-Exupéry was filled with a sense of almost mystic elation—such as he had felt that evening on the Mekong years before as the sun sank through its jungle-web of tropic vegetation. Just below, by the riverbank, a bargeman and his wife were busy watching a mechanic repair their diesel engine.

"Come up and have a drink with us," Saint-Ex gaily called down to them, and the trio gratefully accepted.

"But I know you," said the mechanic, after they had joined them on the terrace. "I've seen your photo in the papers." He disappeared into the indoor dining-room and came back with a postcard which he insisted Saint-Exupéry autograph.

The bargeman and his wife turned out to be Germans, even though their barge was called *Cousance*, after a village in the Jura. They were from the Rhineland, they explained, and felt a Rhenish scorn for Hitler and his swaggering entourage and all this wild war talk.

"We German women," explained the wife, "have no desire to kill French women".

Their proletarian hearts were in the right spot, and they wanted their hosts to know that if ever their leaders were insane enough to start a war between France and Germany, the labouring masses on both sides of the Rhine would rise as one man in revolt. Pacifists? Possibly: though Werth, with his Jewish sensitivity, later could not help wondering if they hadn't been planted there as spies, part of that insidious "fifth column" which was to prove so effective in hastening the *débâcle* of 1940. But the thought did not even occur to Saint-Exupéry, elated by this momentary fraternization between a German couple and a French mechanic. There was something about this Pernod they were drinking, there was a savour to this good peasant bread and country sausage they were eating which he wished the entire world to share. And before lunch was over, in fact almost before it had begun, he was saying to Werth: "Let's motor over and surprise my friend Sallès." Werth, no longer exactly young—he was already in his early sixties —protested, but in vain. A 350 kilometre drive, just to surprise an old school friend, struck him as a rather tall order for a single afternoon. But Saint-Ex was insistent. There was plenty of room in Sallès' charming provençal *mas* —he had been put up there many times—and besides, his friend Henry de Ségogne was staying nearby at Arles. One more reason for making the trip.

That same evening, just as Charles Sallès and his wife were sitting down to dinner two large headlights and a generous blast of a Bugatti's horn beyond the front gate signalled the unexpected arrival of several visitors, at least one of whom was ravenously hungry. The spree lasted several days. Henry de Ségogne was brought over from Arles with his friend Pierre Dalloz, an architect Ségogne had met on his mountain-climbing expeditions. Together they visited the romanesque church of Saint-Gilles, one of the great pilgrimage sites of the Middle Ages, where Saint-Exupéry mysteriously disappeared, only to be discovered, after a few minutes of searching, in a *patisserie*, surrounded by twenty children who were licking the delectable remains of cakes and éclairs from their thumbs and fingers. At Aigues Mortes, as they were clambering over the Tour Constance, Saint-Ex disappeared again—this time to join in a game of bowls with the locals, who were so pleased with his company that in the café to which they repaired, the owner's son, a painter, was willing to part with a small stained-glass pane on which he had painted a black bull. Back at Tarascon one evening, as they sat warming their backs and faces before a blazing hearth, Dalloz's wife entertained them with recitations of Federico Garcia Lorca's poems.

Saint-Exupéry was radiant. "How wonderful!" he kept repeating, "How wonderful to think I've brought together my three best friends"—he meant Werth, Sallès, and Ségogne.

A fourth was missing: Guillaumet, to whom he had dedicated *Terre des Hommes*. Even before Mermoz' death Guillaumet had become Air France's record-holder for the number of flights across the South Atlantic. For most of the past year and a half he and his wife had been stationed at Biscarosse, in the flat fir-studded region of the Landes, south of Bordeaux, where a large inland lagoon provided perfect conditions for seaplane tests and take-offs. It was here, in a quaint country inn—l'Hôtel du Lac et des Pins—that Saint-Ex joined them on May 29—this time a properly invited guest—to celebrate Henri's thirty-seventh birthday. It was a festive occasion, also attended by their friend Jean Lucas, of Port Etienne, Jacques Néri, the radio operator with whom Saint-Ex had once lost his way in "interplanetary space", and Néri's wife, a woman of such remarkable placidity that she was known as "*Tourmente*" (Uproar).

The Latécoère 521, a huge six-engine flying-boat which Guillaumet had been testing for the past eighteen months, was, as he knew only too well, already outdated by the new four-motor clippers Glenn Martin was building in the United States. But the *Lieutenant de Vaisseau Paris*, as it was called, was all Air France had for flying the North Atlantic. The first flight had been scheduled for early July, and Saint-Ex, who had been grounded ever since his Guatemala crash, was determined to make the flight with his friend. For this, special permission had to be obtained from Air France. Louis Castex, whom he rang up on the subject after his return to Paris, was sure it would be refused; but when Saint-Exupéry had set his mind on something, he was not easily stopped. Dragging Castex over to the Air Ministry, he pushed through one office after another straight into the sanctum of sanctums, where the harassed Minister, overwhelmed by his oral vehemence, gave in to the barrage of eloquence and accorded a reluctant authorization.

On July 7th the two friends took off from Biscarosse with three mechanics, two radio operators, and a navigator, reaching New York on the 10th, after a stopover in the Azores. Unwilling, whatever happened, to miss the return flight, scheduled for four days later, Saint-Ex played possum, never leaving his crewmates and refusing to call up any of his New York friends. But he could not help being pleasantly surprised by the impressive piles of *Wind, Sand, and Stars* he saw advertised in bookshop windows. Published a scant ten days before, Lewis Galantière's translation was already a best-seller.

At dawn on July 14th—France's National Holiday—the *Lieutenant de Vaisseau Paris* took off once more, and aided by the prevailing south west winds, made it back to Biscarosse via Newfoundland and Finistère in a single great circle hop. Saint-Exupéry, as Louis Castex was later to write, had brought his friend Guillaumet good luck; for though one engine had to be cut on the way over, the flight—made in twenty eight and a half hours—established a blue ribbon for a trans-Atlantic crossing.

Shortly after landing, Saint-Ex said good-bye to his friends Noëlle and Henri Guillaumet, insisting, however, that they join him that evening at his cousin Yvonne de Lestrange's château at Chitré (near Angoulême). Delayed by an unexpected amount of red tape, Guillaumet and his wife left Biscarosse several hours later than planned. As they approached Chitré that evening, they found a highly anxious Saint-Ex seated on the embankment. Fearful that his friend, who had just triumphantly spanned an ocean, might have been the victim of a car crash, he had spent the last couple of hours between the telephone and the roadside. "He looked like a very unhappy little boy," Noëlle Guillaumet recalls, "and his broad smile only returned, along with the protective, friendly embrace of his long arms, when he realized that we were really and truly there—for as usual, he had imagined the worst."

Even for Saint-Exupéry this was an unusually hectic summer. It had begun some months before with a typical extravaganza in the field of real estate. "I want to have a vacation from being a husband," he had explained to his wife when he moved to the little "bachelor's flat" on the Rue Michel-Ange; and while this was true, he continued to show a solicitous care for Consuelo's welfare. Neither of them were made to resist the temptations which affluence might bring their way, and though he did not have the soul of a proprietor, she did.

Having a place in the country had always been one of Tonio's dreams. One day, during an outing which took them past the Forêt de Sénart, south east of Paris, they drew up by a little church square in the village of La Varennes Jarcy. Across the road was a gate with a sign on it announcing: *Propriété à Louer ou à Vendre Meublée*. In addition to being furnished, the country house being offered for rent or sale brought with it a children's play garden, a park full of handsome trees, and a garden complete with pond in which—if it was not already there when they first saw it—a solitary duck was soon paddling.

"Don't rent that house," they were warned by someone they began questioning, "It brings bad luck".

So it might well have seemed to its owner, a somewhat down at heel widow, but Antoine refused to be put off: the trees surrounding the house were too tempting. They visited it that same day, guided by a café-owner who acted as local estate agent. He led them in through a back door, for which he had the key, and the first thing that struck their eyes—in the kitchen, of all places!—was an outsized chandelier, "big enough for an opera" (in Consuelo's words), whose glass crystals tinkled like the delicate chimes of a carillon. Saint-Ex hardly needed to see anything else: the sight of this "musical chandelier" delighted him as much as the property's leafy name—*La Feuilleraie*.

"This house is yours," he told Consuelo, adding a bit wistfully: "I don't know how I'm going to pay for it."

*Terre des Hommes* provided the answer to this particular dilemma, its soaring royalties soon making it possible to change the rent into outright purchase on the installment plan. As the months passed Consuelo settled down here, attended by a housemaid, a growing brood of hens and rabbits, and a dog called Greco whom Tonio had inherited from the owner of the "Caves Mura" café, who claimed it had been left in his vintner's "cellar" by some unduly careless Yankee topers. Whenever he was in the mood, Antoine would speed out to see her—for he always drove like the wind— sometimes in his Bugatti, at others on a motorcycle. The sight of several automobiles drawn up in front of the house was usually enough to make him turn around and head straight back to Paris; for Consuelo's taste in friends did not always coincide with his own, and on such occasions the only inkling she had of his passage would be a note, often scribbled in the *auberge* across the way, which would inform her: "I'm not coming this evening because you've got too much of a crowd."

Furnishing this spur-of-the-moment acquisition was fortunately less troublesome a task than had been the case with the spacious "void" of the Place Vauban, which was just as well; for Saint-Exupéry would have had little time to devote to it. Hardly had he returned to Paris after his trans-Atlantic flight with Guillaumet than he found himself being bombarded by cables from his American publishers asking him to come to New York to help them in promoting *Wind, Sand, and Stars*. Otis Ferguson, writing in *The New Republic*, had found "Saint-Exupéry's new book on flying . . . more turgid and jumbled, both larger in ambition and less complete in its effect" than *Night Flight*—a criticism which should more justly have been levelled at Lewis Galantière, the translator, for including material the author had wished to scrap; but Bruce Gould, in *The Saturday Review of Literature*, did not hesitate to call Saint-Exupéry the "most articulate airman in the sky" and to place him next to Anne Morrow Lindbergh. Such too had been the opinion of the editors of The Book of the Month Club, who had picked *Wind, Sand, and Stars* for their non-fiction selection in June.

With so much static in the air, the moment was ill chosen for leaving France, but Saint-Ex felt he had to humour the translator and publishers who had done so well by him. Reaching New York by ship, he was put up once again at the Ritz Carlton and spent a number of busy days signing gift copies, giving interviews (which he detested) and having himself photo- graphed. Maximilian Becker, his literary agent, took him on a guided tour of Harlem, a distraction he more than welcomed; but he found the dog-day heat of Manhattan oppressive and was even happier when André Morize, then in charge of the French Summer School, invited him to spend a couple of days in Middlebury, Vermont. He drove up with his friend Yvonne

Michel (a French newspaperwoman he had first met at Jean Prouvost's) and Pierre de Lanux; and on the way he amazed them by talking of the fantastic quantities of energy that were locked up inside an atom. A machine, he said, was already been built to disintegrate the atom, and it might well blow up the planet. It was the first any of the others had heard of "nuclear energy".

At Middlebury a dinner party was given for him, and as it was pleasantly warm outside, he sat under a large tree in front of Forest Hall and entertained some forty students, seated in a large circle around him, with certain of his adventures. Edward Harvey, a summer school student, was particularly amused, as were the others, by his vivid account of the battle with the lion cub in his *Simoun*. "Saint-Ex struck me as tall for a Frenchman, although I have known many tall ones. He had dark balding hair. Was portly and had a round face. He looked like a hearty, jolly tonsured monk. He had intense dark eyes. He spoke with an absurd lisp which did not fit in with the rest of his physical make-up."

The moment he returned to New York, he telephoned to friends in Paris to get their reactions to the international situation. The headlines were growing bigger and darker with each passing day, and so was his concern for his family and his country. Unable to stand it any longer, he embarked on the *Ile de France* on August 20th and six days later he landed at Le Havre. Ribbentrop was in Moscow, putting the final touches to the incredible Nazi-Soviet Pact which was to explode like a bombshell exactly three days later. The fate of Poland had been sealed and within a week Europe was plunged into war.

# 18

## *Pilote de Guerre*

O N September 4th Saint-Exupéry was called up (as a reserve Air Force officer of 1923 vintage) and ordered to report for duty at the military airfield of Toulouse-Francazal. Jean Giraudoux, the playwright, whose novels had exercised such a fateful fascination on his first literary efforts, had sought to enlist his talents for the Information Service just set up by the Daladier government, but Saint-Ex was not interested. He had never felt at home in an office nor could he imagine himself composing facile communiqués and glib exhortations for the boys at the front. He was not going to be one of those pampered intellectuals who, as he later wrote in *Pilote de Guerre*, "hold themselves in reserve, like jam-jars on the shelves of Propaganda, to be eaten after the war".

On September 6th Louis Castex, who had helped him obtain the authorization to fly the Atlantic with Guillaumet, saw him drive up to the Toulouse base in his racy convertible. He was given the temporary rank of Captain and assigned to an air force unit due to undergo training in long-range bombardment. The assignment displeased Saint-Ex almost as much as had Giraudoux' overtures, for the course promised to go on for months, and in any case he had no desire to participate in the kind of indiscriminate bomb-dropping he had witnessed in Spain and seen the Japanese (on the movie-screen) practice in China. The Colonel commanding the Francazal base appears to have been more than cooperative—first by allowing Saint-Exupéry to "keep his hand in" by flying daily "sorties" on a *Simoun*, and then by actively encouraging him to obtain a transfer to a fighter squadron.

It was a strange sort of life while it lasted, as abnormally pacific as was the "phoney war" that was raging between the Maginot and Siegfried Lines where a few stray bullets and an occasional shell disturbed the laundry lines strung between gun casements and barbed wire. While Poland was being ripped to pieces by the German eagle and the Russian bear, Saint-Exupéry and Castex amused themselves skirting the Pyrenean foothills and probing the lovely green valleys once trodden by Charlemagne and his retreating host, before flying on to admire the sparkling turrets and stone ramparts of Carcassonne. But the daily outings completed, Saint-Ex would race back to the Grand Hôtel in Toulouse, where he would put in call after call to Paris imploring his friends to move heaven and earth to have him assigned to a combat unit.

"I am suffocating more and more. The atmosphere of this place is unbreathable, "he wrote to a friend in a letter quoted by his biographer Pierre Chevrier. "I have many things to say about these events. I can say them as a combatant but not as a tourist. It's my one and only chance of speaking out. As you know . . . Save me!" he pleaded, adding: "Don't see Daurat until all the other possibilities for a fighter unit are exhausted."

With the commencement of hostilities Daurat's Air Bleu had been absorbed by Air France and assigned to Supreme Headquarters to fly senior staff officers on top level liaison missions. Daurat would have been only too happy to have his friend join his unit, but Saint-Ex was not interested in ferrying generals or V.I.P.s from one part of the front to another, when it wasn't to London, Brussels, or North Africa. While he fretted in Toulouse, spending the rainy days indoors in front of a blackboard, where even graduate officers of the Ecole Polytechnique were flabbergasted by the ease he showed in dealing with intricate mathematical problems, his friends in Paris kept buttonholing influential officials in an attempt to secure his transfer.

All of ten weeks were needed to break through the barrage of official interdictions. The Air Force doctors who had examined him on induction were of the opinion that a man of thirty-nine with a partially paralysed left shoulder should purely and simply be grounded and used for staff work; and it took the intervention of General Davet, who was in charge of the bomber training programme and fortunately a good friend of Saint-Exupéry's, to get the initial veto waived. But before he was through, Saint-Ex had to carry the battle all the way to the antechambers of the Air Minister, Guy La Chambre, where it was finally agreed that though too old and unfit to be a fighter pilot, he could still fly a reconnaissance aircraft. He was accordingly assigned to the 2/33 Strategic Reconnaissance Group. He celebrated the glad tidings at the Café des Deux Magots, which he had made his unofficial headquarters for the final stages of his bureaucratic *blitzkrieg*, by ordering the waiter to bring him a pack of cards—so that he could dazzle Jean-Paul Sartre's friend Pierre Bost with an uncanny display of wizardry.

The 2/33 Reconnaissance Group—which is to say, the Second Group of the 33rd Reconnaissance Wing—was then stationed in two villages located just south of the Marne canal and the Vitry-le-François—Saint-Dizier highway, 150 miles east of Paris. Bordered by a country lane and a birch wood tufted with mistletoe, the field which the Group had occupied since mid-September was totally bare of hangars. Some of the trucks and mobile equipment had been parked away in nearby barns, others were hidden in the woods, but the fifteen Potez 63s, though camouflaged, had to stay out in the open. The dozen officers had found billets for themselves in the village of Orconte, to the north; the non-coms and enlisted men had nested down in the rustic farmsteads and houses of Hauteville, to the south. A conveniently abandoned farm, some 800 yards from the field had been requisitioned by the photo-interpreting section, the officers' mess had taken over the rear dining-room of Orconte's one and only inn, and the Group's Command Post was set up in a farm building by the field. But the less privileged squadrons had been left to improvise their own "command posts" (essentially a bar and a common-room) from the available resources.

Commanded at the time by an Alsatian, Captain Schunck, the Group consisted of two squadrons: the Third, nicknamed "*La Hache*" (The Axe), and the Fourth, dubbed "*La Mouette*" (The Seagull). The Third, to which Saint-Exupéry was assigned, owed its sobriquet to a swashbuckling Captain called Bordage whose ingenuity in raiding First World War depots, garages, and even factories for his "operational equipment" (everything from planes and guns to trucks and fancy automobiles) inspired the Squadron's emblem—a double-bladed *hache d'abordage* (pirate or boarding axe) which naturally came to be known as *la hache de Bordage* (Bordage's hatchet). True to the freebooting genius of its founder, the Squadron had helped itself to a generous pile of sawn birch logs and timber which a local peasant had carelessly stacked by the roadside and which (to his helpless dismay) shrank to dwarf size overnight. To insulate it from the creeping damp of field and forest, the common-room floor had been raised a foot or two above the moist earth on stilts; and it was here, in a Robinson Crusoe shack roofed with corrugated iron, windowed with mica-glass, and vented by a stove-pipe chimney which elbowed its way out under an eave, that Lieutenant François Laux brought his fellow officers—Israël, Gavoille, and Hochedé—the tidings one late November evening that their already cramped quarters were to receive one more occupant in the person of Captain de Saint-Exupéry.

The news was received with mixed feelings. In addition to the four pilots the tiny shack had to accommodate two regular army officers—Captain Edgar Moreau and Lieutenant Jean Dutertre—who had been assigned to the squadron as aerial observers: to say nothing of the machine-gunners and mechanics who were constantly being called in for consultation in the "map-room". There was the problem of seniority, and there was the problem of age. Saint-Exupéry was considerably older than the rest: he was also a full rank higher than Lieutenant Laux, the Squadron leader, who hardly relished having to break in a man now close on forty. But almost from the moment Saint-Exupéry stepped out of Captain Schunk's car in his somewhat worn uniform and knee-high boots, the apprehensions of the shack-dwellers gave way to curiosity and wonder. To Lieutenant Laux's greeting: "Lieutenant Laux, Squadron Commander" Saint-Ex calmly answered: "Saint-Exupéry, pilot." The ice was broken, and no one needed to fear any longer that the internationally famous author of *Terre des Hommes* was going to high-hat them or "pull his rank".

Saint-Ex's vast fund of stories and his genius for card tricks did the rest. Indeed, when General Vuillemin, the French Air Force's Chief-of-Staff, visited the Group just three days later (December 6th) and was invited to lunch with the officers in the back room of the Orconte *auberge*, Saint-Exupéry dazzled him with a particularly brilliant show of card-calling virtuosity.

Like the other pilots, Saint-Exupéry found himself billeted in Orconte. Fearing that a simple room in one of its village farms would not do for so grand a person, the Group Commander had made plans to move one of his officers out of the local château to make way for him. But Saint-Ex—much to the *châtelaine's* chagrin—refused to indispose a fellow officer, and had himself led instead to a farmhouse, across the way from the church on the village square, where there was an empty ground floor chamber. Madame Cherchell, the farmer's wife, who showed him into it, could not help expressing her surprise that "*Monsieur le Capitaine*" should wish to be lodged in something so humble when princely quarters awaited him in the local mansion, but Saint-Exupéry assured her with a luminous smile that he would just as soon stay here.

"I'm living in a small farm where there's no need of refrigeration," he wrote to his New York literary agent, Maximilian Becker, not long after moving in. "In the morning I break the ice in my water pitcher before washing! We all wear big boots and when it isn't freezing we splash around in the mud up to our knees." Yet this rustic life with its elementary hardships pleased him so much that later, in *Pilote de Guerre*, he painted an idyllic picture of his "monk's cell", into which, with a loud knock on the door, the farmer's wife would bustle in every morning with an armful of logs to start a cheerful blaze in the fireplace, the chilled bedroom's sole source of heat. Slowly the dream world of his semi-conscious being would be scented with the soft fragrance of wood smoke, the gay crackle of sparks and the sizzling of stubborn logs would penetrate through his eiderdown, and when at last he opened one heavy lid, there dancing merrily in the hearth would be a bright fiesta, throwing luminous streamers across the ceiling and winking at him—like his old "friend", the little purring stove of Saint-Maurice.

\*     \*     \*

Bad weather hampered Saint-Exupéry's first training flights on the Potez 63, as several days of steady rain turned the country roads into quagmires. The Group's *Journal de Marche* (log-book) shows that only one war mission was flown for this entire month—on December 21—a mission which ended in disaster when Lieutenant Sagon's Potez was accidentally shot down by two British Hurricanes on its way back from Germany. The machine-gunner and observer were killed almost instantly. A badly burned Sagot managed to parachute to the ground, and Saint-Exupéry's visit to him in the hospital was subesquently recorded in *Pilote de Guerre* (*Flight to Arras*).

A letter written two days after this misfortune gives us a vivid glimpse of Saint-Ex's feelings at the time. He had just come down from his first climb to 30,000 feet, he was deaf in one ear, with a blocked tympanum, though—thank Heaven!—he was spared that awful buzzing in the head that had so troubled him after the Guatemala crash. "I didn't find what I wanted," he wrote. "I found what I was bound to find and I am like the rest. Like them I'm cold and like them I'm afraid. And like the others I suffer from rheumatism . . . And there you have it. I've just come back from ten thousand metres. Another phantom laid to rest. Ten thousand metres, that uninhabitable territory peopled by unknown beasts and from which the earth looks black and concave—and where one's gestures grow as thick as a swimmer's in a syrup. Where the reduced air pressure (1/100th of the normal) threatens to evaporate the life out of you—and where one breathes ice, for the breath at 51° below changes into tiny icicles on the inner surface of the mask—and where one is threatened by 25 different breakdowns, like that of the inhaler which can execute you at a stroke or of the heater which can change you into a block of ice . . . Every now and then one simply presses the little rubber tube leading to the facemask, to make sure it's properly filled, that there's milk in the nipple. And one sucks at the bottle . . ."

To his amazement the heat provided by his flying-suit was marvellously diffused and the wires in the padded lining did not burn his skin. "If only" he thought, "the Eskimos had this!" What a masterpiece of technics, this warm, even bath—save for his gloved fingers, which were cold, particularly when he kept his hand on the machine-gun trigger.

"Well, what was it like up there?" he was asked on landing. "What was the temperature?"

"51 below," he answered.

"You can't have been very warm."

"Yes, but not unpleasantly so. You told me the hot oxygen burned one's nose, yet my nose felt fine. As for the flying boots—"

"No danger of their burning up, your boots," he was told with a laugh. "You forgot to turn on the switch."

Prior to this new baptism of (high) air Saint-Ex had been tormented for hours by the thought of "the slow struggle against fainting. That awful sweat of brow and hands. That sweet, sugary sensation, a sort of perversion of the senses . . ." But no, thirty thousand feet were not as hard to bear as eighteen thousand without oxygen. "And suddenly all my admirations fall flat," he wrote. "Once the ghost has been laid to rest, it becomes a job like any other. Flying at ten thousand metres or stuffing chairs . . . since the ghost is dead already. It's been the same for me each time. Flying the night mail. Drowning at sea. Dying of thirst. And Daurat . . . Daurat didn't teach men courage: he forced them to kill ghosts. I've already said it in *Vol de Nuit.*"

But for the tragic accident caused by the two Hurricanes, this month of December was more cheery than tragic. There were visits to the Théâtre des Armées at Saint-Dizier, and the Group's dreary evenings were enlivened by a magnificent phonograph and a set of records sent to the officers as a gift from Suzy Solidor. The comedian Fernandel turned up on the 16th with his inimitably beaming face and horsemouth grin, made even toothier by the rousing fanfare he was treated to by the Third Squadron's *carabiniers* (ground-crew mechanics) who puffed and tootled away on an extraordinary assortment of horns, fifes, and trumpets fashioned in the repair-shops from brass tubes and metal piping. By the time Joseph Kessel appeared on the scene in his war correspondent's uniform, the first Christmas snows had laid their soft white mantle over the hard mud ruts. New Year saw the usual shenanigans—at any rate for the jovial *carabiniers*, who frightened the life out of poor Madame Renard, the café owner of Hauteville, by suddenly appearing in top-hats and bowlers, armed with lanterns, cutlasses, and pistols, needed, they explained as they forced their way into the premises, to deal with the "bandits" who were hiding inside, under kitchen tables and in pantry closets.

It was the kind of gay horse-play he had indulged in in his youth, but it emphasized the age gap separating Saint-Ex from his younger companions. He complained of it in a letter written to a friend in Paris in which he remarked that getting on with his new *camarades*—who showed a marked preference for the tango over Bach—posed awkward problems. "One is fighting side by side with those who hide away the good music whenever one ventures near the loudspeaker. And yet one finds great, fundamental qualities in them. Those who fight best, the only ones who are really fighting are thus not fighting for the same reasons as I. They are not fighting to save civilization, or rather one should reconsider the notion of civilization and all it contains."

One thing was certain: it was not contained in the pathetic performance put on by a crooner at the Théâtre des Armées who had exasperated him by his vapid songs. Only once during that long wasted evening had he felt the faintest *frisson* of an emotion on hearing two verses:

> *Quand les filles s'en vont au bois*
> *Le Curé est content, ça fera des baptêmes.*

It made him think of those villages where, as in the Middle Ages, there was a sense of duration, transformation, and the flow of time. Where the wheat was sown and rose in its appointed season, and where, if the girls went to the woods, the curate was happy because of the baptisms such outings portended. Where man was part of a lineage and where the dead were present thanks to the church. The dead, elements of duration. "But our dead are empty crates," he wrote. "And our summer has nothing to do with autumn. Seasons which are juxtaposed. The dismantled man of today. And Giraudoux thinking he can save man through the intellect. But the intellect, which takes apart and juxtaposes pieces, when not playfully muddling the arrangement to gain in picturesqueness, loses sight of the essential. When one analyses states, one grasps nothing of man. I am neither old nor young. I am he who is passing from youth to old age. I am something which is being formed. I am a process of ageing. A rose is not something which buds, opens, and fades. That is a pedagogical description, an analysis which kills the rose. A rose is not a series of successive states, a rose is a somewhat melancholy fête . . . I am sad because of this strange planet I am living in. Because of all I fail to understand . . ."

The thought was Henri Bergson's, but expressed in a tone which was to burst forth two years later in *Pilote de Guerre* and *Le Petit Prince*. Try as he might, Saint-Ex could not help but feel an outsider—and even more poignantly now than years before in Toulouse. And the feeling was obviously mutual. It had taken some time for his more rough-hewn companions at Montaudran to get used to this big, bashful aristocrat who had suddenly landed among them, and the same was true once more during these first weeks at Orconte. With the distrust which military professionals are apt to feel for civilians, Lieutenant Laux, the Squadron Commander, had quietly asked Captain Moreau, a graduate of Saint-Cyr, to keep an eye on Saint-Exupéry who, he feared, might prove refractory to military discipline. Moreau found no reason to complain of any lack of application or signs of rebelliousness on Saint-Ex's part, though he and his companions soon detected a tendency to absent-mindedness, which first manifested itself not long after his arrival at Orconte, when he managed to lose his way between billet and Command Post, though he had already made the journey several times.

On a later occasion Madame Cherchell, the farmer's wife, came running across the square with her daughter, crying: "He's dying, he's dying!" And indeed, when his fellow officers hurried over to see what was amiss, the hoarse sound they heard from the other side of the door bore a chilling resemblance to a dying man's final gasps. But when the door was forced open, the bed was empty and there was no sign of a corpse. The death-throes emanated from a Libertyphone radio-record-player which Saint-Exupéry, to dispel his "melancholy", had asked Maximilian Becker to have air freighted from New York via the French diplomatic pouch. He had piled a stack of Bach and Händel records on to the machine, then forgotten to switch it off as he rushed off to some suddenly remembered rendez-vous; with the result that it went on relentlessly playing until the batteries began to give out and the worn needle had scratched the last, hundred times repeated record into an agonizing ruin.

There were other grounds for Lieutenant Laux's suspicions. Not long after the outbreak of the war Saint-Ex's friend Henri Jeanson had been arrested on orders from Daladier (then Minister of War as well as Premier) on the charge of "inciting the military to disobedience through anarchist propaganda". His crime was to have published an article in an organ cryptically entitled SIA (*Société Internationale Antifasciste*) in which he expressed sympathy for the horses killed at Reichshoffen (the last great cavalry charge of modern times) but none at all for their riders, who should have known better than to indulge in such sanguinary heroics. Hailed before a military tribunal, Jeanson had cited a number of witnesses, among them Saint-Exupéry who —so at least Jeanson claims—was refused a twenty-four hour leave of absence from his squadron to come and testify in his behalf.

It is more than likely that Jeanson, in recalling this episode, was yielding to his habitual anti-militarism; for the discipline at Orconte seems to have been relatively lenient at this time, allowing Saint-Ex to make frequent trips to Paris. Be that as it may, one thing is certain: he appeared, with or without permission, . . . and—but let us listen to Jeanson telling the story in his own inimitable style . . . "What did I see march into the court-room, strapped in leather, enveloped in rubber, gloved to the elbows, muddy booted, helmeted, enormous, gigantic, and admirable? A kind of aerial frogman escaped from a futuristic film directed by Fritz Lang . . .

" 'Your name?'

" 'Antoine de Saint-Exupéry.'

" 'Antoine de what?' said the cretin who was presiding the court martial, a certain Colonel Jammes, a kind of scowling, frantic, high-horsing idiot whose sleep at night was ruined at the thought of the prosecutional triumphs being scored by the notorious Colonel Mornet, another pop-eyed buffoon.

"Quite obviously, Saint-Ex and his interrogator did not belong to the same country, the same planet, or the same universe. Three revolutions and a war had been needed to make Saint-Ex meet this sticky, obscene, purulent thing known as a military judge, to establish a dialogue between the Little Prince and Sergeant-Major Cop.

"The bashful Saint-Ex, who hated to appear in public, spoke in a hoarse voice with simple words which added up to sentences of a friendly grandeur. The longer he spoke the rougher, more insistent, more pathetic grew his tone . . . 'But please understand!' he sought to convince that bemedalled hardware. A man was defending a friend and nothing mattered more than this friendship, than this despair at not being understood. He would have liked to find someone behind this uniform, but there was no one, absolutely no one, not even the desert which Saint-Ex had conquered so many times. He didn't lose his temper, he didn't get angry, he didn't implore. He felt sorry for this poor idiot who listened without hearing him while tapping his desk with his pencil-point. Dear Saint-Ex. . . . He was ashamed of the other man . . . He hazarded a final argument, one last anecdote . . . 'But please understand! . . .'

" 'Yes, in short, it's a Jeanson festival!' barked the nonentity.

"Saint-Ex turned his back on him and with a helpless gesture he gave me a sad smile before withdrawing to his heights. He had been unable to crash the sound barrier."

The memory of this dismal scene must still have haunted Saint-Exupéry two years later when, in depicting the chaos of the French war-machine in *Pilote de Guerre*, he told how in a northern *département* a herd of pregnant heifers had been rounded up and sent to the slaughter house. No cog in the military machine, no colonel in the animal requisitioning service had been able to halt the mechanism once it had started to run amok. With the result that the slaughter-house was soon transformed into a "graveyard of foetuses". After which Saint-Ex could not resist adding, with transparent irony: "Perhaps it was a lesser evil. For it might, by running even more amok, have begun slaughtering colonels."

\* \* \*

"You'll tour Germany without machine-guns or controls," Saint-Exupéry
was told shortly after joining the Group. "But don't worry," his new companions had added, just to cheer him up. "You've got nothing to lose. The
fighters always shoot you down before one sees them."

Though the Potez 63s they were using had been conceived for high
altitude flying, their manufacturers had blithely disregarded the mechanical
problems posed by temperatures of 50° to 60° below zero. At 27,000 feet or
higher—the altitude they were designed to fly at—not only machine-guns
but the plane's controls were apt to freeze. Unjamming them, for a pilot,
was no joke; for the slightest muscular exertion at that height could induce
a violent acceleration of the heartbeat, an abnormal sweat, and even a
momentary spell of dizziness. Later, in *Pilote de Guerre*, Saint-Exupéry
was to give a graphic account of these physical hardships, made all the more
painful by his many fractures, unusually sensitive to temperature changes.
But what he did not say, for reasons of modesty, was that it was he who
helped solve the problem of the machine-guns.

Nothing, unbelievable as it may sound, had been done to remedy this
elementary defect when Saint-Ex joined the Group three months after the
outbreak of the war. The torpor which had descended on the French army
during the inactive winter months had now turned into paralysis. Why move,
why do anything, since the *status quo* was comfortably static and there was no
need for it? "This prodigious anarchy," Saint-Exupéry commented in his
notebook. "That other dunderhead who refuses to allow the Americans"—
he meant press photographers—"to take photos"—of what he knew to be
hopelessly antiquated equipment, in the name of "military security". "This
idiot who's scandalized that we should be studying the jamming of machine-
guns." For yes, certain military heads were so dense that they kept insisting
that nothing be done—unless Higher Headquarters specifically demanded it.
Until then they must wait. It reminded Saint-Ex of the German cadets he
had questioned, saying "Yes" or "No . . . As the Führer has told us . . ."
In France there was no Führer, but the sheep were everywhere, waiting for
some other sheep to take the initiative.

By the turn of the year Saint-Exupéry's patience was exhausted and he
decided to look into the matter himself. His interest in scientific problems in
general and in aeronautical mechanics in particular had remained unflagging
throughout the pre-war years. In December 1934 he had taken out a patent
for a night-time or fog landing aid in the form of a goniometric device
designed to measure the angle of reception of radio waves emitted from one
point on a descending plane and capted (after bounding off the ground) at
another point. It was, roughly speaking, an inversion of the process whereby
short frequency radio waves are bounced off the stratosphere. Later

modifications of this idea (also patented) involved the use of photo-electric cells mounted on the landing-gear to measure the height above the ground of an incoming craft, and a two or three-point radio-wave emission system giving the pilot (on a luminous screen) the precise position of his plane with respect to an airfield—a device (derived from other patents) which most modern jets are now equipped with. By 1938—according to A. R. Métral, a French scientist whom Saint-Exupéry frequently consulted about such problems— he was already applying his fertile mind to the invention of a device for recuperating gaseous energy—or what is now commonly known as an "after-burner". He had reached the conclusion that the propeller was a very inefficient means of producing forward motion. When he landed in Algiers three days after Christmas of 1938, bearing the final proofs of *Terre des Hommes* which he wanted to show Georges Pélissier, he asked his friend if he didn't know a hunter who could bag him a couple of seagulls. He had been struck, on his Mediterranean crossing, by the extraordinary economy in the gull's lazy wing-beat, and it had confirmed him in his conviction that the propeller was a fantastically wasteful means of propulsion. Pélissier did not have an opportunity of finding out what conclusions Saint-Ex drew from his Leonardo-like study of seagull wings, for he did not see him again until mid-March of 1939, when both were too upset by the international situation to talk of anything but Germany and Hitler. Saint-Exupéry, however, had already told Pélissier that all the French aeronautic engineers he had talked to in 1938 had *a priori* rejected the idea that aircraft could be powered by anything other than propellers. As Métral was later to write, Saint-Ex by this time was only a step from the jet engine. The solution (the gas turbine) was, in fact, simpler than what he actually conceived: a complex design calling for the use of rockets to induce an accelerated Joukowski effect, doubling or tripling a plane's ascensional force.

The high altitude tests which the 2/33 Reconnaissance Group had under-taken had revealed that the machine-gun on the Potez 63 invariably jammed *after* the first couple of bursts had been fired. This provided Saint-Ex with a clue he was determined to exploit. Climbing into the American de Soto he had swapped for his old Bugatti (not made for a rugged winter), he drove into Paris and straight to the National Research Centre. Here he looked up Professor Fernand Holweck, whom he had met on the *Ile de France* during the return voyage from New York. Tests in the Centre's deep-freeze labora-tory soon revealed the source of the trouble: the condensation of smoke vapour in the barrel after the initial bursts was enough to freeze up the firing mechanism and to jam the machine-gun. The lubricating oil they were using being impervious to water, some substance like glycerine had to be added to absorb the moisture generated by firing. The answer was methyl glycol. On

January 14th (1940) Holweck and several of his assistants from the National Research Centre were warmly welcomed to Orconte. Thanks to Saint-Exupéry's intervention, it took them a couple of weeks to solve a problem which had "bugged" the Group for four long months.

They were lucky, though, to find Saint-Exupéry alive. For just two days earlier he had come close to killing himself. The Group had embarked on night flight training, made more than usually hazardous by the strict black-out which was observed all around the airfield. On January 12 Saint-Ex took off on a night training exercise designed to familiarize him with the airfield's "discreet" beacons. At the briefing session earlier in the day it had been carefully explained that as the plane came down to land over the darkened field a long line of hooded lamps would come into view like the upright of an L, with two other markers, some thirty yards apart, extending to the right to form the base of the L. Saint-Exupéry, his mind perhaps occupied with the scientific problems he would be discussing with Holweck a day or two later, had listened with half an ear, and as he brought down the Potez 63 he had apparently forgotten the instructions. Jean Israël was seated up front in the observer's position, with Saint-Ex at the controls, slightly behind and above him. Normally the plane should have been heading for the dark space between the second and third markers to the right, but Israël noticed that the Potez had drifted towards the left and was headed instead for the interval between the first and second lamps. Assuming that Saint-Ex would correct the drift, he said nothing, only to regret it a moment later. The Potez continued down on its course and suddenly the long line of hooded lamps, stetching down the landing axis, vanished into the night, blotted out by some looming object they could not distinguish in the dark. Israël's reaction—a pilot's instinctive response—would have been to pull back hard on the stick in the hope of clearing the encumbrance. Instead, Saint-Exupéry pushed the stick forward. The Potez nosed down, hit the ground with a resounding thump and bounced straight over the dark obstacle, which turned out to be an emergency searchlight unit, complete with diesel-driven generators. The landing gear of their Potez was damaged, but Saint-Ex and Israël were able to emerge from the shaken machine unscathed. The search-light, which they went back to examine, was more than six feet high and could not have been avoided if Saint-Ex had done the expected thing and pulled back on the stick. Years of rugged experience with the Aéropostale had taught him the rough art of bouncing a plane over logs and ditches and of gunning the engine when crash-landing on a beach to keep the wheels from digging too quickly into the sand. Absent-minded he might be, but in a pinch he was not a veteran for nothing.

\*    \*    \*

Just four days after this close brush with death, the 2/33 Reconnaissance Group was ordered to move to a new airfield at Athies-sous-Laon, a short distance north-east of the city of Laon. The war in Poland was over, the Germans were busy transferring divisions to the western front, and the French High Command wanted to know what forces were being concentrated opposite Belgium and Holland. Officers and men bid a sad good-bye to the sympathetic villagers of Orconte, who seemed as sorry to see them go as they were to leave, and they moved north-west. It was bitter cold and the new, snow-covered airfield looked singularly inhospitable. A "moth-eaten wood"—to quote from the *Journal de Marche*—was all that broke the monotony of the flat white landscape, and almost the only memento the previous unit had left behind was a weird rat-infested dug-out in the middle of the snow. The officers' mess was set up in a large, empty, and (for the first day or two) completely unheated villa. Saint-Ex was given one of the upstairs rooms and passed a particularly frigid night, for the central heating was not yet working and outside it was 25° below zero. With the exception of the Group Commander, who took the room next to Saint-Ex's, the other officers had to find billets for themselves in the village of Montceau-le-Waast, while the enlisted men were bedded down in barns.

"I am so disgusted by my new existence," Saint-Exupéry wrote to a Paris friend a few days later. "This central heating, this mirrored wardrobe, this semi-luxury, this bourgeois life—only now . . . do I realize how much I liked Orconte . . . Once again I feel at sea . . . I didn't want this communal life. I preferred to join them in their silence. I wanted to come in from out of doors, from my farm-house or from ten thousand metres. Holweck was wrong if he thought I was captivated by mess-hall songs. On an equal footing, yes. Without a shadow of condescension. As happy as they to burst into song. With this good earth for my roots. But an entire sky for my branches, and alien winds, and the silence and freedom of solitude. I can perfectly well be alone in a crowd. Upheld by it, but with my head for myself. And my den. Here I no longer have a den . . ."

Two weeks later Captain Schunk was replaced as Group Commander by Major Henri Alias, a short, wiry officer whose crispness of tone was offset by a beguiling Languedoc accent. Most of this month—February—was spent in high altitude training flights, cloudy weather and snowfalls impeding the undertaking of reconnaissance missions. But there was one "hot" moment for Saint-Ex when an order came through from Higher Headquarters, transferring him to Paris, where he was to work with the National Science Research Centre. His restless mind, during these weeks of relative inactivity, had been busy devising a new navigational device designed to give a pilot an accurate idea of his plane's distance from its base. The fundamental principle was simple: the plane emitted an electro-magnetic signal, immediately relayed back to it on another frequency from the ground by the use of a cathode tube. The longer or shorter interval required for the transmission of the impulse was automatically registered by a compass needle, each degree of which represented one kilometre. A reading of 275° would thus mean that the plane was 275 kilometres from its base. A similar device on the ground could permit the Command Post to know exactly how far distant a particular plane was. The idea, for which Saint-Exupéry actually took out patents in the course of this month (February 1940), had been discussed at length with Jean Israël, a graduate of the Ecole Centrale (which made him an ex-*piston*) and Captain Max Gelée, a graduate of the Ecole Polytechnique (and thus a former "*mole*") who had recently taken over command of the Fourth Squadron. Saint-Exupéry had also talked about it with Holweck and high aviation officials in Paris, and this had given them the idea of reassigning Saint-Ex to Paris, where his inventive ingenuity, it was felt (quite rightly), could be put to even more profitable use than in flying reconnaissance missions. But for Saint-Exupéry, who had but one desire—to share the hazards of his front-line comrades—a return to Paris at this time was a catastrophe to be avoided at all cost. His ten weeks with the 2/33 Reconnaissance Group had been exclusively taken up with training flights and he was being transferred before having flown a single mission.

At his urgent request Major Alias agreed to accompany him to higher headquarters. At La Ferté-sous-Jouarre (near Château-Thierry) General Vuillemin, the Air Force's Chief of Staff, received them gladly, but said that the order for Saint-Exupéry's transfer had come from higher up. He would have to inquire at the Air Ministry in Paris. Alias accompanied him to the Ministry, but feeling that it was not his business to walk into the Minister's office, he waited in the antechamber while Saint-Ex went in alone to talk with Guy La Chambre. The door had hardly closed when one of the Minister's aides confided to Alias: "We thought this up—just to get him back." A number of persons had been in on the plot, including apparently Daurat, who did not like the idea of his friend exposing himself to unnecessary risks when he had so much to contribute to his country in other ways.

As others had done before and as others were to do after him, Guy La Chambre gave in to Saint-Exupéry's desperate pleading. He was allowed to return to his Reconnaissance Squadron and there was no more talk of a transfer. As they walked out of the Air Ministry building, a radiant Saint-Ex asked Alias if he wouldn't like to meet Professor Holweck. He had a rendezvous to meet him at a café near the Porte d'Orléans. A white haired gentleman he should have no trouble recognizing—for in the meantime Saint-Ex had someone else he wanted to rush off and see first.

Delighted to meet the man who had helped them clear up their machine-gun problems, Alias, on reaching the café, had no trouble picking out the professor's venerable white mane.

"An extraordinary person, your Saint-Exupéry!" Holweck kept repeating, as they chatted. "Full of breath-taking ideas which we specialists for some reason seem incapable of having. But you'll see for yourself . . ."

And sure enough, when Alias and Saint-Ex later visited the Société des Compteurs' laboratory, it was as though a breath of fresh air had burst into the physicists' cloistral quarters. An expansive Saint-Ex explained what was needed for his cathode tube invention, and a crew of lab technicians just as enthusiastically assured him the device could be made—in a matter of weeks.

Towards the end of February the tedium of a war which was phonier than ever was momentarily disturbed at Athies-sous-Laon when the 2/33 Reconnaissance Group received a visit from its *marraine*, the actress Marie Bell. French military units traditionally arrange to have themselves "adopted" in this way by some fairy godmother who, it is fondly hoped, will generously shower her "godchildren" with gifts. Saint-Exupéry, when the subject had come up, had favoured Michèle Morgan, whom he happened to know; but she was still a relatively unknown star, whereas Marie Bell, with her prestige as a Comédie Française actress, seemed to offer a surer guarantee of affluence. For the dinner given in her honour Alias had placed Saint-Exupéry on one side of her, thinking to honour the celebrated actress with the company of a celebrated author. But the seat remained obstinately empty as the *hors d'oeuvres* appeared, and Alias had to send someone upstairs to persuade Saint-Ex to leave his room. He came down looking obviously grumpy, in an old pair of dark blue trousers which had a small tear above the knee revealing a glimpse of exupérian thigh. Saint-Ex, who could, when he chose, be the life of the party, sat glumly through the meal, letting his fellow officers stoke the fires of a conversation which kept threatening to die. Even the usual round of bawdy barrackroom songs, which Suzy Solidor (on an earlier visit) had improved on with a few of her own, failed to amuse the Juno who had descended among them.

After dinner, as they crowded around the billiard table, Saint-Ex finally decided to try his charm on the goddess. "Pick a card," he said, holding out a pack. After looking at it, she was asked to put it back. There was some quick shuffling, and then Saint-Ex said: "Now tell me what your card was." Marie Bell looked at him for a moment in confusion. "I don't know—" she began, apparently unable to recall if it was a club or a spade. It was the last straw! Flinging the cards on to the table, Saint-Exupéry withdrew in a huff to his own Olympus.

Two days after this *soirée manquée* he and two other officers were ordered to proceed to Marignane, the airfield of Marseille, to receive flight instruction on the new Bloch 174 observation plane. Unlike the Potez, which was little more than a flying death-trap with a maximum speed of 350 kilometres an hour, the new Blochs could exceed 500—enough to give the speediest Messerschmitt a good run for its money. Saint-Exupéry drove down to Marseille in his de Soto, and the next two weeks, though they involved intensive training, bore little resemblance to a war whose chief effect, so far as he could see, was to put most of his compatriots to sleep.

Though it looked fat and heavy, the new Bloch 174 was a definite improvement on the snail-like Potez. The only trouble was—there were far too few of them in production. To his friend Raymond Bernard, the film director, with whom he lunched after his return from the South, Saint-Ex made no attempt to hide his pessimism. *"Mon vieux, nous sommes foutus!"* (Old boy, we're done for!) was the way he put it. France had such and such a plane, as good as anything the Germans had, but only ten had so far come off the assembly line! Then there was the Y—, which was even better. But did he know how many had been produced? Bernard had no idea. "Four, *mon vieux*, exactly four!"

The one cheering piece of news was that the 2/33 Reconnaissance Group was returning to Orconte. Piloting one of the three Bloch 174s which he and the two squadron leaders (Laux and Gelée) had been sent down to Marignane to collect, he landed here on the 18th, only too happy to re-occupy his "monk's cell" in the Cherchells' farm-house. Easter, March 24th, was cold, and four days later they were blanketed by one more snow-storm. But on the 29th Saint-Exupéry was granted the privilege of flying the Group's first mission on a Bloch 174. Accompanied by Captain Moreau (observer) and Adjutant Bagrel (radio operator and tail-gunner), he took the two engined craft on a high altitude reconnaissance aimed at photographing the German lines north of Luxembourg. The machine-guns worked perfectly and so did the cameras (which had been provided with heated covers), but a layer of clouds interrupted the filming, and at 9000 metres—at a temperature of 42° below—the controls froze.

"What shall we do?" asked Saint-Ex, afraid that his observer, Captain Moreau, might think he was getting cold feet.

"No use insisting," came the answer. "Might as well turn back."

The "bugs", or what the RAF was to call the "gremlins", had still not disappeared; but the new plane's superiority was demonstrated two days later when Lieutenant Pierre Lacordaire (Saint-Ex's favourite chess partner) had to turn back in his Potez when cameras and machine-guns froze at 23,000 feet. That same day (March 31st) Saint-Exupéry, again accompanied by Moreau and Bagrel, flew the Group's second Bloch on a successful two hour mission over Aachen, Düsseldorf, and Cologne at a height of 9000 metres, where they were not bothered by German flak or fighters. The only complaint on the ground came from the photo-interpreting section, which discovered that they had inadvertently missed one loop of the Rhine!

The following morning the mishap he had so often feared overtook his Squadron leader, Captain (he had recently been promoted) François Laux, when his oxygen inhaler failed and he fainted dead away. Fortunately he had taken his place on the Bloch as an observer, and the pilot, by diving to a lower altitude, was able to bring the plane safely home. Saint-Ex was asked to step into the breach, and for a second successive day he flew a two hour high altitude mission, this time with Captain Gelée (the Fourth Squadron's commander) as his observer. As they flew over Bonn and Koblenz at 27,000 feet, they were pleased to see that a German fighter they spotted one kilometre to their left and 1500 feet below them could not intercept them.

On April 12th all leaves were cancelled, and to the disgust of both officers and men, the Group was ordered to evacuate "its" little village of Orconte and to return to the field of Athies-sous-Laon. The move brought them bad luck, for just three days later Laux, piloting a Bloch 174, had his rudder control freeze up on him as he was flying over the Ruhr. Jumped by three Messerschmitts, he had the fuel flow to his right engine severed by a burst of machine-gun fire, after which a wild spiralling chase began and he was pursued through several cloud banks over a distance of 100 miles. Adjutant Louis Bagrel, who had accompanied Saint-Ex on all three of his previous missions, bled to death at his post, blazing away with his machine-guns to the last. With his second motor giving way in its turn, Laux was forced to belly-land in Belgium. Severely burned, he managed to work himself free of his flaming craft, but he had to be hospitalized, along with his observer, Maurice Bediez, who died of his wounds that night.

It was a sad day for Saint-Ex's squadron, which Lieutenant Jean Israël was now appointed to command. On the last day of this month (April) the unlucky Third Squadron came near to losing its second commander, when the Bloch in which Israël had taken his place as an observer, crashed during the take-off and he emerged with a broken nose. It caused him considerable pain, and if from then on it had a tendency to turn red (as in Saint-Exupéry's later description of it in *Flight to Arras*), it was probably as much due to Israël's physical as to his mental indignation over the way the war was going.

Saint-Ex, meanwhile, had had to return to Paris for a medical check-up. The two high altitude missions he had flown on two successive days had brought on a new attack of rheumatism, accompanied by fever, and he was anything but well. He thus missed the dawn bombardment at Athies-sous-Laon on May 10th, when half a dozen Dornier 17 bombers flew over the airfield, bombing and strafing, and blew up 150,000 litres of petrol supplies in the station. The "phoney war" was ended; the *blitzkrieg* had begun.

At Athies-sous-Laon, thanks to Alias' elaborate camouflage precautions, only one of the Group's planes was severely damaged by the dawn assault. The bomb craters on the field were hastily filled or covered with metal strips and the first missions ordered. Bad weather conditions obliged Alias to resort almost exclusively to hedge-hopping missions, for which Saint-Exupéry could not have been used in any case. Very dangerous, they required expert skill and a young man's reflexes. Hochedé flew one on May 11th over Maastricht, where the Germans were already busy crossing the Meuse; and that night Gavoille flew a low altitude mission over the Ardennes in which he and his observer saw the roads of this wooded region dotted with faint ribbons of light, indicating the presence of German convoys advancing in the dark with bandaged headlights. Two liaison officers from the 2nd and 9th Armies happened to be at the Command Post when Gavoille came in for the "debriefing" session (more popularly known as "the torture") but with that extraordinary obtuseness which seemed to have descended on the entire French General Staff, from Gamelin on down, they refused to take this information seriously. Dotted ribbons of light in the dark? German convoys moving through the Ardennes? "But gentlemen, let's be serious!" Gavoille and his observer, Captain Pierre Andréva, had been seeing things: they were victims of nocturnal hallucinations!

The next day Hochedé, sent north to reconnoitre the Albert Canal, had his slow-moving Potez badly shot up by machine-gun fire. He managed to make it back to Athies with a dead gunner and a wounded observer—Captain Moreau, the infantry officer who Laux had delegated to keep an eye on Saint-Exupéry. A veteran observer who had flown the first reconnaissance missions of the war, he was a loss the undermanned Group could ill afford.

A second tree-top mission was sent out that same day over the Ardennes. The Potez, braving intense German machine-gun fire, made it back to Athies with 16 bullet-holes and two perforated oil tanks. Hurrying to the Command Post, Lieutenant Henri Chéry, the observer, confirmed what Gavoille and Andréva had seen the previous night. Not only motorcycles and scout-cars, but trucks full of soldiers, armoured cars, and tanks were moving through the Ardennes and encountering no resistance. Alias for a moment was incredulous, but Chéry was a former tank officer who knew what he had seen. The Germans were doing what the French High Command had decided was impossible: they were moving entire armoured divisions through the Ardennes.

Alias, as it happened, had an old school chum from Carcassonne serving in the *Deuxième Bureau* (G2, or Intelligence section) of Ninth Army Headquarters. He rang him up immediately to transmit the news.

"Impossible!" said the Intelligence officer at the other end of the line. "Your man has been seeing things."

"Nonsense," said Alias. "I've just interrogated him. He couldn't be mistaken. He's a tankman himself. Besides, I've also questioned the pilot and the gunner, and they all say the same thing. They saw tanks—hundreds of them—moving through the Ardennes."

The Intelligence Officer still refused to believe him. Alias, who by this time was in a rage, cried: "Here, talk to him yourself!" And he handed the receiver over to Chéry, who had been standing next to him.

If Higher Headquarters were unwilling to believe their reports, what on earth was the point of continuing such risky missions? What indeed? It was the question all the officers in the Group had begun to ask themselves in the face of the staggering ineptitude now encountered everywhere and at every level.

Working straight through the night, the photographic section confirmed what Chéry and his pilot had seen: German tank columns were moving through the Ardennes. But higher headquarters still refused to believe it. Reluctantly Alias found himself obliged to send Gavoille out again to confirm what he had seen two nights before. His orders were: "Establish contact with the enemy." Contact was established, in dramatic fashion. North of Sedan Gavoille's Potez was greeted with a formidable small-arms' barrage. A German observation plane, seeing the French machine coming straight at it, ducked down, only to crash into the woods. Unfortunately a squadron of Messerschmitts was passing at that moment, homeward bound from a mission of their own. Thinking Gavoille's Potez had shot down the observation plane, they peeled off and gave chase. Unable to see behind him—in these machines the pilot, as Saint-Ex was to write later, was "like a pipe in its pouch"—Gavoille had to be guided by his observer, Captain Vésin, who indicated which way the Messerschmitts were coming at him by pressing his left or right hand on his shoulders. A hasty gesture knocked Gavoille's flight helmet down over his eyes for a moment, and in the interval it took him to recover his sight one of the Messerschmitts got in a good burst. With his Potez now beginning to burn, Gavoille had to crash-land on a pasture. Fortunately they were by now behind the French lines, and no one in the plane was badly hurt.

On the road adjoining the pasture a French column was moving north-wards. Suddenly Captain Vésin recognized a former Saint-Cyr classmate he hadn't seen in years.

"Where are you going?" he asked.

"We're going to take up positions north of the Semois river" was the answer.

"But you're out of your minds!" cried Vésin. "The Germans are already in Sedan and headed straight in this direction."

Like the other Doubting Thomases before him, the Saint-Cyr classmate refused to heed the warning. Orders were orders. He and his men moved on northwards—to be caught like fish in the giant drag-net the Wehrmacht was now busily extending. When Gavoille and Vésin got back to the officers' mess that evening, they were received with rejoicing—for they had been given up for lost. Vésin ("of the doleful countenance", as Saint-Ex was to describe him in *Pilote de Guerre*) hardly needed to confirm what the French Army now knew by visceral reaction. Sedan was in German hands, and panzer columns were ripping through General Corap's undermanned Ninth Army like knives through a mound of butter.

From Laon, near which they were based, it was less than 80 miles to Sedan, with the front now breaking wide open. Everyone's nerves were on edge, the mechanics (under Gavoille's watchful eye) working around the clock to patch up returning planes damaged by flak or machine-gun fire. Hochedé, sent out at dawn of the 15th to reconnoitre the Meuse, had to weather not only German but French machine-gunners, who took his Potez for a Luftwaffe plane. (It was probably the first French warplane they had seen.) At 4 o'clock that afternoon Alias returned from a scouting mission to report that the Germans were already at Liart, 40 kilometres to the East. As dusk fell he stopped a *douanier* who was pedalling past on a bicycle weighed down with knapsacks and bundles. What was he doing and where was he going with this extraordinary supercargo? "I'm trying to get away from the Germans," answered the customs official. "They're already at Montcornet"—25 kilometres up the road.

There was not a minute to be lost. Alias ordered the Group's trucks to pack up the mobile echelon's equipment and to be ready to pull out at any moment. Two Dornier bombers flew over, shooting up the field with tracer bullets. Their appearance added to the panic of the villagers, who were already loading their belongings on to farm carts and tractors, getting ready to join the insane exodus. Supper tables were left with the dishes still in place and the soup steaming in the tureens. By nightfall the village was empty; not a soul was left.

At 9 p.m. Gelée returned from a mission to Corap's headquarters at

Vervins to report that the Ninth Army was disintegrating. The roads were clogged with military as well as civilian vehicles, and many troops had even abandoned their arms in flight. The retreat was turning into a stampede. Alias, who had been ordered to send out two more missions for the following day, drove over to the château outside of Laon where General Escudier, commanding the northern air division, had his headquarters. Escudier had shown him the door earlier in the day, but this time Alias was not going to be given the brush-off. He would have one of his pilots fly a final mission the next morning, he told the general, but he had already sent his mobile echelon on its way, with orders to join the planes the next day at the field of Saconin, near Soissons. True to the prevailing form, the general refused to believe that the Germans had reached Montcornet and practically accused Alias of cowardice.

It was close to midnight by the time Alias got back to the field. The trucks had pulled out in convoy at 10.30, moving slowly down the dark highway with their headlights off. The pilots and gunners who stayed behind had been posted to man the machine-guns mounted on the eastern perimeter of the field, ready to defend it against a German attack. They spent a tense night, troubled by the eery clank of diesel engines and the crunch of treads, which sounded as though an armoured division was moving down the road. It was only an army of French tractors, piled with furniture and families, joining the universal rout.

At 3.30 the following morning Hochedé took off into the dark drizzle to see if the Germans had really reached Montcornet. They had. Even in the grey light of dawn the yellow engine bonnets of their trucks were unmistakable. Trucks sandwiched in between tanks, almost bumper to bumper. A little farther on his Bloch was greeted by an arching necklace of tracer bullets. Making a wide loop he put his plane down an hour later at Saconin, where he found the Group miraculously reformed.

It was now May 16th. Six days had sufficed to confirm Saint-Ex's worst forebodings: the French Air Force was non-existent. It was too late now to hope that inadequate factories could possibly make up the difference by a last minute spurt of production. France needed massive help, and there was only one place he could see it coming from—the United States. If necessary, he was willing to cross the Atlantic himself to implore Roosevelt's immediate help.

At 6.30 that evening Paul Reynaud, who had replaced Daladier as Premier, received Saint-Exupéry in his apartment on the Place du Palais-Bourbon, directly behind the Chamber of Deputies. He looked tired, distraught, and harassed as he listened to Saint-Ex's impassioned plea. If he would only let him fly over to see Roosevelt, to ask him to put what planes he had at France's disposal, he (Saint-Ex) would find the French pilots to fly them.

That was all very well, Reynaud answered him shortly, but he wasn't the first who had thought of this. He'd just sent René de Chambrun over on an *in extremis* mission, and there were others already in Washington, trying to work on the President.

Saint-Ex had some difficulty rejoining his squadron, for the 2/33 Reconnaissance Group had moved once again, this time to Nangis, south east of Paris. On the 18th, they were sent up to Le Bourget, from where Hochedé, Gavoille, and Israël flew tree-top missions aimed at keeping track of the German advance. Each reaped a dangerous crop of bullets. On the 19th Lieutenant Mottez, deputy commander of the Fourth Squadron, failed to return from such a mission. On the 20th Hochedé, sent to reconnoitre the region of Amiens and Péronne, almost met the same fate, only just making it back in his bullet-riddled Bloch.

On the 21st the Group moved yet again—to Orly. "I can't understand it," Saint-Exupéry kept repeating, as he and Alias walked to and fro inside one of its bombed out hangars, with the sky staring down at them from above. "What's happened to our reserves? Our High Command doesn't seem to have any." Like so many others, he was vainly trying to refight the First World War, instinctively recasting Gamelin in the role of Joffre, getting ready to stop the Germans on the Marne. He had not breathed a word to Alias about his visit to Reynaud a few days before; but now, with the situation deteriorating by the hour, he sought to talk his Group Commander into accompanying him to the Prime Minister's office. God only knew what the High Command had been telling him about the "front", but a first-hand report from someone whose strategic reconnaissance unit had been in daily contact with the enemy might prove more valuable in stressing the extreme urgency of the situation than a hundred official briefings. Alias, who had more than enough to take care of as it was, brushed the suggestion aside, and no more was heard of it.

The next morning Israël took off on a hedge-hopping mission to find out if the Germans had captured Amiens. Like Mottez, he failed to return. Once again Saint-Ex's Third Squadron was without a commander. Gelée, commanding the Fourth, narrowly escaped disaster in his turn, being chased all the way back from the Somme at tree-top level by three Messerschmitts which he finally managed to shake off in his speedy Bloch. Less fortunate was Lieutenant de Renneville, a newcomer to the Group, who failed to return in a slower moving Potez. Two crews and two planes lost in one day! Though an entire new squadron with 5 Potez 63s had just been added to it, the Group—as Saint-Exupéry was to write in *Flight to Arras*— was melting like wax. The crews were being sacrificed "like glasses of water thrown on to a forest fire".

On the 23rd it was his turn to throw himself into the blaze. Seven weeks had passed since his last reconnaissance and though he was convinced of the growing pointlessness of each new mission, Saint-Ex was not going to be grounded any longer when his companions were daily risking their lives. Major Alias was no less determined to afford him the maximum protection, for this new mission called for his flying at a low altitude over Arras to check on the progress of German tank columns. The group commander he contacted at Chantilly seemed most reluctant to commit any of his fighters to the escort of a reconnaissance plane—they had more urgent problems to take care of—but when he learned that it was to accompany Captain de Saint-Exupéry, the officer abruptly changed his tune. "Ah, that's different", he said. "All right, we're game."

Accompanied by his observer, Lieutenant Jean Dutertre, and a machine-gunner, Sergeant André Mot, Saint-Ex took off from Orly at 7 a.m., landing ten minutes later at Meaux, where Alias was waiting for them. The weather was cloudy, the air charged with thunder, and it was not until after they had lunched that they decided to take off again, flying just under the clouds at a level of 900 feet or lower. The nine Dewoitine fighters detailed to escort them split into two groups. One flew immediately behind them, the other 1500 feet higher up, where the fighters kept disappearing into the dark underbellies of the thunderheads above them. Near Compiègne they ploughed through a rainstorm and as they flew on northwards towards Arras, which was "smoking like a volcano"—as Dutertre later wrote in the *Journal de Marche*—the lightning flashes forking downwards and the columns of dark smoke billowing upwards from the charred ruins below made it look like "a scene from the Apocalypse".

A moment later they were engulfed in another deluge which washed away the world in a hail of bouncing water. Their fighter escort, when they emerged, had vanished, and they were now all alone. In the middle of the blue green landscape ahead of them was a crimson stain, like a bleeding sore. Arras—glowing dark red like an "iron on an anvil", as Saint-Exupéry later described it. Three miles to the south-west a large formation of German tanks were preparing to attack the mutilated city, whose treasures were being melted into twisted braids of smoke.

They were now flying at 600 feet, a perfect target for German machine-guns and anti-aircraft cannon, which let go with everything they had. Suddenly, as though they had kicked over a simmering log, the dark earth beneath them blazed with sparks, which mounted towards them with eery slowness, like golden bubbles rising from a slimy river bottom, like "tear-drops of light" flowing upwards through an oil of silence. Like whipcords snapping about them, the rising chaplets burst into puff-balls of cannon smoke and lances of lightning, which streaked past them like shooting stars. A golden web of tracers was being woven around their Bloch, caught in a vertiginous shuttlework of needles. Above them a diadem of sombre puff-balls framed them, like the crown of an arch. Saint-Ex bore down heavily with his left foot on the rudder-paddle and the diadem slipped off to the right, only to form above them a moment later as the gunners down below readjusted aim. A second powerful thrust with the right foot and the diadem drifted off to the left, while the tracers in hot pursuit sliced past them like swordblades. And then, without his hearing the detonation over the roar of the two engines, the Bloch shuddered and up they rose, as though heaved by a giant hand. An anti-aircraft shell had burst directly beneath them. Saint-Exupéry had no time to be afraid—he was too busy weaving and dodging. But instinctively he glanced at the instrument panel. An oil-gauge was flickering wildly. The flak burst had pierced an oil tank. Putting the plane into a steep bank he ducked into the nearest cloud. There was nothing they could do now but hope to make it back before the overheated engines burned out their bearings. Flying blindly on instruments, according to the compass readings given him by Dutertre, bent over his maps in the forward observer's position, Saint-Ex brought the Bloch out of the clouds as they overflew the Seine. A few minutes later they were taxi-ing to a safe stop on the Orly field. It was 3.30 p.m., and their bullet-scarred plane ("the Germans tried to make a sieve of us," as Dutertre wryly put it) bore visible witness to what Higher Headquarters apparently still refused to believe: that the Germans were south of Arras, now trapped in their iron grip.

That evening at supper Alias brought them the news that three of the escorting fighters had been "jumped" by a squadron of Messerschmitts and shot down. When Saint-Ex learned that one of them was piloted by his friend Jean Schneider (of the famous Le Creusot munitions making family), he was disconsolate. It was he, more than any other, who had been keen to accompany the Bloch when he heard it was being flown by Saint-Ex.

The next days were hectic, with the Group flying from three to six missions daily, more than half of them at low, tree-top levels. Another crew failed to return on May 24th, the day after Saint-Exupéry's flight as far as Arras. He himself went up on his fifth mission three days later, but was forced to turn back after 35 minutes because of engine trouble. On May 30th another of the Group's few remaining Potez was wrecked when a novice pilot landed short of the Orly field in a mud patch. The next day Saint-Ex went up again—this time with Lieutenant Azambre as his observer—and flew an uneventful mission over Amiens, Abbeville, and Péronne at a height of 29,000 feet.

On June 3rd the Group moved from Orly to Nangis (north east of Fontainebleau), narrowly escaping German bomber attacks on each field. On the 6th and again on the 9th Saint-Exupéry flew two more high altitude missions, the second over Soissons and Château-Thierry, which the Germans had now reached. That same day another Potez, sent out on a hedge-hopping mission, failed to return.

Saint-Ex by this time had given up all hope of another Marne. The front, if such it could be called, threatened to envelope them at any moment, and it was time to get Consuelo out of "La Feuilleraie" and on down to the south. She too had been caught up in the general atmosphere of panic, and when Antoine drove over, he found the little canvas-top Peugeot he had given her stuffed with minks and fancy coats and hats she intended taking with her to Pau. She had even intended travelling with her jewel case—a dream Tonio rudely interrupted by taking the precious box out of her hands and going out to bury it under a tree in the garden. The maid was instructed to carry the minks and expensive furs upstairs to "Madame's room", and the thus disencumbered Peugeot was loaded with unaesthetic 5 litre cans of petrol—without which, as Tonio sternly reminded her, "there's no hope of your ever getting to the Pyrenees".

Consuelo's precipitated departure came not a day too soon; for the French army was now in a state of total collapse and the Germans were on the Seine. On June 10th Alias and his bone-weary crews were ordered to move back to an airfield near Blois, a displacement which obliged them to leave behind a disabled Potez and a slightly damaged Bloch. During the next four days Saint-Exupéry paid a hasty visit to Marcel Achard, the dramatist, who had a country-house nearby. He then had himself driven in to Tours, which Reynaud and his ministers and their multitude of camp followers had turned into a highly provisional capital. Unable to find a billet in the overcrowded town, he was guided by a friend to the house of Eve Curie. Here he was given a comfortable mattress to sprawl on. The grateful guest sank almost instantly into a sound, deep sleep, while his snores reverberated through the house so loudly that his enervated hostess was kept wide awake all night.

Depressed by the bureaucratic pandemonium of Tours, Saint-Ex returned to find his Reconnaissance unit battling manfully against the prevailing hysteria. Had Hochedé not volunteered to fly back to Nangis, it would have lost a precious Bloch which a group of agitated "super-patriots" were about to set fire to—to keep it from falling into enemy hands. In the interval two more planes had been lost, though Alias had just been given a second group to command. It was thus two groups, instead of one, which took off on the morning of June 15th for Châteauroux. The recently bombed airbase offered a spectacle of indescribable confusion. The field was littered with damaged planes and the available space between craters had to be shared with a bomber squadron and a dozen fighter planes. Mess facilities were non-existent and harsh words were exchanged before Alias' "newcomers" could get anything to eat. That same day, at the request of Higher Head-quarters, two more missions—over the Seine and the Yonne—were flown, doubtless to reassure the Air Ministry it still had one joint it could move.

As Commandant de Groupement (C.O. of two groups), Alias now found himself the ranking officer in charge of an operational unit: which meant, according to wartime rules, that his was the supreme authority at Châteauroux. The Base Commandant, a Lieutenant Colonel, was damned if he was going to yield control of his fief to an "underling"; but he mys-teriously decamped before the matter could be thrashed out between them. One of his assistants, a Major like Alias, was evidently planning to do the same when he was stopped by the pistol Alias stuck into his midriff. A passing reference to this incident was later made in *Flight to Arras*, where Saint-Exupéry depicted his Group Commander pulling his gun to turn back "the fleers".

Later that same day (June 16th) the Group's trucks were loaded up once more with orders to proceed to Bordeaux, there to be embarked on a ship bound for Casablanca. The planes were to take off the next morning for the airfield of Jonzac, roughly midway between Angoulême and Bordeaux. A final cliff-grazing mission was flown on the 18th (the day of De Gaulle's famous proclamation in London), and when the bullet-scarred Potez, which had been fired on for a good part of the course, finally landed at Royan (having lost its way), pilot and observer were able to inform the bureaucrats and the top brass now comfortably installed in Bordeaux that the Germans had indeed reached the Loire! The "real war" in its own macabre fashion was proving every whit as absurd as the "phoney war" which had preceded it.

On reaching Jonzac Alias sent Saint-Exupéry and half a dozen other pilots down to Bordeaux on several damaged Blochs which they were to get repaired at the aircraft works near the Mérignac field. Though this field had not been bombed, the confusion here surpassed the pandemonium of Châteauroux. To quote General Spears, who had managed to fly out of here the previous day with De Gaulle, "the aerodrome was filled with more flying-machines than I have ever seen in one place either before or since, packed wing to wing as far as one could see". Romain Gary, who narrowly missed being killed here, was later to describe the chaos in *La Promesse de l'Aube* as a one of *chacun pour soi* and "first come, first served". Without waiting to be asked the enterprising airmen of the 2/33 Group helped themselves to a two-engine Goéland (the plane Daurat had helped develop for *Air Bleu*) and a four-engine de Havilland for which there was no longer a British crew. After loading the two planes with all the factory spare parts they could lay their hands on, Hochedé took off in the Goéland, while Saint-Ex's favourite chess partner, Pierre Lacordaire, flew the unfamiliar de Havilland back to Jonzac. "*La Hache*" (The Axe) was once again living up to its pirate tradition.

Saint-Exupéry, meanwhile, had hied himself into Bordeaux to "take the pulse" of the situation. The Reynaud government was in the process of collapsing and the Air Ministry had dissolved into a shapeless "porridge". In the thick of the confusion an Air Force general who was still under the impression there was something to administer was pressing buttons and summoning orderlies to find out what had happened to his, the Minister's, chauffeur, and his, the Minister's, car. More than likely they too had decamped in the wild scramble for the Pyrenees.

The fate of the 2/33 Reconnaissance Group had, however, been decided. It was to proceed to North Africa. Determined to get over as many planes as he could, Alias split the Group into two sections. The larger, which he led himself, took off from Jonzac in the early morning of June 19th, bound for Perpignan and then Algiers. All the planes were crammed with spare parts and Hochedé's Goéland was so overweighted that it took all of his *maîtrise* to get it off the ground.

The smaller section, led by Captain Olivier Pénicault, Alias' deputy commander, consisted of Saint-Exupéry, three other pilots, and a number of observers, radio operator-gunners, and mechanics who drove down to Bordeaux by car to take delivery of any Blochs they could cajole out of the factory foremen in addition to the two which were undergoing repairs. On the Bordeaux-Mérignac airfield it was now *sauve qui peut* and there was a mad scramble to climb aboard anything that could fly before the first Wehrmacht motorcycle platoons roared stolidly down the boulevards. For twenty-four sleepless hours Pénicault and Saint-Ex waited for the factory to ready the four Blochs that were in flying condition. There being an extra pilot available, Saint-Exupéry was offered a four motored Farman, capable of carrying forty passengers. Mechanics and spare parts were crammed into this plane too, but the take-off was delayed by the last-minute arrival of two civilians, an army captain, and a blue uniformed nurse from the S.B.M. (*Secours aux Blessés Militaires*)—the Army's first-aid corps. The captain, an aide-de-camp to General Noguès, the Resident General in Morocco, had been dispatched with two important French industrialists in an *in extremis* effort to persuade members of the government to cross over to North Africa and carry on the war from there. In

Bordeaux they had encountered nothing but indecision and confusion, but they had bumped into an ambulance corps nurse who had volunteered to do her little bit to help them. She was the wife of the deputy and lawyer, Henry Torrès, and she had some experience of ministries and ministers. Camille Chautemps, Vice Premier in the new Pétain cabinet, to whom she introduced them, was his usual inconsequential self ("How is the climate in Algiers? I have a very young daughter—do you think she would fare well there?"). It was soon borne in upon them that they were getting nowhere, that Noguès' exhortations were at cross purposes with Pétain's intentions, and that they would be trapped if they didn't get out of Bordeaux fast.

"Despite the terrifying number of planes upon the field," as Suzanne Torrès was later to write, "there reigned an air of lethargy aggravated by the mid-June heat. A few men, however, were busy fuelling a Farman out of several fuel-trucks. One of them turned to look at us. A well known face. No, we're not mistaken: it's Saint-Exupéry! The great flyer looks worried. 'We're leaving for Algeria,' he says in answer to our query. Ouf! It's our last chance. He must take us, but he seems luke-warm to the idea! The Farman he is to pilot is an 'old crate' which hasn't been looked at or revised, and he's unfamiliar with it. The risks are great! But seeing our desire to leave, come what may, he shrugs his shoulders fatalistically. His observer, Azambre, has us climb aboard, and we sit there anxiously awaiting the take-off and fearful of a last-minute hitch."

The hitch failed to develop, and with Saint-Ex at the controls the "old crate" groaned down the runway and into the air. At the airfield of Perpignan, where they touched down to refuel, the chaos was compounded by the presence of a beleaguered group of Polish airmen who were itching to take off for Algeria in the dozens of idle aircraft that were cluttering the field. Egged on by Noguès aide-de-camp, they made a bee-line for these abandoned "taxis", only to be stopped by a dunderhead of an officer (one more!) who said he would shoot to stop them from taking off, since none of them had French pilots' licences! Charitable as ever, Saint-Ex took pity on their plight and bundled one or two of them on to his Farman.

After the take-off he headed south for Oran. Exhausted by days and weeks of ceaseless movement, work, and worry, Suzanne Torrès dropped off to sleep behind him. Suddenly she was aroused by a hand on her shoulder: it was Saint-Ex shaking her awake. He had not wanted any women passengers on board, but now that there was one, he was going to make sure she shared his anxieties. The Farman, he told her, was slowly shaking itself to pieces in mid-air, it was disintegrating bolt by bolt. It would be a miracle if they could make it across the sea. The news failed to overcome the exhausted woman's need for sleep, and a little later she had to be roused again to be told this time that they had overflown the Balearics and were being chased by Italian fighters. More likely they were Spanish, for the pursuit was soon abandoned. The bolts, or those that were left, held long enough to enable Saint-Ex to bring his "Noah's Ark" (it contained a dog as well as a woman) safely down on the airfield of Oran, which like those they had just left, was as craft-crammed as a car-park.

Captain Pénicault and two other pilots were on the field to greet him. When Alias, wondering what had happened to the rest of his Group, flew over from Algiers the next morning, he found Saint-Ex stretched out in the shade under a wing of his Farman. That afternoon, June 23rd, the Group was once again united at Maison-Blanche, the airport of Algiers.

The officers were put up at the Hotel Alétti, and one of Saint-Exupéry's first acts was to ring up his friend Georges Pélissier, asking him to come over right away. The good doctor had to walk through the blacked-out city, where sentinels with fixed bayonets loomed out of the darkness every time he passed a public edifice. At the Alétti an exhausted Saint-Ex was already in bed, worn out by days and nights of unrelieved tension and activity. "*Ah, la France,*" he said, "*quel désastre!*" In a few vivid sentences he painted a picture of that "prodigiously useless exodus towards the void" which he so graphically described a year and a half later in *Flight to Arras*. "He told me" Pélissier later recalled, "of the horror he felt for the Hitlerian mystique, claiming to found a new age for a thousand years. And gradually his voice sank, the halting phrases wavered, and his words dissolved into a mumble. Totally exhausted, he yielded to sleep. When I saw that he had dozed off, I rose, switched off the lamps, and crept out on tip-toe, leaving him to his infant slumbers."

# 19

# The Wanderer

WHEN Saint-Exupéry awoke, it was to learn that Pétain had sued for an Armistice. The news plunged the Group into a state of gloom, and the *Journal de Marche* for June 25th carried this entry: "Day of National Mourning." Cut off from their families in France, about whom they were justifiably worried, officers and men were further upset by the hostile climate of Algiers. As airmen they were held responsible for the *débâcle* by the locals (many of whom had never left the safe shores of North Africa) and all around them they could hear muttered grumblings: "Look at them . . . You might know they'd get here! But at the front where they were needed, there wasn't a French plane to be seen!"

In fact, having crammed their planes full of spare parts and managed to embark their trucks, the members of the 2/33 Reconnaissance Group were among the few metropolitan units which could still continue operations. For a brief moment—the wildest rumours were in the air—there was even talk of their being sent to Tunisia to participate in a "war of revenge" against Italy. But this wild hope died almost as soon as it was born, and instead, they were ordered to disarm their Blochs, in keeping with the Armistice provisions.

It took Alias and most of his fellow officers some time to accept this humiliating *dénouement*, for their first instinct was to carry on the fight, by one means or another. For some days Alias actually toyed with the idea of flying his entire Group to Gibraltar to join the British. His manifest reluctance to disarm his Blochs led to a flare-up with the colonel commanding the Maison-Blanche airfield, who finally detailed some of his men to dismantle the planes one night when he thought (mistakenly) that the ground crews would be napping. Informed by his men of what was happening, Alias heatedly refused to allow any "outsiders" to touch his planes, claiming —as he had already done at Châteauroux—that he was the ranking officer on the spot in charge of an operational unit. The commandant, who out ranked him, blew his stack, and the resulting row—as we shall see in a moment—went all the way up to General René Bouscat, now the senior French Air Force officer in North Africa.

Suddenly, after weeks of tense animation, the members of the 2/33 Reconnaissance Group found themselves with little to do but to report at the airfield at 8 a.m. and to fill the morning hours with routine chores. The younger pilots, like the mechanics, spent the afternoons sunning themselves on the beaches. In the evening the bar of the Hôtel Alétti would fill up with officers and pilots burning to carry on the fight. "Saint-Exupéry" as Suzanne Torrès was later to recall, "was rarely present. He did not believe in the possibility of a resumption of the struggle from North Africa. His arguments were of a realism made to shatter dreams. He had developed them on the way over and had felt that he was paining these enthusiasts. Such being the case, he preferred not to cast the shadow of his doubt over these hope-charged reunions. He explained his discretion to me with his marvellous, slightly sad smile: 'There's no point trying to snuff out their faith.' "

These differences of opinion were understandable, given the shock of the *débâcle* and its humiliating finale. At the Hôtel Alétti opinions were divided, just as they were at the more elegant Hôtel Saint-Georges further up the hill, between "optimists" who took an immediate dislike to the Armistice and "realists" who regarded it as a necessary evil which at least had the merit of putting an end to the slaughter and of keeping the French fleet and North Africa out of German hands. Faith in such circumstances taking precedence over reason, the disagreements tended to be as heated as the debates were inconclusive. No amount of rational arguments produced by Saint-Exupéry—during the several meals they took together at the Hôtel Saint-Georges—could shake the "fight-on" determination of Edouard Corniglion-Molinier, the madcap airman who had flown Malraux over the wastes of the Hadramaout. The same was true of Sorensen, a wealthy wine-grower of Scandinavian origin with whom Saint-Ex often dined and who declared himself profoundly shocked by the cessation of hostilities.

As the days passed, however, the enthusiasm of the "optimists" began to wane and the ranks of the "realists" to swell. Even as resolute a man as Georges Mandel, the recently replaced Minister of the Interior, who was also staying at the Alétti (one floor above Saint-Ex's), could not make up his mind just what to do next; and instead of seeking to make his way to London, where he would have taken over the direction of the Free French movement from De Gaulle, he let himself be repatriated to France, where he was eventually done in by the pro-Nazi militia.

The situation was particularly troubling for General Noguès, who had done everything he could to try and persuade the Reynaud government to carry on the fight from North Africa. As commander-in-chief of all the French forces in the Maghreb, Noguès had moved his headquarters from Rabat (where he had been Resident General) to a barracks in the Algiers suburb of Ben Aknoun. A brother of the Captain Pénicault with whom Saint-Ex had flown to Oran was on his staff, but Saint-Exupéry had an even better introduction to the General through Paul Creyssel, who had also ended up at the Alétti.

In the twenty years that had elapsed since their first encounter in Lyon back in 1917 Creyssel had risen to become a deputy as well as a lawyer. The war had put him back into uniform and he was on his way to a new assignment in the Middle East as an Air Force captain when the abrupt cessation of hostilities had overtaken him in Algiers. Creyssel's interest in Morocco was of long standing—he had seen Saint-Ex in Casablanca in 1931 when he had come down there to give a lecture on Henry de Montherlant—and he had met Noguès on a number of occasions. It was natural that he should call on him once again; and when the General heard that Saint-Exupéry was also at the Alétti, he sent over a car and a chauffeur to drive him out to his headquarters.

Creyssel recalls at least two such meetings with Noguès, though there may have been more. The General, like almost everyone else, was in a divided state of mind, and no wonder! Loath as he was to give up the fight, he was left with little choice. 150,000 troops of the *Armée d'Afrique* had been sent to France to fight the Germans, but only a handful had returned, leaving him with some 100,000 to defend the whole of the Maghreb—at a time when the Italians were threatening Tunisia and the Spaniards had four divisions poised for an attack in northern Morocco. Woefully under strength in artillery, his soldiers had barely two months' worth of ammunition, with no supporting industry. The arms and equipment he had tried to smuggle over from France at the height of the *débâcle* had been blocked by Darlan, who had even jailed a number of his emissaries. The British, with their backs to the wall, could spare nothing. The response from the United States, where the French Ambassador Saint-Quentin and François Bloch-Lainé had been making desperate pleas for aid, was equally discouraging. A French merchantman, the *Pasteur*, had been rerouted to an English port with one thousand French '75s and thousands of machine-guns, and all the United States had left for immediate delivery was exactly twenty-seven '75s of First World War vintage!

The state of the French Air Force, which would have a major role to play were hostilities to spread to North Africa, was of equal concern to Noguès. In all, some 800 planes had finally made it across the Mediterranean, many of them thanks to a helpful Mistral, but as Saint-Exupéry was only too well aware, many of them had landed without spare parts or ground crews. The information reaching Noguès was that what bomber squadrons there were had exactly one hundred 500-pound bombs for all of them, while the fighters had enough machine-gun ammunition to last half a mission each.

Creyssel at the time was too busy to note down these conversations with Noguès, though he recalls Saint-Exupéry's saying that "we have a living air force which is in danger of asphyxiation—like fish that have just been hauled out of the sea and which are about to die." Just when Saint-Ex produced this typically vivid image is not clear, and it may have been slightly later. But of one thing Creyssel is certain: that Saint-Exupéry was sent—and he thinks by Noguès himself—on a confidential mission to Morocco to ascertain the state of mind of Air Force officers and to check on the available material in Rabat and Casablanca. That Noguès should pick Saint-Ex for such a mission might at first sight seem strange, but for such an abnormal situation an abnormal man might best be fitted; and Saint-Exupéry had the advantage of not being a military professional, nor an administrative official, nor a politician—in the presence of whom otherwise loquacious officers might have felt constrained to "clam up".

The mission was so confidential that his commanding officer, Major Alias, knew nothing about it. Nor did General Bouscat, though he occupied a room on the same floor of the Hôtel Alétti and often joined Saint-Ex and Creyssel in long night talks. Noguès was taking no chances, for already the Armistice Commissions were being set up to report on any warlike activities and Algiers had its fair quota of German spies. From just which unit it was that Saint-Exupéry borrowed a plane is equally unclear; but Creyssel, a flyer himself, remembers that it was in a Potez 63 that they left the airfield of Maison-Blanche. Saint-Ex piloted the plane as far as Rabat, where he took leave of Creyssel, who was travelling on a different mission. From Rabat Saint-Exupéry flew on to Casablanca, where one of his jobs was to visit the Ateliers Industriels de l'Air, to check on the assembling of crated planes recently shipped from the United States. For the sake of secrecy he avoided looking up his old friend Henri Comte, who would have wanted to know what he was doing there; but the private report he brought back to Noguès could hardly have been more disheartening. In all, something like 140 Glenn Martin bombers had been shipped from the United States, but the job of uncrating and assembling them had just begun. To make matters worse, some vital parts were still missing—which meant that it would be weeks before they could be ready for action.

The fate of the 2/33 Group had meanwhile been decided by two almost simultaneous events. The first, occurring on July 3rd, was the disaster of Mers-el-Kébir. This British assault on the French fleet aroused hot feelings, and from then on there was no further question of the Group's joining the R.A.F. The second was General Bouscat's decision to back the airfield commandant at Maison-Blanche and to condemn Alias to fifteen days of *arrêts de rigueur* (a token form of incarceration) on the grounds of "insubordination." France, being now officially in a state of peace, wartime airforce regulations no longer applied; and the 2/33's Blochs were in consequence disarmed.

The Mers-el-Kébir bombardment influenced Saint-Ex's future in one other respect. Almost from the start Creyssel, who had served under Pétain during the First World War, took a dim view of De Gaulle's London broadcasts in which the white-haired Marshal and his entourage were virtually accused of treason. Mers-el-Kébir, though a serious blow to De Gaulle, was justified by the General on the grounds that the Vichy government had been secretly planning to turn over the French fleet to the Germans. Creyssel was outraged by the accusation, while Saint-Ex was dismayed. Though he had no reason for feeling a personal attachment to Pétain, he was put off by the incriminatory tone of De Gaulle's broadcasts, which promised to exacerbate the divisions of his unhappy countrymen at a moment when they needed unity and cohesion above all. It was the beginning of a disenchantment which was to grow deeper and more active with the passage of the years.

\*   \*   \*

In all, Saint-Exupéry spent six weeks in Algiers, waiting for events to decide his future course of action. He continued to labour, as he had done at Orconte during the long, idle hours of the "phoney war" on a new book, for which he eventually chose the title of *Citadelle*. Inspired by the hortatory style of Nietzsche's *Thus Spake Zarathustra*, it differed substantially from his previous writings in being far less autobiographical and to that extent more imaginary, closer to Saint Augustine's *De Civitate Dei* than to his *Confessions*. The parallel is a bold one but not altogether misleading in indicating the new direction of Saint-Exupéry's literary efforts. For if he was so intent on compiling a series of moral and political meditations (taking "political" in its broadest sense as covering everything that has to do with the government of men), it was quite simply, as he explained to Paul Creyssel, because he felt that the crisis which had overtaken France was due, in the final analysis, to a spiritual void—a spiritual void which clamoured for a new Book, such as Pascal in the seventeenth century and Rousseau in the eighteenth had sought to provide. A night owl as ever, Saint-Ex would think nothing of ringing up Creyssel at one or two o'clock in the morning and of reading whole pages to him over the hotel telephone just to have his comments and criticism; and it was also Creyssel who was appointed, by Saint-exuberant fiat, to wake him in mid- or late morning because, as he put it, "I prefer a friendly voice to that of the hotel porter".

Being a reserve and not a career officer, Saint-Exupéry, like Creyssel, was soon demobilized. His Reconnaissance Group treated him to a farewell dinner at the Hôtel de l'Oasis which was graced by the presence of a number of *mignonnes*—as Saint-Ex called the "sweethearts". Ever the *grand seigneur*, he responded by chartering a bus to transport his fellow pilots, observers, and friends (including Creyssel, Dr. Pélissier, and Edouard Corniglion-Molinier) to the property of a Moslem notable, more than a hundred miles to the South, where four splendid *méchouis* (lambs) were roasted over the flames. Towards the end of the *diffa* their Moslem host rose and declared with patriarchal simplicity: "In 1870 we were defeated. In 1918 we won. God has this time willed that the Germans should defeat us. God willing (*inch' Allah!*) we shall take our revenge."

The first pale glimmerings of dawn were beginning to brighten the eastern sky as the chartered bus groaned its way into the suburbs of Algiers. Aroused by the *bachagha*'s oratory and the numerous bottles of heady Algerian wine that had been emptied during the feast, the returning revellers filled the night with bawdy songs which poured generously from the open windows of their conveyance right up to the palm-boxed entrance of the Alétti. A stranger might have mistaken them for drunkards celebrating a victory, but it was simply a close-knit crew trying to drown their anguish and dismay. "With Saint-Exupéry" as Alias had said in his parting toast, "the 2/33 is going to lose its soul".

\*　　\*　　\*

In early August Saint-Exupéry and Paul Creyssel sailed back to France on the *Lamoricière*. The cost of the *diffa*, added to an unexpectedly long stay in Algiers, had so completely emptied his wallet that he would not even have been able to pay for the train fare to Agay had he not been bailed out by his friend Pierre Chevrier, who was in Marseille at the time.

Hearing that Henri Guillaumet was due to fly in from Bizerte the next day, he decided to postpone his home-coming by twenty-four hours. Creyssel was with him when they all met up at the Cintra bar, overlooking the Vieux Port. It was a sad reunion, for no one was in much mood for festivities—least of all Henri and his wife Noëlle, both of whom were in a state of deep dejection. A native of Champagne and thus (in French terms) "*un homme de l'Est*"—an Easterner—Guillaumet had honestly believed, like so many of his countrymen, in the invincibility of the Maginot Line. "It's always the same story for us who come from the East. It's always our lands that are overrun and ravaged—today as in 1914."

"Listen, Henri," Saint-Ex sought to encourage him, "you mustn't get yourself down like this. If France had continued the fight, there would have been nothing left. All our towns and cities would have been destroyed, and the loss of lives would have produced a haemorrhage from which this country would never have recovered."

It was the argument he was to develop at length in *Pilote de Guerre* and which was to lead many of his compatriots to conclude that he had become a Pétainist. In fact, Saint-Exupéry had never been a defeatist in the ordinary sense of that word. But he was too lucid not to realize that the disaster of 1940 was the fruit of years of uninterrupted decline, during which France had simply run downhill. "This country is done for if clear reasons aren't found for its fighting," he had written in a letter from Orconte earlier in the year. "The English are fighting for their customs, their Ceylon tea, their week-ends. All we feel is a vague solidarity. We don't have customs that are as clear-cut and universal. Whence the shallowness of Giraudoux and his philosophical 'cake-mix'. These intellectual artifices to reply to notions like race and unity!"

Saint-Exupéry's de Soto having been swallowed up, like so much else, in the undertow of the *débâcle*, it was a carless Tonio who climbed on to the train at the Marseille terminus. The old coal-burner chugged its way through mountains of pumice and around the bays and inlets of the Bouches du Rhône and the Var, puffing to a halt at last in the deep cutting of Agay. It was a joyful home-coming after all these weeks of uncertain confusion, for his mother was staying with his sister Gabrielle, and besides, he had a special fondness for this old provençal fortress-mansion, immortalized by Maupassant in *De la mer* and which, like any self-respecting castle, could boast a discreet phantom whose periodic manifestations were limited to the creaking of aged doors and the dragging of spectral chains over venerable floors.

Saint-Ex spent several weeks here, in a highly unsettled state of mind, wondering just what to do next. In a nearby villa his friend Nelly de Vogüé had taken refuge from the Germans and been joined by her brother Bertrand and by Alain de la Falaise. Fluent in English, both had served as liaison officers with Lord Gort's Expeditionary Force and been evacuated to Britain during the final stage of the Dunkirk campaign. Having seen the French top brass lie themselves into a paralytic complacency (with fictitious reports on the northwestern extension of the Maginot Line), they were among the rare Frenchmen who were prepared to forgive Churchill and the Royal

Navy for what they had done at Mers-el-Kébir. Both were eager to resume the battle and were debating ways of smuggling themselves out of France and over to London, to join General de Gaulle. But try as they might to talk Saint-Exupéry into joining them, he remained stubbornly luke-warm. Unlike them, he spoke not a word of English and could not see himself enrolled in some R.A.F. unit.

The arguing went on far into each night, interrupted frequently by the card tricks Antoine performed for the amusement of his friends. They were accomplished with such staggering ease and infallibility that Alain de la Falaise finally concluded that some supernatural force was at work and that he was dealing with a *"mage"*, or as we would say, a wizard. Saint-Ex would leave a pack of cards casually lying on the table and Alain de la Falaise, thinking to take him by surprise, would draw out a card. Invariably it was the Queen of Spades! By what magic power could this conjuror force him to choose a card he could not see in a pack he had seemingly not touched? It was like one of those incredible series at roulette, where the same number comes up thirteen or twenty times. There was some kind of spell on this particular pack of cards which made a captive of him. Tonio, of course, remained as mysterious as ever, merely remarking, as though it were the most natural thing in the world: "You will continue to draw the same card until you get the news you are waiting for . . ." For his friend Alain was expecting a letter. And so to his astonishment it happened: the letter arrived and the magic run was ended.

The debate was terminated in a rather different fashion—by the arrival of Nelly's husband, Jean de Vogüé, a French Navy Captain. He had accompanied Admiral Darlan to London on a mission to coordinate the actions of the French and British fleets and had stayed on right through Dunkirk and the *débâcle*. Shortly after De Gaulle's June 18th proclamation calling on the French to continue the struggle, Jean de Vogüé had presented himself at 4, Carlton Gardens. His interview with the General had gone worse than badly, and the picture he painted of De Gaulle was black. "Whatever you do," he said to the others, "don't go to London with the idea of joining De Gaulle. The man's impossible . . . There's only one thing to do—stay here and see what we can do inside of France." Their enthusiasm chilled by this pail-full of cold water, Jaunez and La Falaise finally gave up their original idea and decided to stay on—to Saint-Ex's undisguised relief.

Fitfully and with frequent interruptions Saint-Exupéry continued to work on his book of Nietzschean meditations. But the distractions were multiple, the progress of the Battle of Britain too momentous to be ignored, and the pinch of austerity could already be felt. Gasoline was severely rationed, certain foodstuffs were increasingly difficult to obtain, the trains were jam-packed, and there was hardly a village or a property in southern France that was not still swamped with refugees who had panicked before the German advance.

Before taking leave of Creyssel in Marseille, Saint-Ex had said: "I'll be coming up to Lyon soon. We must arrange to meet at Morateur's and enjoy a plate of carp roe"—one of his favourite dishes. Probably he said it in a spirit of defiance, as though determined to prove, if only to himself, that life in the unoccupied zone could still offer something of the old French *joie de vivre*; but when he reached Lyon several weeks later, it was to Morateur's that both repaired before continuing on that same night to Vichy.

Creyssel, who is in a position to know, claims that Saint-Exupéry made at least three and possibly four trips to Vichy between mid-August and the end of October, when he finally decided to leave France. Many other Frenchmen, wishing to get the "feel" of a bafflingly fluid situation, had already made a bee-line for the famous watering-spa, whose magnetic centre was the luxurious Hôtel du Parc, which Pétain had made his residence and seat of government. One of those thus attracted was Saint-Ex's friend Gaston Bergery, the deputy, who had even joined the Marshal's entourage with the idea of helping him to formulate a new philosophy of government which was eventually to be given the pompous and totally misleading name of "*Révolution Nationale*".

Crowded though the Hôtel du Parc already was, Saint-Ex and Creyssel managed on this first trip to Vichy to find beds for themselves in cramped servants' rooms on the hotel's top floor. Informed of their arrival in "his" capital, Pétain agreed to receive the two recently demobilized airmen, who were treated to a few plain, down-to-earth remarks about the general situation: time was needed to restore order out of chaos, to get the country back on its feet again, and in the meantime nothing "adventurous" could conceivably be attempted. These affable commonplaces were not unforeseen, and they interested the two visitors far less than the two books they saw lying on the Marshal's desk. By resorting to various verbal strategems to keep the monologue going and Pétain's attention focussed on his thoughts, they were able to make out what they were. One was a book called *La Prusse après Iéna*, the other Albert Sorel's study of Talleyrand and Metternich. Like the "resisters" in his entourage—men like Marcel Peyrouton, the Minister of the Interior, Yves Bouthillier, the Finance Minister, Admiral Fernet, who kept the secret cabinet minutes, Jean Borotra, whose tennis-playing talents had been conscripted for the running of the Commissariat of Sport, and Henri Moulin de la Barthète, the head of his civilian secretariat, the white whiskered Marshal was studying the Fabian tactics which Scharnhorst, Gneisenau, and Stein had resorted to after the disaster of Jéna and which eventually permitted a rearmed Prussia to contribute to Napoleon's defeat at Waterloo.

Another prominent "resister" in Pétain's entourage was General Huntziger, who had had the thankless task of negotiating the Armistice with Keitel before replacing Weygand as Minister of War. It is not clear if it was during the first or second of Saint-Exupéry's trips to Vichy that he lunched with Huntziger; but what is certain—we have Charles Sallès' word for it—is that Saint-Ex came away from this luncheon much impressed by Huntziger's evident integrity and determination to stand up to the Germans. In all likelihood this conversation also confirmed Saint-Exupéry in his doubts about De Gaulle; for at the height of the *débâcle* and at a time when the Reynaud government had already withdrawn to Tours, a breathless De Gaulle had suddenly turned up at the headquarters of the Fourth Army Group with what struck Huntziger as a hair-brained scheme for organizing a "Breton front."

If Saint-Exupéry, under the persuasive influence of Creyssel and Bergery, may for a moment have been tempted by the idea of accepting a job in Vichy—"*pour sauver les meubles*" (to save the furniture), as the French picturesquely put it—the idea seems to have palled with each new visit he made to this deceptively somnolent capital. While certain well-meaning Frenchmen were trying to stiffen Pétain's capacity for resistance, there were others, beginning with Laval, who were doing everything they could to ingratiate themselves with the Germans. Indeed, before the month of August was up Laval had reached such a nadir of fawning that he felt obliged to call on Field Marshal von Brauchitsch at his Fontainebleau headquarters in order to offer him the help of French warplanes for the bombing of Britain—a grovelling attempt to kick the bulldog even before he was down which the Field Marshal had the Prussian gall to refuse as unnecessary!

Much as he admired the British, Saint-Exupéry had never believed that Britain alone could rescue France from her plight. The one country that could counter-balance the industrial and military might of Germany was the United States. It was what had been demonstrated in the First World War, and the precedent was bound to repeat itself. His irritation with the military blockheads who had kept American pressmen from photographing (totally antiquated) French military equipment stemmed, as his notebook shows, from his belief that this kind of imbecilic veto could only poison Franco-American relations at a time when everything should have been done to improve them. For the same reason he had hoped that France might go to the aid of Finland, when that country was attacked by Russia, as a way of gaining American sympathy and of getting the United States into the war. Instead, by doing nothing, the French had only strengthened the case of the

American isolationists who, even when they were not outspokenly pro-German or anti-British, could see no reason for helping a country (like France) so manifestly unwilling to fight. It was the same conviction which had moved him to solicit an interview with Paul Reynaud. America was France's only hope.

Now, as though to prove it, came a cable from his New York publishers inviting him to cross the Atlantic. The winner of the National Book Award for the best non-fiction work of 1939, *Wind, Sand, and Stars* had sold a quarter of a million copies and piled up massive royalties for him on the other side of the ocean. Loath as he was to leave his stricken country at such a desperate moment, Saint-Ex found the offer tempting. He was still too close to the dramatic events he had just lived through to know exactly how to write them up, while the book he was working on, *Citadelle*, was years, if not decades, from completion. Besides, was this a time to be writing books in a country where people had more urgent problems to worry about than literature?

More uncertain than ever in his mind, he went to call on his friend Gaston Gallimard, who had pulled part of his publishing company back to Carcassonne, and left him a copy of his new manuscript. It already contained hundreds of pages, but as the canny publisher knew, they were but the *gangue*—the matrix—from which, after endless scraping and polishing, the gem-like brilliance of his prose would finally emerge. Saint-Exupéry's method of writing had by this time assumed a systematic form. Instead of reworking the same passage as originally written, he now preferred to draft a series of "parallel" sketches in which he sought to render the same idea or episode in as many different ways as possible. The process might be compared to an artist's preliminary sketches for a painting, though an even apter simile might be those "variations on a theme" which certain composers, like Bach or Brahms, raised to the level of high art. Of course, theirs were finished works, whereas the final step in Saint-Ex's essentially "horizontal" method of composition was to choose the words and phrases in each version which best conveyed what he wished to express, while the rest was ruthlessly discarded.

Exactly when Saint-Exupéry made up his mind to apply for an American visa is not certain, but it was probably in early October. His decision in any case was heavily influenced by a visit he made to his friend Léon Werth between two trips to Vichy. Suzanne Werth's property at Saint-Amour (near Tournus) had fortunately ended up in the unoccupied zone, where Werth, as a Jew, had less to fear from the vexations to which his persecuted brethren already being subjected in northern France. But even in the southern zone anti-Semitism was now the fashion, already manifested by special travel permits and job prohibitions which boded ill for the future. The mere fact that such discriminations could be officially established was enough to stifle Saint-Exupéry's waning enthusiasm for Vichy—as he took pains to explain to Paul Creyssel during his next trip to that makeshift capital.

When he told his friend about the cable he had received from his New York publishers inviting him to cross the Atlantic, Werth strongly encouraged him to make the trip to the United States, where he could do his country a great service by explaining to Americans that the battle against Hitlerism was not national but international. This, from the very start, had been Saint-Ex's feeling too; but much as he appreciated Werth's encouragement, he was still wracked by misgivings. No matter how one looked at it, leaving France was a privilege reserved for a few: the common lot, the harsh lot, the lot which really deserved to be honoured—was to remain behind.

Back at Agay Saint-Exupéry found it increasingly difficult to concentrate on anything but the international situation, dominated by the R.A.F.'s grim struggle for survival. Anxious to obtain the advice of another old friend, he journeyed over to Tarascon to spend a few days with Charles Sallès in the charming *mas* with the fifteenth century turret which was like a second home to him. Sallès found him troubled, torn between a desire to explain France's calamity to Americans and a reluctance to flee his homeland. But he gave him the same advice as Werth: there was little, given the circumstances, that he could do for France on the spot, whereas in the United States an eloquent new voice might work wonders.

The Mas de Panisse—or as we would say, the Country-house of Panisse, as Sallès' mansion was called in the soft language of Provence—was located three miles south of Tarascon on the road to Arles. Though linked to the town by telephone, the switchboard operator would accept none but local calls, and every day Sallès and Saint-Ex would have to hie themselves in as best they could to put in a call to Vichy from the nearest *commissariat de police*. It must have been close to mid-October when Antoine finally learned that his papers were in order. He decided to leave that very evening. Lacking any better means of locomotion, Sallès borrowed his gardener's tandem. With Antoine's small handbag strapped between them, they pushed off on the unfamiliar machine, zig-zagging drunkenly up the road against a fierce Mistral. As they waited on the platform Sallès was reminded of the evening —a year or was it two before?—when they had come here to meet Consuelo's train. On her way up from Toulouse she got off at Narbonne to snatch a bite at the station buffet, and the train had left without her. Repeated telephone calls had thrown the station into a dither over "*les bagages de la*

*Comtesse de Saint-Exupéry*", now bound for Tarascon without their owner. But what could the harassed station-master do? How, when the crowded train pulled in for a brief five-minute stop, were he and his fellow officials to know just where to start searching for the errant bags? But Saint-Ex, after a rapid walk up the platform, had suddenly made for a door, pushed into a compartment, and said to one of its startled occupants: "Excuse me, but that's my wife's bag you're sitting on." How he had guessed it, Sallès was never able to discover, though he attributed it to that prodigious intuition which guided Tonio in his card-tricks. Still less did he realize now, as he took leave of his friend, that their fond "*Au Revoir*" was to be a definitive "*Adieu*".

*   *   *

A few days before, Saint-Exupéry had rung up Roger Beaucaire from Marseille to say that he would soon be coming up to Vichy and would let him know when he arrived. Pétain's makeshift capital had by now become a labyrinth of spying, rumour, and intrigue, to say nothing of conspiracy and counter-espionage; and one of the focal points of what later was called the Resistance was the Hôtel des Sports, a less than luxurious hostellery where Beaucaire was staying. Located on the periphery of the town a discreet distance from the more fashionable and spied on centre, the hotel had just been hired by an extraordinary Pyrenean firebrand, Major Georges Loustaunau-Lacau (a classmate of De Gaulle's at the Ecole Supérieure de Guerre), who was already knee-deep in anti-German plotting. His "clients" included a strange assortment of army veterans and former flyers—like his Saint-Cyr classmate, Alfred Heurtaux, who had commanded the celebrated "*Cigognes*" (Storks) Squadron in which Guynemer served during the First World War. Another was Pierre Massenet, an aeronautical engineer and gliding enthusiast who had recommended the hotel to Beaucaire. Though Beaucaire, whose sympathies lay to the left, cared little for Loustaunau-Lacau's neo-royalist activities as a pre-war *cagoulard*, he found the Resistance atmosphere of the establishment a refreshing change from the bureaucratic paralysis and stifling conformism of Vichy.

Saint-Exupéry put in a fleeting appearance at the Hôtel des Sports, but it was at the luxurious Hôtel du Parc that he dined with Beaucaire the evening of his arrival. The dining-room, one end of which was cordoned off by a screen so that Pétain could partake of his meals without being exposed to public view, was crowded; and all the *maître d'hôtel* could offer them was an extra table wedged in between two others in the middle of the floor. Undaunted by the presence at the next table of a dignified gentleman and a lady who could hear everything they said, Saint-Exupéry launched into a diatribe against the "suffocating atmosphere . . . this cringing attitude . . . the unbreathable air . . ." of this ersatz capital of a semi-France. At the next table the gentleman said nothing, but Beaucaire noticed that he and his wife were taking in every word. Saint-Ex, who had probably noticed it too, carried on unconcerned, his vehemence rising to a crescendo when he saw a fat, moustachioed little man who looked and probably smelled of garlic walk in through the entrance, smack opposite them.

"Ah!" cried Saint-Ex. "There's a scoundrel for you!"

The scoundrel was Pierre Laval.

The conversation continued in this vein for a minute or two longer, after which Saint-Exupéry said: "Now that we've exhausted the subject, and said enough to get both of us put up before a firing-squad and shot, let's talk about other things."

Outside, in the lobby, as they were leaving the dining-room, they ran into Nelly de Vogüé.

"Well, how did it go?" she asked.

"We had a fine talk," Saint-Ex assured her.

"Ah? I hope you didn't say anything foolish."

"Why?"

"Why? . . . Didn't you realize who was sitting next to you?"

"No."

"De Brinon. And his wife."

A close collaborator of Otto Abetz, who was now German Ambassador in Paris, Fernand de Brinon had long been suspected of being on the Nazi pay-roll—to such an extent that General Weygand refused to shake hands with him, even in public. He was also a close associate of Laval, with whom he was shortly to journey to Montoire to meet Adolf Hitler!

At the brasserie to which they later repaired, Saint-Exupéry suggested that Beaucaire, being an engineer, should think up some pretext—like a trip to inspect American steel-alloy processing at Pittsburg—to justify his leaving Vichy France for the United States. As for himself, it was time to clear out. He had a name which the authorities seemed eager to exploit. Unknown to Jean Borotra (whom Saint-Ex saw briefly during one of these trips to Vichy), Henri du Moulin de la Barthète, the head of Pétain's civilian secretariat, was toying with the idea of having Saint-Exupéry appointed to a senior post in the State Secretariat of Education, where he would have been in charge of Youth as well as Sport. Paul Creyssel, who had broached the idea to a member of Darlan's staff, had found him most receptive to the suggestion; and though there is no proof that such a post was ever actually offered to Saint-Ex, the idea was very much in the air.

Before leaving France, however, Saint-Exupéry was anxious to recuperate the papers and notebooks he had left in his Paris apartment. Access to the occupied zone was limited at this time to returning refugees, who travelled north on packed trains. Otherwise, one needed a special pass from the German authorities. Saint-Ex was wondering how he could procure one when he ran into Drieu La Rochelle, another Gallimard author whom he had befriended in the pre-war years. Drieu, who had a car and who was now something of a V.I.P., offered to drive him up, and Saint-Exupéry accepted with alacrity. Drieu's openly pro-German sentiments were far removed from his own, but with this kind of escort he reckoned he would have less trouble from the occupation authorities. It was a shock, nevertheless, to be halted at the demarcation line near Moulins by steel-helmeted guards who gave his *Ausweis* (exit permit) a close scrutiny.

In Paris Saint-Ex saw a number of people, beginning with his cousin Yvonne de Lestrange. Father Théry, a Dominican he had been introduced to in Léon Werth's apartment on the Rue d'Assas, was struck by Saint-Exupéry's determination to "serve" his country, though just how he did not specify. He was more explicit with Jean Lucas, his old friend from Port Etienne. As they sat at a café watching Wehrmacht officers and soldiers prance up and down an almost carless Rue de Rivoli, Saint-Ex kept shaking his head. He was all for the Armistice, he told Lucas, because France needed a breather and he was certain, absolutely certain that in due course the United States would enter the war. "They'll come to save us—I don't know how or when, but they'll come. As they did the last time." Why, he couldn't say, but there was no shaking his conviction.

"*Ça ne fait pas sérieux*," he added, nodding at the swastika they could see floating from the façade of the Hôtel Continental. The spectacle was too grotesque to seem real.

Grotesque or not, France's occupants were grimly punctilious, as Saint-Exupéry discovered the next day. To obtain the *Ausweis* needed to leave Paris and the occupied zone, he was subjected to detailed interrogation by a senior German official, in the presence of Drieu La Rochelle. The session lasted so long that it was close to 10 p.m. by the time he walked out into the fresh, fumeless air of an unnaturally silent Champs-Elysées. To his consternation he found the entrance grill closed at the Rond-Point *métro* stop. The curfew hour was approaching and there was no time to be lost: he would have to leg it back to the nearest friend's apartment. "The stinkers!" his biographer Pierre Chevrier quotes him as muttering, as he bounded along in his heavy bear-like way, cursing the *Boches*, his sore feet, and his aching fractures, "the stinkers! I'll never let them get my notebooks." For he knew that if the Germans caught him on the street during curfew hours, they would take him back and ransack his apartment before they were through with him.

Determined to leave nothing of value should the Gestapo or the Paris police ever get it into their heads to break into his flat, Saint-Ex had a cyclist pedal a suitcase over to a friend's apartment where he was to lunch the next day. "You'll be surprised when you see what I'm leaving you," he laughed as he opened up the case. He turned a couple of dials and a radio programme came on. It was the Libertyphone radio-record-player which Maximilian Becker had sent him from New York to dispel the snow and mud-bound tedium of Orconte.

October was well into its third week by the time Saint-Exupéry was back on the Côte d'Azur for the final farewells. At Hyères, near Toulon, he spent a few more hours with Gaston Gallimard, a member of whose family had recently been hurt there in an accident. In Cannes he looked in on André Beucler, whom he found crushed, like himself, by the immensity of the catastrophe. They talked about old times and Saint-Exupéry insisted that none of the fundamental problems had changed. Opposed as he was to violence, the war had to be fought. But no less important, even while it was going on, one had to start preparing "*le dessous*"—by which he meant the moral or ideological infra-structure—which would make it possible for people to understand each other at every level of society.

As they parted, Beucler, like his friend Fargue a sedentary urbanite, remarked: "I think one must choose the soil of the *patrie*, even when it's trampled on and sullied."

To which Saint-Ex replied: "I think one must choose withdrawal to a certain distance, for the sake of perspective, and I'm going to look for it in New York."

In the street he ran into Raymond Bernard, who had brought his mother and his famous father (Tristan) down to Cannes in the early days of the German *blitz*. "Come up with me to Cabris," Saint-Exupéry suggested. "I would like you to meet my mother." Bernard was touched by the invitation, which he was unable to accept, and little did he guess, in taking leave of his friend, that he was seeing him for the last time.

The one person who sensed it was his mother, when Antoine turned up to say good-bye in the hillside village near Grasse which she had made her home. As a parting gift he gave her a portable radio—"so that you can keep in touch with the world"—and as she took it from him, holding back her tears, her sixth maternal sense told her with a pang that it was probably the last present from her beloved Tonio she would ever receive.

*     *     *

The Spanish Consulate in Vichy having intimated that he would have difficulty obtaining a transit visa in view of the anti-Franco sentiments he had expressed during the Civil War, Saint-Exupéry sailed from Marseille, bound for Algiers. A day or two later he was in Tunis, to bid good-bye to his friends of the 2/33 Reconnaissance Group, now stationed at the airfield of El Aouina. Alias got the impression that he was going to the United States on some semi-official mission from Vichy, and it is possible that Saint-Ex hinted as much, lest his friends think he was fleeing like a refugee to the plush safety of the New World.

Back in Algiers he checked in once again at the Hôtel Alétti, and as he did so, his eye caught the name of Colonel René Chambe in the registry. An Air Force officer who had made a name for himself as an author of articles and books on aviation, Chambe had first met Saint-Exupéry in the early thirties at the Closerie des Lilas (in Montparnasse) where a literary group known as "The Friends of 1914" would periodically gather under the genial aegis of Paul Fort, the poet. They had since become good friends: good enough for Saint-Ex to order a bottle of champagne immediately brought up to his room.

It was already midnight and Chambe was about to undress when the telephone rang in his room.

"Hallo, Saint-Ex here," said the voice at the other end, without further ado. "Come on over to my room. I've got a bottle of champagne here waiting for you."

By four o'clock in the morning the bottle was empty and both were ready at last to go to bed, pleased to have discovered an extraordinary identity of opinion. One of the first things Chambe had said to the mayor of his little village in the Dauphiné, after his return from the *débâcle*, was: "You'd better start preparing a camp." "A camp?" the startled mayor had asked. "Why yes," was the serene reply. "A camp—for the Americans." For like Saint-Ex, Chambe was convinced that the Americans *had* to get into the war, and this being the case they would.

After the Armistice Chambe had gone to call on Jean Prouvost, the publisher of *Paris-Soir*, who had transferred his operations to the unoccupied zone. He had written many articles for him in the past, and now he proposed a new series—on the morale of the French armed forces in North Africa. Prouvost had immediately agreed to underwrite the costs of the trip, and in Algiers General Testut, the local Air Force commander, had placed a two-motor Goéland at his disposal.

"What! A Goéland?" Saint-Ex's eyes widened and a look of almost childish delight came over his face. "*Eh bien, mon vieux*, I'm coming with you."

Nothing could have pleased Chambe more than to have such a stimulating fellow traveller. From Algiers they flew straight to Rabat, where they were received by General Noguès. The Resident General of Morocco, who was later to grow so cautious, was still making little secret of his anti-German inclinations and his desire to resume the struggle as soon as was possible; and so much did the idea of Chambe's journalistic junket please him that he even offered him a new Goéland, to replace the rickety machine they had flown from Algiers.

In Casablanca Saint-Ex took Chambe to the house of Dr. Henri Comte, where they spent a very literary evening competing in erudite quotations— a game in which, Chambe admits, "I was left very far behind". But this sophisticated fencing was merely a verbal froth on the surface of deeper preoccupations; for when the time came to take leave of his host, Saint-Exupéry said to Comte: "I don't know if I shall have the courage not to join the R.A.F."

At Agadir the two airmen found the local commander (General Henry Martin) favourably disposed towards the idea of resuming hostilities at the earliest opportunity. But such was not the feeling they encountered at their next port of call—the dusty garrison-town of Ksar-es-Souk, on the southern, desert facing slopes of the Atlas. The colonel commanding the Spahi regiment made no bones about it. "We are ready to resume the struggle," he declared over the lunch-table, "provided we get orders. For what matters in the army is discipline."

"Yes," Chambe agreed. "But orders are sometimes cruel."

"We shall obey," answered the Colonel, "even if they are cruel".

"What!" cried Chambe. "Even if you are asked to fire on our erstwhile comrades-in-arms, our friends?"

"Yes," was the uncompromising answer, "even on them".

There was general agreement from the other officers present. No matter what, orders were orders; discipline came first.

The two guests came out appalled.

"But they're mad!" cried Saint-Exupéry, when they were on their own again. It was Chambe's feeling too. For both of them it was the first bitter foretaste of a rigid attitude which was to exacerbate the bitter quarrel between Vichy France and London and lead to much needless bloodshed.

From the red-walled outpost of Ksar-es-Souk they flew north to the royal city of Fez, where they spent a fragrant night among the trumpet lilies and the tiled mosaics of the Palais Jamai. As they sat by the tombs of the Merenide Sultans, watching the dusk settle like a mantle over the great medina, emblazoned by the golden orbs above the darkening minarets, they had to remind themselves that this was 1940, so overpowering was the sense of peace induced by the incomparable vista. Nor was this guilty feeling much attenuated at their next stop—Marrakesh—from whose soft-scented orange-groves and snow-tipped mountains Saint-Exupéry had to tear himself, like a Ulysses from the embrace of a Circe.

Taking leave of Chambe, he made for Tangier, from where he took a steamer to Lisbon. Nothing could have more exacerbated his lurking sense of guilt than the glittering unreality of this city, glowing at night like a jewel on the fringe of a continent which a war had plunged into darkness. What a serenity in these unravaged streets, in these sedate, almost timeless edifices, whose façades seemed attuned to the same discreet measure as the soft lament of the *fados*, which played upon the ear like water flowing from a fountain! But the bright haven, in a world turned dark and angry, had attracted a host of fugitives anxious to escape the storm. In Lisbon there was not a bed to be had, and he had to put up in Estoril, where a strange breed of ghosts, seemingly undisturbed by the chaos which had overtaken Europe, could be seen every evening in their starched shirts and their pearls driving up to the casino in soundless Cadillacs. Watching them, as Saint-Exupéry later recalled it (in *Lettre à un otage*), he experienced neither indignation nor a sense of irony, but only a vague anguish, such as one feels at the zoo before "survivors of an extinct species". Everything about these phantoms was synthetic, beginning with the hope or the despair, the fear, envy, or jubilation they sought to feel as they pressed around the tables and the austere croupiers. The fortunes they were gambling away might already, by virtue of a confiscation or under the hammer-blows of some bombardment which had reduced their factory walls to rubble, have dissolved like smoke. Yet pulling out their cheque-books, "they wrote out cheques on Sirius. By thus clinging to the past, as though nothing on earth had started cracking over the past few months, they sought to convince themselves of the rightfulness of their addiction, of the solidity of their balances, of the eternity of their conventions. It was unreal. Like a puppet ballet. Not gay, but sad."

At the French Embassy Saint-Exupéry met François de Panafieu, the First Secretary. More than ever he was in a divided state of mind, visibly preoccupied by the atmosphere he was going to find on the other side of the ocean. If Lisbon was this unreal, what would he not encounter in New York? Panafieu suggested he call on an old friend of his, now working for the Rockefeller Foundation, a Prince Alexander Makinsky.

"But I know him!" exclaimed Saint-Ex, recalling the evening they had spent at the Brasserie Lipp, discussing Russia and Ivan Moujik.

This time, in going to see the Prince, it was to find out something about America and Uncle Sam. Makinsky found Saint-Ex besieged by doubts far exceeding those that had assailed him on the eve of his Moscow trip. Now that he had come this far and that it was simply a question of getting on to the next boat, he seemed overwhelmed by the idea that he was running away, leaving his family and friends to suffer on in silence without him. "Rarely" recalls Makinsky, "have I seen a person in such an indecisive frame of mind".

Saint-Exupéry's spiritual torments were soon aggravated by a piece of disastrous news. On November 27th his friend Henri Guillaumet had taken off from Marseille in a four-engine Farman—like the one he himself had flown from Bordeaux to Oran—bound for Tunis with Jean Chiappe, recently appointed French Resident General for Syria. But the plane, in which their old friend Marcel Reine was also travelling, had disappeared over the Mediterranean, apparently shot down during a naval-air battle between the British and the Italians. It was a cruel blow which added considerably to his anguished indecision. He had promised to give a talk to the students of the French Lycée in Lisbon, and that evening he did so, devoting most of his address to the memory of the friend he had just lost.

Saint-Exupéry also agreed to give another talk to the students of the Higher Institute of Electricity—on the topic: "Three Agonies": these being his experiences as he flew towards Arras, his sea-plane accident at Saint-Raphael, and his crash in the Libyan desert. As he took his place on the podium, he amused the hall by remarking: "Ah gentlemen, I would rather face a storm than this lecture I have to deliver."

It was one more ordeal, of the kind he dreaded but was now too famous to be able to avoid. Only when it was over could he relax, as he did with the teachers of the French Lycée, and reveal the charm which made him such a captivating guest at small parties. As he sampled a glass of very old port—1830, no less!—which a Mademoiselle Dutheil had managed to unearth for him, he remarked that rarely had he ever tasted anything so fine, even though he flattered himself on being a connoisseur. "This reminds me" he went on, with a dimpled laugh, "of a nightmare which haunted me when I was being tortured by thirst in the Libyan desert. I suddenly began thinking of all the unemptied glasses I had left in bars I had frequented. Such a quantity of liquid stupidly abandoned! I swore that if I managed to save myself this time too, never would I be so casual again. Lest it ever become too crushing a regret."

He also entertained the company that evening with an exercise in hypnotism, something he had been interested in and read many books about since his Cape Juby days. Selecting a victim from among the ladies present, he put her into a trance and had her walk up and down the stairs and through the corridors, in total obedience to his commands. The evening ended with a dazzling display of card tricks, in which by much the same hypnotic and telepathic means this master illusionist could make his captive subjects see a ten of clubs where there was, in fact, an ace of hearts.

But back in his bedroom and alone once more he was in no mood for gaiety. "Guillaumet is dead," he wrote to a friend who had stayed behind in France. "I have the impression this evening that I have no more friends. I don't feel sorry for him: I have never been able to feel sorry for the dead. But this death is something it is going to take me a long time to get used to, and I already feel the weight of this travail. It will last months and months —and I shall need him so often. Does one then age so quickly? I am the sole survivor of the Casa-Dakar team of the old days, of the great team of the Bréguet 14s, Collet, Reine, Lassalle, Beauregard, Mermoz, Etienne, Simon, Lécrivain, Ville, Verneilh, Riguelle"—yes, the same Riguelle who had flown him down on his first flight south from Cisneros, when they had had to crash-land in the dunes near the little fort of Nouakchott: Riguelle too was dead, killed some years before when the plane that was bringing him back to Toulouse had smashed straight into the fog-bound Pyrenees. And now Guillaumet was gone, along with his faithful radio operator Le Duff, who had ditched down nineteen times in the Atlantic and seen a dozen seaplanes disappear beneath the waves . . . And Franques, Guillaumet's mechanic, who had overflown the Andes four hundred times.

"Now they are all dead," Saint-Exupéry went on, "and I have no one left with whom to share my memories. Here I am, a toothless old man rechewing all this for myself alone . . . I thought this only happened to old folk, scattering their friends en route. All of them. If you have known so few of my friends, it's because they are all dead . . . Tell me if I should come back and I'll return."

What the answer was Pierre Chevrier, who quotes this letter in his biography, does not tell us; but presumably it was an encouragement to carry on.

# 20

## The Exile

A T the Technical Institute in Lisbon Saint-Exupéry had found himself sharing the spotlight with another distinguished Frenchman, Jean Renoir the film director; and they were given the same cabin when the American Export Lines' *Siboney* finally sailed for America. They had met once or twice before in Paris on a casual basis, but it took this slow, cramped voyage across a wintry ocean to cement their friendship. With 343 passengers packed into overcrowded cabins that were more like dormitories, all chance of a "discreet adventure" was ruled out. The ship was so small, as Saint-Ex jokingly explained after they had landed, that it was like a life-boat, and "we were fortunate in not meeting a hungry whale: he would have swallowed us, boat and all." It took this rolling tub three quarters of an hour, he went on in the same jovial vein, to climb to the top of each tall wave! Poetic license, to be sure; but if the *Siboney* took so long to cross the Atlantic it was partly due to stormy headwinds, and partly to British warships, which halted the ship twice and forced it to undergo inspection at Bermuda. When they finally pulled in to New York more than a day behind schedule, passengers as well as skipper heaved an immense sigh of relief. The collective thirst had been such that there was not a drop of soda water, beer, or Coca Cola left on board.

It was December 31, 1940, the last day in a catastrophic year. What the new one would bring, Saint-Ex had no idea as he stepped down the gangplank, but there on the dock to greet him was the familiar face of Pierre Lazareff, to whom he had cabled he was coming. There were also several newspapermen, including one from the *New York Times*, who missed Jean Renoir but successfully ambushed the author of *Wind, Sand, and Stars*. Asked (through an interpreter) how long he planned to stay in the United States, Saint-Exupéry answered: "Three to four weeks," adding as an afterthought, "in these days it is impossible to make plans three weeks ahead." What did he think of Marshal Pétain? He declined to say. What was the French attitude towards England? Had the outcome of the Battle of Britain brought about any official change of policy? No, he answered, he'd heard nothing in unoccupied France or in North Africa to support any such idea. On the other hand, he was positive—France would never make war on England. The political situation in France? Well, he still believed in democracy, but not in the kind which the country had known prior to the war, which had produced administrative chaos and paralysis on an unprecedented scale. Were German pilots better than the French? It was hard to say, it being difficult to distinguish between the quality of pilots and the quality of the planes they flew. But Germany won the war through her industrial power, not through the quality of men or machines. And Britain? Did Mr. de Saint-Exupéry think the Germans could bring Britain to her knees through aerial bombardment? No, Mr. de Saint-Exupéry did not. "Night bombardments are not sufficiently effective. They are not decisive," he explained. "Day raids on the other hand, are too costly to be kept up for long, even by the Germans. If the Germans could make a landing in England, with motorized troops and equipment, that would be an unquestionable success, but I don't see how they can do it."

Once again Saint-Ex was put up at the Ritz Carlton, where a suite had been reserved for him by his New York agent, Maximilian Becker, and his publishers, Curtice Hitchcock and Eugene Reynal. Notwithstanding their welcome and solicitude, Saint-Exupéry felt even more lost and out of place here than he had after his Guatemala crash of 1938, even though New York had already attracted a growing colony of French expatriates which included André Maurois, Jules Romains, Saint-John Perse the poet (who finally settled in Washington), Henry Bernstein the playwright, the aircraft manufacturer Michel Wibault, journalists like Robert de Saint-Jean, Geneviève Tabouis, André Géraud (better known as "Pertinax"), Henri de Kerillis, Hélène and her husband Pierre Lazareff, to say nothing of a disordered cohort of surrealist writers and artists led (though that is probably too strong a word) by their still fulminating Pope, His Excommunicated Unholiness, André Breton I.

Pierre Lazareff, as we have seen, was the first Frenchman Saint-Exupéry encountered on disembarking, but when he heard that he had made the crossing with Jean Renoir and that he was proposing they lunch together that same day, Lazareff exploded: "What! With Renoir? Never." In Lisbon, to ingratiate himself with the authorities—it was, after all, Salazar's Portugal—the brilliant director of *La Grande Illusion* had gone out of his way to disclaim any lingering attachment to the radical convictions of his past. Far from harbouring any sympathy for the Communists, he wondered if it might not be possible to come to terms with Adolf Hitler, who was at least doing France a service in ending that Jewish domination which had caused him, Jean Renoir, and so many other Frenchmen endless vexations. Rash words which the Portuguese press was delighted to play up and for which Lazareff was not prepared to forgive him! Saint-Ex, typically enough, came to Renoir's defence—"But Pierre, he didn't mean it seriously!"— and he would not rest until he had dragged a contrite Renoir in to make a stammering apology to a still frowning Lazareff.

Another French newspaperman whom Saint-Exupéry saw soon after his arrival was Raoul de Roussy de Sales, who had been summarily fired from *Paris-Soir* shortly after the establishment of the Vichy régime. Unlike Lazareff, who did not speak a word of English, Sales spoke and wrote English as well as he did French, had married an American wife, and had been living in the United States since 1929. Saint-Ex had seen quite a bit of him in the immediate aftermath of his Guatemala accident, and he was now as eager to hear what Roussy de Sales thought of the present situation in the United States as the latter was to gather his impressions of France.

"He is all right physically," Roussy de Sales noted in his diary (later published under the title, *The Making of Yesterday*) after their first meeting, "but more like a bird than ever, a bird with a tendency to hide its head under a wing. He is, so to speak, weatherbeaten by the war. It is difficult to sum up what he tells me.

" 'The Germans have their hands full with their victory. They are like a man who finds a locomotive in his garden . . .'

" 'In Paris there is an impassable barrier between the Germans and the French. The Germans might well be invisible. No one looks at them, and this makes them very uncomfortable.'

" 'If the Vichy government did not exist, it would have to be invented. It is an ambiguity under cover of which something extremely important may develop . . .'

" 'National sentiment is being reborn. It had not existed since 1914. Everywhere signs of it are to be seen.'

"Yet" he went on, "Saint-Exupéry himself is at a loss. He does not know what to do. He is not sure that France will pull out of the rut, but because of the total nature of the defeat, a resurrection is possible. A halfway defeat, he feels, would have prolonged the decadence for a few more years, and in ten years there would have been nothing left to save. Since the country fell swiftly into collapse without any intermediate stages, recovery is conceivable. In what direction and in what form? He does not know. He admits that the key to the problem lies in the United States, but it is evident that Vichy minimizes American potentialities. They think in terms of production: seven hundred American airplanes a month in January compared with two or three thousand German machines. Laughable. But Vichy is on dangerous ground when it bases its calculations upon American lack of power.

"Speaking of the war, Saint-Exupéry said, 'We did not go on fighting because the whole army understood instinctively that it was no use.' He says that morale could have been restored, but the only result of that would have been the death of two million men, that is to say the extinction of the French race. Like all Frenchmen he evidently accepts the thesis of the irresistible superiority of the German war machine."

The day after Sales made this entry in his diary, it being Sunday (January 5, 1941) Saint-Exupéry and Jean Renoir found themselves in a strangely quiet Manhattan, wondering just what to do with themselves.

"I have an idea," Saint-Ex suggested. "Let's go surprise Bernard Lamotte —we were at the Beaux-Arts together."

Lamotte, who had not seen Saint-Exupéry since the early thirties when he had been raced around Paris in his Bugatti at speeds which had played havoc with his nervous system, had found himself a painter's studio on West 53rd Street in an old New York coach-house which had later served as a laundry. The three upper floors were his, including a terrace which he had made into a roof-garden bordered by potted shrubs.

On hearing the buzzer, he went to the mouth-piece and asked, "Who's there?" in English.

The answer came back in French: "*C'est moi.*" There was silence, and then, as though that weren't mystifying enough, the voice added: "I'm here with Jean."

"Who?" shouted Lamotte.

"It's me . . . Saint-Ex."

"What do you mean—Saint-Ex?"

"Why yes, it's me—Antoine."

"Well, come on up for Heaven's sake!" cried Lamotte, pressing the release button.

It was the first inkling he had of Saint-Exupéry's presence in New York. But an even greater surprise was in store for him; for right behind his friend "*Toi-Toine*" was a kind of double, a second "mastodon" almost as outsized and burly as himself—Jean Renoir.

"*Eh bien, mon vieux*, quite a place you have here!" said Saint-Ex, as he stepped out on to the roof-garden. It reminded him of his old place on the Place Vauban; only this was more bohemian, or as Lamotte put it, more "nomadic", more tramp-like. And indeed, with a five-hole concrete chimney protruding from one corner of the terrace, it could almost have been the deck of a river-barge, except that the bridge-house pavilion they had just stepped out of was not of wood but of glass.

"My friends call it *'le bocal'* "—the "goldfish bowl"—Lamotte explained. "But I wish you'd given me more warning . . . Let me see what I can offer you."

He went back to the ice-box, leaving Saint-Ex and Renoir to admire the view over the neighbouring red brick houses and their ventilating funnels.

When he returned it was with a bottle of chilled Byrrh—a syrupy *apéritif* like Dubonnet or Cinzano.

"I'm afraid this is all I've got," Lamotte apologized. He explained that he'd been designing advertisements for Byrrh, who were anxious to crash the American market, like Dubonnet. They had given him cases of the stuff and the ice-box was full of it.

"Oh, but this is fine," said Saint-Exupéry, who told him how he and Renoir had been reduced, on the *Siboney*, to a diet of biscuits and water after the soda and the Coca Cola had run out.

Soon the first bottle was empty, and Lamotte was dragging a second Byrrh from the refrigerator. It was getting on towards one. Time to be thinking about lunch.

"All I've got in the ice-box is a tired camembert cheese," said Lamotte with a long face. "And this is Sunday, with all the shops closed . . . But I have an idea. There's a nightclub downstairs. Let me see what I can wangle out of the owner."

While Saint-Ex and Renoir sat on the terrace happily enjoying the Byrrh, the skyscrapers, and the intermittent sunshine, Lamotte called on his friend Tony, the nightclub owner. "Do you have anything you could give us for lunch. I've just been landed with a couple of visitors."

"How many of you are there?" asked Tony.

"Two and a half," answered Lamotte. "Two big fellows and a small one—that is, me."

"How about the remains of a *veau marengo*?" asked Tony, opening the refrigerator.

"Splendid."

"With some sardines to start with?"

"Couldn't be better."

"You've got something to drink with it, I take it?"

"Byrrh," said Lamotte.

"Byrrh!" His friend Tony almost reeled. "*Veau marengo* with Byrrh! Why, you poor fellows!"

He was ready to rustle up some wine, but upstairs neither Saint-Ex nor

Renoir would hear of it. They were perfectly happy with their Byrrh, they told Lamotte, when he appeared with two cast-iron stew-pots full of marinated veal. They were put on the stove to be heated. A loaf of bread appeared, followed by butter and sardines. What a feast! It reminded Lamotte of those "lunches" chez Jarras, where they used to say: "Have some bread to put around your mustard."

By now the second bottle was empty. A third Byrrh was collared and brought back from the ice-box.

Sardines with Byrrh! *Veau marengo* with Byrrh! Imagine the look on Bob, the bartender's face at *La Coupole*, if he could but see them now! Or the Père Cazes, chez Lipp! "But *Messieurs*, why not a *pot au feu Saint-Raphaël* or a *choucroute alsacienne au Suze?*" A new gastronomic experience, all right! But none of the victims seemed desperately the worse for it, and even the unprecedented *Camembert au Byrrh* was consumed with surprising relish. They were on to the fourth bottle by now and no one was feeling any pain, far from it. Saint-Ex was bubbling with stories—about the boat-trip, about the war, about the old days at the Beaux-Arts when he was so poor and life was so rich.

By the time the lunch broke up late that afternoon, the sun was sinking fast. Their first New York Sunday had successfully been killed, and there was not a Byrrh left in Lamotte's ravaged ice-box.

"The French, you see, are like herrings," Jean Renoir explained, as he prepared to lumber down the stairs. "They travel in shoals."

\*   \*   \*

It cheered Saint-Ex to know that in New York there was a haven where he could forget his omnipresent cares for an hour or two of jovial fencing with Lamotte, who had lost nothing of his Parigot wit. But such "evasions" were brief and could not still the restless malaise within him. A few days later he was back again at Raoul de Roussy de Sales' apartment, looking gloomier than ever.

"He was exasperated and unhappy," as Roussy de Sales noted in his diary the next day. " 'I am sick and tired,' he said, 'of strolling through the streets of Marseille or New York. I want to do some bombing. What a beautiful sight a plane with eight machine guns can be . . . But what is the use of fighting for a negotiated Anglo-German peace? How would that help France?' He wanted mathematical formulas so that he can bet on a sure thing. He wants to fight, to risk his life, but he wants a sort of reasonable guarantee that it will not be for nothing. I am certainly not in a position to preach sacrifice to others since I have made none myself. I merely note this new French quirk which consists in counting the risks and sacrifices as one counts pennies. Pétain, Weygand and the others had mathematically estimated that the war was irretrievably lost and that England would not last fifteen days after French capitulation. They were wrong. All the French (including Saint-Exupéry) are eating their hearts out, conscious of the fact, without admitting it, that the war is not a question of arithmetic. If today we are the conquered and imprisoned the fault lies in our having approached the war from a mathematical point of view and our having forgotten that 'true realism' includes everything—even imprudence."

As *Pilote de Guerre* (*Flight to Arras*) was to make crystal clear, Saint-Exupéry was as much opposed to the triumph of brute matter, of facts and figures over faith, of Intelligence over Spirit as was Raoul de Roussy de Sales. But he had seen the war from close up and he knew that it takes more than faith to stop a shell or a bullet. Had Sales shown him this particular entry in his diary, Saint-Ex could have answered him with the very argument Sales had used a few weeks before in commenting on Anne Morrow Lindbergh's *The Wave of the Future*, which everyone was then discussing. "Anne Lindbergh invites her readers to go to sleep. Allow yourself to be carried away on the wave of the future, and you will be saved. As she does not explain clearly what the wave of the future is, we can hope for the best. The idea that this wave may be an eighty-ton tank does not seem to occur to some good people." Or as the Swiss writer Denis de Rougemont, who had also taken refuge in the New World, put it in his own journal: "Mrs. Lindbergh, with a discreet art and striking sincerity, urges her compatriots to let themselves be borne away by the 'wave of the future' which is apparently the totalitarian movement—Fascist, Nazi, or Soviet. I think she forgets that waves have never advanced anything, that they rise and fall on the spot, and that he who abandons himself to them emerges with nothing but a serious sea-sickness. And perhaps she forgets that England, in spite of everything, rules the waves, thus saving the future of the human race."

Probably no book published during this winter of 1940–1941 was more hotly debated in New York than Anne Morrow Lindbergh's. This came as a painful discovery to Saint-Exupéry, who had admired her previous work to the point of contributing a preface to the French edition of *Listen, the Wind!* It had been his intimate conviction almost from the opening day of the war that America was France's only hope and that the United States had to enter the conflict, as they had in 1917. But the state of opinion he encountered on his arrival in New York was as passionately confused and divided as it had been in France at the time of the Munich crisis. The Neutrality Act was still in force, and though Roosevelt had pulled off a masterly stroke in negotiating the exchange of 100 American destroyers against a 99 year lease of bases in the Caribbean, the dominant feeling towards Europe in the country was still: "A plague on both your houses!" Wendell Willkie, though he abhorred Nazism, had promised the previous autumn in his acceptance speech that America would "beat Hitler in her own way", without specifying just how this miracle was going to be achieved. Dorothy Thompson, who detested Hitler just as passionately, had been willing to declare that England could defeat Germany "through revolution", causing her friend Raoul de Roussy de Sales to remark in his diary: "The British want airplanes and destroyers; Dorothy offers them a revolution." Even that lucid observer Walter Lippmann could not resist indulging in the same wishful thinking; for a bare two months before Saint-Ex's arrival in New York he had brashly assured his *Today and Tomorrow* readers that never would it be necessary for the United States to send an expeditionary force to Europe.

To Saint-Exupéry all this was distressingly familiar. "They won't be able to keep it up, they haven't the oil!" his countrymen had said of the Germans at the start of the war. "*La route du fer est coupée!*" Paul Reynaud had exulted a little later at the (totally imaginary) idea that the German war machine was going to grind to a halt for lack of Swedish iron-ore. "Have you heard—the United States have entered the war! . . . Russian planes have bombed Berlin! . . ." Any fantasy would do for the haggard refugees he had seen, transmitting fleet-footed rumours which had raced up and down the clogged roads of the *débâcle* a hundred times faster than any of their stalled vehicles. America had been spared such a disaster, but the same psychological mechanisms were at work in the depths of her sub-conscious. Fig-leaves once again were being used to camouflage unpleasant facts, miracles invented to confront the awesome challenge of the morrow. It was the same make-belief world of the "phoney war", uprooted from Europe, like some continental castle, and promised a new and artificial life on the soil of the New World.

Uprooted too and flourishing here as virulently as weeds were the internecine squabbles of his countrymen which Saint-Ex had fondly hoped to leave behind him as he set sail from Lisbon. For the catastrophe of 1940, instead of forging a new unity, had simply led his compatriots to export their petty hatreds, habits, and resentments along with a few of their belongings. In Washington the new French Ambassador, Gaston Henry-Haye, had installed what Raoul de Roussy de Sales called a "kind of informal Gestapo" —made up of a former Versailles police commissioner and a man called Guichard, who had once headed the *Sûreté* (the French equivalent of the F.B.I.)—to report back to Vichy on what the French in America were up to. He was aided by a group of influential New York businessmen, led by a

Frenchman named Aubert, who were busy spreading the Vichy theory of history according to which the British and the Poles, not the Germans, were to blame for France's plight, in having involved her in a war for which she was not prepared. The Gaullists, who had gotten off to a sticky start after the Dakar fiasco of the previous September, had formed into a group called *France Forever*, whose chief financial backer was a French petroleum magnate from Philadelphia called Eugène Houdry. For a while this group was headed by Saint-Exupéry's friend, the aircraft manufacturer Michel Wibault, who, despite his exemplary pluck, was physically too crippled to exert the wholesome influence he might otherwise have done, and who was eventually supplanted by a duumvirate which included Henry Torrès (husband of the Suzanne Torrès whom Saint-Ex had ferried from Bordeaux to Oran in his "Noah's Ark"). Roussy de Sales refused to have anything to do with them— enough to persuade certain British diplomats in Washington that he was a Pétainist! De Gaulle, just to complicate matters, maintained a "personal representative": Jacques de Sieyès, one of his Saint-Cyr classmates who really felt more at home in banking and business than he did in this malodorous welter of intrigue. Even the Jewish community was divided into warring clans, represented on the one hand by André Maurois, who felt sympathy for the old Marshal and France's plight, and on the other by Henry Bernstein, who was soon calling Maurois a "traitor to the cause".

Saint-Exupéry inevitably found himself being solicited by both camps, but as he had no taste for intrigue and disliked politicians, he refused to be drawn into these fratricidal squabbles. He had not been in New York for a fortnight when his misgivings about the Free French movement received emphatic endorsement from a teacher of philosophy named Léon Wencelius. A French liaison officer who had served with the British Expeditionary Force in Brittany, Wencelius was one of a handful of French university teachers whom Paul Reynaud had sent to America in early May 1940 in a desperate attempt to try to talk the United States into entering the war. Before he could return from a hopeless mission, the Wehrmacht had made mincemeat of the French army; and rather than submit to the humiliations of the German occupation, Wencelius had elected to resume his teaching at Swarthmore College. At the conclusion of a lecture delivered at the French Institute in New York, where he had spoken of Saint-Exupéry's books, the historian Paul Hazard had come up to him and said: "If you want to meet Saint-Exupéry, go to the Hotel Ritz and you'll find him there. He's just arrived."

Wencelius followed Hazard's advice, and it was the beginning of a firm friendship, facilitated by the frequent trips into New York he was soon asked to make to teach philosophy at the Lycée Français

Saint-Ex took an instant liking to this anti-Nazi Alsatian whose love of philosophical speculation was anchored by a solid sense of down-to-earth realities. It was refreshing to meet a countryman who was in the United States under something like duress and who was waiting, like himself, for the first favourable moment for returning to the fray. If, Wencelius explained to him, he had not joined *France Forever*, it was for the simple reason that many of its earliest members were Frenchmen who had not waited for the *débâcle* of 1940 to flee their country. One of them, blithely disregarding his country's mobilization orders, had even managed to sail from Holland the day war was declared (September 3rd) and spent an enjoyably quiet year teaching at Hunter College before De Gaulle's proclamation of June 18th had roused him from his unimperilled slumbers. For Saint-Exupéry, as for Wencelius, the super-patriotic vehemence with which such "deserters" now beat the war-drums a good three thousand miles from the nearest front made it all too clear that Gaullism for some was a last refuge made for scoundrels.

From the moment he set foot in the New World Saint-Ex seems to have decided to let others throw the stones and raise the hue and cry for scapegoats; but as long as he was an exile he was going to keep his feelings about Pétain and Vichy to himself. But before this month of January 1941 was over he was forced to depart from this rule in his own defence. Word had reached New York that he had been appointed to the *Conseil National*—a Chamber of some 150 "Notables" which Pétain had recently established in Vichy—and this was enough to set tongues wagging. To dispel all misunderstandings on this score Saint-Exupéry drafted a formal statement saying that he had never been consulted over this "appointment", which for his part was unsolicited, unwanted, and refused. Raoul de Roussy de Sales obligingly translated the communiqué with the help of Lewis Galantière, and it was released to the press at an informal conference held in Saint-Ex's suite at the Ritz Carlton.

To add to the harassing uncertainties of the international situation and the lack of news from home there were the inevitable distractions—like the huge luncheon, attended by 1,500 guests, which was thrown for him in mid-January at the Hotel Astor by the American Booksellers Association and the *New York Herald Tribune*. Elmer Davis, of the Columbia Broadcasting System, who was presiding, presented him with the National Book Award for the Favourite Non-Fiction Work of 1939, and Saint-Exupéry in his reply recalled how news of the award had reached him one year earlier in the snows of Orconte.

There were also the unavoidable interviews, partly inspired by this event, which he had to grant to curious reporters. Robert Van Gelder, who called on him at the Ritz Carlton for the *New York Times Book Review*, was struck by his outlandish size. "His shoes" he wrote in the January 19th issue of that weekly, "are enormous, as large as Carnera's, but it is explained that his feet are not out size. 'He will go into a shoe store,' said his agent, Maximillian Becker, 'and the clerk will measure his foot'. 'You require' the clerk will say, 'size twelve'. So he will put a size twelve shoe on his foot and Saint-Ex will say, 'too small'. The clerk, looking surprised, produces a size thirteen shoe. 'Too small,' says Saint-Ex. The clerk, looking amazed, will produce a size fourteen. That is too small. And so it goes until the clerk, now miserable, had offered him almost the largest shoes in the store. 'Ah,' Saint-Ex will say, 'that is what I want. I like my feet to be comfortable.' "

Van Gelder was also struck by what he described as Saint-Exupéry's "concentration camp haircut"—though, he hastened to add in his article, he had not been taken prisoner by the Germans. His method of writing? Most laborious, Saint-Ex obligingly explained. It was like the work of a sculptor, of a diamond cutter, of a baker. First there was the impression he wished to communicate, though he could never be sure in advance if it was really worth the effort. This impression was conveyed in a first "inclusive" draft that had, somewhere buried inside it, the core of the impression. This first draft was like a crude block of stone or a shapeless lump of dough. "I work at the dough, kneading it over and over," he went on. "Bit by bit the material develops resistance—and then I know I have something to work on." If, he added, he wrote of the desert or of flying, it was because "one must lean on the concrete to reach the abstract".

Before leaving, Robert Van Gelder was shown some manuscript pages covered with fine lines of writing, much of it painstakingly crossed out, with one word standing where there had been a hundred words before, one sentence subsisting from the obliterated ruins of a page. A first draft? Oh, by no means: this was already the third, or maybe even the fourth. It was a lot of work. The interviewer could well believe it. "I work long hours and with great concentration," Saint-Ex explained. That is, when he got going. For, he added with a disarming smile, the hardest thing was getting started.

It was indeed. As in Moscow in 1935 and in Cairo in 1936, it was practically necessary in the end to lock him up in a room to get Saint-Exupéry to write. For such, it soon transpired, was his publishers' fixed intention. Saint-Ex may have fancied he was coming over for a three or four week stay, but his guardian angels on the spot had other ideas on the subject. They had not cabled an invitation and then arranged for his visa and crossing for nothing: they wanted a book on the war, and understandably enough—publishers being what they are (always in a hurry)—they wanted it soon.

To make him feel at home they found him a magnificent penthouse on the twenty-third floor of a building at 240 Central Park South. It was even higher than Maurice Maeterlinck's apartment on the twenty-second floor, and the view from its broad picture window and terrace over the trees of the park put Bernard Lamotte's "goldfish bowl" to shame. As an additional encouragement Saint-Ex was given a secretary to type up what he spent the long sleepless nights composing. But skilled though she was in French, she had frequent trouble decyphering his small and increasingly erratic handwriting.

The solution to this particular problem was hit upon by sheer accident. As he had been wont to do in Paris with his friends, Saint-Ex would think nothing of ringing up Bernard Lamotte at one, two, or three o'clock in the morning, to say: "Hello, Bernard, It's me, Saint-Ex. What are you doing?" As though the last thing anyone should be doing at that hour was to be in bed.

"I'm sleeping," Lamotte would answer. "Theoretically, at any rate."

"Ah, am I waking you?"

"Well, I'm awake now."

"Oh." A pause would follow, and then would come an almost childlike plea. "You wouldn't like me to read you a couple of pages? I'd like to hear what you think of them."

He would read the pages, and Lamotte, who like most painters was an early riser, living by the sun rather than by the moon or the stars, would answer, "fine," or "very good."

"O.K." Saint-Ex would say, "Now sleep."

"I'm wide awake," Lamotte would answer, just to nettle him. "But any way, come by tomorrow and have lunch. I've got some fillets of herring. Do you like them?"

"Do I like them!"

"And we'll grill a steak in the fireplace—"

"I'll be there." Saint-Ex would hang up, his mouth already watering.

One day, on turning up for one of these herring lunches, Saint-Ex said: "Look, *mon vieux*, I'd like you to come with me. I need an interpreter." This too was the source of endless fencing between them; for Saint-Exupéry stubbornly refused to learn a word of English. "All you need know is one word," he explained more than once to Wencelius, astonished to learn that "Hep!" was a universal sesame for all linguistic contingencies. Not being a critical Alsatian, Lamotte could be more easily impressed by the sudden burst of Fribourgeois German with which Saint-Ex would let go in the evident belief that it would shake the locals into a state of semi-comprehension.

"You've lost your bearings," Lamotte would remind him. "We're in America here."

"*Toi, fous-moi la paix!*" (Go jump in the lake!) was the usual rejoinder.

"I speak little," Lamotte would upbraid him, "but at least it's something."

"Exactly," Saint Ex now said. "You have to come with me. Listen, I was walking past a shop today. Inside were organs."

"What?"

"Yes. I want to buy an organ."

"I didn't know you were a musician."

"*Toi, fous-moi la paix!* . . . I want to buy an organ."

"All right," said Lamotte, "we'll go buy an organ. But begin by eating your herrings."

"He wants to buy an organ," interposed Lamotte's uncle, who was staying with him at that moment. "Why stand in his way? He's got a right to buy one if he wants."

It was two against one. Lamotte was forced to acquiesce.

The herrings consumed, Saint-Ex could not wait to drag Lamotte over to his music shop. It was located on 57th Street, a high class establishment proudly advertised as "Aeolian Organ".

The vendor who walked up to them with an ingratiating smile was equally high class.

"May I help you?"

"Yes," said Lamotte. "This gentleman would like to buy an organ."

The vendor looked Saint-Exupéry up and down with evident disbelief. For some reason he did not look like the organ buying type.

"Yes," went on Lamotte, "he wants to buy that organ." He pointed towards the back of the store at an organ large enough to fill a small church.

"That one?" said the salesman, doubting his ears. "You mean the big one?"

"Yes," nodded Lamotte.

Without waiting, Saint-Ex had gone ahead and sat down at the keyboard. He opened the lid and began pulling out stops and pressing buttons.

"Now just a moment," said the vendor, walking over. "This isn't a toy."

It was obvious enough that Saint-Ex had not a clue as to how to make it work. But he was as intent as ever on having it.

"Look," said Lamotte, "I think we're off to a bad start and are going to get ourselves flung out of here".

"But tell him I'll pay for it," Saint-Exupéry insisted.

"We'd better begin by asking the price." Lamotte turned to the vendor. "How much is it—that organ there?"

"Twelve thousand dollars," was the stiff reply.

"Twelve thousand dollars," Lamotte translated. "How do you like that?"

"Well, and what of it?"

"You mean, you've got twelve thousand dollars to burn?"

"I'll pay," insisted Saint-Ex. "But I want to play it first."

"What would you like to hear?" volunteered the salesman, deciding it was high time to rescue the threatened merchandise. "Bach?... Handel?..."

Bach was fine, but Lamotte continued to remonstrate.

"But just where are you going to put it?"

"In my apartment."

"What!" cried Lamotte. "With all those pipes?"

Saint-Ex looked at the pipes, which stretched right up to the ceiling, a tall ceiling at that. For some reason the problem of the pipes hadn't occurred to him. He looked downcast. Suddenly his dream had collapsed and he was like a disappointed little boy.

"Yes, I suppose you're right. I haven't the room."

The salesman, realizing the pointlessness of his continuing for such an audience, closed the lid over the keyboard. They turned to leave, but Saint-Ex's eye lit on a recording machine. One had only to switch it on and the diamond point engraved the record then and there.

"How much is this thing worth?" he asked, his eyes brightening. "Listen, I have an idea. I could write my book on this. I mean by dictating. My book, *Le Caïd.*" (The title he had provisionally chosen for the later *Citadelle.*)

Lamotte turned to the salesman. "How much is this thing?"

"700 dollars," replied the salesman, in a tone of deep disgust. He had wasted enough time on these two jokers already.

"And the records?" asked Saint-Exupéry.

"Thirty dollars apiece," came the curt answer.

"All right," said Saint-Ex. "Tell him I'm taking it."

"The gentleman is interested," Lamotte translated. "He would like to take it."

"I said, Sir, SEVEN HUNDRED DOLLARS!"

Lamotte repeated the figure.

"All right," nodded Saint-Ex. He dug into his pocket and pulled out a thick wad of notes. Hundred dollar bills. He began counting them—one, two, three, . . . five, six, seven. He handed them to the vendor, whose eyes seemed about to leap from their sockets.

"What's the matter?" asked Saint-Ex. "You did say 700, didn't you? Ask him to wrap it up."

The salesman seemed suddenly nervous. "We could have it delivered," he suggested.

"This is Monsieur de Saint-Exupéry," Lamotte explained. But it was as though he had said, "This is Mr. Smith," or "This is Monsieur Dupain." The name meant nothing to the salesman, who seemed more inclined to think they had just looted a bank.

"What's he saying?" asked Saint-Ex.

"He suggests it be delivered."

"Tell him to wrap it up. I'll take it away myself."

Lamotte transmitted the message, and the vendor disappeared into a rear office. The minutes passed. They were doubtless telephoning around to find out what banks had been robbed that morning and if the numbers on these banknotes tallied. Apparently they didn't, for the salesman finally returned, full of smiles and bows.

Saint-Exupéry was allowed to walk out of the store with his new "baby" under his arm. Lamotte accompanied them back to the twenty-third floor penthouse. Triumphantly Saint-Ex set his new toy down on his round dining-room table, the light polished surface of which had been so scarred by the burning cigarettes he carelessly poised on the rims of his ash-trays that it was as mottled as a leopard skin.

"Just think—that's you!" cried Saint-Ex, after recording Lamotte's voice.

"Yes," said Lamotte, "and all you'll have to do now when you want to know what I think of what you've written at three o'clock in the morning is turn on that machine."

\*   \*   \*

The new toy afforded Saint-Ex endless delight and his restless imagination a fertile field for ingenious experimentation. "He would record a Mozart symphony broadcast by Toscanini and then, on the same disc, introduce readings by himself and his friends, of French classical verse scanned to accord with the beat of the music," his translator Lewis Galantière was later to recall. "Hervé Alphand"—still the French Embassy's Commercial Attaché, though he resigned shortly afterwards—"would do his celebrated imitation of a dialogue between the doddering Pétain and a certain senile general descended from the Marquis de La Fayette".

Saint-Exupéry, who would usually have his meals brought up from the restaurant down below, was seldom without a guest or two to share his luncheons or dinners; and rare was the evening when he went out that did not end with his putting on a spell-binding display of card tricks. He was as mysterious as ever about the sources of his wizardry, simply repeating what he had so often said to Léon Werth or Georges Pélissier: "*Je suis le maître de mon cérémonial.*" (I am the master of my ceremonial.)

He needed these innocent divertissements to maintain a *joie de vivre* which was sorely tried by the inner anguish he felt over his country's plight, the deplorable dissensions among French émigrés in New York, and the depressing news from abroad. Saint-Ex was wholeheartedly in sympathy

with the charitable efforts made by Anne Morgan, head of the Coordinating
Council of the French Relief Societies, and by the Quakers to ship foodstuffs
to France. He was particularly incensed at the spectacle of Henry Bernstein
and Eve Curie living it up in de luxe quarters at the Waldorf Astoria, while
passionately holding forth on the "iniquity" of the United States sending
food to France and North Africa. Their argument was that the Americans, in
doing so, were aiding Hitler and undermining the British blockade of the
continent, whereas what concerned Saint-Exupéry, and passionately, was
the extra hardships this might involve for his country. The argument might
have had some justification if, like Simone Weil, they had been willing to
starve themselves to prove the purity of their motives, but coming from exiles
who were not exactly in a sacrificial mood it was positively grotesque. As
Professor Louis Rougier, who had sought to improve relations between
Vichy and London before continuing on to New York, was later to describe
it: "The obesities of Fifth Avenue pitilessly condemned the empty stomachs
of the mother-country. The battle of the resistance in New York manifested
itself above all in a campaign of banquets. Those who were fasting in France
could thus feast by proxy in the United States . . . People living in silk and
honey on the proceeds of propaganda allowances which were not always of
French origin and who had prudently taken out their first citizenship papers
thus managed to convince themselves that they had an option on the France
of tomorrow because they alone had not capitulated. They were intent on
casting aspersions on their unfortunate brethren who had neither planes nor
boats nor visas for leaving France, so that they alone might appear unsullied
to the world."

April, in particular, was a bleak month—with the Germans invading
Yugoslavia and then driving Wavell's British troops, which had come to
the rescue, out of Greece. Charles Lindbergh by this time was openly
proclaiming that the war was lost for Britain and that the New World's
salvation could only be found in a policy of "America First". The United
States' entry into the war seemed remoter than ever, manoeuvre as Roosevelt
might to get around the crippling provisions of the Neutrality Act. What, in
these circumstances, was the use of writing up his recent experiences of the
war? None, so far as Saint-Exupéry could see. He made a few fitful efforts
which only succeeded in depressing him, preferring to do what he had done
at Agay—pour out his innermost thoughts and feelings into his "posthumous
work" (as he jokingly called it) *Citadelle.*

As often as not he was irritable, not to say irascible. He took out his ill
humour on his friends, beginning with Roger Beaucaire, who reached New
York in March 1941 and whose stoic fortitude, under these assaults, soon
caused him to be nicknamed Saint-Ex's "punching-ball". Pierre de Lanux,

who had sailed back to Le Havre with him on the *Ile de France* in August 1939 and who often lunched with him at 240 Central Park South, later wrote: "He wasn't satisfied with being right. He had to prove the other fellow wrong. Was it a lack of certainty which led him to be carried away by the violence of his affirmations (or negations)? Sometimes what he massacred was a mere nothing, an argument which hadn't even been formulated or which he thought up simply to annihilate." At such moments Saint-Ex reminded Lanux of a "malevolent bull, but full of humour". For his fits of repentance were as impulsive and disarming as were his moody silences, his impassioned outbursts, and embittered truculence. One evening he had a violent argument with Lewis Galantière, who lost his temper and called him names before going home feeling most unhappy about their quarrel. But what was Galantière's delighted surprise the next morning to find a seventeen page letter waiting for him! Just as he had done years before after his argument with the Saussine sisters over Pirandello, Saint-Ex had spent part of the night summing up his arguments, then walked over and slipped the lengthy missive under Galantière's door. "To write that letter and bring it to my door in the early morning hours was his way of turning the other cheek."

Such outbursts were the symptoms of an inner malaise which was exacerbated by the slanderous rumours which were soon being woven about him. In May his friend Raoul de Roussy de Sales, deciding that a Frenchman had to take a stand one way or the other, came out with a ringing anti-Vichy statement which he had published by Herbert Agar's group, *Fight for Freedom*. But Saint-Exupéry refused to follow his example. He had decided not to criticize his countrymen in public, no matter what his private sentiments might be. This set Gaullist tongues wagging in a way which, to quote Lewis Galantière again, was "really too poisonous. 'Saint-Exupéry? I saw him yesterday in Washington, lunching with Chautemps, who is here doing a job for Vichy.' Not only had Saint-Exupéry never lunched with Chautemps, he had never talked to the man. 'Saint-Exupéry? He's a Vichy agent, you know. He's here buying planes for Vichy'." And so on it went.

June, for the first time in almost half a year, brought some scraps of good news to relieve the gloom of the preceding months. In an unexpectedly forthright statement issued on the 13th Cordell Hull, the Secretary of State, called upon the French people to revolt against Darlan and Laval, and a day or two later Roosevelt ordered the closing of all German consulates as well as their Information Library and Tourist Office, and the freezing of Italian and German funds in the United States. Though it was only a timid first step, there was no mistaking its direction. Jacques de Sièyes having begun to lose favour with De Gaulle, René Pleven now turned up in New York on a mission to bring some kind of order out of the backbiting chaos in Gaullist ranks. This too was an encouraging sign, prompting Saint-Ex to remark to his friend Beaucaire: "For once De Gaulle has sent someone decent over to clean up the shop here." But the most heartening development by far, overshadowing everything else in its importance, was Hitler's declaration of war on Russia on the 22nd of this same month. The almost unmitigated pessimism he had suffered from since his arrival in New York now gave way to a mild optimism; and as Saint-Ex remarked to Pierre Lazareff that day: "This is the end of the beginning."

It was also the end of the doubts and hesitations which had hampered his literary efforts for so long. Now that Russia was reeling under the shock in her turn, it made sense to convey to readers what it had meant for France. *Citadelle* was laid aside and work on his war book, *Pilote de Guerre*, was begun in earnest. As usual, he worked at night, dressed like Balzac in a dressing-gown and kept awake by a generous pot of coffee which he brewed before sitting down to work at his butt-scarred dining-room table—his desk, as Galantière has noted, serving "merely as a catchall in which his cheque-book could never be found. Now and then he would write in an all-night restaurant, where having eaten a dish of raw chopped beef drowned in olive oil and crusted with pepper, he was likely to scribble from two in the morning until dawn. When he had written himself stiff, he would stretch out at home on a sofa under a lamp, take up the mouthpiece of a dictaphone, and record his copy, revising as he went along. Then, towards seven or eight o'clock in the morning, he would go to bed. The secretary would come in at nine and type while he slept. Often, when friends arrived for lunch at one o'clock, they would ring and pound for twenty minutes before he woke up and let them in." For once submerged in the dream-depths of his sleep, almost nothing could awake him—short of dynamite or shellbursts.

While Bernard Lamotte was recruited to illustrate his new book, Lewis Galantière was put to work translating what came to be *Flight to Arras*. Both, like Yvonne Michel, were deluged by middle of the night telephone calls requesting their reactions to his tortured lucubrations. "At two o'clock in the morning,"—this is Galantière's recollection—"under the half-mocking and half-furious stare of my wife, understanding not a word of what the rapid muffled voice was reciting into the telephone—for I was of course more than half asleep—I would nod my head, interject an appropriate 'Ah!' or 'That's good, that is!' while I sought in vain to catch at the thread of his discourse; and upon his insistent demand, when he was through, that I tell him what I thought, I would repeat mechanically and hypocritically, 'Magnificent! Magnificent!' Generally the session ended with a long silence in which I seemed to hear Saint-Exupéry turning his ideas over in his mind, rhen a sudden 'Good! Sorry to disturb you. Good night,' and he would hang up."

\*     \*     \*

It was partly to get away from the poisoned atmosphere of New York that Saint-Exupéry decided a few weeks later to accept Jean Renoir's invitation to join him in Hollywood. During their Atlantic crossing they had discussed the possibility of making a film out of his South American experiences, and the idea had appealed to Saint-Exupéry immensely. Since *Anne-Marie* he had tried his hand twice at writing new scenarios, though with less success.

In Hollywood Jean Renoir had rented a large house, on the second floor of which Saint-Exupéry was given a room to sleep and work in. Their lives were totally dissimilar: for Saint-Ex, as usual, worked through the night, while Renoir, who was filming *Swamp Water*, had to leave for the studios early in the morning. Between 8 and 8.30, while Renoir was readying himself a breakfast of bacon and eggs, Saint-Ex would come downstairs for his "supper". The one passion they shared in common was for olive oil, a bottle of which Saint-Ex had always kept by his plate when lunching at the Place Vauban or the Rue Michel-Ange. Here it was kept in the ice-box to thicken, and then spread like butter on slabs of toasted bread. Some mornings Saint-Exupéry would go straight back up to his room, where he lay down and slept into the late afternoon. On others he would accompany Renoir to the studios before coming home to turn in. It enabled them to discuss the film they had projected, which would have been built around the first pioneering efforts to overfly the Andes (Mermoz' and Guillaumet's adventures), with an interlude like the Concordia episode thrown in to add a soft, romantic note. But nothing came of these ideas, which were overtaken by the war and Hollywood's demand for more topical subjects.

Saint-Ex's stay on the West Coast would have been happier had he not been plagued by sharp pains in the lower abdomen. Dr. Jean-Louis Lapeyre, the only French doctor in Los Angeles, was summoned to the house, where he found Saint-Ex "in bed in the midst of a magnificent welter of manuscripts, newspapers, and dictaphone recordings. I was lucky enough", he later recalled, "to listen to him read me a few recently completed passages of his book"—*Pilote de Guerre*—"on which he used to work energetically right through each night". Lapeyre sent him to see a specialist, Dr. Elmer Belt, who ran a surgical clinic. Their first encounter was comic; for in the words of his wife, Mrs. Ruth Belt, the doctor's "slight knowledge of French was about equal to Saint-Ex's familiarity with English. Of Spanish each had a smattering of words and phrases but these proved totally inadequate when it came to medical terms. Suddenly Saint-Ex strode across Dr. Belt's consultation room and picking up the hand phone quickly dialed with his big expressive hands. A minute's pause and then he burst into a rippling torrent of French. It ended abruptly and he reached over the desk and pushed the phone into Dr. Belt's hand with a broad grin. A secretary at the other end translated his questions into English and then as Dr. Belt finished the replies he handed the phone back again to Saint-Ex. This went on for several rounds. The subject matter was serious enough but the unusual technique caused both of them to chuckle."

It was finally decided that Saint-Exupéry would have to undergo an operation. He was hospitalized in the surgeon's clinic, and it was an amusing sight to see him, whenever Dr. Belt appeared, reaching for the telephone on his night-table and hurriedly dialing his translator. One day he received a surprise visit from Annabella, the actress who had so charmingly played the part of Anne-Marie and who was now the wife of Tyrone Power. She found Saint-Ex alone, with no flowers to cheer him in his monk-like cell and with nothing but a small book beside him—a copy of Hans Christian Andersen's *Fairy Tales*. "Let me tell you one I've just read," said Saint-Ex, delighted to entertain such a captivating audience. But before he was half-way through the tale, she stopped him, saying, "Now I'll finish it." To his astonishment she did; for she knew all of them by heart!

This was the start of a fervent friendship which brought him often thereafter to Tyrone Power's house. Finally released from the clinic, he went to live in a small apartment in central Los Angeles, where Annabella would find him lying on a couch, trying to recover from the effect of sulpha drugs. While she sat on the floor eating olives, he would reminisce about past experiences in the air and discourse on Life, men, and God. Though both were exiles, they never discussed politics.

His convalescence over, Saint-Exupéry moved into the house which his friend Pierre Lazareff had rented on Fountain Avenue, where he finished *Pilote de Guerre*. In November he returned to New York, followed not long after by his affable host. In Manhattan they saw each other almost daily. On December 7th Saint-Ex had invited Lazareff to join him in his penthouse apartment for Sunday lunch (ordered up from the cafeteria below). With stark drama the radio announced the Japanese attack on Pearl Harbor. Saint-Ex stood for a long moment stunned, without saying a word. Then, his eyes brimming with tears, he seized Lazareff by the arm and said: "In June, when Germany invaded Russia, I said to you: 'It's the end of the beginning.' Now I tell you: 'It's the beginning of the end.' The Americans are obliged to enter the war immediately and we're going to win."

He was right, though for reasons he could hardly have suspected. For the next four days he clung to the radio, like almost everyone else in the United States, waiting to hear the sequel. The Neutrality Act had been abolished only three weeks before by a 15 vote majority in the House of Representatives, and while both Houses of Congress were agreed to declare war on Japan, there was not the same feeling about the other members of the Axis. Then, on December 11th, came the news that both Germany and Italy had done Roosevelt the immense service of declaring war on the United States.

Beaucaire was astounded. "How can Hitler have committed such a blunder?" he kept repeating.

To which Saint-Exupéry, who was no less elated, replied: "There must have been some prior agreement among them about which we know nothing."

The beginning of the end it might well be, but the end at this point seemed as distant as ever—with the Japanese invading Java, sinking British battleships in the South China seas, overrunning Malaya and Singapore, and cornering a General MacArthur, who had carelessly let his air force be wiped out the first day of hostilities despite the warning of Pearl Harbor. Christmas that year was enlivened by the "tempest in a tea-cup" stirred up by De Gaulle's "liberation" of Saint-Pierre and Miquelon—a Lilliputian extravaganza which confirmed Saint-Exupéry in his distrust for "that man who claims to be France". His friend Raoul de Roussy de Sales had by now reached pretty much the same conclusion; for though he had let himself be talked into joining the six-man committee which was formed to oversee the Gaullist movement in New York, by October 1941 he was writing in his diary: "I had one conversation with Pleven which showed me that the abyss between us is so great that one cannot even speak of misunderstanding. We do not use the same language and that is all. I said to him, 'I am not a de Gaullist and I will probably never be one'."

In January 1942 Henri de Kerillis, one of the three non-Communist deputies who had had the courage to vote against the Munich accords, the noted woman journalist Geneviève Tabouis, and Michel Pobers joined forces to launch a French weekly entitled *Pour la Victoire*. Georges Bernanos, living in exile in Brazil, became one of its regular contributors, as did Jacques Maritain, Jules Romains, and other French émigrés, but not, significantly enough, Saint-Exupéry. His own message was contained in the book he had laboured over the previous year, first in New York and then in California, and which was finally published in February. Serialized in three successive issues of *The Atlantic Monthly*, the American version which Galantière had prepared was entitled *Flight to Arras*; the French original, simultaneously published (with Reynal and Hitchcock's backing) by the

Editions de la Maison Française, was entitled *Pilote de Guerre*. Like *Wind, Sand, and Stars, Flight to Arras* was made a Book of the Month Club selection and became a best-seller overnight.

A number of books had already been published on the subject of the *débâcle*, but none of them—not even Jacques Maritain's *A Travers le Désastre*—had made much impact on the American imagination or done much to affect the widely held feeling that France was done for, once and for all. If Saint-Exupéry's surpassed them all in a single bound, it was not only because of the elegance of the style, but also because this was the work of a participant in the struggle. The American reader, as Pierre de Lanux was later to write, was at last brought face to face with Frenchmen who had fought and suffered the torments of the defeat, "who had carried on their job to the end, for the honour of their group, of the country, and of themselves—without this overly solemn word ever being uttered between them". Or as Edward Weeks, editor of the *Atlantic*, commented in his brief review of the book his magazine had serialized: "The credo of a fighting man and the story of a great aviator in action, this narrative and Churchill's speeches stand as the best answer the democracies have yet found to *Mein Kampf*."

In its construction *Pilote de Guerre* was anything but a literal recapitulation of the flight Saint-Exupéry had undertaken on May 23, 1940 with Lieutenant Jean Dutertre (observer) and Sergeant André Mot (gunner and radio-operator). That had been a low altitude mission from start to finish, whereas *Flight to Arras* was the narrative of a high altitude reconnaissance which ends in a low altitude return. The composite experience of several months was thus telescoped into a single flight, symbolic of them all, and the hardships of high altitude flying conveyed to the reader with dramatic density. Interwoven through the book were glimpses of their life at the Command Post—Saint-Ex challenging Lieutenant Pierre Lacordaire to chess, Major Alias subjecting returning crews to what they wryly termed "the torture" (or "debriefing sessions", in contemporary air-force parlance). The farm-house at Orconte was similarly evoked, like the first infant recollections of Paula, the Tyrolean governess, and the dark vestibule at Saint-Maurice, not for the sake of picturesqueness, which Saint-Exupéry abhorred, but to contrast the "sovereign protection" of a life which is well rooted with the deracinated confusion of the *débâcle*. Thus, in describing the *boudin*, or blood sausage, which the farmer had specially prepared for the feast to which Israël, Gavoille and he were invited, Saint-Exupéry was careful to add: "The niece's face grew smooth over its mysterious depth. The farmer's wife sighed, looked about her, and was silent. The farmer, his mind on the morrow, sat wrapped in his earthy wisdom. Beneath the silence of all three there lay an inner wealth similar to a village's—and similarly threatened."

For the central theme or preoccupation of *Pilote de Guerre* was hardly different from that of *Terre des Hommes*: the solidarity which binds human beings together and to the world they inhabit—the farmer to his earth and village, the soldier to his army, the citizen to his country. "Man is but a knot of relationships," Saint-Exupéry reflects, while soaring over his stricken homeland at a height of 30,000 feet, "and now my links are almost value-less". Or, as he adds a little further on, "Civilization is a heritage of beliefs, customs, and knowledge slowly acquired over the centuries, sometimes difficult to justify by logic, but which justify themselves—like paths leading somewhere—since they open an inner realm to man". Again, watching the panic that has overtaken a village where peasants and shopkeepers have piled what they can of their belongings on to tractors, horse-carts, and old jalopes which in some cases they hardly know how to drive, the author feels "a hollow uneasiness at the thought that all these workers and humble folk with such well defined functions and such diverse and precious qualities will by evening have been reduced to parasites and vermin. They will spread over the countryside and devour it. . . . Torn from their environment, their work, their duties, they had lost all significance." Like their uniformed cousins and brothers—"There is no longer an army. There are only men". Men whom the cataclysm has transformed into *"chômeurs de guerre"*—the unemployed, or rather the unemployables, of a war which had engulfed them as remorselessly as that callous economic tide which Saint-Exupéry had seen roll trainloads of uncomprehending miners back to the poverty of their Polish homeland. "This France which is crumbling is no more than a deluge of faceless pieces," he summed up the drama in the final pages. "A cathedral is more than a sum of stones. It is geometry and architecture." For if his country had crumbled so swiftly in 1940, it was not simply due to the baseness and incapacity of its political and military leadership. The baseness and incapacity were merely symptoms of a deeper ill.

The truth, as Saint-Exupéry knew, was complex and contradictory, and he made no attempt to conceal what might be called the defeatist strain in his thinking. "The armaments race could not possibly be won. We were forty million agriculturists confronted by eighty million industrialists! Against the enemy we could pit one man against every three of his. One plane against every ten or twenty; and after Dunkirk, one tank against every hundred." A scorched earth policy could work in Russia, a vast land with a population more than double Germany's, but in France it made no sense. It simply meant consigning to the scrap-heap of war what it had required the painstaking labour of centuries to produce.

Thus France, in going to war, was doomed to be defeated. But did this mean that the war should have been avoided at all cost? Saint-Ex's answer was unequivocal: as clear and unequivocal as that of Georges Bernanos, who had chosen the road of exile, or of Henri de Kerillis, who had voted down the Munich accords. "France" he wrote, "must be judged by her consent to sacrifice. France accepted the war against the truth of the logicians. They said to us: 'There are eighty million Germans. We cannot in one year produce the forty million Frenchmen who are lacking. We cannot change our wheat-fields into coal-mines. We cannot hope for the help of the United States . . . What shame is there in having a land which produces more wheat than machines, and where one is outnumbered, two to one? Why should the burden of shame fall on us rather than the world?' They were right. War, for us, meant disaster. But should France, to spare herself defeat, have avoided war? I do not think so. France, instinctively, felt the same—since such warnings did not keep her from going to war. Spirit overcame Intelligence."

"Life" Saint-Exupéry went on, "always cracks old formulas. The defeat, notwithstanding its hideous scars, may prove to be the only road towards resurrection. I know well that to create a tree the seed is condemned to rot. The first act of resistance, if it comes too late, is always a losing battle. But it is the awakening of the resistance."

It was the argument he had propounded to Raoul de Roussy de Sales during their first New York encounters, and which had left the latter somewhat baffled. It was of course an exaggeration to depict France as a nation of "forty million agriculturists" and Germany an empire of "eighty million industrialists": an argument which could by implication exonerate the French of any deep-rooted blame for the catastrophe which had overtaken them. But it was nonetheless true, as Saint-Exupéry noted further on, that if the French were fighting for democracy, then "we are partners with the Democracies. Let them then fight with us! But the most powerful, the only one which could have saved us, refused yesterday and is still holding back today."

This was the sober truth when these words were written—in the autumn of 1941—but it had ceased to be the truth when *Flight to Arras* was finally published, some ten weeks after Pearl Harbour. Not that this really mattered. For what Saint-Exupéry was ultimately concerned with, in the composition of this book, was not a sterile post-mortem of words like "defeat" or "victory". "I know little how to use these formulas—there are victories which exalt, others which degrade." Logically, his argument that France was right in going to war in 1939 should have made him a Gaullist, but characteristically, it did not: simply because, as he expressed it further on, "The necessities are contradictory. France's spiritual heritage must be saved, without which the race will be deprived of its genius. The race must be saved without which the heritage will be lost. The logicians, lacking a language capable of conciliating these two salvations, will be tempted to sacrifice either the soul or the body."

The Pétainists, in this scheme of things, were those who had sued for peace to save France's body (that is, her population). The Gaullists were those who were battling to save her soul. Both to a certain extent were right; but to the extent that they sought to make of their partial truth a whole, both of them were wrong. For the truth, the bitter and fundamental truth, was simple: "We have all been defeated. I have been defeated. Hochedé has been defeated . . ." And precisely for this reason Saint-Exupéry could not, as he wrote, be "satisfied with polemical truths. What point is there in accusing individuals?" What indeed? "They are only ways and means. I can no longer blame the freezing up of machine-guns on the negligence of bureaucrats, nor the absence at our side of friendly peoples by their selfishness. A defeat, to be sure, expresses itself through individual failings. But a civilization moulds men. If the one I belong to is threatened by the failings of individuals, I have the right to wonder why it has not moulded them into something else.

"A civilization, like a religion," he went on, "condemns itself if it complains of the flabbiness of the faithful. Its duty is to exalt them. Likewise, if it complains of the hatred of the unbelievers, its duty is to convert them. Yet mine, which once inflamed the apostles, curbed the violent, and freed captive peoples, no longer knows how to exalt or to convert. If I wish to lay bare the root causes of my defeat, if my ambition is to live again, I must first rediscover the ferment I have lost."

Seven months later, when *Flight to Arras* was published in England, Philip Toynbee, writing in *The New Statesman and Nation*, complained that "in the flood of words which end the book I could discover only a confused Whitmanism, an affirmation of the value of the individual, far too repetitive to be effective". In fact, though the criticism was well taken, the final pages owed nothing to Whitman. The ferment Saint-Exupéry had lost was the one he had once known in the Aéropostale; it was the faith which had inspired Pierre Latécoère to say to Didier Daurat, in defiance of the "logicians": "My calculations confirm the opinion of the specialists: our idea is unachievable. There's only one thing left for us to do—achieve it." It was the faith he had hoped to find in Soviet Russia and again in Germany, but the inhumanity of which had revolted him. In each of these countries the tyranny of the mass over the individual had resulted in the tyranny of one individual over the mass. But the mere absence of this tyranny, as the case of France had demonstrated, provided no answer—if the result was a will-less aggregate of individual egotisms, too divided by their personal self-centredness and a paralytic bureaucratic superstructure to be capable of purposeful collective action. And if this bureaucratic superstructure was so dangerous, it was precisely because it designed to speak of "the rights of the Collectivity. We have seen the surreptitious onset of an ethos of the Collective which neglects Man. This ethos explains quite clearly why the individual must sacrifice himself to the Community. It no longer explains, without resort to linguistic artifices, why the Community has a duty to sacrifice itself for one sole man. Why it is equitable for a thousand to die to save one being from the prison of injustice. We still recall it, but we are forgetting it bit by bit. And yet it is in this principle, which distinguishes us so clearly from the termite-heap, that our greatness resides.

"For want of an effective principle we have slipped from Mankind—based on the notion of Man—towards this termite-heap which reposes on the sum-total of individuals. What did we have to oppose to the religions of State and Mass? What had become of our great image of Man born of God? It was scarcely discernible any more through a vocabulary emptied of its substance . . . In France we came near to dying of Intelligence without substance."

The thought, like the tone, was unmistakably exalted—and remarkably similar in certain respects to *L'Enracinement*, which another great French mystic, Simone Weil, had begun writing at about the same time. But the exalted texture of Saint-Exupéry's phraseology—with Man, with a capital M contrasted to man, in lower case (to use the language of type-setters)—marred the clarity of the message. The informal annotations in his note-books give us a clearer idea of just where his thought was headed. The Third Republic, in setting up the lycée system, had made a fetish of know-ledge-gathering (in French *"instruction"*) at the expense of that higher category known as "education" which—in Saint-Ex's highly personal language—"founds man". What he meant was what the Greeks called *paideia*—not the mere accumulation of knowledge, but in a deeper sense a "preparation for manhood". "Is it to be a man to know the sum of the angles of a triangle or the longitude of Rangoon?" is a characteristic notebook entry. "To be a man is to be seeded with a fertile treasure of concepts (songs, Man Ray, the universal, etc.); this is what determines human relation-ships—and they are the most important things on earth (thus friendship for Mermoz takes priority over political friendships) . . . It is what makes the difference between the caveman and the British gentleman . . . Stupid modern system of visual education which discovers admirable gimmicks for *effortless teaching*, thus giving the the child, reduced to the role of depositary, a baggage of knowledge, instead of forging a style, and thus a soul." Or again, this entry: "Sole aim of education: style. It's not the baggage which counts (instruction) but the instrument of apprehension . . . People today forget this fundamental problem which pertains to moral problems. Stylo is the soul. And one creates this soul to the extent that one creates a style. (A peasant has style.) Today people receive instruction, but they are no longer educated . . ."

A style presupposes a model, and that was just the trouble. The French, in the levelling process of their unbridled republicanism, had undermined the notion of a valid model around which a style could be built. A rampant egalitarianism had corroded the very notion of excellence and superiority. The cathedral had been torn down so that all its stones could be equal. "The members of a people who possess a queen" as he noted elsewhere in his notebook, "have a few drops of royal blood within them". But his countrymen had turned their back on royalty just as they had turned away from the notion of divinity. They had wanted to be equal citizens in a state which had no kings, but in which everyone was a captain; and the result had been a mob. An aggregate of selfish interests.

"If then they come to me and require me to die for interests," as he wrote in the final pages of *Pilote de Guerre*, "I shall refuse to die. Interest commands one first of all to live. What élan of love would repay my death? One dies for a house; not for objects and walls. One dies for a cathedral; not for stones. One dies for a people; not for a mob. One dies for love of Man, if he is the keystone of the Community. One dies only for that which one lives by."

The French, having had nothing to live by but their individual selves and their petty interests, had refused to fight in 1939 and 1940. There had been no Spirit to blow upon the clay, no leavening ferment to animate the lumpish dough—with the result that there had been no men. Character had been sacrificed to the accumulation of knowledge, Spirit dessicated by the harsh wind of critical intelligence. Robbed of all altruistic tension, the life of the country had grown slack and flabby, its thinking ingrown, maimed, and stunted.

But what was true of France was true because of its universal significance. When the spirit dies, man is doomed to become a mere unit of existence. For if the "Natural Man" of Rousseau is a myth—and of this Saint-Exupéry was profoundly persuaded—there yet lies dormant within each individual a firebird (an image used in one of his notebooks) waiting to be loosed of its shackles. But the bird cannot be freed through the opening of some magic casement. The walls of the prison will not come tumbling down through the sound of some messianic trump. The easy way out—through the arcadian idyll of the "natural goodness of man"—provides no exit, only an impasse. Here the Marxists, like the anarchists, are victims of the same short-sighted myth—the "withering away of the state" being only a collective and typically Germanic magnification of Rousseau's anti-social prejudice. But victims too are the eternal optimists who continue to batten like parasites on the rhetorical illusions of the last two centuries. For the truth, which contemporary politicians and economists strive so desperately to ignore, is that adversity is more vital to man's welfare than any artificially induced felicity. The Garden of Eden may be a myth, but the serpent and the apple are more than ever among us; and no temptation could be more insidiously corrupting than that pursuit of happiness which the modern world has sought to make the be-all and the end-all of human existence.

"To live" as Saint-Exupéry put it in *Pilote de Guerre*, "is to be slowly born. It would be too easy to borrow ready-made souls . . . Man must always make the first steps. He must be born before existing." And this birth, like all births, is necessarily painful. Suffering, sacrifice, adversity alone forge the key needed to unlock the captive soul of human greatness. "I shall fight for Man," as he wrote in the final pages of *Pilote de Guerre*. "Against his enemies. But also against myself."

# 21

## A Solitary Little Fellow

FROM *Pilote de Guerre*, strange as it might seem, it was but a short step to Saint-Exupéry's next work, *Le Petit Prince*, which he began writing in the summer of 1942. For the critique of collectivist thinking and western materialism which emerges in such exalted tones towards the end of *Flight to Arras* was more simply expressed in this later work. The Little Prince of this charming fable for adults is not simply the child Saint-Ex would have liked to father (as he had once written to his mother, back in 1924: "I have such provisions of paternal love stocked up within me. I would like to have a lot of small Antoines."); in his solitary isolation he is a symbol of what modern man has become on a planet where increasingly there is no "gardener for men". "The important thing" as he had written in *Flight to Arras*, "is not exaltation. There is no hope of exaltation in defeat. The important thing is to get dressed, to climb aboard, to take off. What we may think of it ourselves is of no importance. The child who would derive a sense of exaltation from grammar lessons would strike me as suspect and pretentious. The important thing is to conduct oneself with reference to a goal which is not immediately visible." Invisible in just such a way is the goal which leads on K in Kafka's *The Castle*, a book which made a deep impression on Saint-Exupéry when he read it. Like K's, the universe of the Little Prince is full of baffling mysteries, and the frozen note of solitude which haunts it stems from an absence which has made of this lonely child an orphan. What that absence is is never explicitly stated in *The Little Prince*, but it is everywhere implied. As Saint-Ex had written years before in his notebook, à propos of Father Sertillanges' *Sources de la croyance en Dieu* (Origins of the Belief in God): "Too soon deprived of God at an age when one still seeks refuge, here we must struggle for life like little solitary fellows."

For years, in countless letters written on restaurant menus and random sheets of paper, this "*petit bonhomme solitaire*" had been appearing in a variety of disguises: sometimes seated on a cloud with a crown on his head, sometimes posted on a mountain-top—as in the humorous message he had one day sent his *alpiniste* friend Henry de Ségogne, in which the accompanying annotations showed how he was really and truly descended from Adam! Rare was the day at the Café Arnold, on Columbus Circle, where they used to meet for a cup of coffee, that Saint-Ex would not amuse his friends Hélène and Pierre Lazareff covering the paper napkins with pencil drawings of his Little Prince.

It is often difficult in the life of a writer to know at just what point and for what reason a diffuse nebula of ideas suddenly begins to solidify into the nucleus of a book. Such is not the case with *The Little Prince*, whose genesis—as we shall see in a moment—can be traced back to one of these napkin-drawing sessions. It is only fair to add, however, that something of a stimulus was provided by Consuelo's arrival in New York, after an extraordinary series of adventures in southern France which she later described in her book *Oppède* (translated into English as *The Kingdom of the Rocks*). Had they really happened or were they simply the gaudy products of her wild, surrealist imagination? It was impossible to say. But even in their weird implausibility they were spellbinding tales which, like lush flowers, enjoyed a few days of heady glory before beginning to lose their exotic colours. For as Denis de Rougemont was quick to notice, with Consuelo the story-making faculty was essentially spontaneous. Never was the episode livelier and more picturesque than in the first narration; the story shedding something of its aromatic gold-dust with each new telling. Whereas with Saint-Exupéry it was precisely the opposite: each time he repeated the same story it improved, as the tireless craftsman he was strove to model his raw material into an ever more perfect form.

To assure himself a minimum of peace and to give Consuelo a place where she could be free to entertain her surrealist friends Antoine rented an apartment across the hallway on the twenty third floor of 240 Central Park South. In addition to André Breton New York had attracted a number of Surrealists like Joan Miró, Salvador Dali ("Avida Dollars" as Breton sarcastically called him), Yves Tanguy, Max Ernst, André Masson, Marcel Duchamp, René Le Roy, and André Rouchaud, who were as amused by Consuelo's Latin exuberance as she was by their anarchic bohemianism. Some of them Saint-Exupéry was prepared to tolerate—like René Le Roy, whose flute-playing enchanted him. There was also Marcel Duchamp, the real father (before Rauschenberg) of what has come to be known as "pop art", whom Saint-Ex respected as a "decent fellow" and a formidable opponent who was more than a match for him at chess. With André Rouchaud, who spoke English, he was also on friendly terms; and it was to him more than once that he would telephone an urgent S.O.S. from some haberdashery or men's store where he was unable to make the salesman (who doubtless knew no German) understand what kind of tie or shirt it was he wanted. But for Dicton, who was already predicting darkly that the United States after the war would turn into a Fascist state, Saint-Exupéry felt no sympathy. Like Jean-Paul Sartre, who was later to remark in *Qu'est ce Que la Littérature?*, that the horrors of the Spanish Civil War and the Japanese bombardment of Shanghai had shown up the surrealist passion for destruction as the gratuitous and pseudo-revolutionary game it was, he took a dim view of these parasitical literati who spent their time regretting Europe and criticizing the country where they had taken refuge. To be sure, Breton—like Pierre Lazareff, Denis de Rougemont, and others—was now contributing his bit to the common allied effort in the French section of Elmer Davis' Office of War Information (or "the jungle", as they humorously called it) which had been placed under the general management of Lewis Galantière. But when it finally came, Saint-Exupéry's contribution—*Pilote de Guerre*—was harshly judged by Breton and his followers. The French philosopher Alexandre Koyré found it "Fascist" in inspiration, while its underlying philosophy was dismissed as "paternalistic" and "reactionary" in *VVV*, an expatriate surrealist publication put out by Etiemble, who had found a teaching job at the University of Chicago. This particular attack stung Saint-Ex to the quick and moved him to draft an anti-surrealist manifesto in the form of an "Open Letter to André Breton" which for a while he actually contemplated publishing, though nothing seems to have come of the project.

Less critical than the surrealists were the French Canadians—certain of them, at any rate—who now began badgering Saint-Exupéry for a visit. In the end he gave in, agreeing in late April to travel up to Montreal by train and to give a couple of talks about his war experiences to French-speaking groups. He made the trip reluctantly, having no desire to leave the United States, and only after his literary agent, Maximilian Becker, and his publisher, Curtice Hitchcock, had been solemnly assured by the Canadian Consulate in New York and by a highly placed bureaucrat in Washington that Saint-Exupéry could make the two-day trip without requiring special papers. But once in Canada, he found himself debarred from re-entry into the United States because he lacked a visa. Ten days of hectic telephoning and letter-writing followed, during which Saint-Ex suffered nightly attacks of liver trouble due to his more than usually anguished condition. Consuelo bustled up from New York to take care of him, but the episode left a nasty taste in his mouth and confirmed him in the belief that there were persons in Washington, as well as New York, who were out to make trouble for him—either because he was insufficiently Pétainist or because of his ill-feigned distaste for what he liked to call the "Fascism without a doctrine" of General de Gaulle.

Though the liver ailment disappeared after his return to New York, Saint-Exupéry seems to have suffered from recurring bouts of fever over the next few months. To escape from the wilting heat of a Manhattan summer he and Consuelo rented a simple clapboard house at Westport, in Connecticut, where they could cool off in the waters of the Long Island Sound. A chessboard was set up on its wooden porch, and here Saint-Ex spent many long hours pitting his wits against those of Denis de Rougemont, who came out to spend a week with them. To disguise his diabolical cunning beneath an air of nonchalance, Tonio would whistle away with a careless springtime rapture, completely unnerving his exasperated opponent. The remedy, Rougemont finally discovered, was to start a counter-warble, unleashing an unthrushlike cacaphony which was enough to throw a rattled Tonio completely off his game.

One day Antoine returned from New York awkwardly encumbered with a long black box he was carrying under one arm. When the lid was opened out waddled a baby bulldog, all grimacing and trembling—a gift for Consuelo, who missed her little Yuti, the Pekinese of royal lineage: for was he not descended from a Chinese Emperor? The new acquisition was baptized Hannibal, doubtless because he had a touch of Carthaginian in his veins, and Denis de Rougemont, promoted Court Chamberlain Emeritus, was entrusted the delicate task of walking His Imperial Highness up and down the beach.

The gift failed to mitigate Consuelo's dissatisfaction with this clapboard bungalow, apparently not grand enough for her baroque taste. For a few weeks later Denis de Rougemont found them installed at Eton Neck (near Northport, Long Island) in a vast country seat called "Bevin House". Located on a "promontory feathered by windblown trees"—to quote from the Swiss writer's Journal—it enjoyed a proud isolation among its reeds and the sinuous lagoons which surrounded it on three sides "in a landscape of tropic isles and forests".

"I wanted a hut and it's the Palace of Versailles!" Saint-Ex exclaimed crossly the first évening he was dragged off to visit the lagoon-girt marvel. But no less typically, a few days later he was as happy as a clam in this huge shell of a mansion.

"He's back at work, writing a children's tale," Denis de Rougemont noted in his Journal towards the end of September, "which he's illustrating himself with watercolours. A balding giant, with the round eyes of a high-flying bird and the precise fingers of a mechanic, he applies himself to handling tiny schoolboy brushes, the tip of his tongue showing between his lips as he concentrates on not 'washing over the line'. I pose for the *Little*

*Prince* lying on my stomach with my legs in the air. Tonio laughs like a kid: 'Later you'll point to this drawing and say: That's me!' "

The idea of writing a children's fable was not originally Saint-Exupéry's at all. It all started one day over a lunch-table in a New York restaurant. Intrigued by Saint-Ex's doodlings on the white table cloth—which the waiter had been surveying with a frown—Curtice Hitchcock asked him what he was drawing.

"Oh nothing much," was the reply. "Just a little fellow I carry around in my heart."

Hitchcock treated the little fellow to a closer inspection and it gave him an idea. "Now look, this little fellow—what would you think of making up a story about him . . . for a children's book?"

The idea took Saint-Exupéry completely by surprise. He had never thought of himself as a professional writer, still less as an author of children's books. But once the seed of the idea had been planted, it kept steadily growing, nurtured as it was by the gentle prodding of his publisher. A children's book . . . for Christmas? The season of candles he had always loved . . . and children? He who seemed destined never to have any of his own, much as he had longed for them . . . Well, for lack of a real one, why not an imaginary little Antoine? . . . "Just think," he told Léon Wencelius a few days after this luncheon, "they're now asking me to write a book for children! . . . Accompany me to the stationer's would you? I want to buy some coloured pencils."

The pencils bought, Saint-Ex got to work on a few experimental drawings, which were probably intended to "fix" his still nebulous ideas. He then besought the assistance of his old Beaux-Arts colleague, Bernard Lamotte, whose illustrations for *Flight to Arras* had bowled him over for their "telepathic" accuracy of detail. Lamotte responded with a few sample sketches which left Saint-Ex dissatisfied: they were insufficiently naive and dream-like for the effect he wanted to convey. As the days passed and he became more absorbed by his tale, he began to realize that he would have to illustrate as well as write it himself. He continued to solicit his friend's expert advice, but his own ideas had now begun to jell, and one day, after a sleepless night spent painting a baobab tree uprooting a tiny planet, he refused to make the slightest alteration.

"You should straighten it up a bit here, darken it a bit there," began Lamotte.

"Impossible, *mon vieux*," answered Saint-Ex. "If this were a written text, all right—I would agree to modify it, for after all I'm a writer. That's my job. But I can't do better than this drawing. It's quite simply a miracle . . ." And that was that.

September faded into October, the beautiful autumn of the Eastern seaboard "painting the trees in colours of fire", as André Maurois was later to describe it. During a long Sunday afternoon spent at Bevin House he and his wife listened in fascination as Saint-Ex reeled off one magnificent story after another. "He took us from Indochina to the Paris suburbs, from the Sahara to Chile. What a prodigious *raconteur!*"

Maurois was even invited to spend several weeks at Bevin House. In the evenings hosts and guests would play cards or chess and then as midnight approached, Saint-Exupéry would say: "All right, now go to bed. I must work." An hour or so later, just as he was dozing off, Maurois would be woken by shouts from the stairs: "Consuelo! Consuelo!" Thinking the house was on fire the first time he heard the tumult, he slipped into his dressing gown and rushed out on to the landing, only to find Tonio explaining to Consuelo, likewise draped in a bathrobe, that he was desperately hungry and wanted some scrambled eggs. The scrambled eggs consumed, Saint-Ex would resume work for an hour or two, when once again the quiet of the house would be disturbed by more shouts from the stairs: "Consuelo! . . . Consuelo! I've been working for an hour . . . I want some scrambled eggs. . . ." While Consuelo padded off to the kitchen to break a few more yolks, her unsleeping spouse would say to Maurois: "I must talk to someone" or "let's have a walk in the garden." Half an hour later Maurois would be allowed to regain his sheets, but the shouting as often as not recurred an hour or two later, and this time a wide-awake Tonio would insist to Consuelo that "either you or Maurois have got to play chess with me".

Another victim of these nocturnal eruptions was Denis de Rougemont, who used to travel out to Eton Neck every week-end for the thirty-six hours he was allowed away from his job with the Office of War Information. The privileged readings (particularly of *Citadelle*) to which he was treated by the author would often last far into the night, to the dismay of the harrassed guest, who knew that the next morning, while his friend Tonio would be ten fathoms down in the soundless depths of sleep, he, Denis de Rougemont, would have to be very much alive and wide awake amid the wood-pecking typewriters and the nervous chatter of the ticker-tapes at work in the "Jungle". But there was no putting Tonio off; for even after he had retired to his bedroom, he would find himself pursued by his tireless host, who while chain-smoking cigarettes, would continue arguing on every conceivable subject with an inflexible rigour. He gives me" Rougemont could not help adding in his Journal, "the impression of a brain which *can no longer* stop thinking."

Ill health may have contributed to this barrage of words and logic, for part of *Le Petit Prince* seems to have been written in a state of fever which greatly stimulated his imagination. If so, it was a highly productive fever, even though there was hardly a theme in this short work which had not already been sounded in his earlier writings or letters. "I am reading *Dust*" —Rosamond Lehmann's novel—"and I think we all love this kind of book, like *The Constant Nymph*, because we recognize each other," he had written to his mother from Argentina in 1930. Like Margaret Kennedy "we are all part of the same tribe. And this world of children's memories with our language and the games we invented, will always seem to me desperately truer than the other."

The other world, in this autumn of 1942, was the strife-torn world which was edging towards the battle of Stalingrad and that invasion of North Africa which, as we shall see, Saint-Exupéry most ardently desired. But, as Christ had said, what profit it a man if he gaineth the whole world yet lose his soul? It was the message which gleamed through the final pages of *Pilote de Guerre*, which owed more to the Gospel than to Whitman, and it was the central message of The Little Prince, whose only conquests are his friends—the sheep, the sandfox, and the rose. "Reread children's books," Saint-Ex had written years before in his notebook, "entirely forgetting the naive part which has no effect, but noting all along the prayers and concepts carried by this imagery. Study to see if man deprived of this beneficent wave doesn't tend toward the 1936 gigolo." Or, as he put it in another entry: "We are strangely submissive to objects, doubtless because of the long publicitary pedagogy"—Madison Avenue persuasion—"we have undergone. In this respect we are barbarians. And in this respect many barbarians—we vaguely feel—are more civilized than we."

Twenty-five years before the plodding Herbert Marcuse was to "discover" a truth to which he had already been guided by Vance Packard and other analysts of America's "publicitary pedagogy", Saint-Exupéry was already noting that "an industry based on profit tends to create—by education—men for chewing-gum and not chewing-gum for men. Thus from the automobile's need to create the value *automobile* is born the little 1926 gigolo whose only interest in the bars is in pictures and comparisons of bodyworks." His first exposure to American civilization, after his Guatemala accident in 1938, had moved him to write in a letter: "My freedom today is solely based on mass production which castrates all dissident desires, it's the freedom of the horse in blinkers. Lord! in what am I free in my functionary's rut? There's scant originality to be found in the company of today's Babbit, seeing him buy his morning paper, digest this ready-made thought, choose between three opinions because three are proposed to him . . . then lunch at his drugstore where a cast-iron slavery impedes the satisfaction of the slightest individual wish. After which there's the session at the movies where Mr. Z crushes him with his dictatorial silliness . . . But no one seems alarmed by this frightful freedom, which is freedom only not to be. Real freedom consists in the creative act. The fisherman is free when his instinct guides his fishing. The sculptor is free when he sculpts a face. But it is nothing but a caricature of freedom to be allowed to choose between four types of General Motors' cars or three of Mr. Z's films . . . or between eleven different drugstore dishes. Freedom is then reduced to the choice of a standard item in a range of a universal similitude."

Anyone who thinks thus is bound to end up a pessimistic romantic or a romantic pessimist, and this was certainly true of Saint-Exupéry. "The world" as Horace Walpole once observed, "is a comedy to those who think, a tragedy to those who feel." Saint-Ex felt as deeply as he thought, and the resultant allegory in this case proved both humorous and sad. It was also occasionally sharp, as allegories are apt to be, which may partially (but only partially) explain the lack of an enthusiastic response comparable to that which *Flight to Arras* had enjoyed for weeks on end with the American reading public. Though Beatrice Sherman gave it a sympathetic treatment in the April 11, 1943 issue of *The New York Times Book Review*, other reviewers seem to have been at a loss as to just how to interpret a book which could not easily be pigeon-holed. Writing some six months later in *The Commonweal* Harry Louis Binsse was forced to confess, a trifle wistfully, that he was one of the few American critics who regarded this little fable as something of a classic—"a sad classic to make the tears flow, but there is a joy in crying even for childhood, and childhood sometimes does not take as tragic what to me as an adult is tragic indeed. But in this opinion I seem to be somewhat alone. The book has had no tremendous success though it was published last spring, and perhaps my judgment is wrong. What I suspect is that the public does not readily accept something from an author which does not fit into the category in which the public has placed that author, and for an imaginative airman to write what amounts to a fairy story —or at least a fanciful allegory—is perhaps too much for the public to swallow."

It is also possible that certain critics were put off by the ironic digs at American civilization—as in the figure of the *businessman* (the word used in the French as well as the English text) too busy counting his millions of stars to be able to enjoy a single one, or in that of the pharmaceutical salesman whose thirst-curing pills allow one to save exactly fifty-three minutes per week. But they are only two of the protagonists whom the author mocked with a gentle humour which betrays no prejudice or *parti pris*, since the others in this rogues' gallery include an ermine-robed king, a bearded pedant of a geographer, a humble lamp-lighter, a feather-hatted fop waiting for someone to admire the elegance of his attire, and even a lugubrious toper, who when asked by the Little Prince why he drinks, replies: "To forget."

"To forget what?" inquired the Little Prince, already feeling sorry for him.
"To forget that I am ashamed," confessed the drinker, bowing his head.
"Ashamed of what?" asked the Little Prince who wanted to help him.
"Ashamed of drinking!" concluded the drinker, shutting himself into a definitive silence.

This was the kind of circular, self-demonstrating syllogism which Saint-Exupéry in his spare moments liked to try out on friends and particularly on those who took pride in their "logical" turn of mind. It was a trait he shared with Charles Dodgson, better known as Lewis Carroll, an eminent mathematician who enjoyed devising theorems which had a baffling way of disproving their axioms.

Lewis Carroll patterned his Alice after a little girl he knew, and the Little Prince, of course, is Saint-Ex as a child. The Rose it is his duty to tend is a more complex creation, being first of all a symbol, but she is also very feminine and flighty, like Consuelo—that "poppy" who, he had once warned, would end up shorn of her petals if she went on so giddily spinning. The Little Prince's three volcanoes, which he regularly sweeps like a chimney, were similarly inspired by the dead craters Saint-Ex had seen in southern Patagonia. Like all great fables, this one is as full of enchantment for a child as it is rich in nourishment for adults—one of whom, the German philosopher Martin Heidegger, came to regard *The Little Prince* as one of the great existentialist books of this century. It echoes, on a purely lyric plane, many of the themes its author had most to heart: the fragility of joy ("A rose . . . is a somewhat melancholy fête."), the primordial importance of love, without which one is blind—expressed in the little fox's secret: "One sees only with the heart. The essential is invisible to the eye." The importance of a mission, a duty, an obligation in life—exemplified by the lamp-lighter who lights and extinguishes his lamp because that is the way things are—"*C'est la consigne*" (Orders are orders). The vanity of riches and his abhorrence of the collective hurly-burly of metropolitan existence—symbolised by the train-switch operator, routing and rerouting passing expresses full of yawning and dozing passengers who have no idea whither they are bound, save for the little children with their noses pressed to the window-panes. The pleasure which comes not because it is given or received but because it has been earned, like the sweet water of the well "born of the march under the stars, of the chant of the pulley, of the effort of my arms". And not least of all, the feeling that his broken-jointed carcass was done for. "*Le corps, vieux cheval, on l'abandonne*," he had written in *Pilote de Guerre*. "I can't carry off this body. It's too heavy," says the Little Prince as he prepared to return to his tiny star. "But it will be like an old discarded rind." Miraculously his old warhorse of a body had survived the hazards of the *débâcle*, but Saint-Ex could feel it creaking with every step he took—a battered carapace, a mortal coil he could not reel off and which his soaring spirit would have to drag around, like a prisoner's ball and chain, to the very end of his days.

# 22

# Return to the Fray

THEY had argued about it one day in July of 1942, and as Denis de Rougemont wrote it up in his Journal, Saint-Exupéry had undertaken to explain to him that "the Marshal is saving France's 'substance' in agreeing to deal with the occupant, for if he openly revolted, the Germans would only need to cut off all supplies of axle-grease, which would keep the trains from running and block all food supplies. As for the Gaullists, they are not waging war against the Nazis, but against the French elevator boy or the Ritz Hôtel chef who's refused to join their faction and whom they consequently regard as a traitor.

"I replied to Saint-Ex that in our country"—he meant Switzerland—"we would regard it as normal to sacrifice what he calls substance to what I call *raison de vivre*". After which Rougemont was honest enough to add, parenthetically: "The proof is yet to be made, of course, I am only speaking for myself, and neither he nor I for the moment are on the spot or involved."

It was the sober truth and also a sobering truth—at any rate for Saint-Exupéry, who was French, whereas Rougemont could, as a Swiss citizen, have claimed the right to remain neutrally inactive. But the problem for Saint-Ex was—how could he serve? More than once he had lunched with Captain Alexandre de Manziarly, whose crippled leg—from the First World War—had kept him from taking an active part in the Second. He had managed to hobble his way out of France and to join the Free French in London, from where De Gaulle had sent him on to New York as a member of a military recruiting mission. It was not easy for Saint-Exupéry to fend off someone with such impeccable credentials. Besides, "Sasha"—as he was known to his friends (because of his Russian ancestry)—was an acquaintance of long standing and a natural charmer, not to say a troubadour, who was ever ready to enliven a dinner party with drole songs which he accompanied on his guitar. But to the repeated question: "Why don't you join us?"

Saint-Ex's invariable reply was: "To do what? Go over to London and be given a desk job in some office?"

At forty-two Saint-Ex was long past the age for piloting a fighter plane and the idea of flying a bomber—after what he had seen in Spain, to say nothing of the French *débâcle*—was enough to make him shudder. But he had stronger reasons for not wishing to go to London. What Jean de Vogüé had told him about De Gaulle in August of 1940 had been dramatically confirmed to him by General Robert Odic, with whom he had several long talks in the late spring and early summer of 1942. Odic, who had served as General Vuillemin's Chief of Staff in 1939 and 1940, had refused the No. 1 air-force post offered him by Vichy, preferring instead to accompany General Weygand to North Africa. His job, as Weygand's chief air-force officer, had been to prepare for the day when the French could resume the struggle, an assignment which made him naturally sympathetic to Robert Murphy and his assistants. The job was not easy, for North Africa was honey-combed with paid and even unpaid informers, working for the Germans, the Italians, and the more pro-German elements in Vichy. His wife having one day remarked in an Algiers salon that if being anti-German meant being Gaullist, then she was a Gaullist, the remark had got back to Darlan, who had ordered Weygand to "retire" Odic as over-age—an order which caused Weygand considerable embarrassment, since Odic was only 55, while he was well over 70. After making a quick trip back to France to contact air-force officers who shared his own Resistance sympathies, Odic had been helped by Murphy and his assistants to reach Tangier and Lisbon. There, as ill-luck would have it, he had been photographed on the airfield by the Germans. His American mentors, unwilling to run unnecessary risks, had quickly smuggled Odic and his wife on to an American passenger ship, and when the vessel reached New York on October 15, 1941, a senior G-2 officer from the War Department was on hand to escort him directly to Washington. He had been received at the White House and had seen a lot of Alexis Léger (the poet Saint-John Perse), who as the former secretary general of the Quai d'Orsay, was one of Roosevelt's principal advisers for French affairs. Finally it had been decided that Odic should go to London to see if he could not bring his wholesome influence to bear on an increasingly intractable De Gaulle.

By the time Odic reached Scotland, flown over on a bomber, Weygand had been dismissed as French Commander-in-Chief in North Africa and the United States had entered the war, in the wake of Pearl Harbour. There being no further need for discretion, Odic came out with a ringing anti-Vichy statement which was broadcast by the BBC and the Gaullist radio in London. De Gaulle invited him to his headquarters at Carlton Gardens and without more ado offered him the command of all his ground, sea, and air forces in French Equatorial Africa, with headquarters at Brazzaville. The offer struck Odic as a bit off-hand, since these forces were negligible, but in any case he had not come to London to seek a job: of more immediate concern to him was to see what could be done to keep Vichy from drifting into a full-fledged Franco-German alliance, towards which Pierre Laval was now obviously working. "On the contrary," De Gaulle objected, "if such an alliance is formed, the guilt of the Vichy crowd will be established once and for all". Odic was appalled. The welfare of France, it suddenly dawned on him, mattered less to De Gaulle than proving Vichy's guilt and thus the virtue of his own cause. Vichy, not Germany, was his principal antagonist.

Following this first encounter Odic had avoided Carlton Gardens for the next few weeks, anxious to determine if his first, unfavourable impression was mistaken or if it represented a definite attitude and state of mind. The more Frenchmen he talked to the more convinced he grew that what he had heard the General say conformed to a pattern. He had finally gone back to see De Gaulle in the hope of trying to talk him into attempting a rapprochement between the French in London and those he had left behind in Algeria and Morocco. He knew many air-force officers, he told him, who were ready to resume the struggle but unwilling to sign a personal oath of allegiance to the General. At this De Gaulle bristled. Odic went on to point out that just as he himself had refused to sign an oath of allegiance to Pétain, so many Frenchmen in high positions in North Africa whom he had got to know well—like Noguès in Morocco, Yves Chatel in Algeria, Admiral Estéva in Tunis—were ready to resume the fight, provided the moment was ripe and they could count on a really serious Allied intervention to save them from the inevitable German riposte, which could be catastrophic. Like Weygand, who had secretly been building up *l'Armée d'Afrique* for an eventual resumption of hostilities, they were anything but collaborators. De Gaulle cut him short. "Weygand is a traitor!" he summarily declared, adding that as far as he was concerned those who had refused to join him might as well stay where they were, and Odic with them. "For if that's the way you think, you can go back to Africa and I shall fight you."

By March of 1942 Odic and the leader of the Free French were at such loggerheads that De Gaulle asked the British to have Odic arrested. The British politely declined to take action, but Odic now being a liability from their point of view—which was to support De Gaulle at all costs as "their man"—John Winant offered Odic shelter at the American Embassy. A day or two later he was slipped on to a train for Glasgow and placed on a banana-boat for the return trip to America. Such were the harrowing vicissitudes of a man whose one primordial desire had been to check the drift which was carrying Vichy, and North Africa with it, deeper and deeper into the German camp. It seemed unbelievable that such well-meaning and level-headed intentions could produce such violent, not to say hysterical, reactions, but such had been the case. De Gaulle's behaviour, as Saint-Ex could now appreciate, was no different from that of his most fervent supporters in New York, at least one of whom had had the exquisite delicacy of terming Saint-Exupéry a "Fascist"!

Saint-Exupéry's aversion to armchair or microphone propaganda made it equally impossible for him to join his friends Pierre Lazareff, Beaucaire, Rougemont, and Galantière in Elmer Davis's O.W.I. Itch as he might to return to the fray, he was effectively boxed in between his principles and his misgivings. The one occasion on which he broke his self-imposed silence was, characteristically, in answer to a request from Dorothy Thompson, who not being French was not asking him to take sides in a fratricidal quarrel. The "Message to Young Americans" which he wrote at her sugges-tion and which Lewis Galantière translated for the May 25, 1942 issue of *The Sentier Scholastic* was in essence a restatement of the credo expounded at the end of *Pilote de Guerre*. "Liberty" he wrote, "is not a problem which can be separated from others. For man to be free, man must first be"—for once again Saint-Exupéry wished to stress the point that manhood is not a birthright one automatically and effortlessly receives, but rather a precipitate of human action, a quality one develops and even more, contributes. "One is man of a country, a trade, a civilization, a religion. One is not man pure and simple. A cathedral is made of stones. The stones compose the cathedral. In the same way you will only find fraternity in something vaster than yourselves. For one is a brother 'in' something. One is not a brother pure and simple . . ." But here precisely was the rub. For the rise of material progress had obscured this venerable truth: which is that this sense of brotherhood does not spring from what one takes, accumulates, or acquires, but from what one gives. "Mankind's overriding need to wrench man from his bondage, by assuring him the fruit of his labour, focussed attention on work as a value of exchange. On work as merchandise. But we should not forget that one of the essential aspects of work is not the salary it produces but the spiritual enrichment it brings to man. A surgeon, a physicist, a gardener have more human quality than a bridge player. One part of work nourishes and the other founds: and it is what one gives to work which founds."

Implicitly if not explicitly, this was Saint-Exupéry's answer to Marxism and capitalistic economics, a foretaste of the arguments he was to deploy at length in *Citadelle* against the notion of the welfare state. The United States had had to be dragged, prodded, and finally kicked into joining the war, but the sacrifices now being asked of young as well as old Americans were what was going to make a nation of them. "Dorothy Thompson thus asks you to give. She invites you to found your community. When you will bring in the harvest without pay for the good of the United States at war, then you will found the community of the United States. And thus your brotherhood."

For the immensity of the American war effort Saint-Exupéry had nothing but praise; for, as Lewis Galantière has noted, he refused to share the scepticism of so many French exiles, only too ready to dismiss Roosevelt's wartime production goals as so much "American bluff". "Sixty thousand planes and ten million tons of shipping in a single year? Why not? . . . A nation that suddenly stops building five million motorcars a year certainly possesses the manpower, the raw materials, and the skill to carry out Roosevelt's programme."

While the writing of *Le Petit Prince* in the summer and autumn of 1942 kept him occupied for several months, it by no means absorbed all of his energies. His scientific curiosity, which he had kept alive in Hollywood by meeting Theodore von Karman, head of the California Institute of Technology's Aerodynamics Institute, was as lively as ever in New York, where he cultivated the company of French scientists like Lecomte de Nouy as well as members of the American scientific community. His interest in nuclear physics and his inside knowledge were sufficient for him to be able to tell Pierre Lazareff, long before the Manhattan Project was known to the general public, that the Americans were at work on a terrible weapon which, if ever brought into action, could end the war at one stroke. Even the tiny helicopters he fashioned out of strips of paper and launched from his penthouse balcony, far from being simple children's toys, were designed to test his theories about the best exploitation of air currents.

Inexhaustibly inventive as ever, Saint-Ex kept dreaming up schemes which struck Galantière as "worthy of Jules Verne". One such scheme, destined to outwit the Germans' U-boat offensive, called for the construction of huge underwater barges loaded with airplane parts and towed across the Atlantic by giant submarines. Another of his ideas, though bold and romantic in its conception, struck Galantière as feasible enough to warrant his cooperation. General Giraud's dramatic escape from the fortress of Koenigstein filled Saint-Exupéry with jubilation and set his mind to dreaming up ways in which this sensational coup could be exploited. The idea he finally broached to Galantière was simple: he proposed that the War Department send him to North Africa where, precisely because he had refused to join the Gaullists, he would have little trouble getting himself over to France. There he would get in touch with Giraud as the War Department's private emissary and arrange to fly him out on a plane (which he was sure of being able to obtain) for a mid-ocean rendezvous with an American cruiser. Brought to the United States aboard the warship, Giraud could then help the Combined Chiefs of Staff plan an invasion of North Africa, which would be supported by French troops on the spot only too glad, he confidently declared, to place themselves under Giraud's command.

"I was so struck by this plan" Galantière later recalled, "that I went down to Washington and talked it over at dinner with two friends, one from the Combined Chiefs and the other from the OSS. That was in July, 1942. I did not know then that the President and the Prime Minister had just given their approval to Operation Torch, which was to culminate in the North African landings of November 8, 1942, and that, on the French side, Giraud was to be the keystone in the arch of this operation.

"Never have I been the object of such a rebuff—I had better say frankly, bawling out—as at the end of my little speech. My friend Saint-Exupéry might perhaps be a genius, but he was certainly a complete idiot. As for me, what right had I to intervene in matters that did not concern me and about which I could not be more ignorant? If they ever heard that I had repeated a single word of this grotesque pipe-dream to anybody at all, they would take personal and particular pleasure in seeing that I was put away in a Federal penitentiary for a dozen years. And my friend Saint-Exupéry the same."

The next day, in New York, Galantière broke the news to his friend. Nothing doing! the reaction hadn't been negative; it had been positively explosive! There was a long silence, and then Saint-Ex smiled ever so faintly. "Ah?" he said. "So that's how it is! They're cleverer than I had imagined."

What followed was no less gratifying to Saint-Exupéry, whose one desire all along had been to serve, and in some way other than in a sterile war of words. He was already a friend of William Donovan, now promoted to General and made head of the OSS; and in Margaret Hughes' drawing-room, frequented by Dean Acheson, Count Sforza, and a host of influential diplomats and officials, he made contacts which were useful in opening many a Washington office door. One such contact was an aide to Sumner Welles, while others were military men. The upshot of these various overtures and of Galantière's trip to Washington was a visit Saint-Exupéry one day received in his New York apartment from General Spaatz, who had recently made a name for himself by his bombing exploits in the Pacific. Though Saint-Ex did not know it, the general had been selected to direct the United States Air Force in the Mediterranean theatre of operations. Only much later, after he himself had embarked for North Africa on October 3rd, did Galantière discover that "a good deal of what the Combined Chiefs' planners knew of airports, installations, and flying conditions in North Africa resulted from the contact thus established."

This helps to explain the difference between his and General de Gaulle's reaction to the news of the North African landings, on that fateful November 8, 1942. "Have you heard? . . ." Saint-Ex telephoned exultantly to Léon Wencelius. "I feel ten years younger." Whereas De Gaulle, when informed by Colonel Billotte, his Chief of Staff, of what was up, stood for a moment in his pyjamas trembling with rage, before exploding: "Well! I hope those Vichy fellows will throw them into the sea. One does not enter France by housebreaking."

Had this simply been the peevish reaction of a man who was furious because (after the Dakar fiasco) he had been kept in the dark, it could have been dismissed as a fit of momentary pique. But the extraordinary follow-up justified the misgivings Saint-Exupéry had voiced about De Gaulle and his London entourage to Denis de Rougemont and others. The previous June the General had launched a newspaper, *La Marseillaise*, destined to propagate the Gaullist party line. It had been agreed that *Pour la Victoire*, the New York publication with Henri de Kerillis had founded at the beginning of the year with Geneviève Tabouis and Michel Pobers, would reserve two pages of each issue to material cabled over from *La Marseillaise* in London. Unable to attack the British, who were De Gaulle's mentors and financiers, François Quilici, the General's chief editorial hatchet man, had opened a series of snide attacks on Roosevelt and the Americans which by September was already forcing the editors of *Pour la Victoire* to answer with protesting cables. The relations between the two anti-Vichy publications reached the breaking-point six weeks after the North African landings when Quilici published an editorial in *La Marseillaise* which roundly declared: "From the point of view not of our ephemeral generation but of history, the occupation by our American friends of a land which has cost us so much blood hits our country more severely than the occupation of French *départments* by the Hitlerians, because it strikes a blow at its honour." The enormity of this statement was such that the New York editors of *Pour la Victoire* cabled to *La Marseillaise* in London to say that they were not publishing the editorial. They simultaneously requested Adrien Tixier, De Gaulle's representative in Washington, to cable a protest to the General in London. The reply which came back was unequivocal: Quilici enjoyed De Gaulle's full confidence. It was the end of *Pour la Victoire's* brief collaboration with *La Marseillaise*.

All of this had been foreseen with remarkable lucidity and prescience by Saint-Exupéry's friend Raoul de Roussy de Sales, whose feelings on the subject were not so far removed from his own. For months he had gone on hoping, against his better judgment, that the Gaullist movement might move in a more liberal direction, only to see his hopes dashed and Tixier, the most servile of their six-man committee, become De Gaulle's chief representative in North America. In September Jacques Maritain had pleaded with him to stay on as a member of the Gaullist "delegation", and Sales had reluctantly consented. But as he had noted in his Journal: "From the information they have, France is apparently becoming fiercely nationalistic. This nationalism manifests itself in hostility toward everything foreign, whether friend or enemy, and by the Maurrassian* principle that France should seek her salvation in solitude or isolation without looking elsewhere for support. Now that Pétain, who inaugurated this nationalism, has disappointed his faithful followers, it might find its ideal expression in the De Gaulle movement. . . it is probable the defeat and Pétain's doctrine have in fact planted in the French a feeling of despair analogous to that which Hitler exploited in the Germans. It will one day be said that we did not lose this war.

"In other words, what has been called the Pétain myth is actually only a morbid resurgence of nationalism. As the myth tends to disappear, there could be a transfer to De Gaulle, who would thus polarize the chauvinistic aspirations and the mysticism of Vichy. One already sees traces of Pétainism in the present Gaullism: Anglophobia, and even Americanophobia, for example, both stemming from the nationalist and Maurrassian theory which sees in the Anglo-Saxon systems and philosophies such dire perils as democracy, liberalism, commercialism, internationalism, etc."

It was against the background of this prophetic analysis, as valid today as it was when formulated a quarter of a century ago, that Saint-Exupéry had to take a stand. He did. Unhesitatingly and unequivocally. Once again he refused to take sides, to judge, to sit in solemn condemnation. Let someone less guilty than himself cast the first stone. His aim was not to arouse antagonisms but to reconcile. First broadcast in French and then published in Canada, his message entitled "An Open Letter to Frenchmen Everywhere" appeared on November 29th—a couple of days after Quilici's incredible editorial—in the *New York Times Magazine*. It began, in the French text, with three staccato words: "*D'abord la France.*" France first of all. That is, before Pétain and before De Gaulle.

"The German night has finally engulfed our land. For a while we could still know something of those we loved. We could still offer them a tender solace, even if unable to share the poor bread of their tables. From afar we heard them breathe.

* Maurrassian, after Charles Maurras who established the theory and doctrine of the group Action Française, an extreme Right and nationalist movement.

"All that is now over. France is nothing more than silence. She is lost somewhere in the night, all lights extinguished, like a ship. Her consciousness and her spiritual life are gathered together in her depths. We do not even know the names of the hostages Germany will shoot tomorrow."

But, he went on, "it is always in the cellars of oppression that new truths are born. Let us not play the part of braggarts. They are forty million over there, to digest their slavery. We shall not bring the spiritual flame to those who already nourish it, like wax, with their own substance. They, better than we, will resolve French problems. They have all the rights. None of our verbiage in sociology, politics, or even art"—a passing dig at the Surrealists—"will carry any weight against their thinking. They will not read our books. They will not listen to our speeches. They may spit on our ideas. Let us be infinitely modest. Our political discussions are the discussions of ghosts, and our ambitions are comic."

To anyone familiar with the Gaullist creed, according to which they were by definition the Keepers of the Truth, the Guardians of the Holy Writ, this was heresy. But worse was to come. "We do not represent France. We can only serve her. No matter what we do, we shall have no right to gratitude. There is no common measure between a freely consented struggle and the oppression of the night. There is no common measure between the soldier's trade and that of the hostage. They over there are the only true saints . . ."

After paying homage to the "miracle of American action in North Africa", he developed the thesis he had already hinted at in *Flight to Arras* and propounded in more concrete terms to his friends. It had been necessary for a "committee of bankruptcy"—Pétain's Vichy government—to bargain off the conquerors the little axle-grease France needed to keep one hundred thousand French children from starving. The denunciation of the Armistice agreements would have meant a return to a state of war and the automatic imprisonment of the six million Frenchmen liable for military service. Six million Frenchmen would thus have been condemned to death, for the "sink-hole of the German camps yields only corpses". Should or should one not yield to this grim blackmail? Such was the fundamental question which had so long divided the French. But now, with the invasion of North Africa and the total occupation of France, the question was academic. "Vichy is dead. Vichy has carried to the grave its inextricable problems, its contradictory personnel, its sincerities and ruses, its cowardice and courage. Let us for the time being abandon the role of judging to the historians and post-war courts martial. It is more important to serve France in the present than to argue about her history."

All this was in flagrant contradiction with the sectarian spirit of Gaullism; and the exiles who had spent their time jockeying for the best jobs and

476

*Antoine de Saint-Exupéry*

finding themselves cushy nests in the skyscrapers of New York or the leafy
vicinity of Carlton Gardens could not miss the couple of pointed sentences
Saint-Exupéry devoted to their activities: "It is not a question of a race for
offices. The only place to be filled are those of soldiers and, perhaps, quiet
beds in some small North African cemetery."

As though this were not enough, he went on to propound what was in
fact the Giraudist position, the one which had the backing of Roosevelt and
the State Department. "The community I belong to is not a party, nor a
sect, but my country. The provisional structure of France is an affair of
state. Let England and the United States do their best. If our ambition is to
press the trigger of a machine-gun, we shall get needlessly worked up over
decisions that will seem of secondary importance. The real leader is this
France which is condemned to silence. Let us hate parties, clans, divisions."

The exhortation ended with an appeal to his fellow exiles to bury their
sterile feuds and to repair the unflattering image they had given Americans
of themselves. "The French here are looked upon a bit like a basket of crabs.
This is unjust. The polemicists do all the talking. Those who are silent go
unheeded." To correct this impression he proposed that all Frenchmen in
favour of immediate union send a message in this sense to Cordell Hull, the
Secretary of State. After which he closed on a personal note: "Frenchmen,
let us be reconciled. When those of us who have been quarrelling find ourselves aboard a bomber against five or six Messerschmitts, our old quarrels
will make us smile. In 1940 when I returned from a mission on a plane shot
through with bullet-holes, I used to drink an excellent Pernod at the
squadron's bar. And I won my Pernod by winning a round of poker from a
royalist colleague, or a socialist colleague, or from Lieutenant Israël, the
bravest of us all and who was Jewish. And we would clink glasses with deep
fondness."

The tone was unmistakably eloquent, the message, as usual, was charitable, but there were weaknesses in the argumentation, as Jacques Maritain
was quick to point out in an "Open Letter" of his own which he entitled:
"One must Sometimes Judge."

"Saint-Exupéry now tells us that there is only one place possible for the
French who can be mobilized, that of combatant. Why does this thought
only impose itself on him today? Between his deepest wish and the French
people there was the so-called French government, which he took for
France." A "usurped power" had risen from the defeat—Vichy—which had
shut the French people into "the trap of the Armistice". For the argument
that the Armistice was needed to save six million Frenchmen was bogus.
The Belgians had signed no armistice, but Belgian manhood had not been
exterminated in German prison camps, for the good reason that the Germans

needed their captive manpower to work in their factories and on their farms. But what Vichy had done was to corrupt the spirit of France, and in a way which could not simply be ignored or forgotten, as Saint-Exupéry was proposing. All it had been able to contribute to the struggle against Hitler was the ludicrous and typically "defeatist" scuttling of the French fleet at Toulon. The future would judge, to be sure; but in the meantime the, soldiers of Fighting France—those of the submarine *Surcouf*, the heroes of Bir-Hacheim, and first and foremost the man who had rescued France's honour in her darkest hour, General de Gaulle—represented France morally and with far greater right than someone like Darlan, under whose orders the French in North Africa now found themselves disgracefully compelled to serve.

The truth, of course, was that in this debate both Maritain and Saint-Exupéry were right and at the same time wrong. The debate could not be settled on the level of principles or humanitarian feelings to which Saint-Ex had raised it. The Armistice might have saved a few French cities from bombardment, which at the height of the *débâcle* was hardly necessary, so great was the existing panic and confusion. It had to a limited extent allowed the Pétain government, or more exactly the genuine patriots serving it, to limit the damage as regards German exactions. But its supreme contribution had been to keep North Africa out of German hands. The fundamental question was thus not one of right or wrong but of expediency. It was what Washington had understood in refusing to break relations with Vichy while Robert Murphy, the American Ambassador's right-hand man, was delegated to prepare the North African invasion. But was Vichy necessary to save North Africa? Neither Saint-Exupéry nor Maritain could answer that question in any conclusive fashion. Indeed, almost fifty years after the event historians as well as politicians are still divided on the subject.

Maritain's rebuttal upset Saint-Exupéry considerably. His one aim all along had been to avoid polemics and passionate debate and the turgid in-fighting which had turned the French colony in New York into a "basket of crabs", and here he was being sucked into the mêlée. And this precisely at a moment when he had issued an appeal for union. Maritain could at least raise the debate to his own high level, whereas a Gaullist fanatic like Pierre-André Weill could find no better reply than to declare that Saint-Exupéry was an amateur who flew in order to be able to spin out best-selling books!

Having in *Pilote de Guerre* denounced the totalitarian imposition of one system of thought on all others and asserted that the task of a religion, and thus of a philosophy, is not to crush but to convert, Saint-Exupéry felt that he had to see Maritain whom he had met more than once and attempt a public reconciliation. Maritain accepted the proposal, but fearing an explosive reaction from *France Forever*, whose members would not have forgiven his meeting so arrant a "Pétainist", he insisted it be kept secret. A clandestine encounter was accordingly arranged in a small French printing-shop managed by Michel Pobers on Greenwich Street, not far from the fruit market. The debate lasted far into the night, but failed to narrow the gap between their respective positions. For lack of anyone better he had placed his trust in De Gaulle, and this being (as with so many others) an act of blind faith, Maritain could not be swayed by rational arguments.

"One of the things which most set him apart from the Free French" Michel Pobers recalls of Saint-Exupéry, "was his refusal to see the war from a purely strategic point of view. Saint-Ex saw it above all from a human point of view. When the submarine base of Lorient was bombed, for example, his agonized reaction was to ask: 'How many French men and women perished in this raid?' His major preoccupation was: 'Can our people survive all these privations and destruction?' With the possible exception of Simone Weil, who almost starved to death in her desire to share the lot of her compatriots ('I only wish to eat what the French are eating'), I have never known anyone who possessed a greater physical feeling for man and his sufferings."

*     *     *

This feeling found eloquent expression in the last of the three books Saint-Exupéry wrote during his stay in the United States. Like *The Little Prince*, *Lettre à un otage* (Letter to a Hostage) was a creature of circumstance, and indeed of accident. Originally it was not intended for separate publication but only as a preface for a book which his friend Léon Werth had been writing about occupied France. They had corresponded about it and Werth had managed to smuggle out the text before the Germans put an end to the unoccupied zone at the time of the North African landings. When it finally reached New York, its recipient was appalled by the intransigeance of the tone, which struck him as almost "Gaullist". The preface had been intended to develop, on a more poetic plane, the ideas Saint-Ex had expounded in the *New York Times Magazine*; and having gone this far, he needed little persuading to relinquish his little essay to Jacques Schiffrin and Robert Tenger, who had launched a series of Brentano's Books to provide expatriate authors with some badly needed royalties. Schiffrin, who had helped Gide launch the *Pléiade* series of French classics for Gallimard, was naturally known to Saint-Ex, while Tenger, before turning his hand to literature, had acted as Consuelo's lawyer before the war. Both she and Antoine were frequently invited out to the Tengers' country house in Connecticut, where Saint-Ex, as experimentally curious as ever, would entertain the company with spiritualist sessions in which a three legged table was lifted from the floor and made to turn in mid-air.

By far the shortest of Saint-Exupéry's works, *Lettre à un otage* was a kind of prose poem devoted to the intertwining themes of friendship and exile. "Absence" La Rochefoucauld once remarked, "strengthens a strong passion and weakens a feeble one". In Saint-Exupéry's language, which bears an equally close kinship to Keats' ("Heard melodies are sweet, but those unheard are sweeter,") this truth was summed up in this simple sentence: "The presence of a friend who in appearance is far removed, can prove denser than a real presence. As dense as a prayer." The distant presence which had been haunting his spirit in New York was that of Werth, to whom this literary fragment, like *Le Petit Prince*, was dedicated. His friend's plight was in some ways almost as unreal as that of the refugees he had seen flocking to the Estoril casino while the world was crumbling into ruin around their fortunes. But whereas their plush exodus, depicted by Saint-Ex in a few devastating strokes, had left the latter rootless and even more vapid than rich people are apt to get, the "inner exile" now being endured by Werth and his martyred countrymen was dense with significance and substance. As was that moment of joy, that sense of mystic happiness which had filled him that day when they had sat lunching by the Saône, in the riverside restaurant near Tournus, where the German bargeman and his companion had been invited up to join them. As dense with human meaning as was the smile which had enabled him, during a tense moment of the Spanish Civil War, to disarm the menacing suspicions of a group of anarchists who were preparing to shoot him in the belief that he was a spy.

"Is not this quality of joy the most precious fruit of civilization?" he went on. "A totalitarian tyranny might also satisfy us in our material needs. But we are not cattle to be fattened . . . Respect for man! There is the touchstone! When the Nazi respects only what resembles him, he does not respect himself. He refuses creative contradictions, ruins all hope of ascension, and instead of man, he founds—for a thousand years—the robot of the termiteheap. Order for order's sake castrates man of his essential power, which is to transform the world and himself. Life creates order, but order does not create life."

It was his answer to Goebbels and his glib spokesman Otto Abetz finally delivered in written form. But it was accompanied a little further on by an unmistakable lament for the continuing disorder displayed by his compatriots in the face of the monolithic order of the German war machine. "I am so tired of polemics, excommunications, and fanaticisms! I can enter your home without donning a uniform, without having to submit to the recitation of a Koran, without having to renounce a whit of my inner being. With you I do not need to justify myself. I don't have to plead or prove: I find peace, as at Tournus."

How different from New York, where he had to plead and justify and defend the very tolerance he wished to preserve; where the Gaullists, emboldened by Vichy's collapse, were now baying more loudly than ever for immediate power and recognition, egged on by Adrien Tixier, anxious to ape the stiff-necked intransigeance of his master. As Henri de Kerillis was later to note in his book, *De Gaulle, Dictateur*: "We were witnessing an almost exact repetition of one of the most striking political phenomena of the pre-war period, when the firmest, most faithful, most steadfast friends France had in the world—like a Churchill, a Benes, a Titulesco—were being treated by the factions in Paris with the same hatred as the Germans. Similarly, during the long period during which he laboured for the liberation of France, Roosevelt had no more relentless enemies than the Gaullists."

In the same book, which, be it said in passing, no French publisher has dared reprint since the late 1940s, Kerillis summed up the two contrasting attitudes towards the prosecution of the war. On the one hand there was De Gaulle's affirmation of 1940: "France has lost a battle, she has not lost the war." On the other hand, there was Saint-Exupéry's, which amounted to saying: "General, tell the truth. France lost the war. But her allies will win it."

On Christmas Eve Darlan was assassinated in Algiers and General Giraud, whom Saint-Exupéry had volunteered to smuggle out of France, automatically stepped into his shoes. His accession to the top military and administrative post in North Africa was the signal for an all-out campaign of denigration among Manhattan's super-patriots which further outraged, though it no longer surprised Saint-Ex. Paul Winckler, who headed the "Opera Mundi" news syndicate, even had the delicacy to suggest that Giraud's "escape" from Koenigstein had been secretly agreed to by the Germans through the mediation of the Worms bank. The battle on behalf of De Gaulle had now taken precedence over the battle against the Germans simply because, as André Philip (then a rabid Gaullist) one day remarked to Kerillis, "Giraud is a Fascist!" Nor was there any easy way of convincing such self-appointed inquisitors that their hallowed "truth" might be not only over-simplified but warped. When Léon Wencelius invited Philip to lunch with Saint-Exupéry and himself at the Aiglon restaurant, Philip's son Olivier outdid his father's own intransigeance by heatedly declaring that all the "Fascist traitors" had to be executed. The designated victims had changed camp, but Saint-Ex had no trouble recognizing the same fanatic intolerance which had moved Goering to wrath against "the pygmies"; and this and other conversations of the same general kind inspired him, in *Citadelle*, to compose the portrait of the "cross-eyed prophet . . . smouldering with a holy rage" whose righteous zeal demands the purging of all those less righteous than himself.

Now that part of France had resumed the battle, Saint-Exupéry was more anxious than ever to get away from "this basket of crabs", whose abject squabbling depressed him beyond words. "There are times when I simply have to get away from my own countrymen," he would say to Alexander Makinsky, who had returned from Lisbon to occupy an office in Rockefeller Centre. It was galling to realize that Galantière was already in North Africa while he was forced to remain behind twiddling his thumbs. But not until January did the first glimmer of a hope begin to dawn with the arrival in Manhattan of General Antoine Béthouart. The man who had led the French at Narvik and later been arrested by Noguès for helping the Allied landings in Morocco, had been sent over by Giraud at the head of a high level mission to procure weapons for his woefully underarmed soldiers. In Washington Béthouart had been received at the White House, invited to New Year's Day lunch by General Marshall, given an office in the building of the Joint Chiefs of Staff, and offered a warm welcome by top American officials which contrasted singularly with the one offered him by Adrien Tixier—"the plumber", as Franklin Roosevelt liked to call him—who being under the standard Gaullist impression that all Frenchmen in North Africa were collaborators and traitors, found it hard to believe that fifty thousand of them could already be fighting the Germans in Tunisia.

The moment they learned of his arrival, Saint-Exupéry and Léon Wencelius hastened down to Washington. At the Shoreham Hotel, where he had been given a suite, Béthouart assured them that he would get them the highest priority rating so that they could leave for North Africa as remobilized French officers. A little later, when Béthouart came up to New York, he found it almost impossible to climb into a taxi without being asked: "Are you for Giraud or De Gaulle?"—so open had the feuding now become. To which the General, whose aim (like Saint-Ex's) was to reconcile, rather than divide the French, would invariably reply: "I am for both of them. I am French." It was what Saint-Exupéry would also have liked to say—had the behaviour of local Gaullists not put him off completely. Béthouart's optimism on this point seems to have been shared, for a short time at any rate, by Jacques Lemaigre-Dubreuil, a member of the "Committee of Five" (who had helped Robert Murphy prepare the North African invasion) and the only civilian on Béthouart's staff. When Saint-Ex and Léon Wencelius went to visit him at the Saint-Regis in New York, Lemaigre-Dubreuil kept them until four o'clock in the morning, listening in morbid fascination as they explained in detail why they simply could not be Gaullists.

During the several weeks which Béthouart spent in New York, he saw Saint-Exupéry almost daily, and it was indeed in Saint-Ex's apartment that the General was introduced to his future wife, Minou de Montgomery. January faded into February and while Saint-Ex waited impatiently for his orders to come through, there was a new and virulent outbreak of Gaullist crab-clawing. It was occasioned by the arrival in American waters of the French cruiser *Montcalm*, which docked at Philadelphia, and the battleship *Richelieu*, which had managed to escape destruction during the British bombardment of Mers-el-Kébir and which had now crossed the Atlantic to be refitted and modernized for action against the Germans. From his base at Swarthmore Wencelius organized dances with cooperative co-eds to keep the *Montcalm*'s sailors entertained, and one evening Saint-Ex joined him for a visit to the officers' mess, where they were received by the Captain, who answered to the solidly Breton name of de Brannelec.

In New York the *Richelieu*'s officers were given the red carpet treatment by Manhattan hostesses who bent over backwards to make them feel at home with cocktail parties and receptions. But because their commander, Admiral Fenard, had been a close associate of Darlan, the Gaullists in New York whipped up a violent campaign against him. Not content with that, they went to work on the crew, who were intercepted in the bars by emissaries who sought to persuade them that once the ship had been refitted, Fenard (a pro-Nazi) would desert the Allies and go over to the Germans! It was thus their duty as French patriots to join De Gaulle, the only Frenchman who was really fighting the enemy (they forgot to add, from the front-line dug-out of Carlton Gardens). One hundred and twenty of the *Richelieu*'s sailors were gullible enough to swallow these gospel truths, and quietly deserting their ship with the connivance of a "Colonel Brunswick" of the Gaullist forces, they were smuggled up to Halifax, in Nova Scotia, and ferried from there to England, only to discover that De Gaulle had no ships for them to serve in!

Saint-Exupéry, who visited the *Richelieu* with Consuelo, was as scandalized by these incredible goings-on as were André Maurois and Louis Rougier, who accompanied them with their wives. So was General Béthouart, who took the matter up with Pierre de Chevigné, only to hear this dyed-in-the-wool Gaullist say: "I must, after all, tell you, General, that for us yours is a white army, while ours is a red army." An answer which opened the guileless general's eyes to the singular mentality of certain of New York's more frenetic Gaullists.

The dismal upshot of the "*Richelieu* affair" was that the battleship came near to being immobilized for months, while several smaller French warships had their crews so "debauched" by Gaullist agents that they were forced to sail from New York dangerously undermanned. One of them, having lost eight out of ten gunners, was even sunk! For Henri de Kerillis this was the last straw, and as he wrote in his diary: "I desert forever a Gaullism whose actions divide the French, outrage the Allies, and which are now responsible for a German victory over a French ship. *Adieu De Gaulle!*"

Though he was also a veteran aviator, Henri de Kerillis had never been on particularly close terms with Saint-Exupéry, who cared little for politicians and who had probably not forgotten Kerillis's pre-war sympathy for Mussolini's war on Abyssinia and Franco's "crusade" in Spain. But on the subject of De Gaulle they now saw eye to eye. It was time to get away from the poisoned atmosphere of New York and back into the fray. Béthouart had promised him a top priority, but Saint-Ex found it unexpectedly challenged by Adrien Tixier in Washington. What! Give Saint-Exupéry a priority rating and have him flown across the Atlantic to North Africa? Most certainly not, decreed the "Plumber". He would travel in a troop ship, like the infantry. Saint-Exupéry was livid, but could do nothing about it. It was the first Gaullist veto he was forced to endure, but it was by no means to be the last.

\* \* \*

Antoine and Consuelo, meanwhile, had left 240 Central Park South and moved to a four storey brownstone house on Beekman Place which had once been specially furnished for Greta Garbo. "I know nothing more charming in all New York," Denis de Rougemont noted in his Journal. "Tawny wall-to-wall carpeting, large faded mirrors, an old dark green library, a sort of Venetian patina where the ships glide by in front of the windows as though on a level with the carpets."

The view over the East River gave Saint-Exupéry a foretaste of that sea he would soon be crossing, and their new habitat brought him into contact with the East side of Manhattan which he had never properly explored before. One day Michel Pobers accompanied him on a walk down the waterfront as far as the Bowery. An occasional entry in Saint-Ex's notebooks betrays the passing irritation he felt with American civilization ("Horrible American businessman. Horrible distributors and consumers of ugly objects. These crowds are no longer illuminated by their shawls"—a comment elucidated by this other entry: "America needs to be fertilized by a concept capable of carrying a religious movement.") But on this particular day what he saw left him open-mouthed with wonder. At the level of 14th Street he was amused to see a sign advertising a "Labor Temple", where the figure "32" had been crossed out to read "33 Religions Together under one Roof". It struck him as a marvellous demonstration of what today would be called the "ecumenical spirit". And how different from that sectarian pettiness which had turned the French community into a basket of back-biting crabs! In the same way he marvelled to see how in the poverty-ridden area of the Bowery a strangely mixed community of Poles, Jews, Hungarians, and Ukrainians managed to co-exist without friction or apparent animosity. "In Europe" he remarked to Pobers, "if a de luxe car were to drive through here, you would see the envy, not to say hatred on everyone's face. But here people say: 'I don't have one, but my son will.' "

Saint-Exupéry's last days in New York were spent in anxious search of a uniform. He had reached America as a civilian, but he was leaving as a redrafted officer. None of the Army & Navy stores he visited could provide him with what he needed, particularly in the limited time available. A custom-made uniform would take too long to make. Time was beginning to run out and Saint-Ex getting steadily more worried when one of his friends came up with the solution: the one man who could meet his needs was a tailor who made costumes for the Metropolitan Opera. Saint-Exupéry bustled over to see him, and sure enough the tailor had something to offer: a dark blue uniform which he dragged out from his reserves and which was large enough to span his client's massive frame. The brass buttons were plain, instead of bearing the French Air Force insignia, and the gold epaulets were of twisted braid, making him look at first sight more like the chief porter of a Kurhotel in a continental spa than a recently remobilized airman. But it was too late to quibble; and paying cash on the spot he made off with the finery.

Though he had sunk no roots, was anything but a New Yorker, and had made few friends outside of the French colony, now that the time had come to leave Manhattan, he was almost sorry to bid good-bye to the land which had offered him a refuge in exile. It meant saying farewell to a number of good friends—like Maurice Maeterlinck the playwright, and Edgar Varese, the composer of "concrete" music in whose little brick house on Sullivan Street he had been introduced to William Carlos Williams and W. H. Auden. Above all, it meant saying good-bye to Consuelo, and what would his Rose now do, or not do, without him?

It was close to April 10th when he finally received his travel orders for passage across the Atlantic on an Allied transport. He was in a state of such febril excitement that on the eve of his departure he kept Denis de Rougemont up until five o'clock in the morning, talking and arguing about everything. Was he driven by some strange premonition that he might never see him again? Rougemont, in any case, was struck once again by his comments on his "posthumous work" which seemed to imply some kind of death wish. "Later, when you read this," he would say of *Citadelle*, the implication being, "after my death".

When Rougemont returned a few hours later for the final parting, he found his friend Antoine posing for a photographer in his Metropolitan Opera uniform. Pierre Lazareff showed up at almost the same moment and Rougemont could not resist a touch of irony: "My, but you look like your photographs!"—a remark he regretted an instant later when he saw that instead of amusing, it had touched his friend Tonio to the quick. An almost sleepless night had put Saint-Ex on edge and he was visibly nervous about the theatrical ordeal he was going to have to endure when the time came for the parting from Consuelo.

Faithful as ever, Roger Beaucaire accompanied him to the taxi, where Saint-Ex climbed in next to Michel Pobers for the drive down to the dockside and the transport that was to take him overseas. At forty-eight Beaucaire was too old to fly, and he may well have wondered how his friend from the Aéropostale was going to fare in his passionate determination to return to the front.

Adrien Tixier might have been able to keep Saint-Exupéry from being flown across the ocean, but he could not prevent him from being the first French civilian permitted to embark on a troop transport bound for North Africa. The crew and passengers on his ship had been issued winter clothing, leading them to suppose that the convoy in which they were travelling was headed for England. But it did not take Saint-Ex long to realize that this was a subtle artifice aimed, for reasons of security, to obscure their real destination. Using a plumb-line which he stuck to a companionway beam with a piece of chewing-gum, he could roughly measure the angle of displacement made by the sun at high noon; and he was soon able to calculate that they were steering towards Gibraltar.

The seemingly interminable voyage, in a tortoise-paced convoy, took three full weeks, and not until May 4 did the gleaming white kasbah and villa dotted heights of Algiers finally heave into view. The first person Saint-Exupéry looked up, on landing, was his old friend Georges Pélissier, who was delighted to offer him a room in his apartment at 17, Rue Denfert-Rochereau. At French Air Force headquarters he found another friend—Lionel Chassin, his former seaplane instructor at Brest. He had transferred out of the Navy, and was now a Lieutenant Colonel in the Air Force. As for his old squadron, *La Hache*, it was now stationed at Laghouat, near the palm-oasis town of Biskra, in southern Algeria, and commanded by René

Gavoille, since promoted to Captain. Impatient to renew contact with his wartime colleagues of the 2/33, Saint-Ex managed to borrow an air-force liaison plane the very next day, and on the evening of May 5th he put down on the ochre-hued field of Laghouat, where Alain Jourdan, a newcomer to the squadron, saw him climb out of his plane and "walk massively towards us smiling that smile of his which he knew how to make so radiant".

The pilots undergoing training at Laghouat were all lodged at the Hôtel Transatlantique, a small desert caravanserai whose twenty clients—there was hardly room for more—sought refuge from the heat and the glare in the shade of mat-covered corridors and Moslem arabesques. One of them was the airman-author Jules Roy, who had been given a "suite" of two small rooms. He had just gone to bed in the dark—the electric current from the local generator being automatically switched off each evening at 11 p.m.—when he heard voices on the other side of the partition and realized that someone was being installed in the empty room next to his. He could even recognize the muffled voice of Saint-Exupéry, whom he had met briefly at the airfield of Maison-Blanche in late June of 1940. He heard him run the water in the basin and the bed creak as he laid his massive bulk to rest. A moment later there was the sound of a striking match and by and by the sweet scent of American tobacco wafted into his room.

The next morning Roy knocked on the communicating door and found Saint-Exupéry already "seated up in bed, a cigarette between his lips, his night-bird eyes wide open with thought . . . His narrow room was clogged with handsome suitcases opening to reveal fine linen, and on the mantelpiece he had placed a small methyl stove on which he had brewed himself some tea."

Not being a member of the same squadron, Roy, much to his regret, was not invited to the *méchoui* dinner Saint-Ex offered his old comrades-in-arms that evening. Alias, having gone back to France (where he ended up in an air-force resistance network based in Vichy), had been replaced as Group commander by Major Piéchon, but his deputy was the same François Laux (now a Captain) who had welcomed Saint-Ex to the quaint, stove-pipe shack at Orconte in that snow-bound December of 1940. And what a joy to see Jules Hochedé, whose praises he had sung in *Pilote de Guerre*, and that tireless work-horse René Gavoille, his beet-red face forever marked by the burns he had suffered the day he had crash-landed his bullet-ridden Potez some distance east of Laon. "We'll talk about it after the war," Saint-Ex had said to him one day at the height of the *débâcle*, only to hear Gavoille give him this unforgettable retort: "You really don't think, Captain, that we'll still be alive after the war?" And yet here they were, miraculous survivors of an unforgettable adventure. With Gavoille now in charge of the squadron and Saint-Ex, his elder by a good ten years, asking only to serve once again as a *"caporal-pilote"*!

Saint-Exupéry's visit to Laghouat was brief. The squadron had just been attached to Colonel Elliott Roosevelt's Third Photographic Group and ordered to proceed to Oujda, in eastern Morocco, where the United States Air Force had established a training base for Lockheed P-38 pilots. Determined to get himself reassigned to his old squadron, Saint-Ex flew back up to Algiers to take care of the formalities. His squadron mates lined up near the palm-grove, forming a kind of "guard of honour" (in Jules Roy's words) for the take-off, which went off smoothly; but a little later when Roy landed at Bou Saada, he saw a plane with a crumpled landing-gear near the edge of the field. It was the plane Saint-Ex had flown off in from Laghouat, but this mishap at the end of the first hop had not kept the impatient airman from quickly "hitching" a ride the rest of the way up to Algiers.

Another Orconte veteran, Major (he had been promoted) Max Gelée, had just been transferred from Laghouat to Giraud's headquarters in Algiers, but Saint-Exupéry had an even better introduction in the person of René Chambe, who, since he had last seem him in Marrakesh, had added two general's stars to his uniform. He had been part of the network which had helped Giraud escape from Koenigstein and had even hidden him for a whole week in his village in the Dauphiné; but having had trouble getting out of occupied France through Spain, Chambe had only reached Algiers in January, by which time the top air-force job had already been offered to General Bouscat. Determined to keep him by his side, even though he did not always heed his advice, Giraud had refused to let him join an active unit and named him his Director of Information.

Saint-Exupéry found Chambe installed in an office in the quaintly Moorish Palais d'Eté—the "Summer Palace" up on the hill which Giraud had made his headquarters. Chambe could not conceal his surprise when he heard his friend explain that he wanted to rejoin his old squadron and pilot a Lightning, at that time the fastest fighter in existence. Saint-Exupéry wasn't exactly young, and this was considered a singularly "hot ship". Almost certainly it would require special permission and be anything but easy. But Saint-Ex was insistent, and Chambe finally agreed to take the matter up with General Giraud himself.

When Giraud heard that Saint-Exupéry was in Algiers, he said: "Have him come up here for breakfast tomorrow." At the Summer Palace eight o'clock breakfast was an unfailing ritual at which it was often Giraud's custom to "receive".

There were several other officers present the next morning in addition to Giraud and Chambe. The breakfast lasted half an hour—apparently an unusually long time for one of these "receptions"—and Giraud seemed most interested in what Saint-Ex had to tell him about the United States. Saint-Exupéry made no effort to conceal his anti-Gaullist feelings and forebodings, but to his surprise he found Giraud remarkably serene on the subject. Two weeks before he had made a conciliatory gesture by sending General Bouscat, who had once sat on the same bench with De Gaulle at the Ecole Supérieure de Guerre, to open negotiations in London, and it now seemed but a question of time before the Free French leader transferred his headquarters to Algiers. Saint-Exupéry suggested that it might be wiser to let him stay put in London, where the damage he could do was relatively limited, whereas in Algiers there was no telling what might happen. What he had seen in New York—not to mention what General Odic had told him—had robbed him of all illusions. Chambe had given Giraud the same advice, but Saint-Exupéry's suggestions fell on equally deaf ears. Like many well-meaning soldiers, Giraud felt out of his depth in the welter of politics into which he had been thrust, and the constant Gaullist carping at his "dictatorial" inclinations had undermined his will. To prove his critics wrong he intended to play the game; and playing the game meant giving De Gaulle his due and letting him come to Algiers.

Saint-Exupéry came away from this first encounter anything but impressed. "So that is your Giraud!" was all he had to say to Chambe, but the tone was enough.

Just what happened after this is not altogether clear. Chambe claims that Giraud asked him to take up the cudgels for Saint-Exupéry by going to see the Americans, whose word in the field of aviation was law. At the nearby Hôtel Saint-Georges, where Eisenhower had his headquarters, Chambe was informed that the Supreme Commander was too busy to receive him. His Chief of Staff, General Walter Bedell Smith, listened to him politely, said neither Yes nor No, but sought to make it clear that the U.S. Air Force enjoyed a certain autonomy which Higher Headquarters was loath to trample on. Back at the Palais d'Eté Chambe told Giraud that Bedell Smith had been at best luke-warm and that the only chance of Saint-Exupéry's obtaining clearance would rest with an order from the summit.

"All right," said Giraud. "I'll attend to it personally."

He rang up Eisenhower, who may never have heard of Saint-Exupéry—he was not, after all, a Bobby Jones—and Ike was sufficiently impressed by Giraud's insistence to give his agreement.

In all probability these various démarches were spread out over several days, for both Eisenhower and Giraud had more important things to worry about than the future of Saint-Ex. News of the fall of Tunis and Bizerte reached Algiers on May 8th, one day before Joan of Arc's Day (May 9th) which was celebrated with wild rejoicings. One hundred thousand people flocked out to cheer the big military parade, personally led by Giraud and the Foreign Legion's famous slow-pacing band. On the manoeuvre grounds west of Algiers General Eisenhower took Giraud on an inspection tour of the massive quantities of tanks, trucks, anti-aircraft guns, and howitzers which—thanks to the agreement Béthouart had worked out in Washington with Harry Hopkins and General Marshall—were to equip the French as well as American forces in North Africa. De Gaulle was still in London, fuming like a factory chimney over the ovation given his rival (Giraud); but in Algiers for a brief deceptive moment the political bickering was forgotten and the atmosphere recalled the *Union Sacrée* of 1917–1918 and the comradeship which had once bound the soldiers of Pershing and Foch.

Giraud, in the meantime, had been doing some thinking, and the idea had occurred to him, or at least to someone on his staff, that Saint-Exupéry's eloquence might be put to profitable use in the cause of "reconciliation", which was the watchword of the hour. Probably he had been struck by the importance Saint-Exupéry attached to the notion of "*la France d'abord*"— France first of all—and since this sentiment coincided with his own, he asked Saint-Exupéry to undertake a goodwill tour of French army messes in Morocco. The secondary purpose of this trip was to determine how the officers he talked to felt about Giraud, or for that matter De Gaulle. During the victory parade in Tunis General Leclerc, a rabid Gaullist, had refused to let his handful of desert veterans march with the 7,000 soldiers of the *Armée d'Afrique* which Juin had so brilliantly commanded against the remnants of the Afrika Korps, and Giraud was understandably anxious to know if similar frictions were at work in Morocco. The fact that Saint-Exupéry was a civilian who was not identified with any camp might make it easier for otherwise cautious officers to open up on the subject.

Saint-Ex was probably equally curious to take the pulse of army sentiment, and since he needed Giraud's support vis-à-vis the Americans, he was hardly in a position to refuse. Besides, he must have been warned that a week or two at least would be needed for his American clearance to come through, and a trip to Morocco in the interim would be anything but a hardship. What is certain is that he flew down to Casablanca in a *Simoun*, which was made available to him by the French Air Force. From Casablanca he flew on to Marrakesh, where he spent a pleasantly inactive week in the villa of Colonel Georges de Chassey, who was in charge of the local air base and the training of new French units. Informed by a telephone call from higher headquarters that Saint-Exupéry would be arriving, Chassey was much surprised to see him turn up in a dark blue Air Force uniform. Though it was only mid-May, it was already swelteringly hot—with temperatures of 100° Fahrenheit and over in the early afternoon—and Chassey and his fellow officers were all in sun-tan shirts and shorts. Saint-Exupéry amused his host by telling him the story of his Metropolitan Opera gear, but he lost no time shedding the regulation Air Force outfit he had since picked up in Algiers. For when Chassey walked into the villa's living-room early the next morning, he was met by a most extraordinary sight. A completely naked Saint-Ex was walking to and fro with, in his left hand, a book he was intently reading, and, in his right hand, an electric razor with which he was rather absently shaving. A long extension cord had been hooked up to the wall-plug to assure him a maximum of peripatetic movement.

Chassey was under the impression that his famous guest had simply flown down to Marrakesh on a week's leave of absence, and Saint-Exupéry was evidently content to make it appear like a holiday, no more. His job being above all to listen and report, he breathed not a word about any mission Giraud might have entrusted to him, informal or otherwise. But in Casablanca, where he looked up his old friend Henri Comte, he was more confiding. Here as in Marrakesh most officers were solidly Giraudist. The Gaullists, however, had set up an active propaganda centre which was doing its best to lure away soldiers from regular army units and to recruit young men who had recently smuggled their way out of France. Comte had seen Gaullist agents get to work on two of his nephews, and he shared Saint-Exupéry's indignation over these brazen attempts to build up a "simon-pure" army, untainted by the original sin of Pétainism and that insidious corruption of the spirit which made men loyal to Giraud.

On his way back Saint-Exupéry made a slight detour via Oujda, near the Algerian border, whither his old squadron (*La Hache*) had now been transferred from Laghouat. Here, according to the *Journal de Marche*, he spent the evening of May 26th dazzling his pilot friends with several hours of card tricks before turning in for the night. The next morning he flew on to the La Sénia airfield, near Oran, where he caught a brief glimpse of Mermoz' old navigator, Jean Dabry. His *Simoun*, a distinctly weather-beaten "taxi", took to trembling so violently during the last lap back to Algiers that at one point Saint-Ex was afraid the wings were going to snap in mid-air. "*Mon vieux*," he later described the feeling to Dr. Pélissier, "I've never seen anything like it. I was really scared." But the mechanical delirium ended in time for him to put down safely at Maison-Blanche and even to make a luncheon date at the luxurious villa of Anne Heurgon-Desjardins. Here he was greeted by a surprise—in the form of André Gide, who had just been flown in that morning from Tunis.

When Saint-Exupéry rang up the Palais d'Eté to inform Giraud that he was back, he was invited up for another breakfast. This one seems to have been more private than the first, for Chambe was not present. Saint-Ex lost no time expressing his outrage at what he had discovered in Casablanca, almost a carbon copy duplication of the "encouragement to desert" techniques he had seen the Gaullists apply to the crew of the *Richelieu* in New York.

"Eat," said Giraud, nodding at the bread and jam which his guest, in his eagerness to talk, had hardly touched. Between mouthfuls Saint-Ex continued his pessimistic report, predicting the worst if these Gaullist practices were not countered, until finally Giraud stopped him: "Enough! You can have confidence in someone who escaped from Koenigstein."

When Léon Wencelius reached Algiers three months later, Saint-Exupéry gave him an even more dramatic account of how this breakfast ended. According to this version, he ended up telling Giraud: "*Mon Général*, if you have General de Gaulle come here, you will cease to be anything. You will never achieve your dream. You will never enter Metz"—the city of which Giraud had been military governor and which he intended to liberate at the head of his troops. It was too much for Giraud, who flinging his napkin impatiently on to the table, exclaimed: "While you're at it, Saint-Ex, why not call me an idiot?"

Before obtaining his final clearance Saint-Exupéry had to wait out one more week—a particularly critical week which was to mark the high-tide of Giraud's power and the onset of his decline. Algiers was aswarm with airmen and army officers whom Saint-Ex knew and who could fill him in on the momentous feud which was already beginning to tear Algiers to pieces. There was General Odic, who had reached Algiers at about the same time as himself and who, like Chambe, was immediately appointed to Giraud's staff. There was Roger de Sinéty, cousin of the fair Odette he had courted at the Château de Passay, in whose villa at Borj-el-Ahmin, in the outskirts of Algiers, Robert Murphy's assistants Kenneth Pendar, John Boyd, and Felix Cole had set up a radio transmitter to prepare the North African invasion. And there was Major Olivier Martin, a member of the French Air Force mission to London who had been placed under house arrest by the British for refusing to join De Gaulle. He had since joined the staff of Marcel Peyrouton, the Governor General of Algeria, whose company Saint-Ex seems to have found particularly congenial. (The feeling was apparently mutual.)

Saint-Exupéry was still in Algiers when De Gaulle flew in on Sunday, May 30th, and in very short order his worst forebodings were confirmed. The Free French leader had hardly finished shaking hands with Giraud at the airfield than he announced, in a tone admitting of no debate: "*Je veux la tête d'Odic*." (I want Odic's head.) Giraud had been planning to make

Odic a member of the six man "Liberation Committee" which was being established in Algiers, but De Gaulle was determined to get rid of the man he had sought to have arrested in London.

The difference in style between the two French leaders sprang instantly to the eye. Unlike Giraud, whose comings and goings until then had been accomplished in a vehicle which was as "unpretentious and French as a Paris taxi"—to quote Kenneth Pendar—De Gaulle drove down in pomp to the Forum to lay a wreath before the Monument aux Morts. Several thousand Gaullist supporters (probably all Algiers could muster at the time) had been mobilized for the occasion, and their activities were not solely devoted to distributing Cross of Lorraine pins and photos of the General. Odic, who had wandered down to the square in civilian clothes suddenly found himself hedged by three or four men, who began thrusting banknotes at him. "Here, take this and work up a bit of enthusiasm!" The general declined the invitation, but was not overly surprised to hear the crowd take up the chant: "*Un seul chef, De Gaulle!*" with a vigour which was slightly more than spontaneous. Satisfied with this smoothly orchestrated "triumph", De Gaulle climbed back into his car and had himself proudly driven back to his villa on the hill with a noisy motorcycle escort (of the kind Giraud had never used).

What Saint-Exupéry—like Chambe, Odic, and others—had vainly sought to impress on Giraud, now proceeded to happen. The sparks began to fly at the very first meeting of the committee which had been set up as interim caretaker of French national interests. De Gaulle opened with an ultimatum demanding the purge of "Vichy officials", beginning with Marcel Peyrouton, the Governor General of Algeria. General Georges, whom British Intelligence had smuggled out of France at the special behest of his friend Winston Churchill, leapt heatedly to the defence of the man whose crime was to have wanted to continue the battle as Resident General of Tunisia in 1940 and who later, as Pétain's Minister of the Interior, had ordered the arrest of Pierre Laval. The internal Resistance about which De Gaulle claimed to be so well informed? He, Georges, knew something about it, having left France two years after the leader of the Free French. The France that mattered was not one of bickering resistance groups, many of them so rent by jealousies and rivalries that they were not above denouncing each other to the occupying authorities. "There is only one France, and not Pétainists, Gaullists, or Giraudists. All are united in the same hatred of the enemy. This is the union we must achieve."

It was the language Saint-Exupéry had used in New York, but it had no more impact on the monolithic iciness of De Gaulle than *Pilote de Guerre* and his *New York Times Magazine* appeal had had on the super-patriots of

Manhattan. Peyrouton, in a gesture of appeasement, tendered his resignation, asking to be allowed to take his place at the front as a reserve captain of infantry. The resignation was accepted with alacrity by De Gaulle, whose emissaries successfully intercepted the message intended for Giraud, to the latter's profound indignation. This time it looked as though De Gaulle had gone too far and that Giraud had had enough. For suddenly the streets of Algiers reverberated to the rumble of American tanks, French units stationed around the city were placed on the alert, and the guard around the Palais d'Eté was reinforced. For several hours it was touch and go, as the more determined anti-Gaullists sought to unleash a putsch aimed at arresting De Gaulle and forcibly expelling him to Brazzaville or some other remote place —the course Roosevelt and Sumner Welles all but openly favoured. But Giraud, not wishing to appear the "Fascist" the Gaullists had long accused him of being, let the crucial moment pass without giving the fateful order. "*L'affaire du café maure*" (the putsch had been planned in an Arab café not far from the Summer Palace) went up in a cloud of pipe-dream smoke which continued to perfume the hush-hush gossip of the capital for days and weeks thereafter. Peyrouton was allowed to retire and was replaced by General Catroux, who had already subordinated his five stars to General De Gaulle's two; and to show their gratitude for Giraud's moderation, the Gaullists started a whispering campaign insinuating that General Georges, in whom they now recognized an enemy, had been sent to North Africa as a secret agent of the Germans!

The next day (June 4) Saint-Ex was finally able to leave the politics-poisoned city with the authorization he so desperately wanted. He reappeared at Oujda with a smile radiant enough to make his comrades realize at a glance that he had at last been officially reinstated as a member of *La Hache*.

Getting himself reassigned to his old unit would not have been so difficult but for the fact that the squadron was in the process of abandoning the old Bloch 174s for the Lockheed Lightnings which Colonel Roosevelt had offered the French. The P 38, which they were being trained to pilot by their American mentors, was a far more complex and sophisticated craft than the Bloch Saint-Ex had flown three years before. At Orconte he had amused himself staggering the simple-minded farmer in whose house he was billeted by asking: "How many dials and controls do you think I have to keep track of?" The answer being 83. On the Lightning it was closer to 200. The two engines were fed by six different fuel tanks which could be opened or closed by special controls. Two of them were drop-tanks, used to propel the plane on the outbound run and which were jettisoned en route, to lighten the plane for the return. Each motor was equipped with a turbine supercharger which came on automatically at about 11,000 feet to maintain a constant pressure in the air intake; and by pulling a throttle to raise the air pressure even higher the pilot could give his Lightning an extra burst of speed—450 miles an hour on a horizontal course—to enable it to get away if surprised by a German fighter.

Oujda in the summer months sizzles in a desert heat not made to lessen the burdened pilot's tribulations. Simply climbing into one's gear, which each pilot had to do with the help of another, took a good five minutes. The heated flying-suit needed to protect Saint-Ex from the high altitude cold was made of padded and wired silk, which was not too heavy; but over it he had to slip a pair of overalls, the pockets of which were crammed with pencils, erasers, slide-rules, note-pads—all of them attached on lengths of string—as well as silk cloth maps, concentrated K-rations, and even foreign currencies to enable the pilot to subsist if forced to parachute to the ground. As though this were not enough, he also was required to strap on an inflatable Mae West—in case he bailed out over the sea—as well as a Colt revolver (to protect himself from German capture) and an emergency oxygen flask, clamped around his left shin, the tube of which had to be hooked up to the face-mask to keep him from losing consciousness during the first few thousand feet of his fall. The cockpit in these single-seaters was so small and cramped that it was all someone of Saint-Ex's outlandish size could do to squeeze into it, particularly with a parachute and an inflatable dinghy to sit on. The mouth-phone, for communicating with ground control, had to be adjusted beneath the face-mask, itself hooked by tube to an oxygen tank. The functioning of both had to be verified, as did the proper working of the cameras, during the "cockpit check"—an essential but tedious procedure which consumed all of five and sometimes ten perspiring minutes.

To his friends Saint-Ex had often joked about the reluctance of the U.S. Air Force to give clearance to a hoary old-timer whose flowing white beard might get "tangled up in the controls". But now that he had rejoined his old unit, he felt, as he put it in a letter to Curtice Hitchcock, twenty years younger. "I am not too old," he wrote almost gleefully, "since I have succeeded—even with your army—in remaining a pilot! On my arrival in Algiers I refused all other employment—they tried again to put me in the propaganda service"—a reference to Giraudoux's earlier attempt to recruit him in 1939.

"Dear Curtice," he went on, "I have tried with all my might to stick with my colleagues and away from politics, cities, and offices. I share the life in the field of the American army—and I am learning English!"—a spectacle his friend Bernard Lamotte would dearly have loved to witness. "I marvel at your compatriots. They are healthy, fit, and remarkably trained. The relations between them and my colleagues are completely pleasant. Yours is a very great country. As for your war effort, they understand it badly in America. Seen from here it is absolutely overpowering. You can't imagine the impression this avalanche of material creates.

"What I admire, above all, is a certain kind of very simple and noble courage—a kindly courage. I don't quite know how to express it but I shall write you all about it later. I have quite fallen in love with your country."

Which was more, alas, than he could say of his own. For, as he went on, "I was right, I believe, in everything I have been thinking about my country's affairs over the past two years. Today no more than yesterday do I like De Gaulle. He carries the threat of dictatorship, of national socialism . . . When national socialism is elsewhere dying out, it is hardly reasonable to revive it for France. I am terribly worried by that band of men, their appetite for slaughtering Frenchmen, their ambitions with respect to post-war politics (European block) which are likely to bring about a France as weak as Spain, to be no more than a satellite of Russia or Germany. It's not in that direction that the truth for me lies.

"Some day you will be of my opinion too, Curtice. You will smile sadly that I was treated as a Fascist because of my refusal to become Gaullist. Can one believe that De Gaulle represents democracy and General Giraud tyranny? What I hold against Giraud is rather that he has been as weak as a sheep and has yielded on all points to the dictator candidate."

What he carefully concealed from his American publisher was the other side of the coin: the dismay he felt at finding himself lodged three to a room on a large American base where the officers, like the men, had to line up with mess-kits for their food, which they ate standing up. "I feel a bit detached from life, as though in the concourse of the Gare Saint-Lazare," he wrote to Dr. Pélissier on this same day (June 8th). "The basic trouble, dear friend, is that I'm not well, which is sad because my physical state makes each climb as hard as an ascension of the Himalayas, and this additional sacrifice is unfair. Tiny things become pointless tortures. Like all these comings and goings in the heat of the sun. I find them so wearying that at times I feel like leaning my head against a tree and weeping with rage.

"But I prefer this so much to the terrible atmosphere of polemics. All I want is peace, even if it be eternal . . .

"I don't feel I have to indulge in endless self-justifications. I can no longer endure all this explaining, I have no accounts to render to anyone, and those who don't know me are simply strangers. I'm too tired, too weary to change. I have enemies enough to teach me, but I need friends who could be like gardens to rest in.

"*Mon vieux*, this evening I'm really down. It's sad, I would so enjoy liking life a little, but I don't. The other day when I thought I was a goner in mid-flight I regretted nothing.

"Write me about the Giraud-de Gaulle row. I'm appalled for my country."

Fortunately his stay at Oujda was brief. On June 15th the French flyers received orders to move to Maison-Blanche, the airport of Algiers. In all they now had five Lightnings, barely enough to equip a squadron. Their unit was known in official parlance as a "detachment", and Saint-Ex's dream was to have it expanded to a full-fledged Group (with two squadrons), as the 2/33 had been under Alias' energetic command. Major Piéchon, their commanding officer, agreed wholeheartedly—which probably explains why Saint-Exupéry was allowed to leave Oujda a day or two before his colleagues to act as their spokesman in Algiers. He called on Robert Murphy the afternoon of the 16th, and late that night in Dr. Pélissier's apartment he drafted a long letter to the American diplomat summing up his arguments.

He began by explaining that he had refused to become a Gaullist during his years of exile in the United States because he felt that it was the duty of a Frenchman abroad to bear witness for and not against his country. "I let myself be denounced as a 'Fascist' by people of the 'single party' "—he meant, of course, the Gaullists—"and I only broke my silence to write *Flight to Arras* and then a big article in the *New York Times* on the necessity for a French reconciliation at the time of the events in North Africa.

"Right or wrong, I continue to believe that the salvation of my country does not lie in a bloody purge launched by the fanatics of the 'single party', and that the future greatness of my country cannot be founded on the weird ideology of a European block where France, associated with eighty million Germans and one hundred and sixty million Slavs, would only play the role of an impotent satellite. Just as I refused in the name of the salvation of North Africa to criticize the policy of the State Department as regards its representation in France, so in the name of my country I refuse to associate myself with any campaign of distrust towards a future Franco-Anglo–American alliance. Right or wrong, I believe it is the only hope of salvation."

"Chance, which is occasionally favourable," Saint-Ex went on, "has enabled eight pilots of my air group to work in collaboration with your pilots of the Roosevelt Group. I shall write another *Flight to Arras*. In it I shall defend the points of view that are dear to me. But for my book to be effective it is essential that we should participate as soon as possible in your war missions. There are things I have a right to say if my comrades and I return from missions over Italy or France. I can only obtain a hearing if my comrades and myself have risked our lives for our ideas. If I don't take part in the war all I can do is withdraw into silence."

The letter ended with a request that Murphy ask Colonel Roosevelt to join Major Piéchon, another French major, and themselves (Murphy and Saint-Exupéry) for a joint dinner, since "our spiritual interests coincide."

The plea met with a favourable response, for a few days later the French flyers were issued their first Mae Wests and inflatable dinghys and informed that they would soon be transferring to Tunisia for the start of active operations. On June 22nd Saint-Ex and François Laux, the detachment's deputy commander, were both promoted to the rank of Major, and the good news was celebrated the next day with a particularly lively banquet at La Souma (in the suburb of Algiers), where the songs were bawdier than ever.

The solace this offered Saint-Exupéry was only partial. For in that stew-pot of plotting and intrigue known as Algiers the tension and fratricidal back-stabbing were more venomous than ever. One of General Catroux' first acts, as the newly appointed Governor General of Algeria, was to expel Jean Rigault, one of the "Committee of Five" civilians who had helped Robert Murphy and his colleagues prepare the North African landings. Another member of this pro-Allied committee, Jacques de Saint-Hardouin, was summarily dispossessed of his car. General Leclerc was clamouring for a wholesale purge of "traitors"—which is to say, of all those who had failed to join De Gaulle in 1940—to the consternation of Giraud, who remarked that this would mean erecting a guillotine in every village square in France. To which the truculent cavalryman replied: *"Parfaitement, mon général, pas d'hésitation."*

Not to be outdone, other Gaullist officers were busy organizing the *"débauchage"* of Giraud's units. Promised immediate promotions, better pay, and the expectation of being the first to land in France—under the sole banner of De Gaulle—officers and soldiers were smuggled out of Algiers in trucks to a spot with the stimulating name of *"Ravin de la Femme Sauvage"* (Wild Woman's Ravine), where they were clothed in new uniforms and issued new passes as members of the Free French forces. The same scandalous techniques Saint-Exupéry had witnessed in New York and Casablanca were now being employed in Algiers, where De Gaulle now claimed to be "at home" and master of the show. As Kenneth Pendar was to write in his fascinating book, *Adventure in Diplomacy,* "I remember the bitter discussion this caused at the Inter-Allied Club in an old Moorish palace where all Algerian gossip centred. General Béthouart, the man who had tried to help us in our Moroccan landings, and the late Antoine de Saint-Exupéry, the famous aviator and author, were in despair over the spectacle of two rival French Armies at a time when France herself was occupied by her most ruthless enemy." Pendar, who lived through these tense days with a sense of mounting exasperation against his own superiors (who failed to heed Sumner Welles' instructions to take a very firm line with De Gaulle), was for once understating the case. For so great was Saint-Ex's despair over the sordid spectacle of French soldiers squabbling with each other that at one of these lunches at the Cercle Inter-Allié, Pendar saw him vainly fight to stem the tears streaming down his cheeks.

A tragic accident now darkened his already sombre mood. The Group had just received orders to move to Tunis and Gavoille had already gone ahead to prepare the terrain when, on June 28th, Jules Hochedé, who had more war missions to his credit than any other among them, crashed into the sea off Cape Matifou during a training flight on a P-38. As Colonel Karl Polifka was later to admit, the Lightnings the French flyers had been given were "war-weary, non-airworthy craft". It is difficult, otherwise to understand how so seasoned a pilot as Hochedé could have met such an unexpected fate. The entire Group turned out for the funeral, which was attended by two generals and by Saint-Exupéry, for whom this loss was one more sword-thrust in the heart.

In early July the detachment, now designated as "Unit 4" in the NAPRW (North African Photo Reconnaissance Wing), moved to the airfield of La Marsa, not far from Tunis and the site of ancient Carthage. The pilots were given a villa by the shore and charmingly entertained by Madame Mast, the wife of the French general who had engineered the capture of Algiers by the Allies with a minimum of shooting (unlike the bloody hash of things which had been made in Casablanca). By unanimous agreement she was elected the Group's *"marraine"* or godmother, an honour she lived up to with more zeal than Marie Bell.

Gavoille, who had risen to be the detachment's commander since the departure of Major Laux (transferred to Giraud's headquarters), flew the first war mission on July 12th. He was foiled by clouds from taking photographs over France, but he had the satisfaction of outracing the German fighters which climbed up to have a shot at him over Sardinia. The following day André Henry, a former flying instructor from Istres who had just been made a second lieutenant, had better luck, and he was able to come back saying in his modest way: "It's a pleasure to see France again."

Saint-Exupéry was still undergoing training on the Lightning when the detachment was joined by Lieutenant Jean Leleu, a brilliant graduate of l'Ecole de l'Air at Versailles whom Alias had annexed in July of 1940 after Leleu had courageously volunteered to fly across the Mediterranean in an old Potez with a wooden propeller. "I can still see him," Leleu was later to recall his first glimpse of Saint-Ex, "his big awkward body negligently dressed in American suntans, striding with long steps towards our tent, which opened on to the runway. He ducked his head to enter, and I was struck by the extraordinary kindliness and liveliness of the expression in his eyes. He greeted me with a simplicity which surprised me in someone who had so many claims on· one's admiration and who was being talked about in America even more than in France and the French Empire."

It was on July 27th, after seven weeks of training, that Saint-Ex finally flew his first war mission over France. These flights on the Lightning were at least three times as exacting as those he, Gavoille, and the "old timers" had flown in 1939 and 1940 on the Potez 63s and the Bloch 174s. Most war missions in 1940 had lasted between one and a half and two hours; those on the P-38 could last up to six hours, most of which were flown at altitudes close to 30,000 feet where Saint-Exupéry's many fractures caused him intense pain because of the drastically reduced air pressure and the resultant distension of his bones. Leleu was not exaggerating when he described this first mission of Saint-Exupéry's as a "lovely, hard" one. "The Squadron was then operating over France and its job, among other things, was to photograph harbours, airfields, stations, in a word, all the focal points where the enemy was active. It was anything but a cushy job: from Tunis one had to cross the Mediterranean, spend two hours over France, and then regain one's base over the sea again. All of this at a height of 9,000 to 10,000 metres on an isolated, unarmed single-seater. Just to complicate matters Sicily, Sardinia, and Corsica were in enemy hands. Normally offering landmarks, ports of call, or havens for airmen venturing out over the sea, they were now danger spots from which fighters could take off to shoot down planes detected by their coastal radars." The flight route thus chosen lay well to the west of Sardinia and Corsica and took them straight up over the centre of the Mediterranean.

"Wrapped in his heavy padded togs and suffering from the Tunisian heat,"—to quote Leleu again—"Saint-Ex installed himself in the cockpit. He had to labour to do so, for his airplane accidents had played havoc with his bone structure and his muscles revived old pains . . . At midday he took off at last, stirring up the sand of the dried up *sebkha* which the Americans had turned into an airstrip, and disappeared into the blue. He returned six hours later, radiant with joy at having seen France once again and with having brought back the photographs requested of the Rhône valley. In his eyes one could see his spiritual elation at having really resumed his place in the struggle and being able to pursue in action the ideal which had inspired his life as a writer."

Later, in a little basement restaurant in Algiers to which he had invited

Pélissier and several friends, including Jean Gabin, who had followed him over from America, Saint-Ex was still exulting over the glorious sensation of this flight. "You can't imagine what a thrill it is to approach the land of France when one hasn't seen one's country for three years, and to say to oneself: 'I'm overflying my country. I'm mocking the occupying power. I'm seeing things I'm forbidden to see.' My mission required me to hit the coast east of Marseille and to photograph the seaboard all the way to the east of Toulon. But from that height the earth looked naked and dead . . . Our long-range cameras act like microscopes. I looked down and nothing stirred. Not a sign of life. I was deeply disappointed and overcome by a great melancholy. France is dead, I said to myself, growing more and more melancholic. Suddenly little grey puff-balls began framing my plane. I was being fired upon! France was alive! I was happy."

"Well, *mon vieux*," commented Gabin in his gruff but friendly way, "I prefer the melancholy!"

\* \* \*

Saint-Exupéry was less fortunate on his second sortie, which took place on August 1, less than a week after the first. His Lightning developed engine trouble shortly after take-off and he had to turn back to La Marsa. The field, a scant 600 yards long, was unusually short and it took some forceful bearing down on the foot-brakes to bring a P-38 to a halt before the end of the runway. Incoming pilots were instructed to prime them in advance, so that the hydraulic brakes could begin taking effect the moment the wheels touched the ground. It was precisely what Saint-Ex now forgot to do—with the result that he was already half way down the field and pumping madly on the pedals before the brakes began to grip. He ran off the end of the strip and into a neighbouring vineyard, where the plane ended up with a damaged wing and undercarriage.

Colonel Karl Polifka, who took over command of the Mediterranean Photo Reconnaissance Wing from Colonel Roosevelt nine weeks later, was willing to give Saint-Exupéry the benefit of the doubt and to attribute the accident to defective material. But such was not the opinion of Colonel Harold Willis, General Spaatz' mess officer, who happened to witness the mishap. Willis blew up, bawled out Saint-Exupéry in tough trooper terms and drew up a report for General Spaatz recommending that he be grounded forthwith.

Willis, unfortunately, was not the only U.S. Air Force officer who seemed to think that the French were a bunch of undisciplined adventurers who failed in every second mission they undertook because they were too bloody careless and irresponsible. The truth, as Interpreter Fernand Marty was later to write, was that the "five P-38s which had been attached to the French detachment were old. The cockpit heating system was unsatisfactory. The French pilots, in glacial cockpits, often found that their cameras were not working. Due to those facts, several missions had to return without pictures. On the other hand, such men as Colonel Frank Dunn (Roosevelt's second-in-command) and Major Leon Gray, the Group Operations Officer, were frankly against the French detachment. Missions which had been assigned to the French detachment the previous evening were suddenly changed at the last minute, and the pilots had to take off without being briefed about their new mission."

The situation was eventually ironed out when Dunn was sent back to the United States along with Willis and two openly sympathetic officers took over the Wing. But at the time Willis could make out a strong case against Saint-Ex. What was a man of forty-three, someone, that is, who was thirteen years beyond the age limit normally prescribed for this kind of job, doing piloting a Lightning? General Spaatz seems to have been considerably embarrassed to reply. Technically, there could be no doubt about it: Willis was right. Saint-Exupéry, at his age, had no business flying war missions on a P-38. As an initial measure he was grounded, while two new Lightnings were presented to the French detachment on the specific understanding that they were to be reserved exclusively for war missions.

It was several weeks before Saint-Exupéry's case was finally thrashed out. In a desperate endeavour to improve the dramatic deterioration in Franco-American relations, Saint-Ex organized a banquet to which a number of high ranking Americans were invited. Unfortunately many of the invitations reached their recipients too late—though this did not keep the banquet from being a success. Indeed, it was such a success that it overshot the target. The American Air Force Colonel commanding the base at Gammarth was so copiously plied with food and drink that he was hopelessly sick. What began as a Lucullan spree ended in a nightmarish hang-over, and the intended effect boomeranged lamentably. The upshot of this gastronomic fiasco was Saint-Exupéry's transfer to Algiers "pending a new assignment". That could mean anything and nothing; but for the time being at least the axe had fallen.

On August 19th a despondent Saint-Ex reappeared briefly at La Marsa to take leave of his companions. It sounded as though it was good-bye to North Africa and the war, for he spoke to them disconsolately of returning to America. His departure did nothing to dissipate the prevailing gloom in the squadron where, as Fernand Marty was later to describe it, "the spirit of good-will and cheer which had been prevalent began to disappear.

Tents which had been alive with Franco-American friendship only harboured private grudges."

The deterioration in this atmosphere partly explains the desperate tone of a letter Saint-Exupéry penned a few days before his August 1st mishap and which is unquestionably one of the most important he ever wrote. It was apparently addressed to General Chambe, but never mailed, its author, probably feeling that he had yielded to a mood of momentary depression that was a shade too sombre. As it graphically reflects his innermost feelings at the time, parts of it are worth quoting here:

"I have just made several flights on a P-38. It's a lovely machine. I would have been happy to have had such a present for my twentieth birthday. But today I realize with melancholy that at forty-three and with six thousand five hundred flying hours behind me in all the skies of the world, I can no longer find much pleasure in this game. It's nothing more than an instrument of displacement—and here, of war. If I submit to speed and altitude at a patriarchal age for such a job, it's more so as not to refuse any of the vexations of my generation than in the hope of recapturing the satisfactions of bygone times.

"This is perhaps melancholy, but maybe it isn't. I was doubtless wrong when I was twenty. In October of 1940 when I returned to North Africa, whither the 2/33 Group had emigrated, my fuelless car having been stowed away in some dusty garage, I discovered the horse and cart. And through them the grass of the paths. Sheep and olive-trees. Those olive-trees had another role than that of beating time behind closed windows at one hundred and thirty kilometres an hour. They showed themselves in their true rhythm, which is slowly to produce olives. The sheeps' exclusive function no longer consisted of forcing a reduction in speed. They came to life once more. They made real turds and produced real wool. And the grass too had a meaning since they grazed off it.

"And I felt myself coming to life again in this sole corner of the earth where the dust is scented (I'm being unfair, it is so too in Greece as in Provence). And it seemed to me that all my life I'd been an imbecile.

"All this to say that this gregarious life in the midst of this American base, these meals gulped down standing in ten minutes, this moving back and forth between single-seaters of 2,600 horse-power and a kind of abstract edifice where we are stacked three per room, in a word this terrible human desert offers nothing to gladden my heart. This too, like the pointless or hopeless missions of June 1940, is an illness one must endure. I am 'ill' for an unknown lapse of time. But I have no right not to undergo this illness. That's all. Today I am profoundly sad—and in depth. I am sad for my generation which is empty of all human substance. Which having only tho bar, mathematics, and Bugattis as a form of spiritual life, finds itself today in a strictly gregarious action that has lost all colour. People don't even notice it. Take the phenomenon of warfare one hundred years ago. Consider how many of its integrated efforts responded to the spiritual, poetic, or simply human life of man. Now that we are more dried up than bricks, we smile at such idiocies. The costumes, the flags, the chants, the music, the victories (there are no victories any more, nothing which has the poetic density of an Austerlitz. There are only phenomena of a more or less rapid digestion), all lyricism sounds ridiculous and people refuse to awake to the slightest spiritual life. They go honestly about their assembly-line chores. As young Americans say: 'We honestly accept this thankless job', while propaganda, the world over, flays the air in desperation. The ill it suffers from is not a lack of particular talents, but the ban imposed on its falling back, without seeming pompous, on the great refreshing myths. From Greek tragedy mankind, in its decadence, has fallen to the plays of M. Louis Verneuilh (one can hardly sink lower). A century of publicity, mass production, of totalitarian régimes and of armies without bugles or banners or masses for the dead. I hate my epoch with all my strength. Man is dying of thirst."

The rest of the letter is too long to be quoted here in full, though a particularly prophetic slice is reserved for the final chapter. "Ah, what a strange evening, this," Saint-Exupéry concluded, "what a strange atmosphere. From my window I can see the windows light up in faceless buildings. I can hear different radio-sets dispensing their doggerel music to this shiftless crowd from overseas who are not even familiar with nostalgia . . .

"If I am killed in action, I could not care less. Or if I succumb to a fit of rage over these flying torpedoes which no longer bear any relation to flying and which turn the pilot amid his dials and his buttons into a kind of chief accountant . . . But if I come out alive from this 'necessary and thankless job', there will be only one question so far as I'm concerned: what can one, what must one say to men?"

# 23

## The Crab-Pot of Algiers

AFTER much anguished soul-searching Saint-Exupéry finally decided against returning to the United States. He could not bring himself to abandon all the hopes he had nourished for three long years, and much as he detested Algiers and its atmosphere of Renaissance intrigue, he preferred to remain in the Mediterranean sphere of operations rather than put an ocean between himself and the war. Daily life, despite the providential influx of Allied supplies and a flourishing black market, tended to be spartan; for umbilically linked as it had always been to France, Algeria was incapable of providing for even the simplest commodities. Sewing needles, for example, were so scarce that housewives were often reduced to knocking at their neighbours' door to ask if they might be allowed to borrow their one remaining needle for an afternoon or morning. The city, as Diana Cooper was to write in her sprightly *Trumpets from the Steep*, "was totally bereft of any buyable thing—not a plate, hammer or nail, not a sheet of paper could be bought. Glasses were beer-bottles cut down, with jagged lip-sticked edges. Streets and streets of shuttered shops, and the few that were open closed at 11 a.m., cleared of what they had to sell. I tried those first few mornings"—after her arrival with her husband Duff Cooper—"to buy essentials—soap, electric bulbs, candles, pillows, toilet-paper, matches. Not a hope. It was very discouraging." Fuel, of course, was non-existent, and later as autumn turned into winter, the British Ambassador's wife was reduced to sleeping at night in a fur coat.

Such war-time hardships Saint-Exupéry was quite prepared to bear: they were, after all, less artificial than that unreal affluence he had encountered in Lisbon and New York. In Algiers, with the black-out and streets swarming with soldiers of half a dozen nationalities, one at least felt there was a war on. Harder to bear was the spiritual distress. André Maurois, when his ship docked some weeks later, found his friend Antoine terribly downcast—by the petty political intriguing, Hochedé's recent death, and his own elimination from the squadron. The Americans now seemed dead-set against him, and with Giraud losing ground week by week under the pressure of De Gaulle's ruthless drive for power, there was waning hope of effective support from the upper echelons of French officialdom.

In the meantime he had to do something to keep from going out of his mind from sheer frustration and despair. Fortunately he had written to Consuelo, who successfully intercepted Léon Wencelius, just promoted captain after completing a course in U.S. Army methods and materiel at Fort Benning; and on September 7th Saint-Ex was overjoyed to see his friend turn up at Dr. Pélissier's apartment carrying a handsome pigskin suitcase— a present from Consuelo. Inside were several letters from her, a copy of Maurice Blondel's *L'être et les êtres* which he had specially asked for, and the four black bound folders into which he had pressed the 700 pages which his New York secretary had typed up from his dictaphone recordings.

The previous May Dr. Henri Comte had said to him in Casablanca: "Next time you come here, please make this house your home." Saint-Exupéry now availed himself of the invitation. He needed to get away from the political stew-pot of Algiers, and the doctor's pleasant villa in the hilly suburb of Anfa—so much more comfortable than Pélissier's cramped quarters in the very centre of Algiers—beckoned to him like an oasis.

Saint-Ex found the atmosphere so pleasant that he finally stayed one month. As usual, he went late to bed, continuing to labour on *Citadelle* in the small hours of the morning and the early hours of the afternoon. After a busy day at the clinic Comte would often come home so worn out that he could not keep himself from falling asleep over the pages which his anxious guest would thrust upon him at dinner time; and the next day the shame-faced doctor would have to admit that he had been too tired to read more than a few lines. But the book was frequently discussed between them, and Comte very clearly recalls Saint-Exupéry explaining to him how much his portrayal of the Berber ruler who is its central figure owed to the visit they once made together to the caid Tounsi, who had made his home not far from the soaring, rock-perched kasbah of Boulaouane (sixty miles south of Casablanca).

Resourceful as ever, Saint-Ex would amaze his host and his guests by his manual dexterity. Sometimes it took the form of penknife throwing contests, in which he unerringly sank the blade into a wooden door. At other times he would show off his virtuosity on the piano by asking those present, who were not supposed to see what he was doing, if they could identify his rippling arpeggios. "*Mais c'est du Debussy!*" they would cry— only to discover that the strange twelvetone harmonies were caused by oranges and grapefruit rolled successively over the keys while he worked the pedals with his feet. As for his card tricks, they were so uncanny that one evening when Dr. Comte was entertaining some surgeons from an American ambulance unit, a Medical Corps colonel got to his feet in a huff, remarking to his host as he left: "I'm getting out of here. This place is spooky."

The same surgeons were invited on another occasion to an elegant dinner dance with a number of officers from a French *Chasseurs d'Afrique* regiment. The party was in full swing when two Foreign Legionnaires came in through the garden gate to join in the fun. An irate French colonel sought to throw out the intruders, but Saint-Ex intervened, plied them with food, drink, and conversation, and finally made them a present of his lighter.

He had said to Comte, when one day his host was admiring his handsome pigskin bag and toilet case: "Consuelo had them sent to me. She's ruining me with my own money, but I shall always forgive her everything." In the same generous spirit he never failed to contradict the sceptics, hotly defending America's entry into the war as "idealistic" and "disinterested", even going so far as to speak of the G.I.s as twentieth century "crusaders"; and as a token of his gratitude he gave Comte his one and only copy of *Pilote de Guerre*, though it was a unique copy printed on rare paper.

The fearful summer heat had at last begun to wane by the time he returned to Algiers, but it offered him scant relief from his spiritual gloom. Once again he was oppressed by the prevailing climate of squabble and intrigue: so much indeed that he found it difficult to concentrate on *Citadelle*. His distress even affected his handwriting, which for much of this period was so illegible that all attempts to decipher the manuscript sheets after his death had to be abandoned. Even about the pages which had been typed up in New York he now felt qualms, so unsettled was his state of mind. Ever a prey to anxiety as regards the quality of his prose, he exhibited a pathetic and yet tyrannical need to have his friends peruse what he had written. When Nelly de Vogüé reached Algiers in her turn—as a member of a Free French auxiliary unit—she was forced to absorb hundreds of pages of *Citadelle* in one long, almost non-stop session and even to swallow a couple of benzedrine tablets to keep from falling asleep!

Nor was Saint-Ex's gloom merely the product of an embittered imagination; for André Maurois was not long in discovering that the limbo to which his friend had been consigned contained ample room for both. Adrien Tixier having also reached Algiers (where he became a member of the provisional government), De Gaulle was fully informed of their joint unwillingness to join his New York faction; and like the Bourbons Wormwood—as he was universally known to the Anglo-American community—

wa9 in no mood to forget it. Officially debarred by the Gaullists, Maurois
had to appeal to Giraud's Chief of Staff to be able to accompany the French
expeditionary force sent to liberate Corsica from the Germans.

Within days of this first veto Maurois found himself, like Saint-Exupéry,
the target of a second, more sweeping elimination. On October 30th De
Gaulle was to make a speech on the Algiers Forum to commemorate the
sixtieth anniversary of the founding of the Alliance Française. In preparing
the text he asked one of his aides to draft a paragraph devoted to the leading
French writers who had helped save the spirit of France by preferring exile
to the ignominy of Vichy. The list, as readied by this aide, included the names
of André Maurois and Antoine de Saint-Exupéry. But when the General
mounted the podium to speak of those who "as soon as they had escaped the
tyranny, took part in all nobility and, I might add, independence, in the
great spiritual and moral battles of this war," he rolled off the names of
Philippe Barrès, Henry Bernstein, Eve Curie, Father Ducatillon—classed as
among the "greatest writers"!—André Gide, Joseph Kessel, Maritain, and
Jules Romains. Not a word about Maurois, not a syllable about Saint-Ex, or
for that matter Saint-John Perse. Wormwood had taken his pen, dipped it
in his well of gall, and crossed out the names of the three miscreants. The
aide was incensed, as was Léon Wencelius, who understood at once, in
listening to the speech, that if Philippe Barrès headed this extraordinary list
it was simply because this exemplary French author had had the literary
genius to pen a panegyric in honour of De Gaulle.

Joseph Kessel, who had smuggled himself out of France to London and
who now reached Algiers in his turn, added to Saint-Exupéry's dismay by
declaring that in France a blood-bath—after the Liberation—was both
inevitable and necessary. Historically it had always been so: first there were
the wars of religion, and after them an Henri IV was needed to bandage the
wounds.

"Next year" as Saint-Ex wrote to Henri Comte, "there will be a lot of
shooting by firing-squads and it will be rather melancholy. What will this
harvest reap? . . . No matter how much of a genius General de Gaulle may
be (and I have some belief in his political genius), he will one day have to
implement the passions he will have aroused. He will have to mould something. I know what he feels. But truth is not of the realm of feeling. It is of
the realm of the Spirit."

Not the least extraordinary feature of this intolerance—for Saint-Exupéry
at any rate—was its lack of ideological backing: Gaullism being, as he liked
to put it, "a Fascism without a doctrine". Islam, as he wrote to Henri Comte,
"decapitated according to the Koran, the French Revolution guillotined
according to Diderot, Russia resorted to firing-squads according to Marx,

Christianity 'let itself' be beheaded (it comes to the same) according to the Epistles of Saint Paul. The feelings aroused and which authorized these massacres were no more than the means placed at the disposal of the Spirit. Will sentiment for the first time in man's history now use the firing-squad aimlessly, as an end in itself? Passion for me is a blind monster. Even when noble. Even when pure."

*          *          *

During his month-long stay in Casablanca the bitter infighting between Giraudists and Gaullists had spread to the French secret services—represented on the one hand by the Army's D.S.R./S.M. (*Direction des Services de Renseigements et de Sécurité Militaire*) and on the other by the B.C.R.A. (*Bureau Central de Renseignements et d'Action*) which De Gaulle had established in London and entrusted to a high-strung and ambitious ex-ethnologist by the name of Jacques Soustelle. Sent over to look into the disruptive feuding between the two rival intelligence systems, General William Donovan, head of the O.S.S., lost scant time favouring the military professionals of the French Army's G-2 department over Jacques Soustelle's cloak-and-dagger amateurs. But Donovan's brash effort to pressure the French Committee of National Liberation into following his recommendations in this respect had a predictably boomerang effect—in affording the Gaullists a heaven-sent opportunity for smearing their adversaries as "tools of a foreign power."

The confusion was at its height when Paul Dungler, leader of the French Resistance movement in Alsace, turned up in Algiers—where Léon Wencelius soon introduced him to Saint-Ex. Between the massive airman and the powerfully built Alsatian there was an almost instant and total meeting of minds. Like General Chambe, Dungler had been part of the underground network which had engineered Giraud's escape from Koenigstein. In March 1942 he had been arrested by the Vichy police when a radio transmitter was found in his secret Lyon hide-out, but he had soon been released on the express order of Pétain, who had been quietly encouraging his efforts to resist the wholesale incorporation of Alsace into the Third Reich. Informed that Dungler wished to establish contact with Giraud and the Americans in Algiers, Pétain in July 1943 had summoned him to Vichy and entrusted him with an extraordinary mission. On reaching Algiers he was to call on Giraud and De Gaulle and to inform them on his behalf that, inasmuch as the Germans had done away with the French army when they had occupied all of metropolitan France, he, Pétain, was solemnly transferring the allegiance all French officers owed to him as Chief of State to Giraud and De Gaulle.

From now on it would be the duty of all French officers in North Africa to obey the orders of the two men who commanded what French military units still existed. The moment France was liberated, the Marshal went on, he proposed to meet Giraud and De Gaulle under the Arc de Triomphe in Paris and to effect an orderly transmission of his powers to them before retiring to his property at Villeneuve-Loubet.

The problem of reestablishing a normal parliamentary régime after a period of foreign occupation had already arisen during the Franco-Prussian war and been solved by the Treveneuc Law of 1872, which De Gaulle and his supporters had consistently refused to recognize. Pétain would have been on stronger constitutional ground if he had made some reference to this legislation, though it would hardly have affected the outcome of this particular overture. To say that it was coldly received would be an understatement. Giraud, who agreed to see Dungler as soon as he reached Algiers, blew up when he heard Pétain's proposal. After his escape from Koenigstein he had been obliged to write two letters to Pétain: the first to say that he would do nothing to complicate the Marshal's difficult task of appeasing the German occupants, ever ready to exploit a "scandal" of this kind, the second—written at the moment of the Allied landings in North Africa—to say that the new turn of events was too serious for him to be bound any longer by his previous pledge. Technically speaking, Giraud had broken his word, as Marshal Juin was to do shortly afterwards—a pardonable transgression that could be attributed to wartime duress. But what was more serious, and something Dungler did not know, was that Giraud had just been brow-beaten by the Gaullist dominated Committee of National Liberation into signing a decree accusing Pétain of high treason and arraigning him before a court of law to answer for his crimes.

Undeterred by Giraud's negative reaction, Dungler next sought to deliver Pétain's message to De Gaulle. Here the rebuff took a different but even more violent form. The Free French leader, who had not forgiven Dungler for having insisted that the Resistance movement in Alsace operate autonomously (because of the difficulties raised by its forcible incorporation into the Reich), kept him waiting for six weeks before he would agree to receive him.

"Well, and what do you want?" was his brusque greeting when the permission was finally granted.

Dungler introduced himself as the "head of the Alsation Resistance", at which point De Gaulle cut him short with a contemptuous: "Oh, head of the Alsatian Resistance! One of them perhaps, and that's saying a lot!"

"There's only one boss of the Alsatian Resistance," Dungler retorted sharply, "and that's me".

Whereupon a livid De Gaulle leapt to his feet and shouted: "Go, go! Get the hell out of here! Get out!"

Dungler was not even given a chance of mentioning Pétain's name. When Saint-Exupéry heard his account of what had happened from Dungler's own lips, he was once again chagrined but not surprised. Wormwood was running true to form, and Dungler was now getting the medicine that had once been meted out to General Odic. A Frenchman who dared to represent a Resistance movement that he did not personally control had to be combated, neutralized, and eliminated, no matter how or what the cost.

\*　　\*　　\*

Within days of this new flare-up Saint-Exupéry was walking down a dark corridor in Dr. Pélissier's blacked-out apartment building when he failed to notice a flight of six marble steps. "I suddenly found myself floating in space," as he later described it in a letter to Henri Comte. "I heard a tremendous crash. It was me. I found myself gently sprawled out on my back, upheld at two points by two solid angles of false marble. Those two points were the coccyx (? I'll leave the spelling to you) and the fifth lumbar vertebra."

The next morning Pélissier found a note slipped under his bedroom door saying that his lodger was in severe pain, that he had fallen with all his weight on the final vertebra in the spinal column, which he was certain was broken. Pélissier immediately examined his back. All he could find was a serious bruise just above the coccyx which had been inflamed by the rheumatism from which Saint-Ex had been suffering for years. But there was nothing broken, so far as he could see. Antoine refused to believe him. That afternoon, as though to test the doctor's diagnosis as well as his own fortitude, he dragged himself (without telling Pélissier) downstairs and clambered gingerly on to a trolley to attend a reception given by the Russian envoy Alexander Bogomolov. Wracked by pains which raced up and down his back and legs, he suddenly felt so weak that he had to be held up by two friends, who helped him down the stairs and into the car of Admiral Auboyneau, who was kind enough to drive him home. It was all that was needed to convince Saint-Ex that he was right and the doctor wrong.

The next day, November 8th, Saint-Exupéry was suffering too much to contemplate attending the first anniversary celebration of the Allied landings in North Africa—which De Gaulle, true to his splenetic form, boycotted as a "day of mourning". To calm his agitated friend Pélissier sent Antoine to see an X-ray specialist. When he returned there was a gleam of triumph in his dark eyes.

"What did I say?" he exclaimed. "The vertebra is broken."

Pélissier took a long look at the X-ray negatives and shook his head. He could find no trace of a fracture. Saint-Ex had evidently concentrated the full force of his magnetic personality on the specialist, who had ended up seeing a fracture that wasn't there!

A lot of arguing was needed to persuade Saint-Exupéry that Pélissier was right and the specialist wrong, and even so he was less than half convinced. The next day Pélissier had his ageing maid-servant Séverine go in to tell him that her master was expecting *Monsieur le Commandant* for lunch. Antoine interpreted this as an almost sadistic determination to torture him. The ordeal over, he telephoned to a military hospital and had an army doctor come over and prescribe three weeks of immobility. The prescription, as Pélissier realized, was enough to convince his stubborn friend that he really had broken his back and must thus keep to his bed. It was a second diagnosis he was forced to undo, but here too his endeavours met with tenacious disbelief. Night after night, the doctor, worn out from a day spent examining other patients in his consulting room or at the hospital, would be kept up by an insistent Antoine, tirelessly intent on proving—by processes of deductive logic!—that he, Pélissier, was wrong. The debate went on for days until the doctor grew so exasperated that he refused to listen to him any longer. Saint-Ex then took to bombarding him with lengthy epistles in which the same arguments were exhaustively expounded on paper. He was furious to be told that only time could take care of his pains and that enforced immobility would simply aggravate his condition. Six painful weeks thus went by before Saint-Ex was willing to admit, in mid-December, that he had been unjust in his accusations, that the doctor could not be blamed for the blackout or his absent-footedness on the stairs. "I know that your scientific knowledge is incapable of giving me back my hair, my teeth, or my teen-age years," he concluded his letter of apology.

Hardly had this first quarrel been patched up than a new source of controversy opened a second rift between them. One day Saint-Exupéry informed Pélissier that he was suffering from severe intestinal pains. He admitted that he had been taking massive overdoses of sulpha drugs (a novel "cure-all" in those days) in addition to the hotly spiced dishes he insisted on eating. To calm his apprehensions Pélissier sent him to another X-ray specialist, who was troubled by certain shadows which showed up on the negatives. For weeks thereafter Saint-Ex went around persuaded he had cancer, and not until late February of 1944 would he finally admit what all the tests had demonstrated—that his gastric lesions were due to a massive overdose of drugs and spices.

These obsessive ailments, as Pélissier was well aware, owed much to the intense frustration which was eating away at his friend throughout these months of enforced inactivity. Given the acclaim his books had earned in the United States, one of Saint-Exupéry's friends proposed that he be sent to Washington on a material procurements mission for the French Air Force. Back came the answer from André Le Trocquer, a rabidly anti-militaristic Socialist whom Wormwood had named to head the War Commissariat in a move sardonically calculated to clip Giraud's wings prior to his total elimination. Nothing doing. Giraud had already sent General Odic to Washington on just such a mission, and from the Gaullist point of view that was already too much.

Profoundly dispirited though he was most of the time, Saint-Ex could still oscillate from the deepest melancholy to the gayest exuberance with deceptive and disconcerting ease. Probably few of those who came to visit him in the "little grey chamber, as anonymous as a hotel room" which he occupied in Dr. Pélissier's apartment fully guessed the extent of his unhappiness, impressed as they were by his verbal exuberance once he was roused from his lethargy. Robert Bordaz, a fairly frequent caller, has left us a description of this little room—with opened suitcases clogging the floor space, clusters of typed pages, and a table near the window littered with sheets of onion-skin on which he scrawled his latest *trouvailles*, in the form of complex mathematical puzzles. "The work day ended, one often found him in his room stretched out and looking even taller than he was on his tiny bed. Once the conversation got going, Antoine's unforgettable eyes would light up in his half-boyish face and gleam with a bright intelligence . . . But Antoine always greeted you by saying he was tired of life and asking if that wasn't your opinion too."

The faithful Séverine, who watched over him with motherly solicitude and occasionally lectured him like an infant, would answer his summons, shuffling in with plates or basketfuls of dried figs, dates, and oranges which he would distribute to his guests. Antoine and his friends would then slip through the waiting-room, where Dr. Pélissier's clients were awaiting their turn, and take refuge in a corner salon decorated with modern paintings. When at last it was time for dinner they would thread their way through the dark corridors and passageways, escorting Saint-Ex down the stairs—which he never failed to curse as the source of so much physical suffering—before debouching into the city's pulsing streets, alive with their babble of foreign tongues and gutteral Arab greetings.

Often at lunchtime he would take the trolley up the hill to the Cercle Interallié, located not far from the Palais d'Eté and the luxurious Hôtel Saint-Georges, where he would be greeted by the familiar faces of François de Panafieu, Roger de Sinéty, Guy de La Tournelle, Jacques Tiné, General

Bouscat, Léon Wenцelius, Paul Dungler, and a host of Allied diplomats and officers for whom this quaintly Moorish setting provided an international stock-exchange for the peddling of gossip, rumours, and information of a tougher sort. Here too Saint-Ex had frequent occasion to meet two prominent Protestants with whom he immediately hit it off: Pastor André Boegner, head of the Protestant Federation for the Liberated Territories, and Marcel Sturm, Chaplain General for the troops in the field, whose two children Jean Michel and Malou were invariably enthralled by Saint-Exupéry's tricks and inventions.

At the dinner parties he attended he could still be the life of the party, dazzling the company with card tricks which seemed to grow increasingly mysterious the more practised he became. One day, while lunching with General Bouscat and his wife, he suddenly took to swallowing spoons which later turned up in pockets and hand-bags. His stories, of course, were more breath-taking than ever. Max-Pol Fouchet, who for a while shared a room next to his in Pélissier's apartment, remembers them as being "unforgettable numbers"—in a theatrical sense. "For example, he used to reenact the drama of thirst, a non-fiction drama since he had lived it, after an accident in the desert. Everything was mimicked—from the flight of the plane and its engine troubles right down to the hazardous descent towards the ground, with the plane disintegrating on contact and the pilots jumping free, the hours passing, the bodies drying up, and the mucus membranes hardening like stone. The big moment came when he would say: 'When the thirst is extreme and one is about to die, one's tongue comes out of one's mouth.' And Saint-Ex would thrust out a huge tongue, while his eyes rolled wildly in their sockets and the assembled company shuddered, striving hard not to clap."

Minou de Montgomery (the future Madame Béthouart), who had become one of the leading Free French hostesses in Algiers, was particularly struck by the extraordinary tale of a prayer-rug which Antoine had one day acquired in a Casablanca souk (the same rug he had mentioned in a letter to Renée de Saussine, written in the spring of 1927). He had used it to line his cockpit and it had travelled with him everywhere, even as far as South America, almost like a pet. But it had also given him "the soul of a proprietor"— upsetting for someone who felt such a disdain for the goods of this world. And so one day, while flying over the Rio de Oro, he was seized by a sudden impulse: the moment had come for him to divest himself of this earthly attribute which established a material claim from which he wished to be freed. With a generous gesture he had flung the prayer-rug out on to the sands, where it lay waiting to be covered by the wind or rescued by some softly padding caravan.

The same disinterested quality was what most impressed Pierre Cot when he too turned up in Algiers. Anything but insensitive to feminine charm himself, Saint-Ex was irritated by the unsubtle manner in which a pack of young bucks, most of them in uniform, were running after the Swiss ambassador's overly attractive daughter. The spectacle of all these "wolves" vying madly to see which could first toss her on to a bed revolted Saint-Exupéry, who suggested to Cot that they invite her to a quiet lunch—just to reassure her (which they did) that there were some men left in the world who were prepared to take her out with no lecherous *arrière-pensées*.

At Anne Heurgon-Desjardins' villa, where he was a frequent guest, Saint-Exupéry met the cream of the local intelligentsia. Philippe Soupault, the Surrealist, was one of them, though he was overshadowed by André Gide, who held court there, dressed in gaudy striped shirts brought to him by his American admirers. The pointed beret he insisted on wearing over his bald pate gave him an astonishing "resemblance to Holbein the Younger's portrait of Erasmus"—to quote the writer-editor Max-Pol Fouchet, another habitué of Anne Heurgon's literary circle. Fouchet later confessed to being worried by the resemblance, the sage of Rotterdam, "who had let one of his disciples agonize at his door", never having struck him as an exemplary model of humanity. "Gide was there in the middle of this group of writers: Maurois, very talkative, vying with him in general culture; the serious Jean Amrouche, trying to convert Gide to Gaullism; Saint-Exupéry, who exasperated Gide by his *boutades* against De Gaulle; Emmanuel Bove, very human and simple."

"During their joint stay in Algiers" Anne Heurgon-Desjardins was later to write, "I was often saddened by the growing estrangement Gide felt for him, in contrast to the preponderant influence which Amrouche exercised on his thinking. Following the latter, Gide thought or wanted to think himself a Gaullist, and Saint-Exupéry's quips about the General, though often very funny, did not amuse him. Once when Antoine came to lunch and before the usual game of chess he pushed his mockery even further than usual. Gide was silent and Antoine had sensed his exasperation. The next day he rang me up: 'Tell me, I'm afraid I offended Gide yesterday?' 'But no,' I said, 'what on earth makes you think that?' As we talked on Gide walked into the room, listened for a moment with a disapproving air, and then taking hold of the receiver, he said: 'Yes, Tonio, why hide it from you? Yesterday you hurt me.' Not wishing to eaves-drop I closed the door behind me, but I was annoyed with Gide for upsetting this big boy who loved him dearly."

The chess game with Gide, each time he came to lunch at the Heurgons' villa, was an unfailing rite, even though Gide was probably a worse loser than Saint-Ex, who liked to avenge his defeats by inventing ingenious word puzzles. "One day" Max-Pol Fouchet recalls, "Gide was playing against

Saint Exupéry and losing. Suddenly he decided to interrupt the game, it being time for tea, he said. Everyone flocked into the next room, while I remained behind in a corner. A moment later I saw Gide reenter the room and look at the chess-board on the table. I didn't dare show myself, curious to see what he was going to do. I could see his reflection in a window-pane . . . What did he do? Alter the position of the pawns, but in a game of chess surely this would have been noticed? And yet . . . the game was resumed and Saint-Exupéry, who until then had been winning, lost rapidly. When he left I followed him out and told him jokingly what I had just seen. Saint-Exupéry stopped in the middle of the street, more monolithic than ever. Then he burst into an unforgettable laugh. 'But of course,' he cried, 'that's Gide all over'."

Though he could still laugh in public, in private he was more tempted to weep—and not just over his physical travails. The collapse of the Giraudist cause was now complete, with the Gaullist super-patriots fastening their stranglehold on to the political and even military apparatus. Just three days after Saint-Ex's stairway accident De Gaulle had persuaded the Committee of National Liberation to eliminate Giraud and General Georges. Suddenly jolted out of his obtuse complacency, Giraud had locked himself up in his quarters and refused to see anyone for a good twenty-four hours. Finally General Georges had sent Paul Dungler to talk him into appearing for the November 11th Armistice celebrations. Admitted at last into the Presence, Dungler had been dumbfounded to hear the tall white-whiskered general declare without more ado that he had been thinking things over, that Dungler and the others who had tried to reason with him had been right while he was wrong, and that this being the case he was going to put two divisions at Dungler's disposal within the next forty-eight hours "so that you can proceed with the mop-up—by rounding up General de Gaulle and his Committee".

A few months earlier it might have made sense, but this last-minute volte-face only disgusted the Resistance leader from Alsace, who replied that he had not come to North Africa to lead a putsch. "Not two divisions but two companies would be enough to round up all those people down there by the waterfront and to dump them in the sea," he retorted hotly. "But I wouldn't do it with *you*. You've disappointed and let down every single person who's ever done anything for you," he went on, referring to Giraud's step-by-step vacillations and retreats. And with that he walked out, leaving Giraud to his fate. And incidentally . . . Saint-Ex.

"How can America ever have taken this scare-crow seriously?" Saint-Exupéry wrote not long after to his friend Henri Comte. "I understand why he"—General Giraud—"wasn't afraid of noise (it was his only form of

courage) and why he was so afraid of the wind." His own pessimistic pro-
phecies had been fulfilled with a vengeance which inevitably engulfed
himself.

He was made to feel it once again after attending a cocktail party given in
the villa of the Kabyle poet Jean Amrouche. He was standing in the hallway,
visibly bored by the imposing throng of notables whom Gide's friend had
managed to corral when he noticed a Navy captain standing next to him with
a glass of whisky in his hand, and who seemed to feel equally out of place in
this setting. At the sight of the blue lozenge with the red Cross of Lorraine
that was discreetly but plainly displayed on the mariner's chest, Saint-Ex
instinctively frowned.

"So you're a Gaullist?"

"Free French," was the answer. "Commander of the *Curie*."

"Does all this interest you?" Saint-Exupéry asked, waving towards the
nearest group.

The Navy captain shook his head.

"Well, look, I have a Jeep outside," Saint-Ex proposed. "Would you like
me to drive you back?" And he introduced himself—Saint-Exupéry.
Commandant Pierre Sonneville, submarine commander, came the reply.

Delighted to be driven down to the Admiralty jetty, where his submarine
was docked, Sonneville invited Saint-Exupéry on board. Two sailors helped
him down the forward hatch, a routine which had to be repeated each time
he returned. For the moment he was on board he found the political back-
stabbing and intrigue of Algiers forgotten in a *camaraderie* of genuine
combatants. He was invited back for several under-water dinners, and he
entertained Sonneville and his fellow officers by covering pages of the submarine's *livre d'or* with drawings, inscriptions, and ingenious navigation
problems.

The Free French submarine commander and the arrant "Pétainist" got on
so famously that Sonneville finally suggested Saint-Exupéry accompany
them on their next outing. Saint-Ex was elated at the prospect, but a day or
two later back came the answer from the Admiralty: nothing doing. "Saint-
Ex is not a Gaullist!"

*     *     *

Towards the end of November 1943 Pierre Dalloz, the architect whom
he had met with Henry de Ségogne at Arles and Tarascon during the Easter
holidays of 1939, turned up in Algiers. Wishing to establish a regular liaison
with the Allies, he had turned over the command of his Resistance units in
the Vercors to their common friend Jean Prévost and had then had himself

smuggled out across the Pyrenees and Spain with British help. During his two months' stay in Algiers he saw Saint-Ex almost daily. He found him increasingly preoccupied with religious questions—as was evident from the pages of *Citadelle* he was given to read—and particularly by the notion of charity.

Anxious to relieve his friend's immense distress at being grounded and unemployed when so much was going on around him, Dalloz took up his case with Professor Escarra, a Chinese scholar from the Paris Law Faculty who happened to be on good terms with Colonel Billotte, the head of De Gaulle's secretariat. De Gaulle had recently sent General Peshkoff (Maxim Gorky's illegitimate son) to China as his envoy to Chiang Kai Shek, and the proposal they came up with was that Saint-Exupéry be sent to join him in Chungking as Assistant Air Attaché. Though the assignment was remote, Saint-Ex finally agreed to the idea out of sheer desperation: besides, like his sister Simone, he had long been fascinated by the Orient. Dalloz thereupon drafted a note in which it was suggested that if Saint-Exupéry could not be sent to London as Assistant Air Attaché—a proposal that had apparently already met with a rebuff—he be sent to join Peshkoff in China. Finally, if neither of these two alternatives were acceptable, the note proposed that Saint-Exupéry be allowed to resume active service with his squadron. Escarra delivered the note personally to his friend Billotte, who agreed to show it to De Gaulle. Back it came with a comment in the margin in Wormwood's own handwriting: "*Laisser cet officier en réserve de commandement.*" (This officer to be left in reserve status.) To which the General is reported (though possibly on another occasion) to have added the oral comment: "*Il est juste bon à faire des tours de cartes.*" (All he's good for is doing card tricks.) In reporting this withering judgment some twenty years later Jules Roy could not refrain from adding that it came from the same general who had never once, during his thirty-five months in London, deigned to visit the two French bomber groups which night after night were sallying forth with the RAF to hit targets in Germany.

This latest Gaullist veto deepened Saint-Ex's gloom. "I am not in the war, nor working at any particular job, nor healthy, nor ill, nor understood, nor executed by a firing-squad, nor happy, nor unhappy, but desperate," he wrote in a letter which dramatically expressed his misery. The material destruction being wrought by the air war pained him almost as much as his personal plight—particularly after a sombre speech of Churchill's in December warning the British that the *blitz* was not yet over and that worse might still come. "If Hitler has got his hands on uranium," Saint-Exupéry told Dalloz, who had never heard of it, "then the world is done for".

From this mood of black despair Saint-Exupéry was briefly lifted by a cable from Alexander Korda in London proposing that he prepare the scenario for a film to be made of his *Little Prince*. But the day that Korda's emissary was due to fly back to London, Saint-Exupéry absent-mindedly turned up for their luncheon appointment having forgotten to bring along the text. On his return to the apartment he found that his one and only copy of *Le Petit Prince* had disappeared. A heated altercation followed with Pélissier, who was accused of having stolen it away from him to be read by his clients. When the doctor, who was busy giving a patient an intravenous injection, cut him short on the house-phone, Antoine wrote him an angry note saying that he had just caused him a loss of 50,000 dollars by his refusal to sacrifice 30 seconds of his time. Pélissier found the "purloined" volume in his desk and had it brought to Saint-Ex immediately; whereupon the doctor received a charming note of apology in which the grateful recipient declared that "not for a hundred billion would I buy a friend. If it pleases you to read my book and to keep Mr. Korda waiting to the point of giving up, I couldn't care less. I wouldn't buy your friendship with ten of Mr. Korda's films. Korda's money is worth what it's worth, which is to say, what it can procure: not much. Nothing."

Saint-Exupéry's sole satisfaction during this long bleak winter came from Jean Amrouche's generous offer to publish his *Lettre à Un Otage* in the first (February 1944) issue of a new monthly called *L'Arche*, to which André Gide, Jacques Maritain, Pierre Mendès-France, Joseph Kessel also contributed. But it was a minor compensation for the refusal of the Gaullist authorities to permit the publication of *Pilote de Guerre*. One year earlier, in November of 1942, Saint-Ex had managed to have a copy smuggled into France to his friend Henry de Ségogne, who had taken it to Gaston Gallimard. Gallimard had submitted it to a German called Heller, who worked with Ernst Jünger on the *Propanganda Staffel* of Otto Abetz' German Embassy in Paris. Heller, who like Jünger, was a decent fellow trying to do his best in a painful situation, gave his permission for the printing of a limited edition of 2,100 copies—provided that one sentence be knocked out of the text (a sentence in which Hitler was referred to as "*ce dément*"—that madman). Even this was too much for the grovellers. Anxious, like all sycophants, to be more Papist than the Pope, the collaborationist press opened up with a broadside against this "provocation", "this apotheosis of judeo-bellicosity" which, in praising a pilot called Israël, was obviously an instrument of a "judeo-plutocratic International". Aroused by the angry hue and cry, the Nazi authorities had to ban the book, though they could not keep an underground press in Lyon from rolling out another thousand copies. Banned in his own country, Saint-Ex now found himself banned in a supposedly "free" Algeria; and what was more galling, whereas in occupied France more than 3,000 copies of *Pilote de Guerre* had actually been printed, in "liberated" North Africa not a single copy saw the light of day. Wormwood's veto was even more total than the Nazis'.

Saint-Exupéry's state of mind, as the result of slights of this kind, may be judged by the tone of two letters he gave to Pierre Dalloz and to Max-Pol Fouchet to take to a friend of his in London. "Gaullism in a couple of words?" he wrote in the first. "A group of 'particularists' . . . fighting for France, which must save her substance. Which is fine. She must be present in the battle. And the general leading the volunteers of such a foreign legion would have found me in the ranks.

"But this group of 'particularists' takes itself for France. France is D . . . T . . . or Y . . ."—names of friends who had stayed behind in a now totally occupied country—"It claims to profit from a sacrifice less serious than theirs—and there is no real sacrifice save that which is profitless".

"I can no longer stand the slander, the insults, nor this prodigious unemployment," he wrote in the other. "I cannot live except for love. I have never spoken, nor acted, nor written except out of love. I love my country more all by myself than all of them put together. They love only themselves."

* * *

"I feel a vague uneasiness at spending these nights out of time amid this parasitic vegetation," he wrote on another occasion to someone he had met at a dinner party which had brought together the "high-life" of Algiers. "These people give me the impression of mushrooms grafted on to a tree they know nothing about and candidly pursuing their unreal, petty existence. I am thinking above all of that young pseudo-civilian who instead of charm was exuding that kind of ready-made nonchalance, *à la* Fouquet's, which I detest. With his draft-dodging and baccara-fancying vocation he is as foreign to my universe as a goldfish in an aquarium. If my social credo does not embrace a 'purge' of his ilk, it's because he seems to me already completely dead. If the liberation reestablishes this species, it can only mean that the soil of France is rotten to the core, which is not so."

What followed was a continuation of the thoughts he had already expressed in *Pilote de Guerre*, now specifically applied to the intransigeance of rival factions and the damage it was bound to do to France. "*Mon vieux*, you are one of the rare healthy types I have met in this country. At least among those who think. For there are a host of stout fellows to be found on those levels where the mechanism of intelligence has not warped instinct. The difficult thing is to save instinct when one reasons. A certain French bourgeoisie is ghastly, but the pure doctrinaires of marxism are just as bad. (Read my Russian friend Serge's *Il est minuit dans le siècle*.) As for the intellectuals of the University of Paris at the time of Joan of Arc's trial, they were even worse. Read their deliberations!. . . The ironmonger loses his muscles when he becomes a geometrician. If the ignominy of Joan's trial (one of the great documents I know of) had led to the purging of the entire Sorbonne of that time, it would have meant the potential purging of Descartes, Pascal, or Bernouilli, for like a link in the chain, it was their precondition. The man who devotes his life to algebraic simplifications understands nothing about the cultivation of a simple leek, which is complex. He who devotes himself to the growing of leeks is ill prepared to probe the secrets of the nebulae. The contrary of error is not truth, and above all the contrary of the truth is not error. So long as man is not a god the truth, in his language, will express itself through contradictions. And one goes from error to error towards the truth."

It was what he had written earlier under the impact of the Munich crisis, to say nothing of his reaction to the inhuman dogmas of the Spanish Civil War. And it is curious to note—something no one to my knowledge has so far pointed out—to what extent in this respect Saint-Exupéry was a Hegelian. The Marxist pretension to be the ultimate, immutable, unchallengeable truth was what he could not accept, regardless of its actual content; but doubtless this was not the first time (nor probably will it be the last) that Hegel has been used to refute Marx, to say nothing of De Gaulle.

"I have deep reasons" Saint-Exupéry went on, "for hating the myth of the purge . . . the liquidation of a class, or cast, or group buries the evil, to be sure, but also the good, the not always visible good of which they were the depositaries. We were talking yesterday of the French shop-keeper of Louis-Philippe. Perhaps we should reach further back. Melted into the mass through an evolution of the English type, the eighteenth century aristocracy would have fertilized the mass with the idea of greatness of which it was a depository. As with its rites of courtesy. Its prodigality would have become generosity in the little fellow. But it was cut down *en bloc* because of its vices; and with it part of the French nation's heritage was slain.

"France needs a common denominator enabling her to gather her serious qualities around some transcendent image. Her diverse theses. This problem can scarcely be enunciated without raising the conceptual distinction between Intelligence and Spirit. The spirit prescribes the direction, the spiritual point of view . . . Intelligence, governed but not informed by this compass, gropes in its choice of means according to the processes of reason, a reason which is fallible. Which is even always mistaken, for no logical truth is absolutely valid either in space or time, it is only momentary . . . Lieutenant C— and I are fighting for the same greatness of France. And that is enough to make me feel fraternal, even if he is opposed to me in the choice of means. He who has placed the salvation of France in the survival of her two year old children, even if it has meant making compromises on certain points, I cannot consider the spiritual enemy of the man who has based the salvation of France on the purity of principles and, in the name of this absolute, on the acceptance of the liquidation of all children. The truth was contradictory, the two parts of the truth had to be saved. Man's field of vision is tiny, and each only considered his own part. Action demands simplifications. It's in man's nature.

"But once beyond the stage where this problem had a meaning, once France is saved in soul as well as body, I shall divide people not according to the path chosen, not according to the processes of their reason, not according to the function they assumed among necessary functions, but by the sole star they steered by. Not they are my brothers who reasoned like me, but they who 'loved' like me. Thus rendering to 'love' its old meaning of 'contemplation by the spirit'."

For anyone who felt like this the climate of Algiers was bound to be "sordid" and "unbreatheable". His voice was doomed to be a voice in the wilderness. The tolerance he was preaching could cut no ice with the new inquisitors, who having proclaimed themselves *a priori* the guardians of the Truth and the Keepers of the Holy Writ, were out to sit in judgment over and to scourge all those less righteous than themselves with the intransigeant rigidity of Old Testament prophets.

Lionel Chassin, who dropped in on him almost every evening for a game of chess, would often find Antoine absorbed in some new mathematical or physical puzzle he had just dreamed up as a challenge to this restless brain. By adding glycerine to the soap he frothed up in a basin of warm water he could blow up huge bubbles strong enough to be launched out into the street like balloons; and by drawing on a cigarette before puffing through his fingers or a pipe, he could even fill them with grey smoke—to the delighted amazement of the urchins below. His experimentation was not always this frivolous, and Chassin claims to have come upon him more than once engaged in strange hydrodynamic tests involving the use of playing cards in a bathtub full of water. The next day Saint-Ex would have transcribed his findings into algebraic equations which were more than amateurish pastimes. For, to quote Chassin, "behind his nonchalant exterior he was a hard worker and deeply persevering". As for his mathematical brain-teasers, they so impressed a professor at the University of Algiers that he finally told Chassin: "Your friend is a mathematical genius. You should ask him to prove the theorems of Fermat, something no one has been able to do since the seventeenth century. He has it in him to succeed."

While these distractions kept him occupied—for several hours a day, at least—they failed to relieve his inner restlessness; and as the weeks dragged by and turned into months, his wretched state of mind, which was preying on his health, became a matter of growing concern to his friends. Henri Comte, who paid a visit to a shivering Algiers—the city had just been powdered by a freak snowstorm—in January 1944, found Saint-Ex reduced to intriguing with the Gaullist authorities he deep down inside of him despised. Hardly a day would pass without his telephoning to Etienne Burin des Roziers, an influential member of De Gaulle's civilian secretariat, who would have to inform him once again that no new decision had been made on his case. Increasingly perturbed by the bloody purge of "collaborators" and "traitors" which he foresaw as ensuing on the heels of the Liberation, Saint-Exupéry told Comte that he was planning to have himself parachuted into France in an effort to restrain the leaders of the Resistance from unleashing a blood-bath.

The idea of this giant leap in the dark seems to have come to Saint-Ex in the wake of Paul Dungler's final vicissitudes with the Gaullists in Algiers. In his native Alsace, Dungler had made the acquaintance of a German businessman connected with Admiral Canaris's *Abwehr*—the Wehrmacht's Intelligence Service which had become a vast warren of anti-Nazi plotting. Just how William Donovan's O.S.S. got wind of it is not clear, though it was probably through Allen Dulles, who after he had been posted to Berne to head up all O.S.S. activities in Switzerland had been contacted by several anti-Hitler plotters. In Algiers, at any rate, Dungler was introduced to Selden Chapin, who had succeeded Robert Murphy as American Ambassador, and to a Colonel Henry Hyde, of the O.S.S., who explained their great interest in Dungler's reestablishing contact with this particular German businessman. Dungler was dubious about this latter prospect, but he was able to propose an even more interesting contact with members of Canaris's *Abwehr* in Nice, where the Gestapo's surveillance was slightly less oppressive since it lay in the Italians' zone of occupation.

The Gaullists, meanwhile, had been appraised of Dungler's desire to return to his Resistance post in France, after turning down the offer of a safe job in Washington. Immediately an order, issued by De Gaulle and Soustelle, had gone out to all the ports and airfields in Algeria to prevent Dungler's departure. It amounted in effect to a warrant for his arrest, and it was backed up by curious warnings which began reaching him, suggesting that he watch his step at night in returning to his hotel. By December the city of Algiers had grown so uncomfortable for the doughty Alsatian that he left his hotel and took refuge in the villa of Jacques Lemaigre-Dubreuil—the same Lemaigre-Dubreuil whom Saint-Ex and Wencelius had talked to at such length at the Saint-Regis in New York. Lemaigre-Dubreuil, who was now vehemently anti-Gaullist, had also fallen under the local anathema, and there was talk of his being forcibly prevented from returning to France. It was enough to make Dungler realize that the Americans were his only hope. Contact was renewed with Colonel Henry Hyde, of the O.S.S., who now took him under his protection. It was agreed that Dungler should be parachuted back into France, but to guard against a total failure of the mission should an accident overtake him, he was asked to find someone to accompany him. Dungler's choice fell on a young professor called Rivet, whom he had met with Saint-Ex. The three of them met up once again with Léon Wencelius on New Year's Day, and two days later Dungler told Wencelius that he would gladly carry any letters he might have for persons living in France. When Saint-Ex heard of this generous offer, after lunching with Wencelius at the Cercle Interallié, he went back to his apartment and wrote a letter to his mother. It was written on January 5th, entrusted to Dungler on the 7th, and in due course it reached its destination (at Agay)—after Dungler and Rivet had been secretly flown out of Blida on a Flying Fortress and dropped with several special radio sets and their precious crystals over the Massif Central, not far from Clermont-Ferrand.

Saint-Exupéry being a personal friend of "Wild Bill" Donovan, head of the O.S.S., it was only natural that this precedent should arouse similar hopes for himself. Unlike Dungler, however, he did not speak German and had not the slightest underground experience. Donovan, as we shall see, did not flatly discourage his wild hopes; but it seems reasonable to suppose that he was not particularly enthusiastic, Saint-Ex's distinctive size and features making him a singularly poor choice for cloak-and-dagger missions.

Ten days after Dungler's clandestine departure Saint-Exupéry left for Tunis. His old squadron mates had already moved on to Italy, but at La Marsa their "godmother", Madame Mast, kept a number of guest-rooms for them in an old Arab palace which had once served as summer residence for the Turkish Beys. One of them was specially reserved for Saint-Ex, to be used when he wished. Like the others, it had a tiny Arab saloon, which he found utterly enchanting. In this, "one of the few spiritual oases on this sad continent"—as he was later to write to his benefactress—he could forget the "crab-pot of Algiers" and concentrate with renewed energy on *Citadelle*.

Among those whom he met at Madame Mast's was a fellow pilot, Geoffroy de La Tour du Pin, who was at this time undergoing training at the La Marsa airfield. One evening Saint-Exupéry asked if he could drop in on him, and when he appeared at his billet, it was with a suitcase, which turned out to be crammed with typescript pages of *Citadelle*. A bottle of Suze was produced and before Saint-Ex was through with his extended readings from his "posthumous work", he had emptied the entire contents. La Tour du Pin was struck by the incantatory tone of his reading, something he had only heard with one other person, Jules Supervielle the poet. It was evident that he attached great importance to the *sound* of his work: so much so that he insisted on trying it out on the most varied audiences. They included Ramón, a Spanish café owner at La Marsa, who must have been mystified by these "readings"!

Three weeks later Saint-Ex was back in Algiers, where Wencelius found him gloomier than ever. He even declined to introduce his friend to André Gide on the grounds that the latter was "too old now to strike up new acquaintances"; but when Wencelius, disregarding the veto, was well received by Gide, Saint-Exupéry took him to task for going to see Gide without his permission!

Frustration once again was getting the better of his nerves, to the detriment of his physical and mental health. But because they were all he had to sustain him, he would not compromise with his dreams. Offered a headquarters job by General Béthouart, whose army corps was now preparing "Operation Anvil", Saint-Exupéry declined. The invasion of southern France must have seemed too remote a prospect for him to be tempted by a desk job in the intervening months.

He was more receptive to the invitation extended to him by Lionel Chassin, when the latter was given command of a squadron of B-26 Marauders, based in Sardinia. Chassin proposed that he accompany him to Villacidro as one of his staff officers, the understanding being that he would spend part of the time in the air. Notwithstanding his misgivings, he was tempted. At least it would enable him to escape from the "sink-hole" of Algiers. Years later Chassin wrote that Saint-Ex accepted "out of friendship, even though going to bomb works of art in Italy did not represent his ideal". It most certainly did not; and it was why even now he refused to give up his efforts to have himself reassigned to his old squadron.

# 24

# The Veteran

IN the end it was two Americans who helped get him reinstated. The first was Colonel Paul Rockwell, an intrepid North Carolinian who had signed up with the Foreign Legion during the First World War and later flown with the Escadrille de la Garde Chérifienne in the Rif campaign of 1925. Like Colonel Willis, he was one of the senior members of General Spaatz's French liaison section, but unlike Willis he had remained unruffled and serene through the many conflicts and misunderstandings which arose between French and American flyers. During the autumn and winter of 1943–1944 he frequently lunched or dined with Saint-Exupéry in various Air Force messes and in small black market restaurants in and around Algiers. One day, in late March of 1944, on returning from a mission to Italy, Rockwell found a note from Saint-Ex waiting for him at his billet. He was about to leave for Sardinia and asked the Colonel to ring him up because he wanted to see him very much prior to his departure. They met for lunch the next day at an American Air Force mess on the Rue Michelet where, as so often happened, Saint-Exupéry was recognized on the street by a young Frenchwoman who pursued him with a request for an autograph, which he gladly gave her. Over the lunch-table he was more explicit than ever in describing the kind of book he now wanted to write: an Allied rather than an exclusively French *Pilote de Guerre*, designed to extol the *camaraderie* between American and French flyers in the air war. Such a book, he felt, could bring about a better understanding between France and the United States, but it could only be written if he personally shared the experiences and risks of his comrades.

General Spaatz had meanwhile been transferred to London to become Eisenhower's chief air-force aide, and the commander of the United States Air Force in the Mediterranean was now General Ira Eaker. Colonel Harold Willis, who had influenced Spaatz against him, had long since been sent back to the United States, and Saint-Ex wondered if a fresh approach with Eaker might not be tried. Rockwell said he would back him to the hilt, and he promptly sent off a very strong letter of recommendation to Lieutenant Colonel Kenneth Campbell, one of Eaker's liaison officers who had had trouble with Willis himself and who was now stationed at Allied head-quarters at Caserta, near Naples.

The second American who offered to intervene on Saint-Ex's behalf was a *Life* photographer called John Phillips. His father, a Welshman, had chosen to settle in Kabylia before enlisting in the French army in 1914, and his son had been brought up speaking the local dialect as well as French. Returning to Algiers was thus a bit like coming home to John Phillips, for whom the stale aroma of empty wine casks on the wharfs and the smells of leather, oranges, and oil-fried pastries mingled with the damp breath of the sea and an occasional whiff of jasmin, were among his earliest memories.

One day, during a stop-over between two photographic assignments, he heard that Saint-Exupéry was in Algiers and decided to call him up.

"Colonel," he began.

"Major," Saint-Ex corrected him.

Phillips corrected himself. They had a friend in common, he explained, the pilot Rose whom Saint-Ex had one day bawled out in Argentina for having landed next to him instead of carrying the mail on to the next port-of-call . . .

"When I saw him," as Phillips wrote years later in *Odd World*, "he was little more than a silhouette against the window in the early winter dusk. In profile the nose of this twentieth-century Pico della Mirandola stood out with the mocking and insolent air that earned him the nickname Pique-la-Lune.

"Full face, however, Saint-Ex displayed little sign of the many crashes which had broken practically every bone in his body. His worst crash was the one in Guatemala where, as he liked to put it, he 'learned about gravity and remained eight days in coma'. One scar from this accident raised an eyebrow into a permanent look of inquiry, while the other gave his mouth a wry smile."

After reminiscing for a while about Mermoz and Guillaumet—"I'm the last one, and I can assure you it's a very strange feeling"—Saint-Ex went into the kitchen to prepare the drinks. Phillips was intrigued to see him mix sweet muscatel with a harsh alcohol distilled from ordinary wine and then set fire to the concoction instead of shaking it. Back in the drawing-room Saint-Exupéry peered thoughtfully at his glass. He had explained to Phillips that he was unable to write about the war because he was not participating, and "only those who participate have a right to speak". "I want to write," he now continued after a long pause, "and I'll donate what I do to you, for your publication, if you get me reinstated into my squadron".

Incapable of imagining Saint-Ex cooped up like this forever in a gloomy Algiers drawing-room, Phillips promised to do what he could. He saw quite a bit of him over the next few days as they thumbed rides all over town, Saint-Ex "looking elegantly out of place with his summer uniform covered by a large blue raincoat".

Having obtained his priority rating, Phillips was flown to Naples, where he looked up Colonel Tex McCrary, another officer on General Eaker's staff, who agreed that if a man felt that badly about participating in the war, he should be allowed to do so. The colonel broached the subject to General Eaker, who said he would think it over.

Exactly what happened after this is not clear. Lionel Chassin claims that he and Saint-Exupéry flew to Naples from Villacidro, in Sardinia, to see General Eaker, but were unable to get past the aide-de-camps who had apparently never heard of Saint-Exupéry. They were, however, told that Eaker was to fly to Algiers the following week to dine with a French cabinet minister. As both Chassin and Saint-Ex knew the cabinet minister in question, they had little trouble getting themselves invited too. "And it was during this dinner that General Eaker, under the influence of the good food and wines of Algeria, gave Saint-Exupéry a special authorization to undertake five war missions with the 2/33."

John Phillips' account is somewhat different, though not necessarily contradictory: for Saint-Exupéry probably did not wish to discourage Phillips in his efforts by letting him know that he had more than one iron in the fire. On his return to Algiers from Naples Phillips found Saint-Ex in a state of high dudgeon, his own air command having refused to let him be more than a co-pilot (on Chassin's Marauders). "In the hope of convincing General Eaker himself, he followed me back to Italy, AWOL as far as I could see. Helping him pack, I found that most of his belongings amounted to a huge pile of papers, stacked up like a volcano on a low table. He also owned several fountain pens and asked me to carry his inkwell so it would not get lost."

In Naples Phillips had already procured himself an apartment and it was here, in the picturesque old quarter of Vomero overlooking the great port city, that Saint-Ex established residence. While waiting to see Eaker he spent his time reading Kafka and, in Phillips' words, "being a good winner at chess and a poor loser at word games. His competitive spirit was such that he not only disliked losing but refrained from games at which he could not win most of the time. Yet he never let himself get carried away by the games he played well."

Gavoille's squadron was now based at Pomigliano, just outside of Naples, and it was here on April 23rd that Jean Leleu, recently appointed Operations

Officer for *La Hache*, saw a jubilant Saint-Ex walk towards their Lightnings, delighted at the propsect of soon rejoining his companions. Vesuvius had gone into one of its periodic tantrums and Leleu had spent most of that morning flying a geologist from Algiers University round the belching mountain while he snapped photographs. Professor Noetzlin—such was his name —was so pleased by the outing that he invited Leleu, Saint-Exupéry, Chassin, and a British general called Stevens to be his guests that evening. The spectacle, as they dined that night on a restaurant terrace overlooking the cliffs and the bay, was breath-taking. In the distance the volcano glowed like a cone of red-hot iron, as molten lava flowed down its flanks. Billows of reddened smoke rose from the crater, veined with sparks and flashes, and every now and then a brilliant glow would shoot another pillar of smoke far up into the sulphurous heavens. Noetzlin held forth on the subject of volcanoes and earthquakes, after which Saint-Exupéry broadened the discussion to embrace all forms of energy. His statement that the atom bomb was simply a question of time left his listeners dumbfounded; but his intention was less to overawe the company than to meditate aloud on how this sudden magnification of human power to an "astral scale" was going to affect mankind, and not least of all man's relationship to the notion of the divine.

The next day, when Leleu sought him out at the address he had given him in Naples, he found the apartment door ajar with no sign of Saint-Ex. Passing through several empty rooms he stopped by a window overlooking a back court and saw the air filled with fluttering white butterflies. The balconies were choked with laughing and squealing children, who clapped their hands in delight at the sight of these midget helicopters which Saint-Ex and some friends were busy cutting out of sheets of paper.

That evening Saint-Ex, accompanied by Chassin, Noetzlin, and Phillips dined at the American Officers' Mess at Pomigliano. Ham and bottles of white wine specially brought to them by two lady emissaries as a gift from their solicitous *marraine*, Madame Mast, helped alleviate the "monotony of the standard menu,"—to quote from the *Journal de Marche*. The dinner over, all repaired to the *Foyer Français*, a rustic bar decorated with a mosaic of aerial photographs and framed citations and artistically strung bulbs. The non-coms' table, led by a magnificently moustachioed trooper who answered to the name of *"Père"* (Father) Rieutord, vied with the officers' table in the singing of "green" songs, which grew progressively "greener" as the evening wore on and the ladies retired.

It was not until three weeks later—May 16th, to be exact—that Saint-Ex finally rejoined his squadron, which had meanwhile moved from the outskirts of Naples to Sardinia. On May 16th Saint-Ex and John Phillips (who had been assigned to do a photo-reporting job on his squadron for *Life*) flew in to Alghero on a B-26 Marauder. They found Gavoille and his fellow officers billeted in a small fisherman's cottage on a promontory overlooking the sea. The place was so primitive that the rooms were without doors, there was no running water, and their own mechanics had had to install the emergency wiring and bulbs. "Captain René Gavoille"—to quote Phillips again—"greeted our arrival by popping the corks of the best the mess had. Gavoille, a stocky man with a ruddy face and a temper which came to a boil faster than milk on a stove, was considered by Saint-Ex the finest type France had produced. Surrounded by his officers he looked like a triumphant hen. But at briefings he volunteered his squadron, himself first, for the toughest missions. In return, partly in joke, he demanded butter and steaks as rations instead of margarine and Spam."

Spam, however, seems to have been a staple diet for the squadron, already plagued by a local shortage of wine, which in Italy had been in plentiful supply. Lieutenant André Henry did his best to camouflage the raw material behind a variety of culinary disguises, but the taste of pressed beef kept obstinately coming through the thickest of sauces. The meals Phillips shared with the squadron were more remarkable for other reasons, for "happy to be back with *les camarades*', Saint-Ex covered every topic in monologue, turning conversation into a series of essays, which sounded like verbal soufflés to his spellbound listeners".

With the help of Signor Montalto, the amiable pharmacist whose cottage they had taken over, several local shepherds were persuaded to relinquish ten sheep for the slaughter, and on May 28th Saint-Exupéry was at last able to offer everyone a lavish *méchoui*. The ten sheep were skewered on spits and roasted over an open fire, while the shepherds showed Sergeant Major Rieutord how to turn their entrails into blood sausages. The American officers of the neighbouring 23rd Squadron seemed a bit appalled at first at the prospect of having to dig into the skewered lambs with hands and fingers; but warmed by *anisette* and a steady flow of wine, they soon lost all inhibitions. John Phillips had thoughtfully donated a sixty gallon cask of Sardinian *vino*, which kept the company in high spirits for the duration of the feast. Looking grander than ever in his white handle-bar moustaches and his baggy pantaloons, "Father" Rieutord (a Tunisian veteran who had insisted on following the squadron to Italy) climbed on to a wooden table and led a couple of lusty songs. Phillips scrambled over the roof like a chamois for plunging snapshots of the festivities, which rose to a rollicking crescendo when an American chaplain, throwing his cassock to the wind, heaved himself on to the garden table in his turn for a bout of Chaucerian plainsong.

The atmosphere of concord between Americans and French was a far cry from the tense relations which had earlier existed in Tunisia. Instead of treating them as hopelessly undisciplined and irresponsible, the Photo Wing's new commanders, Colonel Karl Polifka and Colonel James Setchell, had come to realize that they could on occasion even learn something from the French.

This is not to say that Saint-Exupéry's arrival did not arouse occasional mutterings from his American and British colleagues. The base commander at Alghero was an RAF Group Captain, and all communication with pilots had to be effected in English. He had difficulty understanding even the simplest instructions from Ground Control to which he replied in a virtually incomprehensible jargon. His absent-mindedness was likewise a source of concern. One day, as Saint-Exupéry was coming in from a practice flight, Phillips saw an ambulance race out on to the field when it looked as though his Lightning was going to land with its undercarriage still up.

Before he left (the day after the *méchoui* banquet) Phillips was granted the rare privilege of watching Saint-Ex at work in his tiny room. "What a strange night" he later described it. "Settling down, I had noticed, was as exhausting for him as struggling into his flying clothes, an ordeal he submitted to with deep sighs. Fitting his large body into a small, squeaky wicker chair, he pressed his feet together like a studious child, crouched over the writing pad resting on his lap and scribbled neat rows of small black characters that slanted hopefully up the page. Next to him lay a watch, at which he frequently glanced to check his speed, as though it were a dial on a plane. The fact that Saint-Ex kept his watch remorselessly ticking at his side did not always mean he would write, though it was one indication of his contradictory attitude toward machinery.

"Saint-Ex sat in one corner of his bare whitewashed room, which was reminiscent in many respects of a monk's cell; only his handsome pigskin suitcase suggested the outer world.

"The wicker chair creaked. 'Funny,' he remarked, rubbing his wrist. 'It hurts only when I write legibly.' He wiggled his fingers, lit a cigarette, and looked at his watch before returning to his black characters."

The eve of Phillips's departure several bottles of Italian *spumante* were opened in his honour, and on May 30th he bid good-bye to his squadron friends and flew off towards other horizons in a Flying Fortress. The kitchen caught fire while they were frying potatoes and it was half an hour before they could smother the flames from the burning oil. But that evening they were able to entertain three RAF officers to a dinner of fried potatoes and lobster, which had by now replaced Spam as the *pièce de résistance* of most meals.

"There was no civilian life at Alghero," recalls Fernand Marty, who served there as liaison and Anglo-French interpreter. "The tempo of life was very leisurely. Gay as usual, shaving when he liked, wearing baggy G.I. clothing and a faded French Air Force cap, Saint-Exupéry seemed to like this Sardinian adventure." The tiny room he occupied on the upper floor of what he liked to call his "*pigeonnier*" (dove-cot) was, as ever, a model of disorder—with money, shirts, cigarettes, and books covering bed, chair, and even floor. "His wardrobe" recalls Jean Leleu, "was limited to several American suntan shirts and trousers in pretty poor condition, but that did not worry him in the least, since he considered himself on vacation. One day, as he was getting ready to take off for Algiers, he noticed that his shirt-sleeve elbows were torn, and for lack of anything better I had to mend them with a stapler. The result was jaunty rather than elegant, but Saint-Exupéry only smiled."

The first such trip was made the day after Phillips's departure (May 31st), when Saint-Exupéry took the Squadron's No. 63 Lightning (exclusively used for training and liaison flights) to Algiers with several dozen lobsters. He had to choose his altitude carefully—not too high or the lobsters would burst, nor too low or they would spoil in the heat. On putting down at Maison-Blanche he telephoned to Madame Guy Monod, the wife of a French diplomat serving in the Cultural section of the Commissariat of Foreign Affairs, telling her to get the mayonnaise ready, as he was bringing her a rich haul of lobsters straight from Sardinia.

Two days later Saint-Ex flew back to Alghero. How happy, he wrote to Madame Mast, the 2/33 Group's "godmother", how happy he was to be flying once more and away from "that crab-tureen known as Algiers . . . I've lost that long white beard I was told six months ago would get wound up in the controls . . ."

On June 4th he hopped over to Villacidro to see his friend Lionel Chassin, and two days later he took off on his first war mission, a "pin-point" assignment calling for the photographing of a number of specific targets in the region of Marseille. A fire in his left motor forced him to turn back before he could reach the target area, and after he had landed at Alghero it was found that the flames had burned a huge hole in the engine casing. That evening everyone crowded around the radio—to hear the exciting news of the Normandy landings.

Bad weather held up all sorties for the next day; but in honour of General Rignault and Colonel Polifka, who turned up on an inspection tour, Lieutenant Henry surpassed himself in the confection of tarts, the crowning touch to a "banquet" which saw a small milk pig and *mousseline* potatoes shunt aside lobsters and thick slices of Spam. The banquet completed, the company withdrew a respectful distance to watch a shooting match between Colonel Polifka and Major de Saint-Exupéry. There were no casualties, and the *Journal de Marche* for this June 7th diplomatically refrains from revealing the identity of the victor; but it does add that the evening ended with "some eye-opening card tricks of Major Saint-Ex".

The diet may have been lacking in variety and their lodgings lacking in luxury, but otherwise life was not too painful. A dip in the sea brought quick relief from the heat, and Saint-Exupéry was soon being initiated into a new sport by Lieutenant Core, who had discovered that the easiest way of bringing up fish was by using small sticks of dynamite!

His second sortie was flown on June 14th. Though hampered by clouds, Saint-Exupéry brought back the photographs requested of the region of Rodez, north of Albi. He took off the next day again to photograph the region of Toulouse and came near to passing out when his oxygen flow stopped working.

On June 17th a major disaster was narrowly averted when Saint-Ex's fishing companion, Lieutenant Core, tipped over on his motorcycle while trying to overtake a truck on a narrow Sardinian road. With him were 400 lbs. of dynamite which fortunately failed to go off. Fernand Marty lost no time getting his hands on the loot, and soon the entire countryside was rocking from explosions and great geysers were rising from the sea. This too brought back familiar memories, and as the *Journal de Marche* noted for June 20, Saint-Ex entertained his squadron mates that evening with "palpitating stories of the Spain of 1937 and the actions of the *dinamiteros*". He also told how the Bedouins who had rescued Prévot and himself when they were dying of thirst in the Libyan desert, had first forced a lentil mash into their parched mouths before allowing them to touch the water which could have split their mucus membranes and killed them. Later, in pondering this experience, it had dawned on Saint-Exupéry that this was the explanation for that strange episode in the Old Testament, where Esau is described as selling his birthright for a "mess of potage". Jacob, having come upon his brother thirsting in the desert, had forced him to part with his share of the heritage in exchange for the lentil mash which alone could save him.

The next evening a group of American officers were invited over for a *méchoui*, everyone got delightfully "fried", the night air echoed with raucous singing until three o'clock in the morning, when Marty, not to be outdone by the *dinamiteros* of Madrid, took it out on the night with a barrage of pistol shots.

Saint-Exupéry's second successful mission was flown on June 23rd when, to make sure that he had "snapped" all his "pin-points" he passed and repassed the target area as though he were ironing a sheet. Though the *Journal de Marche* makes no mention of the fact, it is possible that Saint-Ex made another flying trip back to Algiers before the end of the month; for a few days after this mission Saint-Ex invited Dr. Pélissier and a few friends to a dinner at Châteauneuf (near Algiers), where he kept the company agog with a vivid description of his latest sortie. As he was flying over Avignon, he told them, he had received urgent radio signals instructing him to establish immediate radio contact with Ground Control. Thus alerted, two German fighters had risen to attack him, but by opening the super-chargers and giving his Lightning the gas he had managed to shake them off. "I'm the dean of the world's pilots," was the way he humorously referred to himself. For once he was on the crest of the wave and there was no more talk of broken vertebra or cancer.

The day after his successful mission over Avignon Saint-Exupéry took up a new Lightning for a trial flight. He landed, thinking all was well, when he noticed that one of his propellers had stopped. Only one of the two drop-tanks had been loaded on to the plane and one engine had done all the work. The second propeller had continued turning in the slip-stream sufficiently fast to conceal the trouble. Fortunately no harm was done, but it was one more example of an absent-mindedness which had his colleagues shaking their heads.

Understandably so; for on June 29th it looked as though his luck had failed him. That day Lieutenant Henry and his kitchen crew got to work on an elaborate repast intended to celebrate the Major's forty-fourth birthday. The order in which missions were flown was normally established by Captain Jean Leleu, the Operations Officer, and as a general rule a pilot who had just flown a sortie or returned from a trip away from the base resumed his position at the bottom of the thirteen man roster. Gavoille was scheduled to fly on this particular morning, but when Saint-Ex learned that his assignment was to photograph Annecy, the region of his youth, he pleaded with him to be allowed to take his place. He could enjoy his birthday so much more if he could return that afternoon with the feeling that he had accomplished something!

To humour him Gavoille finally yielded to his entreaties, and Saint-Exupéry took off, headed for Grenoble and the Alps. As he was approaching Lake Annecy his left motor began coughing and spluttering, and he was eventually forced to switch it off completely, to keep the vibrations from shaking his Lightning to pieces. With only one engine to sustain him, Saint-Ex knew that he was an easy target for any German fighter that might wish to climb up and get him. So he turned towards the Alps, where there were fewer enemy bases and he stood a chance of being able to duck down into a valley if he spied a plane in the distance. He apparently followed the valley of the Arc river as far as Saint-Jean-de-Maurienne and then, instead of continuing southward over the region of the Galibier pass (the highest in

France) towards Briançon, he flew on over Modane and the Mont Cenis pass. Beneath him the mountains gradually levelled out into foothills and ripples.

"After threading my way through the valleys and between the snowy peaks," as he later described it to René Gavoille, "I expected to come out over the sea when I saw a huge plain and in this plain a big city surrounded by many airfields". The city, as it happened, was Turin, and instead of heading south, he was headed south east. Suddenly anxious, he glanced at his rear-view mirror and "there like a big black fly, was a fighter". Certain that he had been spotted, he ducked his head down between his shoulders and waited. "*Mon pauvre Antoine,*" he thought, "this time your old carcass is done for". Any moment now and the tracers would be ripping through his cockpit cover, the instrument panel would shatter into a hundred pieces, the wheel in his hands would be seized with a hysterical fit of trembling. "A last thought for everyone, for all those who are waiting for me yonder, beyond the horizon . . . *Mon Dieu*, but it's long! How long death is in coming! . . . I rub my eyes . . . I pinch myself . . . No, I wasn't dreaming, I wasn't asleep . . . I'm wide awake. But then . . . he must have taken me for a friend! How stupid of me. How could he imagine that an enemy would lumber over such a frequented zone?"

An Allied plane flying down the Po valley with one propeller feathered at a height of 8,000 feet, where it was a sitting duck for any German or Italian fighter, was indeed an anomaly. But the extraordinary thing is that Saint-Exupéry does not seem to have realized how fantastically off course he was until he saw the sea and a sprawling city in front of him. "I recognized Genoa" he later told Gavoille, "and in my mind's eye there flashed a vision of the maps in the Operations Tent, with a host of tiny flags pin-stuck around Genoa. Genoa is heavily defended."

It was too late to turn back, so he continued, for better or for worse, overflying the great port city at a height of 8,000 feet. Not an anti-aircraft gun fired, not a plane rose to meet him. He was already some distance out to sea and beginning to breathe more freely when he realized that Ground Control was growing increasingly insistent. Home-coming pilots were instructed to switch on their I.F.F. (Identification Friend or Foe) instruments, which transmitted a recognizable signal indicating that theirs was an Allied and not an enemy plane. In the excitement of overflying Genoa Saint-Ex had forgotten to switch his on, and a squadron of Allied fighters was on the point of taking off to intercept the "hostile" craft. Though Saint-Exupéry had trouble understanding the instructions transmitted from the ground, he could at least make out the word "Borgo"—indicating that he was expected to veer west and to put down south of Bastia, on Corsica's eastern coast, instead of Alghero, in northern Sardinia.

The moment a returning pilot touched down, he had to report to the Operations Tent even before he could climb out of his heavy flying gear and wash off the sweat in the shower-room, to be put through a "debriefing session" by the Group Intelligence Officer. The "debriefing" Saint-Ex was subjected to at the Borgo airfield must have been particularly exacting and have left his American interrogators open-mouthed. But the photographs taken (for he had left his camera going) confirmed his fantastic story—that he had calmly overflown Genoa at a height of 8,000 feet!

That afternoon his anxious squadron mates were relieved to receive a radio message from Corsica informing them that Major de Saint-Exupéry's Lightning had safely landed at Borgo. Jean Leleu took off in another Lightning to find out what had happened; and that evening it was a shame-faced group of gourmets who tucked into the Pantagruelian fare—complete with moka birthday cake and a Mount Everest of ice-cream which *Pâtissier Chef* Henry had prepared to toast the Major's forty-four years.

\*     \*     \*

Not until July 2nd could Saint-Ex fly back to Alghero, and then only on another plane—his Lightning being still immobilized by its defective engine. The next day he was allowed to take off again for Algiers on one of the Squadron's reserve Lightnings in order to stand in at a wedding for Gavoille, who felt that his presence was more urgently needed at the base. That evening (or possibly the next) Saint-Exupéry put in a surprise appearance at the Monods' house at Ain Taya. Gramophone records at this time were so scarce that the little collection Madame Monod had managed to smuggle out of France were deeply appreciated by the connoisseurs, a number of whom were gathered on her terrace listening to Wanda Landowska play Bach's Goldberg Variations. The religious silence was suddenly shattered by the appearance of a jubilating giant in uniform who cried: "Look, touch me, it's a miracle! I'm alive!" The apparition threw the quiet party into a hubbub and made a hash of Madame Landowska's delicate tinkling. Normally a fervent Bach lover himself, Tonio on this particular evening just could not be stilled, but kept repeating: "Touch me! I tell you—it's a miracle!"

Finally, to quiet him down, Madame Monod put three girls on to him with orders to drag him off into a corner and to keep him occupied. The evening air was aswarm with mosquitoes, attracted by the fig-trees, and the silvery tinkle of the harpsichord was interrupted by frequent slaps. The young ladies gleefully had him stretch out under a protective sheet draped over him like a mosquito net. But the corpse refused to be silenced even now, and went right on talking. It explained in detail why mosquitoes were far cleverer than their victims imagined. Their buzzing, for example, was part of a deliberate strategy. When one tried slapping a mosquito, one almost invariably missed, but the slap brought the blood to the surface of the skin, offering the hovering gourmet the rich fare it relished. It was the same way with lions, the cadaver continued, discoursing through its winding-sheet: many were the animals who could outrun a lion any day of the week. Knowing which, old Leo would let out such a formidable, Wagnerian roar that it was enough to paralyse the fleeing prey.

Another person Saint-Ex saw during this two-day stop-over in Algiers was Jacques Meyer, the former managing editor of *L'Intransigeant* and now the director of Radio Algiers. They had lunch together at the villa of Albert Marquet, the painter, high up on the hill overlooking the city. After lunch, while Marquet disappeared for his afternoon siesta, Saint-Ex kept his wife and Meyer goggle-eyed with his card tricks. About De Gaulle he was as caustic as ever, remarking that "I don't speak a word of English, yet De Gaulle doesn't consider me a Free Frenchman". And about himself he was, as usual, fatalistic, repeating what Meyer had already heard him say more than once: "*Un jour ou l'autre je tomberai en croix dans la Mediterranée.*" (One of these days I'll plant my cross in the Mediterranean.)

Saint-Exupéry also had time to call on his friends at Air Force head-quarters, where he was informed that Fernand Grenier, the new Com-missioner for Air, wanted to see him. Saint-Ex had already been introduced to the former Communist deputy at a luncheon specially arranged for him by Henri Frenay, Commissioner in De Gaulle's provisional government for Prisoners and the Deported and a member of the famous "Combat" Resist-ance network in which Albert Camus was active. A number of well meaning Air Force officers had besought Grenier to have Saint-Exupéry transferred to a less dangerous job; but the intended victim was having none of it.

"I have read your pamphlets"—one about the notorious collaborator Alphonse de Châteaubriant, the other about the "*francs-tireurs*" (Resistance snipers)—"what a' people, ours!" remarked Saint-Ex. "Each must fight to hasten the Liberation." After which he added with a gay laugh: "You see, touch wood! I have faith in my star . . ."

Grenier found his optimism so infectious that he didn't have the heart to raise the subject of Saint-Ex's transfer, and as they shook hands on parting, he had to hold back a desire to embrace him.

On the 8th Gavoille took off for Tunis for a glimpse of the son his wife had borne him a couple of weeks before. The following afternoon it was Saint-Exupéry's turn to follow him. He had agreed to be the child's god-father and he was expected in Tunis for the baptism. Baptism or not, he was absorbed in a murder mystery which he refused to stop reading even as the Jeep he was riding in bumped its way out on to the airfield. The Jeep drew up near the Lightning he was to pilot, but Saint-Ex remained stubbornly glued to his thriller.

"Yes, yes," he said, without looking up from the page. "Give me a couple more minutes. I'm practically through."

More prodding was needed to get him out of the Jeep and into the cockpit. He was still clutching the unfinished book, and while someone was sent off for the ear-phones, which had been forgotten, he plunged back into his thriller. He finally agreed to take off, keeping the opened book on his knee, but his colleagues were persuaded that once in the air he went right back to his reading. On touching down at La Marsa, he was told that the baptism of Gavoille's son had been postponed to a later date. Though Saint-Ex seemed in a fairly jovial mood, Madame Mast couldn't help noticing the number of whiskies to which he helped himself after dinner and which she attributed, naturally enough, to some secret malaise.

It was expressed with fewer inhibitions in an undated letter which he probably wrote that night to his friend Georges Pélissier on the official stationery of the Résidence Générale de France en Tunisie. He was returning the next day to his "dove-cot", he wrote, after explaining that the wiring in his plane had caused him some trouble and delay. "A strange job I'm doing at my age. The closest after me is six years younger. I prefer this existence, with breakfast at seven in the morning, the Mess, the tent or the little white-washed room, followed by ten thousand metres' altitude over forbidden territory, to the atrocious inactivity of Algiers. I find it impossible to concentrate and to work for myself in a provisional state of limbo. There I lacked social significance. But I've chosen the maximum of wear and tear and since one must push oneself to one's uttermost limits, I'm not going to give up. I hope this sinister war will end before I've melted away entirely, like a candle in the searing flame of oxygen. Later I have another job to do."

On July 10th Gavoille and Saint-Exupéry flew back from Tunis in their respective planes, the Squadron Leader's well stocked with welcome wines and spirits. During their absence Lieutenant Core had hopped over to Bastia and flown Saint-Ex's stranded Lightning back to Alghero, where everyone was now busy packing and crating their things for the eventual move to Corsica. Indeed, so determined was the hammering that evening inside the fisherman's cottage that part of the ceiling caved in in the lieutenants' room, covering their belongings with plaster—to the amusement of the "elders", who had their quarters upstairs.

The next day, July 11th, Saint-Ex took off on a mission over Lyon. North of Digne he found the earth blanketed by cloud and he was forced to return without photographs.

That night Saint-Ex, Gavoille, and Leleu went off for a farewell dinner in Alghero with Signor Montalto, the friendly owner of their fisherman's cottage. They stopped off on the way for an apéritif with Major Tidswell, of the RAF, and were already feeling scant pain before the dinner got under way. Saint-Ex was in such a loquacious mood that no one could believe that he wasn't as sober as a bishop. He entertained his friends with a new (and doubtless improved) account of his *"échappement par le Po"* (an untranslatable pun roughly meaning his "exhaust-Po escape"), and by giving them an infallible recipe for catching lions in the desert: you take a desert and you take a sieve, you pass the sand through the sieve, and you're left with the lions. The *Journal de Marche* for this day notes that "these officers, albeit distinguished," made a fearful row on returning to the cottage, to which several of the lieutenants, to recover from the shock of falling plaster, had lured a charming damsel with whom they were amiably spending their last Sardinian hours. A booby-trap was laid in the corridor for the tireless Lotharios, but when reveille was sounded at four o'clock the next morning, it was the innocent Fernand Marty (the interpreter) who was drenched.

While the truck detail moved out with the seaborne equipment, Saint-Ex and his fellow pilots stayed on in the cottage, waiting for the final order to leave. The sorties continued as usual, and on the 13th Saint-Ex was to have flown a mission over the Alps had it not been noticed at the last moment that the supply of oxygen aboard his Lightning was insufficient. "Major Saint-Ex" comments the *Journal de Marche* for that day, "is in effect a great consumer". The oxygen supplies having gone ahead with the seaborne echelon, Lieutenant Duriez, the Assistant Operations Officer, who was as small as Saint-Exupéry was big, took the Major's place for this particular mission.

Back at the fisherman's cottage Saint-Ex rolled up his sleeves and volunteered to aid Lieutenant Brillault (appointed Temporary Mess Officer in Henry's absence) in the kitchen. The K and C rations they had now been living off for thirty-six hours had begun to weary his stomach; but the thick covering of spices under which they were blanketed failed to impress Captain Pierre Siegler, inured by four years of Saint-Cyr training to all forms of culinary camouflage. The dinner that evening to which they were cordially invited by a group of Italian officers was more successful: so successful indeed that it led to a heated debate (apparently sparked by Saint-Ex) on the subject of "horizontal steeples". "Major Saint-Ex" adds the *Journal de Marche*, "improvises a song for the occasion which we hear him bawl all night long".

July 14th—France's National Holiday—was, as the log-book noted, "a day with a pox on it". Siegler, on a Lightning borrowed from the American squadron, ran off the tarmac when his landing shutters refused to come down all the way; Core, on another borrowed Lightning, had to turn back prematurely from a photographic mission over Istres and Toulon on discovering that he could not get his right fuel tank into operation; while Saint-Exupéry barely managed to return from a photographic assignment over Annecy after a failure in his oxygen supply brought on a fainting spell from which he had some trouble recovering.

The next day he hopped over to Villacidro to say good-bye to Lionel Chassin, before they moved on to Corsica. On the 16th Lieutenant Henry returned from Mediterranean Air Force headquarters at San Severo with secret information about the southern France invasion which he was instructed to pass on to Captain Leleu, the Operations Officer. Both being now debarred from flying war missions—they knew too much, if shot down and forced to talk by the Germans—they sought in vain to let Saint-Ex in on their secrets, so that he too might be grounded (for his own welfare). "Go away! Go away!" he would say, every time he saw them trying to get him off into a corner to spill the vital beans, "I don't want to hear anything".

July 17th was moving day, and the two pilots flying sorties were instructed to return to the Borgo air strip, south of Bastia, in Corsica. Saint-Exupéry was given one of the older Lightnings to fly over, while a squadron-mate carried the handsome pigskin bag with the typescript of *Citadelle*, to insure against the simultaneous loss of author and opus. That evening the squadron's dozen pilots were all gathered again under a more spacious roof; for instead of a humble fisherman's cottage, they now found themselves housed in a square villa, flanked by two palm trees, overlooking the sea-washed stones of Erbalunga, five miles north of Bastia. Built on the precipitous slope of the *corniche*, it offered little space for their Jeeps and Gavoille finally ordered a garage to be built for them under the villa's terrace. The dirt roadway leading down to it was so steep that the drivers were always afraid that they and their vehicles would roll right on down the embankment and into the sea.

On July 18th Saint-Exupéry flew out on his eighth sortie, returning a few hours later from a flawlessly executed mission. Bad weather kept the Squadron grounded on the 19th, and on the 20th it was still cloudy enough to limit operations to one mission, flown by Gavoille over the region of the Alps. Late that same morning Saint-Ex was sitting on the villa's terrace in his pyjamas playing chess with Jean Lecerf, himself lightly clad in a pair of bathing trunks, when a Captain of Engineers drove up.

"I've come for the pump," he began.

"Ah?" said Saint-Exupéry, without bothering to look up.

"Yes, a water-pump that was picked up yesterday from our depot."

"Water-pump?" said Saint-Ex, moving one of his pieces. "Check . . . what water-pump?"

"Who are you?" exclaimed the officer, irritated by this nonchalance and the unmilitary attire.

"Major de Saint-Exupéry," was the quiet answer. "Check again."

"Oh, excuse me, Major," said the Captain of Engineers. "I take it you're the Commanding Officer here."

"Oh no, it's the Captain."

"The Captain?"

"Yes, Captain Gavoille."

"And where is he, this Captain?"

"Captain Gavoille? Oh, he must be over Macon or thereabouts at this moment."

The officer looked from one to the other, totally bewildered.

"Well . . ." he began, "but . . . but . . . then what are *you* doing here?"

"Me?" said Saint-Ex, finally turning to look at him with a disarming smile. "Oh, I'm just a corporal pilot."

The previous day one of the Squadron's officers had driven down to Bastia with a mechanic and "borrowed" a pump from an ordnance garage where it had been left to be repaired. Installed over a nearby well, it had drawn the water up so beautifully that the boys were loath to part with it. Saint-Ex knew it perfectly well, and as a buccaneering member of *La Hache* he wasn't going to let his fellow pirates down.

"What's this about a pump?" asked Lecerf, after the baffled captain had sulked away.

"Oh nothing," replied Saint-Ex airily. "Just a pump that was left in a garage to be fixed for General de Lattre de Tassigny."

\*       \*       \*

The weather still being bad, Saint-Exupéry took off the next day in a Lightning for Algiers, with one of the Squadron's two sergeant majors (Roussel) riding "piggy-back", as it was called, in the tiny space behind the pilot's seat. Just how long he stayed in Algiers and whom he saw on this trip is not certain; but it seems doubtful that he spent the night here, for his friend Georges Pélissier would almost certainly have remembered it and later recorded it in his book. It is possible that one of the people he saw was General Donovan, Saint-Ex having solid reasons for fearing that he might be grounded at any moment. Whatever the case, we have Donovan's word for it that Saint-Ex called on him at his Algiers office "a short time before he took his last flight. On that occasion he came to see me because of his desire to serve with my command in the Office of Strategic Services. The decision was to be made after his next flight which proved to be a fatal one."

From Algiers Saint-Ex flew on to Tunis to be present for the baptism of Gavoille's son. Madame Mast was struck once again by the amount of whiskies he could consume in one evening and by the simplicity with which he said, almost shrugging his shoulders: "I shall finish like my friends." Several of his squadron mates had had narrow escapes and the latest German planes had rocket boosters which made them a match in speed for the Lightnings. The baptism was scheduled for the next day—July 24th—and that evening as they were talking he said: "I have a small favour to ask of you. It's been so long since I attended a church service I'm afraid of getting mixed up in what I'm supposed to say. Do you think you could give me a small catechism lesson so that I don't look too awkward during the baptism?"

Madame Mast went to get a missal and read him the relevant passages.

"*Mon Dieu!*" he said, when she was through. "It's all my youth coming back to the surface."

They stayed over an extra day and on the 26th Gavoille took off for Corsica, his Lightning loaded with *dragées* which their generous "god-mother" sent to the Squadron's flyers along with another stock of liquor. Saint-Exupéry flew off to Algiers to pick up the sergeant major he had left there. It was a sad parting and almost his last words to Madame Mast were: "It is certain I shall never see you again."

It was still early morning when he landed at the airport of Maison-Blanche. André Maurois had already left Algiers, disgusted by the boycott to which he had been subjected by Wormwood and his entourage; but René Lehmann, a friend of Anne Heurgon-Desjardins', was leaving for New York and Saint-Ex wanted to give him a letter for Consuelo. André Gide was breakfasting with Anne Heurgon when Tonio turned up at eight o'clock. "I've got my car outside," he said to Gide. "It would amuse me to show you my toy"—by which he meant, of course, his Lightning. "Why not drive out with me to Maison-Blanche?"

"Not this morning, *mon vieux*," said Gide. "The next time, yes, I promise you." After which, to convince himself if no one else, he broke into a forced cough. He could not have guessed that he would not have to break his promise since there would not be a next time.

It is just possible that Saint-Ex made one more trip to North Africa, for his friend Lionel Chassin, who had left Sardinia to work on the French General Staff in Algiers, claims to have seen him at the military airfield of Boufarik on July 29th. The Squadron's *Journal de Marche* makes no mention of such a trip, and it seems more likely that Chassin was confusing the 29th with the 26th. Chassin, in any case, undertook to remonstrate with his friend, as had Anne Heurgon and so many others, imploring him to give up a dangerous job for which he was vastly over age. After all, he had flown eight sorties and that really was enough. He had more than earned the right to "speak out after the war".

His friend Antoine smiled but shook his head: "I shall go on as long as I'm allowed to. I can't abandon my comrades. The 2/33 is such a fine team."

Each of Saint-Exupéry's visits to Algiers seems to have left a bitter aftertaste—as regards the future as much as the present. "The politicos" he explained to Alain Jourdan and his fellow pilots, "will hog everything and profit from the situation, leaving the real combatants out in the cold."

Some six months later, in an article written for *Le Figaro*, André Gide claimed that not long before his last flight and during a stop-over in Algiers Saint-Exupéry attended a session of the Consultative Assembly which was addressed by De Gaulle. "He was struck by his calm, the lucidity of his views, the pertinence and persuasive cleverness of his argumentation, and he expressed his astonishment to a close friend he saw on coming away from this session: 'He is obviously stronger, wiser and greater than I expected to see him.'"

The quotation would have been more convincing if Gide had stated openly who this "close friend" was to whom Tonio was alleged to have made this confession. Ever since the day Saint-Ex had hurt Gide's feelings by some particularly sharp cracks against De Gaulle, he had sought to be more tactful; but there can be no doubt what his real feelings were. They found expression in the two last letters we know of and which were apparently written on July 29th.

The first was addressed to Pierre Dalloz in answer to a brief note from his friend informing him that he was just back after five months in London and hoped to see him on his next trip to Algiers. "Dear, dear Dalloz," he began, "how I regret your four lines!"—by which he meant the regret at not having known earlier that Dalloz was in Algiers, where he could have looked him up. "I would have liked to know what you think of our times. I myself despair.

"I imagine you think I was right on all counts, and on all levels. What a stench!" He meant, of course, Algiers. "Pray Heaven you agree with me all the way. How happy I would be with your opinion!

"I myself am plunged in this war as deeply as possible. I am, to be sure, the doyen of the world's war pilots . . . The other day one of my engines broke down ten thousand metres up, above Annecy, at precisely the hour when . . . I was forty-four years old! While I was rowing my way back over the Alps at the speed of a tortoise and at the mercy of the entire Luftwaffe, I had a quiet laugh at the thought of the super-patriots who ban my books in North Africa. How comic!

"I have experienced everything since my return to the squadron (this return is a miracle). I've experienced engine failure, fainting from oxygen malfunctioning, being chased by fighters, and also fire in mid-flight. I'm paying my due. I don't think I'm being over stingy and I feel as wholesome as a carpenter. It's my only satisfaction. This and wandering for hours all alone in an isolated plane, taking pictures over France. How strange!

"Here one is far from the hate mill, but notwithstanding the kindness of the squadron, I suffer from a certain human impoverishment. I never have anyone to talk to, which is already something. I have had people to live with, but what spiritual solitude!

"If I am shot down I shall regret absolutely nothing. The future termite-heap appals me, and I hate their robot virtue. I was made to be a gardener."

The other letter, addressed to a friend in London, was even more explicit in airing his grievances against the "super-patriots" of Algiers. "I have found my Lightning once more. It's a miracle at forty-four to be piloting the fastest single-seater in the world. I spend five hours alone in a solitary plane at ten thousand metres. It's not too wearing on the system. And while I'm wandering over France, I continue to be quarantined and my books forbidden in North Africa . . .

"I'm doing a difficult job. Four times already I almost failed to return. But it's a matter of vertiginous indifference to me . . .

"The hate, muck, and slander factory they call the *redressement* . . . I have no use for. I am exposed to the simplest and purest of war dangers. Absolutely pure. The other day I was surprised by fighters, and just managed to get away. I found it thoroughly beneficial. Not out of any sportive or warlike frenzy which I don't feel. But because I understand nothing, absolutely nothing but the quality of the substance. Their phrases sicken me. Their pomposity sickens me. Their ignominy sickens me. Their polemics sicken me, and I understand nothing of their virtue . . .

"Real virtue lies in saving France's spiritual patrimony by staying on as the curator of the library of Carpentras. It is wandering, naked and unarmed, in a plane. It is teaching little children how to read. It is accepting to be killed as a simple carpenter. They are the country . . . Not I. I am of the country. Poor country."

On July 30th, the day after these two letters were sent off, the skies cleared sufficiently to enable Gavoille to take off on a "mapping" mission over the Alps. Forced to interrupt his "ploughing" by the clouds which formed over the area, he turned and headed for home. Over the Mediterranean he was joined by another Lightning piloted by Eugene Meredith, an American friend from the 23rd Photo Reconnaissance Squadron who had been sent out to photograph the Durance river area north of Marseille. They flew side by side for a moment, and then Meredith waggled his wings and waved at Gavoille to indicate that he was going on ahead. Gavoille, who had a broken knuckle which was painfully sensitive to altitude changes and who was also suffering that day from sinus trouble, let him go, preferring a gentler descent. A moment later he heard a frantic S.O.S. from Meredith, crying: "I'm being fired on . . . I'm going in!"—Air Force jargon for "I'm going to crash in the sea". It all happened so quickly that Gavoille never even saw the German fighter that had surprised his fellow flyer. The commander of *La Hache* had escaped death by a hair.

Dinner at the Erbalunga villa that night was attended by two French Air Force majors as well as by Colonel Davis, the American Group Commander. Several American pilots dropped in after dinner, much upset by Meredith's misfortune. Saint-Exupéry was not present. Earlier in the day he had received a message from Colonel Rockwell saying that he had come up to Bastia specially to see him. They met late that afternoon at a Bastia café. With Rockwell were three friends Saint-Exupéry knew well—Captain Bart Lachelier, a French liaison officer with the British at Dunkirk who had later gone to America with his wife and enlisted in the United States Air Force; Colonel Jean Baradez, a flyer with a passion for archaeology whom Pétain had named Sous-Préfet of Philippeville, where he had greatly helped the British during the North African landings; and Major Olivier Martin, who had served on Peyrouton's staff in Algiers. So far as Rockwell is able to recall—after an interval of twenty-five years—Saint-Ex joined them at the café with the couple he was to dine with that night. For in response to Rockwell's suggestion that he join them that evening for dinner, Saint-Ex begged off, saying he was already taken. Instead, he invited Rockwell and his three friends to dine with him the next evening (July 31st) at the Erbalunga villa—an invitation they joyfully accepted.

With just whom it was Saint-Exupéry dined this night we do not know; but the conversation must have been unusually animated. For at 1.30 the following morning, when Captains Leleu and Siegler returned to the villa after an evening spent with some Italian flying-boat officers who were working with the Air-Sea rescue unit, they passed Saint-Exupéry's door, which was open, and saw the bed unoccupied.

"That's odd," said Leleu. "He was supposed to go out tomorrow on a mission."

These high altitude missions were terribly fatiguing, even for someone far younger than Saint-Ex. The rotation system which had been devised for the flying of sorties was thus designed to allow a pilot several days of rest between them. As Operations Officer, Leleu had strongly urged flyers to get to bed early on the eve of their next sortie. Saint-Ex's absence thus struck him as strange. He had always shown himself most conscientious in the preparation of his missions and his tardiness on this night was abnormal.

They debated for a moment as to what to do, and finally Siegler volunteered to replace him. A graduate of the Military Academy of Saint-Cyr, Pierre Siegler was a first-class pilot who could, if necessary, go for forty eight hours without sleep. He now put his stamina to the test by sitting down at his maps to work out the compass readings and the time measurements required for this mission—one designed to "map" the region of Grenoble. A "mapping" mission, such as the one which had been given Saint-Ex, meant "ploughing" the area to be photographed, much as a farmer ploughs a field. Each run had to be calculated almost to the second, and the 180° turns (in fact, closer to 270° turns) at the end of each furrow or "strip" had to be effected accurately enough to eliminate gaps between adjacent strips, each of which (on the two precision cameras the Lightning carried) were just one kilometre wide. Since there was always the possibility that the primary assignment might be hampered by clouds or rudely interrupted by the appearance of an enemy fighter, pilots were generally given a secondary mission to accomplish as an alternative, should the first prove impossible. Both had to be carefully prepared, with an indispensable minimum of detailed calculation. The pertinent readings were then jotted down on the pad which the outgoing pilot carried on his lap. All of this took a good hour or two of concentrated map-work which was almost always effected the day before the flight. It was what Siegler now had to do before going to bed. It took him something like an hour and a half. At three o'clock, when he finally turned off his light for a few hours of shut-eye, Saint-Exupéry had still not returned.

History, though Siegler could not possibly have guessed it, was repeating itself in a most curious way. The night before his take-off on his abortive Saigon "raid" in December of 1935, Saint-Exupéry had got precious little sleep. He could not have slept much on this fateful night of July 30–31, 1944. Just when he returned to the villa, no one knows. But the next morning, some time after seven, while Pierre Siegler was downstairs having his breakfast, what was his amazement to see Saint-Ex suddenly lumber into the little dining-room. He threw Siegler a dark look, as much as to say: "Thought you'd cheat me out of it, eh?" but said not a word. Siegler too said nothing; and his breakfast completed, he returned upstairs to bed.

At the Erbalunga villa only pilots flying morning missions were obliged to rise early. But each sortie was supervised by the Operations Officer (Jean Leleu) or his assistant (Raymond Duriez), unless the CO (Commanding Officer—René Gavoille) wanted to be present in person. On this morning of July 31st the job fell to Raymond Duriez.

Climbing into the Jeep which they used for running back and forth between their billet and the base, Saint-Ex and Duriez drove down the undulating road that skirts the lovely *corniche*, through the villages of Miomo and Pietranera with their rocky coves and their palm-trees and cypresses and their tiled villas dripping with bougainvillea, mimosa, and hibiscus. Bastia was just waking to its morning animation, and few of the shop awnings were yet down as they drove through the main street and on out past the sloping ramparts of the citadel. Fifteen kilometres of straight roadway, many of them lined with freckled plane-trees, and here they were, turning left on to the little country road that led down to the airfield of Poretta, laid out on the flat sea-bordered plain between the Golo river, the crest-perched village of Borgo, and the Biguglia lagoon.

A mechanic who had driven down in another Jeep was already standing by the Lightning—No. 223—when they drove up. Duriez, a modest Toulousain lieutenant who was much awed by Saint-Exupéry, had little to say to the Major as he helped him into his heated flying-suit, his overalls with the pockets full of K-rations and pencils, and finally the Mae West. The oxygen flask was strapped around his left leg—for the form: Saint-Ex knowing full well that if anything went wrong, he didn't stand a chance. With his left arm partly paralysed, he could hardly hope to open his cockpit cover once the lid was closed above him. The cockpit check was tedious, as usual, and a strain on the sweating pilot; but it failed to reveal any abnormalities. Only after the plane had taken off did Duriez suddenly remember that he had forgotten to see if the battery generators were functioning. But this was something Saint-Exupéry could check from his dials in mid-air.

The US Interrogation Report subsequently drawn up indicates that Lightning 223 took off from the Poretta airstrip at 8.45, destined on a mapping mission east of Lyon. Duriez saw Saint-Ex give him a brief wave from behind the plexi-glass cover he had helped lower over his head, and the wheel-blocks having been pulled aside by the mechanic, the Lightning bumped its way towards the end of the runway for the take-off. For the Assistant Operations Officer this was one more routine mission, and little did it occur to him or to the mechanic that they were to be the last two human beings to see Saint-Exupéry alive.

The flying technique which Leleu and his companions had developed was simple: it was to rise to the altitude at which the Lightning's vapour trail became visible and then to drop 500 or 1,000 feet lower to the level where it disappeared. By flying just below the vapour-trail ceiling the pilot stood a better chance of spotting the enemy if a German fighter climbed up to attack him. For so fast was the Lightning that only if the Messerschmitt or the even speedier Focke-Wulf climbed above it, could it hope to drive home its cobra-like strike;,but this it could not do without unfurling its long white "bridal train", more easily detectable in the rear-view mirror than the fighter's bug-like blackness.

Pilots were thus urged to glance at the rear-view mirror every fifteen or twenty seconds to make sure that all was well behind them. During the early part of the flight this was routine, but it was more difficult when the pilot approached the target. Usually he would have to dip a wing one way or the other to make sure he was directly overhead. One day when Lieutenant Henry said to him: "Major, I hope you look from time to time in the rear-view mirror," the answer he got from Saint-Ex was blunt: "Look, Henry, I do my job. When I'm on top of the target, I haven't time to worry about the rear-view mirror. I'm looking down."

Did Saint-Exupéry concentrate so strenuously on his target that he failed to see the "cobra" (as he had described the Messerschmitts in *Pilote de Guerre*) creep up behind him for its lethal strike? Did an engine fail him once again? Did he exhaust his oxygen supply before he could descend to a lower level? Or was he simply "executed" by a breakdown in the supply system, caused by a disconnected tube? But at noon, when the radar screens should have sighted the first sign of a returning plane, there was no blip and their screens were empty.

The distance from Corsica to France being less than half what it had been from Tunisia, Saint-Exupéry should normally have been back by noon. At 12.30 there was still no trace of his Lightning. On the field René Gavoille began pacing nervously up and down, prey to a mounting anxiety. At 12.45 there was still no sign, and at one o'clock a worried call was put in to radar control. No, their screens had spotted nothing—not even for the outgoing flight! Headquarters were alerted, but there was nothing much they could do. The radar screens being unable to pick up a trace of a plane anywhere in the northern sky, no Air-Sea rescue missions could be ordered.

Two o'clock passed and then the fatal hour of 2.30—fatal because by that time his fuel supplies would have been exhausted, no matter what. At 3.30 p.m. the Interrogation Officer, Vernon Robison, dutifully filled out and signed his Interrogation Report Card. "PILOT DID NOT RETURN AND IS PRESUMED LOST . . . NO PICTURES."

The "doyen of the world's war pilots", the pioneer who had pitted his wits against the Moors and his muscles against the winds of Patagonia, the veteran who had survived the chill waters of Saint-Raphael, agony of thirst in the Libyan desert, the flak of Arras and the fighter-planes of Genoa, had this time not returned. ". . . And after forty be careful of the planes you fly," Madame Pikomesmas, the clairvoyante, had warned him years before. He had probably not forgotten, but faithful to his star, he had refused to heed it.

That evening, when Colonel Rockwell and his three companions drove up to the villa to see their friend Saint-Ex, they were greeted by a dozen long faces. There were no card tricks, no songs, no stories; and the dinner they sat down to was as anguished a repast as any of them could remember.

# 25

# The Prophet

It was years before the mystery of Saint-Exupéry's tragic end was finally and fairly conclusively resolved. When the news of his disappearance first filtered back to Algiers a few days later an extraordinary rumour suddenly began to spread from mouth to mouth. "He's probably landed in Vichy." Even his disappearance was not forgiven him, the insinuation being that it was a camouflaged betrayal. The local papers gave some prominence to his failure to return from his last war mission, a number of commemorative articles were published about him, and then suddenly there was silence, as though in response to a sign from an orchestra conductor's baton. Some concluded that the signal had come, once again, from "the top". Others—and they included General Odic and the Major Olivier Martin who was to have dined with him the evening of July 31—went even further, convinced that Saint-Exupéry had perished through an act of sabotage. Nothing has been found to substantiate the charge, but like the silence which suddenly descended on the Algiers press in August 1944, this hideous suspicion was a typically miasmic emanation of that swamp of political gossip and intrigue.

The German radio, during the days which immediately followed, made no announcement that might have led one to believe that Saint-Ex's Lightning had been intercepted by a Luftwaffe fighter. Among his squadron mates opinions were divided, but Gavoille, Leleu, and Duriez—to name but three—were more inclined to believe that he had suffered once again from oxygen failure. A sixty second stoppage, at a height of 30,000 feet, would suffice to kill a man, and given the area he had been assigned to photograph, the likelihood was that his Lightning had finally crashed in some Alpine peak or glacier. This would explain why the radar screens near Bastia picked up no trace of a returning plane on that fateful July 31.

The years thus passed, without yielding a clue, until one day in March 1948 Gaston Gallimard received a letter from a German pastor, Hermann

Korth, who wrote that he had recently learned the exact date of Saint-Exupéry's last flight from an article he had read in a Göttingen magazine. On checking the wartime diary he had kept from the time when he was serving with the Luftwaffe's Mediterranean headquarters, then located at Malcesine, on Lake Garda, he found that the date tallied with an entry made on July 31, 1944, and which read: "*Anr. Trib. K. Abschuss 1 Auflk. brennend über See. Auflk. Ajacc unver.*" Spelled out in full, the entry read: "*Anruf Tribun Kant Abschuss 1 Aufklärer brennend über See. Aufklärung Ajaccio unverändert.*" Korth's job at Malcesine had been to receive and process the daily reports gathered by Luftwaffe reconnaissance planes not only over Italy, but from the two neighbouring Luftwaffe commands covering the Balkans and southern France. "*Tribun*" was the code-name for the headquarters of the 2nd Luftwaffe command, based near Avignon, and Captain Kant was the Intelligence Officer who telephoned through the results of German aerial reconnaissance missions towards the end of each day. This particular telephone message had reached him, so Korth claimed, late on the evening of July 31, and what it stated was that an Allied reconnaissance plane (*Aufklärer*) had been shot down (*Abschuss*) and sent burning towards its watery grave (*brennend über See*) by a German plane which had then continued on its own reconnaissance mission, which was to photograph Ajaccio (*Aufklärung Ajaccio unverändert*).

For a moment it looked as though the mystery of Saint-Exupéry's end had at last been solved. But not for long. That two Allied reconnaissance planes—Gene Meredith's on July 30 and Saint-Exupéry's on the 31st—should have been shot down into the Mediterranean on two successive days struck certain of his squadron mates as odd. The visits subsequently paid to Pastor Korth by a number of French men and women cleared up at least one point. In July 1944 the Germans, anticipating an impending Allied invasion of southern France, were flying daily photographic missions over the harbours and coasts of northern Corsica. The reconnaissance planes sent out were normally accompanied by a fast Focke-Wulf fighter. One of these fighters had spotted Gene Meredith's Lightning, peeled off, intercepted it, and shot it into the sea on July 30. Meredith had been assigned to photograph the region of the Durance river north of Marseille, and his misfortune was to have crossed the path of the German planes which had been sent out (presumably from Istres) to reconnoitre Ajaccio.

Startling new evidence came to light in 1972, although it was not until 1981 that Jean Lasserre, editor of the French quarterly review, *Icare*, published a report which seems to have elucidated the circumstances of Saint-Exupéry's mysterious disappearance once and for all. In its 725th issue the German magazine, *Der Landser* (The Footslogger), published a letter written by a young Luftwaffe warrant officer, Robert Heichele, to a fighter pilot friend who had recently been shot down twice over the battle front of Normandy. "At this moment" he concluded his letter, "I am piloting a marvellous bird, the FW 190 D9. It is fitted out with a liquid-cooled Jumbo 213 engine. It really is something—1,750 horsepower at the moment of take-off which can quickly be raised for a short period to 2,250 h.p. by injecting a water-methanol mixture. As swift as an arrow, we leave everyone behind us.

"Yesterday, though not yet a full-fledged fighter pilot, I downed a Lightning during a dog-fight . . ."

In the report made to his superiors at the Luftwaffe airbase of Orange, Heichele added these details:

"On July 31, 1944 I took off at 11h02 accompanied by Sergeant Högel, with the mission of checking on the activity of enemy formations between Marseille and Menton and the hinterland.

"We carried out our mission as planned. While circling over Castellane before heading back we met a Lightning P-38. It was very probably a lone reconnaissance plane.

"Since the enemy was flying 1,000 meters above us, we had no possibility of attacking him. To our great surprise the adversary changed his course and attacked us from his altitude at great speed.

"We dodged the adversary's first attack by going into a spiral climb and by outdistancing him thanks to our momentary extra-power. During the dog-fight I managed to place myself in a firing position about 150 to 200 meters behind the Lightning. I fired, but I was too far behind. I missed the P-38. After several manoeuvers I was again able to place myself in a firing position. This time the burst passed in front of the enemy plane. Probably to avoid my fire, the pilot altered his trajectory and began a dive. I pursued him and approached to within 40 to 60 meters and fired with my weapons. I then saw the Lightning going down with a trail of white smoke . . . The P-38 passed over the coastline and flew at very low altitude out to sea. I kept following it. Suddenly flames leapt from the right engine. The right wing plowed into the sea. The plane made several somersaults and disappeared into the water. The crash took place at 12h05 about 10 kilometers south of Saint-Raphaël. We returned to base without meeting any more enemies."

The one puzzling feature in this account is the abrupt change of course Saint-Exupéry apparently decided on while overflying Castellane (about 50 miles northwest of Cannes) and which gave the two Luftwaffe pilots the impression that they were being attacked by the unarmed Lightning. It may be—this is merely a supposition—that Saint-Ex altered course in order to overfly the Esterel and the Château de la Mole rather than Cannes, farther to the east, and he may also have decided to lose altitude because his supply of oxygen was running out. What is certain is that, being armed with 2 machine-guns and capable of flying 450 to 500 m.p.h. at altitudes between 25,000 and 30,000 feet, the new Focke-Wulf 190 was more than a match for the unarmed Lightning.

All of Saint-Exupéry's airmen friends later agreed that the end he finally met was the one he preferred. His miraculous return from his accidental overflight of Turin and Genoa on June 29 had left him with a feeling that he was, as the French put it, *un mort en sursis*—someone whose death has merely been postponed. What was strange was not that he should have disappeared on July 31, but that he should have survived up until then. This is the elementary error made by those who have read a suicidal inclination into his last desperate letters.

*    *    *

Not long after his miraculous escape over Turin and Genoa Saint-Ex had told Gavoille that if ever anything happened to him and he failed to make it back, the fibre suitcase (with a combination lock) in which he kept his manuscripts was to be flown to Algiers and turned over to his friend Georges Pélissier. Gavoille carried out his instructions to the letter, inadvertently touching off an imbroglio which dragged on for months. Normally a vanished flyer's belongings, according to French Air Force regulations, were impounded in a special depot, to be kept and eventually reclaimed by his widow or his nearest kin if and when he was finally given up for lost. Gavoille chose to disregard the letter of the law, preferring to make a special exception in favour of his friend Saint-Ex. The suitcase thus remained with Pélissier in Algiers for a good four months, before being reclaimed—in January 1945— by Jean Leleu, who was sent down specially from Nancy on orders issued by General Chassin.

Saint-Exupéry's last instructions, casually scribbled on the back of an *ordre de mission*, indicated that the rest of his possessions should go to Consuelo. Packed into the handsome pigskin bag she had given him, they too were brought back to Paris, and some time after Consuelo's return to France in 1946, the two bags, containing the flyer's posthumous belongings, were officially unsealed and opened in the presence of a lawyer with the Molièresque name of Tournesac. The contents included several pairs of socks and a shirt, four black bound folders containing the typescript of *Citadelle*, five notebooks in which for years he had carefully inscribed his thoughts on this or that subject, and a number of assorted papers. One of them, consisting of a few mimeographed sheets, was at first thought to be a detached fragment of *Citadelle*; it turned out, however, to be a mimeographed text of Teilhard de

Chardin's which Saint-Exupéry had been given the previous September in Casablanca by one of the Jesuit Father's admirers.

The assorted papers also included the letter Saint-Ex had written from La Marsa but finally never sent to General Chambe. The fact that he had carefully preserved it, even though it was never sent, would seem to indicate the value he attached to its contents; and it is almost certainly no exaggeration to call it, as some have done, Saint-Exupéry's "spiritual testament". As can be judged from this passage:

"Ah General, there is but one problem, one sole problem for the world— how to give men back a spiritual significance, spiritual anxieties. How to rain down on them something resembling a Gregorian chant. If I had the faith, it is certain that once the period of this 'necessary and thankless job' is over, I could no longer bear anything but Solesmes. One can no longer live off refrigerators, politics, bank statements, and crossword puzzles. One can no longer live without poetry, colour, or love. Simply to hear a village song from the XVth century is enough to measure the extent of the decline. All that is left today is the voice of the propaganda robot (pardon my frankness). Two billion human beings have only ears for the robot, understand nothing but the robot, are turning into robots. All the collapses of the past thirty years have sprung from two sources: the *impasses* of the economic system of the XIXth century, and spiritual despair. Why did Mermoz follow his great ninny of a Colonel if it wasn't out of thirst? Why Russia? Why Spain? Men have put Cartesian values to the test; but save for the natural sciences, the result has hardly benefited them. There is one problem, one only: to rediscover that there is a life of the spirit which is still higher than the life of the mind, the only one which satisfies man. This transcends the problem of religious life, which is only one form of it (though the life of the spirit may lead to the other necessarily). And the life of the spirit begins there where an 'integral' being is thought of over and above the materials which compose it. The love of one's house—that love which is unknown in the United States—is already of the life of the spirit.

"And the village fête and the cult of the dead (which I mention, because two or three parachutists have been killed since my arrival here, but they were whisked out of sight—having outlived their usefulness). This is typical of our age, not of America. Man today no longer has significance."

To feel, like Hamlet, that one's time is "out of joint" and to regret that one was not born in an earlier and "brighter" age is not simply the mark of an incurable romantic. Saint-Exupéry's upbringing, in effect that of a monarchist, made him prone to a nostalgia that was tempered, but only momentarily, by the giddy enthusiasm with which he embraced the bright future of aviation. Unlike Baudelaire, he was not ready to condemn steam-engines and railway stations out of hand, but like Baudelaire, he was oppressed by the feeling that the poetry was being squeezed out of modern life by the implacable advance of an ever more soulless and utilitarian technology. His ideal was pre-revolutionary—in the industrial as well as political sense—and this even though, as he once wrote to his mother (during his term of Air Force service in Strasbourg) "the eighteenth century, all pink and rosy, fills me with horror". The age of silk stockings and powdered wigs was too soft and effeminate for his robust taste, and the century which had his preference, the one he would have liked to live in, as he one day confided to Dr. Pélissier, was the sixteenth—the age of Elizabeth and Henri IV, of François Premier and the Chevalier Bayard, the century of Shakespeare, Cervantes, and Rabelais, when France, its mind as yet unravished by the eloquence of René Descartes, was readier to heed the sceptical voice of Michel de Montaigne.

"This poet" as André Maurois once remarked of his friend Saint-Ex, "was a person of the most solid common sense". This judgment is all the more remarkable in coming from someone who must have had ample opportunity in Algiers of taking the measure of Saint-Exupéry's despair. But it stemmed, as he knew, from something deeper than romantic nostalgia for the past; and if, as his letter to General Chambe attests, Saint-Ex was capable of a deep, intuitive, and prophetic understanding of the crisis of our times, it was precisely because—as an aeronautical engineer once said to me —"his feet were very firmly on the ground".

Anyone tempted to doubt it should ponder this paragraph, again drawn from his unsent letter to General Chambe: "What good will it have done to have won the war if we are then to be stuck with one hundred years of revolutionary epilepsy? When the German problem will at last have been solved, all the real problems will arise. It is unlikely that speculation on American post-war stocks will suffice at the end of this war to distract mankind from its veritable cares, as happened in 1919. For lack of a strong spiritual current there will spring up, like mushrooms, thirty-six sects that will divide and split each other up. Marxism itself, having aged, will decompose into a multitude of contradictory neo-Marxisms. It was what we saw in Spain. Unless some French Caesar installs us in a neo-socialist concentration-camp for all eternity."

There is hardly a word that needs changing in this paragraph to make it more relevant to the problems of today, though it was written more than a quarter of a century ago. Even the final sentence—about a French "Caesar" —was singularly prophetic; for while De Gaulle ultimately failed in his tortuous attempt to undermine the power of the French bourgeoisie and to impose a corporate state in France, he did more than any other French politician since the war to promote an increasingly centralized, neo-socialist, and technocratic régime.

It is too easy to dismiss Saint-Exupéry as a reactionary because, like Georges Bernanos, he had the temerity to denounce the collectivized antheap towards which mankind is increasingly tending. For who in this case are the "realists"—those who still have the backbone to condemn the direction that contemporary civilization has taken, or those who are passively resigned to it on the grounds that the massification of mankind represents an irresistible trend, something that we must all of us accept because this is the "way of the world" or represents the "wave of the future", even though this future promises to be less a joyful "opening" than a grim dead-end?

Perhaps it was just as well that Saint-Ex died when he did, being thus spared the spectacle of a world which would have pained him even more than the one he actually experienced. For everything he dimly presaged has come to pass and on a more violent and extensive scale than he imagined. Beginning with the fearful *règlements de comptes*—settling of scores—which accompanied the Liberation, when some 40,000 Frenchmen (some claim it was twice that number) perished: which, unbelievable as it may sound, was about five times as many victims as were claimed by the Robespierre terror of 1793! It is probable, of course, that no voice could then have made itself heard above the clamour of vindictive passions; just as Paris was probably predestined to reenact the same nihilistic follies, to relive the same frivolous philosophical fads, the same café and night-club extravagances which the Berliners went through after the First World War.

What Saint-Exupéry might have produced, what influence he might have had, had he survived the war, it is, of course, impossible to say for sure. *Citadelle*, which Gallimard finally published in 1948 in the unfinished state in which Saint-Exupéry left it, revealed a troubled moralist whom some Frenchmen have not hesitated to compare to Pascal. But just as no one, thumbing through its already typed pages in, let us say, the spring of 1941, could have guessed that within the next two years Saint-Ex would produce three (or at any rate, two and a half) books—one of them a masterpiece—so it is impossible to say what other finished products the tumultuous circumstances of this unlived life would have wrested from him after the war.

Tumultuous rather than pacific it probably would have been, mirroring therein the troubled life of his country. It has been argued—by Herbert Luethy, among others—that it was the super-patriotic inflation of the national ego consciously cultivated by De Gaulle which made it so difficult for France to transform her Empire after the Second World War. France,

already rent by the social antagonisms of the *Front Populaire* of the 1930s
and the German occupation of the early 1940s, was now rent once again
into two hostile camps—the colonialists and the anti-colonialists, each
claiming to be possessors of the *total* truth. For the next dozen years France
was thus condemned to live through a period of phantasmagoric confusion,
with harassed politicians forced to submit to the chronic blackmail of the
super-patriots, ever ready to brand as "treason" any attempt to modify or
remedy the ills of the French Empire, which the leader of these same super-
patriots finally undertook to liquidate in a far more sweeping fashion than
any of their adversaries had dared suggest. Saint-Exupéry would surely have
been solicited by these conflicts, just as he was solicited by the Spanish Civil
War, and out of these new confrontations might have come some badly
needed and dispassionate words of wisdom. They were already there in
*Terre des Hommes*, summing up the pathetic contradiction in the colonialist
experiment: "For the colonialist who founds an Empire, the meaning of life
is conquest. The soldier scorns the settler. But was not the goal of this
conquest the establishment of this settler?"

This perennial conflict between the active and the passive, the nomadic
and the sedentary, the soldier and the civilian, the flyer and the mechanic,
the explorer and the bureaucrat, the conqueror and the conquered, runs
through all of Saint-Exupéry's work, culminating in the monumental
labyrinth of *Citadelle*. He may never have read Ibn-Khaldun, the greatest
of Moslem historians and the one who so influenced Arnold Toynbee, but
Saint-Exupéry had what may be called a Khaldunesque vision of life. The
life of the city, indispensable though it is to the propagation and transmission
of culture, is at the same time essentially corrupting. It softens men and
makes them "sedentary"—a word which recurs often in *Citadelle*—that is,
complacent, self-satisfied, self-centred, slothful, uncreative, and avaricious.
Not everyone, as Saint-Exupéry realized, can choose to live dangerously: not
everyone can be a soldier or a sailor, an adventurer or a pioneer. They also
serve, as the saying goes, who only stand and wait. Such are the "sentinels"
of *Citadelle*, those whose responsibility it is to watch over the "Empire";
but such are also the sedentary artisans—for all obligation involves a measure
of resistance, if only to the unguided whim—like the humble cobbler or
carpenter, to the extent that they remain faithful to their calling, their tasks,
and their traditions. Corruption sets in when these obligations lose their
force in an atmosphere of general facility; which is increasingly the prevailing
climate of the western world. For what conditions man, in the final analysis,
is not that which makes things easier for him; it is, on the contrary, that
which resists him.

It is not easy to do justice to as complex a work as *Citadelle* in a few pages.

Léon Wencelius has distinguished no less than one hundred different themes in this book of 213 chapters and 985 typescript pages (reduced to 531 in the printed text). Many of the chapters—it would be more accurate to call them "sections"—are repetitions or variations on the same theme; for the text which Saint-Exupéry left behind was only a *gangue*—a matrix—from which he intended to carve and polish a book that would probably have been reduced by half had he ever lived to complete it. "It's a torrent which drags too many pebbles," he liked to say to Wencelius. "It will take me ten years to prune it." Nor was he exaggerating when he told Pierre Dalloz, during the last winter in Algiers, that in comparison to this "posthumous work", all his other books were "mere exercises".

Like Nietzsche, speaking of his *Zarathustra*, Saint-Ex would often refer to *Citadelle* as "my poem". But the process of *Citadelle*'s creation was substantially different from Nietzsche's. For Nietzsche *Thus Spake Zarathustra* (which was written in an extraordinary fever of inspiration) was a kind of philosophical pronunciamiento; a symbolic presentation of a philosophy he later set out to comment and expound in a more straight-forward and less hyperbolic style in half a dozen books (*Beyond Good and Evil, The Genealogy of Morals, Ecce Homo, The Anti-Christ*, etc.) published before madness overtook him. Whether Nietzsche really intended to crown the series with a "*magnum opus*", as his opinionated sister, Elizabeth Förster-Nietzsche later tried to claim, is more than a little doubtful and need not concern us here. Saint-Exupéry's *Citadelle* on the other hand, was consciously intended to be his *magnum opus*, already in 1939 and perhaps even earlier. Unlike his previous books, it was stripped of all directly autobiographical references and raised to a "timeless" plane through the use of parables serving to illustrate this or that moral point. The result, even in its rough-hewn, unpolished state, was a work which struck many readers as a radical departure from his earlier crystalline style when in fact it was simply an amplification of the hortatory, Biblical tone already to be found in the Notre-Dame episode of *Courrier Sud* and the final credo of *Pilote de Guerre*.

When Saint-Exupéry first started working on his "poem" in 1936, he thought of entitling it *Reflections of a Berber Lord*. Later he changed this to *Le Caïd*, before finally settling on *Citadelle*, a title chosen from the exhortation: "*Citadelle, je te bâtirai dans le coeur de l'Homme.*" (Citadel, I shall build you in Man's heart.)

In his interesting book, *L'Esthétique d'Antoine de Saint-Exupéry*, Carlo François has compared this quotation to a sentence to be found in an essay written by Elie Faure on Montaigne: "The strange thing is that Pascal . . . evinces a free morality each time he cannot see how the spirit of finesse can slip into the citadel his geometric spirit has constructed, thereby knocking down a wall." If Saint-Exupéry's "citadel" does not suffer from this particular contradiction, it is because it does not strive to be a creation of logic. "Dwelling place of man, who would found you on reasoning? Who would build you according to logic?" is a typical exhortation, which instantly recalls the conflict (established in *Pilote de Guerre*) between Intelligence and Spirit. Saint-Exupéry's "citadel" is not the product of Cartesian logic, it is the product (at least in part) of Pascalian faith—this faith or "fervour", to employ the word he preferred, being synonymous with the creative flame which produced the great Gothic cathedrals of the Middle Ages.

The "citadel" Saint-Exupéry wished to "build in the heart of man" was not simply internal, an echo of the "*Ein fester Burg ist unser Gott*" (A Mighty Fortress is our God) of the Lutherans. It is also an objective, even if obviously symbolic, reality, and the heart of a desert Empire. The brief glimpses Saint-Exupéry allows the reader to obtain of his "father's palace" place it somewhere between a mythical Old Testament palace (with, among other things, a floor of black and golden flagstones) and one of those ramparted Kasbahs he had been able to admire in Morocco. But this "citadel" being, like a Berber kasbah, essentially self-contained, the term embraces all civic activities, much as Hobbes used the symbol of his "Leviathan" to encompass all society.

Though Saint-Exupéry does not seem to have been directly inspired by any oriental source, his *Citadelle* resembles the Koran in being both a treatise on morality and a treatise on government. The author-narrator has just succeeded to the throne of his recently assassinated father, and the meditations which fill the book are based on his father's warnings and exhortations, interspersed with the lessons drawn from his own experience of government. *Citadelle* is to this extent a logical prolongation of *Vol de Nuit*. The Rivière of the novel has here become the late ruler of the realm whose example the son, like Hamlet, is anxious to emulate. For the dead father is not simply an adviser and a model: he is the symbol of an order which, if it has not yet ceased to exist, is now threatened with collapse.

In his intriguing analysis of this book Carlo François has suggested that the "Father-Chief" in *Citadelle* is in part an allegorical representation of Elie Faure. A doctor who later chose to become an art critic and historian, Elie Faure was, curiously enough, a good friend of Léon Werth. Saint-Exupéry apparently never met him—probably because Faure died in 1937, not long after Saint-Ex first met Werth. But he was intimately acquainted with his writings, which marked him so deeply that they even influenced his choice of words and vocabulary. By birth and upbringing Faure was a Protestant who wanted to believe in God in a blatantly positivistic age. The thesis he presented to the Theological Faculty of Montauban in 1909 was devoted to the subject of "Divine Wisdom in the Didactic Literature of the Hebrews and the Jews". Faure by this time had already given up looking for God in the New Testament and had turned his attention to the Old. It only remained for him to carry this process one step further—by renouncing the quest altogether, under the shattering impact of Nietzsche or what he assumed to be Nietzsche. For the next quarter of a century and until the eve of his death, Faure rivalled the young Giovanni Papini in Italy by becoming a rabid French advocate of Nietzschean thought, extolling force as a moral law unto itself, exalting the primacy of aesthetics over ethics, and even going so far as to blame Jesus Christ (in *La Danse sur le Feu et l'Eau*, written in 1920) for having "opened twenty centuries of carnage."

The opening lines of *Citadelle* are an unabashed tribute to the joint influence on Saint-Exupéry of Nietzsche and Elie Faure. "All too often have I seen pity go astray. But we who govern men have learned to plumb their hearts, and we bestow compassion only on what is worthy of our concern."

It was Nietzsche's conviction that if Europe was headed towards what he called "the universal green-meadow happiness of the herd, with safety, security, and alleviation of life for everyone", it was because two tendencies, or perhaps one should call them sentiments, had come to dominate modern political and social thinking: the ideal of equality before the law and the "religion" of sympathy for sufferers. The latter could only make men soft, the former only make men base and stupid—the type of individual Nietzsche contemptuously dismissed as *Pöbelmensch* (mob-man) and *Herdentier* (herd-beast). Christianity, he felt, had encouraged both tendencies—by preaching a doctrine of pity towards the weak and by preaching a doctrine of equality before God. Pascal, in this respect, was typical of a trend which for eighteen centuries had aspired towards the "sublime abortion of man". What modern mankind was most suffering from was a gigantic case of masochism and a superabundant enjoyment in one's own suffering and debasement. The "repentance-spasms" of the Puritans were a good example of it, as, on the philosophical level, was Pascal's deliberate *sacrifizio dell' intelletto*—the sacrifice of Reason on the altar of Faith.

Much as he admired Nietzsche, Saint-Exupéry was too much of a Frenchman to be able to go so far. Even Elie Faure, for all his Nietzschean fervour, could not help feeling a lingering admiration for Pascal. But with Saint-Exupéry it was more than admiration; it was virtually a cult. He could understand but not sympathize with Zarathustra's sigh: "To love, only to love, what a dead-end!" But the man who could write, in *Citadelle*, that the tearful distress of a little child was a focus of universal suffering could not but sympathize with Pascal's feeling that "the heart has its reasons which

Reason is unaware of". Pascal, as Carlo François has pointed out, is present in *Citadelle* in the form of "the only true geometer" whose company the narrator's father used to seek out at night (much as Saint-Ex used to sit up for hours devouring Pascal). So, François claims, is Friedrich Nietzsche—in the person of the "*ennemi bien-aimé*"—the much beloved enemy, whose threatening existence, on the frontiers of his realm, had been the condition of the fitness of his father's Empire. *Citadelle* ends, revealingly enough, with a prayer to God which suggests the possibility of their contradictory philosophies being reconciled—on a higher level.

I do not pretend to be an authority on the works of Elie Faure, or even on those of Nietzsche, but Carlo François' thesis would seem to provide a useful key to the understanding of *Citadelle*. Elie Faure, in addition to being a Nietzschean, had a Hegelian passion for the reconciliation of opposites, and this was certainly true of Saint-Exupéry as well. Other influences are discernible in the composition of *Citadelle*, notably those of Bergson and Plato; but if it had one central aim (which is not certain) it was probably to marry the warring philosophies of Nietzsche and Pascal. It was nothing less than to fuse Christian compassion and Nietzschean hard-heartedness, the cult of Reason and the Gospel of Faith into a higher, one is tempted to say, super-Hegelian synthesis.

"I am appalled by the difficulty of having authority derive from something else than God," is a revealing entry in one of Saint-Exupéry's notebooks. "One seeds from above." Elsewhere he noted: "Difficulty of a morality of man alone. If he is alone there is no longer a frame of reference. Role of God or of the neighbour who judges (but not ourselves)."

Like Nietzsche, Saint-Exupéry felt that a social order had to be hierarchical and to that extent "unjust" to keep man from degenerating. But unlike Nietzsche, who felt that Christian monotheism and the notion of equality before God had helped produce the "herd-beast" individual, Saint-Exupéry was convinced that without a belief in God, or at any rate the divine, human brotherhood is ultimately impossible. If what men admire in each other is simply their "humanity", their human quality, then no matter what that quality may actually be, what they are admiring is inescapably narcissistic and a reflection of themselves. They are holding up for adulation a quality they possess by birthright, and which for that reason is static. If man's destiny in life is simply to be "human", then why should he have to make an effort to be other than he is? Why need he change his ways? And why need he respect the "humanness" of another who has no *a priori* right to merit special respect? When all are equal, the very notion of ascension, of being higher or other than one is, tends to be debased and to lose its meaning. Nor is this all: for unless the cult of universal equality is subordinated to something higher than man, it can only lead to universal selfishness. The satisfaction of each individual ego becomes an end in itself. But the result, instead of being a general increase in human solidarity—"the greatest happiness for the greatest number", that phrase of Bentham's which was enough to make Nietzsche bristle—is precisely the reverse. The cult of universal equality leads to the slow destruction of fraternity. For men can only be brothers in something; and if that something, a something higher than themselves, is missing—because all notion of hierarchy has been scrapped, along with "God" or the "divine" or any force superior to man —then all corporate loyalty begins to dissolve and society disintegrates into an atomistic aggregate which brute force alone can mobilize or hold together.

"Justice and equality, and here is death," as Saint-Exupéry put it in *Citadelle*. "But fraternity is only to be found in the tree"—the symbol (probably borrowed from Nietzsche), he constantly fell back on to suggest a hierarchical, upward-striving society. "And thus came the times when freedom, having nothing left to free, was no more than a dividing up of provisions in a hateful equality.

"For in your freedom you knock up against your neighbour and he knocks up against you. And the state of repose which you encounter is the state of mingled marbles when they have ceased to move. Liberty thus leads to equality and equality to the equilibrium which is death . . . And so came the times when liberty was no longer liberty of the beauty of man but expression of the mass, man having necessarily dissolved within it. And this mass is not free, for it has no direction but is of a leaden weight and remains seated. Which did not keep men from calling freedom this freedom to squat and justice this squatting."

"I am troubled"—to quote another characteristic passage—"that they should have overthrown their truth, blinding themselves to the evidence, which is that the condition of the birth of the ship, and thus the sea, weighs upon the ship, that the condition of love weighs upon love, and that the condition of your ascension weighs upon your ascension. For there is no ascension without a slope.

"But these people say, 'Our ascension is stunted!' And they destroy the obstacles and their space has no slope. And thus are they reduced to a fair-ground rabble, having ruined the palace of my father where all steps had a meaning."

This is a restatement, in Biblical language, of what in an earlier chapter of this biography was termed Saint-Exupéry's "resistencialist" philosophy. The modern cult of facility, he was convinced, far from "freeing" man, has left him more limp and rudderless than ever. For not only has the "permissiveness" of modern society undermined authority, it is gradually sapping it of all value. Where everything is allowed, where "anything goes", nothing ends up having much value any more. For it was the prohibitions surrounding them, the taboos defending them, the obstacles and hardships that had to be surmounted to obtain them, which once gave things their value. If pearls—an image repeatedly used in *Citadelle*—were as common and as easy to find as pebbles, they would have no more value than mere stones.

And so it is with all human relations. As Saint-Exupéry put it more explicitly in his letter to General Chambe: "The bonds of love which today bind man to things as well as beings are so lax, so little taut that man no longer feels absence as he used to. It's the terrible meaning of that Jewish story: 'So you're going over there? How far away you will be!' 'Far from where?' The 'where' they were leaving was simply a vast web of habits. In this period of divorce, one divorces just as easily from things. Refrigerators are interchangeable. So is the house if it is no more than an assemblage. And woman. And religion. And the party. One cannot even be unfaithful; to what would one be unfaithful? Far from where and unfaithful to what? . . .

"And when I think that barely three hundred years ago one could write *La Princesse de Clèves* or shut oneself up in a convent for life for the sake of a lost love, so burning was that love! Today, to be sure, people commit suicide. But the sufferings of the latter are like a tooth-ache. Intolerable. But have nothing to do with love."

The doctrine of courtly love preached by the medieval troubadours— whom Nietzsche so admired—would have been robbed of its content but for the elaborate taboos and prohibitions with which it was surrounded. Juliet would not have been Juliet if Romeo could have had her by simply lifting his little finger. If the Middle Ages were such an intense age, it was precisely because of their inbuilt interdictions and sanctions. Such was "the palace of my father"—by which in *Citadelle* Saint-Exupéry implicitly refers to the Middle Ages—"where all steps have a meaning". But then came the revolutionaries and the levellers and the prophets of facility—Rousseau and Marx calling on man to throw off all social shackles, Proudhon even more succinctly proclaiming the anarchist doctrine of *"Ni Dieu, ni Maître!"*— and the chains having been piled on to the bonfire of History, along with God, masters, and all authoritarian restraints, Man, freed at last, suddenly felt lost and listless, not realizing that it was precisely these restraints, and his struggle against them, which gave life its intensity and meaning.

The notion of the "welfare state" was for this reason as abhorrent to Saint-Exupéry as egalitarian democracy. "Womb-to-tomb" security may, like the abstract notion of Justice, be ideally justified, but it can only produce a flaccid, self-satisfied, challengeless society in which the individual cannot help but degenerate. And this for Saint-Exupéry was all important. He did not care for any -ism as such; what interested him was what kind of man it was likely to produce. "The question" as he put it in *Citadelle*, "is not to know if man, yes or no, will be happy, prosperous, or comfortably sheltered. I ask myself first of all what man will be prosperous, sheltered, and happy."

The idea of justice which emerges from *Citadelle* thus has nothing to do with that "increase in social justice" which has become a major preoccupation of contemporary society. It is much closer to that Spartan notion of Justice which Plato propounded in *The Republic* and which might roughly be defined as "that which preserves a healthy society". But whereas Plato, faithful in this to the deepest strain in Hellenic thinking, could not help imagining his Good or Healthy Society as something essentially static and unchanging, Saint-Exupéry, like Hegel, Nietzsche, and Bergson—to name but three—thought of it as inherently and necessarily dynamic. An absolutely just society would, in fact, be a satisfied society, and thus a dead society. Society, to be dynamic, must therefore be unjust. "For life is structure, line of force, and injustice," he wrote in *Citadelle*, in a Nietzschean phrase which runs through it like a leitmotif. "The cult of ceremonial" must therefore take preference over "the cult of justice, for it is its task to found man, which justice will guarantee. If I ruin the ceremonial in the name of justice, I ruin man, and my justice no longer has an object."

By "ceremonial" Saint-Exupéry meant tradition, and ultimately religion. It was another way of saying that in his (ideal) scheme of things the temporal must be subordinated to the spiritual. Those who have taken issue with *Citadelle* on the grounds that it is really an apologia for "totalitarianism" have completely missed or deliberately ignored this point. The Empire or "citadel" Saint-Exupéry imagined was not a republic nor a parliamentary democracy, any more than was the Aéropostale at its apogee, when it was ruled by the iron will of Didier Daurat. But the ruler-narrator of *Citadelle* is not a totalitarian tyrant, governed only by his own caprice. His rule is patriarchal, to be sure, but subordinated to a spiritual criterion. For the ruler's omnipotence is not an end in itself or even justified *faute de mieux*— as it tends to be in Machiavelli's *The Prince* or Hobbes' *Leviathan*. *Citadelle* abounds in barbed allusions to the "solid stupidity" of generals, to "necessarily stupid" policemen—whose short-sighted endeavours uniformly tend towards the lifeless "museum state". The man who in *Lettre à un Otage* could write, "Life creates order, but order does not create life," found it quite natural to write in *Citadelle* that "Order is the effect of life and not its cause . . . Man entirely free in a field of absolute force and absolute constraints which are invisible policemen: that is the justice of my empire."

One of the fundamental concerns of *Citadelle* is thus not how to impose, but how to *avoid* the police state. It is to find an answer to the burning questions Nietzsche hurled at the twentieth century: how to save the world from general madness and unlimited strife when the belief in God has died; how to rediscover that fervour and communion of purpose which built the great Gothic cathedrals of the Middle Ages; how to instill a spirit of sacrifice in which the arduousness of the effort is its own reward; how to combat the demagogues who would "tear down the temple in the name of the equality of the stones".

The religious tone of *Citadelle* was thus anything but a literary affectation, as André Gide, for one, seems to have supposed; it was basic to its author's purpose. For *Citadelle* is essentially, not accidentally, a religious work—all the more curious for having been written by an unbeliever, by a "mystic without faith", as Clément Borgal has called him. Though he was not a regular church goer, as we have seen, Saint-Ex was imbued with a Christian philosophy of love; a philosophy of love recast in a kind of Platonic mould. For love to be an effective social agent—and this Saint-Exupéry regarded as indispensable for any truly harmonious community—then it must be a living element, and not simply a kind of dead mortar, cushioning the shocks between individual egos. What distinguishes the cathedral from the heap of stones it was built from is the architect's design, itself the product of a special fervour. But this fervour, to be a living force, must, like sap in a tree, act vertically as well as horizontally. It must in the deepest sense be altruistic, tended towards that which is *alter*, the "other" meaning something other than man. For man is so constituted that he cannot unfurl and reach his plenitude if he remains shut up within himself; and he experiences a crippling malaise if, like someone locked into a room full of mirrors, all he is given to contemplate and admire is his own reflection. Even the gods of ancient Greece, though essentially anthropomorphic, were "other", placed as they were on a higher, Olympian plane.

Thus the "pursuit of happiness", or to put it more crudely, the gratification of the masses, if regarded as an end in itself, could only, Saint-Exupéry believed, culminate in a chaotic ant-heap of stunted egotisms—unless subordinated to some higher ordering principle, to a Force or Being superior to Man, whether it be called God, or as repeatedly in *Citadelle*, "the divine knot which binds things together". At the same time he felt no sympathy for the select God of monks and theologians, used to offer believers a kind of psychic crutch, remarking in *Citadelle*, in a passage probably written at the time of his altercation with Jacques Maritain and which clearly defines the limits of his Platonism: "It is too easy to escape and prefer God to the lighting of candles. But I do not know man, but men. Not freedom, but free men. Nor happiness, but happy men. Not beauty, but beautiful things. Not God, but the fervour of the candles." Thus for Saint-Exupéry, as for Goethe, in the Beginning was not the Word, nor even the Faith; in the Beginning was the Act. Or as he put it, even more succinctly, in one of his random notes: "What does it matter to me if God does not exist; God gives man divinity." And elsewhere: "God is true, but created by ourselves." The notion of God may be man-made, as Voltaire suggested, but it is no less essential to the welfare of human society. Without this element of divinity, without a belief in the divine spark inhabiting man's mortal coil, no real human brotherhood is possible, and men end up treating each other as casual objects, irksome obstacles, soulless brutes, or undifferentiated social corpuscles whose ultimate *raison d'être* is simply to nourish the Greater Collectivity.

A good illustration of this truism—for Saint-Exupéry at least—is the phenomenon of Charity, which so occupied his thoughts during the last months in Algiers. Plato implicitly suggested it when, in *The Symposium*, he remarked that "the lover is closer to the divine than the beloved". Christ repeated the same idea in slightly different words when he said: "It is more blessed to give than to receive." This "blessed" presupposes "in the eyes of God", and it raises the question: can Charity be exalted as a purely human ideal independently of some relation to the divine? Saint-Exupéry's answer, given in the credo of *Pilote de Guerre*, was No. "There was a time when the sacrifice which founds human beings took the name of Charity when it honoured God through His human image. Through the individual we gave to God, or to Man. But then, forgetting God or Man, we no longer gave save to the individual. Thenceforth Charity was often made to appear an unacceptable initiative. Society, rather than individual whim, had to assure equity in the parcelling out of the goods of this world. The dignity of the individual could not be reduced to vassalage by the largesse of another. It would be paradoxical to see the 'haves' lay claim not only to their own possessions but to the gratitude of the 'have-nots.'"

The slightly awkward juxtaposition here of God and Man—both deliberately capitalized and offered as alternatives—affords dramatic proof of what it cost Saint-Exupéry in terms of style (and how important that was to him!) to try to wed Christian ethics and Nietzschean psychology. But because he sought to be faithful to both, he found it doubly difficult to swallow the facile notion, popularized by George Bernard Shaw and certain Fabians at the turn of the century, that Socialism is really Christianity in action. It was not the goods to be multiplied and distributed which interested him, but the fervour expended in their manufacture. The utilitarian philosophy which, more or less, has underlain modern socialist thinking—according to which it is the usefulness of the product which confers value on the act—held no appeal for him. Quite the contrary, it was the sheer gratuity of the gift, the spontaneous intensity of the gesture, the love and not the profit, the sacrifice and not the reward which for him were all important. Thus he could even redefine utility, not as that which is convenient and facilitates man's life, but as that which resists one, as that which, by imposing tasks and obligations, draws the best out of man.

This same "resistencialist" criterion likewise underlay Saint-Exupéry's notion of God. Even more than for Pascal, appalled by the inhuman solitude of infinite space, God for Saint-Exupéry is *deus absconditus*, a god who hides his face. At one point in *Citadelle* he has "the only true geometer" (Pascal) say to his chieftain-father: "I would have liked to have discovered in the universe the trace of a divine mantle, and touching a truth outside of me, like a god who had long hidden himself from men, I would have liked to have gripped him by the hem of his coat and to have torn the veil from his face, to lay it bare. But it would not have been given to me to discover aught than myself." Elsewhere Saint-Exupéry wrote: "For I had not touched God, for a god who lets himself be touched is not a god. Nor if he obeys a prayer. And for the first time I understood that the greatness of prayer resides first of all in that there is no answer to it, and that there thus enters into this exchange nothing that hath the sordidness of a bargain."

We are here light years removed from that fatuous notion of God which Norman Vincent Peale has sought to popularize in the United States, by getting God into the office and out on to the golf-links and—after all, why not?—into the kitchen pantry (for an American God can hardly be a misogynist, unwilling to lend a hand with the stacking of the dishes). The *Gott mit uns* philosophy, as Saint-Exupéry realized, is inescapably demagogic and plebeian, conjuring up an illusion of divine intervention in human affairs which is ultimately demeaning to both man and God. For if the greatness of God consists in His shunning such belittling involvements, the greatness of Man resides in his continuing to pray in the knowledge that *never* will his pleas be explicitly answered. The *credo quia absurdum* (I believe because it is absurd) of Nicholas of Cusa has here been transformed into a *Credo quia absconditum* (I believe because the truth is hidden). Were God to relent, even for a moment, and reveal Himself, He would be guilty of "vulgarity" (the word is actually used at one point in *Citadelle*) and condescending indulgence; he would be relenting to the point of absolving man of what is in fact his lot—ascension towards the divine, which is to say, the unknown and unknowable. For, as Saint-Exupéry put it, in a single succinct sentence: *"il n'est point d'amnistie divine qui t'épargne de devenir."* There is no divine amnesty to spare you from becoming. Like K in Kafka's *The Castle*, man's lot is to strive upwards towards a goal he may dimly surmise but will never be allowed to see.

Thus God for Saint-Exupéry was the Great Silent One, what Master Eckhart, the great mediaeval mystic called "the silent wilderness that is God". It is foolish to expect Him to yield to ostentation—simply to reassure man of His presence. In *Citadelle* Saint-Exupéry explicitly condemned all cheap manifestations of the divine—such as visions, archangels etc—as fairground "apparitions" and Punch and Judy antics. The same severity of conception—one is tempted to call it "stoic"—meant implicitly condemning the doctrine of Christian "grace", as bestowed on the pure of heart and the Elect. Even more, though Saint-Exupéry never said so explicitly, it meant rejecting the godhead of Christ, viewed as more than the Son of Man, but as an emanation of God, or at least of the Holy Ghost.

This is, quite obviously, a superhuman conception of God in which—to this extent he remained a Nietzschean—the notion of the divine has been rigorously purified of all human sentimentality. But Saint-Exupéry, being all too human, could only protest at the inhumanity of this conception. *Citadelle*, like the Book of Job, is the work of a sufferer; it echoes with cries and protests. "Appear unto me, Lord, for all is hard when one loses the taste for God." "And I knew the *ennui* which is first of all to be deprived of God. . . . Why do you constrain me, Lord, to this journey through the wilderness? One sign from You and the desert would be transformed." But the sign is not forthcoming and the desert remains. Man is left to fend for himself in a universe where he is radically, essentially alone. Uncertainty and doubt and the anguish that accompany them are thus man's lot. This is the point where Saint-Exupéry joins Heidegger. It is also the point where he joins Ortega y Gasset, who in *El Hombre y la Gente* (Man and People) defines man's radical solitude as fundamental to the human condition. "Our Lady of Solitude" as Ortega remarks, "is the Virgin who remains *solitary* of Jesus, who has been killed; and the sermon preached in Holy Week and called the 'Sermon on Solitude' meditates on the most sorrowful of Christ's words: *Eli, Eli—lamma sabachthani?* 'My God, my God, why hast Thou forsaken me?' Why hast Thou left me solitary of Thee? This is the expression that most profoundly declares God's will to become man—to accept what is most radically human in man, his radical solitude."

\*  \*  \*

It is impossible to pass definitive judgment on a work which was never completed, indeed, which was hardly begun and which remained, after its author's death, a monumental pile of masonry, a not yet constructed ruin. The least one can say is that Saint-Exupéry had not yet succeeded before he died in satisfactorily reconciling the antagonistic philosophies of Nietzsche and Pascal. The endeavour may have been doomed from the outset, but it is this inner and deliberately sought contradiction which gives *Citadelle* its dramatic and at the same time pathetic tension.

It was Saint-Exupéry's belief that Nature being "that which is" and essentially pre-logical and sub-grammatical, the contradictions man finds in life are, in the final analysis, products of his own brain: or more specifically, of the logic and language he uses in his daily speech. This is not the place to debate a highly intricate and complex matter; but if a desire to conciliate antinomies (seeming contradictions) can be said to have been a constant of human thinking from Heracleitus down to Hegel and beyond, then nothing could have been more inherently philosophical than Saint-Exupéry's desperate endeavour to fuse two contradictory doctrines into a higher synthesis. This is something Jean Cau forgot when he wrote some years ago, in the special issue which *Icare* (the French pilots' magazine) devoted to Saint-Ex: "In addition, I have put my finger (easy enough) on an essential piece of trickery: Saint-Exupéry wishes to be warrior (man of war), aristocrat, Nietzschean, and whatever in that genre and *at the same time* he aspires to I know not what mystic, fraternal, and virile communion between 'men'. But one cannot have both: either one proclaims a lordly, Nietzschean ethic—and after all, why not?—or one speaks humbly of man. What irritates me, what strikes me as false, is this mixture of the two. This wish to be a lord who feels himself a brother to his subjects because he discovers that he shares with them the vaguest of common denominators, to wit, that he too is a man."

The exclusiveness implicit in Cau's thinking—one must be this or that, one must do this or that—is a characteristic manifestation of something Saint-Ex particularly abhorred in French thought: the purely logical approach. Faithful in this to the intellectual style established by his one-time master, Jean-Paul Sartre (whose secretary he was for a while), Cau here accused Saint-Exupéry of cheating. This is alas! typical of a whole breed of sub-Sartrians who, wishing to go their idol one better, resort to the age-old method first patented by Diogenes, the prototypic cynic, and which can be summed up in the slogan: "When in doubt, resort to abuse."

Another good example of this style is the paragraph Jean-François Revel, normally an anti-Sartrian, devoted to Saint-Exupéry in his book, *En France, La Fin de l'Opposition*, written in 1965. The author's thesis, which I would personally not quarrel with, is that the French are a politically immature people, a revealing symptom of this immaturity being their childish addiction to pomp and *panache* and a veneration, amounting to a cult, of martial values, drum-beating heroics, and military leadership. Pétain and De Gaulle were thus anything but accidents. Not content with this, Revel went on:

"To measure the hold this imagery has on French civilization, one has only to open one's eyes to the bookshop successes which transcend the world of the literati and even the reading fraction of the bourgeoisie, directly or indirectly impregnating the entire population. The greatest of these successes over the past thirty years has been Saint-Exupéry, the cou-cou man who replaced the human brain with an aeroplane engine. All of his prop-driven platitudes go towards exalting the 'chief' (a word which ought to be restricted, in French, to kitchen *'chefs'*) and the 'team', well led and kept in hand. Saint-Exupéry, who has inundated baccalaureat exams and station bookstalls, de luxe volumes and paperbacks, magazines and weeklies (it takes real genius to fabricate special issues by tirelessly reheating such meagre raw material), Saint-Exupéry has grown into more than an author, he is a saint, a prophet. To understand France one must realize that the influential writer is not Gide, is not Breton, it is Saint-Ex, who has shown the French how an asinine verbosity can become profound philosophical truth if one can have it take off the ground and rise to a height of seven thousand feet. This cockpit cretinism takes on an air of wisdom, a wisdom our young people have imbibed with a fierce avidity . . ." etc.

This is an astonishing statement coming from someone who is anything but stupid. Everything Revel had to say about Saint-Exupéry's extraordinary popularity in the above quoted passage is strictly true; but in his zeal to ridicule the "personality cult" which led his countrymen to admire Pétain and De Gaulle, Revel threw the baby out with the bath water. For to anyone but a Left Bank intellectual it would seem obvious enough that the success of any enterprise, from the humblest to the highest, be it garage, factory, restaurant, magazine—and of this at least Revel has had some personal experience—publishing company, symphony orchestra, museum, railway, shipping company, or ultimately country, depends on the personality of the individual effectively in charge, whether he be called "Boss", "*Chef*", "conductor", "chairman", "prime minister", or "president". Nothing is easier or shallower than denigrating the very notion of leadership in the name of some ill-defined corporate criterion which has no real substance in fact but which permits the debunker to pose as an "authentic democrat".

If Saint-Exupéry was so concerned with the problem of leadership, it was because the need for authority in all fields, material as well as spiritual, has not fundamentally changed since the age of the Greeks. One may deplore the fact in the name of some abstract "democratic" principle, but when the right to dissent is recognized as absolute and as an end in itself, it ceases to be constructive, as healthy criticism always is, and becomes a negative agent of destruction. It may be true, as Dostoevski suggested in "The Legend of the Grand Inquisitor", that the majority of human beings cannot look truth in the face and must therefore be fed myths; but what is certain is that when all authority is called into question, as is increasingly the case today, everything in man's life is condemned to be unsteady and insecure. The authority of parents over their children is contested in exactly the same way as the authority of teachers is contested on the school or university level. The very notion of "authority" becomes so controversial and diluted that parents, yielding to the frivolous fashions of the hour, toss in the sponge, shoving off the problem of education—which is first of all a family problem—on to harassed schoolteachers, who find it increasingly difficult to fulfil their duties in a climate of more or less permanent insurrection. One's feeling of individual responsibility, which Saint-Exupéry regarded as fundamental in anyone claiming to be "man", gradually gives way to a sentiment of collective culpability, as parents seek to atone for their guilt in being parents, teachers ask forgiveness for having to instruct, and religious as well as other leaders ask to be excused for having occasionally to lead. Like the nineteenth century French demagogue, Ledru-Rollin, who was once asked where he and his party were headed, they are ready as one man to reply: "I do not know, but I am their leader, so I must follow them." This is the "revolutionary epilepsy" Saint-Exupéry spoke of in his letter to General Chambe, and which cannot but thrive in a climate of universal abdication. Each, instead of trying to determine what is objectively called for, first seeks to find out what the other desires, as though these desires, being desires, were in themselves categorically imperative. That ascensional or aspirational force, which Saint-Exupéry felt was vital for the functioning of a healthy society, is thus inverted and becomes *descensional*. Parents abdicate before their children, teachers before their pupils, and priests before their congregations. Everyone ends up retreating before something or someone. The tillers of the soil flee the problems of the land, just as, paradoxically, the city-dwellers flee the increasingly nightmarish congestion of the cities: forgetting that they have inherited a legacy it is their privilege and should be their obligation to defend, they surrender to those perennial parasites—the speculators, the get-rich-quick operators, the wreckers, and their political camp-followers— and flee to the country, in search of something that can give them back a sense of lost solidity and attachment. Just how far this particular process will be carried—in the land which is presently looked up to as the leader and model of the western world—there is no telling; but it may be America's final destiny to fulfil Nietzsche's sombre phophecy, according to which the dominant man of tomorrow will be a nomad species, an ever more collectiv-ized camper.

Judged by the criterion Saint-Exupéry regarded as essential—"What kind of man is it going to produce?"—Western civilization today would probably have to be regarded as almost as crass a failure as the spirit-warping dictator-ships of the East. For it is one of the great (and greatly overlooked) ironies of our age that while the last war was fought by the western democracies in the name of liberty and the "dignity of the human individual", the values which are now everywhere in the ascendant are unindividual, quantitative, and collective. In a world where what counts is how many automobiles were manufactured last year, how many houses built, how many more miles of asphalt were laid down, how many brassieres and bathing-suits were sold, refrigerators distributed, cigarettes smoked, fuel burnt, movies seen, ice cream eaten, Coca Cola drunk, and barbiturates consumed, there is no room for purely qualitative qualms. The distinction Saint-Exupéry carefully established in *Citadelle* between the "urgent" and the "important"—"It is urgent, to be sure, that men eat . . . but love and the sense of life and the taste for God are more important"—can thus be dismissed as irrelevant. Since love and the sense of life (that is, of Nature) and the taste for God cannot be tabulated, they can be declared statistically non-existent, and the world can go its way without them.

All this Saint-Exupéry felt and foresaw. The numeromania to which contemporary man, and not least of all the contemporary Frenchman, has succumbed was something he deplored as much as what Lewis Mumford has, a bit too mildly, termed "the myth of the machine". Nor, had he lived longer, would Saint-Ex have been unduly startled to hear General de Gaulle, in the mystical *élan* of his "robot virtue", exalt as a national ideal a "France of one hundred million Frenchmen"—as though the doubling of its present citizenry would suffice to make it twice as estimable a land. In a congested world whose population is expected to double (from three and a half to seven billion) by the end of the century, France's role, it appears, is here too to lead the way. As Ledru-Rollin might have said: we have no idea where we're headed, but we must remain in the van.

Other Frenchmen (and they include Georges Pompidou) have suggested that it should be France's destiny to become a Latin Sweden. Perhaps she will. But at the present rate of development she seems more likely to go the way of an overcrowded Holland, with a predictable loss of what Saint-Exupéry most valued—that priceless asset known as "charm". Charm, being an imponderable that can neither be weighed nor measured, presents a standing challenge to the technocrat, for whom the only things that matter are things that can be counted, weighed, and added. Unable to cope with something so inherently baffling, the technocrat avenges his wounded susceptibility by dismissing charm as superannuated and *"peu rentable"*—unprofitable. His reaction is Cartesian in the profoundest sense—to the extent that anything which appeals to the senses is fundamentally suspect.

"I hate this epoch" Saint-Exupéry wrote in his letter to General Chambe, "in which, under the sway of a universal totalitarianism, men become soft, polite, and quiet cattle. We are asked to regard this as moral progress! What I hate in Marxism is the totalitarianism it leads to. Man is defined in it as producer and consumer, and the essential problem is one of distribution. So it is on the model farms. What I hate in Nazism is the totalitarianism it lays claim to in its very essence. Ruhr workers are made to file past a Van Gogh, a Cézanne, and a cheap print. They naturally vote for the print. This is the people's truth! The potential Cézannes, the potential Van Goghs, all the great non-conformists are solidly locked into a concentration-camp and the subjugated cattle are fed cheap prints. But where are the United States going, and where are we too going in this epoch of universal bureaucratization? Robot-man, termite-man, man oscillating between assembly-line and the bowling alley. Man castrated of all his creative power, and who no longer even knows, from the depths of his village, how to create a new dance or song. Man fed on ready-made culture, on standardized culture, much as cattle are fed on hay. That's what man is today."

Yes, it was perhaps just as well that Saint-Exupéry died when he did; for the spectacle of the contemporary "human zoo"—as Desmond Morris has graphically described it—would have been too much for him to bear. "Evolution through mechanization is, in some respects, a disaster for the human species," he once wrote in his notebook. "It pulls man out of his conceptual civilization, it changes the type of man too rapidly for him ever to become one." The thought could have been better phrased, though the meaning is crystal clear. But if Saint-Exupéry was in error on this point—and as one can see, his attitude was ambivalent (he was after all a pilot who had once been mad about machines)—it was only in thinking that the source of contemporary man's predicament could be looked for in "the *impasses* of the economic system of the nineteenth century." For that system was not simply a technological phenomenon, arising by a process of spontaneous generation; it was the result of a revolutionary change in Europe's intellectual climate. The Industrial Revolution, like the antagonistic philosophies that grew out of it, was only the prolongation of what had been started in the previous century. And it was the eighteenth century which gave the world the two ideas which have sustained the economic and social thinking of modern mankind. The first was the idea of human progress, as something unlimited and never-ending, which was invented by two Frenchmen,

Turgot and Condorcet. The other, conceived at roughly the same moment (in the 1760s) by the Scotsman Adam Smith, was the idea of unlimited growth and ever-increasing wealth, as the result of expanding trade. Today it sounds a commonplace, but at the time it was a revolutionary idea. Prior to Adam Smith's day it was taken for granted that a country's wealth was something fixed and static. Exports were thus regarded as more likely to be a danger than an asset, a kind of economic haemorrhage which had to be carefully counterbalanced by imports (particularly of gold bullion) to keep a country from perishing of anaemia. Which is why both were controlled by what any businessman (west of the Iron Curtain) would today consider intolerable—state licences and charters.

Together these two ideas have fused to form what may be called the Principle of Unlimited Expansion: a principle which today underlies the economic and social thinking, and thus the practice, of all modern economies, whether capitalistic or marxist. The principle might have continued to be valid if, as the world's industrial expansion grew, with an ever increasing output of concrete and metal (the basic ingredients for automobiles and houses), the surface of the planet had similarly grown, like that of an inflated balloon. But this has not happened.

Saint-Exupéry's generation was the first to discover this radical, new, and awful truth—that the size of our planet is limited. Nay, that the Earth is relatively small. The astronomers had already guessed it, but it took the airplane to bring this sobering truth home to the general public. An ocean ceases to be vast when it can be overflown in half a day; and even a large continent like America shrinks when it can be crossed in a matter of hours. Saint-Exupéry, precisely because he was a flyer, understood this instinctively. Our planet, he knew, was shrinking, and far faster than is generally realized. This is the price man has had to pay for speed. It is also the price he is paying for his prolific industry. For the tireless churning out of more concrete and more metal cannot be continued indefinitely if man is to be left with any room in which to breathe.

Yet this truth, one of the basic truths of our age, has so far failed to make much impression on contemporary economic thinking. We should not be particularly surprised by this. The economist is a person trained to keep his nose to the statistical grind-stone; he is trained to be short-sighted. He is the specialist of the short run; for as Keynes sagaciously remarked, "In the long run we are all dead". But Keynes, who was a great economist precisely because he was more than an economist, was also careful to point out that the economist's task is to deal with the "how"; he cannot be asked to deal with the "why". Economics is a science of means, not ends.

But it is the ends, not the means, which are ultimately all-important.

Man, precisely because he is being made to live by bread alone, is now threatened with mass starvation. This is the ironic revenge which History is exacting of a mankind which has turned its back on its lessons. For it was asking too much of the economist to entrust the welfare of society to his safe-keeping. It is asking too much of the engineer, it is asking too much of the scientist. This too Saint-Exupéry understood, and more deeply than might be suggested by the caricatures he sketched, in *The Little Prince*, of the businessman and the mathematician. For already he could write, in 1939, a sentence which Jean-François Revel may dismiss as a "prop-driven platitude", but which Plato, who knew what philosophy really is, would not have gainsaid:

"*J'admire la Science, bien sûr. Mais j'admire aussi la Sagesse.*"*

---

\* "I admire Science, to be sure. But I admire Wisdom as well."

# Notes and Acknowledgements

The quotations in this biography are drawn from the following works of Antoine de Saint-Exupéry:

*Courrier Sud* (Gallimard 1929)
*Vol de Nuit* (Gallimard 1931)
*Terre des Hommes* (Gallimard 1939)
*Pilote de Guerre* (Gallimard 1942, reprinted 1962)
*Lettre à un Otage* (Gallimard 1944)
*Le Petit Prince* (Gallimard 1946)
*Citadelle* (Gallimard 1948)
*Carnets* (Gallimard 1953)
*Lettres de Jeunesse*, 1923–1931 (Gallimard 1953)
*Lettres à sa Mère* (Gallimard 1955)
*Un Sens à la Vie* (Gallimard 1956)

The latest *Quid?* almanach for the year 1970 lists the following books as the best sellers of recent years in France:

| | | | |
|---|---|---|---|
| 1. *Le Petit Larousse* (dictionary) | 31,000,000 | copies published | |
| 2. *Le Tour de la France par deux enfants* by Bruno | 8,328,500 | ,, | ,, |
| 3. *Le Grand Meaulnes*, by Alain Fournier | 2,300,000 | ,, | ,, |
| 4. *Vol de Nuit*, by Antoine de Saint-Exupéry | 2,242,600 | ,, | ,, |
| 5. *La Peste*, by Albert Camus | 2,198,400 | ,, | ,, |
| 6. *Les Malheurs de Sophie*, by the Comtesse de Ségur (1882) | 1,905,793 | ,, | ,, |
| 7. *L'Etranger*, by Albert Camus | 1,884,000 | ,, | ,, |
| 8. *Terre des Hommes*, by Antoine de Saint-Exupéry | 1,822,100 | ,, | ,, |
| 9. *Le Petit Prince*, by A. de Saint-Exupéry | 1,760,600 | ,, | ,, |
| 10. *Maria Chapdelaine*, by Louis Hémon | 1,752,000 | ,, | ,, |

11. *Les Carnets du Major Thompson,* by
    Pierre Daninos                         1,670,000 copies published
12. *Bonjour Tristesse,* by François Sagan   1,521,000   „      „


Saint-Exupéry is thus the only French author of this century to have three books among the first ten.


## Chapter 1. THE LINDENS OF SAINT-MAURICE

For information about Antoine de Saint-Exupéry's childhood years I am first of all deeply indebted to his mother, Madame Marie de Saint-Exupéry, who has been generosity personified, and to his two sisters, Simone and Gabrielle. Mademoiselle Anne-Marie Poncet was also a priceless source, as were Madame Le Bély and Mademoiselle Richer, Monsieur Chancharme, director of what is now the Internat Saint-Exupéry at Saint-Maurice-de-Rémens, and Colonel Charles de Fonscolombe, who was kind enough to take me on a guided tour of the Château de la Môle.

The quotations in this chapter are drawn from *Pilote de Guerre, Courrier Sud, Citadelle, Le Petit Prince,* and *Terre des Hommes,* and are, as throughout this book, in the author's own rendition.

pp. 9–10   For Simone de Saint-Exupéry's reminiscences see article entitled "*Antoine, mon Frère*", included in the anthology published by Hachette (Collection "*Génies et Réalités*") in 1963.

pp. 12–13   Pierre Chevrier, *Antoine de Saint-Exupéry* (Gallimard 1949, p. 13) As indicated in a letter written from Casablanca in 1921 (*Lettres à sa Mère,* p. 87), the tiny armchair was green, rather than blue. The garbled story of Abraham and Isaac was repeated by François, not Antoine. Otherwise Pierre Chevrier's account is correct.

pp. 13–14   For this second reminiscence of Simone de Saint-Exupéry see her article in the special issue of *Confluences* (Nos 12–14) published in 1948 in honour of her brother.


## Chapter 2. POET AND PRANKSTER

For the genealogical background in this chapter I am indebted to Antoine's first cousin, Guy de Saint-Exupéry, to his niece, Mireille des Vallières, and to General and Madame Joseph du Pontavice. I am most grateful to Paul Gaultier, Claude de Castillon, and Max de Villoutreys for details about the Collège Notre-Dame de Sainte-Croix, as I am to Roger de Sinéty for information about the Château de Passay and to Madame Odette de Sinéty for permission to quote from her drawing-book.

p. 22    The statement about Antoine and his grandfather was made by Mademoiselle Charlotte Churchill. See Helen Elizabeth Crane, *L'Humanisme dans l'oeuvre de Saint-Exupéry* (Principia Press, Evanston, Illinois, 1957, p. 250.)

pp. 23–4    *Lettres à sa Mere*, pp. 34–5. Text includes erratic spelling of the original.

pp. 25–7    Antoine's handwritten copy of "The Odyssey of a Top Hat" was long kept by Abbé Launay, who used to read it to his class as a model of what an imaginative French composition could be.

pp. 30–1    Helen E. Crane, *op. cit.*, pp. 262–4.

pp. 31–3    I owe special thanks to the widow of Dr. Paul Michaud for being allowed to quote from these unpublished Saint-Exupéry poems and from the text of the speech her late husband delivered at Chambéry on 26 April, 1966.

For information about the Villa Saint-Jean I am first of all deeply indebted to Charles Sallès, who has been kind enough to let me quote from the unpublished letters Saint-Exupéry later wrote to him. I also owe thanks to Jean Ihler, Father Jean de Miscault, Abbé Boulet (who was kind enough to supply the photo of *Le Malade Imaginaire*), and Brother Terrence O'Connor, who was good enough to let me look over the school's grade-books.

p. 39    See "Books I Remember", *Harper's Bazaar*, April 1941, pp. 82, 123.

p. 40    For François' death see *Pilote de Guerre*, pp. 170–1.

pp. 40–1    For information about her father and the photo of Fernand de Saint-Exupéry I am much indebted to Mlle. Charlotte Churchill.

I owe special thanks to Henry de Ségogne and to Chanoine Garand of the Ecole Bossuet for information concerning Saint-Exupéry's Paris studies.

p. 42    *Lettres à sa Mère*, p. 43. Other quotations in this chapter are taken from subsequent letters included in this collection.

pp. 45–6    The text of this poem can be found in the 1951 issue of the Ecole Bossuet's annual *Bulletin*.

## *Chapter* 3. BAPTISM OF THE AIR

For the aeronautical information contained in this chapter I am first of all grateful to Colonel Rougevin-Baville, director of the Musée de l'Air in Paris, and to his assistant, Monsieur Bénard, for kindly permitting me to use their library. I am also indebted to Father Raymond de Castillon for his precious recollections of the "Aéro-Club" at the Collège de Sainte-Croix, to Charles de Vries for his amusing reminiscences of First World War piloting, and to General René Bouscat for his first encounter with a stunt pilot over the Casablanca airfield.

pp. 48–9   See Gabriel Voisin's delightful autobiography, *Mes* 10,000 *Cerfs-Volants* (Table Ronde, 1960).

pp. 57 forward   *Lettres à sa Mere*, pp. 54–91.

p. 57   Marcel Migeo, *Saint-Exupéry* (Flammarion 1958, pp. 24–42) is particularly informative on this period of Saint-Ex's life.

## Chapter 4. ADRIFT

I owe special thanks to Mademoiselle Renée de Saussine for all she had to tell me about the Hôtel de Créquy, to Madame Louise de Vilmorin for a most entertaining afternoon partly devoted to her cousin Antoine, to Madame Scapini for her recollections of the town-house on the Rue François-Premier at a time when she was Lucie-Marie Decour, and to Madame Yvonne de Lestrange for many valuable glimpses of her impecunious relative.

pp. 69 forward   Many details in this description of Verrières-le-Buisson and the house on the Rue de la Chaise are drawn from André de Vilmorin's book about his sister (*Poètes d'Aujourd'hui*, 91, Seghers 1962).

pp. 73–4   Louise de Vilmorin, "*Ma Fièvre me raconte de belles histoires d'amour*" (*Marie-Claire*, October 1955).

The quotations in this chapter are most of them drawn from Antoine's letters to Renée de Saussine, published under the title *Lettres de Jeunesse*.

pp. 87 forward   On the subject of the Rue de l'Odéon see Sylvia Beach, *Shakespeare and Company* (Harcourt, Brace 1959), Adrienne Monnier, *La Rue de l'Odéon* (Albin Michel 1960) and *Les Gazettes*, 1925–1945 (Julliard 1953), and Ernest Hemingway, *A Moveable Feast*. Other details have been drawn from Jean Prévost' self-portrait in *Les Caractères* (Albin Michel 1948).

pp. 91–2   Beppo de Massimi, *Vent Debout* (Plon 1948, p. 295).

## Chapter 5. THE MAIL-CARRIERS OF TOULOUSE

The account herein given of the early years of the Latécoère company is based on Beppo de Massimi's *Vent Debout* (previously mentioned), Didier Daurat's *Dans le Vent des Hélices* (Seuil 1956), and Jean-Gérard Fleury's *La Ligne* (Gallimard 1949).

pp. 102–4  Jean Mermoz's description of his first encounter with Daurat was published after his death in an anthology of his writings entitled *Mes Vols* (Flammarion 1937, pp. 25–30). See also Joseph Kessel's biography, *Mermoz* (Gallimard 1938, pp. 92–4).

pp. 107–8  The Spanish map session and description of the bus ride to Montaudran come from *Terre des Hommes*.

p. 109  Raymond Vanier, *Tout pour la Ligne* (France-Empire 1960, pp. 134–5).

## Chapter 6. Sea and Sand

p. 114  Five letters written to Lucie-Marie Decour, published in *Le Figaro*, 8 July 1950. One of them describes his room on the Rue Alsace Lorraine (see p. 115).

pp. 117 forward  Description here given of Rozès and Ville's shooting match with the Moors, like other incidents of the same kind, follows Jean-Gérard Fleury's account in *La Ligne*.

pp. 121–6  I am indebted to Madame Guillaumet, Henri Guillaumet's widow, for much invaluable information, including the exact dating of Saint-Exupéry's first trip down the African coast and the vivid description of the propeller-whirling episode.

pp. 123–5  Saint-Exupéry wrote several versions of this crash-landing and of the night at Nouakchott which followed. One appeared at the end of *Courrier Sud*, another in *Terre des Hommes*, and still another (probably taken from a previously published account in a French aviation weekly) in *Wind, Sand, and Stars*. Jean-Gérard Fleury gives yet another version in *La Ligne* (pp. 93–5). There is also an unpublished letter Saint-Exupéry wrote not long after the event which antedates them all.

p. 127  Madame Guillaumet's account of this first meeting can be found in the special issue of the French pilots' magazine, *Icare*, devoted to Saint-Exupéry (No. 30, Summer 1964).

p. 128  This description of Boulimit is based on a documentary film which Edouard Bobrowski was kind enough to project for me. I am also grateful to Mr. Bobrowski for letting me listen to a fascinating tape-recording made of a number of former Latécoère pilots and mechanics, including Léon Antoine, Henri Delaunay, André Dubourdieu, Rolland, and Jean-René Lefèbvre.

p. 129  For Spanish sentinel episode see *Lettres à sa Mere*, p. 135.

pp. 129–30  This description of the Dakar hospital is taken from a letter written to Charles Sallès.

### Chapter 7. A Year among the Moors

p. 133    I am grateful to Monsieur Renac, of the Public Relations department of Air France, for letting me see the report filed by Didier Daurat with Pierre Latécoère on 24 September 1927 regarding Ould Haj'Rab's visit to Juby. The Latécoère files were dispersed during the last war and have not yet been reassembled and processed.

p. 134    See Joseph Kessel, *Mermoz*, p. 131.

pp. 136 forward    Many details in this description of Juby are taken from Henri Delaunay's splendid *Araignée du Soir* (France-Empire 1968, pp. 101–2).

p. 142    From Jean-René Lefèbvre's recollections, as tape-recorded by Bobrowski.

pp. 143–6    See Saint-Ex's own account of this adventure in a letter addressed to Albert Tête, *Icare* (summer 1964), pp. 27–28.

p. 148    The text of this report on the Rio de Oro can be found in René Delange's *La Vie de Saint-Exupéry* (Seuil 1948, pp. 203–13).

### Chapter 8. Southern Mail

p. 150    For Rouveyre's onslaught against Valéry see Jean Galtier-Boissière's highly entertaining *Mémoires d'un Parisien*, Vol. II (Table Ronde 1961, pp. 159–62).

p. 152    Monsieur Gaston Gallimard, who was gracious enough to talk to me about his friend Antoine, could not recall having sent him to Beucler, but we have Beucler's word for it in a radio broadcast he did for the R.T.F. (French Radio Television) in 1954. Beucler had already written up this first meeting with Saint-Ex in an article published by *Le Figaro Littéraire* (30 July 1949).

p. 154    Edmond Jaloux, *Les Nouvelles Littéraires* (6 July 1929).

p. 155    Georges Mounin, "*L'espérance de l'homme*", included in René Tavernier's *Saint-Exupéry en Procès* (Belfond 1967, p. 126).

### Chapter 9. The Winds of Patagonia

pp. 160–2    Lionel Chassin's first account of this celestial navigation course was printed in *Confluences* (summer 1948) and a second account in *Icare* (summer 1964).

p. 165    *Araignée du Soir*, pp. 71–73.

p. 166    Letter to Lucie-Marie Decour (*Figaro Littéraire*, 8 July 1950).

pp. 167–70    For the biographical information on Almonacid I am most grateful for the copious material sent to me by his daughter, Señora Esmeralda de Carballido, and by Señor Antonio Biedma, editor of the *Revista Nacional de Aeronáutica* in Buenos Aires. I am also indebted to Miguel Riglos and Señora Lasra for letting me see the several essays Joaquín Gonzales devoted to his friend Almonacid.

pp. 172 forward   A detailed description of Saint-Ex's first flight south can be found in Rufino Luro Cambaceres' valuable little book, *Rumbo 180°—Huellas en el Cielo Austral* (Buenos Aires 1956), which Commandant Jean Dabry was kind enough to lend me.

pp. 178–9   See Chapter IV, "The Elements" in *Wind, Sand, and Stars*, and the French original in *Un Sens à la Vie* ("*Les Puissances Naturelles*").

### Chapter 10. *Hijos de Francia*

pp. 180–2   See Fleury, *La Ligne* (pp. 150–218).

p. 183   *Terre des Hommes*, p. 26.

p. 184   Raymond Vanier, *Tout pour la Ligne*, p. 165.

p. 184   Didier Daurat, *Dans le Vent des Hélices*, p. 155.

p. 186   The incident with Rose is to be found in John Phillips' *Odd World* (Simon & Schuster 1959, p. 157). Madame Guillaumet can recall no French pilot by that name in South America, but he may possibly have been an Argentinian.

p. 186   For the story about the virtuous youth see Dr. Georges Pélissier, *Les Cinq Visages de Saint-Exupéry* (Flammarion 1951, p. 30).

pp. 189–92   I have followed Guillaumet's own report of his accident, as given to Didier Daurat (*Dans le Vent des Hélices*, pp. 135–8), and added a couple of things told me by Madame Guillaumet. I am likewise grateful to her for letting me listen to the Chilean ballad, as sung by "*Los Huasos de Pichidegua*", which gave me the name for this chapter.

### Chapter 11. *Ma Sorciére*

pp. 194–5   *Lettres de Jeunesse*, pp. 103–7.

pp. 197–8   These pages are based on a visit to San Carlos and an interview with the two Fuchs sisters filmed by Edouard Bobrowski.

p. 198   *Lettres de Jeunesse*, pp. 111–14.

p. 199   Nino Frank, *Mémoire Brisée* (Calmann Levy 1967, Vol. I, p. 37). See also Richard Ellman's *James Joyce*, where there are many references to Benjamin Crémieux.

pp. 199 forward   The biographical details on Enrique Gomez Carrillo were most of them obtained from Gonzales Porto-Bompiani's *Diccionario de Autores*.

pp. 200–4  Xenia Kouprine's reminiscences are taken from an article published in *Spoutnik*.

p. 205  André Gide, *Journal*, 1889–1939 (Gallimard, Pléiade, pp. 1040–1).

## Chapter 12. INTO THE NIGHT

I am indebted to the late Didier Daurat, as I am to Roger Beaucaire and Prince Charles Murat, for helping me to supplement the account of the Aéropostale crisis which is to be found in Fleury's *La Ligne* (pp. 240–50) and in Daurat's own book, *op. cit.*, pp. 171–80.

pp. 216–17  Jean-Gérard Fleury, "*Saint-Exupéry, l'aviateur du désert*", article published in *Candide*, 9 January 1936.

pp. 215–17  I am grateful to Dr. Henri Comte for supplying me these little known details about Saint-Ex's life in Casablanca.

p. 217  *Terre des Hommes*, pp. 26–32.

pp. 218–20  Letter to Benjamin Crémieux published in *Les Annales Politiques et Littéraires*, 15 December 1931.

pp. 220–1  André Dubourdieu, article in *Forces Aériennes Françaises*, July 1947.

p. 221  On Gide see Jean Prévost, *Les Caractères*, p. 100.

p. 222  *Lettres à sa Mere*, pp. 160–2.

p. 231  Julien Benda, *La Trahison des Clercs* (Grasset 1927, Chapter 3 entitled "*L'exaltation du courage*").

p. 232  Gide, *Journal*, pp. 1041–2.

## Chapter 13. ADRIFT ONCE MORE

p. 233  I am indebted to Antoine's sister, Madame Gabrielle d'Agay, for the detail about Madame Pikomesmas, the fortune-teller.

pp. 234–6  See Caresse Crosby, *The Passionate Years* (Southern Illinois University Press, 1953).

pp. 236–7  I owe thanks to the late Stuart Gilbert and his widow for the details contained in these pages.

p. 237  Peter Quennell, *New Statesman and Nation*, 3 December 1932. *Times Literary Supplement*, 5 January 1933. L. A. G. Strong, *The Spectator*, 16 December 1932.

p. 237  Clifton Fadiman, *The Nation*, September 7, 1932.

p. 240  *Dans le Vent des Hélices*, p. 161.

p. 244  Letter quoted in Pierre Chevrier's biography, p. 100.

p. 244  *Terre des Hommes*, pp. 129–30.

p. 245  For full text of Saint-Exupéry's letter to Raoul Dautry see Daurat, *Dans le Vent des Hélices*, pp. 176–80.

p. 247  I am indebted to M. Charles Ford for the information about Clarence Brown's film of *Night Flight*.

pp. 247–8  forward I owe thanks to Victor Rescanières, André Dubourdieu, and above all to Gilbert Vergès for their recollections of Saint-Ex's test-pilot exploits.

p. 249–50  Letter quoted in Chevrier's biography, p. 102.

pp. 253  Text of this letter can be found in Daurat, *op. cit.*, pp. 241–44.

p. 254  Caresse Crosby, *The Passionate Years*, p. 321. No date is given for the visit made to "The Mill", in the forest of Ermenonville, by Consuelo, Mermoz, and Saint-Ex. "Antoine de St. Exupéry was a quiet, heavy man with a round, deliberate gaze, almost a stare. He talked little, his volatile wife talked most, but when he did talk, everyone listened. He had the great quality of suppressed drive and wonder too.

"Mermoz, who was a sinewy 'tough guy' in comparison to his friend, was full of activity and charm. He fell in love and romped with the schnautzer pups and begged to take one of them with him . . ." etc.

p. 255  Text of letter notifying him of his admission to Air Force can be found in Chevrier's biography, pp. 118–19.

p. 256  See Daurat, *op. cit.*, pp. 185–8.

pp. 257–9  Pierre Gaudillère, *Forces Aériennes Françaises*, July 1947.

p. 259  Luro Cambaceres, *op. cit.*, p. 126.


### *Chapter* 14. TWO CRASHES

For the details concerning Saint-Ex's journalistic activities I am much beholden to Pierre Lazareff, Hervé Mille, and Jacques Meyer, as I am to Comtesse Marthe de Fels and Prince Alexander Makinsky for the many interesting things they had to say about Léon-Paul Fargue and Saint-Ex. Colonel Frédéric Loiseau was as irresistible as ever in relating the story of the Avenue Montaigne encounter, *chez* Bugatti, and Georges Kessel was most entertaining in his account of his friend's Muscovite tribulations.

p. 262  This and subsequent quotations from Henri Jeanson are taken from a brilliant *in memoriam* article which deserves a place in an anthology (*Constellation*, September 1968).

p. 264  Joseph Kessel, *Gringoire* 10 January 1936.

p. 265  For preface to Maurice Bourdet's *Grandeur et Misère de l'Aviation* see *Un Sens à la Vie*, pp. 243–6.

p. 266   I am grateful to Monsieur and Madame Gaston Bergery for their reminiscences of Saint-Ex and their kindness in letting me consult their personal collection of *La Flèche*.

p. 268   Fargue's two retrospective articles about Saint-Exupéry were published in *La Revue de Paris* (September 1945) and *Confluences* (summer 1948).

pp. 272 forward   Saint-Ex's six Russian articles can be found in *Un Sens à la Vie*, pp. 35–79.

p. 282   *Marianne*, 7 August 1935.

pp. 283–6   I am most indebted to Raymond Bernard for kindly letting me read the copy of the original scenario of *Anne-Marie*.

p. 290 forward   I owe thanks to M. Laclavière for information about his father's dealings with Saint-Ex.

p. 293   Jean Lucas was his usual generous self in filling me on this and other episodes in his friend's life.

pp. 294 forward   For detailed account of this abortive flight see *Wind, Sand, and Stars*.

pp. 296–7   The text of his report on the crash can be found in Chevrier's biography, pp. 130–4.

## Chapter 15. THE AGONY OF SPAIN

I am beholden to Robert Bresson for the interesting things he had to say about the filming of *Courrier Sud*, and to Consuelo de Saint-Exupéry for the details about Boris, the butler. I also wish to thank Alexandre de Manziarly for his recollection of the dinner party that was saddened by the news of Mermoz' disappearance, and Geoffroy de la Tour du Pin for the account of Saint-Ex's experience with the grenade-throwing *desesperado* which he heard from him years later in Tunis.

p. 303   For Werth on Saint-Ex's ill-humour, see his essay *"Tel que je l'ai connu"*, included in Delange's *Vie de Saint-Exupéry*, pp. 187–8.

pp. 312 forward   Saint-Exupéry's five articles on the Spanish Civil War appeared in the 12, 13, 14, 16, and 19 August 1936 issues of *L'Intransigeant* and can be found in *Un Sens à la Vie*, pp. 82–112.

p. 320   See Gide, *Journal*, 4 September 1936 entry (Pléiade, pp. 1253–4) for Malraux' intended offensive on Oviedo.

p. 320   See Chapter 9, *"Embarras et Echec du Front Populaire"* in Jacques Chastenet's *Histoire de la Troisième République*, Vol. 6 (Hachette 1962).

p. 320   The quotations from his notebooks can be found in *Carnets*, pp. 23–4.

p. 321   *Marianne*, 7 August 1935.

pp. 321–2  The three articles on Mermoz appeared in *L'Intransigeant* of 10 December 1936, *Marianne* ot 16 December 1936, and *L'Intransigeant* ot 22 January 1937, and are included in Jean Mermoz, *Mes Vols*, pp. 192–200.

p. 323  For details about the lion cub and Saint-Ex's narrow escape at Algiers see Pélissier, *op. cit.*, pp. 27–8.

pp. 324–5  André Gide, *Retour de l'U.R.S.S.*, published by Gallimard in November 1936.

p. 324  *Voltaire*, 30 January 1937.

pp. 325  See *Carnets*, pp. 85, 59.

pp. 326–7  According to Pierre Chevrier (biography p. 152), Franco's Nationalists later sought to claim that Saint-Ex had flown down a plane to be turned over to the Republicans.

p. 327  See Carlos Baker, *Hemingway* (Collins 1969, p. 371).

pp. 328 forward  The three articles published in *Paris-Soir* (27, 28 June and 3 July 1937) can be found in *Un Sens à la Vie*, pp. 114–142.

p. 333  Chevrier, *op. cit.*, pp. 152–3.

### *Chapter* 16. BETWEEN SICKLE AND SWASTIKA

I am grateful to André de Fonscolombe for what he had to tell me about his cousin's attitude towards Gide and Communism, to Bertrand Piémore for the many interesting things he had to say about his First World War friend Léon Werth, to Julián Gorkín for the background concerning *Monde* and Victor Serge, and to General Paul Stehlin for his description of a memorable Sunday at Tempelhof.

pp. 334 forward  The quotations from Saint-Exupéry's notebooks concerning Gide's *Retour de l'U.R.S.S.* and his general attitude to Communism can be found in the fourth section of *Carnets*, devoted to social and economic problems.

p. 335  *Retour de l'U.R.S.S.*, pp. 60–1. *Carnets*, pp. 53–4, 62, 85–7.

pp. 340–1  On the *Journal du Peuple* see Jean Galtier-Boissière, *Mémoires*, Vol. II, p. 66, and Henri Jeanson, "*Celle qui peut parler de la bande à Bonnot*" (*L'Aurore*, 2 April 1968). For Valéry's remark see Malraux, *Antimémoires* (Gallimard 1967, p. 13).

pp. 341–2  See Galtier-Boissière, *op. cit.*, Chapter 44 on Victor Serge.

p. 343  Gide, *Journal*, 29 August 1933 (Pléiade, pp. 1181–2).

pp. 343–4  *Carnets*, pp. 96, 23.

pp. 344–6  Chevrier, *op. cit.*, pp. 155–59.

p. 347  *Les Ailes*, 23 September 1937.

p. 347  Madame Paul Ghali, to whom I am indebted for the mention of Saint-Exupéry's lecture trip to Rumania, could not recall the exact date, but it must have been some time in 1937.

p. 348   A letter describing this ocean clipper feeling is quoted at some length in Chevrier's biography, pp. 165–6.

p. 349   For the "sheet that heals wounds" episode see "Books I Remember", *Harper's Bazaar*, April 1941, p. 123.

p. 349   I am indebted to Jean Israël for the story of the non-amputated hand.

p. 350   André Gide's advice with regard to Conrad's *Mirror of the Sea* is quoted by Pélissier, *op. cit.*, p. 68.

p. 351   See Lewis Galantière, "Antoine de Saint-Exupéry", *Atlantic Monthly*, April 1947.

p. 352   The preface to the French translation of *Listen, the Wind!* (*Le Vent se lève*) can be found in *Un Sens à la Vie*, pp. 247–256.

p. 354   *Carnets*, p. 131. On the Abyssinian war, p. 75, on Alain, pp. 16–17.

pp. 354–9   The three articles entitled "*La Paix ou la Guerre?*", published in *Paris-Soir*, can be found in *Un Sens à la Vie*, pp. 147–182.

p. 355   Galtier-Boissière, *Mémoires*, Vol. 3, p. 9.

p. 358   Fargue, article in *Confluences*, reprinted in René Tavernier's *Saint-Exupéry en Procès*, p. 30.

p. 359   The winter 1935 issue of *Minotaure* contained Saint-Ex's lyrical recollection of "Moisy" folding the linen sheets at Saint-Maurice (later included in *Terre des Hommes*) and an interesting analysis of the palm-prints of Saint-Ex and Aldous Huxley.

pp. 360–1   Galantière, *Atlantic Monthly*, July 1947.

pp. 361–2   Pélissier, *op. cit.*, p. 68. On Saint-Ex's talent for story telling see Galtier-Boissière, *Mémoires*, Vol. 2, p. 297.

p. 362   Werth, *op. cit.*, p. 153.

p. 362   Jacques Baratier, *Nouvelles Littéraires*, 11 March 1939.

pp. 363 forward   For German trip see Chevrier, *op. cit.*, pp. 175–7. I am indebted to Charles Sallès for the account of the visit to the Berlin picture gallery.

pp. 364–5   Henri Bordeaux, *Ecrits de Paris*, September 1948. René Delange, *op. cit.*, p. 79, claims that Goering wanted to see Saint-Ex. Presumably the invitation reached him through Otto Abetz.

p. 365   Pélissier, *op. cit.*, p. 33.

## Chapter 17. MAN'S EARTH

p. 368   The term "resistencialist" appears in *El Hombre y la Gente*, a series of lectures first delivered at the Institute of the Humanities in Madrid in 1948–9 and later translated into English under the title, *Man and People*.

p. 368   *Carnets*, pp. 69, 43, 55  They owe much to Nietzsche.

p. 371   Saint-Ex on Valéry, see Chevrier, *op. cit.*, pp. 48–9.

p. 372   Edmond Jaloux, *Nouvelles Littéraires*, 8 April 1939.

pp. 372–3   Henri Bordeaux, *Etapes Allemandes*, published after the outbreak of war, carried this dedication: "In memory of our encounter in Berlin and in homage to the author of that *Terre des Hommes* I so admire."

pp. 373 forward   A full account of this riverside meal can be found in *Lettre à un Otage*.

p. 374   See Pierre Dalloz's account of this visit to Aigues Mortes in *Confluences* (summer 1948).

p. 375   Louis Castex, *De Clément Ader à Gagarine*, (Hachette 1967, p. 184) devotes an entire chapter to Saint-Ex.

p. 375   This blue ribbon flight was later written up by the navigator, Paul Comet, in *Icare*, No. 37 (spring 1966).

pp. 376–7   Most of the details concerning "La Feuilleraie" are drawn from an RTF (state radio) interview of Consuelo made in 1954.

p. 377   Otis Ferguson, *The New Republic*, July 5, 1939; Bruce Gould, *Saturday Review of Literature*, June 17, 1939, and in the same weekly, Anne Morrow Lindbergh, October 14, 1939.

pp. 377–8   See H. E. Crane, *op. cit.*, pp. 276–8.

## Chapter 18. *Pilote de Guerre*

I owe a great debt of thanks to Saint-Ex's fellow airmen for their unstinting efforts to help me piece together a complex mosaic—beginning with Colonel Henri Alias and General René Gavoille. Jean Israël was more than kind in lending me a copy of the Group's *Journal de Marche*, as were Major Edgar Moreau-Berillon and Robert Dutordoir in supplying the photos of Orconte and Montceau-le-Waast.

pp. 379–80   Chevrier, *op. cit.*, pp. 215–6.

p. 380   See General Davet's introduction to Daniel Anet's *Antoine de Saint-Exupéry, poète, romancier, moraliste* (Corréa 1946).

p. 380   Pierre Bost, *Figaro Littéraire*, 9 July 1964.

pp. 380 forward   See the four articles written by Jean Israël, Jean Dutertre, François Laux, and Dr. Dominique Picard in *Icare* (summer 1964).

p. 382   I am grateful to Mr. Maximilian Becker for being allowed to see a copy of this letter.

pp. 383 forward   This and other letters quoted elsewhere in this chapter were published in *Le Figaro Littéraire*, 27 July 1957.

p. 388   *Carnets*, pp. 21–2.

pp. 388–90   A. R. Métral, in *Confluences* (summer 1948). Pélissier, *op. cit.*, devotes one fascinating chapter to Saint-Ex's ingenuity as an inventor.

pp. 399–400   On the Reynaud interview, see Chevrier, *op. cit.*, p. 223.

p. 403   These details on Consuelo's departure from "La Feuilleraie" are drawn from the previously mentioned broadcast of 1954. The property was subsequently occupied by the Germans, French *maquisards*, and the U.S. Army, and it is hardly surprising that many things disappeared never to be seen again, including, apparently, some of Tonio's letters.

pp. 403–4   Sir Edward Spears, *Assignment to Catastrophe*, Vol. 2 (London 1954, New York 1955, pp. 44, 321).

pp. 405–7   Suzanne Massu (now wife of General Massu), *Quand j'étais Rochambelle* (Grasset 1969, pp. 10–11).

p. 407   Pélissier, *op. cit.*, pp. 36–7.

## Chapter 19. THE WANDERER

For the information in this chapter, much of which has never appeared in print before, I am first of all indebted to Paul Creyssel. In addition to those already mentioned who have helped me with previous chapters and again with this, I would like to express my thanks to Alain de la Falaise, Pierre and Marthe Massenet, Jean Borotra, General René Chambe, and François de Panafieu for the precious details and advice they furnished me about a troubled period.

pp. 410 forward   See Chapter "General Noguès' Ten Days" in Claude Paillat's *L'Echiquier d'Alger* (Laffont 1966).

pp. 411–12   General Lionel Chassin, who was too ill to receive me during my initial researches, was kind enough to send me a message from his sick-bed as this book was going to press. Then a lieutenant colonel, he commanded a group of light Glenn Martin bombers at the time of Saint-Exupéry's stop-over in Rabat. Saint-Ex said nothing at all about a mission and Chassin had the impression he had simply hopped over to see him, profiting from the "general confusion" then reigning in Algiers. Two groups of Glenn Martins —about forty planes in all—had been readied for action and were then in Morocco. The other 100 were presumably waiting to be uncrated and assembled at the Ateliers Industriels de l'Air in Casablanca. General Georges Grimal, who was involved in French Air Force purchases in the winter and spring of 1940, has assured me that this latter figure is not exaggerated.

p. 413   For this farewell dinner, see Pélissier, pp. 37–8.

p. 413   See Chevrier, *op. cit.*, p. 226.

p. 414   Letter quoted in *Figaro Littéraire*, 27 July 1957.

pp. 415–17   For situation at this time see Robert Aron, *Histoire de Vichy*, 1940–1944 (Fayard 1958, p. 254).

pp. 420–1   On the Hôtel des Sports see Georges Loustaunau's lively *Mémoires d'un Français Rebelle* (Laffont 1948) and Marie-Madeleine Fourcade's *L'Arche de Noé* (Fayard 1968).

pp. 422–3   See Chevrier, *op. cit.*, pp. 227–9.

p. 426   From Saint-Exupéry's own beautiful description of Lisbon in *Lettre à un Otage*.

p. 427   The French historian Alain Decaux has published a detailed investigation of the curious circumstances surrounding this last flight of Guillaumet and Jean Chiappe. There is little doubt that their Farman was shot down by Italian fighters, frustrated by the beating they had just been administered by the R.A.F. and the Royal Navy. See *Nouveaux Dossiers Secrets* (Académie Perrin 1967).

pp. 427–8   See H. E. Crane, *op. cit.*, pp. 278–283.

p. 428   Quoted by Chevrier, *op. cit.*, p. 230.

## *Chapter* 20. The Exile

Of those who helped me with this chapter I wish first of all to thank Jean Renoir for kindly receiving me at a very busy moment; my friend Eugene de Thassy for tape-recording Bernard Lamotte's priceless reminiscences; Denis de Rougemont for supplementing what he had already noted in his Journal; Madame Yvonne Michel, Pierre Lazareff, and Roger Beaucaire, to whom I am already deeply indebted; and last but not least, Michel Pobers and Professors Louis Rougier and Léon Wencelius—all three of whom were kind enough to go through the English text and to suggest valuable corrections.

pp. 429–30   See *New York Times*, January 1, 1941, p. 20. "France's Fall laid to Military Chiefs."

p. 430   For the notable French exiles in New York see Guy Fritsch-Estrangin, *New York entre De Gaulle et Pétain* (Table Ronde 1969).

pp. 430–1   On Saint-Ex's mediation between Renoir and Lazareff see Henri Jeanson, *L'Aurore*, 5 November 1968, p. 2.

pp. 431–2, 434–5   Raoul de Roussy de Sales, *The Making of Yesterday* (Reynal & Hitchcock 1947): entry dated January 4, 1941 (pp. 175–6), January 14, 1941 (p. 178). On *The Wave of the Future*, November 30, 1940, (p. 169).

p. 435   Denis de Rougemont, *Journal d'une époque* (Gallimard 1968, pp. 462–3), entry dated 21 January 1941

pp. 436–7   R. de R. de Sales, *op. cit.* On Dorothy Thompson, August 5,

1940, pp. 153–4; on Walter Lippmann, October 22, 1940, p. 165; on Henry-Haye, October 4, 1940, p. 162; on Houdry and *France Forever*, September 14, 1940, p. 158.

p. 437   On the feud between Bernstein and Maurois see Rougemont, *Journal*, p. 519; and also the curious correspondence published by *Aujourd'hui* in February 1941, in Jean Galtier-Boissière, *Mémoires*, Vol. III, p. 54.

pp. 438–9   *New York Times*, 31 January, 1941. "Saint-Exupéry dislikes Vichy appointment: says he would have refused if asked." See also Pélissier, *op. cit.*, pp. 164–5. For Book Award lunch, *New York Times*, 15 January 1941, p. 6.

p. 439   Robert Van Gelder, *New York Times Book Review*, 19 January 1941.

p. 444   Louis Rougier, *Mission Secrète à Londres* (Paris 1948, pp. 107–8).

pp. 444–5   Pierre de Lanux in *Confluences* (summer 1948).

p. 445   Lewis Galantière, *Reader's Digest*, December 1957, and *Altantic Monthly*, April 1947. Most of the quotations from Galantière in this chapter are drawn from the latter.

p. 447   The two scenarios, entitled *Igor* and *Sonia*, were both melodramatic thrillers taking place on shipboard.

pp. 447–8   For Saint-Ex's medical troubles see H. E. Crane, *op. cit.*, pp. 284–9.

p. 449   R. de R. de Sales, *op. cit.*, p. 226.

p. 450   Edward Weeks, *Atlantic Monthly*, April 1942.

pp. 454–5   *Carnets*, pp. 118–9, 199.

## Chapter 21. A Solitary Little Fellow

p. 457   *Lettres à sa Mere*, p. 104.

p. 457   *Carnets*, p. 35.

p. 458   Consuelo de Saint-Exupéry's *Oppède* was first published by Brentano's in 1945 (with 19 illustrations by the author) and later in a cheaper edition by Gallimard.

p. 459   Jean-Paul Sartre, *"Qu'est ce que la Littérature?"* in *Situations*, Vol. II (Gallimard 1948, pp. 218–229, 317–326).

p. 459   The text of an anguished letter Saint-Ex wrote to Curtice Hitchcock from Canada was included in the special issue of *Icare* (summer 1964).

p. 460   Rougemont, *Journal*, pp. 519–521.

p. 461   I am indebted to Léon Wencelius for this account of the genesis of *Le Petit Prince*.

p. 462  André Maurois, *Nouvelles Littéraires*, 7 November 1946. Other details come from an RTF (state radio) interview made in 1954.

p. 463  *Lettres à sa mere*, p. 160.

p. 463  *Carnets*, pp. 28–9, 32.

pp. 463–4  Letter quoted in Chevrier, *op. cit.*, pp. 170–1.

p. 464  H. L. Binsse, *Commonweal*, November 19, 1943.

*Chapter* 22. RETURN TO THE FRAY

p. 467  Rougemont, *Journal*, p. 519.

pp. 468–70  I am indebted to General Odic's widow for this account of her husband's tribulations in London. See also Kenneth Pendar, *Adventure in Diplomacy* (London 1966, pp. 197–200), and a shorter account in Robert Mengin's illuminating *De Gaulle à Londres, vu par un Français Libre* (Table Ronde 1965, p. 245).

pp. 470 forward  Again, Galantière, *Atlantic Monthly*, April 1947.

p. 473  In French: "*Eh, bien! J'espère que les gens de Vichy vont les flanquer à la mer. On ne pénètre pas en France par éffraction.*" As quoted in Jean-Raymond Tournoux' *Pétain et De Gaulle* (Plon 1964, p. 297).

p. 473  François Quilici, *La Marseillaise*, 27 November 1942.

pp. 473–4  R. de R. de Sales, *op. cit.*, p. 290 (September 26, 1942).

pp. 476–7  The full text of Maritain's rebuttal can be found in Pélissier, *op. cit.*, pp. 219–227.

p. 477  On Pierre-André Weill, see Rougier, *op. cit.*, p. 126.

pp. 478–9  I am most grateful to Robert Tenger for his recollections of life as a wartime publisher in Manhattan.

p. 480  Henri de Kerillis, *De Gaulle, Dictateur*, p. 145.

p. 480  On Paul Winckler see Rougier, *op. cit.*, p. 119. On Philip see Kerillis, *op. cit.*, p. 145.

pp. 481 forward  General Béthouart's own account of his mission to America can be found in his *Cinq Années d'Espérance* (Plon 1968, ch. 10). I am indebted to him for adding a few details for this and the next chapter.

p. 482  *Cinq Années d'Espérance*, p. 192.

p. 483  Kerillis, *op. cit.*, pp. 211–222.

p. 483  Rougemont, *Journal*, p. 526.

p. 484  General Georges de Chassey was kind enough to tell me of this Metropolitan uniform, as of a later Saint-Ex stop-over in Marrakesh.

p. 485  For Saint-Ex's Atlantic crossing see Pierre Sonneville, *Les Combattants de la Liberté* (Table Ronde 1968, p. 269).

pp. 485–6  Pélissier, *op. cit.*, p. 39, and the articles by Chassin and Jourdan in *Icare* (summer 1964).

pp. 486 forward  Jules Roy, *Passion et Mort de Saint-Exupéry* (Julliard 1964, pp. 51–3, 59–62).

pp. 486 forward  I am beholden to Alain Jourdan, General René Gavoille, and General Hayez of the Service Historique de l'Armée de l'Air, for their kindness in letting me consult their copies of the 2/33's *Journal de Marche* for the years 1943 and 1944.

p. 488  See Bouscat's own account of his London mission in his *De Gaulle–Giraud: Dossier d'une mission* (Flammarion 1967).

pp. 488 forward  For the situation in Algiers at this time see Ch. 11 *"La Pagaille d'Alger"* in René Chambe's *Le Maréchal Juin, Duc du Garigliano* (Presses de la Cité 1968); Claude Paillat, *L'Echiquier d'Alger*, Vol. II, chs. 9–10; Kenneth Pendar, *op. cit.*, chs. 13–14.

p. 490  See Dabry's article in *Icare* (summer 1964) and Pélissier, *op. cit.*, p. 39.

p. 490  Gide, *Journal*, 1939–1949 (Pléiade 1954, p. 246).

pp. 492–3  K. Pendar, *op. cit.*, p. 170. For a fascinating account of why Murphy disregarded Sumner Welles' instructions regarding De Gaulle, see Lilian Ernoul's interview with Pendar in *Rivarol*, 25 May 1967.

pp. 493 forward  For these details about the Lightning I am particularly indebted to Jean Leleu, who was kind enough to run through this and the next two chapters for technical errors.

p. 494  Maximilian Becker was kind enough to let me have a photo copy of this letter to Curtice Hitchcock.

pp. 495–7  The letters to Pélissier and Murphy can be found in Pélissier, *op. cit.*, pp. 40–4.

p. 497  On Leclerc see Paillat, *op. cit.*, pp. 278–9, and for "Wild Woman's Ravine", *ibid.*, pp. 280–4.

pp. 497–8  Pendar, *op. cit.*, pp. 182–3. I am grateful to Kenneth Pendar for adding something to his description of that tearful scene at the Cercle Interallié.

p. 498  For Polifka's statement, see Crane, *op. cit.*, pp. 309–312.

pp. 498–9  See Leleu's article in *Confluences* (summer 1948), reprinted in Tavernier's *Saint-Exupéry en Procès*.

pp. 499–500  Pélissier, *op. cit.*, pp. 45–46.

p. 501  See Marty, in H. E. Crane, *op. cit.*, 295–300.

pp. 502–3  For full text of *"Lettre au General X——"*, see *Un Sens à la Vie*, pp. 223–231. Though General Chambe is not certain the letter was really destined for him, I think it more likely that he was the intended recipient rather than General Bouscat.

p. 504   Diana Cooper, *Trumpets from the Steep* (Hart-Davis 1960, p. 173).

p. 504   Maurois, *Nouvelles Littéraires*, 7 November 1946.

p. 507   On Maurois and Corsica, see Paillat, *op. cit.*, Vol II, pp. 339–40; also Ch. 8 in Maurois' *Mémoires* (Flammarion, 1970), in which he tells how he had himself appointed liaison officer on General Henry Martin's staff.

p. 507   Charles de Gaulle, *Discours et Messages, 1940–1946* (Paris, Berger-Levrault, 1946, p. 360). The aide asked me not to reveal his name.

pp. 507–8   I am most grateful to Dr. Henri Comte for being allowed to quote from this letter.

p. 508   On the rivalry between French intelligence services see Michel Garder's authoritative book, *La Guerre Secrète des Services Spéciaux Français* (1935–1945) (Plon 1967).

pp. 508–10   The story of Dungler's mission to Algiers is told in full, fascinating detail by Gabriel Jeantet in *Pétain contre Hitler* (Table Ronde 1966).

pp. 510–12   A blow by blow description of these physical torments is given by Pélissier, *op. cit.*, pp. 137–150.

p. 512   I owe thanks to Pierre Dalloz for an accurate account of Saint-Ex's vicissitudes with members of De Gaulle's government and secretariat.

p. 512   Bordaz, *Forces Aériennes Françaises* (July 1947).

p. 513   For Saint-Ex's relations with the Protestants I am indebted to Léon Wencelius.

p. 513   I owe a second debt of thanks to General Bouscat for kindly lending me the copy of *Terre des Hommes* in which he pasted the self-portrait which "Pépino" did of himself in the course of this same lunch and which can be found among the photos in this book.

p. 513   Max-Pol Fouchet, *Un Jour je m'en souviens* (Mercure de France 1968, pp. 153–6).

pp. 513–14   I am indebted to Madame Béthouart for the story of the prayer-rug, and to Pierre Cot for the episode which follows.

pp. 514–15   Fouchet, *op. cit.*, pp. 127–9. Anne Heurgon-Desjardins, preface to *Entretiens avec André Gide*, edited by Marcel Arland and Jean Mouton (Mouton 1967).

pp. 515–16   Jeantet, *op. cit.*, ch. 10.

p. 516   See Pierre Sonneville, *op. cit.*, pp. 267–9.

p. 517   Jules Roy, *op. cit.*, p. 90. The comment of De Gaulle's also figures in Migeo's biography, but with no mention of the source.

p. 517   Letter quoted in Chevrier, *op. cit.*, p. 268. The words "nor executed by a firing-squad" refer to the just completed trial and execution of Pierre Pucheu, Pétain's one-time Minister of the Interior, who had obtained Giraud's permission to volunteer as a simple soldier in *l'Armée d'Afrique* in order to fight the Germans, but who was arrested on Gaullist orders the moment he reached Morocco.

p. 518   For details about Korda see Pélissier, *op. cit.*, pp. 153–5.

pp. 518–19   I am grateful to Jacques Meyer for letting me see the number of *L'Arche* in which *Lettre à un Otage* was published, and to Henry de Ségogne and Gaston Gallimard for the details about Heller and the *Propaganda Staffel*. For excerpts from the collaborationist press, see Chevrier, *op. cit.*, pp. 240–1.

See also Pélissier, *op. cit.*, p. 122.

p. 519   These letters are quoted in Chevrier, *op. cit.*, pp. 259–261.

pp. 519–21   For full text of this letter, see *Le Monde*, 29 July 1950.

p. 521   Chassin, article in *Confluences* (summer 1948).

pp. 522–3   See Jeantet, *op. cit.*, p. 74. I am indebted to Paul Dungler and Colonel Henry Hyde for confirming the account herein given. Jacques Soustelle, as might be expected, dismissed Dungler as someone "imbued with rabidly reactionary political ideas" when he wrote up this affair in *Envers et Contre Tout, D'Alger à Paris* (1942–1944) (Laffont 1950, p. 328).

pp. 523–4   I am most grateful to Madame Mast and to Geoffroy de La Tour du Pin for their reminiscences of La Marsa.

p. 524   Chassin, article in *Icare* (summer 1964).

### *Chapter* 24. THE VETERAN

In addition to those who helped me with previous chapters I am indebted to Colonel Paul Rockwell, André Henry, Madame Guy Monod, Ambassador Jean Chauvel, Fernand Grenier, and Raymond Duriez for their contributions to this one.

pp. 526 forward   See the chapter devoted to Saint-Exupéry in John Phillips' *Odd World* (Simon & Schuster 1959).

p. 527   Chassin, *Confluences*, already cited.

pp. 530–1   Marty, in H. E. Crane, *op. cit.*, pp. 295–300.

See Chassin and Leleu articles in *Confluences* (reprinted Tavernier, *op. cit.*).

p. 532   For the explanation of the meaning of the Biblical "mess of potage" I am beholden to Alain Jourdan's keen memory.

p. 533   Pélissier, *op. cit.*, p. 50.

p. 534   See Gavoille's account of the Genoa overflight in *Forces Aériennes Françaises*, July 1947.

p. 536   See Fernard Grenier's book, *C'était ainsi . . .*, pp. 194–6.

p. 537   Pélissier, *op. cit.*, pp. 47–8.

pp. 539–40  For pump episode see Tavernier, *op. cit.*, p. 90.

pp. 540–1  Donovan's letter is quoted in Crane, *op. cit.*, p. 276. In a letter sent to the author as this book was going to press, Colonel Henry Hyde recalls having seen Donovan in Washington on 15 July 1944. It is possible that Donovan was back in Algiers by the 21st, but equally possible that Saint-Exupéry saw him during an earlier visit to Algiers.

p. 541  Anne Heurgon-Desjardins, *op. cit.*

p. 542  In his first article (*Confluences* 1948), Chassin quoted Saint-Ex as saying: "Impossible. Now I'll go on to the end. It isn't very far off, I imagine. I'll stick with my comrades—to the end." The phrasing is ambiguous, but it was almost certainly the end of the war he meant.

p. 542  Gide, *Le Figaro*, 17 February 1945.

pp. 542–3  I am grateful to Pierre Dalloz for a copy of Saint-Ex's letter to him. Excerpts from the other are quoted in Chevrier, *op. cit.*, p. 278. For a singularly parallel opinion on the subject of one's "real" country, when in exile, see Queen Wilhelmina, as quoted in Mengin, *De Gaulle à Londres*, p. 298.

## Chapter 25. THE PROPHET

p. 551  The pertinent passage in Herr Noack's letter states: "The wartime record-books of the Luftflotte 2 are missing, as are the record-books of the airbases in southern France. They were presumably destroyed. The only surviving record-book is that of the Fliegerhorstkommandatur at Istres-le-Tube. The entries for 30 and 31.7.1944 indicate: Strong enemy reconnaissance activity over the whole southern France area, without further comments." I am indebted to General Mark Bradley, General Keeling, Major Jack Tebo, John Bross, Dr. Maurer Maurer, and Mr. W. M. Mills for helping me to establish contact with the military archives department of the West German Defence Ministry.

p. 552  Henri Bordeaux, in *Ecrits de Paris*, September 1948.

p. 554  Maurois, in *Nouvelles Littéraires*, 7 November 1946.

pp. 558–60  Carlo François, *L'Esthétique d'Antoine de Saint-Exupéry* (Delachaux & Niestlé 1957). Professor Léon Wencelius, who is an authority on *Citadelle*, is, however, distinctly dubious about François' suggestion that the "*ennemi bien-aimé*" is Nietzsche.

p. 567  José Ortega y Gasset, *Man and People* (Norton 1957, p. 50).

p. 568  Jean Cau, in *Icare* (summer 1964).

pp. 568–9  J.-F. Revel, En France, *La Fin de l'Opposition* (Julliard 1965).

p. 574  The final quotation is drawn from a preface written for the French magazine *Document*, which devoted a special issue to test pilots. Reproduced in *Un Sens à la Vie*, p. 259.

# Index

597